HEALTH AND THE LAW

HEALTH AND THE LAW

A Handbook for Health Professionals

Tom Christoffel

THE FREE PRESS
A Division of Macmillan Publishing Co., Inc.
NEW YORK

Collier Macmillan Publishers
LONDON

THE FREE PRESS
A Division of Macmillan Publishing Co., Inc.
866 Third Avenue, New York, N.Y. 10022

Collier Macmillan Canada, Inc.

Library of Congress Catalog Card Number: 82-70808

Printed in the United States of America

printing number

1 2 3 4 5 6 7 8 9 10

Library of Congress Cataloging in Publication Data

Christoffel, Tom.
  Health and the law.

  Includes index.
  1. Medical laws and legislation—United States.
2. Public health laws—United States. I. Title.
[DNLM: 1. Legislation—United States. 2. Public health
—United States—Legislation. WA 33 AA1 C5h]
KF3821.C57   1982   344.74′04   82-70808
ISBN 0-02-905370-6   347.3044   AACR2

Chapters 6–9 contain several quotes from Steven Jonas, ed., *Health Care Delivery in the United States*, 2d edition. Copyright © 1981 by Springer Publishing Co., Inc., New York. Used by Permission.

To Harold and Ann Christoffel, my parents

Contents

PART III: Clinical Practice and the Law

Preface and Acknowledgments

A LEGAL MYSTIQUE—what one observer has called a "veil of dignified mystery"—often deters nonlawyers from attempting an understanding of legal principles and concepts. Many nonlawyers tend to believe that the law, like the theory of relativity, is beyond their ken, and that legal principles and concepts can be understood only by those who have dedicated their professional careers to the task. Thus while acknowledging the importance of such understanding to their personal and professional lives, they make little effort to inform themselves in this area. (Similarly, most people without training in the health professions know amazingly little about how their bodies work or about disease processes, and many are convinced they cannot possibly learn enough to really understand the subject.)

There are legal aspects to virtually every facet of health care in this country: whether the issue is immunization policy, new drug testing, organ transplants, decisions to terminate life-support, intervention in cases of child abuse, or the funding of health care for the poor, health and law are becoming more and more intertwined. Yet most health care practitioners have little knowledge of specific laws or understanding of the legal system within which they function. More often than not, their perceptions are based on misinformation or on a few atypical cases that have caught the attention of the media. The result of such ignorance can be serious—on the one hand, the possibility of blundering into substantial legal problems, and on the other, the avoidance of permissible medical decisions and actions for fear of legal difficulties.

Yet the law is far from the mystery the nonlawyer believes it to be. "On the contrary," wrote one well-known iconoclastic law professor, "law deals almost exclusively with the ordinary facts and occurrences of everyday business and government and living. . . . Lawyers would always like to believe that the principles they say they work with are something more than a complicated way of talking about simple, tangible, non-legal matters; but they are not."[1]

The legal profession, by and large, is not unhappy with the mystique that surrounds their work, since it underscores their indispensability. There are several things that help maintain this mystique. First, legal jargon—the fact that most legal sentences "have a way of reading as though they had been translated from the German by someone with a rather meager knowledge of English"—helps to obscure for the layman the law's underlying logic.[2] Second, lawyers serve as the interpreters of law to nonlawyers, and do so at all levels of the legal process. Judges—who are lawyers—interpret and apply the law. Lawyers write the history of the law and serve as the teachers of the law. And, until recently, whenever law was studied using the tools of the sociologist, the philosopher, or the political scientist, it was lawyers who did the studying.[3] Finally, lay confusion is compounded by the everchanging nature of the law and the lack of consensus among the experts themselves as to what the law is at any particular time.

Nevertheless, there is a certain predictability about the law, and it is quite possible for intelligent, educated nonlawyers to inform themselves regarding the basic legal concepts underlying subjects of interest to them.

This book is intended to provide health professionals with these basics by presenting an overview of the many areas of law that relate to health and health care delivery: underlying legal theories and basic principles are explained, current issues reviewed, and future trends predicted. The specific objectives of the book are:

- to provide an understanding of the place of law in the health professions
- to survey the basic concepts and content in the major areas of health law
- to explain the sources of legal authority and the relationship between them
- to develop some familiarity with legal language and thinking

Such a general introduction necessarily focuses on basic concepts rather than on detail. Not only do each of the subject areas covered deserve—and have—volumes of detailed exposition, but the specifics in each area change rapidly and vary from state to state. It is *not* intended that the general knowledge offered here be used as a substitute for legal skills and training with respect to specific legal problems.

Health professionals can approach the law in one of two ways. One is simply to ask how the law might directly affect the individual's day-to-day professional activities; the broader view is to examine how the law might help or hinder the overall effort to improve the health of patients and the general society. The general background in this book is intended to provide a useful framework within which to carry on one's own work confidently, and to ask legal questions intelligently. Non-lawyers can maintain a working knowledge of those legal issues most important to their areas of activity. They can use legal counsel effectively, for advice rather than directives. They can avoid panic and inaction. And they can work with law as a permanent and important part of the environment in which they function, rather than reacting with acquiescence to a set of absolutes.

Who Should Read This Book

This book is aimed at all health professionals and students in the health professions. It assumes no prior familiarity with legal study on the part of the reader, and was developed as a handbook, with each chapter providing a comprehensive and self-contained review of a particular area of law.[4] Part I defines law and health law and describes the legal system in the United States. Part II focuses on how law is used to protect and enhance health, through health professional licensure, facilities regulation, public financing, and areas of public law dealing with pure food and drugs, occupational and environmental health. Part III deals with those areas of health law that are particularly relevant to the individual, such as consent to treatment, abortion, mental health law, and malpractice.

Obviously, by the time this book is off the press, new statutes and court decisions will have changed some of the specifics in many of the chapters. Thus one of its important tasks is to alert readers to the importance of keeping abreast of the law. Chapter footnotes and the Appendix provide information on how to read a legal decision, how to use a law library, and how to interact effectively with various parts of the legal system.

Use of this book will vary from reader to reader. Those with little previous training and information about the law will find it a useful primer. Those with a background in certain areas of health law may be particularly interested in the reference materials for the chapters dealing with those areas, using the rest of the book to supplement their existing background. Some readers will confine themselves largely to the text; others will want to review the footnotes thoroughly. Sharp differences in time, interest, and need determine that what is adequate for one person may be incomplete for the next. The sources listed offer a quick reference for those who want to delve more deeply into a given subject.

Acknowledgments

Thanks go first of all to the students in my health law classes at the University of Illinois School of Public Health. Over the past several years they have helped to form the scope and approach of this book and have provided feedback on early draft chapters. For reviewing and commenting on portions of the manuscript, as well as for providing information, my thanks to Gary Albrecht, James Anderson, Wendy Burgess, Katherine Christoffel, Ruth Dick, Mitchell Drexler, Linda Edwards, David Finkelhor, Bruce Goldstrom, Diana Hackbarth, William Hallenbeck, Joseph M. Healey, Jr., Stephanie Hoffman, Rob Holmes, Steven Jonas, Dean Timothy Jost, George Kaufer, Robert Kirschner, Naomi Klein, Kristin McNutt, James Melius, Gregory Nigosian, Clare Barret Obis, Paul Q. Peterson, Steven Polan, Madeleine Ruekberg, Edward Sabljak, Susan Sawyer, Gregory Storch, Daniel Swartzman, Ellen Wachtel, Michael Walker, Barbara Weiner, Sherry Weinstein, Kenneth Wing, and many others who helped in ways large and small. Special thanks to George Annas and Ruth Roemer, both of whom read the manuscript in its entirety and offered valuable comments. The primary goal in writing this book was to make the material as understandable as possible. Therefore my greatest debt is to Sonya F. Kaufer, without whose considerable editorial skills this would have been a hopeless task. I am, of course, responsible for any errors or confusion that persist. This publication was supported in part by NIH Grant LM 00027 from the National Library of Medicine, for which I am sincerely grateful.

NOTES

1. Fred Rodell, *Woe Unto You, Lawyers!* (New York: Berkeley, 1980), pp. 4, 6. Interest in the study of the general principles of law by nonlawyers is hardly new. For centuries law teachers have favored such study as part of a general program of liberal education, but with little effect. See Harold J. Berman and William R. Greiner, *The Nature and Functions of Law*, 3d ed. (Mineola, N.Y.: Foundation Press, 1972), pp. 1–5. There is a rationalization for the legal mystique that is less self-serving than monopolistic fees: namely, the belief

that the less people know about how the law actually operates, the more they will respect and uphold it. Bismark is credited with the observation that laws are like sausages, the more one learns about the making of them the less one appreciates them. The major criticism of the book *The Brethren* by members of the legal profession was not that the book was inaccurate, but rather that it was not good to have the Supreme Court exposed warts and all. Bob Woodward and Scott Armstrong, *The Brethren: Inside the Supreme Court* (New York: Simon & Schuster, 1979).

2. Rodell, *Woe Unto You, Lawyers!*, p. 121.

3. A useful collection of writings illustrating the trend away from the lawyer's monopoly on legal scholarship is Lawrence M. Friedman and Stewart Macaulay, *Law and the Behavioral Sciences*, 2d ed. (Indianapolis: Bobbs-Merrill, 1977). As regards history: "One of the most important characteristics of the writing of American legal—as opposed to constitutional—history is that it has almost exclusively been written by lawyers." Morton J. Horwitz, "The Conservative Tradition in the Writing of American Legal History," *American Journal of Legal History* 17:275 (1973), reprinted in Philip Shuchman, *Cohen and Cohen's Readings in Jurisprudence and Legal Philosophy*, 2d ed. (Boston: Little, Brown, 1979), p. 722. A notable exception is Jerold S. Auerbach, *Unequal Justice* (New York: Oxford University Press, 1976).

4. However, some understanding of how the health care delivery system operates is assumed. The most valuable single source of information on this subject is Steven Jonas, *Health Care Delivery in the United States*, 2d. ed. (New York: Springer, 1981).

Part I

LAW AND THE LEGAL SYSTEM

1 | What Is Law? What Is Health Law?

As soon as law is defined in terms of a set of actions and ideas, instead of in terms of a set of rules, it becomes possible to study its interrelationships with other types of patterned behavior and thought. Thus by a study of the part which law plays in the total social process, one may acquire fuller understanding both of law and of the nature of society itself.
—Berman and Greiner[1]

What Is Law?

THE QUESTION of what is law has been debated as long as laws have existed; it is a subject that intrigued ancient Greek philosophers and continues to intrigue late twentieth-century thinkers. One reason the question cannot be answered categorically is that the query itself means different things to different people. From a functional perspective it asks what purpose is served by law. From a philosophical perspective it asks whence legal rules are derived. And from a political perspective the question concerns structure and process.[2]

There is broad general agreement that in every society the functions of law are to meet the twin purposes of social control and conflict settlement.[3] (Some argue that all functions, including conflict settlement, are basically subsumed under social control.)[4] There are, of course, other social control mechanisms as well, including religion, customs, education, media, physical force, and the like; but in contemporary society, the legal system plays a crucial role in social control. Roscoe Pound, one of

3

America's leading legal scholars, defines the function of law quite simply as "social control through the systematic application of the force of politically organized society."[5]

Pound and most other experts on the law believe that it represents the social consciousness of society, emerging out of a pluralistic political process. Others argue that, rather than representing social consensus or compromise, law signifies the victory of particular interests over the rest of society.[6] Resolution of these conflicting views is ultimately crucial to understanding the legal system, but this task is beyond the scope of this book. The question is basically "Who governs?"—i.e., what model best describes the exercise of power and control in society? Three models exist: the pluralist, the elitist, and the class. The pluralist model is one in which power is seen as widely diffused among various interest groups and coalitions of interest groups that change as issues change, with no single group ever achieving permanent dominant control.[7] In the elitist model, power is concentrated in a dominant, ruling minority elite or set of elites whose membership may change over time, although elite control is constant.[8] The class model has power originating in economic production; in capitalist societies this power resides in a small, relatively static ruling social class which controls most of the wealth, and government serves primarily to protect the interests of this dominant class.[9] An individual's perception of who exercises power and control in society obviously determines his or her perception of why the legal system operates as it does.

Another way of defining what law is focuses on the principles and the process involved. There are a number of different approaches to jurisprudence (the science and philosophy of law),[10] all relating fairly closely to one or another of three basic concepts: natural law, positivism, or historical jurisprudence.

The *natural law* concept sees law as an embodiment of "right reason"—moral imperatives derived either from "divine laws" or "human nature." Thus Cicero wrote of law as "the highest reason, implanted in Nature, which commands what ought to be done and forbids the opposite,"[11] and this concept of law as a set of moral ideals reigned virtually unchallenged for many centuries.

The *positivism*[12] concept, which emerged in the nineteenth century, sees law simply as the commands or will of the state.[13] In this view, as John Austin, one of the founders of positivism, explained, "A law . . . may be said to be a rule laid down for the guidance of an intelligent being by an intelligent being having power over him."[14]

The concept of *historical jurisprudence* sees law as rooted in the traditions and customs of a society, almost an organic part of a people's history. As one leading American exponent of this view put it:

Law is not a body of commands imposed upon society from without, either by an individual sovereign or superior, or by a sovereign body constituted by representatives of society itself. It exists at all times as one of the elements of society springing directly from habit and custom. It is therefore the unconscious creation of society.[15]

There have been many variants of the three views outlined above.[16] In the United States, sociological jurisprudence, a combination of the positivist and historical approaches, has exercised great influence, particularly during the first third of this century. Closely associated with such noted figures as Oliver Wendell Holmes, Jr., Roscoe Pound, and Benjamin Cardozo, this pragmatic approach, as Justice Holmes made clear, focuses on the law in action and the interplay between law and society:

The life of the law has not been logic; it has been experience. The felt necessities of the time, the prevalent moral and political theories, intuitions of public policy, avowed or unconscious, even the prejudices which judges share with their fellow-men, have had a good deal more to do than the syllogism in determining the rules by which men should be governed.[17]

This perception of law as common sense influenced by political and public policy considerations is likely to have particular appeal to non-lawyers, more so certainly than a formless set of "principles" derived from "natural law" or ancient tradition.[18]

Unfortunately, lay study of the law often consists either of memorizing long series of rules or of pondering abstract philosophical principles. But in fact law is best understood as a political mechanism and approached with common sense. As one distinguished federal judge put it:

I believe the truly important constitutional decisions are exercises in pragmatics often clothed in legalistic syllogisms and that the controlling principle, seldom expressed, is expediency: What is best for the nation? Sometimes the true rationale of decision is never mentioned. Worse, it may be covered up and buried beneath page after page of legalese.[19]

This could be confusing and boring, but illumination is possible and rewarding. As one of the leading legal philosophers of this century observed: "If the Law of the State be seen . . . not [as] a 'code' nor a body of Rules, but as in first essence a going institution, it opens itself at once to inquiry by the non-technician."[20]

Perhaps the most important fact about the legal system—and one that most people do not realize—is its relatively small direct impact on the functioning of society. Most nonlawyers tend to think of the law as reaching into every single nook and cranny of life. (These perceptions are reinforced by news of the filing of bizarre lawsuits, such as the case of the man who sued a woman for standing him up for a date, even though such lawsuits are generally thrown out of court.) The truth is that a large proportion of our day-to-day activities are not affected by statutes or amenable to settlement by lawsuits and that many important issues are effectively beyond the reach of the legal system.[21] In addition, many problems are not reached by the legal system for practical reasons, even though existing law theoretically could affect the problem. This may be the case because the individual involved cannot afford the costs of entering the legal system. Or the stakes involved may be too low for any single individual to justify the costs of litigation. Or the individual confronted with a problem may simply assume—often with cause—that the law in practice would not do what, in principle, it should do.[22]

What Is Health Law?

How, then, does all this relate to health law? Philosophical inquiry aside, the question "What is law?" can be viewed the way many lawyers view it: Law is what is learned in law school and practiced by lawyers. From this perspective, law becomes simply a composite of different subject areas, in the same sense that medicine could be viewed as a combination of pediatrics, internal medicine, obstetrics, psychiatry, radiology, et al. This analogy points up another aspect of law often ignored by the non-lawyer—that contemporary law, like medicine, involves areas of special-ization (though there are still many lawyers involved in "the general practice of law"). Thus attorneys may specialize in tax law, environmen-tal law, antitrust law, patent law, criminal law, municipal bond law, and a host of other discrete areas of practice.

Health law is another subcategory of law; but unlike those just cited it is not defined by legal practice. Historically the interaction of law and medicine dates back thousands of years, and for the most part con-cerned itself with the investigation of deaths and injuries. By the time of the Emperor Justinian, A.D. 483–565, the law provided that "Physicians are not ordinary witnesses, but give judgment rather than testimony." A multivolume *Quaestiones Medicolegales* was published in the 1600s by the medical consultant to the Papal Court of Appeals, and in 1788 the first systematic English work on this subject was published by Samuel Farr under the title *Elements of Medical Jurisprudence; or, a succinct and compen-dious description of such tokens in the human body as are requisite to determine the judgment of a coroner and courts of law, in cases of divorce, rape, murder, etc. To which are added directions for preserving the public health.*[23]

Although health has always been an object of governmental concern, the last decade in the United States is without precedent in the expan-sion of health-related statutes and regulations. Lawyers have become so involved in practically all aspects of health and health care that they could be considered a new category of health professional.[24] It has become almost routine for lawyers to be involved as advisers in matters ranging from termination of treatment to approval of experimental protocols. Yet there really are no generic health law practitioners—that is, individual attorneys are not likely to be involved in all the health-related areas of law. There are lawyers who specialize in hospital law[25] or food and drug law; there are personal-injury lawyers who handle significant numbers of malpractice claims, and others who are especially knowledgeable about Medicaid or worker's compensation benefits. There are lawyers, especially those employed by various government agencies, who concentrate on mental health, or substance abuse, or licensure and regulation. But no attorney can master all of these areas. Yet health care professionals—both providers of service and researchers—well may find themselves concerned with several of these aspects at one time or another.

William J. Curran has proposed that the term "health law" be used to identify "the wide range of legal aspects of medicine, nursing, dentistry, and other health service fields including public health and the environment." His precise definition of the term is "a specialty area of law and law practice related to the medical and other health fields—such as dentistry, nursing, hospital administration, and environmental law."[26] And George J. Annas suggests that, just as astronomy and physics can be viewed as applied mathematics, health law can be viewed as applied law, concerned with a particular area of human endeavor.[27] It could be said that health law refers to the ways in which the law serves as a tool or restraint in achieving health objectives. Although the goals are health oriented and defined in terms of health care, the experts are the attorneys.[28]

Table 1.1 lists some of the major topics generally included under health law. (Several of these, such as drug abuse, children's rights, and battered persons, involve social problems that are not primarily health related, but have certain aspects that fall within the purview of the health care system.) Most, but not all, of the topics listed are touched on in this book, though many receive only cursory attention. To keep the contents to a reasonable length, the pages that follow concentrate on those areas that are incontestably a part of health law, or have a direct and important impact on the work of large numbers of health professionals, or are subjects widely discussed or debated by the general public, such as abortion, human experimentation, and the like.

Almost all aspects of health law have undergone a great deal of change in recent years, some of it—regarding abortion and the treatment of mental patients, for example—quite revolutionary. In some areas, such as termination of treatment, the courts are quite openly

TABLE 1.1   Major Topics Included under Health Law

*Abortion (42)
 Adoption
 Aging
*Alcoholism and drug abuse (30)
 Allied health professionals and the
    law
 Battered persons
 Behavior modification
*Business and financial aspects of
    practice (16)
*Child abuse and neglect (40)
 Children's rights
*Confidentiality (55)
*Consent to treatment by minors
    and incompetents (48)
*Death and dying (46)
 Dentistry and the law
 Developmental disability
 Discrimination
 Drafting legislation and regulations
*Drug abuse and controlled sub-
    stances (22)
*Drug regulation (29)
*Duty to warn (29)
*Emergency treatment (53)
 Environmental health
*Euthanasia (39)
*Forensic medicine (13)
 Genetics
 Handicapped persons
 Health insurance
 Health maintenance organizations
 Health planning
*Health professional as trial witness
    (42)
*Hospital and medical staff issues
    (33)
*Human experimentation (41)

*Informed consent (66)
*Introduction to the legal system
    (57)
 Labor relations
 Laboratory medicine
 Long-term care
*Malpractice (64)
 Medical devices
*Medical records (51)
*Medicare/Medicaid (23)
*Mental health law (43)
 Nursing and the law
 Occupational safety and health
 Patient's rights and advocacy
 Pharmacy and the law
 Podiatry and the law
*Practitioner-patient relations (57)
 Preventive medicine
*Professional licensure and disci-
    pline (46)
*PSROs, audit, and quality control
    (21)
 Public health law
*Rape (6)
*Refusing treatment (51)
*Reporting requirements (40)
*Reproduction (32)
 Risk management
*Role of government in financing
    and delivery of health care (34)
 Sterilization
 Toxic substance regulation
*Transplantation (34)
*Treatment against parental beliefs
    or wishes (34)
 Working with legal counsel

*Those items preceded by an asterisk are taken from a 1978 study of health law courses offered in medical schools.[29] The figure in parentheses indicates how many of the 101 schools responding included the topic in their courses (ranging from informed consent, which was included in 66 courses, to rape, which was included in only 6).

making up new law as they go along. And many topics barely covered in the legal literature a few decades ago—such as child abuse reporting, human experimentation, patient's rights, and data confidentiality—are now receiving considerable attention.

It is important to understand the legal prohibitions, requirements, and options in the area in which you work. It is equally important to realize that these constraints exist because of various statutes, regulations, and court decisions, all of which are constantly changing. The goal of this book is not so much to focus on what the law *is* on any particular issue, but rather to explain the general legal thought on each subject and to describe the direction of the changes that are taking place.

NOTES

1. Harold J. Berman and William R. Greiner, *The Nature and Functions of Law*, 3d ed. (Mineola, N.Y.: Foundation Press, 1972), p. 7.
2. The philosophical and political perspectives are especially difficult to distinguish in commentary written in English, which—unlike many other languages—uses the same word, law, to refer both to law as "rules prescribed under the authority of the state or nation" and law as "a system or collection of [and] controlling influence of such rules." *The Random House Dictionary of the English Language* (New York: Random House, 1967), p. 812.
3. See, for example, Ronald L. Akers and Richard Hawkins, *Law and Control in Society* (Englewood Cliffs, N.J.: Prentice-Hall, 1975); Lawrence M. Friedman, *Law and Society: An Introduction* (Englewood Cliffs, N.J.: Prentice-Hall, 1977); Lawrence M. Friedman, *The Legal System: A Social Science Perspective* (New York: Russell Sage Foundation, 1975); Laura Nader, *Law in Culture and Society* (Chicago: Aldine, 1969).

    Just as many physicians are unaware of the principles of the allopathic medicine they practice, many lawyers pay little attention to the nature and function of the legal system of which they are part. Practicing attorneys must be particularly well grounded in the current and technical specifics of law and in the procedure and politics of legal practice; theories and concepts do not settle cases and conflicts. The reverse is true for the layperson; it is the theories and concepts that provide insight into the legal process.
4. See Friedman, *Law and Society*, pp. 10–14. On the other hand, Laura Nader would include additional, latent "extralegal" functions, e.g., status gaining, therapy, and continuation of conflict. See Akers and Hawkins, *Law and Control*, p. 6.
5. Roscoe Pound, "Sociology of Law," in George Gurvitch and Wilbert Moore, eds., *Twentieth Century Sociology* (New York: Philosophical Library, 1945), p. 300. Legal rules not only specify proper conduct for the citizen (so-called primary norms), but also contain a set of secondary norms, intended as guides to the conduct of the various officials charged with enforcing rules. See Akers and Hawkins, *Law and Control*, pp. 14–16.

6. See, for example, Richard Quinney, "The Social Reality of Crime: A Sociology of Criminal Law," reprinted in Akers and Hawkins, *Law and Control,* from Quinney, *The Social Reality of Crime* (Boston: Little, Brown, 1970).

7. From the essays of James Madison through the observations of Alexis de Tocqueville to the works of Robert Dahl, Nelson Polsby, and other contemporary political scientists, pluralism has served as the orthodox political model. See *The Federalist Papers,* Numbers 10 and 51 (New York: New American Library, 1961); Alexis de Tocqueville, *Democracy in America* (Garden City, N.Y.: Doubleday, 1969); Robert A. Dahl, *A Preface to Democratic Theory* (Chicago: University of Chicago Press, 1965); Robert A. Dahl, *Who Governs?* (New Haven: Yale University Press, 1961); Nelson W. Polsby, *Community Power and Political Theory* (New Haven: Yale University Press, 1963).

8. Sociologists such as Vilfredo Pareto, Gaetano Mosca, Robert Michels, and, more recently, C. Wright Mills are particularly identified with the elite model. See C. Wright Mills, *The Power Elite* (New York: Oxford University Press, 1959); also G. William Domhoff, *Who Rules America?* (Englewood Cliffs, N.J.: Prentice-Hall, 1967).

9. The political philosopher Karl Marx was so instrumental in outlining the class model that it can as readily be called the Marxist model. In addition to the standard works of Karl Marx and Frederich Engels, see Ralph Milibard, *The State in Capitalist Society* (New York: Basic Books, 1969) and T. B. Bottomore, *Classes in Modern Society* (New York: Pantheon Books, 1966). Specifically on law, see Maureen Cain, "The Main Themes of Marx's and Engels's Sociology of Law," *British Journal of Law and Society* 1:136 (1974), reprinted in Lawrence M. Friedman and Stewart Macaulay, *Law and the Behavioral Sciences,* 2d ed. (Indianapolis: Bobbs-Merrill, 1977), pp. 653–659. One benchmark that can be used in assessing political developments from the perspective of whose interests are most consistently being favored is the effect of a development, if any, on the pattern of income and wealth distribution in society. Recent summaries of relevant data in this regard can be found in Richard H. deLone, *Small Futures: Children, Inequality, and the Limits of Liberal Reform* (New York: Harcourt Brace Jovanovich, 1979), and William Ryan, *Equality* (New York: Pantheon, 1981).

10. Although "jurisprudence" and "philosophy of law" are often used interchangeably, the former is most accurately applied to the systematic study of law from the perspective of the legal profession, while the latter applies to the philosopher's attempt to define the role of law from the perspective of society. For general readings see Joel Feinberg and Hyman Gross, *Law in Philosophical Perspective* (Encino, Calif.: Dickenson, 1977).

11. Cicero, *Laws,* in Michael M. Foster, *Masters of Political Thought,* vol. I (Boston: Houghton Mifflin Co., 1941), p. 183. Aristotle described law as "reason unaffected by desire." Aristotle, *Politics,* in ibid., p. 159. The natural law concept is also sometimes labeled with the frightening amalgam term: philosophical jurisprudence.

12. Also known as analytic jurisprudence or imperative theory.

13. In a book of this sort the word "state" provides considerable problems. Sometimes—as here—the word refers simply to the political authority or

sovereign government. At other times it is used to refer, in general, to a political subdivision of the United States, i.e., one of the fifty states.

14. John Austin, "The Province of Jurisprudence Determined" (Lecture I), in Philip Shuchman, *Cohen and Cohen's Readings in Jurisprudence and Legal Philosophy*, 2d ed. (Boston: Little, Brown, 1979), p. 13. Positivism works least well as a theoretical description if applied within the pluralist model. It also is time specific, not focusing on why the law is the way it is or on what changes can be expected. By removing ideals from the definition of law, positivism highlights the separateness of ethics as an area of study.

15. James Coolidge Carter, "The Ideal and the Actual in the Law," *American Law Review* 24:752 (1890), in Ervin H. Pollack, *Jurisprudence: Principles and Applications* (Columbus: Ohio State University Press, 1979), p. 360.

16. See Shuchman, *Cohen and Cohen;* Pollack, *Jurisprudence;* Edgar Bodenheimer, *Jurisprudence: The Philosophy and Method of the Law*, rev. ed. (Cambridge: Harvard University Press, 1974); and similar collections and reviews.

17. Oliver Wendell Holmes, Jr., "The Common Law," in Shuchman, *Cohen and Cohen*, p. 397.

18. The extreme version of the pragmatic approach to law was articulated in the 1920s and 1930s by the legal realists, who viewed law primarily in terms of the behavior of the law enforcers—courts, etc.—rather than in the contents of specific laws. "What these officials do about disputes . . . is the law itself," wrote a leading realist, Karl N. Llewellyn, in *The Bramble Bush* (Dobbs Ferry, N.Y.: Oceana Publications, 1960), quoted in Pollack, *Jurisprudence*, p. 792. (Llewellyn later bemoaned the distortion—through overemphasis—that "this lone lorn sentence" brought about. See Llewellyn, *The Common Law Tradition* [Boston: Little, Brown, 1960], quoted in Shuchman, *Cohen and Cohen*, p. 227.) As a characterization of law itself, realism is not particularly prominent today; but its primary focus—the legal order as it actually operates—has been receiving increasing attention by social scientists. This is true, for example, of studies of the impact of different legal *structures* on results or output (and therefore on how a society functions), as well as on how different actors—especially judges and lawyers—affect results. See Friedman and Macaulay, *Law and the Behavioral Sciences*, pp. 888, 905–907. Unfortunately, there is only a limited literature analyzing the effectiveness of particular types of legal *systems* in maximizing specific societal goals. See ibid., pp. 574–575.

19. J. Braxton Craven, Jr., "Paean to Pragmatism," *North Carolina Law Review* 50:977 (1972).

20. Karl N. Llewellyn, "The Normative, the Legal, and the Law-jobs: The Problem of Juristic Method," *Yale Law Journal* 49:1355 (1940), quoted in Berman and Greiner, *Nature and Functions of Law*, p. 6. Otherwise, as Berman and Greiner note (p. 6): "To seek in a liberal arts course a summary of the vast body of legal rules which are to be found in the statute books, the court reports, the blackletter treatises, and the host of other legal materials which make up a law library, is to seek that which is unattainable and which, if it were attained, would be useless."

21. This is not to deny that areas long considered unreachable by the law can suddenly come within its purview as a result of new legislative action or court decisions. It should also be noted that the pattern of what is and what is not within the legal system's purview varies from society to society. In one society failure to aid a stranger in distress may violate a statute or be grounds for a lawsuit, while in another society it may be considered to be strictly a private matter. In one society health care and housing may be viewed as basic legal rights; in another society they may not be.

22. On the latter point, see Howard Zinn et al., *Justice in Everyday Life: The Way it Really Works* (New York: Morrow, 1974).

23. "The History of Legal Medicine," in Francis E. Camps, ed., *Gradwohl's Legal Medicine*, 3d ed. (Chicago: Year Book Medical Publications, 1976), chap. 1. Also see the chronology by Jaroslav Nemec, *Highlights in Medicolegal Relations*, rev. and enl. ed. (Bethesda, Md.: National Library of Medicine, 1976) (DHEW Pub. No. (NIH) 76-1109), as well as William J. Curran, "History and development," in William J. Curran, A. Louis McGarry, and Charles S. Petty, *Modern Legal Medicine, Psychiatry, and Forensic Science* (Philadelphia: F. A. Davis, 1980).

24. Why this increase in health-related law? Clearly a variety of factors are involved, among them: a more litigious society; a widespread loss of trust in experts; a growing awareness of the effects of environmental and occupational hazards on health; a heightened interest in the public's right to information, especially the right to information on oneself; mushrooming federal expenditures on health care, with a variety of regulatory strings attached; and the willingness of courts to deal with matters they had largely ignored in the past (e.g., mental health, juvenile, and abortion rights). In addition, the health care industry's size (over 9 percent of the GNP; the largest single employer) and complexity escalated dramatically in recent decades. Sheer size and complexity in any industry will increase the role played by law and lawyers. Certainly this is the case when the matters dealt with—health, illness, and death—are very much both public and individual concerns.

25. Hospital attorneys probably come the closest to being health law practitioners in that they are from time to time drawn into quite a number of the subtopic areas of health law.

26. William J. Curran, "Titles in the Medicolegal Field: A Proposal for Reform," *American Journal of Law and Medicine* 1:10 (1975). Curran also offers the following related definitions:

> *Forensic medicine:* The specialty areas of medicine, medical science and technology concerned with investigation, preparation, preservation, and presentation of evidence and medical opinion in courts and other legal, correctional, and law-enforcement settings.
>
> *Forensic pathology:* a sub-specialty of pathology concerned with medicolegal autopsies and with primary emphasis on investigation, preparation, preservation and presentation of death-case evidence in law and law-enforcement settings. The forensic pathologist may also be the operational head of a public death investigational program including other forensic medical specialists and forensic scientists.
>
> *Legal medicine:* the specialty areas of medicine concerned with relations with substan-

tive law and with legal institutions. Clinical medical areas—such as the treatment of offenders and trauma medicine related to law—would be included herein.

Medical law: a specialty area of law and law practice related to legal regulation of medicine and medical practice and other legal aspects of medicine.

27. Annas, personal communication.

28. This is in contrast to legal medicine, an area of medicine defined by the ways in which medicine serves as a tool in achieving certain legal objectives. Here the goals are law oriented and defined in terms of law, but the experts are the health professionals.

29. Barbara Ruhe Grumet, "Legal Medicine in Medical Schools: A Survey of the State of the Art," *Journal of Medical Education* 54:755–758 (1979). Also see "A Recommended Medical-Legal Curriculum," *Journal of Legal Medicine* (February 1977), pp. 8EE–8GG. For a review of health law courses offered at law schools, see Carl J. Schramm and Mary S. Hencke, "The Teaching of Health Law in 1980: Results of a Survey," *Journal of Health Politics, Policy and Law* 6:558–561 (1981).

2

The Legal System in the United States

We are under a Constitution but the Constitution is what the judges say it is.

—Charles Evans Hughes[1]

THE "WHAT-IS-LAW?" DISCUSSION in the previous chapter would apply with equal validity to any legal system: ancient or modern; French or Chinese; centralized or decentralized.[2] However, although the basic nature and function of law may remain the same in all legal systems, the rules and structures will vary widely. In order to understand the operation of a particular legal system, it is therefore necessary to know something about its basic components. This chapter will provide this basic operational information on the legal system of the United States, with particular emphasis on the judicial system.

Actually there is no "legal system of the United States." Instead there are fifty-one legal systems, those of the fifty states plus the federal system, and much of constitutional law is concerned with defining the relationship between the federal and state systems. Each of these systems evolved in its own way, each with its own constitution, its own legislation, and its own judicial decisions. The result is a complex and voluminous set of laws, but the basic components are similar enough that generic discussion is possible.

The U.S. legal system is best understood if viewed in terms of a system that divides the powers of government into three separate branches—legislative, executive, and judicial[3]—with the constitution establishing the framework. Each of the three branches creates law in varying form, so that on both state and federal levels four different "types" of law can be distinguished, based on the origin or authority for each: constitutionally based law, legislatively based law, regulations, or administratively based law, and judicially based, or common, law.[4]

1. *Constitutional law,* under which the Constitution of the United States provides the basic authority for the U.S. legal system, stands above all other types of law, including individual state constitutions and legal systems.[5] The Constitution defines the functions, powers, and limits of government. State constitutions provide the same basic definitions of authority on the state level.[6]

The U.S. Constitution is a short and generally worded document. That there shall be a president who will serve a four-year term, that legislative power will be vested in a House and Senate, and that the states shall not coin money are straightforward provisions. But nothing is said about the structure of the judicial system other than declaring that there shall be a Supreme Court. The states are guaranteed a republican form of government, without any explanation of what that means. Numerous key terms are left completely undefined; for example, general welfare, necessary and proper, due process, cruel and unusual punishment, unreasonable search and seizure. This ambiguity has made it possible for the Constitution to be, in Charles Beard's words, "a living thing."

2. *Statutory law* is that created by legislative bodies—the Congress, state legislatures, and city councils—which govern a wide variety of human endeavors, usually with the purpose of declaring, commanding, or prohibiting something. These enactments are known as statutes or, on a municipal level, ordinances, to distinguish them from the three other types of law. Statutes must be consistent with the U.S. Constitution (and, in the case of state and local statutes, with the individual state constitutions), and may be repealed or revised by later legislation. Through statutory law government is supposed to make policy choices, translating public needs and demands into official programs and restrictions.

3. *Administrative law* consists of the rules and regulations issued by departments, offices, and bureaus to translate the broadly worded federal, state, and local statutes into operating standards. Legislators rarely have the technical expertise to develop detailed laws on the wide range of human activities on which they legislate. Moreover, if a legislative body were to attempt to enact laws detailed enough to anticipate and deal with all possible applications of any law, they would face two insurmountable problems. First, they would find that setting all the specific

standards for a single statute—especially one as broad in impact as the Medicare law or the Federal Food, Drug, and Cosmetic Act—would take all their time (and even then likely remain unfinished), leaving no time to devote to any other subject. In addition, they would produce an extremely rigid set of laws; the legislative process is one of political maneuvering and compromise; once agreement is reached, modification is difficult.

The solution is for legislatures to enact broadly worded statutes establishing basic goals, policies, and ground rules and then to delegate the task of working out the details to administrative agencies. This involves developing regulations. Regulations have the force of law; they control what government does and does not do, and what individuals may and may not do.[7] Thus, for example, a state statute may authorize pharmacists to substitute generic equivalents in filling prescriptions unless specifically instructed not to. It then becomes the responsibility of an administrative agency, such as the State Department of Public Health, to develop regulations listing acceptable generic equivalents and to specify what a physician must do if he or she wants to prohibit such substitution. In explaining this filling-in-the-blanks function, Supreme Court Justice Robert H. Jackson once described statutes as "unfinished law which the administrative body must complete before it is ready for application."[8]

Although law most often is thought of in terms of legislative enactments and judicial decrees, administrative or regulatory law has become so vast in scope that three decades ago Justice Jackson could already observe that "The rise of administrative bodies has been the most significant legal trend of the last century and perhaps more values today are affected by their decisions than by those of all the courts. . . ."[9] Chapter 3 explores administrative law and the regulatory process in some detail.

The fact that administrative agencies are not directly responsible to the public—i.e., not elected—periodically provokes outcries regarding the influence of "faceless bureaucrats." There are three important rejoinders to such concern. First, there is no realistic alternative; elected bodies cannot cope with the sheer magnitude of the regulatory task. Second, administrative agencies must follow specific rules and processes in developing regulations. Third, just as statutes must be consistent with statutory law, the agency issuing a regulation must have proper statutory authorization, and the regulation must not violate either the general purpose or the specific provisions of the relevant statute.

4. *Common law*, perhaps the most difficult type of law to define, is judge-made law, as opposed to law created by legislative or administrative bodies, and theoretically derives from earlier decisions (legal precedent) and custom and tradition dating back to "immemorial antiquity" in England.[10] The entire body of judicial decisions therefore constitutes an important type of law.

One could envision a different type of legal system: one in which courts called upon to resolve legal disputes in areas where no statutory law applied would reach a decision based simply on logic and fairness. What any other court had said about a similar dispute would be irrelevant. In such a system, a judicial decision would affect the parties involved but would have no continuing significance; the judge's reasoning could be forgotten. Such a system could be fair, efficient, and maybe even predictable. It would also make it desirable to develop statutes and regulations to cover as many areas of human activity as possible, thereby minimizing the need for judges to make decisions without recourse to statutory and regulatory law.

This type of approach, the civil law system, characterized classical Roman law and is strongly reflected in the current legal systems of Western Europe, Latin America, and the French-influenced parts of the world (including Quebec and Louisiana). But it is not the approach adopted from England by the United States. Most of the English-influenced countries of the world follow the common law system, wherein a court called upon to resolve a legal dispute in an area where no statutory law applies will look to and be guided by what other courts—or the same court—have previously decided in similar disputes. Thus, past decisions—*precedents*—become a type of law in themselves. The principle is that a past decision, i.e., the rationale for its outcome, must be followed by a court when it next confronts the same question, as well as by all subordinate courts.[11]

When past decisions serve as an authoritative set of guidelines, there is less need for statutes and regulations. During the early history of the United States, common law principles—developed over centuries by courts in England and the United States—served as the relevant law; statutes were not at all the favored mechanism for social control and conflict resolution. Even though statutes will supersede it, common law is still the basis for much of the law in the United States, especially as regards private law, such as personal injury (torts), contracts, and property. In most states today, if one person sues another for malpractice, libel, or breach of contract, the legal principles governing the outcome will not be found in any statute book but in the common law as contained in reported judicial decision. Similarly, the courts have been guided by common law in deciding recent cases involving the termination of medical treatment for the hopelessly ill.

Every state has its own body of common law, developed independently by its own courts, although a few states—especially Louisiana and to a lesser extent California and Texas—have been influenced by the European civil law system. Civil law emphasizes a statutory *code* "systematically arranged into chapters, subheads, table of contents, and index [to make a] complete body of laws designed to regulate completely subjects to which they relate."[12] Several other states have a partial type of codification in which the common law for certain subjects areas, such as criminal law, is arranged into a "code" which is then enacted by the legislature as a statute. The code approach makes it considerably easier to determine what the law is on a particular point; with common law the authority to be consulted is the gigantic and disparate collection of all past court decisions.

Because published court decisions run into the millions, because the reasoning behind these decisions is often less than clear or succinct, and because common law adopts Anglo-American custom and tradition as influential, common law is amorphous. Court A may write an opinion explaining the rationale for a decision. Court B may rely on the earlier opinion of court A in reaching a decision on a similar issue. Yet the two decisions may be different enough to provide subsequent courts with two different rationales to choose from when applying "established precedent." Still, as Fred Rodell noted, "The common law is actually closer to the Law with a capital L than any constitution or statute ever written."[13] It is that part of law which remains most obscure to nonlawyers and, therefore, most requiring the skills of a lawyer for interpretation: "The ultimate expression of the domination of the legal profession in the legal order."[14]

As might be imagined, this collection of constitutions, statutes, regulations, and judicial opinions makes for an overwhelming body of written law. Legal research is very much a matter of locating the relevant parts of this mass, and many of the tools of legal research consist of guides, indexes, summaries, and digests. A major objective of the lawyer using these tools is to locate authoritative materials—statutes, prior cases, etc.—that will persuade a particular court hearing a particular case that it has no clear choice but to decide in favor of the lawyer's client. This can be a detailed and exhausting research enterprise if done well. Yet the nature of this task does not mean that a law library cannot be a useful source of information to the nonlawyer seeking general information on a particular topic.

How the System Works:
The Key Role of Judges

In order to understand how the U.S. legal system works, it is necessary to explore the way in which constitutional, statutory, regulatory, and common law—the basic building blocks of the system—are used and how they interrelate. As already explained, common law bows to relevant statutes, if any; regulations are only valid when consistent with authorizing statutory law; and all three must be consistent with state and federal constitutions. However, this is not a self-enforcing procedural hierarchy. If it were, one could program into a computer all the constitutions, statutes, regulations, and court decisions extant (along with rules of judicial and administrative procedure) and the computer would determine what the law is for any given situation. In fact, however, the real legal system is fraught with disagreement, with the law on any particular point varying considerably, from place to place, from time to time, and from lawyer to lawyer. Sholom Aleichem noted, "Lawyers are just like physicians; what one says, the other contradicts." The reason for the ambiguity is that applying law to a specific dispute means applying abstract principles to a definite set of facts, i.e., legal interpretation. Someone has to decide what the true meaning of the law is, and that someone will be a judge.

Interpretation takes the form of a written judicial opinion. Lower level courts most often render a decision without offering any elucidation of the reason. Of course if all courts did this, the precedent-based legal system could not function, since the explanation for a decision is in many ways as important as the outcome. But appellate courts do issue opinions—often several on the same decision, reflecting the differing views on a multijudge court.[15] This judicial power to interpret and decide the law is undeniably a tremendous one. Moreover, the scope afforded judges in interpreting the law can be quite broad. If the interpretation is of the common law, the opportunity for controlling the outcome is considerable; for despite what was said earlier about the value attached to adhering to prior decisions, only a higher court—or a legislative change in the law—can effectively call a court to task for ignoring precedent. Even when interpretation is of a statute or regulation, courts will have considerable latitude in determining what a legislature or administrative body "really" meant when writing laws. Most significant of all, however, is the area of constitutional law, where judicial power truly reigns supreme.

That the judiciary should have such considerable power was not at all evident at the outset. The U.S. Constitution merely provides that "The judicial Power of the United States, shall be vested in one Supreme Court, and in such inferior Courts as the Congress may from time to time ordain and establish . . ." and then goes on to explain that "The judicial Power shall extend to all Cases, in Law and Equity, arising under this Constitution, the Laws of the United States, and Treaties . . . ." Not a word is mentioned suggesting Supreme Court authority to void as unconstitutional statutes passed by Congress or state legislatures.[16]

In the Judiciary Act of 1789 Congress chose to "ordain and establish" a system of inferior federal courts, a system that has survived with remarkably little change to the present day. Except for some specialized courts, such as the U.S. Tax Court and the Court of Customs and Patent

Appeals,[17] the federal courts constitute a simple three-tier system: on the lowest tier are the federal district courts, with the nation currently divided into ninety-seven judicial districts;[18] these, in turn, are grouped to fit under one of twelve federal appeals courts, which have authority to review and alter the decisions of the district courts under them; at the top, the U.S. Supreme Court carries out the review function over appellate decisions.[19] When hearing appeals, these higher courts consider only written and oral arguments regarding legal issues; they do not usually review the facts involved in a case. Some controversies, such as those between two state governments, can be brought directly to the Supreme Court, but most cases reach the highest court after a losing party asks the Justices to review a lower court decision. With very few exceptions the Court is free to pick and choose among such requests, agreeing to accept about three hundred cases annually out of some twenty-seven hundred it is asked to consider.[20]

Not until several years after the federal judicial system was established did the Supreme Court consider the extent of the federal courts' authority when confronted with a statute seemingly in conflict with the Constitution.[21] *Marbury v. Madison*,[22] decided in 1803, has come to stand for two propositions that are today taken for granted:

1. That it "is emphatically the province and duty of the judicial department to say what the law is."
2. "That a law repugnant to the constitution is void; and that courts, as well as other departments, are bound by that instrument."

Taken together these propositions lead to an implied conclusion: It is up to the courts, especially the Supreme Court, to determine whether or not a statute is valid. Inherent in this conclusion is a tremendous power.

However, it was not until over half a century later that the U.S. Supreme Court again held an act of Congress unconstitutional. By contrast, in the twentieth century the power to void federal and state statutes as being unconstitutional has been used with increasing frequency, with many such decisions—for example, those regarding abortion laws—of tremendous political and social impact. This exercise of *judicial supremacy* has consistently generated criticism. One of the first to complain was Thomas Jefferson, who wrote:

> Our Constitution . . . intending to establish three departments, coordinate and independent, that they might check and balance one another, . . . has given [according to recent developments] to one of them alone the right to prescribe rules for the government of the others, and to that one, too, which is unelected by and independent of the nation. . . . The Constitution, on this hypothesis, is a mere thing of wax in the hands of the judiciary which they may twist and shape into any form they please.[23]

Jefferson's words are repeated anew today every time the Court invalidates congressional legislation, although it is highly unlikely that judicial supremacy will be significantly altered.[24]

Complaints about judicial usurpation would be quite silly if the Supreme Court was merely applying logic and a constitutional template in a more-or-less computerlike fashion. But in reality judges—at all levels—have considerable leeway in interpreting constitutions, statutes, regulations, and the common law. And this leeway is exploited, often quite effectively. As Justice Holmes pointed out, "The true grounds of decisions are consideration of policy and of social advantage, and it is vain to suppose that solutions can be attained merely by logic and the general propositions of law which nobody disputes."[25]

This is all quite understandable. Law consists of written words, many of which are ambiguous. Judges are human beings, not computers, and are influenced by their individual backgrounds, including their education (both general and legal), family and personal associations, wealth and social position, legal and political experience, political affiliations and opinions, and intellectual and temperamental traits.[26] The result is that judicial decisions are exercises in political pragmatism. As one distinguished federal appeals judge put it:

> I believe that there are only two kinds of judges at all levels of courts: those who are admittedly (maybe not to the public) result-oriented, and those who are also result-oriented but either do not know it or decline for various purposes to admit it.[27]

There is nothing sinister in this. Decisions rendered by courts—especially those rendered by the highest level of courts and especially decisions involving constitutional questions—are basically policy decisions. As Judge Craven notes, "The controlling principle, seldom expressed, is expendiency: What is best for the nation?"[28]

The only reason that this point is worth belaboring is that nonlawyers tend to have an idealized view of the Court or, perhaps more accurately, tend to accept both the myth and the reality simultaneously. Robert Dahl points out:

> As a political institution, the Court is highly unusual, not least because Americans are not quite willing to accept the fact that it is a political institution and not quite capable of denying it . . . frequently we take both positions at once.[29]

The mythical view of nonpolitical judges who "find" rather than "make" the law is sustained in large part by the mystique surrounding the judicial process, particularly the Supreme Court. Judges wear long robes, sit on elevated platforms in templelike surroundings, and are referred to in respectful terms. Although the several members of appellate courts will often disagree on both the result and rationale of a decision, courts are often viewed as having but one voice. An "opinion of the court" seems consistent with the view that judges find rather than make law; the blunt fact that five judges outvoted four others to decide a case is far less awesome. Although it is difficult to determine how many people actually believe it, the national political folklore includes the idea that upon donning judicial robes and ascending to the bench, formerly politically active men and women become politically impartial, indifferent to the factors that had previously guided their ideological outlook. As a result, even though courts are frequently lambasted over unpopular decisions and even though courts depend entirely on the other branches of government to enforce their decisions and provide their financial support, the Supreme Court, as well as the lesser courts, has been remarkably successful in maintaining respect and, with it, political authority. (Of course one aspect of the political astuteness of the Supreme Court has been extreme care in never going so far out on a limb as to provoke actual confrontation with the executive and/or legislative branches—a stance reflected in a general policy of deciding cases on the narrowest possible grounds.)

How is judicial policymaking carried out? The greatest latitude for rationalizing a judicial outcome is found when constitutional issues are involved in a case. Sometimes this broad latitude results in judicial flipflops, such as the *Brown v. Board of Education* reversal of the Court's previous approval of "separate but equal." Sometimes the Supreme Court creates entirely new areas of law, as with the series of privacy right decisions launched by *Griswold v. Connecticut.* More common than either reversal or originality, however, is the positive use of precedent, carefully choosing those earlier decisions consistent with a desired result and asserting that, unlike any inconsistent decisions, they were based on factual situations most like those in the present case. Since any lawsuit will involve innumerable facts, there is always considerable opportunity for picking and choosing the "most relevant" facts. The converse of this approach—to be used when precedent is uniformly nonsupportive—is to focus on the specific facts of the case under consideration, arguing that they are so unique as to require an entirely new legal approach. Judges can also rely on legal *principles,*[30] i.e., general statements distilled by legal scholars from the totality of decisions involving a particular issue. The trouble with legal principles, however, is that, like the precedents from which they are derived, they can be used selectively to justify virtually any argument. So, for example, one common principle of negligence law is that people should not be liable for reasonably unforeseeable consequences of their negligence, while another common principle is that negligent persons must take existing circumstances as they find them. Finally, courts also have broad latitude when called upon to interpret the meaning of specific statutory language; by focusing on different aspects of the legislative history and by relying on different legal principles, judges can often arrive at diametrically different conclusions.[31]

The important point to be grasped in all of this is that courts are one type of political body and laws the formal enunciations of these bodies. Judges decide what the law is, but the judicial process neither is magical incantation nor based on intellectual insight unattainable by lesser mortals. Rather, the power of judicial pronouncement lies in the speaker, not the statement, and accurate prediction of judicial outcomes requires political understanding. Laurence Tribe, a leading constitutional scholar, concludes:

> As Justice Robert Jackson once observed of the Court, "We are not final because we are infallible, but we are infallible only because we are final." And the Courts that held slaves to be nonpersons, separate to be equal, and pregnancy to be non sex-related can hardly be deemed either final *or* infallible.[32]

The Court System

Most disputes are resolved without resort to the courts. Similarly, most lawsuits are settled while awaiting trial and most of the remainder decided with finality at the lowest rung of the judicial system: the trial courts. Appellate level courts are important, but they are merely the tip of the iceberg. State and federal trial judges are more involved in the day-to-day handling of straightforward disputes than in the fashioning of new legal doctrine. In fact, state trial court judges usually do not prepare written opinions. Trial courts therefore function somewhat according to the classical model of "applying" the law. This does not mean, however, that they are not recognized as political bodies in their own right. The author of a basic introduction to the court system notes that as recently as the mid-1960s "the proposition that courts are part of the political system was a relatively daring one. . . . Now that proposition is part of the accepted wisdom."[33]

The structure of the court system is complex, especially on the state level. Moreover, the judicial structure of every state differs from that of the other states—and of the federal court system. Fortunately, most of the complexity—in terms of jurisdiction, rules for appellate review, and actual court procedure—need not preoccupy the nonlawyer, for anyone brought face-to-face with the court system should be there with the assistance of legal counsel, who will be familiar with these technical aspects. However, several major features of the court system should be noted here:

1. Because of the dual state-federal nature of the U.S. legal system, an initial question in any legal dispute is whether it should be brought into federal or state court. A dispute involving federal law would be handled in federal court and a dispute involving state law in state court. But disputes involving state law in which the parties are from different states may be heard in federal court. Disputes involving both federal and state law may be brought into either court system. Generally, federal courts decide questions involving the U.S. Constitution and state courts decide questions involving state constitutions. Because the two systems have different politics, different procedures, and different substantive law, getting into the right court can make a significant difference. The great majority of both criminal and civil cases are brought in state courts, since they involve state constitutions, statutes, regulations, and common law and do not involve federal questions.

2. The state court systems follow a hierarchy similar to that of the federal system, with trial courts at the bottom and a supreme court at the top,[34] although only twenty-three states have an intermediate appellate court level. The complexity found at the trial court level generally reflects population size. A large city in a populous state is likely to have an array of different trial courts. Inferior courts, often called municipal courts, handle minor disputes, traffic offenses, and the like. (In rural areas the counterpart of the inferior courts are justice-of-the-peace courts.[35]) These minor trial courts usually function without juries and rarely keep a permanent record of proceedings. Circuit, superior, county, or district court is the name often given to the type of trial court that handles more serious cases, involving more money in civil cases and longer potential prison terms in criminal cases. Very large cities often have additional specialized courts, such as family court, small claims court, traffic court, or probate court. In some jurisdictions separate criminal and civil (noncriminal) courts exist, while elsewhere both criminal and civil cases may be handled by the same court.

3. Although trial court decisions can be appealed, only a small fraction are. The time and money required discourage even the strongest case for appellate reversal. For most lawsuits, therefore, the trial court judge has the final word. That is why it makes an important difference as to which judge hears a case. One of the trial lawyer's key skills is getting cases before those judges most likely to reach a desired outcome. This is a tricky enterprise; some judges are strict, some lenient; some innovative, some rulebound; some honest, some on the take; some fair, some highly prejudiced.

4. Finally, the fact that courts are predominantly political institutions is most apparent at the trial court level (and more apparent in the state

rather than federal court systems). The political nature and function of courts make them the object of considerable political maneuvering.

Courts, Law, and Legal Rights

Although they may be forbidding places to most people, courts are also popularly viewed as guarantors of fundamental rights. "Rights" is an ambiguous term. "To have a right," wrote John Stuart Mill, "is . . . to have something which society ought to defend me in the possession of." To be meaningful, such a right must be one that a court would recognize and enforce.[36]

There are two bases on which a court may recognize individual rights. First, there are *civil rights,* granted and defined by statute and common law, which belong to every citizen of the state or nation by virtue of their citizenship. These rights are positive in nature; they can be asserted by one person against another and redressed or enforced in a civil action, e.g., a lawsuit by an unsuccessful applicant to a school of nursing who asserts that his rights under the Federal Rehabilitation Act of 1973 have been denied.

A second basis for legal rights, more correctly termed civil liberties, is found in various provisions of the U.S. and state constitutions. These rights, which are negative in nature, can be traced back to the first ten amendments of the Constitution—the Bill of Rights; they define those things government cannot do to the individual, but do not provide anything that the individual can positively invoke.[37]

Because health measures can lead to government control of many aspects of life, civil liberties protections have a clear relevance to health law. The Fourth Amendment prohibition on unreasonable government searches has been held to limit the way in which health inspections can be conducted, and the Eighth Amendment ban on cruel and unusual punishment has been used to define an acceptable minimum level of medical care provided to prisoners. On the other hand, the free exercise of religion provision in the First Amendment has not prevented government from enforcing health measures, such as vaccination, against individuals who objected on religious grounds. Nor have any of the provisions of the Bill of Rights prevented government from carrying out involuntary sterilization programs.

Two quite general provisions in the amendments to the U.S. Constitution have played especially important roles in defining how laws are created and enforced. These provisions can be found in the Fourteenth Amendment, which specifies that "No State shall . . . deprive any person of life, liberty, or property, without due process of law; nor deny any person within its jurisdiction the equal protection of the laws." The *due process* provision requires basic fairness in the procedural application of the law (such things as notice, hearing, and a right to defend oneself). *Equal protection* requires an evenhandedness in the application of the law, with similarly situated individuals being similarly treated by government. Equal protection does not mean that laws can never make differentiations between categories of people, but rather that such differentiations must have a rational basis, being substantially related to an important and legitimate governmental objective. Zoning law that requires that apartment buildings contain a minimum percentage of tenants over sixty-five years old may be upheld as consistent with a legitimate governmental interest. But a governmental health clinic that treated whites only would clearly violate the equal protection clause.[38]

What happens if Congress or a state legislature enacts a law in disregard of any of the provisions just described? In principle the law is invalid as being "repugnant to the Constitution." But only the courts can make such a determination. This means that an individual or group must challenge the law, in many cases by violating it and then claiming, in defense, that the law should be declared invalid.[39] Everything said earlier about judicial interpretation will of course apply in such situations: results can be fluid, inconsistent, subjective, and—always—political. Thus it is very important to keep in mind that "constitutional rights" are not guarantees cast in stone; they vary with the times.[40] Several of the chapters that follow will illustrate this fact with health examples, involving such disparate topics as abortion, mental hospital admission, health inspections, and physician advertising.

Conclusion

Oliver Wendell Holmes, Jr., in an oft-quoted sentence, once remarked that "The prophecies of what the court will do in fact, and nothing more pretentious, are what I mean by law."[41] Charles Evans Hughes's observation is repeatedly quoted: "We are under a Constitution, but the Constitution is what the judges say it is."[42] These renowned Supreme Court justices offer nonlawyers an important antidote to the vision of law as a force in itself, to the myth of law as a combination of principle and logic. Such idealized views of law make it difficult to understand what is really going on—and why. Understanding is possible; appreciation of a less idealized view of law will make the succeeding chapters more helpful.

NOTES

1. Charles Evans Hughes, *Addresses and Papers* (1908), quoted in Louis Fisher, *The Constitution Between Friends* (New York: St. Martin's Press, 1978), p. 6. Charles Evans Hughes served as a justice of the United States Supreme

Court (1910–1916) and as chief justice (1930–1941). He was also governor of New York (1907–1910), the Republican presidential nominee in 1916, and U.S. secretary of state (1921–1925).

2. See Lawrence M. Friedman, *The Legal System: A Social Science Perspective* (New York: Russell Sage Foundation, 1975), esp. chaps. 1 and 6. Also see Lawrence M. Friedman, *Law and Society, An Introduction* (Englewood Cliffs, N.J.: Prentice-Hall, 1977), esp. chaps. 1, 4, and 5.

3. As will be discussed later in the chapter—and in Chapter 3—even this is not quite accurate because of the quasi-"fourth branch" status of administrative agencies.

4. These four constitute the more formal sources of law. (For the sake of completeness, treaties might be added as a fifth type, but it is obviously a highly specialized and limited type.) Informal sources of law include standards of justice, principles of reason, individual equity, public policy, moral convictions, social trends, and custom. See Edgar Bodenheimer, *Jurisprudence: The Philosophy and Method of Law*, rev. ed. (Cambridge: Harvard University Press, 1974), pp. 324–325.

5. Specifically, the Constitution fulfills four fundamental functions; establishing a national government, controlling the relationship between the national and state governments, defining and preserving personal liberties, and enabling the national government to perpetuate itself. See Jerre S. Williams, *Constitutional Analysis in a Nutshell* (St. Paul: West, 1979), pp. 33–36.

6. State constitutions are similar to the federal Constitution in defining powers and functions of government. But state constitutions will usually be more detailed than is the federal Constitution, outlining mechanisms for local government, financing of various state activities, and the like.

7. Although primarily a matter of administrative practicality, delegation to administrative agencies is also a way in which legislators can avoid having to make some politically sensitive decisions by leaving them for the more politically insulated agencies to make.

   In developing regulations, administrative agencies are engaging in what is often described as a "quasi-legislative" function. Administrative agencies also engage in determining—on a case-by-case basis—how regulations are to be applied to specific situations: a "quasi-judicial" function.

   In its proper usage in the U.S. legal system (European usage is broader) the term "administrative law" refers only to the procedural aspects of administrative agency activity and regulations; it does not include the substantive law contained in the body of regulations. See Kenneth C. Davis, *Administrative Law Text*, 3d ed. (St. Paul: West, 1972), p. 2. But it is not uncommon for administrative law to be used to refer generally to all the law that has its origins in administrative agencies.

8. *Federal Trade Commission v. Rubberoid*, 343 U.S. 470 (1952) (dissent) at pp. 485, 487. In any citation of a judicial decision, the first number following the names of the parties refers to the volume of collected opinions in which the decision is to be found; the letters in the middle of the reference indicate the particular series of volumes involved; and the final number gives the page on which the decision begins. The year in which the case was decided usually follows in parentheses. Thus 343 U.S. 470 (1952) indicates a 1952 decision which can be found beginning on page 470 of volume 343 of the *United States*

Reports, the officially published decisions of the U.S. Supreme Court. For more on citation form, see the Appendix.

9. Ibid.

10. See, for example, Daniel Oran, *Law Dictionary for Non-Lawyers* (St. Paul: West, 1975), p. 67. Common law is also defined by being distinguished from equity law. Early English law evolved to a point of such procedural rigidity that many legitimate complaints could not be remedied by existing law simply because they did not fit into the proper procedural cubbyhole. The king's chancellor, and later a separate Chancery Court system, came into being in order to deal with such problems in terms of "equity" rather than "law." In the United States this dual system has usually become simply two different sets of rules followed by the same court. While a court sitting in law in a civil suit is limited largely to the awarding of damages as a final order to the parties before it, a court sitting in equity has broader powers, especially direct orders to do or not do something (in the form of an injunction). This is obviously of critical importance if the complaint is a repeating one, such as the draining of sewerage onto a neighbor's land. Equity has developed its own set of established rules and procedures, but the guiding principle is supposed to be that no legal right should be without an adequate legal remedy.

11. The principle is not applied horizontally between states; an Illinois court will not be bound by what a Michigan court has decided. As will be discussed later in this chapter, the highest court of a jurisdiction can specifically overrule a prior decision, and a lower court can ignore an earlier decision of a higher court, by distinguishing the facts from the case it is considering or by noting the changed nature of the times.

12. *Black's Law Dictionary*, 4th ed. (St. Paul: West, 1951), p. 323.

13. Fred Rodell, *Woe Unto You, Lawyers!* (New York: Berkley, 1980), p. 20.

14. Morton Horwitz, in Philip Shuchman, *Cohen and Cohen's Readings in Jurisprudence and Legal Philosophy,* (Boston: Little, Brown, 1979), p. 728. One question unlikely to occur to the nonlawyer is whether the federal courts follow state or federal common law when considering "diversity of citizenship" cases, i.e., civil cases brought to federal court because the parties are from different states. In 1842 the Supreme Court held that the federal courts were to follow "general principles of common law," which established the basis for a unique set of federal common law principles. This system was abandoned in a 1938 Supreme Court decision. The federal courts now look to the common law of the state in which the issue in contention occurred. In the 1870s about 40 percent of litigation reaching the Supreme Court involved common law; today virtually none does.

15. Sometimes a majority of an appellate court will agree not only regarding a decision, but also on the rationale, so that the opinion written by one judge can be characterized as the opinion of the court. At other times the majority may disagree so much over rationale that there is no opinion "of the court" but only a collection of opinions, each representing the view of one or more judges. For an interesting description of political infighting over the assignment of opinion writing on the U.S. Supreme Court, see Bob Woodward and Scott Armstrong, *The Brethren: Inside the Supreme Court* (New York: Simon & Schuster, 1979).

16. Some people—e.g., Roul Berger—continue to argue that the Supreme Court acquired its power of judicial review through usurpation. Others, such as historians Charles Beard and H. Allen Smith and Supreme Court Justice Byron White argue that this power was an intended part of the Constitution. Of course it is a moot point; whatever its origins, the Court's power of judicial review is permanently established. Moreover, this point should not be confused with the founders' intentions regarding the superior federal role. As made clear in creation of the federal court system, the emphasis—as with all of the Constitution—was on a strong national government.

17. Other special courts are the U.S. Court of Claims and the U.S. Court of Military Appeals. See William C. Louthan, *The Politics of Justice* (Port Washington, N.Y.: Kennikat Press, 1979), pp. 55–56.

18. Federal district courts hear three main types of cases: (1) criminal cases involving violations of federal criminal statutes; (2) civil cases involving a "federal question," i.e., requiring an interpretation of the U.S. Constitution or federal statute; (3) civil cases (with more than $10,000 involved) where the parties are citizens of different states.

19. This appellate jurisdiction is authorized, not required, by the Constitution. Congress could limit the scope of Supreme Court appellate review sharply— or completely.

20. See Louthan, *Politics of Justice*, pp. 53–55.

21. The Court actually decided that statutes were unconstitutional and therefore invalid on two earlier occasions, but was too timid to put such an idea in a written opinion.

22. 1 Cranch 137, 2L.Ed.60 (1803).

23. Letter to Judge Spencer Roane, September 6, 1819. In Merrill D. Peterson, ed., *The Portable Jefferson* (New York: Viking Press, 1975), pp. 562–563.

24. Technically this would merely require an act of Congress eliminating the Court's appellate jurisdiction, a proposal currently being advanced by conservative Senators Helms and Thurmond.

25. Holmes, dissenting, in *Vegelahn v. Guntner*, 167 Mass. 92, 105–106 (1896).

26. This list is derived from C. G. Haines: General observations on the effects of personal, political, and economic influences in the decisions of judges. *Illinois Law Review* 17:96 (1922); reprinted in Shuchman, *Cohen and Cohen*. To this list can be added efforts to manipulate judicial thinking after the judge assumes the bench. Interestingly, the behavior of juries has been studied more fully than the behavior of judges.

27. J. Braxton Craven, Jr., "Paean to Pragmatism." *North Carolina Law Review* 50:977 (1972). Judge Craven qualifies this observation somewhat by granting that there is a "group of cases, perhaps thirty to forty percent of the total volume, that can be decided but one way." (He notes that Justice Benjamin Cardozo once estimated 50 percent for this group.) These cases with less leeway for judicial decision making more likely would involve statutory rather than constitutional law, more likely would be cases decided in lower level courts.

28. Craven, "Paean to Pragmatism." It is at this point that the differences between the three models of political power and control become crucial, since the elite and class models are not consistent with the concept of a unified

"national interest." See Chapter 1. Craven also goes on to note that "Sometimes the true rationale of decision is never mentioned. Worse, it may be covered up and buried beneath page after page of legalese."

29. Robert A. Dahl, "Decision-Making in a Democracy: The Supreme Court as National Policymaker," *Journal of Public Law* 6:279 (1967). In Joel B. Grossman and Richard S. Wells, *Constitutional Law and Judicial Policy Making* (New York: John Wiley, 1972), p. 4.

30. *Black's Law Dictionary*, p. 1357, defines principle as a "fundamental truth or doctrine; a comprehensive rule or doctrine which furnishes a basis or origin for others; a settled rule of action, procedure, or legal determination. A truth or proposition so clear that it cannot be proved or contradicted unless by a proposition which is still clearer."

31. Karl Llewellyn discusses the "very real leeway" the plethora of legal principles affords the highest courts and provides several examples regarding the interpretation of statutes, such as "A statute cannot go beyond its text" vs. "To effect its purpose a statute may be implemented beyond its text." See Llewellyn, "Remarks on the Theory of Appellate Decision and the Rules of Canons About How Statutes Are to Be Construed," *Vanderbilt Law Review* 3:395 (1950). In Ervin H. Pollack, *Jurisprudence: Principles and Applications* (Columbus: Ohio State University Press, 1979), p. 853.

32. Laurence H. Tribe, *American Constitutional Law* (Mineola, N.Y.: Foundation Press, 1978), p. iii.

33. Herbert Jacob, *Justice in America: Courts, Lawyers, and the Judicial Process*, 3d ed. (Boston: Little, Brown, 1978), pp. v, vii. Also see Louthan, *Politics of Justice*, chap. 3, and John A. Robertson, *Rough Justice: Perspectives on Lower Criminal Courts* (Boston: Little, Brown, 1974).

34. Terminology varies, however. In New York the state's highest court is called the Court of Appeals, while the major trial courts are called Supreme Courts.

35. Louthan, *Politics of Justice*, pp. 42–43.

36. Or, at least, that there is a strong likelihood that a court would enforce it, even though the right previously has not received judicial acceptance. See the further discussion of a "right" to health in Chapter 9, particularly at note 44.

37. A conceptually similar categorization of rights distinguishes between positive "claim rights"—e.g., government entitlements—and negative "liberty rights"—e.g., freedom not to be interfered with.

38. In addition to the direct effect of the Due Process and Equal Protection clauses on the states, the Fourteenth Amendment has had two other legacies. First, in attempting to define what is meant by due process, the Supreme Court has determined that the most useful guidance can be found in the first ten amendments to the Constitution. The Court has therefore applied most—but not all—of the Bill of Rights restriction on federal action to the states. Thus neither the states nor the federal government can pass laws establishing religion or restricting the free exercise of religion; abridging the freedom of speech, press, or assembly; or limiting a fair, impartial public trial and the assistance of counsel in serious criminal cases. And the states are also held to the strictures against unreasonable search and seizure,

self-incrimination, and cruel and unusual punishment. Second, the Court has in turn used the Fifth Amendment Due Process provision to require that the federal government refrain from discriminatory treatment of different groups of individuals, effectively applying an Equal Protection requirement (not contained in the original Bill of Rights) to the federal government.

39. The Supreme Court has always followed a policy of deciding only real controversies, on the theory that only parties actually faced with dire consequences can be depended upon to honestly and effectively argue their side of a question. Thus in the main the Court will not simply advise Congress or the president whether a law could be or is constitutional.

40. See generally Stuart A. Scheingold, *The Politics of Rights: Lawyers, Public Policy, and Political Change* (New Haven: Yale University Press, 1974).

41. O. W. Holmes, Jr., "The Path of the Law," In *Collected Papers* (New York: Harcourt, Brace, 1920), pp. 167–175; also *Harvard Law Review* 10:457–462 (1897); or any collection on legal thought, such as Shuchman, *Cohen and Cohen*, pp. 59–63.

42. See note 1, Hughes, *Addresses and Papers*.

3 | Administrative Agencies and the Regulatory Process

The rise of administrative bodies probably has been the most significant legal trend of the last century and perhaps more values today are affected by their decisions than by those of all the courts. . . . They also have begun to have important consequences on personal rights. . . . They have become a veritable fourth branch of the Government, which has deranged our three-branch legal theories much as the concept of a fourth dimension unsettles our three-dimensional thinking.
—Robert H. Jackson[1]

THE DICTIONARY DEFINES *administer* as "to manage (affairs, a government, etc.); have executive charge of: *to administer laws.*"[2] This function is so obvious and necessary for any government, that in defining the roles of the three branches of the federal government the U.S. Constitution does little to describe the executive function other than to outline the president's appointive powers. Nor has the administrative authority of government and administrative law ever been precisely defined by the courts. Yet the federal government's administrative functions today are mammoth and are carried out by an extensive, powerful, and often confusing bureaucracy.

"Administrative agency" is a generic term embracing not only those bodies that function as direct arms of the executive branch, but also commissions or boards that have been established by law as independent administrative agencies of government.[3] The first type of administrative agency is generally an executive department or a division of a major executive department—such as a state department of public health, the U.S. Public Health Service, or the U.S. Occupational Safety and Health

Administration.[4] Its chief executive is appointed by, and usually serves at the pleasure of, the president or a state governor, or their cabinet-level appointees. Thus, for example, the head of OSHA is an assistant secretary of labor, who can be replaced by the secretary of labor at any time, just as the secretary can be replaced by the president at any time.[5] Independent administrative agencies, on the other hand—such as state professional licensing boards or the Federal Trade Commission[6]—are not considered part of the executive branch. Such agencies are usually headed by a board whose members are appointed by the president or state governor to fixed terms, set by the Congress or state legislature, and cannot be removed at the whim of the chief executive. The laws that establish such independent administrative agencies also define their functions, which often include legislative and/or judiciallike operations, along with purely ministerial tasks.[7] Some administrative agencies that are parts of the executive branch have taken on most of the attributes of an independent agency, the Food and Drug Administration being the prime example.

A leading legal text on administrative law[8] defines an administrative agency as "a governmental authority, other than a court and other than a legislative body, which affects the rights of private parties through either adjudication or rule making." Whether such an agency is an executive department or an independent body, its basic function is to carry out statutory mandates. When the relevant law is clear and complete, this task involves straightforward investigation and enforcement.[9] But often, as explained in Chapter 2, the laws enacted by Congress and state legislatures are "unfinished," in the sense that legislative bodies can not foresee and deal with all the contingencies likely to develop under the new statute. Nor can they devote adequate attention and expertise to complex, technical problems. Thus the Occupational Safety and Health Act, the National Health Planning and Resources Development Act, or the Professional Standards Review Organization Amendments, will establish a basic goal or program and leave it to the administrative agencies involved to work out specific criteria, standards, and regulations. It has been observed that "laws usually are stated in quite broad terms and are relatively permanent, while regulations usually are more detailed and are changed more frequently."[10]

The keystone of this arrangement is flexibility; for example, if Congress, in enacting OSHA, had set specific noise standards for foundries or, in legislating on interstate commerce, had set rail rates for steel strapping tape, the law would have been so rigid that there would be no allowance for exceptions, variations, and the like. Administrative agencies, when they engage in decision making, can take the time to consider on a case-by-case basis how particular statutes and regulations will be applied and can change those decisions on the basis of experience.

A number of medical schools stage mock malpractice trials in order to familiarize budding health professionals with a situation they may possibly experience in the course of their practice. The fact is, however, that the health care practitioner is more likely to appear before an administrative body than in a malpractice courtroom.[11] Public hearings to consider proposed new rules and policies are becoming more and more common. On the federal level, for example, administrative trials outnumber federal district court trials six to one.[12] As a former Federal Communications commissioner put it:

> While the courts handle thousands of cases each year and Congress produces hundreds of laws each year, the administrative agencies handled hundreds of thousands of matters annually. The administrative agencies are engaged in the mass production of law, in contrast to the courts, which are engaged in the handicraft production of law.[13]

The output of this administrative agency activity is administrative law in the substantive sense—environmental law, occupational health and safety law, labor law, utility law, communications law, and so forth. The field of administrative law could be said to include both this substantive law, as developed by administrative agencies, and the procedural law which defines and controls the administrative process itself. The present chapter focuses on the procedural aspects only, as does the formal study of administrative law. Although most administrative law has been developed in the context of the independent regulatory agencies, the principles generally apply to all types of governmental administrative bodies. Administrative agencies exist on both the federal and state levels, but states tend to follow the federal government's lead in developing their own administrative law.[14]

How Administrative Agencies Function

Most federal and state administrative agencies have regional field offices that provide information to the public, receive complaints, conduct investigations, and carry out other functions assigned them. The regional offices of the Food and Drug Administration, for example, have investigation units, which conduct inspections of manufacturing and processing plants; research units, which analyze samples obtained by the investigators; and compliance units, which determine whether there has been a violation of the Food, Drug, and Cosmetic Act requiring enforcement action.

The food and drug law itself is long and detailed, with numerous definitions and extensive lists of prohibited acts, penalties, and enforcement measures. Nevertheless, the statute cannot cover every contingency. For example, the law stipulates that food must not be "prepared, packed, or held under insanitary conditions." What exactly does this mean? Is a food-processing plant with cigarette butts on the floor unsanitary? Such determinations must be made by the FDA, which must develop specific guidelines that will make clear to those subject to the law just what they must do to comply with it. Usually a statute will specifically authorize—in some cases direct—the agency to develop such regulations. (A regulatee can always challenge regulations it believes are inconsistent with the statute on which it is based.)

> To explain what is needed to maintain sanitary conditions in food establishments FDA has published a set of Current Good Manufacturing Practice Regulations. These tell what kind of buildings, facilities, equipment, and maintenance are needed, and the errors to avoid, to insure sanitation. They also deal with such matters as building design and construction, lighting, ventilation, toilet and washing facilities, cleaning of equipment, materials handling, and vermin control.[15]

In the same way, the Federal Communications Commission must develop rules spelling out what the Federal Communications Act means when its states that broadcasting licenses should be awarded on the basis of "public convenience, interest, or necessity." From the point of view of those affected by the law, the impact of statute and regulation is the same: do's and don'ts are established and made known, and they must be abided by under threat of penalty.

Administrative agencies have both informal and formal mechanisms for detailing and interpreting the statutes they are implementing. Informal mechanisms include advisory opinions, policy announcements, negotiations with regulatees, voluntary compliance agreements, nonbinding directives, and publicity. Formal mechanisms include: (1) rule making, which is quasi-legislative in nature; and (2) adjudication, which is quasi-judicial in nature.[16]

1. "Rulemaking involves the formulation of a policy or interpretation which the agency will apply in the future to all persons engaged in the regulated activity."[17] It is a process that determines what those covered by the law in question will be required to do to meet its requirements. It operates prospectively, applies generally, results in sanctions against regulatees only after a further procedure, and involves general, not specific, facts.

The product of administrative agency rule making is correctly termed a *rule:* "an agency statement of general or particular applicability and future effect designed to implement, interpret, or prescribe law or policy or describing the organization, procedure, or practice requirements of an agency."[18] (The more commonly used term is the synonym "regulation": many lawyers prefer the redundant expression "rule and regulation.") There are several types of rules: substantive rules, with the general force of law; rules governing grants and benefits; interpretive rules; procedural rules; guidelines; and policy statements.[19]

2. Adjudication is similar to a court trial, but conducted less rigidly and without a jury. It is used for "deciding disputed questions of fact, determining policy in a precise factual setting, and ordering compliance with specific laws and regulations."[20] Adjudication is generally initiated by an agency which files a complaint against a specific party deemed in violation of the law. The hearing officer is asked to examine a specific situation, and to decide, for example, that a statute has been violated or that a license should be granted. Adjudication operates primarily retrospectively, applies only to specific parties and facts, and results in immediate actions (often penalties). But, as in a judicial proceeding, the decisions establish precedents with implications that reach beyond the immediate parties. For example, the Federal Trade Commission's prolonged efforts to establish that the American Medical Association's ban on solicitation of business constituted conspiracy to restrain competition was part of an FDA drive to increase competition in the professions. And a state licensing board's hearing on the possible revocation of Dr. Jones's license to practice podiatry can have a deterrent effect reaching well beyond Dr. Jones.

Regulating the Regulators

In the mid-1930s, the U.S. Supreme Court invalidated two New Deal measures on the grounds that Congress's delegation of administrative authority had been too broad and nonspecific. As one commentator recently observed:

> Today the opinions in those cases seem written from another world. The courts have all but abandoned the view exemplified in them—that laws delegating power must be invalidated unless they contain limiting standards. Wholesale delegations have become the rule in our administrative law.[21]

Sometimes this delegation is made directly to the executive branch—the broad authority given the president to implement gasoline rationing, for example; more often it is left to independent agencies to decide, for instance, how "public convenience, interest or necessity" is to be interpreted.

Does this mean that administrative agencies can do basically anything they want to, without limit or recourse? Though this image is vividly projected by many editorial writers and campaigning politicians,[22] there are rules limiting the power of administrative agencies.

Administrative Procedure Act. In 1946 Congress adopted an Administrative Procedure Act,[23] designed both to protect the rights of individuals in their dealings with administrative agencies and to restrict the regulatory power of government. The act specifies the procedures federal administrative agencies must follow when they engage in rule making and adjudication. These procedures are similar to those used in courts, but less rigid. However, the act contains a number of exceptions that limit its impact, among them matters relating to the military and foreign policy, internal personnel rules and practices, trade secrets and confidential financial information, medical and investigatory files, and matters "specifically exempted from disclosure by statute."

A major thrust of the Administrative Procedure Act is to promote public input into the process of rule making.[24] A notice of a proposed rule must be published in the *Federal Register,* which is published regularly to acquaint the public with all federal regulatory developments having general applicability and legal affect.[25] The agency proposing a new rule must allow interested parties time to submit comments, and those comments are supposed to be considered before final adoption of the regulation. In some instances, public hearings, with an official record and formal rules of evidence, must be conducted. The final rule must be published at least thirty days before it is to take effect, and then included, according to subject matter, in one of the fifty titles of the *Code of Federal Regulations (CFR),* which contains all federal regulations in force.

This formal rule-making process, however, is mandatory only when the statute under which an agency operates specifically requires it—and most do not. In fact, the Administrative Procedure Act, 5 U.S.C. Sec. 553(b)(3)(B), provides that, unless mandated by another statute, the notice and hearing requirement is not necessary "when the agency for good cause finds . . . that notice and public procedure thereon are impracticable, unnecessary, or contrary to the public interest." Nevertheless, many agencies voluntarily follow the more formal procedure (at least regarding notice and comment), primarily because it helps them secure the cooperation of regulatees.

The Administrative Procedure Act also calls for agencies engaged in adjudication to notify affected parties of the matters of fact and law to be considered at a hearing, the time, place, and nature of the hearing, and the legal authority for it. Affected parties are entitled to representation by counsel and to confrontation and cross-examination. In a series of cases during the 1970s[26] the U.S. Supreme Court held that individuals have a due-process right to a full adversary proceeding, governed by the adjudicatory requirements of the Administrative Procedure Act, whenever their medical and other governmental benefits are threatened with denial, withdrawal, or curtailment.

Administrative agency adjudication functions very much like a court trial, with some important differences. One is the kind of judge who sits on such cases. The Administrative Procedure Act has established a category of administrative law judges, employed and supervised by the Civil Service Commission, to serve as impartial hearing officers for the various administrative agencies.[27] Unless appealed to the agency board members, their decisions become the decisions of the agencies themselves. Administrative law judges occasionally conduct rule-making hearings for the agencies, but most of their work involves adjudicatory hearings.[28] Also unlike judges in a regular courtroom, administrative law judges deal with similar subject matter a good deal of the time, and individual administrative law judges often become quite expert in drug regulation, banking job safety, or other fields they habitually cover. The decisions of agency adjudication affect not only the party or parties directly involved in the proceedings but all individuals, organizations or companies under the agency's jurisdiction. Thus the policy implications of adjudication are of clear importance.

Judicial Review. Administrative agency activity must be consistent with the rest of the legal system: the Constitution, relevant statutes, and the common law. Judicial review of agency activity is therefore important, and standards for judicial review are outlined in the Administrative Procedure Act. Such review is not aimed at whether the administrative agency acted wisely, but at whether the agency has (1) exceeded its constitutional or statutory authority, (2) properly interpreted the applicable law, (3) conducted a fair proceeding, (4) avoided arbitrary, capricious, and unreasonable action, and (5) reached a decision supported by substantial evidence on the record.[29] The U.S. Supreme Court has held that, although the standards courts are to follow in reviewing agency decisions are technically narrow ones, they should include a searching and careful inquiry to determine "whether the decision was based on a consideration of the relevant factors and whether there has been a clear error of judgment."[30] Although most judicial review involves requests by affected parties to alter an agency decision, judicial intervention may also be asked to order an agency decision where one has been avoided.

In actual practice, however, judicial involvement in the activities of an administrative agency is relatively rare. The broad powers delegated to most agencies give them wide latitude; most courts tend to defer to an agency's specialized expertise; and even when an agency has clearly abused its authority or discretion, the affected party may hesitate to go over the heads of the agency personnel with whom they are likely to have ongoing contact. In addition, much of the informal power of an agency is beyond judicial reach. As one observer explains:

While an occasional instance of judicial review may send shock waves through an agency, administrative law "principles" by and large have a marginal impact, if any, on the policymaking process of agencies and on the dealings between lawyers and agency officials.[31]

As Fritschler observes, "The extent to which a court will consent to fully substitute its judgment for that of an administrative agency is one of the . . . most tangled areas in American jurisprudence."[32] Thus, most attorneys who specialize in representing clients before administrative agencies do not concentrate on the due process and abuse of authority questions with which a court would be most concerned. Instead, "the administrative lawyer does most of his work . . . in [the] various low-visibility byways of . . . constituency influence, congressional oversight, [and] executive appointment."[33] "Even in agencies with highly formalized procedures," note the editors of a leading administrative law textbook, "the great bulk of official business (including that in which lawyers for private interests participate) is disposed of informally."[34]

In the final analysis, the most meaningful external control over administrative agency activities and decisions comes from the legislature, which can:

1. Restrict an agency's authority and mandate (as Congress specifically restricted the FDA's authority over saccharin);
2. Mandate specific action (such as congressional instructions to the FDA to regulate hazardous household substances and dangerous toys, or the requirement that all federal agencies develop environmental impact statements as part of their decisions);
3. Exercise continual supervision or periodic investigations, usually through committee hearings but also—as has been the case with the FTC—by providing for congressional veto of agency decisions;
4. Reduce or increase appropriations to show approval or disapproval of agency behavior;
5. Influence the makeup of an agency through approval or disapproval of new appointees; and
6. Intercede informally with a good word from one or more legislators on behalf of a particular regulatee or issue.

Public Access: Information and Funding

The health practitioner's involvement with administrative agencies is most likely to take the form of "public citizen" input into rule-making hearings. Two issues are especially relevant to such participation. The first concerns how one learns what administrative agencies are, are not, and can be doing; the second concerns how one can become involved in the administrative process.

Before the *Federal Register* was established in 1936, no single published document existed that reported the offical actions of administrative agencies. Someone who wished to know what new regulations were under consideration by a particular agency would have to contact that agency directly at the appropriate time. Enactment of the Administrative Procedure Act ten years later helped to open the regulatory process even further by requiring notice to the public and open hearings for certain agency actions. But although the final stage of rule making and adjudication became visible, the public still had little knowledge of what federal agencies were up to most of the time. Many materials that might be of interest and concern to the public such as a report on conditions in federally supported nursing homes, for example, remained, and to some extent still remain, closed. But the situation was improved considerably in 1966 when Congress added the Freedom of Information Act (FOIA) to the Administrative Procedure Act.[35]

Before passage of the FOIA, there was little clear legal support for an individual seeking access to government records and information, and the burden was on the seeker to prove his or her need for such material. The FOIA, which was enacted to create a uniform federal policy on information release, requires that a federal agency must promptly make available at reasonable cost, upon the request of any person, copies of any records in its possession unless the information requested has previously been published and made available for sale, or falls within one of nine specific categories of exempted material.[36] Individuals do not have to explain why they want the information.

Persons seeking information under the FOIA do, however, have to have some clear idea of what they want and where it is. The Act does not require that a document be specified by name or title, but the request must "reasonablly describe" the information sought. The act also requires that federal agencies publicize their central and field organizations and where FOIA requests should be sent. But there is no assurance that if an inquiry is misdirected, the agency will forward it to the appropriate source, and the search for information can often be a time-consuming and frustrating undertaking.[37]

In addition to obtaining information from administrative agencies, individuals and organizations may also want to provide information at agency-conducted public hearings—and virtually anyone who wishes to testify on the subject of the hearings usually can[38] if he or she has the time and money to do so. Cost may not be a major consideration if a single individual appears at a state administrative agency hearing, or before a federal agency holding a local hearing. Nor is it likely to be a problem for large corporations and organizations, which are generally prepared to send several lawyers and top officials to offer testimony wherever the hearings may be held. But small organizations—a state society of physician assistants, for example, may not have the funds to send a representative to Washington to testify, let alone to pay attorney and expert-witness fees for such testimony.

Because public participation in regulatory functioning is considered important, some thought has been given in recent years to the notion of public funding for participation in agency proceedings. A few agencies—the Federal Trade Commission and the National Transportation Safety Administration, for example—have done so on a voluntary basis,[39] but most have not. Generally, those that do require that applicants for funds demonstrate (1) that they are unable to finance participation on their own and (2) that they represent an interest that otherwise would not be adequately represented before the agency. The agencies have considerable discretion in making these determinations, and presumably the practice has been significantly restricted under the Reagan administration.

Conclusion

The role of administrative agencies is likely to remain dominant in the governmental structure in the future. Certainly the health practitioner's contact with the legal system is likely to occur most often at the administrative level. Whether by choice—as with testimony at rule-making hearings—or by compulsion—as with meeting relicensure requirement—the world of the administrative agency will be close at hand. Although this world is often a cumbersome bureaucracy, it is one in which health practitioners, with a little time and effort, can learn to find their way around and make valuable contributions. Whether it be a Civil Aeronautics Board hearing on rules limiting second-hand smoke on aircraft or a state rate-setting authority considering patient education costs as a factor in establishing per diem hospital rates, health professionals will often wish to be heard. Formal testimony should offer the most convincing arguments possible; but it should also be remembered that persuasion not only consists of clearly reasoned testimony, but also depends upon the ability to indicate significant support for the position being advocated.

NOTES

1. Justice Robert Jackson dissenting, in *Federal Trade Commission v. Rubberoid,* 343 U.S. 470 (1952), at 487.

2. *The Random House Dictionary of the English Language* (New York: Random House, 1967), p. 19.

3. A standard legal encyclopedia explanation is: "Some cases recognize that administrative power is distinct from the executive power. Very often, however, administrative power is taken to be the same as executive power. . . . Administrative agencies are often described as 'executive' or as 'executive or administrative.' . . . The distinction between 'executive' and 'administrative' is that the former involves carrying out a legislatively completed policy while the latter involves legislative discretions as to policy in completing and perfecting the legislative process." *American Jurisprudence 2d*, (Rochester, N.Y.: Lawyers Cooperative, 1968), vol. 1, Administrative Law, Sec. 82, p. 877. Another distinction is historical. The independent agencies were for the most part created many decades ago to carry out economic regulation. With the exception of the Federal Trade Commission and the National Labor Relations Board, they were established to regulate a particular industry. The executive agencies generally date from the mid-1960s; they tend to focus on broad social problems, including welfare and environmental concerns. See Bernard Schwartz, "Administrative Law: The Third Century," *Administrative Law Review* 29:291–319 (1978).

4. Other examples would include the Department of Health and Human Services, as well as all other cabinet departments and their subdivisions, the FDA, FBI, and so forth.

5. This is an oversimplification since Cabinet officers receive Senate confirmation and that body may have some limited ability to restrict a completely free presidential hand. But in practical terms, such Cabinet officers serve only at the pleasure of the chief executive.

6. Other examples would include state public service or utilities commissions, industrial or worker's compensation commissions, civil service commission, the Interstate Commerce Commission, Federal Trade Commission, and Securities and Exchange Commission. At the federal level there are some fifty-one independent administrative agencies. Each one is described in the *United States Government Manual*, an annual directory available from the Government Printing Office. On independent administrative agencies in general see Marvin Bernstein, *Regulating Business by Independent Commission* (Princeton: Princeton University Press, 1955).

7. The true role of the independent administrative agencies has long been a topic of debate among political scientists. The textbook model is that these agencies function to protect the public in areas where the market system and individual choice do not suffice as a protection against powerful and/or irresponsible forces. An alternative view is that agencies are created to protect the people but over time are "captured" by the very forces they are supposed to regulate, taking on almost an identity of interests. A third model is that the major regulatory agencies were not created for the purpose of protecting the public but rather to rationalize the regulated industry to the benefit of the dominant forces in the industry. A classic historical presentation of the third model is Gabriel Kolko, *The Triumph of Conservatism: A Reinterpretation of American History, 1900–1916* (New York: Free Press, 1963).

8. Kenneth C. Davis, *Administrative Law*, 3d ed. (St. Paul: West, 1972). Also see

Walter Gellhorn, Clark Byse, and Peter L. Straus, *Administrative Law*, 7th ed. (Mineola, N.Y.: Foundation Press, 1979).

9. Agency investigatory powers can be extensive. The FTC, for example, can direct corporations to file annual or special reports or answer specific questions in writing, obtain access to corporate files for examination and reproduction of their contents, and subpoena the attendance of witnesses and the production of documentary evidence.

10. *Regulations and Health: Understanding and Influencing the Process* (New York: National Health Council, 1979), p. 1. This booklet is a very useful introduction to the federal regulatory process. It includes an extended example of the evolution of a rule, with reprints from the *Federal Register*. Also see *Federal Regulation, Hospital Attorney's Desk Reference* (Chicago: American Hospital Association, 1980).

11. See Chapter 16 for statistics on the likelihood of being involved in a malpractice suit.

12. Ernest Gellhorn, *Administrative Law and Process in a Nutshell* (St. Paul: West, 1972), p. 132. Gellhorn uses 1963 statistics, but it is unlikely that the contrast has changed markedly in the years since then (except, perhaps, toward an even more lopsided ratio).

13. Lee Loevinger, "The Administrative Agency as a Paradigm of Government—A Survey of the Administrative Process," *Indiana Law Journal* 40:305 (1965); cited in A. Lee Fritschler, *Smoking and Politics: Policymaking and the Federal Bureaucracy*, 2d ed. (Englewood Cliffs, N.J.: Prentice-Hall, 1975), pp. 56–57. Fritschler presents an excellent description of the administrative process in action, using an important health-related case study.

14. See Gellhorn, Byse, and Strauss, *Administrative Law*, chap. 1.

15. *Requirements of Laws and Regulations Enforced by the U.S. Food and Drug Administration* (Rockville, Md.: Food and Drug Administration, 1979), p. 14 (HEW Publication No. (FDA) 79-1042).

16. Although most administrative law deals with rule making and adjudication, most administrative decisions are based on informal mutual consent (with the threat of coercion always a motivating force). On agency decision making regarding which path to pursue, see Gellhorn, Byse, and Strauss, *Administrative Law*, pp. 210–213.

17. Gellhorn, *Administrative Law and Process*, pp. 121–122. See Gellhorn's chap. 7 for a summary discussion of rule making.

18. Federal Administrative Procedure Act, 5 U.S.C. 551(4).

19. See *Regulations and Health*, pp. 31–33, for definitions of these basic types. The most important types, substantive rules, "impose duties or requirements on individuals or organizations in the private sector."

20. Gellhorn, *Administrative Law and Process*, p. 132. See Gellhorn's chap. 8 for a summary discussion of adjudication.

21. Schwartz, *Administrative Law*, p. 295. Also see Gellhorn, Byse, and Strauss, *Administrative Law*, pp. 50–68.

22. A more thoughtful critique is offered in Charles A. Reich, "The New Property," *Yale Law Journal* 73:733 (1964).

23. 5 U.S.C. Secs. 551–559, 701–706, 3105, 3344, 4301 (2)(E), 5335 (a)(3)(B), 5362, 7521 (1970). Many states have passed their own Administrative Pro-

cedure acts. See Appendices A and B in Gellhorn, Byse, and Strauss, *Administrative Law.*

24. Of course in many instances the agency would seek some input even if not required. Agency staff may confer with members of Congress instrumental in passing a statute, congressional committee staff who helped draft it, other agencies, state and local governments, and private interests.

25. This is no mean task. In 1978 the *Federal Register* ran to 61,261 pages. For a more detailed description of the *Federal Register,* see the Office of the Federal Register publication, *The Federal Register: What It Is and How to Use It* (Washington, D.C.: U.S. Government Printing Office, 1980). The Office of the Federal Register also offers workshops in selected cities on using the *Federal Register.* For information call (202) 523-5235. Also see the discussion of how to use a law library in the Appendix of this text.

26. Beginning with *Goldberg v. Kelly,* 397 U.S. 254 (1970).

27. In the mid-1970s there were over eight hundred administrative law judges, over half of them assigned to the Social Security Administration. See Schwartz, *Administrative Law,* p. 307.

28. Administrative law judges function without a jury. Since much of a trial court's formal rules of evidence are intended to protect juries from unreliable evidence (such as hearsay), such rules are unnecessary in adjudication hearings where the person ruling on the acceptability of evidence is the same person rendering the final decision. Thus the proceedings can be significantly less formal than those employed in a court of law.

29. See Robert L. Rabin, "Administrative Law in Transition: A Discipline in Search of an Organizing Principle," in Robert L. Rabin, *Perspectives on the Administrative Process* (Boston: Little, Brown, 1979), pp. 1–14.

30. *Citizens to Preserve Overton Park, Inc. v. Volpe,* 401 U.S. 402 (1971). Also see discussion of the scope of judicial review in Chapter 12.

31. Rabin, "Administrative Law in Transition," p. 9.

32. Fritschler, *Smoking and Politics,* p. 110.

33. Rabin, "Administrative Law in Transition," p. 8 (sequence altered). Fritschler's book is an illustration of this point.

34. Gellhorn, Byse, and Strauss, *Administrative Law,* p. xix.

35. 5 U.S.C. Sec. 552.

36. These are matters that are (1) related to national defense or foreign policy, (2) internal personnel rules and practices, (3) exempted by specific statute, (4) trade secrets and commercial or financial information, (5) interagency and intra-agency memoranda and letters, (6) personnel and medical files, (7) investigatory files, (8) agency financial institution records, and (9) "geological and geophysical information and data, including maps, concerning wells."

37. Basic information on agencies can be found in the *United States Government Manual* and also can be requested from an agency's Public Information Office. In filing a FOIA request, a letter should be sent to the agency's Freedom of Information Officer, with a specific description of the information desired. For detailed FOIA instructions, see *A Citizen's Guide on How to Use the Freedom of Information Act and the Privacy Act in Requesting Government Documents* (Washington, D.C.: U.S. Government Printing Office, 1977). On

directions from Attorney General Bell during the Carter administration, FOIA requests were liberally construed and honored. The Reagan administration has reversed that policy and has been seeking to repeal parts of the act in order to narrow its applicability.

38. The rules regarding standing are quite liberal. See Ernest Gellhorn, "Public Participation in Administrative Proceedings," *Yale Law Journal* 81:359 (1972). Going even further, the rules under which the Illinois Pollution Control Board operates allow anyone in the hearing room audience to cross-examine witnesses after each witness has presented testimony.

39. The authority for such funding is not completely clear. See Susan B. Flohr, "Funding Public Participation in Agency Proceedings," *American University Law Review* 27:981–1010 (1978).

Part II | PUBLIC HEALTH AND THE LAW

4 | Federal Authority in the Health Field

This Government is acknowledged by all to be one of enumerated powers. The principle, that it can exercise only the powers granted to it . . . is now universally admitted. But the question respecting the extent of the powers actually granted is perpetually arising, and will probably continue to arise, as long as our system shall exist.

—*McCulloch v. Maryland[1]*

IN 1787, WHEN REPRESENTATIVES of the original states gathered to draft a national constitution, they were determined that the new federal government should not become so powerful that it could usurp state sovereignty or trample on individual freedoms.[2] The result was a document which carefully defined the power of the federal government and (in the Tenth Amendment, added a short time later as part of the Bill of Rights) reserved to the states all powers not delegated to the federal government. Under the resulting system of government, known as federalism, the national government and the states each have their own areas of supremacy; over the years a sizable portion of constitutional law has been devoted to defining and redefining this relationship and to settling the conflicts and rivalries between the states and the federal government.

At the time the Constitution was adopted, the existing state governments possessed all the powers traditionally inherent in government, foremost among which is found the power "to enact and enforce laws to protect and promote the health, safety, morals, order, peace, comfort, and general welfare of the people." In contrast, under the federal government's constitutionally enumerated powers, Congress and the President can do only those things the Constitution says they can do.[3] Yet given the current size of the federal government and the wide range of its activities—from the assurance of consumer product safety to the bailout of financially failing corporations—there is obviously more here than meets the eye.

McCulloch v. Maryland,[4] an 1819 Supreme Court decision written by Chief Justice John Marshall, analyzed the federal-state relationship and pointed the way for the development of federalism. Many consider it the most important Supreme Court decision of all time. In *McCulloch* the Court decided that Congress had the authority to charter a national bank, although no such power is mentioned in the Constitution. The Court also decided that the states could not tax local branches of the Bank of the United States. Marshall construed the constitutional delegation of powers to the national government as a broad one of *implied* as well as *expressed* powers, noting that the Constitution provides: "The Congress shall have power to make all laws necessary and proper for carrying into execution the foregoing powers. . . ."[5] Thus, concluded Marshall, the framers of the Constitution did not intend to set down a rigid legal code, but rather they wanted a document that could survive for ages through continuing interpretation. "Let the end be legitimate, let it be within the scope of the Constitution, and all means which are appropriate, which are plainly adapted to that end, which are not prohibited, but consist[ent] with the letter and spirit of the Constitution, are constitutional."[6]

McCulloch also stands for the proposition that when two constitutional powers conflict—as with a state tax on the Bank of the United States—then "the Constitution and the law made in pursuance thereof are supreme . . . they control the Constitution and laws of the respective states, and cannot be controlled by them." One part of a superior whole cannot stand in the way of what other parts collectively wish to do, so that any conflict between a valid federal law and a state law voids the latter. "If any one proposition could command the universal assent of mankind," Marshall wrote, "we might expect it would be this—that the Government of the Union, though limited in its powers, is supreme within its sphere of action." This means that when the federal government "preempts the field" by passing laws in a certain subject area, the states are precluded from legislating the same specific area.[7] The way in which this principle is applied continues to have important implications, as, for example, in environmental law.

By far the greatest portion of federal-state conflict has involved the federal government's constitutional authority to regulate interstate commerce, based on Article I, Section 8: "The Congress shall have power to . . . regulate commerce with foreign nations, and among the several states. . . ." The importance of this commerce clause should not be at all surprising, since commerce is critical to the nation ("The business of America is business"), and the United States Constitution was brought into being primarily to provide a central government with power to regulate commerce in a uniform manner.[8] The federal government's commerce power has been important in justifying federal authority in the health field, so it is necessary to understand the nature of that authority. In a series of cases in the mid-1800s the Supreme Court laid down the rule that, in the absence of specific legislation by Congress, the question of whether regulation of a particular area of commerce lies exclusively with the federal government or can also involve the states will focus on the subject of the regulation and will depend upon the need for uniformity in that particular area. Said the Court in a leading case, "Whatever subjects of this power [to regulate commerce] are in their nature national, or admit only of one uniform system or plan of regulation, may justly be said to be of such a nature as to require exclusive legislation by Congress."[9] What happens, then, in those areas that have traditionally been the undisputed subjects of state governmental action to protect the public's health, safety, and general welfare, but that may have a negative impact on interstate commerce (e.g., state highway safety or pollution control laws that impinge on interstate trucking)? In the absence of any specifically conflicting federal laws, the Supreme Court has tended to balance the burden of interstate commerce against the importance of the state law as a means to some legitimate end. However, if Congress has passed specifically conflicting legislation, the states are precluded from regulating the area themselves. The Supreme Court has been less than consistent in applying these principles, so it is impossible to accurately predict what will happen as states become more intent on restricting hazardous waste dumping and nuclear power plants.[10]

Health Authority

The authority of *state* government to regulate in the area of health and health care is extremely straightforward, since this has been an area of governmental concern for thousands of years. Chapters 5, 6, and 7 discuss the traditional areas of state health legislation and regulation in some detail. One of the most complete affirmations of this state authority is found in *Jacobson v. Massachusetts*, in which the U.S. Supreme Court upheld the state's authority to compel smallpox vaccination against the claim that it went too far in restricting individual constitutional rights. The opinion explained that:

> The authority of the State to enact this statute is to be referred to what is commonly called the police power—a power which the state did not surrender when becoming a member of the Union under the Constitution.

Although this court has refrained from any attempt to define the limits of that power, yet it has distinctly recognized the authority of a State to enact quarantine laws and "health laws of every description"; indeed, all laws that relate to matters completely within its territory and which do not by their necessary operation affect the people of other States. According to settled principles the police power of a State must be held to embrace, at least, such reasonable regulations established directly by legislative enactment as will protect the public and public safety. . . . The mode or manner in which those results are to be accomplished is within the discretion of the State, subject, of course, so far as Federal power is concerned, only to the condition that no rule prescribed by a State, nor any regulation adopted by a local government agency acting under the sanction of state legislation, shall contravene the Constitution of the United States or infringe any right secured by that instrument.[11]

The basis of *federal* authority in health and health care is less straightforward. The Constitution does not mention health or a federal health power, nor is a federal health authority implied. Health and health care were public concerns in the late 1700s, and a literal reading of the Constitution would suggest that this is an area of governmental concern "reserved to the states respectively." But one need only look at Medicare, Professional Standards Review Organizations, Health Systems Agencies, the Food and Drug Administration, the Occupational Safety and Health Administration, and a host of other federal health activities to see that this interpretation obviously is not the accepted one.

In fact, however, for the first century of its existence the federal government enacted virtually no health measures. This was in part due to the fact that when the Constitution took effect, most of the states already had a considerable body of health legislation.[12] Since no strong national purpose was served by a federal role in health, the views of state's rights proponents prevailed in this area. They were aided by the Supreme Court's leading interstate commerce decision[13] wherein, in an aside, Chief Justice Marshall described "inspection laws, quarantine laws, health laws of every description" as being clearly within the sphere of state, not congressional, concern. Although this view—especially as regards quarantine as a defense against the international spread of epidemics—would be rejected today, it prevailed for a very long time. With very few exceptions (and those spurred only by emergencies, such as the great yellow fever epidemic of 1878)[14] Congress and the presidents took Marshall's charge so much to heart that by 1886 the Supreme Court of that day went out its way to criticize the lack of federal health action. The Court said:

For the period of nearly a century since the government was organized, Congress has passed no quarantine law, nor any other law to protect the inhabitants of the United States against the invasion of contagious and infectious disease from abroad; and yet during the early part of the present century, for many years the cities of the Atlantic Coast, from Boston and New York to Charleston, were devastated by yellow fever. In later times the cholera has made similar invasions; and the yellow fever has been unchecked in its fearful course in the Southern cities. . . . During all this time the Congress never attempted to exercise this or any other powers to protect the people from the ravages of these dreadful diseases. No doubt they believe that the power to do this belonged to the states. . . .

But it may be conceded that whenever Congress shall undertake to provide for the commercial cities of the United States a general system of quarantine . . . all State laws on the subject will be abrogated, at least so far as the two are inconsistent.[15]

Slowly Congress begin to legislate on matters affecting the public's health. The Pure Food and Drug Act of 1906, for example, established what today is an extensive federal regulation of foods, drugs, medical devices, and cosmetics. The Venereal Disease Act of 1918, as another example, made use of federal grants to states for health purposes. Today, of course, federal health regulation is virtually all pervasive. But the sharp contrast from the previous hands-off policy of the federal government to today's hands-on approach makes it all the more relevant to look at the Constitutional authority used by Congress in legislating in the health field.

There are several provisions of the Constitution that provide authorization for federal health activity in rather special circumstances. Thus the federal government's postal authority[16] allows it to exclude injurious materials and misleading information—such as quack remedy advertisements—from the mails. The federal war powers,[17] which also authorize permanent maintenance of an army and navy, provide the basis for extensive health care provisions for servicemen and their dependents and veterans. Federal governmental authority in the District of Columbia and federal territorial areas and on U.S. property permit direct involvement in those specific geographical areas.[18] And federal treaty powers[19] provide a basis—not extensively used—for health-related agreements between the United States and other nations, agreements that could take precedence over state laws. But far and away the bulk of federal health legislation is based on two very general powers of the national government: the commerce power and the spending power.

The Commerce Power

Since commerce lay at the heart of the Constitution, it should not be surprising that it serves as the basis for broad federal authority. The logic underlying this power, it will be recalled, was the need for a uniform, uninterrupted system of commerce among the several states. This power, the Supreme Court noted early on, "is complete in itself, may be exercised to its utmost extent, and acknowledges no limitations other than are prescribed in the Constitution."[20] The commerce power has been used extensively to justify federal health-related legislation. Thus, for example, the Federal Food, Drug, and Cosmetic Act (21 U.S.C. Sec. 331) centers about a prohibition on the "introduction or delivery for introduction into interstate commerce of any food, drug, device, or cosmetic that is adulterated or misbranded." And the Federal Occupational Safety and Health Act (29 U.S.C. Sec. 651) begins by stating:

> The Congress finds that personal injuries and illnesses arising out of work situations impose a substantial burden upon, and are a hindrance to, interstate commerce in terms of lost production, wage loss, medical expenses, and disability compensation payments.

These extensive regulatory programs aptly illustrate the fact that the commerce power is used not merely to regulate actual commerce itself, but also to affect the goods that pass through interstate commerce and anything with a significant impact on those goods. The judicial history of the commerce clause has been one of expansive definition of commerce, which includes everything, literally, from soup to nuts, along with such things as radio waves, air pollutants, and people. Moreover, within any of these categories the reach of the commerce clause can be extensive, perhaps best illustrated by the Court's upholding the application of commerce-power-based agricultural marketing controls to wheat intended solely for on-farm consumption (the rationale being that if such wheat were not grown, the farmer would have purchased flour, thereby affecting the overall national commerce in wheat.) The federal government's authority over commerce is almost complete. A useful illustration is the substance laetrile, which the Food and Drug Administration (FDA) considers an unapproved drug. Although several states passed laws in the late 1970s specifically "legalizing" this substance, the effect of such state legislation is so limited as to be virtually meaningless. In order to get around the FDA prohibition in any of these states, a seller of laetrile would have to be selling a substance made entirely in that state from raw materials from that state and without relying on important supplies or equipment from outside that state, and would have to be selling the substance only for use in that state. Even when an effort is made to do so, it is almost impossible to meet such rigid requirements of purely intrastate activity.[21]

The Spending Power

Article I, Section 8, Clause 1 of the Constitution of the United States provides: "The Congress shall have power to lay and collect taxes, duties, imposts and excises, to pay the debts and provide for the common defense and general welfare of the United States." In other words, the federal government can raise money and it can spend it. The power—and ability—to spend large amounts of money is an influential one, which the federal government uses in two important ways. First, it spends money directly, through such programs as Medicare. Second, it establishes expenditure programs with the states, either through joint funding arrangements, such as with Medicaid, or through outright grants to states for their administration, such as with the Hill-Burton hospital construction program. This second approach is especially significant, because funds almost always come to the states with strings attached: he who pays the piper calls the tune. By making grants to states (as well as those to individuals and corporations) contingent on meeting certain conditions, the federal government is able to achieve indirectly many things it lacks the authority to accomplish directly. For example, the federal government could not order the states to institute certificate-of-need programs. But by making millions of dollars in federal funds available to a state *if* the state institutes certificate-of-need, it becomes almost a foregone conclusion that the state will comply with federal wishes. This mechanism for "buying compliance" has been repeatedly upheld by the courts against the claim of unconstitutional federal control over sovereign states. The states always can refuse to take the money, although they rarely do. The latest decision on this point upheld the certificate-of-need requirement in the National Health Planning and Resources Development Act. Said the court in upholding the requirement:

> We perceive nothing unconstitutional either in the purposes of the Act or in the condition thereby attached to health grants made to the States under federal health programs. Without question Congress in making grants for health care to the States, should be vitally concerned with the efficient use of the funds it appropriates for that purpose. It had a perfect right to see that such funds did not cause unnecessary inflation in health costs to the individual patient. It certainly had the power to attach to its grants conditions designed to accomplish that end. . . .
>
> It must be remembered that this Act is not compulsory on the State. . . : it gives to the states an *option* to enact such legislation and, in order to induce that enactment, offers financial assistance. Such legislation conforms to the pattern generally of federal grants to the states and is not "coercive" in the constitutional sense.[22]

Conclusion

Although the doctrine of enumerated federal powers continues as a valid constitutional principle, it is not a meaningful limit on the activities of the federal government. Yet it is still useful to understand the theoretical bases of federal authority in health. Such an understanding helps the nonlawyer in untangling some of the legal niceties surrounding current health regulations; e.g., how is it that the federal government and some states prohibit and "legalize" laetrile simultaneously? Furthermore, in developing new ways of dealing with significant health problems—epidemic venereal disease or pedestrian safety, for example—an understanding of the most appropriate way to frame a federal, or state, role is important; e.g., is regulation, "buying compliance," or direct funding the best approach? Likewise, at a time of considerable discussion of whether federal regulation—particularly health-related regulation—has exceeded its proper role, it is helpful to know that the need for uniform national approaches to problems is what brought the Constitution into being in the first place. Finally for those called upon to work with legal counsel and/or to peruse the legal literature themselves, it is important to realize that lawyers think in these "basis-of-authority" terms.

NOTES

1. *McCulloch v. Maryland*, 17 U.S. (4 Wheat.) 316, 4 L. Ed. 579 (1819).
2. Although the debate over the new Constitution usually is portrayed as primarily a contest between federalists and states' rights advocates, it might be characterized better as a major step by the country's economic elite to assure control over a sometimes rebellious populace. However, since the latter were spectators rather than participants, the "debate" was rather one-sided. See Michael Parenti, *Democracy for the Few*, 3d ed. (New York: St. Martin's Press, 1980), chap. 4. Also see Arthur Selwyn Miller, *Democratic Dictatorship: The Emergent Constitution of Control*, (Westport, Conn.: Greenwood Press, 1981).
3. It is not clear whether the drafters actually intended the enumeration of federal powers to be limiting. A strong case can be made that they intended the federal government to have broad general powers on all matters of common interest to the Union, the enumeration simply listing everything this broad language was understood to mean. See David E. Engdahl, *Constitutional Power: Federal and State* (St. Paul: West, 1974), pp. 1–3; also see William B. Lockhart, Yale Kamisar, and Jesse H. Choper, *Constitutional Law* (St. Paul: West, 1970), pp. 139–141.
4. *McCulloch v. Maryland*.
5. Marshall disposed of the Tenth Amendment provision that "powers not delegated to the United States . . . are reserved to the States" by noting that the Amendment does not say "expressly delegated" (as had the Articles of Confederation as well as a recommendation rejected by the Constitutional Convention). Moreover, argued Marshall, if the drafters of the Constitution had not intended a broad grant of implied federal powers, why would they have included in Article I, Section 9, a list of specific limitations of federal powers?

6. Twenty years earlier Thomas Jefferson ridiculed this logic in a letter to Edward Livingston. "Congress are authorized to defend the nation. Ships are necessary for defense; copper is necessary for ships; mines necessary for copper; a company necessary to work the mines; and who can doubt this reasoning who has ever played at 'This is the House that Jack Built?'" In Charles Warren, *The Supreme Court in United States History* (Boston: Little, Brown, 1922); reprinted in Lockhart, Kamisar, and Choper, *Constitutional Law*, p. 141.

7. If Congress has passed laws regarding some aspects of a subject matter but not others, does this mean the members of Congress intended to preempt the entire field or, conversely, to allow state legislation where no direct conflict occurred? This can become the basis of some rather creative statutory interpretation by the courts.

8. For example, "Finance, commerce, and business assembled the historic Philadelphia Convention. . . ." Albert J. Beveridge, *The Life of John Marshall* (New York: Houghton, Mifflin, 1916); "The Constitutional Convention was called because The Articles of Confederation had not given the Federal Government any power to regulate commerce." Robert L. Stern, "That Commerce Which Concerns More States than One," *Harvard Law Review* 47:1335 (1934). Both in Lockhart, Kamisar, and Choper, *Constitutional Law*, pp. 160–162. Also see Michael Conant, *The Constitution and Capitalism* (St. Paul: West, 1979).

9. *Cooley v. Board of Wardens of Philadelphia*, 53 U.S. (12 How.) 299, 13 L.Ed. 996 (1851). Actually applying this "subject matter" approach has not worked very well, but the basic principle has been retained. "*Cooley* has been repeatedly cited for the proposition that whether a state regulation which impinges upon interstate commerce is invalidated by the commerce clause depends (at least in part) upon whether the regulation is justifiable in terms of local peculiarities and necessities, or whether state regulations of that sort are so disruptive of the uniformity that is necessary, as a practical matter, for a viable national business economy as to be unjustifiable in view of the commercial unity of the nation contemplated by the commerce clause." Engdahl, *Constitutional Power*, p. 266. Most readily invalidated are state restrictions that have the effect of favoring a state's own trade and commerce over those of other states.

10. An instructive example of the federal-state power balance can be found in two somewhat similar Supreme Court decisions. In *Huron Portland Cement Co. v. City of Detroit*, 362 U.S. 440 (1959), the balance lay between a city smoke abatement ordinance—a health protection measure clearly within the state's usual powers—and the fact that enforcement of the law would prevent some noncomplying Great Lakes ships from entering the Port of Detroit—thus clearly affecting interstate commerce. Making the balancing more difficult was the fact that Congress had created a system of ship inspection and licensing which the noncomplying ships had satisfied, *but* this system was concerned with assuring the seaworthiness of vessels, not their smoke output. In deciding which laws prevailed, the majority of the Court concluded that the city and the federal government were regulating different things and could do so simultaneously. But to reach this conclusion they had to ignore the fact that by upholding the ordinace they effectively barred

certain ships from using the port. In dissent, Justice Douglas—a renowned environmentalist—pointed to the clear hindering of interstate commerce that would result unless the ordinance gave way. In addition, he suggested that by enacting a program for vessel certification Congress had completely preempted, i.e., taken over, the field and that failure to include smoke emission levels among the standards indicated a congressional decision not to institute such restrictions, thus barring any contrary local policy.

In a more recent decision, *Dixy Lee Ray v. Atlantic Richfield Company and Seatrain Lines, Inc.*, 435 U.S. 151 (1978), the state of Washington had passed laws regulating the size, design, and movement of oil tankers in Puget Sound in order to protect the surrounding environment from oil spills—again something clearly within the state's normal power to do. Yet this clearly could affect interstate commerce. Moreover, Congress had established comprehensive standards in the Federal Ports and Waterways Safety Act of 1972 that clearly overlapped the state laws. The Court majority, therefore, invalidated most of the state provisions, with three dissenters arguing that the state requirements were nondiscriminatory—i.e., were not attempts to favor Washington over non-Washington ships or trade—and also reasonable environmental protection measures within the authority of state power. See the discussion of state police power following in this chapter and in Chapter 5.

11. 197 U.S. 11 (1905). The first use of the term "police power" was by Chief Justice John Marshall in *Brown v. Maryland*, 25 U.S. (12 Wheat.) 419, 6 L.Ed. 678 (1827). In the *License Cases*, 46 U.S. (5 How.) 504, 12 L.Ed. 256 (1847), Chief Justice Roger Taney wrote: "But what are the police powers of a state? They are nothing more nor less than the powers of government inherent in every sovereignty to the extent of its dominions . . . the power to govern men and things within the limits of its dominions." (To which Fred Rodell responded: "What 'state police power' really meant in Taney's day and has meant ever since is the use of state laws to do things that a majority of the justices, at any given time, do not strongly disapprove of the states doing—nothing more, nothing less.") Justice Roberts wrote of police power: "It means the power to regulate the conduct and relations of the members of society. In effect, it means the general power of legislation." All are quoted in Ruth Locke Roettinger, *The Supreme Court and State Police Power: A Study in Federalism* (Washington, D.C.: Public Affairs Press, 1957), pp. 10–11.

12. See Carleton B. Chapman and John M. Talmadge, "The Evolution of the Right-to-Health Concept in the United States," in M. Visscher *Humanistic Perspectives in Medical Ethics* (Buffalo: Prometheus Books, 1972), pp. 72–134 at p. 74. Also see Morris Kagan: "Federal Public Health: A Reflection of a Changing Constitution," in C. Burns, *Legacies in Law and Medicine* (New York: Science History Publications, 1977), pp. 206–229.

13. *Gibbons v. Ogden*, 22 U.S. (9 Wheat.) 1, 6 L.Ed. 2d 23 (1824)—The New York–New Jersey Steamboat Case.

14. The 1878 epidemic took an estimated 30,000 lives in the Mississippi Valley, and the resulting outcry induced Congress to create a national health authority, the National Board of Health. The board was given half a million dollars to fund research grants and also given authority to implement a

national quarantine system. But political opposition—especially within the government from what was to become the Public Health Service—led to the board's elimination in 1884. See Chapman and Talmadge, "Evolution of the Right-to-Health Concept," pp. 85–89. Another notable exception to federal noninvolvement in health matters was a law passed by Congress in 1813 which required the federal government to guarantee the efficacy of cowpox vaccine and to distribute vaccine without charge to anyone requesting it. See Chapman and Talmadge, "Evolution of the Right-to-Health Concept," pp. 79–80.

15. *Morgan's Louisiana and Texas R.R. and Steamship Company v. Louisana State Board of Health*, 118 U.S. 455 (1886); quoted in Kagan, "Federal Public Health," pp. 216–217.
16. Article I, Section 8, Clause 7.
17. Article I, Section 8, Clauses 11–16.
18. Article I, Section 8, Clause 17, and Article IV, Section 3, Clause 2.
19. Article II, Section 2, Clause 2, and Article VI, Section 2. It has also been argued that Article I, Section 2, Clause 3, which calls for a federal census every ten years, could provide authority—never used—to collect health statistics on a national basis, rather than having the federal government merely compile data provided by the States. See Kagan, "Federal Public Health," p. 213.
20. *Gibbons v. Ogden.*
21. On the commerce clause in general, see Paul R. Benson, Jr., *The Supreme Court and the Commerce Clause, 1937–1970* (New York: Dunellen, 1970). And on both the commerce and spending powers, see Kenneth R. Wing and Andrew W. Silton, "Constitutional Authority for Extending Federal Control over the Delivery of Health Care," *North Carolina Law Review* 57:1423–1479 (1979).
22. *North Carolina ex rel. Morrow v. Califano*, 445 F. Supp. 532 (E.D.N.C. 1977), *affd mem.*, 435 U.S. 962 (1978).

5 | Traditional Public Health Activities of State and Local Governments

*Public health is the science and art of preventing disease,
prolonging life, and promoting physical health and efficiency
through organized community efforts for the sanitation of the
environment, the control of community infections, the
education of the individual in principles of personal hygiene,
the organization of medical and nursing service for the early
diagnosis and preventive treatment of disease, and the
development of the social machinery which will ensure to every
individual a standard of living adequate for the maintenance
of health; organizing these benefits in such fashions as to
enable every citizen to realize his birthright of health and
longevity.*

—C.-E. A. Winslow[1]

IF THE CONCEPT of public health is a mystery to the general public, it is
not much clearer to the majority of the health community. The role of
state and local health departments in carrying out traditional public
health functions is poorly perceived and understood. Even those engaged in a specific public health function may lack an overview of state
public health activity, and few will be familiar with the legal authority
underlying it. The long history and clear legal basis of these governmental efforts, in fact, may be why public health is taken for granted.

History records the systematic efforts of many ancient civilizations to
protect the health of the community. As social, scientific, and medical
knowledge increased and as an emerging capitalist class became more
dependent on a healthy workforce, approaches to public health became
more clearly defined. By the late eighteenth century—around the time
of the American Revolution—the idea that government should undertake to create and implement a national medical policy was becoming
popular in Europe, i.e., the concept of "medical police." (With sanitation

so rudimentary, diseases so undifferentiated, and health records virtually nonexistent, there were few early successes for this concept.) The great names in public health—Chadwick, Shattuck, Virchow, and others—were active during the nineteenth century, and their work helped involve government more deeply in public health protection.[2]

In the United States, the landmark period was from 1869 to 1909 when the state boards of health were established. (Schools of public health were not organized until the twentieth century.) An early treatise on the law of public health and safety in the United States spelled out the government's responsibility in this regard as follows:

> One of the legitimate and most important functions of civil government is acknowledged to be that of providing for the general welfare of the people by making and enforcing laws to preserve and promote the public health and the public safety. Civil society can not exist without such laws; they are, therefore, justified by necessity and sanctioned by the right of self preservation. The power to enact and enforce them is lodged by the people with the government of the State, qualified only by such conditions as to the manner of its exercise as are necessary to secure the individual citizen from unjust and arbitrary interference. But even under these restrictions, the power exists in ample measure to enable government to make all needful regulations touching the well-being of society.[3]

The federal government plays such a predominant role in financing and regulating health care delivery and health-related research in this country that the role of the state governments in this area is easily overlooked. Most health issues—from swine flue and legionnaires' disease to occupational health and hospital-cost containment—receive public attention as national problems. Yet it is the states that have traditionally developed and exercised the most clearly established public health powers.

Table 5.1 lists some of the most widely accepted state public health activities. Although much of this work is educational and does not require the force of law, other activities clearly depend on the potential for enforcement for their effectiveness; thus the laws mandating state public health activities generally include such enforcement mechanisms as permits, licensure, and registrations; injunctions; inspections; embargoes, seizure, condemnation, and destruction; nuisance abatement; and penal sanctions.

The power of the state to enact and enforce laws to protect the public's health, safety, and general welfare, known as the state's "police power," is a vague concept broadly encompassing the traditional functions undertaken by all governments in regulating society.[4] Generally, public health regulations will be upheld if it can be reasonably shown that they are needed to protect and promote the public's health, safety, and general welfare, and if they are reasonably drawn to accomplish that

TABLE 5.1   State Public Health Activities*

Abatement of nuisances	Health personnel licensure and
Air pollution control	registration
Alcohol and addiction control	Health planning/needs and resource
Ambulance service	assessment/certificate of need
Anatomical gift regulation	Home health care
Blood donation regulation	Housing inspection
Business regulation (restaurants, bar-	Immunizations
bers, dry cleaners, etc.)	Laboratory services
Campground and swimming regula-	Maternal/child health
tion	Mental health
Care of indigent	Migrant labor camp regulation
Chronic disease control	Milk inspection
Clean water and sewage	Mosquito abatement
Communicable disease control	Nursing care
Compulsory examination	Nutrition programs
Compulsory treatment hospitaliza-	Occupational health
tion	Operate hospitals and clinics
Crippled children services	PKU/metabolic screening
Dental health	Plumbing codes
Disease reporting and recording	Poison control
Emergency medical services	Prevention of blindness
Extermination services	Quarantines
Facilities inspection	Rabies control
Facilities licensure	Radiological health
Family planning	Refuse disposal
Food and food service inspection	School health
Funeral/burial requirements	Sexually transmitted disease control
Hazardous substances control	Tuberculosis control
Health education	Vital statistics recording
	Water/stream pollution control

*Adapted, with additions, from C. A. Miller et al., "Statutory Authorizations for the Work of Local Health Departments," *American Journal of Public Health* 67:940–945 (October 1977).

end. But the courts will not go beyond the legislature's finding that a particular regulation was the best means toward a public health end.[5]

The state's authority over public health has been sustained not only in regard to actions aimed at protecting the public's health in general, but also in regard to actions designed to protect and enhance the health of individuals. The rationale is the state's interest in a healthy citizenry whose members can support themselves, contribute to the economy, and bear arms if need be. Thus courts have upheld the state's public health power even when no immediate public health danger threatens (e.g., compulsory vision testing of schoolchildren) and even when individual and private property rights are significantly infringed by the operation of that power (e.g., compulsory physical examination or destruction of dangerous goods or structures without compensation).

The state legislature, in turn, may delegate authority to legislate and regulate certain aspects of public health to political subdivisions of the state, such as counties and municipalities. Under the U.S. Constitution, these political subdivisions have no independent powers; they derive their authority by specific mandate of the state legislatures. The state also may delegate authority to administrative agencies, such as the state department of (public) health. Grad explains:

> In delegating power, the state legislature may, and usually does, place limits on its exercise. The person or agency to whom the power is delegated may be specified in some detail, the manner in which the power is to be exercised, and the consequences of failure to exercise it, or the consequences of its improper exercise, may be specified. The delegation may be . . . a mere delegation of administrative functions—such as the power and duty to enforce the state health code—or it may include a delegation of regulatory or rule-making powers.[6]

As the American population expanded and the nation became increasingly urbanized it became evident that many health-related problems were handled best on the local level. To avoid the need for specific police power authorization each time a new need arose, most states—either through legislation or by constitutional amendment—gave local governmental units "home rule," that is, authority to carry out public health and other functions without having to seek legislative authority anew for each activity.[7] For example, the revised Constitution of the state of Illinois, which was adopted in 1970, provides:

> A County which has a chief executive officer elected by the electors of the county and municipality which has a population of more than 25,000 are home rule units. Other municipalities may elect by referendum to become home rule units. Except as otherwise limited by this Section, a home rule unit may exercise any power and perform any function pertaining to its government and affairs including, but not limited to, the power to regulate for the protection of the public health, safety, morals and welfare; to license; to tax; and to incur debt.[8]

Of course the home rule provisions of the individual states differ considerably, as do the ways in which particular legislatures view whether public health problems are dealt with best on a centralized or decentralized basis.

The first state law authorizing establishment of local boards of health was passed in Massachusetts in 1797. Seventy-five years later there were still only thirty-seven local health departments in the entire country. The first state board of health was created—also in Massachusetts—in 1869, but by 1909 all states had state boards.[9]

Although Table 5.1 lists most of the major activities of concern to states and local health departments, it should be kept in mind that individual departments may be involved in only some of the activities listed. In addition, some functions may be handled on the state level, some by the county, and some by local municipalities, or cooperatively in multi-county, county-city, or other forms. This parceling-out of function may also vary from county to county; a large city may itself carry out what is a county function in counties made up of small towns and unincorporated villages. And on each level, public health functions may be divided among a number of departments: health, environmental affairs, registration, and so on. For example, local boards of education have principal responsibility for conducting school health programs in forty-five states; in only five instances does responsibility rest with local health departments. At the state level, twenty-four education departments have primary regulatory responsibility for school health services, and twelve state health departments have primary responsibility (however, in many states, more than one agency is usually involved).[10]

Nor are the authorizing laws themselves, which were generally enacted piecemeal over several years, very neatly organized. Even when an overall health code brings all the obvious public health laws together into one organized section, it may not include necessarily all the state statutes or local ordinances that affect public health. Often, if one were to inquire regarding some well-accepted public health requirement, "Where does the law say that this is required?" a difficult search would ensue. For example, some state public health codes include laws regulating food and drugs, protection of the environment, or health facility licensing, whereas in another state such laws might be found separately codified. Laws establishing state reimbursement for medical services to the sick poor are not likely to be part of the public health code, but the operation of state health facilities for the sick poor well may be included. Although a state medical practice act could be considered as public health protection, it generally appears separately in the statute books. Finally, many statutes of importance to the public health function, such as those outlining state administrative and judicial procedures, have nothing directly to do with public health at all.

Unfortunately it is not easy to revise the cumbersome and dated maze of public health laws that accumulates over the decades. Probably the most up-to-date state public health code at present is that of Michigan, where seven years of "blue ribbon" committee studies, followed by four years of intensive political support-building, led to a new code in 1978. The success of this revision lay in an extensive, carefully built coalition, representing business, labor, consumers, providers, and agencies of state and local government (including both executive and legislative branches), that drafted legislation and shepherded it through the legislature.[11] The Michigan experience serves as a useful example to other states, but it also highlights the amount of work needed to update the law on a subject that is far from being the most controversial to face society.[12]

Even on the local level, where the public health role can be more clearly defined, there is seldom a truly consolidated public health code. New York City's Metropolitan Health Law, adopted in 1866, was a model for other municipalities; but it was seldom updated despite the constant accretion of relevant advances. A new code in 1959 was the first revision in almost half a century.

Local public health activities, though not quite as broad as those authorized on the state level, are still extensive. The 1959 New York City Health Code, for example, regulates virtually every phase of human endeavor, from reporting of births and ritual circumcision to reporting of deaths, disposal of human remains, and location of cemeteries.[13]

On both the state and local levels, the codification of existing public health laws and the development of new statutes is an increasingly complex and sophisticated process that ideally calls for a creative partnership between lawyers and health care professionals. Such a partnership is only possible when all involved have a basic understanding of how the law can further or impede public health goals.[14] The pages that follow will explore the role of public health laws in the maintenance of an overall health-quality control mechanism. As with any such mechanism, there are a data base, standards, measurement, and feedback, all leading to corrective and/or preventive steps. The discussion will also explain some of the legal limits on the state's broad—but not absolute—powers to protect the public's health.

Data Base/Reporting Laws

In order for states and municipalities to undertake meaningful public health programs, they must have reliable information regarding the existing state of the public's health. Thus, all states have had, for many years, public health reporting requirements obligating health professionals and patient care facilities to provide information on three basic areas: vital statistics, communicable diseases, and child abuse. Vital statistics recording goes back to very early Colonial America, and communicable disease recording at least to the Michigan law of 1883, while reporting on child abuse is a much more recent requirement dating largely from the 1960s. (There are, or course, other types of reporting requirements that apply to other groups, such as regulated industries, businesses, and professions. Also, there are other reporting requirements which, although imposed upon health professionals and related to public health in the broadest sense, are primarily concerned with criminal law; examples include reports of gunshot wounds and prescriptions involving controlled substances.)

The reporting and recording of vital statistics data such as birth, fetal deaths, deaths, marriages, and divorces are important to public health planning and evaluation. Collection of such information is relatively noncontroversial[15] and, because of the involvement of the National Office of Vital Statistics and the World Health Organization,[16] relatively uniform.

Reporting of communicable diseases is far less universal, both because practitioners are often hesitant to report certain diseases and because officials are reluctant to force such reporting. States vary somewhat in the way in which they frame the requirement. California, for example, specifies by statute which diseases must be reported, while Illinois simply provides the state department of public health with such broad powers to "adopt, promulgate, repeal and amend rules and regulations and make such sanitary investigation and inspections as it may from time to time deem necessary," thus permitting the department to develop its own list of reportable diseases. Other states specifically require reporting but leave it up to the department to establish the reportable diseases.[17] States also may vary as to who, besides physicians, must report communicable diseases, e.g., dentists, nurses, laboratories, hospital administrators, or school authorities.

Although the various reporting laws contain penalty provisions, compliance is fairly low. A New Haven, Connecticut, study in 1974 found that only 35 percent of viral hepatitis cases had been reported,[18] and an earlier study in Nassau County, New York, found only 4,917 out of 20,184 cases of streptococcal sore throat properly reported.[19] Several reasons have been advanced for such underreporting. One is widespread ignorance of the specific requirements of the reporting laws. Another is the fact that certain "sensitive" diseases, such as gonorrhea and syphilis (the most common reportable diseases), can cause embarrassment and inconvenience to the patient; therefore private practitioners in particular tend to neglect reporting them. In addition, numerous health care providers are eager to avoid both the added paperwork and any possible legal harrassment by angry patients—though, short of malice, this is not a realistic worry.[20] Conversely, skepticism as to whether any useful action will result from disease reporting can undermine routine reporting. Finally, violations can be difficult to discover, penalties are often light, and enforcement efforts are often virtually nonexistent.

This state of affairs is not likely to change significantly in the near future, unless a preventable public health crisis discovered too late increases public and legislative demands for strengthened enforcement of reporting requirements. Such a crisis could also generate civil suits charging that failure to fulfill reporting requirements caused preventable harm to the plaintiff. There have been a few such suits, based on failure to report communicable disease and child abuse.[21]

With child abuse and neglect, what is reported is usually suspicion, rather than fact, and these reports need to be investigated. Under-reporting is also widespread in child abuse. But child abuse is currently of considerable social concern, and there is much pressure for more adequate abuse and neglect reporting. Possibly, improvement in child abuse reporting may carry over to the area of communicable diseases as well.[22]

Setting Standards

To protect the public's health, states set standards to be met by people (individuals and groups of individuals), places, and things. Standards for *people* are the requirements for licensure in the professions, occupations, and businesses.[23] Grad defines licensure as "limiting certain fields of endeavor that may involve hazards to the health and safety of the people to persons who are properly qualified, who have the necessary equipment and facilities, and who, by reason of their training or experience, are least likely to create danger to the public." He adds:

> The field of public health law, as one of the earliest fields of administrative law, has used licensure effectively for hundreds of years. The occupations and callings which fall into the general sphere of public health law are probably among the earliest of licensed occupations.[24]

Licensure laws take one of two forms: they either declare that only those meeting specified requirements may engage in a particular endeavor (such as the practice of medicine) or that only those meeting the requirements may use a particular designation (such as Certified Public Accountant or Licensed Practical Nurse), although anyone can perform the functions involved. Health professional licensure will be discussed in Chapter 6 and health facilities licensure in Chapter 7.

There are other occupations, professions, and businesses not involved in health care delivery which are also regulated through licensure or permit requirements in order to protect the public's health, including, among others, barbers, food-establishment operators, undertakers, tattoo parlors, plumbers, rooming-house operators, and waste-dump operators. An example of a licensing standard relating to food establishments, for example, is the relatively recent requirement that managers, or perhaps all food-handling employees, complete a course on sanitary food handling.

Health standards applicable to *places* include operational licensure and code requirements and limits on the emission of various pollutants. Building codes may prohibit lead-base paint or asbestos insulation, set safety-related fire and electrical standards, and incorporate plumbing codes and similar measures that affect both health and other functions.

Standards applicable to *things* include not only food and drug laws, but also regulation of hazardous products. Since things can be moved easily from state to state, most regulation in this area is done on the federal level, though states and local governments do play a supplemental role.

States vary as to whether standard-setting authority will be delegated to local health departments, retained by the state, or exercised concurrently. If strict local standards come into conflict with more lax state health standards the state standard can usually be expected to prevail, but there are instances where higher local standards have been upheld.

Measurement and Feedback

Inspections.   Most health standards are prospective controls; they specify that certain things cannot be legally done, used, or sold, unless these standards are met first. This is true especially with regard to licensure. As Grad notes, "The purpose of a licensing statute in relation to public health is generally to exclude from activities which may adversely affect the health and safety of the public those entrepreneurs who will not or cannot conform to desirable standards."[25] Such prospective controls are, in a sense, self-enforcing, since it is up to the would-be licensee to demonstrate that the standards have been met. A statute that simply declares a particular practice illegal, on the other hand, requires the government, whether it be a federal department or a local or state agency, to seek out and punish violations. This policing approach requires authority on the part of appropriate officials to determine, often by inspection, if there is compliance with the law. "Inspections are the staple of public health enforcement . . ."[26] writes Grad in his *Public Health Law Manual.* Although the goal of inspection is to ascertain that specified standards are being met, rather than to uncover evidence of a crime, a public health inspection often involves intrusions similar to those of a police search. But the legal rights involved have been defined somewhat differently under the law.

The Fourth Amendment to the U.S. Constitution provides that "The right of the people to be secure in their persons, houses, papers, and effects against unreasonable searches and seizures shall not be violated, and no Warrants shall issue, but upon probable cause, supported by oath or affirmation, and particularly describing the place to be searched, and the persons or things to be seized." If in interpretations of this amendment, public health inspections of restaurants, factories, stores, residences, and the like were equated with police searches, it would be necessary for health inspectors to go before a judge and describe the premises to be searched, the purpose of the search, and what they expected to find. Most important of all, they would have to provide reasonable grounds for suspecting that some violation of the law was occurring. The judge would then decide whether there were "reasonable ground of suspicion, supported by circumstances sufficiently strong in themselves to warrant a cautious man in the belief that the party is guilty of the offense with which he is charged,"[27] and thus justifying such a search. If the judge decided there were reasonable grounds, a warrant would be issued to the health inspector, just as to a policeman seeking a warrant to search for stolen goods in an apartment when there are reasonable grounds for believing they are hidden there. But there is a great deal of difference between the two situations. Most public health inspections are conducted as routine checks of compliance with health and safety standards, not because there is specific reason to suspect noncompliance; hence there is no "probable cause" basis justifying a warrant to intrude into a citizen's private domain.

It has been argued that where the public purpose is clear and the possible penalties light, there is no need to follow the guidelines of criminal law. But regardless of benefit or penalty, Anglo-American law protects private homes and property against uncontrolled state intrusion; and public health inspection, with or without warrant, is not necessarily a trivial incursion since discovery of noncompliance can lead to penalties as severe as restaurant or building closure or condemnation.

Because of this dilemma, the United States Supreme Court has had considerable difficulty in applying the Fourth Amendment to inspections. In the leading case, decided in 1967,[28] the Court held that it would "surely be anomalous to say that the individual and his private property are fully protected by the Fourth Amendment only when the individual is suspected of criminal behavior." The Court held that if an inspector is refused entry, he must obtain a warrant in order to carry out his inspection. But the Court went on to outline special inspection warrant requirements, much easier to satisfy than those established for police searches, insisting only that the inspection be part of a legitimate inspection program, that the premises to be entered fall into the category or geographical area covered by the inspection, and that entry has been refused;[29] and for commercial premises, even this latter requirement can be dispensed with. Three dissenting justices felt that the majority was requiring a "paper" warrant—a meaningless formality, and argued that legal inspections did not require a warrant in order to meet the constitutional requirement of reasonableness.

To a large extent these conflicting views among the justices represent a dispute between pragmatism and principle. The majority, while aware that their insistence is somewhat formalistic, is guarding against an interpretation that might lead to more serious erosion of Fourth Amendment protection. The Court has allowed warrantless inspections where very specific and unique fact situations limited the application of the holding. These involved commercial operations in industries with long histories of extensive government regulation, such as the sale of liquor or firearms.[30] These "carefully defined classes of cases" represent the farthest the Court has been willing to go in compromising the basic constitutional protection. When the Federal Occupational Safety and Health Administration (OSHA) conducted its inspections without warrants, the Court—in 1978—reaffirmed its earlier ruling requiring warrants whenever inspectors are refused voluntary admission.[31]

It is safe to assume that further exceptions to the warrant requirement will be very limited, and that most inspection programs, whatever their aegis or purpose may be, will require either the owner's consent or a warrant to enter. It may be, as the 1967 dissent predicted, that warrants "will be printed up in pads of a thousand or more—with space for street number to be inserted—and issued by magistrates in broadcast fashion as a matter of course," but they will be required nevertheless.

Corrective action.   In addition to verifying and enforcing compliance with legal standards affecting public health, the states and municipalities also have the responsibility to deal with specific public health problems that may reveal themselves by inspection or by analysis of health data. Although public health is strongly biased toward educational responses to health problems, it may be necessary to take corrective actions, medical and/or legal, to eliminate the cause of a problem or to limit its impact. Such actions, too, may affect people, places, and things.

When *people* constitute the source of the problem—as with communicable diseases—corrective action involves limiting contagion (by isolating the source) and treating the disease. The most extreme version of isolation is quarantine—the forced restriction of sick and/or exposed individuals to specific premises. With advances in mass vaccination to help prevent epidemics and a host of new medications to deal with outbreaks when they occur, quarantine is seldom used today. But not many decades ago, it was an important public health tool; and when the public's health was weighed against individual freedom, the rights of the individual were often forced to yield. In the case of *People v. Robertson,*[32] in 1922, for example, Jennie Barmore, a boardinghouse-keeper in Chicago was found to be a carrier of typhoid. The city's commissioner of health quarantined her house and restricted her to one room; the closing down of her boardinghouse effectively halted her source of income. Yet Barmore's application for a writ of *habeas corpus,* challenging this severe loss of freedom and livelihood, was turned down on the grounds that the quarantine constituted a reasonable exercise of police power to preserve the public health.

Corrective action directed against *places* generally involves the abatement of "public nuisances."[33] Nuisance is a common law action dating back many centuries. Today most states have laws defining what is meant by a public nuisance and outlining what may be done to deal with them. Usually such laws stipulate that in an emergency public health officials may act first and ask (and answer) questions (in court) afterward. In nonemergency situations, property owners have the opportunity to contest the actions of the public health officials in court. It is significant that if the abatement measures are upheld, the state need not pay compensation to the owner for loss of property as it would have to if the land were taken under the state's eminent domain power.

Public health officials also generally have the authority to seize things, e.g., goods, and, where appropriate, to embargo them. This is analogous to quarantine, in which the goods are left with the owner but cannot be disposed of or used.[34] After judicial proceedings, the owner may be given the opportunity to bring the goods in question into compliance with the standard they violated, either by altering the goods themselves or by altering the purpose for which they are made available. If this is not, or cannot be, done the goods may be destroyed. The seizure power, as with quarantine and nuisance abatement, is quite broad.

Prevention. The corrective actions discussed above all involve existing problems. But the primary focus of public health has long been prevention. State and federal courts have made it clear, for example, that the state's police power gives it the power not only to *offer* vaccination to the public, but actually to *require* it. The leading decision is *Jacobson v. Massachusetts*, in which the U.S. Supreme Court upheld the validity of a compulsory smallpox vaccination statute, explaining that "the liberty secured by the Constitution of the United States to every person within its jurisdiction does not import an absolute right in each person to be, at all times and in all circumstances, wholly freed from restraint. There are manifold restraints to which every person is necessarily subject for the common good. On any other basis organized society could not exist with safety for its members."[35]

All the states today have compulsory immunization laws, most of them requiring that at a particular age (or prior to school attendance) a child must be immunized against diphtheria, whooping cough, and polio. In addition:

- Twenty-seven states require screening for vision and hearing.
- Sixteen states require that children have physical examinations when they start school or at other specified times.
- Ten states require dental examinations.
- Fourteen states require schools to maintain health records for schoolchildren.[36]

Legislatures often provide an exemption for those for whom vaccination would violate religious principles; however, there is no constitutional requirement for such an exemption. The Supreme Court has made it quite clear that the First Amendment guarantees freedom of belief, not freedom of action, and any current challenge of compulsory vaccinations laws, whether based on religious or other grounds, will be dismissed with brief reference to the well-settled authority of the states in this area.[37]

Other compulsory preventive measures have been similarly upheld. For example, in a suit challenging the right of the state to require that motorcyclists wear helmets, a federal court in Massachusetts declared:

> While we agree with plaintiff that the act's only realistic purpose is the prevention of head injuries incurred in motorcycle mishaps, we cannot agree that the consequences of such injuries are limited to the individual who sustains the injury. In view of the evidence warranting a finding that motorcyclists are especially prone to serious head injuries, see Statistical Division, National Safety Council, *1971 Motorcycle Facts*, the public has an interest in minimizing the resources directly involved. From the moment of the injury, society picks the person up off the highway; delivers him to a municipal hospital and municipal doctors; provides him with unemployment compensation if, after recovery, he cannot replace his lost job, and, if the injury causes permanent disability, may assume the responsibility for his and his family's continued subsistence. We do not understand a state of mind that permits plaintiff to think than only he himself is concerned.[38]

Court have also upheld state and local authority to fluoridate water, a preventive measure which affects everyone, including even the toothless nonbeneficiary.[39]

Compulsory medical examinations have also withstood legal challenge, although within more narrowly drawn limits. The state's authority to require physical examination of schoolchildren is quite clear (another set of equally valid laws, requiring school attendance bolster this authority). It is also clearly legal for the state to require medical examinations for food handlers, nursery school teachers, or other occupations clearly related to the public's health. Beyond such special groups, however, compulsory medical examination is generally only legally defendable when a specific problem is suspected; it cannot be looked upon as a routine preventive screening device.

Conclusion

In *People v. Robertson*,[40] the Illinois court declared that "among all the objects sought to be secured by governmental laws none is more important than the preservation of public health." This importance has led courts to interpret the public health powers of the states broadly. But the legal authority described in this chapter represents potential rather than realized fact. Actually, the commitment by state governments to enforcement—and education in behalf—of many public health laws is shockingly slack. The contrast between the law in the books and the law on the streets is as sharp in the public health area as elsewhere—and perhaps even more so, since there is no organized lobby with a stake in seeing public health law effectively enforced.

NOTES

1. C.-E. A. Winslow, "The Untilled Fields of Public Health," *Science* 51 (n.s.):23 (1920); also *Modern Medicine* 2:183 (March 1920), as quoted in James A. Tobey, *Public Health Law*, 3d ed. (New York: Commonwealth Fund, 1947), p. 4. More recently, the Report of the Milbank Memorial Fund Commission, *Higher Education for Public Health* (New York: Prodist, 1976), p. 4, developed the following definition: "Public health is the effort organized by society to protect, promote, and restore the people's health. The programs, services, and institutions involved emphasize the prevention of disease and the health needs of the population as a whole. Public health activities change with changing technology and social values, but the goals remain the same: to reduce the amount of disease, premature death, and disease-produced discomfort and disability."

2. On the history of public health see George Rosen, *A History of Public Health* (New York: MD Publications, 1958); George Rosen, *From Medical Police to Social Medicine: Essays on the History of Health Care* (New York: Science History Publications, 1974); and Colin Fraser Brockington, "The History of Public Health," in W. Hobson, *The Theory and Practice of Public Health*, 4th ed. (London: Oxford University Press, 1975). Also see Jaime Breilh, "Community Medicine Under Imperialism: A New Medical Police," *International Journal of Health Services* 9:5–24, (1979), and Knut Ringer, "Edwin Chadwick, the Market Ideology, and Sanitary Reform: On the Nature of the 19th Century Public Health Movement," *International Journal of Health Services* 9:107–120 (1979).

3. L. Parker and R. H. Worthington, *The Law of Public Health and Safety and the Powers and Duties of Boards of Health* (Albany: Bender, 1892), Sec. I., as quoted in Tobey, *Public Health Law*, p. 5.

4. See Chapter 4, especially note 11.

5. *American Jurisprudence 2d*, (Rochester, N.Y.: Lawyers Cooperative, 1968), vol. 39, "Health," sec. 20. However, if a fundamental constitutional right is involved, the state must show a compelling interest for exercising its police power.

6. Frank Grad, *The Public Health Law Manual* (Washington, D.C.: American Public Health Association, 1975), pp. 6–7. Also see *Kesler & Sons Const. Co. v. Utah State Division of Health*, 30 Utah 2 90, 513 P.2d 1017 (1975) (statute authorizing Department of Health to promulgate regulations that are reasonable and proposed to protect the public's health is not an improper delegation of legislative authority) and *State v. Kelsall*, 523 P. d 1334 (Ariz. App. 1974) (state legislature's delegation of authority to the board of health to prescribe reasonably necessary measures for controlling communicable disease transmittible to man is not unconstitutional).

7. On home rule in general, see *American Jurisprudence 2d*, vol. 56, "Municipal

Corporations," etc., secs. 126–138 (1971). Also see Grad, *Public Health Law Manual*, pp. 18–19.

8. Art. VII, sec. 6(a).

9. Tobey, *Public Health Law*, pp. 9–12.

10. M. A. Kohn et al., *School Health Services and Nurse Practitioners: A Survey of State Laws* (Washington: Center for Law and Social Policy, 1979).

11. William Clexton, Janice Ruff, and Stuart Paterson, *Michigan's Public Health Code—First Year of Implementation* (Lansing: Michigan Department of Public Health, 1979).

12. To avoid a more controversial area, public support for health care services for the needy—Medicaid—was excluded from the revision package.

13. Howard N. Mantel, "New Horizons for Local Legislation: The New York City Health Code," *Brooklyn Barrister* 10:216 (1959).

14. Some understanding of legislative drafting is important here. See Reed Dickerson, *The Fundamentals of Legal Drafting* (published for the American Bar Foundation by Little, Brown, Boston, 1965). Also see William J. Curran, "The Preparation of State and Local Health Regulations," *American Journal of Public Health* 49:314–321 (1959), and William J. Curran, "The Architecture of Public Health Statutes and Administrative Regulations," *Public Health Reports* 79:747–754 (1964).

15. See Chapter 13.

16. Jon R. Waltz and Fred E. Inbau, *Medical Jurisprudence* (New York: Macmillan, 1971), pp. 312–316; Grad, *Public Health Law Manual*, pp. 200–220.

17. Waltz and Inbau, *Medical Jurisprudence*, pp. 316–320. The Illinois provision is found at Ill. Rev. Stat., ch. 111½, sec. 22.

18. Center for Disease Control, "Current Trends: Viral Hepatitis Reporting," *Morbidity and Mortality Weekly Report* 24:165–166 (May 10, 1975).

19. Reuben Tizes and Douglas Pravda, "Proposed Toll-free Telephone Reporting of Notifiable Diseases," *Health Services Reports* 87:633–637 (1972).

20. For example, Ill. Rev. Stat., ch. 126, sec. 1, provides that "any medical practitioner or other person making a required communicable disease report in good faith shall be immune from suit for slander or libel based upon any statements contained in such reports."

21. Nathan Hershey, "Putting Teeth into the Public Health Reporting Laws," *American Journal of Public Health* 66:399–400 (1976).

22. Child abuse and neglect reporting requirements are discussed in Chapter 20. Other areas in which reporting may be required include diseases in newborns, animal and human bites, gunshot and knife wounds, etc.

23. Although licensure of personnel is based on public health grounds, this does not mean that a state's department of public health will exercise this function for every—or any—profession. Departments of education, registration, boards of regents, and other such agencies may be involved.

24. Grad, *Public Health Law Manual*, p. 54.

25. Ibid., pp. 58–59.

26. Ibid., p. 76. Often the authority to conduct inspections is limited by constitutional and statutory prohibitions, with local and state agencies having no jurisdiction over state and federal institutions. Thus, for example, while food poisoning is not uncommon in state treatment facilities, prisons, and

college dormitories, authority for local health inspectors to enter such governmental facilities may be lacking.

27. See *Dumbra v. U.S.*, 268 U.S. 435 (1924) at p. 441.

28. *Camara v. Municipal Court of the City and County of San Francisco*, 387 U.S. 525 (1967). Also see companion case, *See v. City of Seattle*, 387 U.S. 541 (1967).

29. Justice White, writing for the Court, stated: "Probable cause to issue a warrant to inspect must exist if reasonable legislative or administrative standards for conducting an area inspection are satisfied with respect to a particular dwelling. Such standards, which will vary with the municipal program being enforced, may be based upon the passage of time, the nature of the building (e.g., a multi-family apartment house), or the condition of the entire area, but they will not necessarily depend upon specific knowledge of the condition of the particular dwelling."

30. *Colonade Catering Corporation v. United States*, 397 U.S. 72 (1970) (dealers in alcoholic beverages) and *United States v. Biswell*, 406 U.S. 311 (1972) (dealer in firearms).

31. *Marshall v. Barlow's, Inc.*, 436 U.S. 307 (1978). During an eighteen-month period following *Barlow*, warrants were demanded for OSHA inspections 2.6 percent of the time. See Mark A. Rothstein, *Occupational Safety and Health Law* (St. Paul: West, 1981 Supplement), sec. 226.

32. 302 Ill. 422 (1922).

33. "A public nuisance is distinguished from a private nuisance in that a public nuisance obstructs or causes inconvenience to the public in general, while a private nuisance adversely affects the property rights or obstructs or causes inconvenience to a neighbor or other person in the vicinity of the condition." Grad, *Public Health Law Manual*, pp. 122–123.

34. Because the proceedings are actually directed against the goods rather than the owner, one finds court decisions in this area with interesting names such as *People v. 532 cases, more or less, "Aunt Polly's Better Buttercookies."*

35. 197 U.S. 11 (1905).

36. Kohn, *School Health Services*. Also see Grad, *Public Health Law Manual*, p. 45, and Eugene W. Fowinkle, Steven Barid, and Clara McD. Bass, "A Compulsory School Immunization Program in Tennessee, *Public Health Reports* 96(1):61–66 (1981).

37. However, there is a legal problem area involved in public immunization programs: legal liability for adverse effects of such immunization. See, for example, Chap. 7 of Richard Neustadt and Harvey V. Fineberg, *The Swine Flu Affair: Decision-Making on a Slippery Disease* (Washington, D.C.: Department of Health, Education, and Welfare, 1978). Note: "Apportioning Liability in Mass Innoculations," *New York University Review of Law and Social Change;* 6:239–262 (1977); and Marc A. Franklin and Joseph E. Mais, Jr., "Tort Law and Mass Immunization Programs: Lessons from the Polio and Flu Episodes" *California Law Review* 65:754–775 (1977).

38. *Simon v. Sargent*, 346 F. Supp. 277 (D. Mass., 1972), affirmed without opinion, 409 U.S. 1020 (1972). Legal authority notwithstanding, a number of states have repealed their compulsory helmet laws under pressure from irate cyclists.

39. Preventive intervention by government to reduce the incidence of so-called

"self-inflicted" death and disease—i.e., the effects of cigarettes, alcohol, highway travel without protective devices, etc.—is discussed in Chapter 12. For an analysis of the philosophical justification for such intervention see Dan E. Beauchamp, "Public Health and Individual Liberty," *Annual Review of Public Health* 1:121–136 (1980).

40. See discussion in text accompanying note 32.

6

Licensure, Certification, and Accreditation

Health care delivery systems are not solely concerned with medical practice. They provide for payment for care, construct and operate institutions, provide employment, and carry out educational and research activities; however, the major purpose of all these activities is to make it possible for medical practice to be carried on. . . . Whoever controls medical practice, therefore, controls the keystone upon which all the rest depends. . . . In the United States, because of the way the medical licensing laws are written, the physicians have a virtual hammerlock on medical practice.

—Steven Jonas[1]

HEALTH PERSONNEL CREDENTIALING—licensure, certification, and accreditation—is so much a part of health care delivery that it is taken for granted. Even the health professionals themselves generally think of credentialing as a series of hurdles to be jumped rather than a rationalizing mechanism for the health care system—perhaps because they are in a better position than others to observe how inadequately credentialing fulfills its idealized role of protecting the public. In the past two decades, however, there has been a growing movement, both among health professionals and in the society at large, to reassess the procedures and scope of credentialing programs in the health field.[2]

Several factors prompted the increasing concern. The emergence of new categories of health workers has been accompanied by a proliferation of credentialing programs. In 1890 there were only about ten occupations licensed in one or more states. Today there are well over one hundred; some thirty-five of them are health related.[3] Another new phenomenon is the explosion of knowledge in the medical sciences and the realization that even the most thorough training can no longer assure a lifetime of adequacy as a health care professional.

Medical licensure dates back to the Middle Ages, when the medical faculties of European universities approved the physicians who trained under them. (As skilled craftsmen, surgeons were members of guilds, a certification rather than licensure type of credentialing.) Later, licensure came under the joint aegis of the government and the professional medical societies.[4]

In the United States medical licensure went through the same stages, but more quickly. During the colonial period, physicians were in such short supply that little control was imposed; an individual needed only the approval of the physician with whom he had served his apprenticeship to set up in practice himself. Not until the colonies became a nation did the states begin to require either a medical school diploma or examination by the state medical society as a prerequisite to medical practice, requirements soon nullified by the development of medical diploma mills offering little training but impressive certificates of completion.

By the mid-1800s many states had abandoned licensure requirements. But after the Civil War the states tackled the problem again, ultimately establishing the system of medical licensing boards in effect today. Texas enacted what is generally considered to be the first modern medical practice act in 1873, and most other states followed suit during the next two decades.[5] West Virginia's law, enacted in 1882, provided a legal test of this exercise of state police power. This statute allowed a person to practice medicine in the state if: (1) he was a graduate of a medical school approved by the state board of health; or (2) had been in the continuous practice of medicine in West Virginia for the ten years preceding the act; or (3) passed an examination prepared by the state board of health. One individual, a Dr. Dent, engaged in the practice of medicine although he met none of these criteria. Convicted of violating the medical practice act, he challenged the law on due-process grounds, pressing his case all the way to the U.S. Supreme Court, which upheld the constitutionality of the law.[6]

New medical practice acts played an important role in dealing with the cultists and incompetents of the day. But they also fostered an elite profession, frequently insensitive to society's less fortunate. Following the European example, the state governments implemented their licensure systems in close cooperation with the state medical societies. The professional societies readily assumed the dominant role.[7]

Licensure of other health professionals parallels the development of the professions themselves over the years. Pharmacists were first licensed in 1816 and dentists in 1841. The first nurse licensing law was enacted in 1903; opticians were first licensed in 1935; medical technicians in 1936; psychologists and social workers in 1945. By 1970, at least forty-five health professions and occupations were licensed in one or more states, fourteen of them in all states.[8] In 1971 the U.S. Department of Health, Education, and Welfare recommended what became a four-year moratorium "on the enactment of legislation that would establish new categories of health personnel with statutorily defined scopes of functions." Yet despite the moratorium, eleven new licensure bills were enacted into law in 1972 and thirty new laws in 1974.[9] On the other hand, some important functions have remained outside the licensing system. (In forty states anyone can operate medical X-ray equipment. It is estimated that only half of the country's 130,000 to 170,000 X-ray operators are covered by either mandatory or voluntary state credentialing programs.[10]) In addition, many health professionals who do function under a licensing statute routinely act beyond their authorized scope of practice—with the tacit approval of all concerned. And since any change in licensure laws is apt to disturb a delicate balance of power among the various health professionals, in most cases no one is eager to rock the boat.

The Credentialing System

What exactly is licensure? How does it differ from certification? From accreditation? And how do they interrelate? Of the three, licensure stands out as the product of laws, not private action, and it will be discussed in greatest detail. Many of the points common to all three will be developed primarily in terms of licensure. While these three credentialing concepts—licensure, certification, and accreditation—are clear and distinct, the same is not true of the words used to describe the concepts. It is not uncommon to find a state applying the word "certification" to the licensure process. Similarly, in some states "registration" is used to describe licensure, in others it means certification, and in still others it has yet a third application.

Webster's New World Dictionary defines "license" as "a formal permission to do something; esp., authorization by law to do some specified thing."[11] In the context of professional licensure such authorization generally comes from the state, acting under its police power. Implicit in the definition is the suggestion that doing the specified thing without the formal permission is proscribed; otherwise there would be no point in the formal permission.

There are two different types of things permitted by license: the practice of a particular profession and/or the use of a particular title. The first approach, known as *mandatory licensure,* prohibits the carrying out of a specified task or series of tasks (such as representing clients in court) to all but those licensed to do so. The second approach, known as *permissive licensure,* does not bar any particular activity, but allows only licensed individuals to use a title that is recognized by the public as a mark of special expertise; for example, anyone can charge a fee for preparing a financial accounting but only a certified public account can hold himself out as a CPA.[12]

The assumption underlying licensure is that the general public is not in a position to adequately judge whether professional practitioners are competent in their professions. Thus, the purported purpose of licensure is to protect the public by assuring that those practicing the licensed profession or occupation, or using the title, are competent to do so.[13] "An agency of government grants permission to an individual to engage in a given occupation upon finding that the applicant has attained the minimal degree of competency necessary to ensure that the public health, safety, and welfare will be reasonably well protected."[14]

Licensure, then, is a prospective control, a determination made before the individual begins practicing that he or she has the knowledge, skill, and experience necessary to function at a minimally competent level. Theoretically, licensure programs also enforce performance standards, permitting the withdrawing of a license if the licensee performs below a minimal level. But this aspect of professional licensure is universally acknowledged as a failure.[15] Traditionally licensure has looked at credentials, rather than at track records.[16]

The major difficulties in implementing licensure programs involve determining what constitutes "qualified" and defining the scope of authorized activity. There is no Platonic ideal of the competent health professional, for example, nor do state legislators generally have the expertise to develop a standard. Of course the legislature could establish a body of outside experts to whom they could turn for advice; but this is not, for the most part, what has happened. Instead, legislatures have turned to already existing bodies, the professional societies. The result, many believe, has been to foster more of a self-serving monopoly rather than a mechanism to protect the public.

Health Professional Licensure

"The main objectives of licensing laws are to control entrance into the occupation and to support and enforce standards of practice among licensed practitioners," stated a 1971 report by the secretary of Health, Education, and Welfare on health personnel credentialing. According to the report, the major activities involved in accomplishing these objectives are:

- Examination of applicants' credentials to determine whether their education, experience, and moral fitness meet statutory or administrative requirements.
- Investigation of schools to determine whether the training programs meet requisite standards.

- Administration of examinations to test the academic and practical qualifications of applicants to determine if preset standards are met.
- Issuance of regulations establishing professional standards of practice; investigation of charges of violation of standards established by statutes and regulations; suspension or revocation of violators' licenses; and restoration of licenses after a period of suspension or further investigation.[17]

The easiest way to determine how the licensure mechanism works is to examine the dominant portion of the system, physician licensure. All states have medical practice acts that prohibit the unlicensed practice of medicine. The New York statute, for example, states that "the practice of the profession of medicine is defined as diagnosing, treating, operating or prescribing for any human disease, pain, injury, deformity or physical condition."[18]

This is a clearly mandatory, or compulsory, licensing statute; only a person licensed under the act is allowed to practice medicine. Unlicensed practice can result in criminal prosecution and is punishable by fines, imprisonment, or both. Courts may also be asked to order a person to stop unauthorized practice. And persons with a valid license in a related area, but one more limited than a medical license, could lose that license for engaging in the unauthorized practice of medicine.[19]

State regulation of chiropractors, dental hygenists, dentists, opticians, optometrists, osteopaths, pharmacists, podiatrists, and veterinarians also uses the mandatory approach to licensure. However, in a major study of health occupational licensure, Pennell and Stewart point out that "exclusions and exceptions from licensure requirements are always made for Federal employees in the course of their employment and frequently for state and municipal workers. Personnel engaged in research or educational pursuits are sometimes excluded, as are students and auxiliary personnel working under the supervision of a licensed practitioner."[20]

Although the trend is away from the permissive approach to licensure, some examples are still found in the health field. For example, in many states anyone can legally function as a "practical nurse," although only those properly licensed can use the title "licensed practical nurse." This is also true, in a number of states, for physical therapists, psychologists, sanitarians, and social workers.

The most difficult aspect of any professional licensure law is defining which activities are prohibited to all but the properly licensed. Except for Massachusetts, where it is defined by regulation, all state medical practice acts contain some definition of the practice of medicine.[21] These statutory definitions generally conceive of medicine in terms of diagnosis, treatment, and prescription, but the scope of practice allowed is virtually unlimited. Thus, an individual who qualifies for a physician's license may legally practice not only general medicine, but surgery, psychiatry, oncology, pediatrics, or any other specialty with or without additional training in these areas.[22]

Since, generally speaking, the scope of a physician's license allows the licensee to do whatever doctors customarily do, problems arise whenever innovations in practice or technology appear on the scene that do not readily fit the rubric of "what doctors traditionally do." Acupuncture, for example, is an ancient art, but not one that American physicians have customarily practiced. Is it nevertheless to be considered part of the practice of medicine? Many physicians argue that it is; many laymen, including those who have practiced acupuncture for many years here and in other countries, argue that it is not. As of this writing several states have defined acupuncture as the practice of medicine, but there is no definitive answer.[23]

A similar problem concerns the practice of other health practitioners. If physicians have an unlimited scope of practice and only physicians may legally do what physicians do, how can any other health care practitioner function without violating the medical practice act? One answer lies in *exemptions* to the statute; another lies in *delegation*.

Health professionals whose work is quite independent of physicians—dentists, psychologists, podiatrists, chiropractors and the like—usually are exempted by virtue of their own practice acts, which define and limit the tasks and duties related to their specific professional role and function. In some states such statutes explicitly exempt the professions they define from the medical practice act; in others there is a general exemption for persons legally practicing another profession licensed by the state.[24]

Physicians and other independent licensed practitioners are legally able to delegate some functions and duties, provided they are carried out under the control and supervision of the delegator. ("Control and supervision" is a term subject to a variety of interpretations, it does not necessarily require physical presence.) The authority to delegate may come from specific statutes or from court interpretations. Frequently, the authorization will also specify the type(s) of health professional who can be delegated to, often persons licensed—or certified—in their own profession.[25] Absent some specific statutory exemption from the medical practice act, diagnosis, treatment, and/or prescription functions performed by *unlicensed* personnel could be violations of the medical practice act even when performed under supervision and control of a licensed physician.[26]

Exemption and delegation sometimes exist in tandem, as in the nursing profession. Most of what nurses do would be a violation of medical practice acts without some special provision to the contrary. In twenty-nine states and the District of Columbia, the lawful practice of nursing is specifically exempted from the medical practice act. In six states, nursing practice is authorized only under the supervision and control of a physician. And in thirteen states that neither exempt the practice of nursing from the medical practice act nor provide for delegation by the physicians, "custom and usage have long since established that a physician may delegate certain medical acts to a nurse acting under his supervision and control, and the chances of the act being interpreted in an appropriate case as prohibiting this part of the traditional role of the nurse are virtually nonexistent."[27]

All states have nurse practice acts,[28] but there is some variation in how the professional nursing role is defined. The traditional approach, based on a model definition adopted by the American Nurses' Association and still followed in several states, provides:

> The term "practice of professional nursing" means the performance, for compensation, of any acts in the observation, care and counsel of the ill, injured or infirm or in the maintenance of health or prevention of illness of others, or in the supervision and teaching of other personnel, or the administration of medications and treatments as prescribed by a licensed physician or a licensed dentist; requiring substantial specialized judgment and skill and based on knowledge and application of the principles of biological, physical and social science. The foregoing shall not be deemed to include acts of diagnosis or prescription of therapeutic or corrective measures.

The first sentence provides a fairly broad authority; but the second sentence bars nurses from any independent performance of medical practice. Some states have specified "medical diagnosis" in the second sentence, but the definition remains a sharply restrictive one.

In recent years the growing complexity in medical care has considerably expanded the nursing role. Some of the new tasks nurses perform—including emergency room and critical care nursing, and other tasks requiring independent judgment and action—do not seem to be authorized by the traditional nurse practice act. Some states have dealt with this issue by amending their nurse practice act to permit "additional acts" beyond those traditionally authorized, leaving it to the state board of nursing or jointly to the medical and nursing boards to determine what "additional acts" should be covered; other states have simply defined "additional acts" as those recognized by the medical and nursing professions as properly performed by registered nurses; and still others require that the "additional acts" be delegated by a physician.[29] A number of states require additional education and training for those nurses performing "additional acts."

Several states, including New York and California, have entirely rewritten their nurse practice acts to provide a more rational and sophisticated definition of professional nursing.[30] The New York law authorizes diagnosis and treatment by nurses, but only according to statutory definitions of these terms, which limit diagnosis and treatment to the context of "nursing regimens" and the "execution of any prescribed medical regimen."[31] California provides for a somewhat broader and independent nursing role, but only according to "standardized procedures," defined as "policies and protocols developed . . . through collaboration among administrators and health professionals, including physicians and·nurses." It should be noted, however, that these breaks with older definitions also open the door to unpredictable interpretations of the new acts by the courts.[32]

Beside the traditional nursing role, states have statutes that authorize nurse practitioners. While their permissible scope of practice varies from state to state, it often includes performing diagnostic tests and physical examinations, initiating treatment and managing chronic illnesses, and dispensing and prescribing drugs (the latter is prohibited in three states). In all instances, however, some level of physician supervision of the nurse practitioner is required.[33]

Physician assistants also perform medical procedures with a certain amount of independence, but under closer physician direction, supervision, and control than is the case with nurse practitioners. Some states regulate physician assistants under a credentialing system, establishing minimum qualifications in addition to requiring the supervision of a physician. Other states simply exempt physician assistants from the medical practice act and require physician supervision, but leave it to the physician to determine qualifications. Often physicians will be limited to one or two physician assistants working under them.[34]

For all such licensed health professionals, practicing beyond the scope of one's license can lead to prosecution for violation of the medical practice act. In some states, however, the risk is even greater, for under those statutes, the courts may presume malpractice negligence if a person is found to be functioning beyond the scope of the relevant licensing act.[35]

Powers and Duties of Licensing Boards

According to Pennell and Stewart,[36] "About half of the occupational licensing statutes require that *all* board members be licensed practitioners in the occupations regulated by the boards on which they serve." In those states only physicians serve on medical licensing boards, only dentists on dental boards, only pharmacists on pharmacy boards. (Common exceptions are dental hygienists, licensed by dental boards made up of dentists; practical nurses (LPNs) licensed by boards made up of registered nurses (RNs); and midwives.)

In other states the board that licenses physicians also licenses osteopaths, podiatrists, and/or physical therapists. These boards may have a mixed membership, usually drawn from related health professions. Lay representatives of the general public are usually not included on these boards.[37]

The number of members on a licensing board can vary widely. Some have as few as three; others as many as twenty. In some states the boards for the different licensed professions operate quite independently of one another; in others their functions are coordinated by a central board or agency.[38] In most states board members are appointed by the governor, although a few provide for appointment by the State Department or Board of Health or of Education. Some statutes require the governor to appoint from lists submitted by the relevant professional society. Derbyshire reports that "regardless of minor differences the laws of 23 states provide that the medical society shall have a direct voice in the appointment of members."[39] And most governors consult with professional societies on licensure board appointments even if they are not legally required to do so. In several states the governor's selection must be confirmed by the state senate.

After a thorough study of medical licensure in the United States, Derbyshire developed the following composite picture of a medical licensing board member:

> He is a Caucasian man, a little over 58 years of age . . . ; most likely a general practitioner; if not, a general surgeon or an internist. He is a leader in the medical community and well known to the members of his state medical society. He possesses no singular attributes which qualify him to judge the academic attainments of applicants for licensure, but he is sincere in carrying out his duties and may seek help in formulating his examination questions. He is a graduate of an approved American medical school and is better qualified to carry out the disciplinary duties of his office than the educational and examining functions. He does not serve with thought of financial gain.[40]

Licensing boards function under and according to their authorizing statues, adopting their own rules and regulations. Their functions generally include:

1. Examination of applicants.
2. Issuance of licenses.
3. Suspension, revocation, and restoration of licensure.
4. Enforcement of the licensing statute (including discipline).
5. Approval of professional schools.[41]

In addition, licensing boards determine the personal, educational, experience, and examination standards that must be met in order to be eligible for licensure. Usually these will include: (1) good moral character; (2) graduation from an approved training program; (3) completion of some period of supervised practice; and (4) passing of an examination.

A 1967 survey of state requirements for medical licensure carried out by Ruhe[42] indicated that forty-two states required graduation from high school; twenty-nine states specified the necessary number of college credits that had to go into college graduation; and twenty-six states detailed the amount of work required in the applicant's medical school curriculum. Twenty-six states required that the licensing board itself must approve the medical school from which the applicant graduated, in one case through its own inspection (the remainder accepted approval by the American Medical Association and/or the Association of American Medical Colleges);[43] thirty-nine required internships, some specifying the exact nature and content of the internship; and all required an examination of some sort. Two-thirds of the state statutes specified the subjects to be covered by the examination, and over half specified the acceptable passing grade. Similar requirements are set for the licensing of other health professionals.

All states accept the results of examinations conducted by the National Board of Medical Examiners and/or the Federation Licensing Examination, rather than relying upon questions developed by their own board members, as they once did. The trend for all health professions is in the direction of greater national uniformity, which means growing acceptance of national examinations and professional degrees, as well as internships from institutions approved by national bodies rather than a state board itself.[44]

The trend toward uniformity in licensure helps to simplify the credentialing of someone already licensed in another state. Almost all states provide a licensing shortcut for such individuals, often through *reciprocity*, an arrangement under which two states with similar licensing requirements agree to recognize each other's licensure for a particular profession, thus eliminating the need for reexamination. A second approach, *endorsement*, relies on a discretionary determination by a state licensing board that the licensure requirements of another state at the time the applicant received his or her license to practice were substantially equivalent.[45]

Usually licenses are for a fixed period of time; a licensed professional must periodically renew his or her license, or reregister. But renewal requirements are largely pro forma, involving payment of a fee and updating of general information. A considerable number of states have recently instituted continuing education requirements for licensure renewal by physicians, nurses, dentists, pharmacists, and dental hygienists.[46] But seldom is there a reassessment of the renewing practitioner's qualifications to function in the particular profession. Pennell reports that about three-quarters of all health professional licenses must be renewed annually, most others biennially. A few have renewal or registration periods of three to five years and a small number are permanent registrations.[47] Failure to renew could cause a license to lapse.[48]

One of the most potentially important functions of a licensure board is its power to suspend and revoke licenses.[49] But this power is rarely invoked. Derbyshire, studying the period 1963 through 1967, found a total of 938 disciplinary actions against physicians taken by boards nationwide, 375 of them involving probation and 334 revocations of licenses. Of the 938 actions, 440 involved narcotics.[50] A *New York Times* study in 1976, covering the period 1971 to 1974, disclosed an average of 72 medical licenses revoked annually, a figure consistent with the average of 66 revocations annually found in a Federation of State Medical Boards study covering thirteen years.[51] A 1980 American Medical Association study found a significant increase, with 685 disciplinary actions in 1977 and 1,476 in 1978, with 216 revocations.[52] Still, these figures are for the nation as a whole; they represent at most about 0.027 percent of the close to 400,000 licensed physicians in the country. In a review of this problem, Steve Jonas offers several reasons for this low level of activity:

> One reason is the professional dominance of medical licensing boards . . . and the possible "reluctance to enforce sanctions against fellow practitioners (perhaps in part because of close professional and social interrelationships)." . . . A lack of graduated means of discipline has been another problem. . . . By 1978, more states were adding more graded sanctions to the list available. . . . Some medical boards may be reluctant to act because they do not want to get involved in litigation. . . . Other boards would like very much to act much more vigorously than they do, but find themselves hamstrung by lack of funds, lack of staff, and lack of enough readily available, qualified legal counsel. . . . Finally, many instances of gross medical misconduct are simply not reported to state boards.[53]

Generally, a licensing statute will specify some of the grounds on which a license may be suspended or revoked, including such things as conviction of a crime that is a felony and/or involves moral turpitude, and including so-called generic or general offenses, under the broad rubric of "unprofessional conduct."[54] Licensing boards considering a charge of unprofessional conduct will often be guided by the ethical codes adopted by relevant professional societies. Since the determination tends to be a subjective one, it is likely to be subject to close court scrutiny.[55]

Because "few medical practice acts are specifically directed to ensuring that some level of professional competence is maintained,"[56] incompetence is rarely a cause of license revocation.[57] Part of the problem is a failure of practitioners to report incompetent colleagues to appropriate authorities. (The AMA considers it unethical not to do so,[58] but this ethical guideline has obviously not been persuasive.) At least eleven states have adopted "snitch" laws that require physicians to report incompetent colleagues and grant immunity from suit to the reporting physician. Failure to report is statutorily defined as unprofessional conduct. (In Arizona the number of reports quadrupled after the law was passed.)[59] Roemer writes that, in addition, "some states require physicians to report malpractice claims, judgments, or settlements against them, and eleven states require insurers to report malpractice judgments and settlements to the disciplinary authority."[60]

One area of some progress involves impaired or disabled physicians, including those with alcohol or drug dependency problems. During the past decade over two-thirds of the states have enacted "sick doctor" laws allowing the state medical board to require mental and physical examinations of physicians whose mental or physical ability or ability to practice with reasonable skill and safety have been called into question. Failure of such an examination, as well as refusal to submit to examination, can lead to licensure suspension, restriction, or revocation.[61] But there is little evidence that state boards are taking this problem very seriously.

There has long been debate as to whether a license to practice a profession constitutes a right or a privilege. The professional who has spent years qualifying for the license, and whose livelihood depends upon it, may well view it as a valuable property carrying with it all the rights of property ownership, including the right to use without interference. But the states, as regulators and protectors of the public health, prefer to view a license as nothing more than an administrative lifting of a legislative prohibition,[62] a privilege that can be granted or taken away in the public interest. The distinction is important because it affects the legal burden a state licensing board faces in seeking to revoke a license to practice. If a license is viewed as a privilege, the courts are likely to allow licensing boards somewhat more discretion in procedural matters. Recognition of a license as property, however, limits the state's procedural discretion, because U.S. law attaches great importance to property rights.

It is clear that in the face of immediate threat to the public's well-being, licenses can be revoked summarily. Generally, however, a state licensing statute—or its administrative procedures act—will set various due-process requirements that must be met before a license can be revoked, including requirements for notice and hearing, evidentary standards of reliability, authenticity, and fairness, a written record, and an appeals process.[63] Often these can be cumbersome and time consuming and, through overreaction more than necessity, can be a deterrent to disciplinary action.

There is still some debate about whether a license confers a right or a privilege, but the trend seems to favor observance of the due-process panoply. Grad and Marti argue that recent Supreme Court decisions requiring due-process safeguards in the granting and revocation of professional licenses have "virtually laid to rest the right-privilege distinction as applied to occupational choice and the right to practice a profession."[64] According to Annas et al.:

> It has been suggested, for example, that words like *privilege, property,* and *liberty* be "put to one side" and that the real question is how actions taken by the government against a licensee can be reconciled with the dictates of justice. It strikes us that this is the proper question. Regardless of the label, courts will strive to treat professionals fairly, and will go to great lengths to provide them due process of law, because their licenses are viewed, at the very least, as something of "tremendous value to the individual."[65]

Why Licensure?

There are two opposing theories as to why occupational licensure systems exist. The *idealistic* theory holds that licensure is intended primarily to protect the public from incompetent, perhaps dangerous, professionals, and that government must assume this function because the general public is not able to assess professional competency. The *acquired* theory holds that licensure is designed and operated primarily for the benefit of the licensed professions, creating legal monopolies restricting the number of practitioners in each licensed field and making it impossible for consumers to go to anyone other than the licensed professional in the field covered by the license.

Though the perceived view, for the most part, upholds the idealistic approach, there is considerable evidence to support the acquired theory,[66] particularly in the health field, where the impetus for licensing generally comes from the professional societies, some of them expressly organized as a prelude to a lobbying for licensing laws.[67]

Of course, such efforts may well be prompted, at least in part, by a desire to protect the public from incompetent practitioners and assorted quacks. But since disciplinary actions by licensure boards are rare, and few licensing statutes even specify incompetency as grounds for license suspension or revocation, this can hardly be looked upon as a quality assurance mechanism. The close relationship of state licensure boards and the professional organizations, and the almost complete failure of such boards to discipline licensees, point to other motivations as well. The impact of licensure on health manpower supplies and utilization has been well documented. Certainly it bolsters the monopoly position of a profession and boosts the income of its practitioners.[68] But besides making it easier for the state to regulate practice and for the professionals to maintain fee schedules, licensure can retard innovation in education, training, and practice, because such advances might threaten the power of those already in professional practice.[69]

Not surprisingly, licensure has been under increasing attack, both within and without the health professions. Among the many suggested reforms, the most extreme approach, and one which will certainly not be accepted, is that offered by Friedman, Illich, and others, which is simply to abolish all licensure laws and rely on the "free market" factors that supposedly control other industries supplying goods and services.[70] A less extreme reform (also predicated on the "free market" approach) would utilize the antitrust laws to limit excessive professional control over the delivery of health services.[71]

Since most licensed health professionals (including physicians on at least a part-time basis) practice in hospitals and other institutions, one suggestion that received considerable attention during the early 1970s is the concept of *institutional licensure*, which would concentrate on state licensure of these institutions, and leave it to the institutions to "credential" the health professionals they employ.[72] In effect, state practice acts would exempt from board oversight anyone practicing within a licensed institution, and the threat of malpractice liability and possible loss of licensure would compel institutions to check and supervise carefully all who work for them. Institutional licensure was a major recommendation in HEW's 1971 *Report on Licensure and Related Health Personnel Credentialing*,[73] but there was such widespread and vociferous opposition that the suggestion was not pursued. The concept has been criticized on the grounds that institutional licensure would give hospitals excessive control over professional employment in the health field.

A number of reforms that involve strengthening the current system without making structural changes are, in fact, already being slowly implemented. In many instances these are reforms that can be undertaken with a minimum of legislative action. One is an increased attention to disciplinary action. This requires not only a change in administrative priorities, but increased appropriations for licensing boards as well, because investigations and disciplinary hearings cost money and so does the pursuit of contested disciplinary action in the courts. It may also require changes in the licensing statutes and/or regulations, to define more clearly the grounds for suspension and revocation of licenses.[74]

Another nonstructural reform is the substitution of a time-limited license, requiring periodic reassessment of qualifications, for the currently widespread system of licensing for life. Such programs usually involve either relicensure examinations or mandatory continuing education requirements. (There is still considerable debate as to whether examination scores or hours of study correlate with professional competency; but since the existing licensing mechanism is based on the assumption that the successful completion of prescribed professional courses and the ability to pass an examination signify a minimal level of competence it seems unlikely this assumption will be soon abandoned.) In recent years, twenty states have amended their medical practice acts to add continuing education requirements for physicians. Forty-two states require evidence of continuing qualifications for license renewal by optometrists, thirty-one by dental hygienists, eight by registered nurses, seven by pharmacists, and six by dentists.[75]

A third nonstructural change, adopted by an increasing number of states, is the provision for consumer representatives on professional licensing boards. By 1980 this had been done with medical licensing boards in twenty-four states.[76] This is an easy change to make—in some cases it requires legislative action, in others it is simply a matter of selecting appointees from a broader list—but it has won few accolades from critics of the licensure system; because of the intimidating effect of professional expertise the impact of the lay minority on such boards is usually virtually unnoticeable.

Certification

The Public Health Service's report on health-manpower credentialing defines certification as the process "by which a nongovernmental agency or association grants recognition to an individual who has met certain predetermined qualifications specified by that agency or association."[77] Because of the parallel between licensure and certification, it is important to understand their relationship to each other.[78]

Certification requirements, like those of licensure, usually cover personal character, education, experience, and successful completion of an examination. Unlike licensure, however, certification programs usually apply uniform national standards. Individuals must be graduates of an approved training program and, in some cases, also a member of the relevant professional association. A number of programs—especially those concerned with medical specialty certification—require several years of postgraduate experience before certification is granted. A growing number of certification programs also require periodic reexamination and/or continuing education to make certain that certificands keep up with advances in their profession.[79]

In some cases certification is carried out by the professional associations themselves; in others separate certifying boards are established.[80] Certification is a voluntary system; there is no legal penalty for practicing a profession without certification by a professional association (although individuals who falsely assert that they are certified could face legal difficulties). But it carries a great deal of weight, particularly with hospitals and other institutions and job registries, which use it as a major screening device for professional job applicants. Although for due-process reasons employers cannot make certification an absolute job requirement, it is often a de facto requirement.

Certification is especially relevant where a profession is not licensed, or where—as in medicine—the profession has become extensively specialized beyond the basic license. Since a medical license allows the holder to practice all aspects of medicine and surgery, it is of little help to the hospital considering whether to grant a particular licensed physician the privilege of performing neurosurgical operations. For this reason, hospitals at one time required those seeking certain staff privileges to have specialty certification as well as a medical license. Today the requirement is generally that the physician be either board-certified or board-eligible (meaning that he or she has met all the educational and experiential requirements but has not taken and passed the examination for certification.)[81]

Where no license system exists, or where that system is too basic for the specialization involved, certification serves as an unofficial licensing system. It also facilitates new approaches to credentialing, such as the use of reexamination and requirements for continuing education. And it is likely that it takes some of the public pressure off a lax licensing system. At the same time, certification programs are vulnerable to the same criticisms leveled at licensure: They are run by the professions themselves, they have the effect of limiting competition (and raising prices), and there is no proof that they protect the public. In addition, since certification lacks the mantle of state law, it is possible that it constitutes an illegal conspiracy in restraint of trade.[82]

Accreditation

Also part and parcel of health personnel credentialing is accreditation, which is directed at institutions rather than at individuals. The Public Health Service defines accreditation as the process "by which an agency or organization evaluates and recognizes an institution or program of study as meeting certain predetermined criteria or standards."[83]

Both licensure and certification rely heavily on the educational credentials of applicants, generally requiring graduation from an approved school or training program. State licensure boards and certifying bodies could, of course, investigate schools and training programs and issue their own approvals; but such an approach would be costly and burdensome,[84] and would make reciprocity and endorsement very difficult. Accreditation obviates this task by providing an entity to investigate and approve schools and training programs whose findings will be acceptable to most credentialing agencies.

Institutional accreditation covers an entire institution, such as a university or college. Specialized accreditation covers specific programs, departments, or curricula within an institution. Usually specialized accreditation of a part of an institution requires that the entire institution be accredited. Though most accreditation programs focus on educational institutions,[85] such as colleges and universities, there are also programs covering hospitals and related institutions.[86] HEW's *Report on Licensure and Related Health Personnel Credentialing*[87] describes the following steps as basic to the accreditation process:

1. The accrediting agency, in collaboration with professional groups and educational institutions, establishes standards.
2. The institution or program desiring accreditation prepares a self-evaluation study that provides a framework for measuring its performance against the standards established by the accrediting agency.
3. A team selected by the accrediting agency visits the institution or program to determine firsthand if the applicant meets the established standards.
4. Upon being satisfied through the information obtained from the self-evaluation and the site visit that the applicant meets its standards, the accrediting agency lists the institution or program in an official publication with other similarly accredited institutions or programs.
5. The accrediting agency periodically reevaluates the institutions or programs that it lists to ascertain that the standards are being met.

The American Medical Association plays a key role in accrediting a variety of education programs for the health professional. The AMA, together with the Association of American Medical Colleges, accredits U.S. medical schools. These two organizations, along with the American Hospital Association and the specialty societies and boards, review and approve residency training programs. The AMA's Council on Medical Education, in collaboration with the allied health professions and the medical specialties concerned, also accredits training programs for certified laboratory assistants, cytotechnologists, histologic technicians, inhalation therapy technicians, medical assistants, medical record librarians, medical record technicians, medical technologists, nuclear medicine technologists, occupational therapists, orthopedic assistants, physical therapists, physician assistants, radiation therapy technologists (or technicians), and radiologic technologists (formerly X-ray technicians).

As Jonas points out: "The basic principles of accreditation are similar to those of licensure in that it is assumed that if the institution meets certain standards of physical and organizational structure at one point in time, then: (1) good quality health care, or health personnel education, is being delivered at that point in time; and (2) it can be predicted that the care will continue to be of good quality for a discrete period of time."[88]

Conclusion

Licensure, certification, and accreditation have functioned together in the health care field as means of assuring professional well-being and control while maintaining the overall dominance of the medical profession. Changing economic relationships, with power shifting from health care practitioners to corporate managers, suggest that in future decades health professionals will function in a more open system, exercising less of their own control. The most likely result will be less job autonomy, with even physicians ceasing to be independent, becoming instead a category of highly paid technicians. If this change should come about, the moving forces will be economic but the mechanism will be alterations in the credentialing process.

NOTES

1. "Measurement and Control of the Quality of Health Care," in Steven Jonas et al., *Health Care Delivery in the United States*, 2d ed. (New York: Springer, 1981), p. 406.
2. For an important and useful review of the courts' involvement in credentialing, see William A. Kaplin, "Professional Power and Judicial Review: The Health Professions," *George Washington Law Review* 44:710–753 (1976).
3. As of 1977, thirty-five health professions and occupations were licensed in one or more states, sixteen in all states and the District of Columbia. *Health Resource Statistics, 1976–1977 Edition,* (Hyattsville, Md.: National Center for Health Statistics, 1979), p. 473 (DHEW pub. no. (PHS) 79-1509). Paul R. Torrens and Charles E. Lewis report that: "Of the 665 primary or alternate job titles in health care that could be identified by the Department of Labor in 1975, more than 150 of them were subject to separate certification or professional designation by various professional organizations or agencies." Torrens and Lewis, "Health Care Personnel," pp. 256–286 at 257, in Stephen J. Williams and Paul R. Torrens, *Introduction to Health Services* (New York: John Wiley, 1980).
4. Henry M. Sigerist, *Medicine and Human Welfare* (New Haven: Yale University Press, 1941 (reprinted College Park, Md.: McGrath, 1970); R. H. Shryock, *Medical Licensing in America, 1650–1965* (Baltimore: Johns Hopkins, 1967).
5. In part in acknowledgment of the fact that no one, regardless of credentials, could accomplish much in terms of curing or ameliorating disease. See Steven Jonas, *Medical Mystery: The Training of Doctors in the United States* (New York: W W Norton, 1978), pp. 168–169.

6. *Dent v. West Virginia,* 129 U.S. 114 (1888). See K. C. Sears: "The Medical Man and the Constitution," *Annals of Internal Medicine* 25:304–323, (1946); cited in Robert C. Derbyshire, *Medical Licensure and Discipline in the United States* (Baltimore: Johns Hopkins, 1969), p. 15.

7. Dr. William Osler, originally a strong supporter of state licensing boards, later came to view them as "provincialism run riot." Derbyshire, *Medical Licensure and Discipline,* p. 151.

8. National Commission for Health Certifying Agencies, *Perspectives on Health Occupational Credentialing* (Washington, D.C.: Health Resources Administration, April 1980), p. 7 (DHHS pub. no. (HRA) 80–39).

9. *Ibid,* p. 8.

10. *Washington Report on Medicine and Health* 33(30):4 (July 30, 1979). However, under the Omnibus Reconciliation Act of 1981 (P.L. 97–35) the secretary of Health and Human Services is to promulgate minimum standards for X-ray technicians, dental hygienists, and other health care personnel. The states will then have three years to comply with the standards.

11. *Webster's New World Dictionary* (New York: World, 1972), p. 815. Rick Carlson describes occupational licensure as "legal boundaries around manpower categories." See Carlson, "Health Manpower Licensing and Emerging Institutional Responsibility for the Quality of Care," in Clark C. Havighurst, ed., *Health Care* (Dobbs Ferry, N.Y.: Oceana Publications, 1972), p. 386.

12. In some states the mandatory licensure restriction applies only if the person performing the otherwise prohibited task is paid or expects to be paid for so doing. See note 18. Although "mandatory" and "permissive" are the terms most often used in describing the two types of licensure, some writers use "compulsory" and "voluntary." See, for example, M. Y. Pennell and P. A. Stewart, *State Licensing of Health Occupations* (Washington, D.C.: U.S. Department of Health, Education and Welfare, 1968).

13. Or as Grad puts it: "To exclude from activities which may adversely affect the health and safety of the public those entrepreneurs who will not or cannot conform to desirable standards." Frank P. Grad, *The Public Health Law Manual* (Washington, D.C.: American Public Health Association, 1973), pp. 58–59. A similar purpose is found in facilities licensure, discussed in Chapter 7.

14. *A Proposal for Credentialing Health Manpower* (Public Health Service: U.S. Department of Health, Education and Welfare, June 1976), p. 1.

15. See notes 56–61.

16. Licensure is not the only method by which government seeks to protect the public against incompetent practitioners. Chapter 16 will discuss the way in which the malpractice lawsuit has functioned as a judicially controlled protection device. Chapter 8 looks at how the government's power as the purchaser of health care services gives it control over the way in which that care is delivered, an approach taken in the Professional Standards Review Organization (PSRO) system. Government also makes use of privately operated protective mechanisms, as will be discussed later in this chapter.

17. *Report on Licensure and Related Health Personnel Credentialing* (Washington, D.C.: U.S. Department of Health, Education and Welfare, June 1971), pp. 10–21, (DHEW pub. no. (HSM) 72-11). Two other activities listed are grant-

ing of licenses on the basis of reciprocity or endorsement to applicants from other states or foreign countries and collection of various types of fees.

18. New York Consolidated Laws Service, Education Law, Sec. 6521 (1979). Article 4510 of Texas Revised Civil Statutes Annotated provides: "Any person shall be regarded as practicing medicine within the meaning of this law: (1) Who shall publicly profess to be a physician or surgeon and shall diagnose, treat, or offer to treat, any disease or disorder, mental or physical, or any physical deformity or injury, by any system or method, or to effect cures thereof; (2) or who shall diagnose, treat or offer to treat any disease or disorder, mental or physical or any physical deformity or injury by any system or method and to effect cures thereof and charge therefor, directly or indirectly, money or other compensation. . . ." Derbyshire, *Medical Licensure and Discipline*, p. 19, says that in twenty-three states to practice medicine a person must be paid or expect to be paid a fee directly or indirectly; two states say that payment is irrelevant, and the rest are silent regarding the effect of compensation. Derbyshire also reports that at least one state goes so far as to specify that attaching "Dr." "Doctor," "MD," or "Healer" to one's name constitutes the practice of medicine.

19. Jon R. Waltz and Fred E. Inbau, *Medical Jurisprudence* (New York: Macmillan, 1971), p. 27.

20. Pennell and Stewart, *Licensing of Health Occupations*, p. 6.

21. Virginia C. Hall, *Statutory Regulation of the Scope of Nursing Practice* (Chicago: National Joint Practice Commission, 1975), p. 34.

22. Physicians may not, of course, claim to be board-certified in a particular specialty unless they have actually received such certification.

23. See, for example, *Acupuncture Society of Kansas v. Kansas State Board of Healing Arts*, 602 P.2d 1311 (Kan., 1979), in which the Supreme Court of Kansas held that acupuncture was not surgery and a chiropractor performing acupuncture was not illegally practicing medicine. In *Andrews v. Ballard*, 498 F.Supp. 1038 (S.D. Tex., 1980) a federal district court held that the Texas Medical Practice Act unconstitutionally infringed upon the decision to obtain acupuncture treatment, which was protected by the right to privacy.

24. An approach that is followed in California, Illinois, Indiana, Maryland, Michigan, Minnesota, Nebraska, and New York. Hall, *Regulation of Nursing*, p. 34.

25. For example, by 1973 forty-four states had authorized "expanded functions" for licensed dental hygienists and dental assistants. See Ruth Roemer, "Regulation of Health Personnel," in Ruth Roemer and George McKray, *Legal Aspects of Health Policy: Issues and Trends* (Westport, Conn.: Greenwood, 1980), p. 110.

26. See, for example, *Whittaker v. Superior Court of Shasta County*, 68 Cal.2d 357, 438 P.2d 358, 66 Cal.Rptr. 710 (1968). Also see Carlson in *Health Care*, pp. 398–401. One reason for such a requirement is to protect the public by assuring that only qualified individuals engage in these activities, which is the classic objective of licensure. It could be argued, however, that requiring supervision and control by a *licensed* physician should in itself provide adequate protection. Another reason for the requirement may be to protect the monopoly position of those individuals who meet the requirements, because

only they can be hired to carry out these functions. Regardless of reason, the frequent requirement of delegation only to licensed or certified individuals has resulted in a tremendous proliferation of credentialing categories for allied health personnel.

27. Hall, *Regulation of Nursing*, p. 37. The information on how many states exempt or don't exempt nursing from the medical practice act also comes from Hall, pp. 34–37. She does not provide information on Washington and Wyoming.

28. Practical nurses are licensed in almost all states, although in a sizable minority of these states the permissive approach, limiting use of the title only, is employed. A confusing note is added by the fact that it is common for states to use the term "registration" for licensure of RNs (i.e., registered nurses). Properly used, registration means to record in a registry kept by a regulatory agency, a technique employed to keep track of the registered individuals. But one may find it used in licensing acts as a synonym for licensure, or in the redundant phrase "licensed and registered," or—to compound the problem—as a synonym for certification. See Jonas, et al., *Health Care Delivery*, p. 413; Grad, *Public Health Law*, pp. 55–56.

29. See Hall, *Regulation of Nursing*, pp. 12–18. Also see Nathan Hershey, "Defining the Scope of Nursing Practice: Actors, Criteria and Economic Considerations," *Nursing Law and Ethics* 1(7):3, 10–12 (August/September 1980); American Nursing Association, *The Nursing Practice Act: Suggested State Legislation* (Kansas City, Mo.: The Association, 1980); and Daniel A. Rothman and Nancy Lloyd Rothman, *The Professional Nurse and the Law* (Boston, Little, Brown, 1977), chap. 7.

30. New York provides that:

   1. The practice of the profession of nursing as a registered professional nurse is defined as diagnosing and treating human responses to actual or potential health problems through such services as casefinding, health teaching, health counseling, and provision of care supportive to or restorative of life and well-being, and executing medical regimens prescribed by a licensed or otherwise legally authorized physician or dentist. A nursing regimen shall be consistent with and shall not vary any existing medical regimen.
   2. "Diagnosing" in the context of nursing practice means that identification of and discrimination between physical and psychosocial signs and symptoms essential to effective execution and management of the nursing regimen. Such diagnostic privilege is distinct from a medical diagnosis.
   3. "Treating" means selection and performance of those therapeutic measures essential to the effective execution and management of the nursing regimen, and execution of any prescribed medical regimen.
   4. "Human Responses" means those signs, symptoms and processes which denote the individual's interaction with an actual or potential health problem.

   N.Y. Ed. Law Secs. 6901-6902 (1979)

   Under the California statute, nursing functions are defined to include:

   (a) Direct and indirect patient care services that insure the safety, comfort, personal hygiene, and protection of patients; and the performance of disease prevention and restorative measures.
   (b) Direct and indirect patient care services, including, but not limited to, the admin-

istration of medications and therapeutic agents, necessary to implement a treatment, disease prevention, or rehabilitative regimen ordered by and within the
scope of licensure of a physician, dentist, podiatrist, or clinical psychologist.

(c) The performance of skin tests, immunization techniques, and the withdrawal of
human blood from veins and arteries.

(d) Observation of signs and symptoms of illness, reactions to treatment, general
behavior, or general physical condition, and (1) determination of whether such
signs, symptoms, reactions, behavior, or general appearance exhibit abnormal
characteristics; and (2) implementation, based on observed abnormalities, of appropriate reporting, or referral, or standardized procedures, or changes in treatment regimen in accordance with standardized procedures, or the initiation of
emergency procedures. "Standardized procedures" . . . means . . . policies and
protocols developed . . . through collaboration among administrators and health
professionals including physicians and nurses.

Calif. Code, Business and Professions Sec. 2725 (1981)

31. For a discussion of nursing diagnosis as contrasted to medical diagnosis see
George J. Annas, Leonard H. Glantz, and Barbara F. Katz, *The Rights of
Doctors, Nurses and Allied Health Professionals: A Health Law Primer* (New York:
Avon, 1981), pp. 24–25.

32. See Hall, *Regulation of Nursing*, pp. 18–20. Also see "Credentialing in Nursing: A New Approach," Report of the Committee for the Study of Credentialing in Nursing. *American Journal of Nursing* 79:674–683 (April 1979).

33. See Bonnie Bullough, ed., *The Law and the Expanding Nursing Role* (New
York: Appleton-Century-Crofts, 1975), esp. chapts. 5, 8, 10, 12; Philip C.
Kissam, "Physicians' Assistant and Nurse Practitioner Laws: A Study of
Health Law Reform." *Kansas Law Review* 24:1–65 (1975); Ann A. Bliss and
Eva C. Cohen, *The New Health Professionals: Nurse Practitioners and Physician
Assistants* (Germantown, Md.: Aspen Systems Corporation, 1977. Warren
notes: "A nurse is generally recognized as functioning within professional
nursing practice if, in carrying out a physician's instruction or standard
procedures, the nurse is allowed to determine whether specified conditions
exist, indicating the need to execute orders. This is sometimes referred to as
'following standing orders,' although technically 'standing orders' usually
refer to a particular patient, rather than general physician's instructions or
standard procedures." David G. Warren, *Problems in Hospital Law*, 3d ed.,
(Germantown, Md.: Aspen Systems Corporation, 1978), p. 79. Separate and
special problems apply to midwives and nurse anesthetists. Bullough reports
that: "The legal status of midwives varies. In 19 jurisdictions nurse midwifery is recognized either in the laws or the regulations. Four states require
certification by the College as a prerequisite to practice. In the Virgin Islands there is even a separate midwifery board. In 22 jurisdictions their
status is ambiguous with some permissive regulations; but nurse-midwives
are not differentiated from the lay midwives of an earlier era. In 13 jurisdictions the law is definitely prohibitive or restrictive." "Nurse anesthetists are
in a somewhat similar situation. Although they have been a recognized
specialty throughout the country, there has been considerable discussion
about their legality because they often carry out diagnostic and treatment
functions." Bonnie Bullough, "The Third Phase in Nursing Licensure: The
Current Nurse Practice Acts," in Bullough, *Expanding Nursing Role*, p. 167.

34. See Annas, *et al.*, *Health Law Primer*, pp. 51–54; Kissam, *Health Law Reform;*

Bliss and Cohen, *New Health Professionals;* National Center for Health Services Research, *Review and Analysis of State Legislation and Reimbursement Practices of Physician's Assistants and Nurse Practitioners* (1978), (DHEW pub. no. (HRA) 230-77-0011). Annas, *et al., Health Law Primer,* at p. 27, note that in *Washington State Nurses' Association v. Board of Medical Examiners,* 605 P.2d 1270 (Wash. 1980) state regulations allowing physician assistants to write medical orders and prescriptions were upheld. "The court held that physician assistants are *agents* of the physician, and therefore nurses executing orders issued by physician assistants would not be exposed to any liability, since the order was legally the order of the physician."

35. See Annas, *et al., Health Law Primer,* chap. 3, for brief discussions of the licensure and liability status of physical therapists, social workers, pharmacists, optometrists, respiratory therapists and technicians, and X-ray technicians. Also see D. B. Hogan, *The Regulation of Psychotherapists: A Study in the Philosophy and Practice of Professional Regulation,* vol. 1 (Cambridge, Mass.: Ballinger, 1979).

36. Pennell and Stewart, *Licensing of Health Occupations,* p. 7.

37. Twenty-four states provide for public or lay membership on physician licensing boards, including Alaska, Arizona, California, Colorado, Connecticut, Delaware, Hawaii, Iowa, Kansas, Maine, Massachusetts, Michigan, Minnesota, Ohio, Pennsylvania, South Dakota, Vermont, Washington, and Wisconsin. See Jonas et al., *Health Care Delivery,* p. 173. Also see Frank P. Grad and Noelia Marti, *Physicians' Licensure and Discipline: The Legal and Professional Regulation of Medical Practice* (Dobbs Ferry, N.Y.: Oceana Publications, 1979), p. 57. Also see Jonas, *Medical Mystery,* p. 175 and Pennell and Stewart, *Licensing of Health Occupations,* pp. 7–9. In a quite dramatic break with tradition, California's Governor Jerry Brown has appointed a chiropractor to the state's medical board and an MD to the chiropractic board.

38. Colorado: Department of Regulatory Agencies; Florida: Department of Professional and Occupational Regulation; Hawaii: Department of Regulatory Agencies; Illinois: Department of Registration and Education; Massachusetts: Division of Registration; Michigan: Department of Licensing and Regulation; Montana: Department of Professional and Occupational Licensing; Utah: Department of Registration; and Wisconsin: Department of Regulation and Licensing. Grad and Marti, *Physicians' Licensure and Discipline,* p. 212.

39. Derbyshire, *Medical Licensure and Discipline,* p. 33. Grad and Marti, *Physicians' Licensure and Discipline,* p. 57, put the figure at thirty, including Alabama, Maryland, and North Carolina, in each of which the state medical society selects board members.

40. Derbyshire, *Medical Licensure and Discipline,* pp. 44.

41. Pennell and Stewart provide extensive information on how each of these functions is handled for each licensed health profession in each of the states. See their entire report, *Licensing of Health Occupations,* as well as text at pp. 9–11. For physicians, see Derbyshire, *Medical Licensure and Discipline,* and Grad and Marti, *Physicians' Licensure and Discipline.* Also see H. S. Cohen, "On Professional Power and Conflict of Interest: State Licensing Boards on Trial," *Journal of Health Politics, Policy and Law* 5:291–308 (1980).

42. Described in Derbyshire, *Medical Licensure and Discipline*, pp. 20–26. Also see Grad and Marti, *Physicians' Licensure and Discipline*, pp. 60–65.

43. This provides part of the difficulty in licensing graduates of foreign medical schools. New York State's announcement in 1981 that it would review the adequacy of off-shore medical schools produced widespread protest within the medical education community. See Steven Jonas, "State Approval of Foreign Medical Schools: Ensuring the Quality of the Training of the Students and Graduates from Foreign Medical Schools Entering New York State," *New England Journal of Medicine* 305:45–48 (1981).

44. But for physicians the trend could be reversing. At least one state, California, has been experimenting with its own supplemental examination. See *American Medical News* (June 27, 1980), p. 1. *A Discursive Dictionary of Health Care*, Subcommittee on Health and Environment, Committee on Interstate and Foreign Commerce, U.S. House of Representatives (Washington, D.C.: 1976), p. 91, points out: "There is no national licensure system for health professionals, although requirements are often so nearly standardized as to constitute a national system." For an analysis of *medical* education in the United States—past, present, and future—see Jonas, *Medical Mystery*.

45. Licensure by waiver and examination represent alternative shortcuts that are not commonly used. The willingness of a state to afford reciprocity as a shortcut often correlates with its need for more physicians.

46. See Roemer and McKray, *Legal Aspects of Health Policy*, p. 104.

47. "In Accreditation, Certification and Licensure," in E. T. McTernan and R. O. Hawkins, eds., *Educating Personnel for the Allied Health Professions and Services* (St. Louis: Mosby, 1972), p. 81.

48. Periodic reregistration differs in that a failure to register means that the individual is no longer licensed to practice, but registration at any time restores the license. The Licensure Information System, a computerized data base containing complete texts of state licensing laws and board regulations affecting more than forty health occupations in the fifty states, the District of Columbia, Puerto Rico, and the Virgin Islands, is operated by the Health Resources Administration in conjunction with the Council of State Governments. Inquiries about state laws concerning licensure requirements, professional board regulations, continuing education requirements, etc. can be sent to Licensure Information System, Council of State Governments, P.O. Box 11910, Iron Works Pike, Lexington, Kentucky 40578.

49. Grad and Marti, *Physicians' Licensure and Discipline*, p. 56, report that all but the following states combine licensing and disciplinary functions in the same governmental body: Alabama, California, Connecticut, Idaho, Illinois, Maryland, Nebraska, New York, Rhode Island, South Carolina, and Washington.

50. Derbyshire, *Medical Licensure and Discipline*, pp. 77–78.

51. "Few doctors ever report colleague's incompetence," *New York Times*, 29 January 1976, p. 13.

52. American Medical Association, news release: "Disciplinary Actions against Physicians Continue Upward Trend" (Chicago, February 11, 1980); as reported in Jonas et al., *Health Care Delivery*, p. 407.

53. Jonas et al., *ibid*, p. 408.

54. See the valuable series of eight articles on medical discipline by Bruce E.

Vodicka in the *Journal of the American Medical Association* 233:1106–1107, 233:1427–1428, 234:327–328, 234:642–643, 234:1062–1063, 235:302–303, 235:651–652, 235:1051–1052 (1975–1976).

55. These—along with the licensure requirement of "moral fitness"—are very malleable criteria and subject to abuse, especially political abuse. One leading example involved the U.S. Supreme Court's upholding the revocation of a medical license solely on the basis of the physician's conviction for refusing to produce names before the House Un-American Activities Committee. *Barsky v. Board of Regents*, 347 U.S. 442 (1954).

56. Vodicka, *JAMA*, part 4, "The Offenses" 235:303 (January 19, 1976).

57. In Derbyshire's study of 938 disciplinary actions, seven actions were attributed to gross malpractice. In the *New York Times* study (note 51), an average of 1.5 revocations a year for the nation as a whole were due to extreme incompetency. In the past, one disincentive to disciplinary action was the severity of the punishment. Suspension and revocation are still the most common sanctions taken against physicians. But as Grad and Marti report, *Physicians' Licensure and Discipline*, pp. 174–175, "the trend is toward a more flexible and rehabilitative approach." They explain: "The sanctions that may be authorized by law include reprimand or censure; probation with or without conditions; fines; limitations of practice to certain areas of medicine, or to certain specialties, procedures or certain designated facilities; requirement of practice under the supervision of another physician in a clinic or other controlled setting; limitation of practice by forbidding the use of certain medical procedures or the prescription of certain medications without consultation with another physician; imposition of educational or retraining requirements, including the requirement that the licensee undergo an examination or other qualifying procedure to demonstrate the successful completion of retraining; imposition of significant money penalties; the requirement that, as a condition of probation, or of termination of license suspension, the licensee devote time to uncompensated public service; license suspension, and license revocation."

58. *New York Times Study*, p. 12.

59. Ibid. Grad and Marti, *Physicians' Licensure and Discipline*, pp. 139–141, report that Arizona, California, Connecticut, and Oregon have the most detailed reporting requirements. Also see William C. Felch and Abraham L. Halpern, "Coping with Physician Incompetence," *New York State Journal of Medicine* 79:1921–24 (1979).

60. Roemer and McKray, *Legal Aspects of Health Policy*, p. 117.

61. See Grad and Marti, *Physicians' Licensure and Discipline*, pp. 160–163. Also see Annas et al., *Health Law Primer*, pp. 10–13 and George J. Annas, "Who to Call when the Doctor is Sick," *Hastings Center Report* 8(6):18 (December 1978). Also see "Symposium-Medical Discipline: Dealing with Physicians Who are Unscrupulous, Disabled, and/or Incompetent," *New York State Journal of Medicine* 79:1018–41 (June 1979).

62. Grad, *Public Health Law*, p. 54.

63. See Grad and Marti, *Physicians' Licensure and Discipline*, pp. 141–59, on State Administrative Procedure Acts, the right to a hearing, notice, and other due-process rights.

64. Grad and Marti, *Physicians' Licensure and Discipline*, p. 142. Kenneth Culp

Davis, *Administrative Law Text*, 3d ed. (St. Paul: West, 1972), p. 184, observes: "Many licenses that were once regarded as privileges have become rights. The movement is strong and clear, although some traces of the privilege doctrine remain in the state courts." He goes on to state: "Occupational licenses in the dignified callings have always been regarded as rights, so that they cannot be denied or revoked without trial-type hearings on issues of adjudicative facts." A similar view can be found in Walter Gellhorn, Clark Byse, and Peter L. Strauss, *Administrative Law*, 7th ed. (Mineola, N.Y.: Foundation Press, 1979), pp. 420–424. Yet Derbyshire, *Medical Licensure and Discipline*, pp. 13–14, recounts how the Federation of State Medical Boards, in recommending a model Medical Practice Act in 1956, included a preamble that began: "Recognizing that the practice of medicine is a *privilege* granted by legislative authority and not a *natural right* of individuals . . ." On this point also see Vodicka, *JAMA*, part 8, "Procedural Matters," 235:1051–1052 (March 8, 1976); Jonas, *Medical Mystery*, p. 173; Grad, *Public Health Law*, pp. 62–66, 70–76; and Charles A. Reich, "The New Property," *Yale Law Journal* 73:733–786 (1964).

65. Annas, et al., *Health Law Primer*, p. 4.

66. See, for example, Ronald L. Akers, "The Professional Association and the Legal Regulation of Practice," *Law and Society Review* 2:463–482 (May 1968), reprinted in Akers and Richard Hawkins, *Law and Control in Society* (Englewood Cliffs, N.J.: Prentice-Hall, 1975); Jeffrey Lionel Berlant, *Profession and Monopoly: A Study of Medicine in the United States and Great Britain* (Berkeley: University of California Press, 1975); Elton Rayack, *Professional Power and American Medicine: The Economics of the American Medical Association* (Cleveland: World, 1967); William D. White, *Public Health and Private Gain: The Economics of Licensing Clinical Laboratory Personnel* (Chicago: Maaroufa Press, 1979); James G. Burrow, *Organized Medicine in the Progressive Era: The Move Toward Monopoly* (Baltimore: Johns Hopkins University Press, 1977).

67. Akers, "Legal Regulation of Practice."

68. See, for example, K. B. Leffler, "Physician Licensure: Competition and Monopoly in American Medicine," *Journal of Law and Economics* 21:165–186 (1978), and Neil A. Paloma, "The Role of Law in Achieving Efficient Health Care Delivery," *Labor Law Journal* 24:733–738 (1973). Also see Rayack, *Professional Power and American Medicine*.

69. The main losers when innovation is retarded are patients. Licensure clearly serves to restrict access by the public to alternative sources and means of health care, not always to the public's advantage. The controversy often generated by such professional restriction has been especially prominent as regards midwifery. See, for example, Cynthia Watchorn, "Midwifery: A History of Statutory Suppression," *Golden Gate University Law Review* 9:631–643 (1978–1979). A similar controversy has surrounded denturism. See Richard A. Abrams, "Denturism and the Dentists," *New England Journal of Medicine* 299:1131–1133 (November 11, 1978), and H. Barry Waldman, "The Reaction of the Dental Profession to Changes in the 1970s," *American Journal of Public Health* 70:619–624 (1980). Because medical practice acts tend to be very broadly drawn, a literal application of the law could mean that self-care and mutual aid constituted the illegal practice of medicine. See Lori B. Andrews and Lowell S. Levin, "Self-care and the Law," *Social Policy*

9(4):44–49 (January/February 1979), and Ellen L. Hodgson, "Restrictions on Unorthodox Health Treatment in California: A Legal and Economic Analysis," *UCLA Law Review* 24:647–696 (1977).

70. See, for example, Edwin A. Locke, Arthur S. Mode, and Harry Binswanger, "The Case against Medical Licensing," *Medicolegal News* 8(5):13–15, 28 (October 1980); followed, at p. 20, by George J. Annas, "The Case for Medical Licensure."

71. See the discussion of antitrust in Chapter 8. Also see Andrew K. Dolan, "Antitrust Law and Physician Dominance of Other Health Practitioners," *Journal of Health Politics, Policy and Law* 4:675–690 (1980), and Philip C. Kissam, "Applying Antitrust Law to Medical Credentialing," *American Journal of Law and Medicine* 7:1–31 (1981).

72. See W. Randolph Tucker and Burtchaell G. Wetterau, *Credentialing Health Personnel By Licensed Hospitals: The Report of a Study of Institutional Licensure* (Chicago: Rush-Presbyterian-St. Luke's Medical Center, 1975). Also see Rick J. Carlson in *Health Care* and Nathan Hershey, "Institutional Licensure for Health Professionals?" *Hospital Progress* 57(9):75–80, 124 (September 1976). Health facilities licensure is discussed in Chapter 7.

73. *Report on Licensure*, pp. 65–70, 77.

74. On procedural aspects of disciplinary proceedings see Grad and Marti, *Physicians' Licensure and Discipline*, pp. 141–159; on judicial review of disciplinary hearings, ibid., pp. 177–190. Jonas believes that "the single most salutary change that could occur in state licensing laws would be the clear embodiment in the laws of the concept of the medical license as a privilege, under the ultimate control of the people, who grant the privilege." *Medical Mystery*, p. 173.

75. Roemer and McKray, *Legal Aspects of Health Policy*, p. 104; Grad and Marti, *Physicians' Licensure and Discipline*, pp. 71–81. The idea of imposing additional restrictions on those who do not practice at a certain volume level or who return to work after a prolonged period of not practicing has received little support.

76. See note 37.

77. *A Proposal for Credentialing Health Manpower*, p. 1.

78. This chapter focuses on licensure and certification as the two major types of health professional credentialing (with accreditation—an important component of both—to be discussed later). It should be noted that there are yet other credentialing mechanisms, although they are generally not labeled as such. See, for example, the *discussion of hospital staff privileges* in Chapter 7 and the discussion of *controlled substances prescribing* in Chapter 11.

79. Roemer and McKray, *Legal Aspects of Health Policy*, p. 104; National Commission on Health Occupational Certifying Agencies, *Health Occupational Credentialing*, pp. 27–28.

80. There are 22 medical specialty boards and more than 100 health certifying agencies. The number of health professionals certified by each varies tremendously: 200 hold certificates from the Child Health Associate Program, 200,000 from the Board of Registry of the American Society of Clinical Pathologists. See National Commission on Health Occupational Certifying Agencies, *Health Occupational Credentialing*, pp. 9, 23.

81. At least in public hospitals, complete reliance on specialty board certification

is arbitrary, and deprives the applicant of an opportunity to challenge lack of certification and directly demonstrate competence. This may even be the case when the requirement is "board certified or board eligible." See *Armstrong v. Board of Directors of Fayette County General Hospital,* 553 S.W.2d 77 (Tenn. App; Western Section, 1976), *cert. denied,* Tenn. Supreme Court (1977). Arbitrary and discriminatory certification procedures have also been successfully challenged by suing the specialty society directly. See *Higgins v. American Society of Clinical Pathologists,* 51 N.J. 191, 238 A2d. 665 (1968). Also see Kaplin, "Professional Power and Judicial Review."

82. See references, note 71.
83. *A Proposal for Credentialing Health Manpower,* p. 1.
84. See note 43.
85. In many, if not most, other countries, the review and regulation of educational and training programs is a governmental activity, not a voluntary one. In the United States the governmental role is limited to reviewing the acceptability of such voluntary programs, because the flow of public funds to private and public institutions is often dependent on accreditation. The U.S. Department of Education plays a major federal role in accreditation. Its acceptance of an accreditation program has been crucial to receipt of health manpower training capitation funds; the ending of capitation eliminates outside pressure for more stringent accreditation. (There is, however, a private National Council on Post-secondary Accreditation, an "umbrella organization representing recognized accrediting bodies and the post-secondary educational institutions whose activities they accredit." See Roemer and McKray, *Legal Aspects of Health Policy,* p. 99.
86. See Chapter 7.
87. *Report on Licensure,* pp. 9–10.
88. Jonas et al., *Health Care Delivery,* p. 410.

7

The Operation and Regulation of Hospitals

The United States of America is a large nation with great diversity among its 50 state jurisdictions and a high measure of independence in its general hospitals. While most of the hospital beds for mental disorder and other long-term disease are under government auspices, most of the beds for general care—which receive by far the great majority of patients each year—are under the auspices of nonsectarian or religious voluntary bodies.

Despite the individual sovereignty of these voluntary general hospitals, their construction and operation have come increasingly under the influence of public authorities. Standards for construction and operation are prescribed in state laws, and the implementation of these standards is becoming more rigourous.

—R. F. Bridgman and M. I. Roemer[1]

THE FIRST COUNT of hospitals in the United States, compiled by the U.S. Bureau of Education in 1873, listed 178 institutions. By 1909, however, a Bureau of the Census survey showed 4,359 hospitals of various types.[2] Today, most analysts would agree that the nation's more than 7,000 hospitals form the hub of the American health care system, encompassing a vast array of inpatient, outpatient and ancillary health care facilities.[3] In 1979 some 40 percent of all health dollars, or $85 billion went toward hospital care.[4] Almost two million health professionals, some 37 percent of the total, work in hospitals, virtually all physicians and nurses receive part of their training there and, of course, it is the hospital that delivers critical emergency care for most patients. The modern hospital is also a legal entity with all of the complexities that this implies.

The legal aspects of facility ownership, operation, licensure and liability vary markedly from state to state and, within each state, depend on differences in sponsorship and organization. But certain basic principles governing the general hospital apply, with variations, to other facilities

105

as well. (A truly comprehensive review focusing separately on every type of health facility is beyond the scope of this book. Tables 7.1 and 7.2 indicate how many types of health facilities there are.) Hospitals are classified in many ways: by length of stay (short-term or long-term); by major type of service (psychiatric, tuberculosis, other special,[7] or general); by type of ownership (public, nonprofit, or proprietary); and as teaching or nonteaching hospitals. The short-term, general, nonprofit hospital, generally referred to as a "voluntary" hospital, predominates.

Today's voluntary hospitals are not only medical facilities, they are also multimillion-dollar businesses, whose functions are of interest not only to their patients and employees but to the state and federal governments and courts as well. Hospital law, which barely existed as a distinct field twenty years ago, is now one of the most developed areas of health law.[8] And the legal status of the hospital—what it may and may not do, and who bears the ultimate responsibility for its actions—needs to be understood by every health professional.

Organizational Structure

The first important legal question regarding hospitals relates to ownership. Public hospitals may be under federal, state, or local jurisdiction. Nongovernment hospitals may be proprietary—investor-owned and operated for profit—or voluntary, not-for-profit facilities.

Except for public facilities, which may be administrative divisions of some unit of government, most hospitals are corporations.[9] A corpora-

TABLE 7.1   Inpatient Health Facilities

General hospital
Specialty hospital
Nursing care home
Personal care home with nursing
Personal care home without nursing
Domiciliary care home
Facility for the mentally retarded
Orphanage
Home for dependent children
Home for the emotionally disturbed
Home for unwed mothers
Facility for alcoholics or drug abusers
Home for the blind or deaf
Home or school for the physically handicapped
Other resident facilities

SOURCE: Master Facility Inventory, *Health Resources Statistics.*[5]

**TABLE 7.2 Outpatient and
Nonpatient Health Facilities**

Ambulance services
Blood banks
Clinical (medical) laboratories
Comprehensive health services programs
Dental group practices
Dental laboratories
Family planning services
Health maintenance organizations
Home health services
Kidney disease treatment centers
Medical group practices
Opticianry establishments
Pharmacies
Poison control centers
Psychiatric outpatient centers
Rehabilitation facilities
Suicide prevention centers
Surgical centers

SOURCE: *Health Resources Statistics.*[6]

tion is an artificial legal entity, separate and distinct from those who own
or operate it, which means—and this has been one of its primary advantages—that the corporate owners and operators are not personally liable
for the contracts and torts of the corporation. Instead, it is the corporation itself that owns property, employs agents, is sued or sues others, and
conducts such other legal transactions as individuals or partnerships
might in other circumstances. In fact, the courts have often treated
corporations as if they were persons, with the legal rights of individual
persons. And since a corporation has an independent, perpetual existence, it can survive despite the death or resignation of its owners and
operators.

Corporations are established under state law and have only the authority granted to them under these laws. In some states all hospitals are
incorporated under the general incorporation laws of the state; in other
states there are separate laws authorizing for-profit and not-for-profit
corporations. Some of the corporation's authority to act will be expressly
stated in the relevant statute; others are inferred from it. Many court
decisions regarding corporations center on whether authority to perform a particular act is implicit in those corporate objectives that are
clearly proper under state law. (Often these cases involve operation of
nonhealth-related businesses to earn income for the hospital.) As part of
the incorporation process a corporation adopts bylaws, which are rules
to which the corporation binds itself. More detailed than incorporation

laws, they have legal status and specify just how the corporation must function.[10]

Corporate power to act is vested in a board of directors, usually elected by and responsible to the corporation's shareholders. Nonprofit corporations, however, do not have shareholders, although some do have "members," who select the governing body of the institution.[11] In nonprofit corporations without members, the governing boards are basically self-perpetuating; but this does not mean that they are free to do entirely as they wish. In fact, some courts have held the boards of nonprofit hospitals to a higher standard of responsibility than those of for-profit corporations.

The hospital board, however it is selected, has a fiduciary duty to the institution—that is, corporate power is entrusted to its members *for the benefit of* the hospital, and it is their duty to exercise prudence, skill, and diligence appropriate to circumstances and to put the interest of the corporation above their own.[12] In fulfilling its duties to the institution the hospital board has several key functions. First, it appoints administrative officers and delegates to them the authority to carry out the day-to-day business of the hospital. Second, it delineates and awards medical staff privileges. Third, it develops operating policies and long-range plans. And fourth, it supervises, controls, and evaluates the performance of administrative and professional staff. In his text on *The Law of Hospital and Health Administration,* Southwick details these functions as follows:

> [The board] handles the major financial matters for the hospital, making certain that assets and funds are properly used. It acquires hospital property, preserves it from destruction and loss, and provides for adequate insurance, both casualty and malpractice. It arranges for the repair of plant and equipment and for the payment of debts and taxes, as well as enforcing and collecting payments due the hospital. It selects and appoints the major administrative officers, and it also selects the medical staff and defines each individual's clinical privileges, upon the receipt of appropriate professional advice. The board establishes and regularly reviews the hospital's relations with other hospitals in the community, as well as its relations with other institutions and with governmental agencies. Finally, and above all, it regularly reviews and appraises the hospital's overall accomplishment, including the quality of professional care rendered by the hospital's medical staff.[13]

The relationship of the corporate governing board to the administrative staff is clear: The board selects the senior administrator who, in turn, hires and supervises assistants and all other employees and is responsible to the board for their performance. This corporate hierarchy is common to both for-profit and not-for-profit corporations. But hospitals have one additional factor—the medical staff. The Joint Commission on Accreditation of Hospital's (JCAH) *Accreditation Manual for Hospitals*, reflecting existing organizational patterns, requires: "There shall be a single organized medical staff that has the overall responsibility for the quality of all medical care provided to patients, and for the ethical conduct and professional practices of its members, as well as for accounting therefor to the governing body."[14]

Unlike the nursing staff, which relates to the governing board through the administration,[15] the medical staff is directly responsible to the governing board, and unlike nurses, physicians are not necessarily employees of the hospital. Thus there is a medical organizational hierarchy distinct from and parallel to the administrative hierarchy, but under the same ultimate authority. This confusing and not very satisfactory arrangement derives in part from the special status of physicians in American society and from the fact that most physicians are not employees of the hospitals where they have clinical privileges. But an even more important reason for the anomalous position of the medical staff in the organizational structure stems from the nature of medical practice. While courts have long held corporations to be "persons" in a legal sense, state medical practice acts take a much narrower view. Only an individual can be licensed to practice medicine; a hospital corporation cannot. It is the physician practicing in the hospital, not the hospital itself, who makes judgments regarding the diagnosis and treatment of patients. Certainly hospital boards can influence those judgments through the policies and procedures they establish, but the boards must rely on an organized group of licensed physicians to oversee physician performance.

Considerable attention is therefore paid to medical staff structure by accrediting agencies and regulatory bodies. The Joint Commission on Accreditation of Hospitals, for example, requires that the medical staff "establish a framework of self-government,"[16] including adoption of bylaws, rules, and regulations and the creation of a functioning organizational structure for the medical staff. The JCAH requires "an executive committee of the medical staff that is empowered to act for the staff in the intervals between medical staff meetings. The committee . . . shall serve as a liaison mechanism between medical staff and hospital administration. . . ."[17] Other important medical staff committees are the credentials committee, which makes recommendations regarding the granting, suspension, and revocation of medical staff privileges, and the medical audit committee, which reviews the quality of professional care provided in the institution. Still other medical staff committees oversee medical records, tissue review, pharmacy and therapeutics, and blood and antibiotic utilization. Infection control committees are hospitalwide and interdisciplinary, but are responsible to the medical staff. Finally, the JCAH (and, less formally, Medicare) require:

> A formal means of liaison should be established among the governing body, administration, and medical staff. The liaison function may be performed by means of a joint conference committee when one exists.[18]

The number and responsibilities of medical staff committees relate primarily to the size of the institution. But all can be expected to have a medical staff executive committee and a multidisciplinary medical staff or hospitalwide infection control committee.

Public Control and Accountability

If a hospital were simply a "doctor's workshop," made up of independent practitioners who shared the rent on a well-equipped building, only the practitioners, as independently functioning individuals, could be held responsible for the level of professional performance within that institution.[19] The fact that the hospital is a legal entity makes it possible to exert public control and accountability over its functioning.

How hospitals operate is important to the public not only because they are at the center of the nation's health care delivery system; but also because a large portion of their income comes from government sources. If all hospitals were public institutions, public control and accountability would be easier and more orderly. But although only 800 of 6,361 general hospitals are operated for profit, only 2,220 of the remaining 5,561 not-for-profit hospitals are governmentally owned and operated.[20] Yet despite the "private" nature of most hospitals, public regulatory control over hospitals is increasing. Over a century ago the U.S. Supreme Court concluded that when "one devotes his property to a use in which the public has an interest, he, in effect, grants to the public an interest in that use, and must submit to be controlled by the public for the public good. . . . Property does become clothed with a public interest," the Court held, when it is "used in a manner to make it of public consequence, and affect the community at large."[21]

More recently the Supreme Court of Hawaii suggested:

> If the proposition that any hospital occupies a fiduciary trust relationship between itself, its staff and the public it seeks to serve is accepted, then the rationale for any distinction between public, "quasi public" and truly private breaks down and becomes meaningless, especially if the hospital's patients are considered to be of primary concern.[22]

The significance of this view is that it provides a rationale for public accountability, without which hospital decisions to deny a physician or podiatrist staff privileges or to bar husbands from delivery rooms would be entirely private matters impervious to court challenge by affected individuals.

An additional basis for a public role on the part of nonprofit hospitals is the fact that they are generally exempt from local property taxes, state sales and income taxes, and federal income taxes. Some of the statutes creating such exemptions, as well as some court decisions, require a public service role on the part of qualifying hospitals. At the very least, these exemptions from tax obligations can provide further justification for regulatory and judicial intervention in hospital operation.[23]

Fiduciary responsibilities and public accountability aside, hospital governing boards are constrained by the institution's corporate charter and bylaws (in some states, for example, incorporation statutes deny hospitals the right to own real estate purely for investment purposes), by the danger of civil damage suits—especially those involving liability for malpractice negligence—by federal and state regulatory bodies, and by the policies and practices of numerous professional associations. Of all these constraints, government and professional regulation is the most pervasive.

A study by the Hospital Association of New York State found that 164 different regulatory bodies were involved with hospitals in that state, including 96 state agencies, 40 federal agencies, 18 city and county agencies, and 10 voluntary and quasi-public agencies.[24] Although this may be an exaggeration, there is no doubt that a great many government and professional bodies have some regulatory functions designed to insure the quality and efficiency of hospital services. Some of the regulations concern hospital-patient relations, others deal with professional standards and other relations between hospitals and the health care professionals who work in and/or for them. It is often charged that these various inspections are overlapping and duplicative, yet a 1980 study by the U.S. General Accounting Office concluded:

> Although hospitals are subjected to many inspections and are requested to complete many forms and reports, our work indicates that the degree to which they are duplicative or similar is not as great as other studies on this subject have reported. Further, we believe that efforts by Federal, State, and private organizations currently underway to reduce the existing duplication and similarity of inspections and information requests are improving the situation. . . . Twenty States currently accept Joint Commission accreditation, either in whole or in part, for licensure or participate in cooperative inspection activities with the Joint Commission. Sixteen States and the District of Columbia are considering such arrangements.[25]

There are many reasons that government might wish to survey and regulate health care institutions. These include protecting the public from unsafe or unsanitary conditions and incompetent care, establishing standards of performance where the public is unable to make its own judgments, encouraging high quality care practices, rationalizing the system, conserving limited health resources, and assuring the provision of adequate health services. And as government is paying for a larger and larger portion of hospital care, there has been a growing interest in evaluating that which is being paid for. Voluntary regulation, such as accreditation, may have some of the same objectives, and may also be used to stave off more rigorous governmental regulation. Many other regulatory goals could be listed, but all would fall under one of three broad headings: assuring quality, controlling costs, and providing for equity in access.[26] The first is the subject of the remainder of this chapter; the second forms part of the general discussion of cost control in the chapter that follows; and the third is the focus of Chapter 9.

Quality Control

The quality of hospital care is regulated by state and federal governments, the courts, the industry itself, and patient action.

Governmental regulation.   The main quality assurance mechanism employed by the states is licensure. Licensing statutes prohibit operation of a health facility without a license and establish minimum requirements for obtaining and keeping a license. Before World War II few states licensed hospitals or other health facilities, and those that did had only rudimentary requirements.[27] The postwar Hill-Burton Act encouraged such licensure by limiting the availability of federal hospital construction funds to those states that had minimum standards of maintenance and operation for hospitals.[28] Today every state but Ohio licenses general hospitals, all fifty states and the District of Columbia license nursing homes, and forty-two states license hospitals and homes for the mentally retarded.[29] Jonas reports:

> Licenses are usually granted on an annual or biennial basis. Although the statutory boards involved in institutional licensing usually include representatives from the health care field, they are much less likely to be completely dominated by providers from the type of institution being regulated than are statutory boards in individual licensing. . . . [Moreover] in institutional licensing, unlike individual licensing, the state departments usually have more control over the actual licensing process than do the statutory boards.[30]

Authority for overseeing licensed health facilities is usually vested in the state department of health. Although the trend has been toward licensing statutes with greater detail, most statutes concentrate on general policy.[31] The Illinois Hospital Licensing Act, for example, provides:

> Upon receipt of an application for a permit to establish a hospital the Director shall issue a permit if he finds (1) that the applicant is fit, willing, and able

to provide a proper standard of hospital service for the community with particular regard to the qualification, background, and character of the applicant, (2) that the financial resources available to the applicant demonstrate an ability to construct, maintain, and operate a hospital in accordance with the standards, rules, and regulations adopted pursuant to this Act, and (3) that safeguards are provided which assure hospital operation and maintenance consistent with the public interest having particular regard to safe, adequate, and efficient hospital facilities and services.[32]

Implementing regulations will usually establish specific, measurable requirements regarding qualifications of personnel, space allocation per patient, fire safety standards,[33] and a host of other specifics.[34] But however detailed these requirements may be, a common problem of enforcement remains, because most states have many hospitals, detailed licensing requirements, and only a handful of inspectors to check on compliance. Unless the penalties for violation of statute and regulations are extremely severe, the impact of licensure requirements is very limited. Usually, however, any penalty severe enough to jeopardize the functioning of a hospital will jeopardize a needed public resource and therefore may not be used short of the very grossest violations.[35]

Nor have regulatory bodies found a way to relate standards for physically measurable things such as staffing and equipment, important as they are, directly to quality care, although there is ample evidence that inadequate, low quality input precludes such care. The considerable and growing literature on the subject suggests that it is far more useful to analyze the process of patient care and/or the outcomes of that care than to focus on the structural inputs so basic to the licensing approach.[36] But such a focus would be difficult to legislate and even harder to enforce.

The federal regulatory role in relation to nongovernment hospitals is exercised largely through its ability to reimburse—or to refuse to reimburse—patients for health care services covered by Medicare and other federal programs.[37] When Congress established the Medicare program in 1965 it mandated the Department of Health, Education and Welfare (HEW) to establish standards for facilities receiving Medicare reimbursement. HEW developed national Medicare certification standards, entitled Conditions of Participation for Hospitals, drawing heavily on the standards set by the voluntary Joint Commission on Accreditation of Hospitals and accepting JCAH accreditation as constituting compliance with federal requirements.[38] Popko explains:

> In the past, most government programs, i.e., Workmen's Compensation and public assistance, had made little or no effort to specify the quality of care they were purchasing. In the Medicare program, Congress rejected such a laissez-faire attitude and set minimum requirements for participating hospitals. These requirements included such items as maintenance of clerical records, medical staff with bylaws, twenty-four-hour nursing services, utilization review plan, state licensure, and any other requirement that the

Department of Health, Education, and Welfare (HEW) deemed necessary to assure health and safety of individuals receiving services in the institution. There was one mitigating factor. These HEW requirements were not to be higher than those prescribed by the Joint Commission on Accreditation of Hospitals (JCAH).[39]

In 1972 amendments to the Social Security Act permitted HEW to develop even more rigorous standards than those of the JCAH by augmenting the Conditions of Participation, most significantly by adding a national medical peer review system. The Professional Standards Review Organization (PSRO) program[40] was designed to assure that all such federally funded medical services—especially those delivered in hospitals—were necessary, appropriate, and of satisfactory quality. It divided the country into 195 PSRO areas and required that PSROs be established in each area to assume responsibility for the review of the professional activities for the purpose of determining whether

—such services and items are or were medically necessary;
—the quality of such services meets professionally recognized standards of health care; and
—in case such services and items are proposed to be provided in a hospital or other health care facility on an inpatient basis, such services and items could, consistent with the provision of appropriate medical care, be effectively provided on an outpatient basis or more economically in an inpatient health care facility of a different type.[41]

Under the PSRO program the federal government does not regulate patient care directly; instead, it requires and oversees physician review.[42] Applications were solicited within each area from groups seeking to be recognized as the local PSRO, with preference given to physician groups.[43] In many areas the group selected was a "medical foundation" established by the local medical society but open to all local physicians without regard to society membership. Recognized PSROs function under grants or contracts from the Department of Health and Human Services, and are charged with reviewing all federally reimbursable care in order to verify that such care is appropriate, necessary, and of good quality. PSROs do not determine the eligibility of specific patients under federal entitlement programs.

PSRO review involves three approaches: utilization review (including concurrent admissions review and length of stay review), audits (called medical-care evaluation studies), and data profiles compiled on physicians, hospitals, and patients. The PSRO is obligated to apply these three approaches to those patients in a hospital for whom federal reimbursement will be sought. The utilization review and audit functions, however, may be delegated to the hospital itself, subject to retrospective analysis by the PSRO, if the hospital can demonstrate its competence to carry them out. Moreover, under a concept known as "focused review," diagnoses, physicians, or even entire hospitals that demonstrate continuing adherence to review criteria may eventually be exempted from all but retrospective scrutiny.

At present the major thrust of the PSRO program is directed at the physician component of inpatient hospital care; but as the law now stands several expansions of the review process are slated, first to include evaluation of long-term and ambulatory care (already underway on an experimental basis) and gradually to include the work of other health professionals (who would also become part of the review apparatus). Such expansion of program impact can mean potential refusal of federal reimbursement for any aspect of care adjudged inadequate by PSRO standards, as well as penalities for the individual practitioners who repeatedly fail to meet PSRO norms. There has been also a lingering concern that PSRO screening criteria may be used by judges and juries to define the proper standard of care in malpractice suits, although this has not come to pass.[44]

Expansion of PSRO functions would bring to the fore a question already puzzling many observers: Are PSROs public or private bodies? On the one hand, they are key components of a major governmental regulatory program; on the other hand, they are privately incorporated organizations selling their services to the federal government, much as a university sells research capabilities or Chrysler sells tanks. The question is important for several reasons, not the least of which is the fact that if PSROs are agencies of government, the federal Freedom of Information Act could apply to the data they collect from and about health care providers. This issue has been the subject of prolonged litigation, with one federal district court ruling that the act does apply and with that holding recently being reversed by the Court of Appeals.[45]

Almost a decade after enactment of the PSRO law, it is still not clear whether it is working successfully. The *Professional Standards Review Organization 1979 Program Evaluation*[46] concluded: "With respect to the quality assurance objective, the PSRO program appears to be producing increased physician compliance with quality of care criteria and facilitating the implementation of information about efficacious medical procedures and treatments." Not all evaluations of the program, however, have been as positive in their findings.[47]

The Reagan administration would like to eliminate completely the PSRO program, but has been unsuccessful in doing so. In mid-1981 Congress rejected a complete phaseout of the program, voting instead to allow the secretary of Health and Human Services to close as many as 30 percent of existing PSROs by October 1983. In addition to keeping the PSRO program alive, Congress also authorized PSROs to contract with the states for Medicaid review, with the federal government paying three-fourths of the costs.

It would seem that as long as the federal government continues funding hospital care, the opponents of the PSRO program face a dilemma. For the alternatives to PSRO are either: (1) for the federal government to pay for health care with no check on the quality or cost of what is being paid for; or (2) to have quality and cost review performed by government employees. Since both are unpalatable options, it seems quite possible that, despite its unpopularity, the PSRO program will continue in some form for the foreseeable future.

Litigation.   Another quality-assurance mechanism that regulates the actions of hospitals and other health care facilities is the lawsuit, particularly by a patient claiming to have suffered harm for which the institution is alleged to be responsible.[48] The regulatory mechanism involved in this instance is not professionalism, but fear—the risk of dire consequences to institutions and individuals who fail to exercise due care in the treatment of their patients.

Hospital liability for harm suffered by a patient has received increased attention in recent years.[49] In part this reflects the general increase in litigation, especially malpractice litigation (see Chapter 16). In addition, hospitals have become more vulnerable as certain legal defenses that formerly protected them have disappeared. Foremost among these is the doctrine of charitable immunity, which protected nonprofit hospitals from legal liability, even when they were clearly at fault, on the theory that money paid to a successful plaintiff would be money taken away from the hospital's valuable contribution to the community. In recent years, however, virtually all states have abandoned the charitable immunity protection. A related doctrine—that of governmental immunity—bars suits against federal, state, and municipal governments on the basis of the ancient common-law rule that the soverign could do no wrong (or, in a supposedly more palatable logic, that the government that makes and enforces all laws cannot be made vulnerable to those laws). This doctrine, too, places a severe burden on the negligently injured patient; and although it remains legally valid, both the federal and state governments have passed laws waiving this immunity. The federal Tort Claims Act,[50] for example, specifies situations in which the government will allow itself to be sued, making it easier for a malpractice suit to include a government-owned hospital as a defendent.

There are two basic grounds on which hospitals can be held liable for damages of inadequate or incompetent care. One involves negligent (that is, careless) treatment of the patient by a hospital employee, making the institution liable as the responsible employer. The other involves negligence by the hospital itself in carrying out some institutional obligation to the patient. In neither instance is the hospital required to guarantee a perfect outcome for the patient; only negligent, careless performance creates liability.[51]

The legal doctrine of *respondeat superior* ("let the master answer") is well established. The theory behind it is that because an employee works in the employer's behalf and is subject to the latter's supervision and control, persons injured through the employee's negligence should have access to the employer's greater resources when seeking compensation. (Aggrieved persons can also sue the employee, since a person is always responsible for his or her own negligence; but unless the employee has considerable assets or insurance there is little to be gained by such suits. Similarly, an employer found liable on a *respondeat superior* basis may seek indemnification from the employee, but will likely gain little.) From the plaintiff's perspective the *respondeat superior* theory makes a good deal of sense when applied to a hospital: The patient came to the *hospital*, not to the negligent nurse, X-ray technician, or intern for care; therefore the *hospital* should bear the responsibility for a careless injury. From a social perspective such "vicarious" liability also makes sense because it not only assures adequate compensation to the injured but provides a strong institutional incentive to prevent carelessness.

Institutional (or corporate) negligence involves the failure of the institution to reasonably meet specific corporate duties or obligations to the patient, including:

1. *The duty to maintain the physical condition of the premises.* This "brick and mortar" obligation is similar to that owed a visitor by any building owner. But because it is known that many persons in hospitals are infirm or disabled, the institution will be held to a particularly high standard.

2. *The duty to maintain equipment.* It is the responsibility of the institution to make certain that all its equipment—from thermometers to CAT scanners—are reasonably fit for their intended uses. The obligation relates not only to proper maintenance, but also to care in selecting equipment. Again, it is not perfection that is required, but the same reasonable and ordinary care and diligence generally exercised by similar facilities.[52] In determining whether such a standard has been met (both as regards equipment and premises), a court may attach great weight to the relevant licensing and accreditation standards.

3. *The duty to select carefully and to supervise employees.* This obligation goes beyond the *respondeat superior* situation described above, which applies only when the employee is carrying out his or her prescribed duties. The hospital may be liable if an employee physically attacks a patient, if it could be shown that previous problems with the same employee were carelessly ignored. If a patient's injury can be shown to have resulted from assigning tasks beyond the known capabilities of employees, the hospital may also be liable. In both instances the hospital has failed to fulfill an institutional obligation to the patient.

4. *The duty to implement appropriate policies and procedures.* If a hospital administration cannot guarantee perfection in either patient outcome or

employee performance, it can anticipate problems, establish policies, procedures, and protocols to minimize them, and make certain that they are followed. A classic example of failure in this regard was a patient with a head injury brought to the hospital at the beginning of a holiday weekend. A possible skull fracture was detected by the hospital radiologist, who dictated to that effect. Because the hospital had no special procedure for dealing with such a situation, the report lay untranscribed and unacted upon for several days; meanwhile the patient died. The hospital was held liable for failing to have had a mechanism for dealing with such an anticipatable and avoidable delay.[53]

Nosocomial infections represent another area of possible hospital liability. Although infection is a common, and often unavoidable, risk of hospitalization, a hospital can be found liable for those infections that demonstrably result from negligence—whether it be negligence in maintaining the premises and equipment, selecting and storing supplies, screening and training of personnel, or implementing aseptic policies and procedures. The institution may also be liable under the *respondeat superior* doctrine for infections traced to the negligence of employees.[54]

5. *The duty to select carefully and to credential the medical staff.* While the courts have expanded their interpretation of liability in a number of directions in recent years, the area that has received most attention has been the hospital's obligation to carefully oversee the patient-physician match.

Since physicians are not usually employees and the hospital itself cannot practice medicine, hospitals have only limited authority over how physicians treat patients. For this reason, courts for a long time accepted the argument that the quality of patient care was the hospital's responsibility only if the physical facilities, equipment, or hospital employees were at fault. Any problem involving medical treatment was a matter entirely between the physician—an "independent contractor"—and the patient. Today this view is no longer generally accepted. This change has not come about simply because treatment is increasingly hospital oriented; it is due primarily to the organizational structure of hospitals—their corporate identity and legally defined responsibilities and authority, professional administration, and organized medical staff.

Every patient-physician encounter in the hospital is thus made possible by the fact that the hospital has awarded the doctor staff privileges. Many patients today rely on the hospital to "select" a physician. In emergency situations and outpatient care, patients often come to the hospital without physician referral; in other instances the patient's choice of a physician often is influenced by the fact that the physician has admitting privileges at a particular hospital, and one doctor's referral to another may be influenced by the fact that both have staff privileges at the same hospital. Hospitals therefore have an obligation to their patients to award admitting privileges carefully,[55] and the judicial trend during the past two decades has been to find them liable if they fail to carry out this duty properly. As hospital attorney Lee J. Dunn, Jr. has observed:

> The days of hospitals being seen simply as hotels are definitely over. What we are now seeing is not simply the academic discussion of a theory of responsibility for the quality of care practiced within the hospital, but the vigorous enforcement of that theory.[56]

Decisions in several states highlight this legal trend. In the most famous, *Darling v. Charleston Community Memorial Hospital*,[57] a hospital was held liable because, among other things, it had failed to review the treatment of a patient and require consultation as needed. In *Joiner v. Mitchell County Hospital Authority*[58] the court held that a hospital that awarded staff privileges simply on medical staff recommendations, without sufficient review and documentation, could be liable for granting privileges to an incompetent physician whose lack of skill allegedly caused the plaintiff harm. In *Purcell v. Zimbelman*[59] the court held that a surgical staff's failure to adequately assess a physician's competence and recommend limitations could be imputed directly to the hospital. Perhaps the most instructive case of all is *Hull v. North Valley Hospital*,[60] in which the hospital involved was found *not* liable, although the plaintiff had been harmed by an error committed by a physician with hospital privileges. The court found that the hospital had fulfilled its obligation to the patient by making an adequate—although imperfect—effort to supervise the quality of medical practice in the institution; its bylaws set forth procedures for delineating and reviewing privileges, and it used these procedures. The most notorious case is *Gonzales v. Nork*,[61] in which the trial judge found the hospital liable despite the fact that its medical staff was doing what the judge admitted was a better-than-average job of evaluating the quality of patient care by members of the medical staff. The judge found that at the time in question (the late 1960s) medical care evaluation techniques were so primitive that better-than-average application still failed to fulfill the hospital's quality-control duty to the patient. The judge concluded:

> The hospital has a duty to protect its patients from malpractice by members of its medical staff when it knows or should have known that malpractice was likely to be committed upon them. Mercy Hospital had no actual knowledge of Dr. Nork's propensity to commit malpractice, but it was negligent in not knowing. It was negligent in not knowing, because it did not have a system for acquiring knowledge.[62]

Finally, in *Johnson v. Misericordia Community Hospital*[63] the court drew on these earlier cases in similarly holding that a hospital owes an independent duty to its patients to exercise reasonable care in granting privileges to physicians, and that the hospital's failure to verify the accuracy of an application for privileges constituted constructive knowledge of incompetence—incompetence that could forseeably lead to unreasonable risks of danger for patients.

The lessons of these decisions are clear—and less demanding than they may seem at first glance. Hospitals are *not* forced to share in liability for any malpractice committed by a physician with staff privileges. Rather they are held to have an *independent* duty to make certain that privileges are awarded and maintained on the basis of proven competence.[64] From the hospital's perspective this duty creates certain problems. Physicians, traditionally viewed as the hospital's "customers" and entitled to every consideration, do not take kindly to having their privileges limited. Unfortunately those who object most strenuously to such limitation are often in greatest need of limitation. Thus while exercising its responsibility to patients, hospitals are also very sensitive to their responsibility to physicians.

The authority of the hospital governing board over staff privileges is clear. Arthur Southwick, a leading commentator on hospital law, notes that "neither case nor statutory law . . . has ever given a licensed physician an absolute legal right to attain or retain medical staff membership or privileges."[65] He goes on to note elsewhere that

> Courts have generally upheld as reasonable and non-arbitrary any rule or standard bearing a rational relationship to professional standards of patient care, the objectives of the hospital, or the character and ethical behavior of the individual physician.[66]

What the courts have not allowed are hospital privilege decisions that are "arbitrary, capricious, or unreasonable" or based on other impermissible grounds or reached without affording the physician adequate procedural due process.[67]

Of course, the courts can only intervene in hospital credentialing decisions if they first determine that they have jurisdiction to do so; otherwise it remains a private matter. In the case of hospitals owned or operated by a unit of government, constitutional due process and equal protection principles apply directly and the courts will step in to assure that they are adhered to.[68] Even private hospitals, if they have received significant federal support, would be in violation of the Civil Rights Act of 1964 if they discriminated in medical staff appointments on the basis of race, color, or national origin.[69] And, as stated earlier, some courts have viewed all hospitals as quasi-public, assuming from this the jurisdiction needed to scrutinize the awarding of staff privileges and similar actions of a governing board. Southwick concludes that

> The duty of the governing board in rendering decisions with respect to staff appointments and in delineating clinical privileges is the same for public and private hospitals. . . . The result is that the range of the hospital's discretion

in appointing physicians to its medical staff has been narrowed, while the rights of physicians have been expanded by a standard of reasonableness and a recognition that physicians are entitled to a fair evaluation of their credentials and competence. . . .[70] In a nutshell, what the courts and statutes are saying is this: individuals must be judged as individuals in light of their training, experience, current demonstrated clinical and professional competence, ethical attitudes, and ability to function effectively with patients and colleagues.[71]

Although corporate negligence in granting and limiting staff privileges has been a major issue in hospital law in recent years, it is far from the only basis for legal suits against hospitals. The hospital is also obligated to provide an environment—building, equipment, staff, and procedures—aimed at assuring quality patient care (as well as safety for all who visit or work in the hospital). Risk management, a concept that has gained prominence in recent years, is a systematic effort to assure such an environment and to reduce the danger of harm to patients, thus reducing lawsuits.[72]

Voluntary control.   Voluntary control generally refers to self-regulation by the hospital industry, although it can also include efforts by patient groups to influence the quality of hospital care without involving government and the courts. Private accreditation is an important mechanism used by the industry to regulate hospital quality. The Joint Commission on Accreditation of Hospitals (JCAH) is the best-known accrediting agency, but hospitals may also be affected by the accreditation programs of the American Osteopathic Association, Liaison Committee on Medical Education, or other accrediting bodies.

Accreditation, like licensure, stresses a structural approach to quality assurance. The process differs from licensure in that it is private and voluntary, and there is no legal need to meet the standards promulgated. But the pressures for compliance are very strong; since Medicare reimbursement, capitation payments, and other sources of funding are for the most part made only to accredited institutions, accrediting bodies take on a quasi-public function. The Joint Commission on Accreditation of Hospitals, for example, is a joint enterprise of the American Medical Association, the American Hospital Association, the American College of Surgeons, the American College of Physicians, and the American Dental Association. It was organized in 1952 to take over the American College of Surgeon's hospital standardization program,[73] and until the late 1960s the commission functioned in an almost casual manner, its accreditation primarily a mark of prestige and a means of access to consultation and advice for hospitals that did not have a professionally trained administrative staff.

When Congress enacted the Medicare law, it used the JCAH accreditation standards (plus utilization review requirements) as the government's maximum standards for qualifying for Medicare reimbursement. This section of the law was challenged in a suit charging illegal delegation of government authority, because, in effect, it permitted a private body to determine, without any public input, how public funds were to be dispersed. But before the suit was decided, Congress amended the law to make JCAH accreditation an alternative and partial way of qualifying for Medicare payment. But because it remains the most convenient alternative, the JCAH accreditation process still effectively retains a "quasi-public" role.[74]

Joint Commission standards—and accreditation programs in general—tend to be nonspecific, designed to encourage "optimal achievable" levels of care, rather than to set definite, rigorous requirements.[75] In defining acceptable services and staff, for example, JCAH states that

A well-defined plan for emergency care, based on community need and on the capability of the hospital, shall be implemented by every hospital.[76]

The nursing department/service shall be directed by a qualified nurse administrator and shall be appropriately integrated with the medical staff and with other hospital staffs that provide and contribute to patient care.[77]

The pharmaceutical department/service shall be directed by a professionally competent and legally qualified pharmacist. It shall be staffed by a sufficient number of competent personnel, in keeping with the size and scope of services of the hospital.[78]

During the JCAH's earliest days, when state licensure of hospitals was very weak and federal review mechanisms nonexistent, the accreditation systems served to screen out institutions with the gravest inadequacies while helping mediocre hospitals to improve themselves. Today the JCAH is one of several review systems, including state licensure, federal Conditions of Participation, and the PSROs, that check on whether hospitals have quality-care evaluation mechanisms in place (but do not attempt to assess that quality themselves). Critics of this approach argue that it is readily circumvented by concentrating on form rather than substance, while defenders argue that it strengthens the hand of those who want to use it to achieve greater quality control and that undue rigor will simply force those institutions most in need of improvement to opt out of the system.[79]

The JCAH is entirely a provider organization, and a narrow one at that. Only physician, dental, and hospital administrator organizations are represented on the JCAH board; nurses and other hospital-based health professionals have no formal input. And while quality assurance, whether through accreditation, licensure, or PSROs, is aimed at protecting the patient, patients are not included in the process, which has traditionally been viewed by health professionals as a province solely for peer evaluation and judgment.

In the 1960s and 1970s, however, this perspective was challenged by the emergence of a "consumer perspective" on health care.[80] The intent of this development is clear—to represent and protect the interest of the patient in the health care system; but the mechanisms for implementing the intent are sparse. While the patients are obviously the most directly concerned about the quality of patient care, they are also, in most cases, least able to assess and influence that quality, and must rely on providers and professionals, the federal government, state licensure, PSROs, and the courts for protection. In most instances, this reliance serves the patient well; sometimes it is woefully inadequate.

Because it is next to impossible for individual patients—or even organizations of patients—to assess and assure quality of care, patient groups have concentrated on efforts to increase and improve the degree of information and control provided to patients. As Louise Lander has pointed out:

> Reform in the consumerist mold . . . came to mean issuing doctors' directories and shoppers' guides, arguing for a right of access to one's medical records, and generally attempting to increase the availability of information on medical professionals, institutions, and procedures. . . . The theoretical implication is that well-informed individuals, as individuals, can protect themselves against inferior quality. Similarly, patients' rights activities, which were originally directed at systematic abuses of the sick poor, developed into mechanisms—patients' bills of rights, sometimes accompanied by institutionalized grievance procedures—for individual patients to assert their rights vis-a-vis individual professionals.[81]

Applied to hospitals, these perspectives mean a concern for privacy and confidentiality, respectful treatment, and adequate dialogue and clear designation of the physician in charge of the patient's hospital care. They also support patient-access to records, adoption of patient bills of rights, and notification at the time of admission as to what those "rights" are and to whom (patient representative or other official) the patient can turn if they are violated.

Hospitals have generally responded to such consumer pressures by adding "consumer" members to the governing board, hiring "patient representatives," and adopting the American Hospital Association's Patient Bill of Rights (which in most instances is not legally enforceable against a hospital or any individual provider).[82] Only five or six states have written a patient's bill of rights into law, and so far these have had little practical impact. One of the more recent, the Massachusetts law, is perhaps the most advanced, but even it does not go much beyond the protections already existing under common law and accepted hospital practice.[83]

The one area where patients may be able to assert enforceable rights and affect important change is in opening up hitherto tightly held information to their own scrutiny and that of the public at large. As noted elsewhere (see Chapter 17), a number of courts and legislatures in recent years have affirmed the patient's right of access to his or her own medical record, although it still often requires a good deal of persistence on the part of the patient for the record to be made available. Information on a hospital's performance record (outcome data) is also likely to become more available as time goes on. Regulations issued under the PSRO law require local PSROs to reveal data they have collected on hospital performance (hospitals may include an explanatory note regarding their performance). And as noted earlier, the same principle may be applied to individual physicians, under the Freedom of Information Act.[84] Federal regulations issued in 1979 also provide for public disclosure of information on health facility ownership, state survey reports, and notification of deficiencies based on the reports.[85]

Patients may also seek information about hospital and physician track records—that is, their successes, complications, failures, etc.—directly from their physicians, although they are unlikely to get it. It has never been tried, but it would seem reasonable, in a malpractice liability trial, to argue that failure to provide such data is a negligent denial of informed consent, since it would seem more relevant for the patient to know the complication rate for a particular procedure in the hospital to which he or she is being admitted or at the hands of a particular surgeon than to have such figures for the nation as a whole.[86]

Interestingly, some of the more meaningful patient rights legislation of late has concerned nursing home patients, a response to the fact that these patients are particularly dependent upon the facilities in which they reside. Illinois has one of the more far-reaching patient rights acts applying exclusively to nursing homes. The law narrowly limits involuntary discharges and transfers, requires that facilities provide for protection of residents' property, guarantees the right to refuse treatment and to inspect records, and affords access to residents by public officials, legal services attorneys, and members of community organizations. The law requires written contracts between facility and patient and lays down requirements for managing residents funds. Most important, the law allows patients to designate individual advocates; provides for advisory councils of residents, friends, and community advocates; requires extensive disclosure of information to the public; provides for a variety of intermediate sanctions; and provides for a private right of action, so that patients and/or their representatives can pursue violations of the law should the responsible state agencies fail to do so.[87]

Business and Labor Problems

Hospitals are businesses, and like any other business enterprise a hospital will be involved in a wide variety of situations involving the law. A contract is signed with a supplier, and the supplier fails to conform to his part of the bargain. A passerby slips on an icy sidewalk and sues. The trustees decide to purchase the apartment building immediately adjacent to the hospital. For the most part these are straightforward legal matters unaffected by the fact that one of the participants is a nonprofit health care provider.[88] The focus of this chapter has been on those legal concerns that are relatively unique to the hospital industry; for more general business law matters the interested reader can consult a standard introduction to business law.[89] However, there is one area of business-related law unique enough in its health care context to have become an area of specialization: health care labor law.

The health care industry is the largest single employer of people in the United States, and four-fifths of the nation's seven million health industry personnel work in institutions—primarily in hospitals.[90] Despite the humanitarian purpose and professional commitment involved, the fact is that health workers—including, to an increasing extent, physicians—function in an employee-employer relationship. This relationship has legal implications ranging from corporate liability for employee negligence to worker's compensation coverage; of special concern is the way in which the employee-employer relationship is specifically defined under federal labor law and in a number of state laws.

Until the 1960s the number of hospital employees covered by union contracts was small; but in the past two decades that number has increased sharply, and in 1974 the National Labor Relations Act (NLRA) was amended to bring the 1.4 million people employed by private, nonprofit hospitals, clinics, nursing homes, extended care facilities, and health maintenance organizations under the jurisdiction of the National Labor Relations Board (NLRB).[91] Only institutions operated by the federal government or by state or local governments are still exempt from the National Labor Relations Act, and they may be covered by the Federal Labor Relations Authority or by state labor relations acts.

The NLRA was enacted to reduce the turmoil and disruption of economic conflict between employers and workers by guaranteeing and protecting the employees' right to organize and bargain collectively and preventing certain unfair labor practices by both employers and unions. The Health Care Institution amendments, which extended the act's coverage to health care institutions, also imposed special procedural requirements on collective bargaining in the health industry, in recognition of the public interest in uninterrupted health care. These requirements include mandatory fact-finding and mediation, and ten days' advance notice to employers before any strike or other job action disruptive to patient care can be carried out.[92]

Probably the most important coverage granted health care employees under the NLRA is the right to a representation election. Any labor union that has secured signed authorization cards from 30 percent of the workers involved in an organization effort can ask the NLRB to conduct a secret-ballot representation election. If the union wins a majority of votes, it is certified as the workers' bargaining representative, and management may not refuse to bargain with that union over wages, hours, and conditions of employment. An impasse in labor-management negotiations automatically triggers federal mediation machinery aimed at reaching a settlement without the disruption of a strike. Any party seeking to terminate or modify an existing labor contract must give the other party at least ninety days' notice of intent and give the Federal Mediation and Conciliation Service (FMCS) at least sixty days' notice.

Labor law is an excellent example of legislation as "unfinished law." The NLRA provides the authority of the NLRB to act in labor disputes. But the accumulated decisions of the NLRB in specific labor disputes and the rulings of federal courts that review certain NLRB decisions constitute a sizable portion of American labor law.[93] This is particularly evident in the way the board has defined appropriate bargaining units in health care institutions and determined what constitutes permissible activity under the NLRA in the health care industry.

After determining that it has jurisdiction over a particular group of employees,[94] the board must decide on appropriate collective bargaining units or groupings—that is, who will be allowed to vote in a representation election. With some exceptions, the board has defined six basic bargaining units in health care institutions: employee physicians, registered nurses (including graduate nurses), all other professionals, technical employees (including LPNs), business office clerical employees, and service and maintenance employees.[95]

In defining permissible activities and unfair labor practices under the Health Care Institution amendments, the board has decided that hospitals can prohibit union solicitation and distribution of organizing literature, but only according to general rules that apply to all solicitation in the hospital and only in work areas closed to visitors and ambulatory patients.[96] The board has also ruled that the ten-day advance notice provision covers not only institutional employees, but also employees who only happen to be working temporarily at a health institution site—such as construction workers—even if their job actions do not interfere with the institution's business.[97]

The board decision that has gained the most notoriety in the health care field involved the question of whether or not interns and residents were employees within the meaning of the NLRA. The board ruled that they were not, and after a series of appeals the Supreme Court let stand the board's decision was not reviewable. The legislative history of the amendments and earlier decisions defining an employee as "someone who works or performs a service for another from whom he or she receives compensation," show this decision to be clearly in error. However, it remains, in effect, a testimony to the highly politicized nature of judicial decision making.

States have their own labor laws and labor relations boards, and before the NLRA was extended to cover voluntary hospitals these laws often governed labor relations in such institutions. Federal law now takes precedence over state labor laws for these institutions, but the state laws remain important in labor relations between public hospitals and their employees.[98]

Conclusion

Significant changes in hospital law can be anticipated in the near future, but these will relate primarily to cost control efforts (the subject of the next chapter). It seems quite likely that the hospital corporate liability trend will extend to more and more states and that hospitals will rely increasingly on in-house legal counsel.

The legal concerns facing hospitals have their parallel with other types of health care institutions, such as long-term care facilities and health maintenance organizations. Perhaps the major distinction between hospitals and other types of health care institutions is one of timing; whatever the problem and whatever the approaches suggested for their solution, hospitals often have confronted them first.[99]

NOTES

1. R. F. Bridgman and M. I. Roemer, *Hospital Legislation and Hospital Systems* (Geneva: World Health Organization, 1973), p. 87.
2. *Health Resources Statistics*, 1976–1977 ed. (Hyattsville, Md.: National Center for Health Statistics, 1979), p. 303 (DHEW pub. no. (PHS) 79-1509). On the cottage industry nature of turn-of-the-century health care delivery see Sander Kelman, "Toward the Political Economy of Medical Care," *Inquiry* 8(3):30–38 (1971). On the history of hospitals in the United States, see Bridgman and Roemer, *Hospital Legislation;* John Gordon Freymann, *The American Health Care System: Its Genesis and Trajectory* (Baltimore: Williams and Wilkins, 1974); and Robin O'Connor, "American Hospitals: the First 200 Years," *Hospitals, JAHA* 50(1):62–72 (January 1, 1976).
3. *Health Resources Statistics*, p. 317 (7,271 hospitals, of which 6,361 are general hospitals). For a description of the hospital today, see Michael Enright and Steven Jonas, "Hospitals," in Steven Jonas, et al., *Health Care Delivery in the United States*, 2d ed. (New York: Springer, 1981), and William L. Dowling and Patricia A. Armstrong, "The Hospital," in Stephen J. Williams and Paul R. Torrens, *Introduction to Health Services* (New York: John Wiley, 1980).
4. *Health, United States, 1980* (Hyattsville, Md.: National Center for Health Statistics, December 1980), p. 101 (DHHS pub. no. (PHS) 81-1232).

5. *Health Resources Statistics*, pp. 297–298. For reimbursement purposes under Medicare and Medicaid, nursing facilities are classified into various levels of Skilled Nursing Facility, Intermediate Care Facility, and Residential Facility.

6. *Health Resources Statistics*, p. 349.

7. "Other special" includes narcotic addiction; maternity; eye, ear, nose, and throat; rehabilitation; orthopedic; chronic disease; mental retardation; and alcoholism. See Enright and Jonas, "Hospitals."

8. Those readers interested in more detail on hospital law than is presented here can profit from two useful general texts on hospital law: Arthur F. Southwick, *The Law of Hospital and Health Care Administration* (Ann Arbor: Health Administration Press, 1978) and David G. Warren, *Problems in Hospital Law*, 3d ed., (Germantown, Md.: Aspen Systems Corporation, 1978). Aspen also markets a detailed looseleaf manual to hospital attorneys and administrators, *The Hospital Law Manual*.

9. Some public hospitals may have a corporate structure.

10. See *Guide for Preparation of Constitution and By-Laws for General Hospitals* (Chicago: American Hospital Association, 1973). Currently many hospitals are involved in corporate reorganization, aimed at retailoring the corporate structure (often by spinning off one or more separate corporations) to better achieve hospital goals without running into difficulty with tax, liability, licensing, and other laws.

11. In not-for-profit hospitals the term "board of directors" is rarely used, and one is more likely to hear about the governing board or governing body. In fact, because voluntary hospitals have their antecedents in the legal construct known as the charitable trust, members of hospital boards are commonly referred to as trustees. (Technically they are not trustees, because title to hospital property is not vested directly in them as trustees.) It should be noted that a not-for-profit hospital is not necessarily a charitable institution. Nor are all charities incorporated, although in some states they must be and in all states most are. See, generally, Southwick, *The Law of Hospital and Health Care Administration*, chaps. 2 and 3. In recent years, hospital trustees have had to become increasingly sophisticated regarding the legal issues confronting the hospital. An example of the growing number of law-related handbooks and workshops aimed at trustees is Arthur H. Bernstein, *A Trustee's Guide to Hospital Law* (Chicago: Teach 'Em, 1981).

12. Eugene T. Hackler, "Hospital Trustees' Fiduciary Responsibilities: An Emerging Tripartite Distinction" *Washburn Law Journal* 15:422–434 (1976).

13. Southwick, *The Law of Hospital and Health Care Administration*, p. 42.

14. *Accreditation Manual for Hospitals* (hereafter referred to as *AMH*), 1981 ed. (Chicago: Joint Commission on Accreditation of Hospitals, 1980), p. 93. The role and authority of the Joint Commission is discussed later in this chapter.

15. However, it is noteworthy that the JCAH standards no longer provide that the director of nursing "should be responsible to the chief executive officer." *AMH*, 1976 ed., p. 121. Instead the lines of authority are left to the hospital to define, but with "a written organizational plan that delineates lines of authority, accountability, and communication" required. *AMH*, 1981 ed., p. 116.

16. *AMH*, 1981 ed., p. 103.

17. *AMH*, 1981 ed., pp. 101–102. The federal Medicare Conditions of Participation do not specifically require an executive committee, but do require that the executive committee *functions* are carried out.

18. *AMH*, 1981., p. 54. Another formal type of bringing together of governing board and medical staff occurs when physicians sit on the governing board, sometimes by virtue of their administrative office (e.g., chief of staff), sometimes as an elected representative of the medical staff, and sometimes simply as an individual who also happens to practice in the hospital. At one time this practice was frowned upon and, in some instances, prohibited. Now it is generally viewed as a good idea. Nurses may occassionally sit on hospital governing boards, but this seems to be an even rarer practice.

19. Although in *Coreleto v. Shore Memorial Hospital*, 350 A.2d 534 (N.J. Super. 1975), a trial court held that a medical staff was an unincorporated association that could be sued as a group. This approach, which has not been followed by other courts, is criticized by J. F. Horty and D. M. Mulholland, "The Legal Status of the Hospital Medical Staff," *Saint Louis University Law Journal* 22:485–500 (1978).

20. Calculated in terms of the number of beds the ratio favors nongovernmental, nonprofit hospitals even more. Only 82,519 of 1,069,828 general hospital beds are in proprietary hospitals, only 316,471 of 937,301 not-for-profit beds are in government hospitals. See *Health Resources Statistics*, p. 317.

21. *Munn v. Illinois*, 94 U.S. 113 (1877).

22. *Silver v. Castle Memorial Hospital*, 53 Hawaii 475, 497 P.2d 564 (1972). Also see *Pinsker v. Pacific Coast Society of Orthodontists*, 12 Cal.3d 541, 526 P2d 253, 116 Cal. Rpt. 245 (1974). Courts are just beginning to look at hospitals in this way, although the idea of treating certain private businesses as if they were public is not new. Under English common law, courts applied this "quasi-public" view to any businesses providing an indispensable service with significant impact on the public's health and safety. For an excellent general discussion of this subject see John J. McMahon, "Judicial Review of Internal Policy Decisions of Private Nonprofit Hospitals: A Common Law Approach," *American Journal of Law and Medicine* 3:149–181 (1977). Also see Arthur F. Southwick, "The Physician's Right to Due Process in Public and Private Hospitals: Is There a Difference?" *Medicolegal News* 9(1):4–9, 29 (February 1981), beginning with his discussion of *Greisman v. Newcomb Hospital*, 40 N.J. 389, 192 A.2d 817 (1963).

23. On tax exemptions, see pp. 303–314 in Warren, *Problems in Hospital Law*. Also see discussion of IRS definition of charitable in Chapter 9 of this book. The Fourth Circuit Federal Court of Appeals has held that receipt of Hill-Burton and other federal funds cloaked a private hospital with sufficient public role to justify judicial intervention, but other federal courts have not followed suit. *Simkins v. Moses H. Cone Memorial Hospital*, 323 F.2d 959 (4th Cir. 1963), *cert. denied*, 376 U.S. 938 (1964); *Sams v. Ohio Valley General Hospital Association*, 413 F.2d 826 (4th Cir. 1969).

24. *Report of the Task Force on Regulation* (Albany: Hospital Association of New York State, 1976).

25. "Information on Hospital Inspections, Reporting Requirements, and Life Safety Code Enforcement (HRD-80-94)," General Accounting Office Report, Human Resources Division, July 2, 1980, B-199186.

26. The American Hospital Association, in its report on hospital regulation, employs four categories: access, planning, quality of care, and payment. The latter is an aspect of cost control (perhaps the only aspect palatable to the AHA), while planning draws together some aspects of both cost and access considerations. See *Hospital Regulation: Report of the Special Committee on the Regulatory Process* (Chicago: American Hospital Association, 1977).

27. Homes for unwed mothers, dependent children, and residential treatment centers for emotionally disturbed children were the earliest health-related facilities to be licensed by a significant number of states; about half of the states enacting laws between 1900 and 1930, the remainder since then. All states currently license nursing and convalescent homes, forty-five of those laws being passed between 1940 and 1960. See *State Licensing of Health Facilities* (Hyattsville, Md.: National Center for Health Statistics, 1972), p. 6 (DHEW pub. no. (HSM) 72-1757). The number of states requiring licensure prior to the 1946 Hill-Burton Act is given as ten by Milton I. Roemer and Jay W. Friedman, *Doctors in Hospitals* (Baltimore: Johns Hopkins, 1971) and as "fewer than a dozen" by William Worthington and Laurens H. Silver, "Regulation of Quality of Care in Hospitals: The Need for Change," in Clark Havighurst, ed., *Health Care* (Dobbs Ferry, N.Y.: Oceana Publications, 1972), p. 76.

28. Most of the states that responded to the Hill-Burton minimum standards requirement adopted the Model Hospital Licensing Act, which was developed at the initiative of the American Hospital Association. A 1950 federal requirement similar to that of Hill-Burton prompted most of those states lacking nursing home licensure laws to adopt such legislation. See Louise Lander, "Licensing of Health Care Facilities," in Ruth Roemer and George McKray, *Legal Aspects of Health Policy: Issues and Trends* (Westport, Conn.: Greenwood, 1980), pp. 131–132.

29. *Health Resources Statistics*, pp. 303, 328, 339. In 1974 there were close to 500 state agencies that "licensed, approved, certified, supervised, and otherwise regulated inpatient health facilities." Three-quarters of these were health and/or welfare departments. Ibid., p. 299.

30. Steven Jonas, "Measurement and Control of Health Care Quality," in Jonas, et al., *Health Care Delivery*, p. 409.

31. Hospital licensing statutes provide a good example of statutes as "unfinished law." See Chapter 3.

32. ILL. ANN. STAT. ch. 111½, sec. 147(a).

33. In many instances a state will simply adopt the requirements of the National Fire Protection Association's Life Safety Code. Hospital compliance with the code is a requirement for JCAH accreditation, as well as for participation in Medicare and Medicaid. "Generally, hospitals are one of the safest places in terms of risk of death by fire." General Accounting Office Report, note 25. Also see Rich Feeley, Diana Chapman Walsh, and Jonathan E. Fielding, "Structural Codes and Patient Safety: Does Strict Compliance Make Sense?," *American Journal of Law and Medicine* 3:447–454 (Winter 1977–1978).

34. Lander, in Roemer and McKray, *Legal Aspects of Health Policy*, pp. 139–142, describes "The system of licensure within licensure" that has been developing in several states, including California, New York, and Pennsylvania. These states have developed separate standards and a separate permit system for specialized technology-intensive facilities within the hospital, such as burn centers, cardiac surgery services, renal dialysis units, kidney transplant services, radiation therapy, emergency centers, and intensive-care newborn nurseries.

35. An obvious way out of this dilemma is to avoid the all-or-nothing approach in favor of meaningful, targeted penalties. Ibid., pp. 145–147, explains how an operating license could be temporarily suspended or limited by withdrawing state approval to operate in the specific areas of deficiencies. The withholding of state funds for noncompliance with licensing requirements could be a potent tool also. And in extreme cases, rather than close a deficient facility, the institution could be placed in state receivership. Some states have experimented with these approaches, but the fact is that in most states hospital licensure activities are underfunded, understaffed, and of quite limited impact. The receivership idea originated with Frank P. Grad, "Upgrading Health Facilities: Medical Receiverships as an Alternative to License Revocation," *Colorado Law Review* 42:419–436 (1971). Under the Illinois Nursing Home Reform Act of 1979, intermediate sanctions available to the State Department of Public Health include imposition of a correction plan, limitations on state agency referrals, conditional licensure subject to immediate revocation, transfer of residents, placement of monitors in a facility, receivership, various civil and criminal penalties, and injunctive relief. See note 87.

36. See Jonas, "Measurement and Control of the Quality of Health Care." The distinction made in quality of care evaluation among structure, process, and outcome is a conceptual paradigm developed by Avedis Donabedian. See Avedis Donabedian, "Evaluating the Quality of Medical Care," *Milbank Memorial Fund Quarterly* (Part 2) 44:166 (1966), and Avedis Donabedian, *The Definition of Quality and Approaches to its Assessment: Exploring in Quality Assessment and Monitoring*, vol. 1 (Ann Arbor: Health Administration Press, 1980). Also see James P. LoGerfo and Robert H. Brook, "Evaluation of Health Services and Quality of Care," in Williams and Torrens, *Introduction to Health Services*, and Charles M. Jacobs, Tom H. Christoffel, and Nancy Dixon, *Measuring the Quality of Patient Care* (Cambridge: Ballinger, 1976).

37. An exception—important because compliance can be a major cost item for hospitals and nursing homes—is the accessibility requirement of the Architectural Barriers Act of 1968 (42 U.S.C. 4151 et seq.), which was aimed at insuring that certain federally funded buildings were designed and constructed so as to be accessible to the physically handicapped.

38. The Conditions of Participation were applied primarily to unaccredited hospitals in inspections and were usually conducted by state health departments under federal contract. No similar certification program was included under Medicaid; some state Medicaid plans simply required that qualifying hospitals be licensed, others that the Medicare requirements be met. See Lander in Roemer and McKray, *Legal Aspects of Health Policy*, p. 135. In 1972

Congress changed the law to make JCAH accreditation one alternative and partial, but still the major, way of qualifying for Medicare payments. See discussion later at note 74. In spring 1980 the Health Care Financing Administration (HCFA) completed a series of eleven public hearings throughout the country as part of a comprehensive evaluation of certification procedures for Medicare and Medicaid providers. See National Health Standards and Quality Information Clearinghouse, *Information Bulletin*, June 1980, pp. 1–6. On June 20, 1980, HCFA issued the first major modification of the Conditions of Participation since their inception in 1966. They are intended to be more flexible, with general, simplified standards. See Proposed Rules, 45 Fed. Reg. 41794-41818, June 20, 1980.

39. Kathleen M. Popko, *Regulatory Controls: Implications for the Community Hospital* (Lexington, Mass.: Lexington Books, 1976), p. 8.

40. 42 U.S.C. 1320c-1 et seq.

41. 42 U.S.C. 1320c-4(a)(1). Clark Havighurst observes that the "initial limitation of PSRO jurisdiction to 'services provided by or in institutions' . . . strongly suggests that Congress saw the statute as primarily cost-oriented. Excessive utilization of resources occurs primarily in inpatient care, whereas quality concerns would probably be greatest with respect to outpatient care, where existing peer-review mechanisms are least effective." Clark Havighurst, "Coping with the Cost/Quality Trade-offs in Medical Care: The Role of the PSRO," *Northwestern University Law Review* 70:6 (1975). The PSRO law was challenged as being unconstitutional on several grounds in *Association of American Physicians and Surgeons v. Weinberger*, 395 F.Supp. 125 (N.D. Ill. 1975) affirmed without opinion, 423 U.S. 975 (1975). None of the challenges were accepted by the court.

42. The *PSRO Program Manual* explains that the law is "based on the concepts that health professionals are the most appropriate individuals to evaluate the quality of medical services and that effective peer review at the local level is the soundest method for assuring the appropriate use of health care resources and facilities."

43. If a significant number of physicians objects to being "represented" by a particular prospective PSRO, a poll of all local physicians is conducted on the subject; official designation as a PSRO then requires support from at least half the physicians in the area. PSROs have been almost exclusively physician-sponsored; in 1980 only four were sponsored by nonphysician groups.

44. PSRO criteria were not developed—and are inappropriate—for this evidentiary purpose. General guidelines and recommendations are rarely accepted as evidence in defining a professional standard of care. See Henry E. Simmons and John R. Ball, "PSRO and the Dissolution of the Malpractice Suit," *Toledo Law Review* 6:739–763 (1975). Also see John D. Blum, Paul M. Gertman, and Jean Rabinow, *PSROs and the Law* (Germantown, Md.: Aspen Systems Corporation, 1977), chap. 7.

45. *Public Citizen Health Research Group v. DHEW et al.*, 449 F.Supp. 937 (D.D.C. 1978); reversed, 668 F.2d 537 (1981). But see *St. Mary Hospital v. Philadelphia Professional Standards Review Organization*, no. 78-2943 (E.D. Pa. 1980). It is widely believed that if the *Health Research Group* decision should

be successfully appealed to the Supreme Court, Congress would then legislate a reversal by specifically removing PSROs from coverage by the Freedom of Information Act. Congress has already exempted PSROs from FOIA coverage until one year after final judicial resolution of the question. See Douglas A. Hastings, "Professional Standards Review Organizations and Confidentiality: The Question of Public Access to Medical Peer Review Data through the Freedom of Information Act," *Journal of Health Politics, Policy and Law* 16:136–158 (1981). For a general discussion of the Freedom of Information Act, see Chapter 3.

46. *Health Care Financing Research Report: Professional Standards Review Organization 1979 Program Evaluation* (Washington, D.C.: Office of Research, Demonstration, and Statistics, Health Care Financing Administration, May 1980), p. 14 (DHEW publication no. (HCFA)-03041).

47. See *The Impact of PSRO on Health Care Costs: Update of CBO's 1979 Evaluation* (Washington, D.C.: Congressional Budget Office, 1980). Helen L. Smits, who as director of the Health Standards and Quality Bureau was responsible for managing the PSRO program in the late 1970s, notes: "Almost from its inception, the PSRO program has been subject to a series of rigorous annual evaluations. . . . They are a model of assessment of a new government program. However, they are also proof that even massive amounts of data analyzed with sophistication do not yield the kinds of answers that Congress and the Office of Management and Budget demand. The 1977, 1978, and 1979 evaluations served as major topics of debate at Departmental budget hearings. The result was described by Hale Champion, former Undersecretary of the Department, as illustrative of the federal tendency to 'pull programs up by the roots to see if they are still growing.' Complex data analyzed with complex methods yield complex and often equivocal results. Congress, on the other hand, wants a 'yes' or 'no' answer, and much is lost in translation." Helen Smits, "The PSRO in Perspective," *New England Journal of Medicine* 305:253–259 (1981).

48. Health care facilities may also be sued by visitors and employees for harm for which the institution is alleged to be responsible, but the focus in the following discussion will be on patient-initiated lawsuits. Also, there are several types of legal actions in which the institution might be a party, including those involving contracts, property rights, discrimination, and violations of criminal law. The discussion that follows will be limited to the area of tort liability (an area of law that is explained at the beginning of Chapter 16).

49. For discussions of hospital liability in much greater detail than that presented here the reader should consult Southwick, *The Law of Hospital and Health Care Administration*, pp. 346–423. Also see Warren, *Problems in Hospital Law*, pp. 99–121.

50. 28 U.S.C. 1346 et seq.

51. Negligence: "The omission to do something which a reasonable man, guided by those ordinary considerations which ordinarily regulate human affairs, would do, or the doing of something which a reasonable and prudent man would not do." *Schneeweisz v. Illinois Central Railway Co.*, 196 Ill. App. 248, 253, in *Black's Law Dictionary*, 4th ed. (St. Paul: West, 1951).

Negligence and negligence of an employee attributable to the employer are discussed more fully in Chapter 16.

52. *American Jurisprudence 2d*, vol. 40: Hospitals and Asylums, sec. 26 (Rochester, N.Y.: Lawyers Cooperative, 1968), p. 869. If equipment is obviously defective and is still used, the user would also be guilty of negligence.

53. *Keene v. Methodist Hospital*, 324 F.Supp. 233 (N.D. Ind. 1971). See, generally, Marguerite R. Mancini and Alice T. Gale, *Emergency Care and the Law* (Rockville, Md.: Aspen Systems Corporation, 1981).

54. See Warren, *Problems in Hospital Law*, pp. 117–121. Also see Sheila Cram, "The Hospital's Obligation to Protect Patients from Carriers of Infectious Diseases," *Medicolegal News* 7(3):8–12 (Fall 1979). Cases include *Kapuschinsky v. United States*, 248 F.Supp. 732 (D.S.C. 1966) and *Suburban Hospital Association, Inc. v. Hadary*, 22 Md. App. 186, 322 A.2d 258 (1974).

55. See Anthony J. J. Rourke, "The Credentials Committee," in C. Wesley Eisele, ed., *The Medical Staff in the Modern Hospital* (New York: McGraw-Hill, 1967).

56. Lee J. Dunn, Jr., "Hospital Corporate Liability: The Trend Continues," *Medicolegal News* 8(5):16–17, 29 (October 1980).

57. 33 Ill.2d 326, 211 N.E.2d 253 (1965), *cert. den.* 383 U.S. 946 (1966). The hospital was also found to have failed to have a sufficient number of trained nurses to properly monitor patient care. The *Darling* court quoted at length from an even earlier opinion, *Bing v. Thunig*, 2 N.Y.2d 656, 143 N.E.2d 3 (1957), where it had been observed that:

> The conception that the hospital does not undertake to treat the patient, does not undertake to act through its doctors and nurses, but undertakes instead simply to procure them to act upon their own responsibility, no longer reflects the fact. Present-day hospitals, as their manner of operation plainly demonstrates, do far more than furnish facilities for treatment. They regularly employ on a salary basis a large staff of physicians, nurses and interns, as well as administrative and manual workers, and they charge patients for medical care and treatment, collecting for such services, if necessary, by legal action. Certainly, the person who avails himself of hospital facilities expects that the hospital will attempt to cure him, not that its nurses or other employees will act on their own responsibility.

58. 299 Ga. 140, 189 S.E.2d 412 (1972).

59. 500 P.2d 335 (Ct. App., Arizona, 1972). This appellate court decision was noted with approval by the Arizona Supreme Court in *Tucson Medical Center v. Misevch*, 545 P.2d 958 (1976).

60. 498 P.2d 136 (Montana, 1972). There is some disagreement as to the true meaning of *Hull*. In *Nork*, note 61, below, the judge distinguished *Hull* from the post-*Darling* trend of decisions. Southwick, *The Law of Hospital and Health Care Administration*, pp. 413–417, points out that the *Hull* court clearly misinterpreted *Darling*, but still finds that facts and results of *Hull* fit logically into the trend.

61. No. 228566 (Sup. Ct. Calif., Sacramento County, November 19, 1973), *reversed on other grounds*, 131 Cal. Rptr. 717 (1976). The *Nork* decision was issued by a trial-level court, so it has no direct precedential value. Moreover, the hospital reached an out-of-court settlement before the decision was handed down—but after it had been written—further limiting the decisions

status. But the decision is so well done, thorough and well reasoned, that it has received considerable attention and has an indirect influence.

62. *Nork,* see note 61, above, p. 194.

63. 301 N.W.2d 156 (Wis. 1981).

64. The hospital governing board cannot simply delegate review "away" to the medical staff. The board can delegate the review *task,* asking the medical staff for recommendations, but the board retains the ultimate *responsibility* for effective review. In both *Joiner* and *Purcell* the hospitals argued "its not our fault, we asked the docs to take care of it." The defense failed in both instances. However, this does not mean that a plaintiff cannot sue the medical staff—as well as the hospital—for failure to properly carry out staff credentialing. This approach was accepted in *Corleto v. Shore Memorial Hospital,* 350 A.2d 534 (N.J. Super. 1975), a decision regarded as "the key case" in Thomas R. Mulroy, *Hospital Liability Revisited: How Governing Boards Can Protect Themselves and Improve Patient Care* (Chicago: Blue Cross Association, 1980), p. 5. But see the criticism of this decision in John F. Horty and Daniel M. Mulholland, "The Legal Status of the Hospital Medical Staff," *Saint Louis University Law Journal* 22:485–500 (1978).

65. Southwick, *The Law of Hospital and Health Care Administration,* p. 430.

66. Southwick, "The Physician's Right to Due Process," p. 6.

67. Procedural due process would involve providing a written explanation of the reasons for denial or restriction of privileges, a timely and impartial hearing, an opportunity to present evidence and witnesses, a hearing decision reasonably based on the evidence with a written explanation thereof, and an opportunity to appeal. Much of the law regarding physician's hospital privileges is currently emerging. Only New York has a statute specifically requiring due process safeguards in hospital bylaws and providing physicians with judicial recourse. See "ABA Debates Due Process in Hospitals," *American Medical News* (August 15, 1980), p. 3. Also see Jay A. Epstein: "Physician-Hospital Conflict: The Hospital Staff Privileges Controversy in New York," *Cornell Law Review* 60:1075–1104 (1975).

68. See *Moore v. Board of Trustees of Carson-Tahoe Hospital,* 495 P.2d 605 (Nev. 1972).

69. As noted earlier (see note 23), only one federal court of appeals has held that receipt of federal funds also subjects the hospital to more general due process obligations. And as will be discussed in Chapter 9, Civil Rights Act enforcement against hospitals has been minimal. For a review of several theories of judicial jurisdiction, see David Hejna, "Hospital Medical Staff: When Are Privilege Denials Judicially Reviewable?" *University of Michigan Journal of Law Reform* 11:95–109 (1977).

70. Southwick, "The Physician's Right to Due Process," pp. 5–6.

71. Southwick, *The Law of Hospital and Health Care Administration,* p. 432. On hospital staff privileges, generally, see Laurence W. Kessenick and John E. Peer, "Physicians' Access to the Hospital: An Overview," *University of San Francisco Law Review* 14:43–76 (Fall 1979); Barbara Cray, "Due Process Considerations in Hospital Staff Privilege Cases," *Hastings Constitutional Law Quarterly* 7:217–262 (Fall 1979); and Sheree Lynn McCall, "A Hospital's Liability for Denying, Suspending, and Granting Staff Privileges," *Baylor*

Law Review 32:175–214 (Spring 1980). A relatively new area of the law on hospital staff privileges involves applications for privileges by podiatrists, clinical psychologists, midwives, chiropractors, and other practitioners. In the past, lawsuits brought by such practitioners when privileges were denied were usually based on constitutional grounds and failed. Now such lawsuits present antitrust arguments against hospitals and seem more likely to succeed. See the discussion of antitrust law in Chapter 8.

72. See, for example, Bernard L. Brown, Jr., *Risk Management for Hospitals: A Practical Approach* (Germantown, Md.: Aspen Systems Corporation, 1979).

73. The American College of Surgeons program was begun in 1918. It was logical for surgeons to institute the first such accreditation program, since they rely on the hospital to function. Interestingly, the results of the first accreditation surveys in the United States were so abysmal that both results and standards were destroyed. See Carl P. Schlicke, "American Surgery's Noblest Experiment," *Archives of Surgery* 106:379–385 (1973).

74. Close to three-quarters of all general hospitals are accredited, which somewhat attenuates the prestige aspect of accreditation. What with different— and less expensive—routes to Medicare qualification being available and with a diminishing need for outside administrative "consultation," some hospitals—including some of the better ones—are beginning to question the value of Joint Commission accreditation. One view holds that only a more rigorous JCAH, that is, one whose findings would be accepted by some of the myriad of other hospital inspection agencies, can really be worthwhile.

75. JCAH patient-care audit requirements, which generated considerable physician and hospital complaining in the mid-1970s because they were considered too definite, have become progressively less specific.

76. "Emergency Services Standard I," *AMH*, 1981 ed., p. 23.

77. "Nursing Services Standard I," *AMH*, 1981 ed., p. 115.

78. "Pharmaceutical Services Standard I," *AMH*, 1981 ed., p. 137.

79. The 1972 Medicare-Medicaid amendments directed HEW to survey a sample of accredited hospitals in order to assess the validity of the JCAH accreditation process. This was not done for several years, but when finally carried out the results made headlines. The HEW surveys disclosed many more violations of standards than had the JCAH surveys of the same hospitals. The differences were due to HEW's more rigorous look at safety problems, especially those relating to fire safety. As a result, the JCAH tightened up its activities in this area. Ironically, however, the number of fire-related hospital deaths is so low that this danger should really be on the bottom of the list of things for hospitalized patients to worry about. The safety area aside, the HEW validation surveys uncovered *fewer* problems than did the JCAH surveys.

80. See E. Riska and J. A. Taylor, "Consumer Attitudes Toward Health Policy and Knowledge about Health Legislation," *Journal of Health Politics, Policy and Law* 3:112 (1978). The following discussion does not apply to rights of mental patients, discussed in Chapter 19, nor individual authorization of care, discussed in Chapters 14 and 15.

81. Louise Lander, "Doctor-Patient Models: Reformist Dilemmas," *Health Law Project Library Bulletin* (January 1979), pp. 1–8.

82. The Patient Bill of Rights was affirmed by the board of trustees of the American Hospital Association on November 17, 1972. Although this document was merely offered for voluntary adoption by hospitals and, if adopted, has little binding effect on the institution, it has been widely republished. See, e.g., Appendix B in Harry I. Greenfield, *Accountability in Health Facilities* (New York: Praeger, 1975), and George J. Annas, *The Rights of Hospital Patients* (New York: Avon, 1975), pp. 26–27. The document is replete with subjective, unenforceable terms such as "considerate and respectful care" and "reasonable continuity of care." It seems highly unlikely that such ambiguous wording would be used as a standard by a court in a suit against a hospital, although such a fear was expressed by some members of the hospital industry. See the discussion of the concept of "rights" in Chapters 2 and 9. The best source on the rights of hospital patients is the aforementioned book by Annas, bearing that title. Also see George J. Annas and Joseph M. Healey, Jr., "The Patient Rights Advocate: Redefining the Doctor-Patient Relationship in the Hospital Context," *Vanderbilt Law Review* 27:243–269 (1974), and Barbara Huttman, *The Patient's Advocate: The Complete Book of Patient's Rights* (New York: Viking Penguin, 1981).

83. On the Massachusetts Patients' Bill of Rights see George J. Annas, "How to Make the Massachusetts Patients' Bill of Rights Work," *Medicolegal News* 8(1):6–8 (February 1980); Patrick R. Carroll, "What's Right with Patients' Rights?," *Medicolegal News* 8(1):9–11 (February 1980); and William J. Curran, "Massachusetts Patients' Bill of Rights: Cabbages, Kings, Sausages, and Laws," *New England Journal of Medicine* 301:1433–1435 (1979). The most unusual—and controversial—provision in the Massachusetts law declares a right "in the case of a patient suffering from any form of breast cancer, to complete information on all alternative treatments which are medically viable." This provision would seem to merely underscore existing informed consent principles. See Chapter 14.

84. See discussion of *Public Citizen Health Research Group v. DHEW et al.*, note 45.

85. 42 C.F.R. 431.115, Disclosure of survey information and provider or contractor evaluation.

86. Over sixty years ago E. A. Codman wrote: "Every operation done, in any public or private hospital, is an experiment. I do not claim that such experiments are wrong, but privacy in regard to them is wrong. The public is entitled to know the results of the experiments it must endure. Both the successful and unsuccessful experiments and experimenters should be advertised (made public)," Codman, *A Study in Hospital Efficiency*, 1916. Reproduced by University Microfilms (Ann Arbor: 1972), p. 12.

87. ILL. REV. STAT. ch. 111½, sec. 4151-101 et seq. See Richard M. Daley and Dean Timothy Jost, "The Nursing Home Reform Act of 1979," *Illinois Bar Journal* 68:448–454 (1980). Also see three articles by Patricia A. Butler in October 1980 special issue of *Clearinghouse Review:* "A Long-term Care Strategy for Legal Services," 14:613–622; "Nursing Home Quality of Care Enforcement: Part I—Litigation by Private Parties," 14:622–663; and "Nursing Home Quality of Care Enforcement: Part II—State Agency Enforcement Remedies," 14:665–702. Of the various statutory nursing home patient protections, the private right of action is the most crucial. In

addition to Illinois, nineteen other states have adopted comprehensive nursing home patient's bill of rights legislation. A potentially key enforcement device, effective use of which is just being explored, is receivership. See Butler; Part II, pp. 668–676.

88. The major exception is the exemption from federal and state income taxes, local property taxes, and sales and use taxes for certain categories of charitable enterprises, such as nonprofit hospitals. See, for example, "Exemption from Property, Sales, and Income Taxation," chap. 15 of Warren, *Problems in Hospital Law*. For a criticism of this public policy favoring the voluntary hospital, see Robert Charles Clark, "Does the Nonprofit Form Fit the Hospital Industry?," *Harvard Law Review* 93:1416–1489 (1980). Other areas of business law common to health care delivery are collections and insurance. See Warren, *Problems in Hospital Law*, pp. 297–299 (collections) and pp. 287–289 (insurance).

89. See, for example, Alfred F. Conrad, Robert L. Knauss, and Stanley Siegel, *Enterprise Organization*, 2d ed. (Mineola, N.Y.: Foundation Press, 1977); Robert C. Corley and William J. Robert, *Dillavou and Howard's Principles of Business Law* (Englewood Cliffs, N.J.: Prentice-Hall, 1971); John W. Wyatt and Madie B. Wyatt, *Business Law: Principles and Cases*, 4th ed. (New York: McGraw-Hill, 1971); George J. Siedel, ed., *The Lawyer and Business: An Anthology* (St. Paul: West, 1976); and Bernard D. Reams, *Law for the Businessman* (Dobbs Ferry, N.Y.: Oceana, 1974). Hospital and clinic administrators need to be familiar with business law and usually have had one or more courses on the subject during their training. For other health professionals, however, it is not a crucial area of concern. There is some variation, but most books dealing with health or hospital law do not include standard business law topics.

90. Hospital wages have risen faster during the past twenty-five years than have those in other parts of the economy, but much of this is attributed to catching up by traditionally underpaid workers. But wages have *not* been a major component of hospital cost inflation, accounting for approximately one-fourth of hospital cost increases in excess of inflation and representing a declining percentage of the overall hospital budget. Kenneth R. Wing and Burton Craige, "Health Care Regulation: Dilemma of a Partially Developed Public Policy," *North Carolina Law Review* 57:1165–1195 (1979), at 1178–1179, citing data from the Council on Wage and Price Stability, *The Rapid Rise of Hospital Costs*, staff report (1977).

91. In 1961, 224 voluntary hospitals (3.2 percent of all voluntary hospitals) had collective bargaining agreements with one or more unions. In 1967 the figure was 555 hospitals (7.7 percent); in 1970, 1,046 (14.7 percent); and in 1976, 1,327 (23.1 percent). Unionization is more likely in large hospitals, especially public hospitals. Dowling and Armstrong, in Torrens, *Introduction to Health Services*, pp. 157–159. The National Labor Relations Act, as originally enacted in 1935, excluded only governmental hospitals, but in 1947 this was changed to explicitly exclude private, nonprofit hospitals as well. This did not mean that workers in the excluded hospitals could not organize unions and engage in job actions, but only that the special protections, assistance, and restrictions of federal labor law did not apply to them.

92. For fuller descriptions of the 1974 amendments see Ira M. Shepard, "Health Care Institution Amendments to The National Labor Relations Act: An analysis," *American Journal of Law and Medicine* 1:41–53 (1975), and Yvonne N. Bryant, "Labor Relations in Health Care Institutions: An Analysis of Public Law 93-360," *Journal of Nursing Administration*, pp. 28–39 (1978).

93. The circumstances under which NLRB decisions can be reviewed by the federal courts have been narrowly defined by Congress, in order that appeals to the courts not be used by employers as a means of delaying the obligation to bargain in good faith with unions certified as bargaining agents by the board. A discussion of federal court jurisdiction can be found in *Physicians National Housestaff Association v. Murphy*, 443 F.Supp. 806 (D.D.C. 1978); 642 F.2d 492 (D.C. Cir. *en banc* 1980); *cert. denied*, 101 S.Ct. 1360 (1981).

94. In determining whether it had jurisdiction, the NLRB has had to decide whether particular employers were health care institutions, whether institutions were political subdivisions of state or municipal government, and whether institutions were involved in interstate commerce.

95. In some instances service employees and maintenance employees have been placed in separate units. See Bryant, "Labor Relations in Health Care Institutions," pp. 34–35. A separate question, after bargaining units have been determined, is who may be excluded from the unit, e.g., supervisory personnel.

96. See *NLRB v. Beth Israel Hospital*, 437 U.S. 483 (1978).

97. Reviews of legal developments under the Health Care Institution Amendments to the NLRA include Ira M. Shepard, "Health Care Institution Labor Law: Case Law Developments, 1974–1978," *American Journal of Law and Medicine* 4:1–14 (1978); Robert W. Mulcahy and D. W. Rader, "Trends in Hospital Labor Relations," *Labor Law Journal* 31:100–114 (1980); Cathy Schatz Glaser, "Labor Relations in the Health Care Industry—The Impact of the 1974 Health Care Amendments to the National Labor Relations Act," *Tulane Law Review* 54:416–455 (1980); D. A. Zimmerman, "Trends in NLRB Health Care Industry Decisions," *Labor Law Journal* 32:3–12 (1981); and Ira M. Shepard and A. Edward Doudera, eds., *Health Care Labor Law* (Ann Arbor: AUPHA Press, 1981).

98. A related area of concern is discrimination in employment. Federal law—including Title VII of the Civil Rights Act of 1964, the Age Discrimination in Employment Act, and the Equal Pay Act—as well as state equal employment opportunity laws apply to health care institutions. See Warren, *Problems in Health Law*, pp. 245–246. Also of special note is the impact of state rate review activities on hospital labor relations. See Carl J. Schramm, "Regulating Hospital Labor Costs: A Case Study in the Politics of State Rate Commissions," *Journal of Health Politics, Policy, and Law* 3:364–374 (1978); Paul A. Weinstein, "Impact of Hospital Cost Review on Industrial Relations," *Labor Law Journal* 30:503–513 (1979); and George W. Bohlander, *Impact of Third Party Payers on Collective Bargaining in the Health Care Industry* (Los Angeles: University of California, 1980).

99. Several works dealing with the legal aspects of nonhospital health care in-

stitutions are available. For example, on nursing homes see Lander, "Licensing of Health Care Facilities," pp. 148–155. Also see *Legal and Business Problems of Health Maintenance Organizations* (New York: Practicing Law Institute, 1974); Valerie La Porte and Jeffrey Rubin, eds., *Reform and Regulation in Long-Term Care* (New York: Praeger, 1979); John R. Kress and James Singer, *HMO Handbook* (Rockville, Md.: Aspen Systems Corporation, 1975); George Reardon, "Note-Medical Clinics—Legal and Political Structure in Group Practice," *University of Florida Law Review* 28:68–87 (1976); Philip C. Kissam and Ronald M. Johnson, "HMO's and General Law: Toward a Theory of Limited Reform Mongering," *Vanderbilt Law Review* 29:1163–1232; William J. Curran and George B. Mosley. III, "Malpractice Experience of HMOs," *Northwestern Law Review* 70:69–89 (1975).

8 | Controlling Health Care Costs

*In an economy relatively free of other inflationary controls,
governmental regulation of hospital operating budgets is
analogous to plugging a hole in a dike and expecting this to
keep down the rising flood. If any money is saved, it will be at
the cost of reduced services.*

—John Gordon Freymann[1]

HEALTH CARE COSTS in the United States have escalated more rapidly
during the past decade than almost any other item on the consumer
price index. Most efforts to curb these increases, particularly in hospital
costs (which account for 40 percent of the health dollar and have been
rising at close to 15 percent annually), have concentrated on improving
the efficiency and/or the structure of health care delivery. Both state and
federal governments have sought to increase the rationality and efficiency of health care services by requiring more careful planning, providing
incentives for resource reallocation, and encouraging alternative delivery modes and rate and utilization review.[2] Cost-control efforts, like
quality-control approaches, concentrate on structure, process, and outcome. Structural approaches seek to restrict expansion and capital investment or to strengthen the "free market" system. Process approaches
question the need for specific services or types of services. And outcome
approaches simply place an overall dollar limit on hospital and other
health charges.

Planning

A recent volume on hospital cost control notes that "attempting to control hospital operating costs without controlling capital investment is futile, since capital borrowing, amortization, interest, and depreciation are translated into per diem costs, and, more important, influence manpower and the use and volume of services."[3] Nevertheless, efforts to restrict hospital expansion (or to force closure or conversion of unnecessary facilities) are frequently opposed both by individual facilities eager to "grow" and by communities and neighborhoods eager to develop "their own" health care facilities.

One of the earliest attempts to encourage health planning was the Hospital Survey and Construction Act of 1946 (Hill-Burton),[4] which, while aimed primarily at ameliorating a shortage and maldistribution of hospital beds, required states participating in the funding program to develop an annual construction plan, appoint a State Hospital Planning Council, survey and report hospital construction need, and designate a single state agency to oversee plan implementation.[5] Billions of Hill-Burton fund dollars poured into the states for hospital construction under this act, but while the hospital bed shortage was ended the act's planning requirements had little effect. Planning councils were unrepresentative, understaffed, and unable to deal knowledgeably with competing requests for construction funding.[6] Thus, instead of increasing rationality or efficiency, the Hill-Burton Act may well have made it possible to create more hospital beds than were needed.

The Regional Medical Program (RMP),[7] enacted in 1965, and the Comprehensive Health Planning (CHP) program,[8] enacted in 1966, were other attempts by Congress to encourage a more rational hospital system. Under the Regional Medical Program the federal government spent over a billion dollars to fund cooperative projects, generally between universities and provider groups, aimed at improving various aspects of health care services. The major thrust of the voluntary program was to make the latest scientific advances in treating heart disease, cancer, and stroke available at the local level. But, as Kenneth Wing has observed:

> It is generally agreed that RMP . . . failed to achieve its purposes. . . . Regional agencies [became] deeply involved in the medical politics of the communities . . . and though a great deal of money has changed hands, there is little evidence that it has been well spent.[9]

The Comprehensive Health Planning program, a major, largely unsuccessful, effort at nationwide health planning, provided funds for state and local health planning agencies. Wing notes that:

With very few exceptions, the CHP program established a complete network of local and state health planning agencies for the whole country. However, these agencies were given very limited authority with which to enforce compliance with the plans they developed. The amount of money that CHP agencies were given to offer as incentives for compliance was insignificant. The only comprehensive authority was to "review and comment" on requests for federal funds coming from their areas. . . . Whatever the potential effect of this authority, most CHP agencies have been so ineffective, understaffed, and administratively inept that this review and comment process has been little more than added paperwork for the funding applicants.[10]

While the federal government was pursuing its ineffective efforts at planning, about half the states—with strong support from the American Hospital Association—developed certificate-of-need laws. In general, these laws empower a designated state agency to approve or disapprove all proposed hospital or other health facility construction and/or expansion, after determining the need for such expanded resources.[11] Third-party reimbursements can be tied to certificate-of-need determinations. In the Social Security amendments of 1972, for example, Congress declared that in calculating the basis for Medicare, Medicaid, and Maternal and Child Health reimbursement, hospitals could only include the costs of those capital expenditures that had been approved by a designated state planning agency. At the same time, certificate-of-need laws are rather limited in scope—for example, physicians' offices are usually not affected—and have generally proven to be manipulatable.

The most ambitious federal effort in this area to date has been the National Health Planning and Resources Development Act of 1974,[12] an attempt to consolidate the various federal health planning programs. The act establishes that "the achievement of equal access to quality health care at a reasonable cost is a priority of the federal government." Of the three concerns involved—access, quality, and cost—it seems fair to say that the last named is first among equals. The planning law divides the country into 205 health service areas with a local Health Systems Agency (HSA) for each area.[13] The HSAs have as their legislatively assigned purpose:

1. improving the health of residents of a health service area;
2. increasing the accessibility (including overcoming geographic, architectural, and transportation barriers), acceptability, continuity, and quality of the health services provided them;
3. restraining increases in the cost of providing them health services;
4. preventing unnecessary duplication of health resources;
5. preserving and improving competition in the health services area.[14]

HSAs are also assigned certain functions in working toward these generally worded purposes:

1. to assemble and analyze data;
2. to establish a statement of goals and an annual implementation plan indicating objectives and priorities;
3. to provide technical assistance and/or financial support for projects necessary for the achievement of HSA goals;
4. to coordinate activities, with PSROs and other planning and administrative agencies;
5. to review and approve or disapprove applications for federal funds under certain programs;
6. to make recommendations to the states concerning the need for newly proposed "institutional health services," the appropriateness of existing services, and projects for the modernization, construction, and conversion of medical facilities.[15]

A close reading of these purposes and functions reveals that they almost entirely limit the local HSAs to advice and recommendations. Only in relation to some categories of Public Health Service funds do HSAs have any direct regulatory power. Since the act provided for phasing out the Hill-Burton and RMP funding programs, it was believed that the HSAs would assume these functions; but Congress never appropriated enough money to make this possible. And despite the legislative rhetoric, there was no effective mechanism or leverage in the act that gave the HSAs a significant quality-control role. Thus, with respect to Hill-Burton funds and state certificate-of-need decisions, HSAs can make recommendations, but cannot enforce them. Nor do the HSAs have anything to do directly with Medicare and Medicaid, the two most costly federal health expenditures.[16]

To the extent that power is exercised in the system, it is at the state and federal levels. Under the National Health Planning and Resources Development Act, the states are required to establish certificate-of-need programs and designate state bodies to operate them; to develop a state health plan and oversee HSA plans and activities; and to review the appropriateness of existing health facilities (a negative review places the facility on an excess-capacity listing). The federal role is to develop national health-planning guidelines and regulations and to coordinate the state and local components of the program.

Considerable debate and litigation has been prompted by the provision of the act that requires that HSA boards be broadly representative of the communities in which they exist (the major concern being to prevent providers from dominating board discussions and decisions).[17] Given the limited authority possessed by these boards, the significance of this controversy is somewhat obscure.

The National Health Planning and Resources Development Act, like earlier federal health planning programs, has disappointed those who expected it to have a major impact on cost control, access to, and quality of, health care.[18]

Antitrust

An entirely different structural approach to cost control rejects planning and regulation in favor of "free market" competition. It is not at all clear that increased competition in the health sector will lead to lower health care costs, and there is some reason to suspect that it will not.[19] Be that as it may, the late 1970s and early 1980s have seen rapidly growing support for competition as a way to control costs.[20] This approach has taken two different forms: one is an effort to eliminate anticompetitive practices, the other, an effort to encourage and enhance competition.

Elimination of anticompetitive practices could be achieved through voluntary efforts by health care providers, but most attention has focused on the use of federal and state antitrust laws. On the federal level, the basic legal tool is the Sherman Act, enacted in 1890 and strengthened through passage of the Clayton Act in 1914. It prohibits contracts, combinations, and conspiracies in restraint of trade, and also outlaws monopolization. Since almost any commercial transaction could be said to restrain trade, the courts have developed a "rule of reason," applying the Sherman Act only to the more egregious instances of monopoly control and trade restraint. Certain specific anticompetitive practices, however, such as price fixing, division of markets, group boycotts, and tying arrangements,[21] are considered inherently, or per se, violations of the act. The Federal Trade Commission Act is primarily concerned with unfair methods of competition; the commission has authority to police unfair, and especially deceptive, trade practices.[22] State antitrust statutes tend to be less inclusive than the federal laws, and use of the state laws has been more limited.

A decade ago the mention of antitrust laws in connection with health care delivery would have seemed bizarre to most lawyers; today antitrust has become an important concern of both health care providers and antitrust enforcers. Health care delivery in the United States is extensively regulated, not only by government but also through such private mechanisms as accreditation, specialty certification, hospital credentialing and peer review, all of which, in one way or another, restrict competition (for example, by making it difficult or impossible for persons with inadequate credentials to treat patients). Other mechanisms that would appear to violate antitrust law prohibitions on monopolization and restraint of trade include restrictive licensure and privileges, prohibitions on advertising, reimbursement and practice limitations, AMA accreditation activities, and even health-planning efforts themselves.

The reason antitrust laws have not been applied to health care practices in the past is not because they failed to meet the statutory definition of prohibited practices, but because several established legal defenses protected health care providers. The most important of these is the fact that federal antitrust laws were written to apply specifically to "trade or commerce," and the practice of the learned professions were not considered "trade or commerce." In addition, activities required or regulated by state government—as is much of health care delivery—were expressly exempted from federal antitrust law,[23] and most health care delivery was considered unrelated to the interstate commerce underlying the federal government's antitrust authority. Finally, the business of insurance was specifically exempted from federal antitrust law, an important factor in an industry in which third-party payment predominates.

Recently, however, the law regarding each of these defenses has been changed, and there is now some questions as to how much, if at all, health care providers are protected from the application of antitrust laws. In 1975 the U.S. Supreme Court declared that there is no learned profession exemption from federal antitrust law;[24] and since 1975 the Court has continually narrowed the protection of the state-action exemption.[25] In 1976 the Court decided that local hospital business has sufficient effect on interstate commerce to made federal antitrust law applicable.[26] And two other Supreme Court decisions, in 1978 and 1979, significantly limited the insurance industry's exemption from the antitrust laws.[27] The result has been a spurt of antitrust activity in several quarters, which is likely to continue despite the Reagan administration's general de-emphasis of antitrust enforcement.

Violation of antitrust laws can lead to various legal actions, both criminal and civil. The antitrust division of the U.S. Department of Justice has exclusive authority to prosecute criminal charges under federal antitrust laws. In addition, under the Sherman Act, any person injured as the result of an antitrust violation may initiate private litigation against the violator and, if successful, collect three times the actual damages. State attorneys general, who have their own enforcement role under state antitrust statutes, can also bring federal antitrust suits on behalf of affected individuals residing in their states. Finally, the Federal Trade Commission (FTC) has authority to investigate, prosecute, and issue rules in the broad area of deceptive trade practices, as well as some antitrust enforcement powers. However, the FTC's jurisdiction does not extend to not-for-profit corporations or associations; thus a not-for-profit hospital would not come under FTC jurisdiction. But the Supreme Court recently decided that professional organizations such as the AMA do come under FTC jurisdiction since they operate for the economic benefit of their members. Where it has been active, [28] the FTC role has been important because of the resources the agency can bring to investigatory and corrective efforts.

The application of the antitrust laws to the health sector has only just begun.[29] Perhaps the greatest change to date has been the loosening of prohibitions on professional advertising, although the First Amendment has provided a stronger legal basis than the antitrust laws in this instance.[30] Other areas of current or likely antitrust developments include:

Limitations on patient access to potential providers and services. Antitrust laws were first invoked in the health field in the 1940s, in an effort to halt physician boycotts of prepaid health plans. Today, any organized attempts to interfere with some innovative delivery mode could easily lead to antitrust action, either by the parties involved[31] or by government. Antitrust laws may also be used in efforts to challenge the denial of hospital privileges,[32] especially to nonphysician practitioners,[33] to eliminate restrictions on the advertising of prescription drugs and eyeglasses, or the sale and servicing of dentures by nondentists, or to end physician boycotts of Medicaid patients. More speculative are antitrust challenges of mechanisms that limit patient options in securing health care, such as licensure, peer review,[34] educational accreditation,[35] and antisubstitution laws.

Reimbursement and the provider-insurer relationship. The FTC has been particularly interested in the dominance of Blue Cross/Blue Shield in health insurance, as well as in the close relationship among Blue Cross/Blue Shield, physicians, and hospitals.[35] At the same time, nurse-midwives, clinical psychologists, and other health care professionals who have been routinely denied third-party reimbursement for covered services have been exploring the use of antitrust remedies.[37] And despite their lack of success in litigation, the Justice Department and the FTC have managed to convince several medical specialty societies and associations to abandon their restrictive relative value scales.[38]

Various hospital practices. Antitrust questions may well be raised about shared services arrangements,[39] mergers,[40] opposition to new entrants before regulatory agencies,[41] voluntary rate review, medical staff privilege practices,[42] and arrangements tying staff privileges to agreements to use hospital laboratories and/or rent office space from the hospital.[43]

Health planning. Though health-planning requirements clearly run counter to the "free market" thrust of the antitrust laws, thereby constituting an intentional restraint on trade,[44] it was generally accepted until recently that the state-action exemption and government regulatory programs, such as the National Health Planning and Resources Development Act of 1974, constituted an "implied repeal" of antitrust laws.[45] But in 1976 the Supreme Court held that activity approved under a state regulatory program is only immune from federal antitrust law if such immunity is necessary and was consciously intended.[46] In the recent case of *National Gerimedical Hospital and Gerontology Center v. Blue Cross of Kansas City*, the Court also considered the extent of the implied-repeal doctrine. National Gerimedical had been excluded from the Blue Cross reimbursement program because it had not received a certificate of need from the local HSA. The hospital brought suit under federal antitrust laws, charging that Blue Cross and the HSA were conspiring to boycott the hospital in order to protect existing market control. The lower courts found that the National Health Planning and Resources Development Act was in clear conflict with the antitrust laws, and that no specific exemption from those laws was contained in the planning act. But the lower courts did accept the idea of an implied exception in Congress's establishment of a certificate-of-need planning system. On appeal, the Supreme Court rejected the implied-repeal defense, noting that the planning law "is not so incompatible with antitrust concerns as to create a 'pervasive' repeal of the antitrust laws as applied to every action taken in response to the health-care planning process."[47]

It is too early to predict what these recent antitrust decisions auger for the health-care delivery industry, since the extent of antitrust activity depends on both legal developments and on their impact. Most of these actions are premised on the belief that "free market" forces can benefit the health consumer by reducing costs and improving quality of care. If this premise should begin to appear incorrect, more pinpointed regulation may be viewed as the only promising alternative.

The use of antitrust laws to spur competition in the health field has encouraged the federal government to support other mechanisms toward the same end, such as health maintenance organizations,[48] various federal health manpower training programs,[49] and innovative reimbursement formulae. Since the major purpose of such efforts is to reduce costs rather than to increase access, additional steps are needed to prevent competition from pricing the poor out of the health delivery market.

Utilization Review

A somewhat different approach to hospital cost control is utilization review. This effort, aimed at influencing process, is designed to make certain that patients receive only those medical services that are really needed. Such scrutiny may take place prior to or during the patient's hospital stay, or after discharge. If a proposed treatment is adjudged unnecessary before, or in the early stages of, admission, the treatment may be withheld; if such a determination is made later, the provider may be denied reimbursement by a third-party payer. (A review designed solely to determine if reimbursement is justified is known as claims review.)

The main difference between utilization review and other resource-allocation mechanisms is that the former focuses on aspects of health care directly under the control of the individual physician, who decides whether patients should be admitted to the hospital, what tests, procedures and treatments will be provided for them, and how long they should stay.

Pressure for utilization review has come primarily from third-party payers, particularly the federal government. It is considered essential in containing Medicare, Medicaid, and Maternal and Child Care programs, for without some control mechanism every licensed physician could bill the national treasury for any service rendered to patients covered by such programs. Many hospital-based utilization review programs involve only patients with these particular kinds of third-party coverage.

When the government first mandated a utilization review system for Medicare in 1965, it did not specify how the system should operate.[50] As a result, many early utilization review programs did little to control rapidly accelerating costs, while retroactive denial of benefits caused hardships for hospitals, physicians, and patients. In 1972 a U.S. Senate report concluded that "utilization review activities have, generally speaking, been of a token nature and ineffective as a curb to unnecessary use of institutional care and services."[51] To overcome these shortcomings Congress established the Professional Standards Review Organization (PSRO) program, specifying that payments under federally sponsored medical reimbursement programs will be made:

1. only when, and to the extent medically necessary, as determined in the exercise of reasonable limits of professional discretion; and
2. in the case of services provided by a hospital or other health care facility on an inpatient basis, only when and for such period as such services cannot, consistent with professionally recognized health care standards, effectively be provided on an outpatient basis or more economically in an inpatient health care facility of a different type, as determined in the exercise of reasonable limits of professional discretion.[52]

The PSRO program (which is discussed more fully in Chapter 6) has developed national norms, criteria and standards for use in the utilization review process, including indications for admissions and continued-stay norms (although local PSROs may be allowed to develop their own parameters). Admission review "certifies" an admission as medically necessary and appropriate to the facility in question. The Department of Health and Human Services requires that such certification take place within forty-eight hours of actual admission, and guarantees reimbursement for this initial period, regardless of final certification status. (A more selective version, "focused review," requires admission certification only for those diagnoses, physicians, or institutions with a history of inappropriate admissions, as demonstrated by earlier utilization review results or through retrospective review.)

Continued-stay review uses predetermined criteria to assess the need for continued hospitalization, requiring special justification for a hospital stay that exceeds a designated time period (such as the fiftieth percentile of all patient length-of-stays for a particular diagnosis). If the attending physician cannot provide such justification, reimbursement for the extended stay beyond the two or three days needed to arrange discharge may be withheld.

Both admission and continued-stay reviews are initially conducted by a review coordinator (not a physician) who uses the relevant norms, criteria, and standards to determine whether or not admission certification or continued stay is in order. But the coordinator can only make a positive determination; rejections must be corroborated by a physician reviewer; and attending physicians who disagree with the findings can appeal to the utilization review committee and/or the local PSRO (in a process that is cumbersome and seldom resorted to).[53] These utilization review functions may be carried out by PSRO staff or may be delegated to the hospital itself, subject to retrospective analysis by the PSRO, if the hospital can demonstrate competence to carry them out.

Although almost a decade has passed since Congress established the PSRO program, it is still not clear whether it has been successful in controlling health care costs. The Department of Health and Human Services, evaluating the PSRO program as of the end of 1978, concluded:

> With respect to the cost control objective, the PSRO program has shown the ability to make a modest impact on reducing or slowing down increases in Medicare beneficiary hospital utilization, with an estimated savings in Medicare expenditures $21 million greater than the cost to administer the PSRO program. The impact on hospital utilization is not uniform, but varies in different parts of the country.[54]

As indicated in the previous chapter, as long as the federal government continues to fund hospital care, some type of federally mandated utilization review program will be continued—whether called PSRO or by some other name.

Another process approach to escalating costs encourages second opinions whenever expensive medical procedures are contemplated. This approach assumes (1) that a significant proportion of recommended surgery is unnecessary and (2) that a second opinion is likely to disclose such instances. Of course, second opinions have long been recommended and sought on a voluntary basis; but only recently have campaigns been launched to promote their widespread use. In the least intrusive of such programs, third-party payers agree to pay for a second opinion if the patient desires one, but there are also programs under which third-party insurers (or employers paying the insurance premiums) will not reimburse for nonurgent surgery unless a second opinion as to its need has been obtained.

Rate Setting

Yet another approach would control medical costs by imposing financial ceilings, such as maximum allowable charges, leaving it to the providers to find ways to deliver care within those limits. On the federal level there have been two attempts at such outcome control: the wage-price freeze under the Nixon administration's Economic Stabilization Program, and the Carter administration's unsuccessful efforts to enact a "cap" on hospital charges.[55] Most outcome controls, however, have been imposed at the state level, primarily through rate setting or limitations on the reimbursement hospitals can expect to receive.[56]

Technically, rate setting involves external review and approval or disapproval of hospital charges or per diem rates, but the term is often used to include any prospective determination by an external body as to what will and will not be reimbursed. (A determination by Blue Cross, for example, that it will "disallow" that portion of hospital costs attributable to a hospital addition constructed without relevant certificate-of-need would be a type of rate setting.) A growing number of states have undertaken to regulate hospital rates,[57] some establishing independent commissions for this purpose, others vesting the authority with the state budget director or with the departments of health, social service,[58] or insurance.

There are several ways in which rates can be established, ranging from a simple percentage limit on year-to-year increases to a detailed review of hospital budgets. Some rates are based on norms developed through hospital-to-hospital comparisons; others are negotiated between the hospital and the rate setter. Rate reviewers must also determine whether institutions that do better in controlling cost increases than they were required to should be rewarded in some way. The wide diversity of rate-setting programs and the short time they have been in place (as well as the severe inflation experienced during this period) make it difficult to know how successful the process has been as a cost control.[59]

The policies described above all relate to efforts by the federal and state governments and by private insurers to encourage or mandate medical cost containment. Another aspect of this issue involves fiscal restraint by the hospitals and health care professionals themselves. Unfortunately, there seems to be little incentive for such voluntary moves by the individual facility or practitioner and scant inclination for united action to control costs. The most visible effort in recent years has been the American Hospital Association's Voluntary Effort, which sought to stave off more restrictive federal hospital cost-containment measures by helping member hospitals institute cost-containment programs.[60]

Possibly the greatest potential for voluntary cost control lies with the private third-party payers—especially the Blue Cross plans—which are relatively free to disallow charges attributable to inappropriate institutional expenses. Until recently, however, most efforts by Blue Cross to force hospitals into cost savings were forced upon it by private litigation and/or by aggressive state insurance commissioners.[61]

Conclusion

There is nothing to suggest that health care cost inflation will not continue in the years ahead—and continue at a rate that outpaces the rest of the economy. Since none of the cost-control approaches discussed above has produced dramatic results, it is likely that the experimentation, change, debate, and frustration that has characterized past efforts will continue into the future.[62]

NOTES

1. John Gordon Freymann, *The American Health Care System: Its Genesis and Trajectory* (Baltimore, Williams & Wilkins, 1974), p. 388.
2. See such reviews as David A. Pearson and David S. Abernethy, "A Qualitative Assessment of Previous Efforts to Contain Hospital Costs," *Journal of Health Politics, Policy and Law* 5:120–141 (1980); David S. Abernethy and David A. Pearson, *Regulating Hospital Costs: The Development of Public Policy* (Ann Arbor: AUPHA Press, 1979); Marc J. Roberts and Ted Bogue, "The American Health Care System: Where Have All the Dollars Gone?" *Harvard Journal on Legislation* 13:635–686 (1976); Michael Zubkoff, Ira E. Rankin,

Ruth S. Hanft, eds., *Hospital Cost Containment—Selected Notes for Future Policy* (New York: PRODIST, 1978); and Gordon K. MacLeod and Mark Perlman, eds., *Health Care Capital: Competition and Control* (Cambridge: Ballinger, 1978). Most cost-control mechanisms are premised on the belief that the U.S. health care system is irrational and inefficient. An exception involves alternative payment modes—such as deductibles and copayment on insurance coverage—premised on the belief that demand for health care services is artificially inflated because neither patient nor provider has any financial incentive to forgo care.

3. Zubkoff, Rankin, and Hanft, *Hospital Cost Containment*, p. 5.

4. 42 U.S.C. 291 et seq. (P.L. 79–725).

5. In order to receive Hill-Burton funds through the state, hospitals had to comply with their state plans and had to agree to provide a reasonable volume of care to those unable to pay and not to discriminate in the provision of care. See discussion of these requirements in Chapter 9.

6. Moreover, existing facilities and construction undertaken without Hill-Burton assistance were not influenced by the law; only 25 percent of the nation's hospital beds were affected. See Kathleen M. Popko, *Regulatory Controls: Implications for the Community Hospital* (Lexington, Mass.: Lexington Books, 1976), pp. 306. For a less critical account see J. R. Lave and L. B. Lave, *The Hospital Construction Act: An Evaluation of the Hill-Burton Program, 1948–1973* (Washington, D.C., American Enterprise Institute for Public Policy Research, 1974).

7. 42 U.S.C. 299 et seq. (P.L. 89–239).

8. 42 U.S.C. 246 et seq. (P.L. 89–749).

9. Kenneth Wing, *Law and the Public's Health* (St. Louis, C. V. Mosby: 1976), p. 134. For more information on the Regional Medical Program, see Carol McCarthy and Steven Jonas, "Planning for Health Services," in Steven Jonas et al., *Health Care Delivery in the United States*, 2d ed. (New York: Springer, 1981), and Thomas W. Bice, "Health Services Planning and Regulation," in Stephen J. Williams and Paul R. Torrens, *Introduction to Health Services* (New York: John Wiley, 1980).

10. Wing, *Law and the Public's Health*, pp. 134–135.

11. It has been observed that "certification of need is a negative rather than a positive health planning tool. It allows a health planning agency to prevent particular changes proposed by institutional health care providers that do not accord with established health plans. It does not increase the agency's ability to implement desired changes. . . ." McCarthy and Jonas, in Jonas, *Health Care Delivery*, p. 385. In one state, North Carolina, the state supreme court held a certificate-of-need statute to be unconstitutional under the state constitution. *In re Certification of Need for Aston Park Hospital Inc.*, 282 N.C. 542, 193 S.E.2d 729 (1973). But this type of ruling is unique to North Carolina. There is considerable literature on certificate-of-need. See, for example, David S. Salkever and Thomas Bice, *Hospital Certificate-of-Need Controls: Impact on Investment, Costs, and Use* (Washington, D.C.: American Enterprise Institute, 1979); Clark C. Havighurst, ed., *Regulating Health Facilities Construction* (Washington, D.C.: American Enterprise Institute, 1974); *Symposium: Certificate-of-Need Laws in Health Planning, Utah Law Review*, vol.

1978, no. 1 (1978); Herbert Harvey Hyman, ed., *Health Regulation: Certificate of Need and Section 1122* (Germantown, Md.: Aspen Systems Corporation, 1977); Urban Systems Research and Engineering, *Certificate of Need Programs: A Review, Analysis and Annotated Bibliography of the Research Literature* (Washington, D.C.: U.S. Department of Health, Education and Welfare, 1978).

12. 42 U.S.C. Sec. 300K et seq. (P.L. 93-641). "Ambitious" is used advisedly. Like earlier health planning efforts, P.L. 93-641 contains ambitious legislative pronouncements but quite limited enforcement mechanisms. For an illuminating discussion of this dichotomy in several congressional programs, see Rand E. Rosenblatt, "Health Care Reform and Administrative Law: A Structural Approach," *Yale Law Journal* 88:243–336 (1978).

13. Governmental or private nonprofit entities (excluding educational) entities were able to apply for designation as the HSA for their area. Existing Comprehensive Health Planning and Regional Medical Program agencies, as well as local health departments, received HSA designation in many instances.

14. 42 U.S.C. Sec. 300l-2(a).

15. 42 U.S.C. Sec. 300l(2)(b)–(g).

16. However, the act did carry over the linkage between certificate-of-need approval and calculation of a reimbursement base for Medicare, Medicaid, and Maternal and Child Health funding.

17. See, for example, Rosenblatt, "Health Care Reform," pp. 304–336.

18. On the other hand, Drew Altman concludes that "local planning agencies have embraced the task of health regulation somewhat more fully than had generally been expected." He notes that "the controlling factors in health planning are political, not technical, and there is more occurring at the state and local levels than many had predicted, although any impact is not likely to be dramatic." Altman, "The Politics of Health Care Regulation: The Case of the National Health Planning and Resources Development Act," *Journal of Health Politics, Policy and Law* 2:560–580 (1978), at 560. There is a growing literature regarding the ability or inability of HSAs to accomplish anything. See, for example, Nancy N. Anderson and Leonard Robins, "Observations on Potential Contributions of Health Planning," *International Journal of Health Services* 6:651–666 (1976); Sam Cordes, "Can P.L. 93-641 Accomplish Its Goals?" *Health Law Project Library Bulletin* 3(7):1–6 (July 1978).

19. See, for example, Philip Caper, "Competition and Health Care—Caveat Emptor," *New England Journal of Medicine* 304:1296–1299 (May 21, 1981).

20. See, for example, Warren Greenberg, ed., *Competition in the Health Care Sector: Past, Present, and Future* (Germantown, Md.: Aspen Systems Corporation, 1978).

21. For a full discussion of these anticompetitive practices, as well as of antitrust law in general and its specific application to the health sector, see Martin J. Thompson, *Antitrust and the Health Care Provider* (Germantwon, Md.: Aspen Systems Corporation, 1979), esp. chap. 1; Arnold J. Rosoff, "Antitrust Laws and the Health Care Industry: New Warriors into an Old Battle," *St. Louis University Law Journal* 23:446–490 (1979); Andrew K. Dolan, "Antitrust Law and Physician Dominance of Other Health Practitioners," *Journal of Health*

Politics, Policy and Law 4:675–690 (1980); Dennis J. Horan and Robert E. Nord, "Application of Antitrust Law to the Health Care Delivery System," *Cumberland Law Review* 9:685–719 (1979); Robert P. Borsody, "The Antitrust Laws and the Health Industry," *Akron Law Review* 12:417–463 (1979); Phillip E. Proger, ed., *Antitrust in the Health Care Field* (Towson, Md.: National Health Publishing, 1979); "Symposium on the Antitrust Laws and the Health Services Industry," *Duke Law Journal* 1978:303 (1978); Andrew Lichtman, "Recent Antitrust Price Fixing Decisions: Impliciations for the Health Care Industry," *Whittier Law Review* 2:659–665 (Summer 1980); and Philip C. Kissam, "Antitrust Law, the First Amendment, and Professional Self-Regulation of Technical Quality," in Roger D. Blair and Stephen Rubin, *Regulating the Professions* (Lexington, Mass.: Lexington Books, 1980), pp. 143–183. More generally, see David F. Drake and David M. Kozak, "A primer on Antitrust and Hospital Regulation," *Journal of Health Politics, Policy and Law* 3:328–344 (1979), and the special issue on "Competition and Regulation in Health Care Markets," *Milbank Memorial Fund Quarterly/Health and Society* 59:107 (1981).

22. The Federal Trade Commission also has some antitrust enforcement powers, but this area of authority came under attack by the Reagan administration in 1981 and could be eliminated.

23. See references collected in footnote 21, including James F. Blumstein and Terry Calvani, "State Action as a Shield and a Sword in a Medical Services Antitrust Context: *Parker v. Brown* in Constitutional Perspective," in *Duke Law Journal* Symposium, at p. 389.

24. *Goldfarb v. Virginia State Bar,* 421 U.S. 773 (1975). A subsequent decision, *National Society of Professional Engineers v. United States,* 435 U.S. 679 (1978), held that a professional society's ethical prohibition on price bidding competition was illegal per se; the Court rejected the argument that such a prohibition was a professional quality-control measure.

25. *Goldfarb, Cantor v. Detroit Edison Company,* 428 U.S. 579, (1976) (plurality opinion); *City of Lafayette, Louisiana v. Louisiana Power and Light Co.,* 435 U.S. 389 (1978) (plurality opinion).

26. *Hospital Building Company v. Trustees of Rex Hospital,* 425 U.S. 738 (1976).

27. *St. Paul Fire and Marine Insurance Company v. Barry,* 438 U.S. 531 (1978); *Group Life and Health Insurance Company v. Royal Drug Company,* 440 U.S. 205 (1979). Also see Note, Robert P. Rothman, "The Definition of Business of Insurance under the McCarran-Ferguson Act after *Royal Drug,*" *Columbia Law Review* 80:1475 (1980).

28. The FTC has been concerned with such financing and delivery issues as provider dominance of open-panel health care plans, provider resistance to insurer cost-control efforts and to closed-panel HMOs, potential reduction of competition through merger, and lack of adequate consumer information. Health manpower supply issues addressed by the FTC have included physician versus nonphysician provision of optical care, anesthesia and primary medical care, denial of hospital privileges, accreditation of medical schools, restrictions on dental practice and the provision of dentures, and restriction on veterinary practice. Under the influence of the Reagan admin-

istration the FTC is considerably less aggressive than it had been, but the federal government's extreme concern over escalating health care costs may prompt continued FTC activity in the area of health care delivery.

29. See, for example, Rosoff, "Antitrust Laws and the Health Care Industry," pp. 481–490.

30. See Paul N. Bloom and Ronald Stiff, "Advertising and the Health Care Professions," *Journal of Health Politics, Policy and Law* 4:642–656 (1980).

31. See, for example, *Feminist Women's Health Center v. Mohammad*, 586 F.2d 530 (5th Cir., 1978), reversing in part 415 F.Supp. 1258 (N.C. Fla. 1976); *cert. denied*, 444 U.S. 924 (1979).

32. See Thompson, *Antitrust and the Health Care Provider*, chap. 6. Also see J. Peter Rich, "Medical Staff Privileges and the Antitrust Laws," *Whittier Law Review* 2:667–681 (1980).

33. Antitrust law has also been used to challenge the denial of nonphysician privileges, a charge pressed against the Joint Commission on Accreditation of Hospitals by clinical psychologist and others. See, generally, Herbert Dorken and James T. Webb, "The Hospital Practice of Psychology: An Interstate Comparison," *Professional Psychology* 10:619–630 (1979). Also see Edward E. Hollowell, "The Growing Legal Contest—Hospital Privileges for Podiatrists," *St. Louis University Law Journal* 23:491–508 (1979).

34. See, for example, Frank P. Grad, "The Antitrust Laws and Professional Discipline in Medicine," *Duke Law Journal* Symposium, at p. 443, as well as Thompson, *Antitrust and the Health Care Provider*, pp. 31–32, 107–147; and Dolan, "Antitrust Law and Physician Dominance," p. 686. Also see Philip C. Kissam, "Applying Antitrust Law to Medical Credentialing," *American Journal of Law and Medicine* 7:1–31 (Spring 1981).

35. See Michael Allan Cane, "Restrictive Practices in Accreditation of Medical Schools: An Antitrust Analysis," *Southern California Law Review* 51:657–694 (1978).

36. In 1979 the FTC charged that one state medical society's negotiations with Blue Cross and Blue Shield on cost containment and reimbursement policies amounted to price fixing. In 1980 the FTC explored the need for action to limit the anticompetitive effect of physician control of Blue Shield plans (See 45 Fed. Reg. 17019–17024, March 17, 1980). See, generally, Thompson, *Antitrust and the Health Care Provider*, chap. 7. *Arizona v. Maricopa County Medical Society*, 50 U.S.L.W. 4687 (U.S. June 15, 1982), held that U.S. antitrust laws apply to *maximum* fee schedules.

37. *Blue Shield of Virginia v. McCready*, 50 U.S.L.W. 4723 (U.S. June 22, 1982), allowed antitrust suit *by patient* when psychiatrists' services, not those of psychologists', were reimbursed.

38. Under a relative value scale program a professional association establishes a schedule which, while not specifying fees for particular procedures, does provide relative weighting based on median charges (e.g., if the fee for a tonsilectomy is two units the fee for a cholecystectomy might be five units.) See Note, "Relative Value Rule Guides and the Sherman Antitrust Act," *Vanderbilt Law Review* 33:233–249 (1980), and Clark C. Havighurst and Philip C. Kissam, "The Antitrust Implications of Relative Value Studies in

Medicine," *Journal of Health Politics, Policy and Law* 4:48–86 (1979). Also see *United States v. American Society of Anesthesiologists, Inc.*, 473 F.Supp. 147 (S.D.N.Y. 1979), and Andrew Lichtman, "Recent Antitrust Price Fixing Decisions: Implications for the Health Care Industry," *Whittier Law Review* 2:659–665 (1980).

39. See Thompson, *Antitrust and the Health Care Provider*, p. 138.

40. See, for example, *City of Fairfax v. Fairfax Hospital Association*, 562 F.2d 280 (4th Cir. 1977), vacated 435 U.S. 992 (1978).

41. See, for example, *Hospital Building Co. v. Trustees of Rex Hospital.* 425 U.S. 738 (1976).

42. Thompson, *Antitrust and the Health Care Provider*, chap. 6.

43. *Traveler's Insurance Company v. Blue Cross of Western Pennsylvania*, 298 F.Supp. 1109 (W.D. Pa. 1969). The U.S. Supreme Court has already held that some aspects of the pharmaceutical manufacturers' practice of offering a preferred price on drug purchases by nonprofit hospitals is illegal price discrimination. *Abbott Laboratories v. Portland Retail Druggist Association, Inc.*, 425 U.S. 1 (1976). Also see A. J. Rosoff and T. W. Dunfee, "A 'Fix' for the Retail Pharmacy: The Supreme Court Redefines Application of Robinson-Patman Act to Drug Sales by Nonprofit Hospitals," *California Western Law Review* 1:195, 1977; as well as chap. 8 of Thompson, *Antitrust and the Health Care Provider*.

44. See Thompson, *Antitrust and the Health Care Provider*, chap. 3.

45. Moreover, it has long been held that efforts to influence government policymaking decisions would not bring private parties, such as those cooperating with government agencies, into conflict with antitrust law. This so-called *Noerr-Pennington* doctrine is explained in the general introductions to antitrust and health care collected in note 21, including Note, "Physician Influence: Applying *Noerr-Pennington* to the Medical Profession," in, *Duke Law Journal* Symposium, at p. 701.

46. *Cantor v. Detroit Edison Co.*, 428 U.S. 579 (1976).

47. 101 S.Ct. 2415 (1981).

48. For example, the Health Maintenance Organization Act of 1973, 42 U.S.C. Sec. 300e et seq. Although HMOs are usually portrayed in a pro-competitive role, it can be argued that closed-panel arrangements and favorable hospitalization, equipment, and supply contracts sought by HMOs can actually restrict competition. (A similar limitation can occur regarding price discrimination in pharmaceutical sales to particular groups of purchases; see Thompson *Antitrust and the Health Care Provider*, pp. 189–212.) On HMOs and antitrust in general see Phillip C. Kissam, "Health Maintenance Organizations and the Role of Antitrust Laws," in, *Duke Law Journal* Symposium, at p. 487.

49. For example, the Health Professions Educational Assistance Act.

50. This nonspecific utilization review requirement was extended to Medicaid in 1967.

51. Senate Report No. 92-1230 to accompany H.R. 1, to amend the Social Security Act, and for other purposes; 92d Congress, 2d Session, September 26, 1972, pp. 255–256.

52. 42 U.S.C. Sec. 1320c, Declaration of Purpose. While the PSRO program has focused on both cost and quality, it seems clear that cost concerns are what prompted Congress to create the program. See Chapter 7, note 41.
53. The appeals process also allows for further appeal of a denial to the secretary of Health and Human Services (provided that the reimbursement involved exceeds a certain amount).
54. *Professional Standards Review Organization 1979 Program Evaluation Health Care Financing Research Report* (Baltimore: U.S. Department of Health and Human Services, May 1980), p. 14 (HCFA pub. no. 03041). But see also *The Impact of PSROs on Health Care Costs: Update of CBO's 1979 Evaluation* (Washington, D.C.: Congressional Budget Office, 1980).
55. See Pearson and Abernethy, "A Qualitative Assessment," pp. 120–125.
56. See Abernethy and Pearson, *Regulating Hospital Costs.* Alternating payment modes, including insurance mechanisms such as deductibles and copayments, might also be viewed as a type of outcome control, although they do not affect providers directly. Instead, they create an incentive for patients to apply cost-saving pressure on providers.
57. By the end of 1978 twenty-seven states had rate-setting programs. See American Hsopital Association, *Report on Budget/Rate Review Programs* (Chicago: AHA, 1978).
58. A practice opposed by hospital associations, since this means a major purchaser of services—Medicaid—is determining the price at which it buys the service. On the other hand, a few states have received waivers from the Department of Health and Human Services allowing the state rate-setting body to establish Medicaid and Medicare rates directly.
59. One recent study found "a statistically significant reduction in average annual cost increases in rate-setting states as compared with non-rate-setting states from 1976 to 1978," See Brian Biles, Carl J. Schramm, and J. Graham Atkinson, "Hospital Cost Inflation under State Rate-setting Programs," *New England Journal of Medicine* 303:664–668, (1980). On hospital rate setting in general, see Katherine G. Bauer, "Hospital Rate Setting—This Way to Salvation?" *Milbank Memorial Fund Quarterly/Health and Society* 55:117–158 (1977); Lawrence S. Lewin, Anne R. Somers, and Herman M. Somers, "State Health Cost Regulation: Structure and Administration," *Toledo Law Review* 6:647–676 (1975); Michael L. Ziegler, "Health Planning Goals and Rate-setting Provisions: A Brief Overview," *Health Law Project Library Bulletin* 3(11):23–29 (November 1978); Roger G. Null, "The Consequences of Public Utility Regulation of Hospitals," in Institute of Medicine, *Controls on Health Care* (Washington, D.C.: National Academy of Sciences, 1975), pp. 25–48; and Zubkoff, Rankin, and Hanft, *Hospital Cost Containment.*
60. The Voluntary Effort was begun in January 1978 as a direct response to administration efforts to impose tighter controls on hospitals. See Abernethy and Pearson, *Regulating Hospital Costs,* pp. 147–155. The fact that the industry acted only in the face of threatened federal action would seem to be as much an argument for federal cost-control regulation as against it. The Voluntary Effort sought an antitrust clearance from the Justice Department, but without success. See Ibid., pp. 154–155.
61. Herbert Denenberg of Pennsylvania was the most aggressive and dramatic

state insurance commissioner. See, for example, Sylvia A. Law, *Blue Cross: What Went Wrong?* (New Haven: Yale University Press, 1974), pp. 98–102, 110–113. More recently similar cost-control pressures were applied by the Michigan State insurance commissioner, who reduced a Blue Cross rate increase request by the amount he felt Blue Cross would have saved had it adopted various cost-saving measures he had recommended. The Michigan Supreme Court restored this amount, however, stating that the commissioner only had authority to approve or reject rate requests, not use them to tailor the industry. In other instances, however, private litigation has been aimed at forcing unwilling state insurance commissioners to more actively impose cost-control requirements on the Blues. See, for example, *Thaler v. Stern,* 44 Misc. 2d 278, 253 N.Y.S. 2d 622 (1964). In a few instances, state statutes mandating Blue Cross cost-containment efforts have required a showing of compliance at state insurance rate increase hearings.

62. For a more far-reaching approach to the cost problem, see Milton I. Roemer, "National Health Insurance as an Agent for Containing Health-Care Costs," *Bulletin of the New York Academy of Medicine* 54:102–112 (1978).

9 | Access, Discrimination, and the Right to Health Care

One of the most basic of human rights is the right to good health care. In recent years we have come to understand that health care is not merely a technical problem for medical specialists. It is a vital concern for all who help shape the economic, social, and political processes of our communities and nations.

—Jimmy Carter[1]

HEALTH CARE DELIVERY in the United States accounts for 9 percent of the gross national product and employs close to seven million people, more than any other industry.[2] Americans have come to view access to this vast system of health care services as a basic "right" and Congress and the states have enacted various entitlement programs assuring such access for an increasing number of people. Nevertheless, there continues to be wide differences in access to health care, and the health status of Americans differs considerably according to income, race, and geography;[3] the availability of care and the issue of who pays for it are serious political and legal concerns.

From the perspective of the provider, whether salaried or working on a fee-for-service basis, the important question is, How is payment received for work done?[4] From the patient's perspective, the important question is, *Who pays?* The answer depends very much on the type and aspect of health service involved. As Donabedian indicates, "the scope of benefits and the conditions governing eligibility are so intimately related that it is difficult to speak of one feature without becoming involved, to some extent, in the other."[5] Although virtually everyone has some out-of-pocket health care expenses, most Americans carry some kind of health care coverage, either through private insurance contracts, government third-party payment programs, and/or by qualifying for the direct provision of health care services through the Veterans Administration, the Defense Department, state and local hospitals and clinics, and the like. In addition, a small group of people may receive as professional courtesy or as charity, services that normally would be billed for.

In 1976, it is estimated, approximately 89 percent of the civilian noninstitutionalized population had some form of health care coverage. Most had private insurance only (often paid for by their employer), others were covered by Medicare or Medicaid, still others carried some combination of Medicare, Medicaid, and private insurance. But some 11 percent of the population—approximately 23,200,000 people—had no insurance coverage of any kind, public or private.[6] As might be expected, the majority of those without such coverage were the poor or near-poor. Davis and Schoen note:

> About 8 million to 10 million people below the poverty level, or about one-third of the poor, are not covered by current federal health care programs and their receipt of basic health care services lags behind that of the rest of the population.[7]

Government Health Prgorams

The state and federal governments have been involved to some degree in health care delivery for a long time. The Marine Hospital Service (later renamed the U.S. Public Health Service) was established by an act of Congress in 1798. The first proposal for a national health insurance system appeared in a national political platform in 1912. However, most early governmental health programs concerned themselves with persons under special government protection, such as members of the military, Native Americans, and the most indigent of the population. Even today, the United States government is less involved in health care than the governments of most other industrialized countries.

In 1935 Congress enacted the Social Security Act, which created both a federally administered social security insurance program, including retirement and disability benefits financed by a payroll deduction system, and a cooperative federal-state welfare program for three special categories of the poor: the blind, the elderly, and families with dependent children. Over the years some payments for medical care have been added to the welfare program.

By 1964 considerable political support had developed for expansion of these benefits to provide more comprehensive coverage for the medical care needs of the elderly. Wing explains:

> The central issue in the congressional debate was not whether there should be a program, but whether it should be—like social security—an entirely federal program or—like the welfare programs—primarily state administered with federal financial assistance. The result was a compromise.[8]

In 1965 Congress expanded the Social Security Act, adding to it two new medical care programs. One was Medicare, a health insurance program for the elderly or disabled Social Security recipient, which, like monthly Social Security payments, is financed by payroll deductions and administered by the federal government. The second was Medicaid, a medical assistance program for welfare recipients and other poor people, administered jointly by the state and federal governments. These two extremely complex programs[9] are probably best described in terms of what they are not.

Medicare and Medicaid are not health care service programs; they are a means of reimbursing private sector health care delivery programs for services rendered. Nor are they universal or comprehensive programs; both stipulate specifically which individuals are eligible for coverage, which services are reimbursable, and what portion of the bill will be paid.

Despite these limitations, the creation of Medicare and Medicaid sharply increased the public funds spent on health care and reduced the medical costs borne directly by the elderly and the poor. In 1965 government (federal, state, and local) accounted for 21.9 percent of total personal health care expenditures—$7.9 billion out of $36 billion. In 1979 the governmental share was 40.2 percent—$75.8 billion out of $188.6 billion.[10] Over 38 million people—17.9 percent of the population—were covered by Medicare and Medicaid in 1978.[11]

Medicare[12] provides hospitalization and medical insurance for persons aged sixty-five and over who are entitled to Social Security or Railroad Retirement benefits, as well as those receiving Social Security disability benefits for two years or more.[13] In addition, the small number of elderly who do not qualify for Social Security can buy into the Medicare system. Unlike Medicaid, eligibility for Medicare has nothing to do with financial need.

Medicare is divided into two parts: Part A, Hospital Insurance, is financed by payroll tax deductions collected under the Social Security system, and covers hospital, extended care, home health, and hospital outpatient diagnostic services. Part B, Supplemental Medical Insurance, covers physicians' and home health services, outpatient therapy, and a number of related services. Participation in Part B is voluntary; anyone eligible for Part A may enroll in Part B by paying a monthly premium, which is matched by the federal government.[14] Part B pays participants 80 percent of "allowable" expenses after a yearly deductible, but the participants themselves must pay any charges above this amount.

Both Part A and Part B include various deductibles, coinsurance requirements, and ceilings on the number of days covered during any one spell of illness and calendar year as well as during the participant's lifetime.[15] As a result, as McCarthy describes, Medicare coverage is neither complete nor uniform. In 1977, for example:

> 74% of hospital care costs was covered; 56% of physicians' charges; 52% of "other professional services" and only 3% of nursing home expenses. Even after other government programs and supplementary private health insurance were taken into account, the 1977 per capita out-of-pocket expense for the elderly was $613, approximately 35% of costs.[16]

Since Medicare is solely a federal program, it is theoretically uniform throughout the United States. But the actual handling of claims is performed by private insurers, such as Blue Cross/Blue Shield, which contract with the federal government to serve as "fiscal intermediaries," and these insurers make the initial determination as to whether a particular service is reimbursable. Health care providers wishing to participate in the Medicare program must file with the secretary of Health and Human Services an agreement to comply with the fiscal, accounting, administrative, and coverage provisions of the law,[17] and then nominate an intermediary as fiscal representative. As explained in Chapter 7, state agencies monitor hospital compliance with the Medicare Conditions of Participation for Hospitals (or accept private accreditation findings), and similar monitoring systems exist for other providers. Reimbursement under Part A is based on reasonable costs; reimbursement under Part B is based on reasonable charges, which cannot exceed a certain percent of the average fee charged for the same service in the geographic area.

Medicare has not generated very much legal controversy during its decade and a half of existence. For the individual provider the only decision that need be made is whether or not to participate directly in the Medicare program by accepting "assignment," that is, by agreeing to handle Medicare billing and accept the allowable charge as payment in full. (By the late 1970s only about 50 percent of physicians did so.) Physicians also have the option of billing a Medicare-eligible patient directly without limitation on the fee (the patient is then reimbursed by Medicare for whatever portion of the bill the program will cover). Hospitals and nursing homes may also refuse to accept Medicare as payment-in-full for services rendered, but Medicare will not reimburse patients for *any* services received at those institutions.

Medicaid[18] differs from Medicare in several key respects. It is operated jointly by the federal and state governments, so the details of the program differ tremendously from state to state. Eligibility for Medicaid is based on income and other factors, and is considerably more complicated and controversial than the eligibility determination for Medicare. Funding for Medicaid comes primarily from general revenues, rather than from an insurance "transfer." And payment to providers is more restrictive (and quite often slower) than for Medicare, prompting many providers to opt out of the system.

Medicaid has been described as a "sleeper" that burgeoned into a massive health program. According to Wing, it "was actually conceived in a hurried congressional compromise. While the controversy over Medicare had been waged for several years and its details tediously debated, the Medicaid program was almost thoughtlessly appended to the Medicare bill, and Congress, ironically, gave it relatively little consideration."[19] In addition, the program suffered from the onset from the fact that it was framed as a welfare program rather than a health program. The allowing of variation from state to state also served to make a successful overall program unlikely.[20] Medicaid has aided almost twice as many individuals as has Medicare, but since Medicaid beneficiaries are poor and mainly children it has lacked the political support Medicare has had.

States can choose whether or not to participate in Medicaid, but since the federal government contributes 50 to 80 percent of the cost (depending upon the state's per capita income) all states have opted in.[21] In return for its fiscal contribution, Congress has established various guidelines that the states must abide by. But within these guidelines the states have considerable flexibility to decide who shall be eligible for Medicaid, the types and levels of services to be covered under it, and the levels of reimbursement for health care providers. As a result, there are fifty-four different Medicaid systems,[22] each with its own complex eligibility and benefits structure.

Because the program is aimed at the poor, eligibility for Medicaid is linked to eligibility for welfare, although only 59 percent of those who meet the federal government's definition of poverty qualify for Medicaid. The Medicaid law requires that all participating states include in the program the "categorically needy"—that is, persons who fall into certain categories defined by characteristics other than income alone, namely families covered by aid to families with dependent children programs (AFDC), as well as aged, blind, and disabled persons receiving Supplemental Security Income.[23] In addition, states may include individuals who would meet the "categorically needy" definition except for some particular factor, such as residence in a nursing home or failure to meet AFDC school attendance requirements. States also have the option of including in Medicaid "medically needy" aged, blind, or disabled individuals and families with dependent children who do not meet the "categorically needy" requirements, but whose incomes, *after medical expenses have been subtracted,* are 133 1/3 percent or less of the AFDC eligibility income level for the state. These persons, however, are subject to various deductibles and copayments.

The result of these complex restrictions, as Davis and Schoen explain, bar most of the following low-income individuals from Medicaid assistance:

—widows and other single persons under sixty-five and childless couples;

—most two-parent families (which constitute 70 percent of the rural poor and almost half the poor families in metropolitan areas);

—families with a father working at a marginal, low-paying job;

—families with an unemployed father in the twenty-six states that do not extend welfare payments to this group; and unemployed fathers receiving unemployment compensation in other states;

—medically needy families in the twenty-two states that do not voluntarily provide this additional coverage;

—single women pregnant with their first child in the twenty states that do not provide welfare aid or eligibility for the "unborn child";

—children of poor families not receiving AFDC in the thirty-three states that do not take advantage of the optional Medicaid category called "all needy children under 21."[24]

The Medicaid benefit structure is as complex as its eligibility requirements. All participating states must cover inpatient hospital care, outpatient hospital and rural health clinic services, physician services, family planning, laboratory and X-ray, care in a skilled nursing facility, home health care for individuals twenty-one and older, early and periodic screening, diagnosis, and treatment (EPSDT) for those under twenty-one, and transportation for medical needs. However, states can set their own limits on the "amount, scope, and duration" of these services; for example, the number of hospital days paid for per year or per admission, or the number of physician visits covered. States may, if they choose, include additional benefits, for which they may impose deductibles and copayments, such as drugs, dental services, eyeglasses, intermediate-care facility services, inpatient psychiatric care for the elderly and the young, emergency hospital services, private duty nursing, clinic services, physical therapy, prosthetic devices, and other services. Obviously, these options result in a wide variation in coverage from state to state. Medicaid payments per child recipient in 1970 ranged from $43 in Mississippi to $240 in Wisconsin.[25]

Except in an emergency, Medicaid recipients must receive care from a provider who has been certified as eligible to receive Medicaid payments, and neither institutions nor practitioners can charge a Medicaid patient any fee in addition to the Medicaid payment. For a number of reasons, far fewer physicians accept Medicaid than Medicare in payment for their services, a fact that limits promised benefits for many eligibles.[26] Medicaid allows the states to choose between the "usual and customary fee" standard of Medicare and an indemnity schedule set at significantly lower levels. And although private insurer fiscal intermediaries are allowed under Medicaid, most states have chosen to handle claims payments through their own bureaucracies. Delayed and/or low reimbursement, along with often nightmarish bureaucracy, have—intentionally or not—served to save the Medicaid program money by discouraging providers from participating, and thereby making it less likely that eligible recipients will receive needed care.[27]

The amount of Medicaid funds that states receive from the federal government constitute a fixed—and since 1981, shrinking—pie, so changes in eligibility requirements, scope of benefits, and reimbursements rates represent tradeoffs. Most states have been tinkering with their Medicaid programs for years in efforts to reduce overall costs, and significant cutbacks have been occurring for almost a decade. Now, under the compromise Omnibus Reconciliation Act of 1981, the federal component of Medicaid will—with some exceptions—be reduced by 3 percent in fiscal 1982, 4 percent in fiscal 1982, and 4.5 percent in fiscal 1984.

There are other federal, state, and local programs designed to help people obtain and pay for needed health care services. For example, maternal and child health (MCH) programs provide federal matching grants to states for medical services directly to mothers and children, especially crippled children, without regard to income; but Medicare and Medicaid account for most of the public funds expended for health care.[28] (In 1976, MCH funds totaled $593 million compared to $17,777 million for Medicare and $15,320 million for Medicaid.)[29]

Despite the vast amounts spent on Medicare and Medicaid, governmental health benefits still show large gaps in eligibility and coverage. In 1976, 21 percent of those with incomes below $7,000 and 15 percent of those with incomes between $7,000 and $10,000 lacked any form of health insurance;[30] in the latter half of the 1970s there was virtually no increase in the number of Medicaid recipients.[31]

Three factors are primarily responsible for these gaps. One is that, despite the rhetoric, Congress and the states never intended Medicare and Medicaid to provide universal, comprehensive health care benefits.[32] Second, the states have sought to relieve the burden of escalating Medicaid costs by controlling the number of Medicaid beneficiaries (a) by not establishing a medically needy program, (b) by not increasing medically needy income levels or AFDC levels to keep abreast of inflation, and (c) by erecting administrative barriers to participation. The third major factor responsible for gaps in Medicare and Medicaid is discrimination, particularly racial discrimination. Davis and Schoen report:

> Nursing home services are the most inequitably distributed, with average payments almost five times as high for white Medicaid recipients as for nonwhites. Recent data from the Georgia Medicaid program indicate that whites receive an average Medicaid payment of $587 for all services, but blacks and others receive only $271.[33]

It is hardly surprising, then, to find significant differences in health status figures comparing nonwhites and whites in terms of infant mortality, birth weight, Apgar scores, immunization rates, and total life expectancy.[34] Various groups have sought to challenge discriminatory delivery of health care services directly; but for the most part these efforts have not succeeded. A leading law review article on the subject explains:

> Title VI of the Civil Rights Act of 1964, which prohibits racial discrimination by recipients of federal funds . . . was enacted primarily to prohibit segregation in publicly-funded schools, but it applies to all recipients of federal funds, including institutions that provide health care. . . .
> For a health facility to comply with Title VI usually requires only that the facility sign a non-discrimination agreement. . . .
> Because of the inadequate manner in which the Title VI enforcement program has been administered, there is little monitoring of health facility compliance and virtually no available data generated on the services delivered to minorities.[35]

Legal Services attorneys have also gone to court in efforts to ease state eligibility requirements for Medicaid and to challenge state determinations of medically needy income levels,[36] although little can be done regarding the amount, duration, and scope of Medicaid coverage. As one commentator has observed:

> Because the Medicaid program is an exercise in cooperative federalism, participating states retain broad discretion to shape and alter their coverage plans, subject only to vague federal requirements of reasonableness. Title XIX contains no express indication that states must fund all medically necessary services. Instead, the statute requires only that limitations on funding for such services be reasonable. Since it supplies no general formula for evaluating reasonableness, the validity of state funding restrictions can only be ascertained on a case-by-case basis.[37]

Patricia Butler notes: "Over the last few years, Legal Services programs have begun to challenge these limitations, based on various statutory or regulatory authorities. Results have been mixed."[38] Butler outlines the following legal arguments for such challenges:

—mandatory services should not be so limited as to eliminate conditions entirely from treatment;

—optional services, if offered, must be reasonably sufficient to
achieve their purpose;

—after a state designates a condition for which care is necessary, it
should avoid limiting physician discretion as to the type of care to
be provided, and should afford comparable care to both the categorically and medically needy.

Other efforts to obtain health care benefits for individuals and classes
of individuals have focused on other federal statutes, specifically those
that set conditions under which providers qualify for federal funds or
tax benefits. One such statute is the Hill-Burton Act; another involves
the IRS definition of charity.

The Hill-Burton hospital construction act requires of recipient hospitals both a pledge of nondiscrimination and an assurance that "there will
be made available in the facility or portion thereof to be constructed or
modernized a reasonable volume of services to persons unable to pay
therefore."[39] The act also required that HEW promulgate regulations
implementing this requirement and enforce the regulations. For a quar-
ter of a century after passage of the act in 1946 (during which approximately one-third of the hospital beds in the nation were built with Hill-
Burton funds), HEW did nothing to fulfill this mandate. Only in the face
of a series of lawsuits[40] were the necessary regulations promulgated, and
these have given rise to further litigation involving HEW, the hospital
industry, and Legal Services attorneys in the 1970s.

As they now stand, these "free service" regulations stipulate that for
twenty years after completion of construction with Hill-Burton-assisted
funds, a hospital must either (a) provide the lesser of 3 percent of operating costs or 10 percent of federal assistance in uncompensated services
or (b) have an open-door policy under which no individual will be excluded from admission because of inability to pay. Potential recipients of
such uncompensated care must be advised of their possible eligibility
when they seek admission (the hospital cannot include bad debts as part
of their obligatory volume of uncompensated care). However, no individual patient may claim a specific entitlement to Hill-Burton care.

The Federal Internal Revenue Code bears, indirectly, on health care
delivery. Section 501(c)(3) of the code exempts from federal taxation
any corporation organized and operated exclusively for charitable purposes, and contributions to such corporations are deductible from individual income, estate, and gift-tax obligations. The rationale for this
provision, which obviously represents the loss of considerable tax revenues to the government, is that the operation of such charitable enterprises—including not-for-profit hospitals—spares the government a public burden. But the tax law does not define charitable purpose: this is left

to the commissioner of Internal Revenue in promulgating regulations. Prior to 1969 these regulations stated that to qualify for charitable status a hospital

> Must be operated to the extent of its financial ability for those not able to pay for the services rendered and not exclusively for those who are able and expected to pay. . . . It must not, however, refuse to accept patients in need of hospital care who cannot pay for such services. Furthermore, if it operates with the expectation of full payment from all those to whom it renders services, it does not dispense charity merely because some of its patients fail to pay for the services rendered.[41]

In 1969 the regulations were amended, and a hospital could qualify as charitable

> By operating an emergency room open to all persons and by providing hospital care for all those persons in the community able to pay the cost thereof either directly or through third-party reimbursement.[42]

Thus a hospital could qualify as a charitable enterprise if (a) it participated in Medicare and Medicaid and (b) it operated an emergency room that was open to all regardless of ability to pay. This change, which many viewed as a significant limitation in service to the poor, was challenged in *Eastern Kentucky Welfare Rights Organization v. Simon*. Although the plaintiffs succeeded in the Federal District Court, the decision was reversed by the Court of Appeals, and the U.S. Supreme Court dismissed the entire challenge on procedural grounds. Thus, the 1969 tax regulation remains in effect.[43]

A Right to Health?

As indicated earlier, there are individuals and medical needs not covered by any of the programs outlined above. Is society obligated to provide comprehensive health care for everyone? Can there be said to be such a thing as a "right to health?" As Annas and Healy have explained:

> The statement "I have a right" performs several functions and has several different meanings. The particular function and meaning are generally not made clear to the listener and may not even be clear to the person making the statement. Possible meanings include:
> I. "Because I am a citizen of this country, I possess x as a legal right created by the Constitution, by legislative action, or by prior court determination."
> II. "Because of my relationship with another party, there is a strong possibility that a court of law would recognize x as my legal right."
> III. "I believe that x should be recognized as a right even though a court of law would probably not recognize it as such."[44]

In the final analysis, it is what the courts recognize and uphold as a right that gives the term legal meaning and force. And as Annas and Healy indicate, the courts make their determinations on the basis of common law, statutes, and federal and state constitutions.

Though no provision of the U.S. Constitution states that health or health care is a constitutional right—or even mentions the word *health*—it has been argued that under the equal protection clause of the Fourteenth Amendment unequal access to medical care for reasons of income constitutes invidious, unconstitutional discrimination.[45] The equal protection concept has been held to mean that individuals similarly situated must be similarly treated by government, and that laws cannot be applied one way to one group of people and another way to a different group of people unless there is a rational reason for doing so. Thus, government cannot say that people with white skins are entitled to drivers' licenses while people with black skins are not, because the differentiation bears no reasonable relationship to the law involved. It can, however, say that people with physical handicaps are entitled to automobile license plates that provide preferential parking privileges, while those with no physical handicaps are not, because government can claim a legitimate interest in assisting handicapped citizens lead more productive lives.

The U.S. Supreme Court over the past decade or more has issued a confusing chain of decisions regarding the extent to which the equal protection umbrella may require positive government actions in support of certain categories of people. Wealth, or the lack of it, was not considered a valid basis for equal protection support until the Court decided, in 1956, that all indigent criminal defendants must be furnished stenographic trial transcripts necessary for appellate review.[46] Later the Court extended this concept by requiring the government to provide counsel for the indigent in appeals guaranteed by law,[47] and broadened the concept still further when it was held that a poll tax was an invidious and impermissible discrimination by reason of wealth.[48] Most important, in 1969, in *Shapiro v. Thompson,* the Court found invidious discrimination in a state denial of welfare assistance to persons who had resided in the state for less than a year, and held that such a residency requirement served no compelling governmental interest.[49]

One specific application of the equal protection clause to medical care is found in *Memorial Hospital v. Maricopa County,*[50] which deals with an Arizona statute requiring county governments to provide necessary nonemergency hospital and medical care for their indigent sick. In *Maricopa,* an indigent was denied free treatment at an Arizona county hospital on the basis of a one-year residency requirement for nonemergency medical care. Writing for the Court, Justice Thurgood Marshall held that this requirement created an invidious classification that infringed upon the right of the indigent to travel from state to state. In the *Maricopa* case, Justice Marshall also referred to medical care as a "basic necessity of life":

> Whatever the ultimate parameters of . . . *Shapiro* . . . it is at least clear that medical care is as much a basic necessity of life to an indigent as welfare assistance. And, governmental privileges or benefits necessary to basic sustenance have often been viewed as being of greater constitutional significance than less essential forms of governmental entitlements.

Despite this broad language, however, *Maricopa* does not obligate state governments to provide nonemergency medical care to indigents or others, because the case is limited to an existing entitlement program; it simply says that if the state chooses to establish such a program, its benefits cannot be limited according to duration of residency. There is nothing in the equal protection clause or elsewhere in the Constitution, however, to keep states from dispensing with such programs altogether. As of the present, most experts feel it is unlikely[51] that the Court will place medical care in the same category of "fundamental rights," as the right to vote or the right to travel, thereby requiring legislatures to enact and/or administrators to carry out new and very costly programs for the equitable distribution of health resources.[52]

Still another effort to extend and broaden federally sponsored health care services has focused on the due process clauses of the Fifth and Fourteenth Amendments. At one time, government social welfare benefits were viewed as privileges that government could bestow or withhold at will, and potential beneficiaries were not considered to have any legal claim regarding the way beneficiary decisions were made. But in 1970, in the case of *Goldberg v. Kelly*, the U.S. Supreme Court for the first time equated an individual welfare right with a traditional property right.[53] "It may be more realistic today," the Court declared, "to regard welfare entitlements as more like 'property' than a 'gratuity.' " While this conclusion did not result in court-ordered payment of benefits, the Court did decide that due process requires a state to provide a welfare recipient with an opportunity for a hearing before terminating his or her benefits.

A ruling that such statutory entitlements as Medicaid must be viewed as a property right is vastly important in the U.S. legal system, which affords property such procedural respect. But it should be emphasized that the protection involved is limited to individual due-process rights, such as notice and hearings. Efforts to assure prior hearings when governmental agencies are acting in a policymaking capacity have not been successful.

Common law support for a general right to medical care is also limited, except in emergency situations. Some courts have held that hospitals with emergency rooms risk legal liability if they turn away true emergencies.[54] Similarly, once treatment is undertaken by a hospital or physician, the patient cannot be abandoned.[55] But neither of these rules covers a right to medical care in the absence of an emergency.

Since both the federal and state governments are already heavily involved in health care through entitlement programs, licensure requirements, tax exemptions, and the like, advocates of increased public responsibility for the health care of the disadvantaged look to expansion of existing statutory governmental health roles. Thus, whenever a health-related statute is enacted, there is a rush of maneuvering, politicking, and legal challenge over its interpretation and implementation.

When all is said and done, therefore, any claims to a legal right to health care are limited. Those who advocate such rights may well have to look toward measures that help prevent illness, rather than those that assure medical care, a trend consistent with the generally growing emphasis on health education, improved nutrition, immunization, screening and detection, accident prevention, environmental and occupational safety, and other aspects of health preservation.

NOTES

1. Statement of November 11, 1977, as quoted in *The Nation's Health* 7(11):9 (November 1977).
2. In 1979, $212.2 billion was expended on health care in the United States ($91.4 billion of it by government), a total 9 percent of the GNP. See *Health, United States, 1980* (Hyattsville, Md.: U.S. Public Health Service, December 1980), table 60, p. 206, and table 65, p. 211 (DHHS pub. no. (PHS) 81-1232). Paul R. Torrens and Charles E. Lewis, "Health Care Personnel," in Stephen J. Williams and Paul R. Torrens, *Introduction to Health Services* (New York: John Wiley, 1980), p. 257, list the health care industry as "the largest single employer of people." Sue S. Moyerman and Robert D. Eilers, "Financing," in Anthony R. Kovner and Samuel P. Martin, *Community Health and Medical Care* (New York: Grune and Stratton, 1978), pp. 201–262, describe health care delivery as the second largest industry, after the food industry.
3. See Institute of Medicine, *Health Care in a Context of Civil Rights* (Washington, D.C.: National Academy Press, 1981), pp. 23–82, and *Health of the Disadvantaged, A Chartbook* (Washington, D.C.: Health Resources Administration, 1977) (DHEW pub. no. (HRA) 77-628). Also see Melvin H. Rudov and Nancy Santangelo, *Health Status of Minorities and Low-Income Groups* (Washington, D.C.: Health Resources Administriation, 1979) (DHEW publication no. (HRA) 79-627); LuAnn Aday, Ronald Anderson, and Gretchen V. Flemming, *Health Care in the U.S.: Equitable for Whom?* (Beverly Hills: Sage Publications, 1980); the special issue on narrowing the gaps in health status between the poor and the nonpoor, *Medical Care* 15:611 (1977); and Pierre Devise, ed., *Slum Medicine: Chicago's Apartheid Health System* (Chicago: University of Chicago Community and Family Study Center, 1969).
4. See William A. Glaser, *Paying the Doctor: Systems of Remuneration and Their*

Effects (Baltimore: Johns Hopkins, 1970); William A. Glaser, *Health Insurance Bargaining: Foreign Lessons for Americans* (New York: Gardner, 1978).

5. Avedis Donabedian, *Benefits in Medical Care Programs* (Cambridge: Harvard University Press, 1976), p. 3.

6. "Health Care Coverage: United States, 1976," *Advance Data from Vital and Health Statistics of the National Center for Health Statistics*, no. 44 (September 20, 1979) (DHEW pub. no. (PHS) 79-1250). A more detailed analysis of health care coverage can be found in "Health Care Coverage under Private Health Insurance, Medicare, Medicaid, and Military or Veterans Administration Health Benefits: United States, 1978," *Advance Data from Vital and Health Statistics of the National Center for Health Statistics*, no. 71 (June 29, 1981) (DHHS pub. no. (PHS) 81-1250).

7. Karen Davis and Cathy Schoen, *Health and the War on Poverty: A Ten-Year Appraisal* (Washington, D.C.: The Brookings Institution, 1978), p. 2.

8. Kenneth Wing, *Law and the Public's Health* (St. Louis: Mosby, 1976), p. 71.

9. An indication of the extent of that complexity is the statement by Leonard Schaeffer—then head of the Health Care Financing Administration, which oversees Medicare and Medicaid—to the National Conference of State Legislatures: "I'm not sure we understand where all the money is going. . . ." *American Medical News* (December 7, 1979), p. 4.

10. *Health, United States, 1980*, table 67, p. 213.

11. "Health Care Coverage under Private Health Insurance, Medicare, Medicaid, and Military or Veterans Administration Health Benefits: United States, 1978, tables 1, 2, pp. 2–3.

12. Title 18 of the Social Security Act, P.L. 89-97, 42 U.S.C. Sec. 1395 et seq.; regulations found in 20 C.F.R. Sec. 404 and 42 C.F.R. Sec. 405. For history and description of Medicare see Herbert M. Somers and Anne R. Somers, *Medicare and the Hospitals: Issues and Prospects* (Washington, D.C.: The Brookings Institution, 1967); Theodore R. Marmor, *The Politics of Medicare* (Chicago: Aldine, 1973); Robert N. Brown, *The Rights of Older Persons* (New York: Avon, 1979) chap. 6; Patricia Butler, "An Advocate's Guide to the Medicare Program," *Clearinghouse Review* 8:831 (1975); and *Medicare and Medicaid Guide* (Chicago: Commerce Clearing House, 1980/81).

13. Medicare also provides benefits for younger persons with chronic renal disease. See Brown, *The Rights of Older Persons*, p. 189.

14. States may pay the Medicare premium—as well as deductibles and coinsurance amounts—for their Medicaid recipients who also qualify for Medicare.

15. The Part A hospital care deductible roughly equals one day of hospital care. For each illness episode the first sixty days are covered completely, the next thirty days are reimbursed at a 75 percent rate, the next sixty days at 50 percent, then coverage stops. There is also a "lifetime reserve" of sixty days, with copayment. See William C. Richardson, "Financing Health Services," in Williams and Torrens, *Introduction to Health Services*, p. 314. Also see Davis and Schoen, *Health and the War on Poverty*, p. 95. Because of the limits and gaps in Medicare coverage, nearly two-thirds of the nation's elderly have purchased supplemental private health insurance, so-called medigap policies. *American Medical News*, August 15, 1980, p. 19.

16. Carol McCarthy, "Financing for Health Care," in Steven Jonas et al., *Health*

Care Delivery in the United States (New York: Springer, 1981), p. 278, citing R. M. Gibson and C. R. Fisher, "Age Differences in Health Care Spending, Fiscal Year 1977," *Social Security Bulletin* 42:3 (1979).

17. Institutional providers must execute a nondiscrimination assurance and a facility compliance report. See Kenneth Wing, "Title VI and Health Facilities: Forms Without Substance," *Hastings Law Journal* 30:139–190 (1978), footnotes 74, 75. In 1978 individual physicians declined to accept "assignment" of Medicare claims (and Medicare "reasonable" fees) for 51 percent of services rendered. See Thomas P. Ferry et al., "Physician's Charges under Medicare: Assignment Rates and Beneficiary Liability," *Health Care Financing Review* 1(3):49–73 (1980).

18. Title 19 of the Social Security Act, P.L. 89-97, 42 U.S.C. Sec. 1396 et seq.; regulations found in 42 C.F.R. 430 et seq. For more on Medicaid see Brown, *The Rights of Older Persons*, chap. 7; Davis and Schoen, *Health and the War on Poverty;* Patricia Butler, "The Medicaid Program: Current Statutory Requirements and Judicial Interpretations," *Clearinghouse Review* 8:7 (1974); Patricia Butler, "Legal Problems in Medicaid," in Ruth Roemer and George McKray, eds., *Legal Aspects of Health Policy: Issues and Trends* (Westport, Conn.: Greenwood Press, 1980), pp. 215–241; and *Medicare and Medicaid Guide.*

19. Wing, *Law and the Public's Health*, p. 71. Also see Allen D. Spiegel, *The Medicaid Experience* (Germantown, Md.: Aspen Systems Corporation, 1979), p. 1, who points out that the Medicaid "sleeper" was premised on the beliefs that (1) the Medicaid population would be small, and (2) Medicaid would simply be a stopgap until national health insurance was enacted. Also see Rosemary and Robert Stevens, "Medicaid: Anatomy of a Dilemma," *Law and Contemporary Problems* 35:348 (1970).

20. See Butler, "Legal Problems in Medicaid."

21. In turn, state and local governments join in meeting the "state" share of Medicaid costs. In late 1981 Arizona became the last state to enter into the Medicaid program.

22. Fifty states plus the District of Columbia, Puerto Rico, Guam, and the Virgin Islands.

23. The states are actually given two options regarding recipients of supplemental security income. They may cover all such recipients—all but fifteen states have chosen this option—or they may use a set of more restrictive eligibility requirements that were applied to the aged, disabled, and blind before Aid to the Totally Disabled, Aid to the Blind, and Old-Age Security welfare programs were federalized under Supplemental Security Income in the early 1970s.

24. Davis and Schoen, *Health and the War on Poverty*, p. 53. They then go on to look at who is actually covered by Medicaid: "The stereotype of a Medicaid recipient is a black welfare mother. This does not fit with the facts that almost half the recipients of Medicaid are children and that three out of every five people covered are white. Twenty-seven percent of the recipients are aged or disabled. For them Medicaid is largely supplementary to the Medicare program. Almost two-thirds of recipients, however, are female, and three out of every four recipients are on welfare" (p. 54).

25. Karen Davis, "Achievements and Problems in Medicaid," *Public Health Reports* 91, no. 4 (July–August 1976), as cited in Spiegel, *The Medicaid Experience*, p. 19. Also see Patricia Butler, "State Limitations on the Amount, Scope, and Duration of Services under Medicaid," *Clearinghouse Review* 11:456 (1977).

26. Nearly 60 percent of Medicaid patients receive care in a relatively small number of group practices. A study published in the *Journal of the American Medical Association* (*JAMA*) found no evidence that these practices, often called "Medicaid mills," were characterized by fraud or improper care. See Janet B. Mitchell and Jerry Cromwell, "Large Medicaid Practices and Medicaid Mills," *JAMA* 244:2433–2437 (1980). The Omnibus Reconciliation Act of 1981 permits the states to request waivers from the Medicaid freedom-of-choice-in-provider provision; if granted, the waiver would allow the state to require that beneficiaries who overutilize the program use providers chosen by the state, not the beneficiary. The act also allows the states to restrict Medicaid participation by providers known to have abused the program.

27. See Davis and Schoen, *Health and the War on Poverty*, p. 55. Also see Michael W. Jones and Bette Hamburger, "A Survey of Physician Participation in and Dissatisfaction with the Medi-Cal Program," in Spiegel, *The Medicaid Experience*, pp. 277–289.

28. In 1977, for example, Medicare and Medicaid accounted for 62 percent of all public funds expended on health services and supplies. Public Health Service hospitals and state and local expenditures for hospital (largely psychiatric) care accounted for 13 percent and the military and Veteran's Administration health systems for another 12 percent. See *Health, United States, 1978* (Hyattsville, Md.: U.S. Public Health Service, December 1978) (DHEW pub. no. (PHS) 78-1232).

29. Davis and Schoen, *Health and the War on Poverty*, p. 121. In 1981 maternal and child health became part of a federal block grant available to the states, rather than a separate, categorical program.

30. Lynn Naliboff and Dorothy T. Lang, "Expanding Access to Health Care: Written Eligibility Standards for the Medically Indigent," *Clearinghouse Review* 13:848–857 (1980).

31. *Data on the Medicaid Program* (Washington, D.C.: Institute of Medicaid Management, 1978); as cited in "Checking the Legality of Your State's Medically Needy Income Levels," *Clearinghouse Review* 13:755–757 (1980).

32. One long-term strategy behind the legal challenges described below was aimed at highlighting this incomplete coverage by making the patchwork system so expensive that a new, more comprehensive welfare program would have to be enacted. Only the first portion of the strategic goal was achieved.

33. Davis and Schoen, *Health and the War on Poverty*, p. 208. The Institute of Medicine Study on the Health Care of Racial/Ethnic Minorities and Handicapped Persons "reached the general conclusion that race is associated with differences in the use of health services and that these differences do not mirror differences in need. The causal relationships behind these associations are complex and poorly documented." Institute of Medicine, *Health of the Disadvantaged*, p. 4.

34. See Institute of Medicine, *Health of the Disadvantaged,* pp. 23–82; *Health, United States, 1979* (Hyattsville, Md.: U.S. Public Health Service, 1980), chap. 1 (DHEW pub. no. (PHS) 80-1232); and *Health, United States, 1975* (Washington, D.C.: Health Resources Administration, 1976), pp. 225, 353, 371, 373 (DHEW pub. no. (HRA) 76-1232). Early in 1981 the Children's Defense Fund released a report, *Portrait of Inequality: Black and White Children in America,* further bearing out this differential. *New York Times,* 7 January 1981, p. 7.

35. Wing, in *Hastings Law Journal,* pp. 137, 138, 140. The Institute of Medicine study, *Health of the Disadvantaged,* pp. 15, 17, noted of federal antidiscrimination enforcement that the "necessary implementing structure is not as well developed in health as in such areas as education, employment, housing, and voting rights. . . . Although more than 15 years have elapsed since the passage of the Civil Rights Act, there still remains little guidance as to its application in health care." Nor has private enforcement been particularly helpful in this area, although some of the litigation surrounding the Hill-Burton obligation not to discriminate may have some effect. See Hill-Burton discussion at notes 39 and 40. Also see Marilyn G. Rose, "Access for Minorities into Mainstream Hospital Care," *Clearinghouse Review* 13:83–86 (June 1979), and Kenneth R. Wing and Marilyn G. Rose, "Health Facilities and the Enforcement of Civil Rights," in Roemer and McKray, *Legal Aspects of Health Policy,* pp. 243–67.

36. See, for example, "Checking the Legality of Your State's Medically Needy Income Levels." Also see Frank S. Bloch, "Cooperative Federalism and the role of Litigation in the Development of Federal AFDC Eligibility Policy," *Wisconsin Law Review* 1979:1 (1979). One long-running and complicated area of litigation has involved the Early and Periodic Screening Diagnosis and Treatment (EPSDT) program. See Butler "Legal Problems in Medicaid," pp. 224–227, 233–235.

37. Lucinda M. Finley, "State Restrictions on Medicaid Coverage of Medically Necessary Services," *Columbia Law Review* 78:1491–1516 (1978), at p. 1516.

38. Butler in Spiegel, *The Medicaid Experience,* p. 35. On a somewhat different but related issue, see the discussion of Medicaid funding of abortions in Chapter 18.

39. The Hospital Construction and Survey Act of 1946, 42 U.S.C. Sec. 291 c(e)(2).

40. See Rose, "Access for Minorities." *Cook v. Ochsner,* 319 F.Supp. 603 (E.D.La. 1970) has been the flagship lawsuit in a decade of litigation aimed at enforcing the uncompensated care and community services provisions of the Hill-Burton Act, as well as applying Title VI of the Civil Rights Act of 1965 to racial discrimination on the part of hospitals. For a history of these legal developments, see pp. 159–181 of Institute of Medicine, *Health of the Disadvantaged.* Also see James T. Cowdery, "Hill-Burton Hospital Must Afford Procedural Due Process in Its Statutory "Free Care" Obligation: *Newsome v. Vanderbilt University,*" *Connecticut Law Review* 11:248–272 (1979).

41. Revenue Ruling 56-185, 1956-1 CUM. BULL. 202.

42. Revenue Ruling 69-545, 1969-2 CUM. BULL. 117.

43. *Eastern Kentucky Welfare Rights Organization v. Simon,* 370 F.Supp. 325 (D.D.C. 1973). The Court of Appeals considered the merits of the argument

and held that the challenged revenue ruling was not contrary to congressional intent, 506 F. 2d 1928 (D.D.Cir. 1974). The Supreme Court's order of dismissal was based on the grounds that plaintiffs had failed to establish their standing to sue as affected parties, 426 U.S. 37 (1976). See Marcia Cypen, "Access to Health Care Services for the Poor: Existing Programs and Limitations," *University of Maimi Law Review* 31:127–159 (1976).

44. George J. Annas and Joseph M. Healey, Jr., "The Patient Rights Advocate: Redefining the Doctor-Patient Relationship in the Hospital Context," *Vanderbilt Law Review* 27:243, footnote 27. Also see Stuart A. Scheingold, *The Politics of Rights: Lawyers, Public Policy, and Political Change* (New Haven: Yale University Press, 1974).

45. See, in general, Norman L. Cantor, "The Law and Poor People's Access to Health Care," *Law and Contemporary Problems* 35:901 (1970); Sarah C. Carey, "A Constitutional Right to Health Care: An Unlikely Development," *Catholic University Law Review* 23:492 (1974); William T. Blackstone, "On Health Care as a Legal Right: An Exploration of Legal and Moral Grounds," *Georgia Law Review* 10:39 (1976); Edward V. Sparer, "The Legal Right to Health Care: Public Policy and Equal Access," *Hastings Center Report*, 6(5):39 (1976), and Tom Christoffel, "The Right to Health Protection," *Black Law Journal* 6:183 (1980). More generally, see Frank I. Michelman, "The Supreme Court, 1968 Term, Foreword: On Protecting the Poor through the Fourteenth Amendment," *Harvard Law Review* 83:7 (1969), and Robert Lanon White, *Right to Health: The Evolution of an Idea* (Ames, Iowa: University of Iowa Press, 1971). There is an extensive philosophical literature on a right to health; see, for example, the entire June 1979 issue of the *Journal of Medicine and Philosophy* 4, no. 2.

46. *Griffin v. Illinois*, 351 U.S. 12 (1956).

47. *Douglas v. California*, 372 U.S. 353 (1963).

48. *Harper v. Virginia Board of Education*, 383 U.S. 663 (1966).

49. *Shapiro v. Thompson*, 394 U.S. 618 (1969). In each of these cases the Court was dealing with what it determined to be fundamental constitutional rights: in *Shapiro*, the right to travel from state to state; in *Harper*, the right to vote; in *Griffin*, the right of equal access to the criminal appellate process.

50. 415 U.S. 250 (1974).

51. Especially in light of another Supreme Court decision, *Rodriquez v. San Antonio School District*, 411 U.S. 1 (1972), which held that education is not a fundamental right. Perhaps the sharpest indiciation of the Supreme Court's unwillingness to expand the fundamental rights category was *Dandridge v. Williams*, 397 U.S. 471 (1970). Also see *United States Railroad Retirement Board v. Fritz*, 101 S.Ct. 453 (1980).

52. This has been done for mental patients confined by the state, although not by the U.S. Supreme Court. But that is obviously a much narrower situation, since these patients are involuntarily confined and the confinement is justified—in principle—by a need for treatment. See discussion in Chapter 19, at note 39. In *Estelle v. Gamble*, 429 U.S. 97 (1976), the Supreme Court affirmed a cause of action for prisoners where a "deliberate indifference" to the prisoner's serious illness or injury can be shown. The petitioner in that case was unable to demonstrate that he had been unconstitutionally denied

medical attention, since he had been examined and treated on several occasions. The Court decided that his complaint of lack of diagnosis and inadequate treatment of a back injury raised issues of malpractice, rather than failure to provide care within the meaning of the standard outlined. The case does take a small step in the direction of recognizing a right to medical care, however, even though it is limited to a class of persons whose claims to treatment can be distinguished from that of the general population. In addition, *Estelle* was based on the Eighth Amendment, rather than on an implied right to medical treatment, or even on another explicit constitutional provision that could be applied outside the prison walls. See Wendy K. Mariner, "Medical Care for Prisoners: The Evolution of a Civil Right," *Medicolegal News* 9(2):4–8 (1981).

53. 397 U.S. 254 (1970). See the discussion of right versus privilege in the context of professional licensure, Chapter 6, at note 55.

54. See *Wilmington General Hospital v. Manlove*, 54 Del. 15, 174 A.2d 135 (1961); *Guerrero v. Copper Queen Hospital*, 112 Ariz. 104, 537 P.2d 1329 (1975).

55. See Jon. R. Waltz and Fred E. Inbau, *Medical Jurisprudence* (New York: Macmillan, 1971), pp. 142–151.

10

Occupational Health Law

> *It may not be wise to continue placing sole reliance on experts to solve our occupational health problems. In a sense, the experts got us into the trouble we are in by claiming to have a monopoly on the requisite knowledge. The fact is that all too often medical experts have not been interested in the prevention of occupational disease, and safey experts have not been interested in health. Scientific researchers seeking "objective truth" are employed principally by management and quite naturally reflect its view. And the lawyers who administer many government programs all too often act as advocates and present biased views.*
>
> —Nicholas Ashford[1]

THE MAJORITY of this country's adult population—more than 90 million people—spend a considerable portion of their waking hours at work. Conditions of employment, therefore, play a vital role in the physical and mental well-being of large numbers of Americans. Many improvements in working conditions have been achieved during the past century; however, the workplace is still hazardous to the health and safety of so many workers that the Center for Disease Control warns that the United States is "on the threshold of an epidemic of occupational illness."[2]

Tragically, even the dimensions of the problem are uncertain. In the early 1970s—in what is probably a low estimate—the U.S. Public Health Service estimated that there were some 390,000 new cases of occupationally induced diseases annually, with as many as 100,000 deaths each year. Close to 2.5 million disabling work injuries, and three to ten times as many serious injuries overall are estimated to have taken place in one year, and on-the-job deaths are estimated at 14,200 to 45,000 annually.[3]

Occupationally induced injuries and illnesses are not only the concern of the doctors and nurses specializing in occupational medicine or of the physical, respiratory, or occupational therapists. Internists and family practitioners must also be alert to possible connections between their patients' work and their presenting complaints (as well as to the compensation implications of diagnoses and treatment entered in their patients' records). And because workers may, in some instances, bring some of the hazards of the workplace home with them—toxic residue on clothing, for example—problems of occupational safety and health are relevant even to pediatricians, whose practices usually involve no direct contact with occupational diseases and injuries. Moreover, if a considerable portion of the nation's health care resources are devoted to treatment of occupationally induced ailments, fewer resources are available for other health needs. Although this fact may seem irrelevant to the individual practitioner treating an individual patient, the magnitude of the occupational health problem and its tremendous toll in death, disease, disability, and finances make it a concern of all health professionals.[4]

The knowledge and technology to eliminate or significantly ameliorate the hazards of the workplace already exist. Until quite recently, however, the legal machinery needed to enforce these improvements has been lacking.

Before the 1970s health and safety hazards on the job were largely ignored by existing legal doctrines. At the turn of the century on-the-job accidents were exceedingly common;[5] but employers were generally protected from legal liability for injury and death. Hence there was little incentive to improve job safety and health conditions.[6] Even when an accident could be shown to result from employer negligence, employers could escape legal liability by showing contributory negligence, however slight, on the part of the employee, by arguing voluntary assumption of risk on the part of the worker or by demonstrating that another employee had helped cause the accident. It is estimated that 70 to 94 percent of all job accident and death claims during this period were uncompensated.[7]

Worker's compensation laws, adopted by most states between 1910 and 1921, were one effort to deal with this problem, by providing payment for job-related injuries, regardless of fault.[8] But these statutes impose stringent limits on such payments and often fail to cover diseases, (such as those stemming from long exposure to dangerous substances).[9]

The first worker safety law was enacted by Massachusetts in 1877; within the next two decades most of the industrialized states had followed suit. But the laws were weak and enforcement weaker still. An AFL-CIO survey of twenty-five states in 1968 found one-and-a-half times as many state game wardens as safety inspectors.[10] The situation regarding occupational health was even more dismal. "The general pattern of neglect on the part of the states," wrote Nicholas Ashford in his Ford Foundation report, "eventually led to federal action and the passage of the Occupational Safety and Health Act of 1970."[11]

Nor was the federal record prior to the 1970 act spectacularly better than that on the state level. In 1936 Congress began regulating working conditions to some degree on those jobs for which the employer had a federal contract.[12] But even then, Congress gave the Department of Labor fairly narrow authority over job health and safety, and the department made the least of what authority it had. Thus for all intents and purposes, the Occupational Safety and Health Act of 1970[13] was really the first meaningful occupational health and safety law in the United States.[14]

The Occupational Safety and Health Act of 1970

Congress based its authority to legislate on job safety and health on its constitutional power to regulate interstate commerce.[15] The Occupational Safety and Health Act of 1970 applies to any person "engaged in a business affecting commerce who has employees." This is very sweeping coverage, since virtually every business, however small, can be found to have some relation, direct or indirect, to interstate commerce. The act declares that since "Congress finds that personal injuries and illnesses arising out of work situations impose a substantial burden upon, and are a hindrance to, interstate commerce in terms of lost production, wage loss, medical expenses, and disability compensation payments . . . Congress declares it to be its purpose and policy . . . to assure so far as possible every working man and woman in the Nation safe and healthful working conditions. . . ."

Toward this goal, the act establishes mechanisms for developing and enforcing job safety and health standards, and sets certain legal responsibilities for both employers and employees. Employers must comply with three major provisions of the act: Their places of employment must be free of recognized hazards likely to cause death or injury;[16] they are required to comply with the safety and health standards developed under the act;[17] and employers bear record keeping and reporting responsibilities.[18]

The only employees in the U.S. work force not covered by the Occupational Safety and Health Act are: (1) those employed by federal, state, or local governments; (2) those protected by a small number of other federal statutes;[19] (3) those employed in domestic service in a residence, in agriculture on a family-owned-and-operated farm, or in a religious service; and (4) the self-employed. Federal employees are covered by a parallel program under an executive order[20] based on a provision in the act, and the act also directs that state and local government employees be covered under a state's occupational safety and health plan to the "extent permitted by law." Thus the great majority of workers in the United States—over 70 million—are protected by the act.

The Reagan administration's occupational safety and health policy has been one of gutting the statutory program, particularly through administrative inaction. Thus any description of the law's framework and of agency responsibilities under the law portrays a largely empty shell. But given the increased worker awareness of the magnitude and severity of job health and safety problems—and of the means to deal with them—that developed in recent years, any long-term retreat from the prior governmental occupational safety and health role seems unlikely.

Congress assigned the responsibility of carrying out the intent and provisions of the new law to three agencies. The primary administrative role was placed in a new Occupational Safety and Health Administration (OSHA), located within the Department of Labor and headed by an assistant secretary. OSHA is responsible for establishing occupational safety and health standards, assuring compliance with these standards by means of a workplace inspection program, and assessing penalties for violations. Even before the Reagan administration, the resources available for carrying out these tasks were quite limited.

The act also elevated the already existing Bureau of Occupational Safety and Health to national institute status, within the then Department of Health, Education and Welfare. This agency, the National Institute for Occupational Safety and Health (NIOSH), is a research body charged with developing the medical criteria that OSHA can use to set and enforce standards. NIOSH also has the responsibility for fostering "education programs to provide an adequate supply of qualified personnel to carry out the purpose of this act" and of training "employers and employees in the recognition, avoidance, and prevention of unsafe or unhealthful working conditions."

Finally, the act created the Occupational Safety and Health Review Commission,[21] a quasi-judicial three-member board appointed by the president and independent of both the Department of Labor and the Department of Health and Human Services, whose task is to review any contested enforcement actions of OSHA. This review takes the form of a hearing by an administrative law judge,[22] whose report to the commission stands as the final order of the federal government, subject only to appeal to the U.S. Court of Appeals, unless one of the commissioners calls for full commission review.

Besides laying the groundwork for health and safety standards and providing mechanisms for their enforcement, the Occupational Safety and Health Act also creates a set of legal rights and responsibilities for both employers and employees[23] (enforcement of which is an important new development in law). Other than complying with the OSHA standards themselves, the most important employer responsibility under the act is the *general duty clause* (Sec. 12): "Each employer . . . shall furnish to his employees employment and a place of employment which are free from recognized hazards that are causing or are likely to cause death or serious physical harm to his employees . . ." In addition, employers must: (1) conduct regular self-inspections; (2) post informational notices for employees; (3) keep records of work-related injuries and illnesses and report serious accidents promptly to OSHA. They are also prohibited from taking reprisals against employees for engaging in activities protected under the act. At the same time, employers are entitled to OSHA consultative services and have the right to take disciplinary action against employees who refuse to comply with safety standards.

Most of the employee rights specified in the act are designed to assure that its intent is carried out. Thus employees are authorized to file complaints with OSHA and to accompany OSHA inspectors during their inspections, and can call on the Federal District Court to compel the secretary of Labor to take action in case of imminent danger. If violations are discovered by OSHA during an inspection, workers must immediately be notified, and they have a right to challenge the length of time their employer is given to correct violations. They must also have access to personal medical records and to all toxicity monitoring records assembled by their employer.[24] And their employer may not fire or otherwise retaliate against workers who exercise the rights granted them under the act.[25]

Because Congress recognized that upgrading occupational health and safety practices would be a lengthy and complicated task, the act also provided for some shortcuts. One shortcut permits OSHA to skirt the elaborate standard-setting machinery and establish temporary emergency standards if its inspectors determine that exposure to toxic substances or other hazards place workers in grave danger. Such standards take effect immediately upon issuance, although the formal procedure must still be completed within six months.[26]

Since any interested party may petition OSHA to adopt a particular standard, the advisory role of NIOSH may seem insignificant.[27] But the act gives NIOSH considerable authority for carrying out its research *in the workplace,* including the right to conduct inspections and question employers and employees; to require employers to measure, record, and make reports on the exposure of employees to substances that may be dangerous to health; and "to establish such programs of medical examinations and tests as may be necessary for determining the incidence of occupational illnesses and the susceptibility of employees to such illnesses." This is a very important provision; without it only the employer could determine which researchers, if any, would have access to the workplace for data collection[28]

In promulgating occupational safety and health standards, OSHA is under certain restraints. The act's purpose—assuring "so far as possible" safe and healthful working conditions—means that standards must be technologically feasible. This does not mean that the technology must be readily available, but rather that the standard is not clearly impossible of attainment. The courts have also held OSHA standards to a test of economic feasibility. But the fact that the costs of meeting a standard may put some companies out of business is not sufficient evidence of infeasibility. Only if an entire industry would be financially jeopardized in attempting to meet a standard would this test be failed.

In 1980 the Supreme Court added a "threshold determination" requirement to the OSHA standard-setting process, holding that before issuing any standard the secretary must "determine that it is reasonably necessary and appropriate to remedy a significant risk of material health impairment." This decision, however, did not find a majority of the justices agreed upon the rather convoluted rationale; that fact, plus the scientific uncertainty inherent in many health-effect determinations, makes the impact of this decision less than clear.[29]

More straightforward and more significant was the decision by the Court in a case involving OSHA cotton dust standards. For toxic substances and other harmful physical agents in the workplace, the act requires "the standard which most adequately assures, to the extent feasible, on the basis of the best available evidence, that no employee will suffer material impairment of health or functional capacity even if such employee has regular exposure to the hazard dealt with by such standards. . . . .'"[30] In adopting a standard for permissible exposure limits to cotton dust in textile mills, OSHA had determined that a significant health risk was involved and that the standard was both technologically and economically feasible. But the textile industry argued that OSHA must also demonstrate that the reduction in health risk brought about by the standard would be significant in light of the costs of attaining that reduction. Since the Reagan administration had been advocating just such a cost-benefit balancing for all federal regulations, the case had a particularly far-reaching importance. By a 5 to 3 vote the Court rejected a cost-benefit requirement, noting that in enacting the Occupational Safety and Health Act "Congress itself defined the basic relationship between costs and benefits by placing the 'benefit' of worker health above all other considerations save those making attainment of this 'benefit' unachievable."[31]

Once standards have been adopted, all businesses covered by the act must adhere to them. An employer may, however, apply to OSHA for a temporary variance when additional time is needed to comply with a standard. The employer must show that every effort is being made to comply as quickly as possible, but that for reasons beyond the employer's control—and not including lack of money—some delay is necessary. An employer may also seek a permanent variance if he or she can demonstrate "by a preponderance of the evidence that the conditions, practices, means, methods, operations, or processes used or proposed to be used by an employer will provide employment and places of employment to his employees which are as safe and healthful as those which would prevail if he complied with the standard" (Sec. 6[d]).

Once the standard has been established, OSHA has statutory authority to make certain it is adhered to. To verify compliance, OSHA is authorized:

> (1) to enter without delay and at reasonable times any factory, plant, establishment, construction site, or other area, workplace or environment where work is performed by an employee of an employer; and (2) to inspect and investigate . . . all pertinent conditions, structures, machines, apparatus, devices, equipment, and materials therein, and to question privately any such employer, owner, operator, agent or employee.[32]

When the law was first passed, OSHA took the position that its inspection was an administrative search of a type that did not require a search warrant, but the U.S. Supreme Court rejected this view in *Marshall v. Barlow's Inc.*[33] However, the issue of a warrant only arises if an employer refuses entry to OSHA compliance officers. OSHA expects this will rarely happen, and that when it does, securing a warrant will not be difficult.[34] The real difficulty lies in the magnitude of the inspection task. Some five million businesses are covered by the act, many of them enormous and complex. Even though states have assumed about half of the inspection responsibility,[35] effective periodic inspection of all work sites would be a Herculean undertaking. And since some of the worst health and safety problems are associated with smaller businesses, it would not do to simply inspect the largest workplaces. As the Ford Foundation report points out, "inspection of all U.S. workplaces is neither a goal of the Act nor a numerically feasible possibility."[36] Instead, OSHA has established priorities for inspection: (1) situations involving an imminent danger of death or serious physical harm; (2) investigations of catastrophes, fatalities, and accidents resulting in hospitalization of five or more employees; (3) valid employee complaints; (4) a "special emphasis" program—now disbanded—which was aimed at high-hazard industries, occupations, and substances; (5) some random inspections;

and (6) reinspections where serious violations had been found. The major focus of inspections is on uncovering serious violations; thus first-instance other-than-serious violations do not lead to penalties unless the employer has ten or more violations.

Since it is clear that only a small portion of the five million workplaces will be visited under this system of priorities (less than 60,000 OSHA inspections in 1979), effectiveness of the act is officially tied to voluntary compliance on the assumption that improved occupational health and safety is in the long-term best interest of both employees and employers, that businesses can be convinced of this, that OSHA can assist businesses in a voluntary compliance program, and that the threat of possible OSHA inspection will serve as an impetus to voluntary action.[37]

How effective has this approach been? OSHA offers figures indicating a significant positive impact. According to former Secretary of Labor Ray Marshall,

> Injury and illness rates published by the Bureau of Labor Statistics . . . are one indication of OSHA's effectiveness. The overall rate has dropped from 10.6 injuries per 100 workers in 1973 to 9.2 in 1978, a 13 percent improvement. This means that *there were almost 4 million fewer injuries between 1973 and 1978 than would have occurred at the 1973 rate.*[38]

However, others argue that progress has not been all that encouraging, especially as regards health hazards with long-term effects. More to the point in assessing the act's impact is the degree of commitment on the part of the government agencies administering it and the willingness of Congress to appropriate adequate funds for such administration. Prior to 1977 OSHA—and its dependence on voluntary compliance—were widely criticized as ineffective.[39] During the Carter administration, OSHA and NIOSH became more efficient and more aggressive. Among other things, OSHA: (1) revised and simplified existing occupational safety and health standards, eliminating many of the trivial standards—unnecessary for worker protection—that had been the basis of much ridicule and scorn; (2) filled a critical gap by developing new standards for serious health hazards; (3) reduced paperwork burdens; (4) focused enforcement on areas of serious violations calling for significant penalties; and (5) improved training for OSHA compliance officers, especially in the health hazards area. The Reagan administration is committed to moving things back in the other direction, by changing and withdrawing regulations and altering enforcement policies, with the likely result of eliminating OSHA and NIOSH as meaningful mechanisms for worker protection. Thus if the act is to have anything more than a minimal impact, the force for change will have to come from somewhere outside of the federal government. The only two prospects for such a likelihood are the states and workers themselves.

The State Role

The Occupational Safety and Health Act preempts all conflicting state laws.[40] But the act also allows the secretary of Labor to cede jurisdiction back to those states that have satisfactory job safety and health programs of their own. In applying for approval for its own program, a state must meet federal requirements by demonstrating that its workplace safety and health standards are "at least as effective as" OSHA's, that there is a state agency to enforce the plan, with procedures corresponding to those of OSHA to provide for variances, emergency standards, employee complaints, and the like. State plans must also include adequate funds and the qualified personnel necessary for enforcing the standards.[41] States with approved occupational safety and health programs may receive federal grants to cover up to 50 percent of operating costs.

Liberal approval policies under the Nixon administration led to a total of thirty-one states with approved plans, but several states subsequently withdrew their plans and the secretary has moved to withdraw approval in a few instances. By 1980, twenty-three states, with 40 percent of the nation's workers, had approved plans. A few states, notably California, have strong programs, but most of the states' programs have been weaker than that of OSHA. States seem to be finding their own plans expensive to implement, and businesses operating in many states are unhappy with the lack of a uniform program, so it seems unlikely that the number of state occupational safety and health programs will increase. With a few possible exceptions, it seems highly unlikely that any increase in worker safety and health protection will occur on the state level.

The Worker Role

As indicated earlier, the Occupational Safety and Health Act gives employees a considerable role in its enforcement. Employees can request and participate in an OSHA inspection. They can challenge the abatement period allowed for violations and they can challenge OSHA standards and any employer variances with respect to those standards. They can observe onsite monitoring of hazardous materials and can ask NIOSH to provide information on the potential toxic effects of workplace substances. But all of these rights are meaningless unless workers have some reason to suspect that they may be in some danger on the job. Two types of information can help provide the necessary warning signals: information on the nature, exposure patterns, and potential health effects of the work environment (including chemicals, noise, and radiation) and information on actual health effects, as documented in employees' health records.

Even before 1970 employers had a common-law duty to warn their employees of unquestionable but not readily apparent workplace hazards, and to inform employees of adverse results of job-related medical examinations. In both instances, however, it is a meaningful duty only when an employee can demonstrate harm resulting from a failure to warn.[42] But there was no system for nationwide monitoring of occupational injuries and illness. Today all businesses employing ten or more people must keep, and periodically post, job injury and illness statistics and report serious accidents involving deaths or multiple hospitalizations to OSHA.

The Occupational Safety and Health Act detailed the informational duty. Section 8(c)(3) directs the secretaries of Labor and of Health and Human Services to issue regulations "requiring employers to maintain accurate records of employee exposures to potentially toxic materials or harmful physical agents . . . with . . . appropriate provision for each employee or former employee to have access to such records as will indicate his own exposure to toxic materials or harmful physical agents." The resulting regulations, promulgated a decade after passage of the act, provided for access to four types of exposure records: environmental monitoring records, biological monitoring records, material safety data sheets, and any other record disclosing the identity of a toxic substance or harmful physical agent. However, exceptions in the regulations allowing the withholding of "trade secret" data greatly limit their potential. Employees may designate a representative to exercise their right of access to exposure records, with certified labor unions automatically receiving such designation without individual employee consent. OSHA also has a right of access to these exposure records. Exposure records must be preserved for at least thirty years. But the Reagan administration withdrew the toxic substances regulation and may eliminate other provisions, so the worker's "right to know" is currently cloudy at best.

A similar, but more limited, right of access to employee medical records is provided for under the same regulations. Individual employees have virtually unrestricted access to their employer-held medical files, but union access requires specific written consent. OSHA's access to personally identifiable medical records is more limited than is its access to exposure records. Employers must also preserve employees' medical records for at least thirty years.[43]

Exposure and medical records are important to the individual employee when seeking outside medical treatment, but they are even more important from an epidemiological perspective. Patterns suggesting occupationally induced health problems can only be revealed if relevant records are accessible and can be followed up. Implementation of the access to records regulations is too current an issue to allow for any assessment of their possible impact.

Conclusion

There is little doubt that effective occupational health and safety laws can reduce the number of workers who suffer injury or work-related illness on the job. A 1981 study by the Council on Economic Priorities documented a 23 percent reduction in illnesses and injuries in the chemical industry during the first eight years of OSHA enforcement, at an estimated cost of $140 per employee.[44] At the same time, injury rates seem to be increasing in those areas in which the agency has had the least impact. OSHA's future, as of this writing, is cloudy; the Reagan administration is clearly dedicated to curtailing the agency's activities. The injury tax, increasingly suggested as an alternative to the OSHA regulatory approach, is primarily suited to accident prevention rather than the more critical area of occupationally caused disease. Nevertheless, as research traces more and more serious illnesses to conditions in the workplace, the demand for federal protections is likely to grow, and health professionals are certain to play an important role in the policy debated in this area.

NOTES

1. Nicholas A. Ashford, *Crisis in the Workplace: Occupational Disease and Injury, A Report to the Ford Foundation* (Cambridge: MIT Press, 1976), p. 542.
2. Bureau of National Affairs, *Occupational Safety and Health Reporter* 8(16):463 (September 14, 1978).
3. A major reason that the figures are so imprecise is that the employer, who is in the best position to collect dependable data, has the least incentive to do so. The 14,200 deaths and 2.3 million injuries are figures for the year 1971 from the National Safety Council, a private body often criticized for having an industry bias. The higher figures can be found in Senate testimony on the Occupational Safety and Health Act of 1970 (Hearings before the Subcommittee on Labor of the Committee on Labor and Public Welfare on S. 2193 and S. 2788, Part I, p. 188) and in Ashford, *Crisis in the Workplace*, pp. 83–96. Until quite recently the health impact of the workplace was particularly ignored, so that occupational disease estimates are even more likely to be understated than are injury/accident figures.
4. Basil Whiting, then deputy assistant secretary of Labor for Occupational Safety and Health, noted that Congress passed the Occupational Safety and Health Act after recognizing that "voluntary efforts in themselves had

proved insufficient because employers could shift the costs of job-related injuries and disease to workers and society, which paid for them through higher health insurance premiums, social security and welfare payments, and other social programs. Furthermore, workers' compensation, as presently structured under State law, does not provide much of an incentive to employers to take preventive steps." Statement before the Committee on Labor and Human Resources, United States Senate, March 21, 1980.

There are some other reasons that health professionals should be concerned with occupational health—and law—even though their professional concerns seem far removed from this area. First, most health professionals are directly affected by the Federal Occupational Safety and Health Act because they are covered under the act—either as employees or employers. This could be the case even with a solo practitioner employing only one or two people in an office practice. Certainly the modern hospital is not without its own health and safety hazards. Secondly, health professionals—both clinicians and researchers—are frequently called upon as professional experts in dealing with regulatory questions in this area. At one time that pool of experts was predominately industry-oriented, a situation that seems to be changing.

5. As many people were being killed fortnightly on the job as went down in the *Titanic*. Crystal Eastman's *Work-Accidents and the Law* became a best seller. See Joseph A. Page and Mary-Win O'Brien, *Bitter Wages* (New York: Grossman, 1973), pp. 47–48.

6. See Chapter 16 for a discussion of the deterence function of tort law.

7. Page and O'Brien, *Bitter Wages*, p. 51. On the employer bias of the courts and the emergence of the worker's compensation system, see Ashford, *Crisis in the Workplace*, pp. 47–57, 388–423, as well as National Commission on State Workman's Compensation Laws, *Compendium on Workmen's Compensation* (Washington, D.C.: Government Printing Office, 1973), document no. 496-632.

8. Worker's compensation statutes are often portrayed as a salvation for workers from the oppressiveness of existing tort law. But this assumes a static state of affairs when, in fact, the law was already beginning to change. The statutes were, in fact, a business response to this change. See Ashford, *Crisis in the Workplace*, pp. 388–389.

9. The Occupational Safety and Health Act of 1970, which is discussed later in this chapter, established a National Commission on State Workmen's Compensation Laws. Ashford, *Crisis on the Workplace*, pp. 338–423, criticizes the commission's report, especially its failure to deal with one of the major weaknesses of the worker's compensation program—nonattention to occupational *disease*. For a followup on the commission's recommendations see Irvin Stander, "The Future of Workers' Compensation," *Medicolegal News* 8(2):7–9 (April 1980).

10. Page and O'Brien, *Bitter Wages*, p. 71. Also see Ashford, *Crisis in the Workplace*, pp. 46–56.

11. Ashford, *Crisis in the Workplace*, p. 51.

12. The Walsh-Healey Public Contracts Act of 1936 apparently had little impact on occupational safety and health. In 1965 two laws containing health and

safety provisions were enacted: the McNamara-O'Hara Public Service Contract Act and the National Foundation on the Arts and Humanities Act. Other relevant federal legislation included the Federal Metal and Nonmetalic Mine Safety Act of 1966, the Construction Safety Act of 1969, and the Federal Coal Mine Health and Safety Act of 1969. All, however, were limited in scope. For the earlier years in particular, enforcement was negligible.

13. 29 U.S.C. Sec. 651 et seq. The act was signed into law on December 29, 1970. According to Rothstein, "As the legislative history clearly indicates, OSHA was the result of numerous compromises, a fact evidenced in two important ways. First, the Act is not well drafted: various sections of the Act are vague, redundant, and even paradoxical. Second, in construing the Act, the legislative history is seldom conclusive because the members of Congress never considered the Act in its present form until after the Conference Report. Thus, Commission and judicial resort to the legislative history as an aid in interpreting the Act has often proved fruitless." Mark A. Rothstein, *Occupational Safety and Health Law* (St. Paul, Minn.: West, 1978), p. 8.

14. The medical profession's failure to perceive occupational standards as a health issue and to join the drive for effective health and safety laws was one reason, among many others, for the long delay in getting such legislation passed.

15. See Chapter 4 for a discussion of federal health authority.

16. Sec. 5(a)(1).

17. Sec. 5(a)(2).

18. Sec. 8(c).

19. Such as the Federal Coal Mine Safety Act, the Federal Metal and Nonmetalic Mine Safety Act, and the Atomic Energy Act. But these areas are not totally exempt, the other acts applying only to the extent that parallel protective authority is exercised.

20. Executive Order No. 12196, 45 Fed. Reg. 12, 769 (February 26, 1980). Regulations, to be codified at 29 CFR Part 1960, in 45 Fed. Reg. 69, 796 (October 21, 1980). An executive order is a directive issued by the president to the administrative departments and agencies of the federal government. As to them it has the force of law. The act itself makes it "the responsibility of the head of each federal agency to establish and maintain an effective and comprehensive occupational safety and health program which is consistent with the [OSHA] standards."

21. In addition to the three principle agencies described in the text, the act also creates a National Advisory Committee on Occupational Safety and Health, consisting of twelve "representatives of management, labor, occupational safety and occupational health professions and of the public. . . . The Committee shall advise, consult with, and make recommendations to the Secretary [of Labor] and Secretary [of Health and Human Services] on matters relating to the administration of the Act." Nicholas Ashford was committee chairman in 1980. The act also empowers the secretary of Labor to appoint advisory committees to assist him in setting standards.

22. See Chapter 3 for a discussion of administrative law judges.

23. See Rothstein, *Occupational Safety and Health Law*, chap. 8. Also see Baruch A.

Fellner and Donald W. Savelson, *Occupational Safety and Health-Law and Practice* (New York: Practicing Law Institute, 1976), pp. 24–28, and *All About OSHA* (Washington, D.C.: U.S. Department of Labor, 1980) OSHA 2056 (revised), pp. 39–45.

24. On records, see the discussion later in this chapter.

25. Section 11(c)(1) of the act provides that: "No person shall discharge or in any manner discriminate against any employee because such employee has filed any complaint or instituted or caused to be instituted any proceeding under or related to this Act or has testified or is about to testify in any proceeding or because of the exercise by such employee on behalf of himself or other of any right afforded by this chapter." The secretary of Labor issued a regulation in 1973 that provided that among the protected rights "afforded by this chapter" was a right to withdraw from extreme hazard. The regulation provided that "when an employee is confronted with a choice between not performing assigned tasks or subjecting himself to serious injury or death arising from a hazardous condition at the workplace . . . [and] . . . with no reasonable alternative, refuses in good faith to expose himself to the dangerous condition, he would be protected against subsequent discrimination." This regulation was challenged as going beyond the scope of rights Congress intended to protect when it enacted Section 11(c)(1). But in a unanimous decision the Supreme Court upheld the regulation as clearly conforming to the fundamental objective of the act—to prevent occupational deaths and serious injuries—and as an appropriate means of assuring that the general duty clause requirement is met. Thus employees who refuse to work in the face of extreme hazard cannot be fired, disciplined, or docked in pay. The Court noted, however, that "any employee who acts in reliance on the regulation runs the risk of discharge or reprimand in the event a court subsequently finds that he acted unreasonably or in bad faith." *Whirlpool Corp. v. Marshall*, 445 U.S.1(1980).

26. This emergency approach has rarely been used. Emergency temporary standards were issued for asbestos, vinyl chloride, pesticides, and a package of fourteen carcinogens. The failure to make wider use of this authority is not for want of potentially harmful toxic substances warranting such use. See, for example, Ashford, *Crisis in the Workplace*, p. 252.

Another shortcut written into the act permitted OSHA, before April 1973, to establish "interim" standards that did not have to go through the formal rule-making procedure. These standards, which could be based on either an "established federal standard"—an occupational safety or health standard previously established by other federal agencies or previously contained in federal law—or on "national consensus standards"—an occupational safety or health standard which "(1) has been adopted and promulgated by a nationally recognized standards-producing organization under procedures whereby it can be determined by the Secretary that persons interested and affected by the scope or provisions of the standard have reached substantial agreement on its adoption, (2) was formulated in a manner which afforded an opportunity for diverse views to be considered . . ."—could remain continuously in effect unless and until OSHA moved to change them.

Most standards have been of the "specificiation" type; for example, requiring that for a certain type of walkway the employer must provide guardrails of a specified height and specified construction. An employer with a different but equally effective safety system would still have to meet these specifications. "Performance" standards ignore the specific means and concentrate on adequacy of protection. But such standards are much harder to enforce because of the subjective measurements involved. See Ashford, *Crisis in the Workplace,* pp. 179–180.

27. In *Industrial Union Department, AFL-CIO v. Hodgson,* 499 F.2d 467 (D.C. Cir. 1974), the Court of Appeals rejected the argument OSHA is bound by NIOSH recommendations in the area of toxicity standards.

28. But see Marjorie Sung, 'NIOSH under Siege," *Science* 213:315 (July 17, 1981).

29. *Industrial Union Dept., AFL-CIO v. American Petroleum Institute,* 448 U.S. 607 (1980). Also see discussion of scientific uncertainty, Chapter 10.

30. Section 6(b)(5). More generally, Section 3(8) of the act provides: "The term 'occupational safety and health standard' means a standard which requires conditions, or the adoption or use of one or more practices, means, methods, operations, or processes, reasonably necessary or appropriate to provide safe or healthful employment and places of employment."

31. *American Textile Manufacturers Institute v. Donovan,* 101 S.Ct. 2478 (1981). Also see discussion of cost-benefit analysis in Chapter 10.

32. Sec. 8(a).

33. See Chapter 5.

34. From October 1978 to April 1980, warrants were required in only 2.6 percent of OSHA inspections. When needed, OSHA can obtain a warrant without prior notice to the business to be searched, and can then conduct an unannounced inspection. To secure the warrant OSHA need merely show that the premises had been selected for inspection in a reasonable and objective manner. See Rothstein, *Occupational Safety and Health Law,* 1981 supplement, chap. 10.

35. See discussion of state plans at note 41.

36. Ashford, *Crisis in the Workplace,* p. 456. Rothstein reports, *Occupational Safety and Health Law,* 1981 supplement, p. 88, that "as of January, 1981, OSHA conducted over 500,000 inspections, alleging over 1.7 million violations. . . ." He also notes, p. 85, that health inspections have become increasingly more important, although still only accounting for 18.7 percent of all 1980 inspections.

37. Despite this emphasis on voluntarism, lawyers concerned with the Occupational Safety and Health Act spend perhaps the greatest portion of their time on compliance issues. A somewhat unique aspect of the act is the fact that initiation of the formal enforcement procedure is up to the employer, rather than the government. After an inspection an employer will receive a *citation* describing any violations of OSHA standards and regulations and setting a time limit within which to correct them and a *notification* of proposed penalty. The employer has fifteen working days to file a Notice of Contest, challenging the violations cited, the abatement time allowed, and/or the penalties assessed. Unless such a Notice of Contest is filed, the citation

and notification become final orders not subject to any judicial or administrative review. The number of cases contested has steadily and sharply increased over the years, reaching 21 percent in 1979. See Whiting statement, at note 4.

38. Statement before the Committee on Labor and Human Resources, United States Senate, April 1, 1980. Emphasis in the original. Whiting (statement, at note 4) adds that the improvement was even greater for small businesses (a decline of 26 percent) and for hazardous industries (construction: 19 percent; primary metals manufacturing: 18 percent; machinery: 19 percent).

39. For example, Ashford, *Crisis in the Workplace*, p. 498, concluded that:

> The "voluntary compliance" which OSHA hopes to encourage on the part of industry is ineffective because (1) regulations and standards do *not* exist for most serious health hazards; (2) the inspection force is *not* large enough to present a serious possibility of random inspection; (3) significant penalties are *not* being levied; (4) the inspectors are poorly qualified; and (5) employees are *not* well informed on their rights.

40. See discussion of federal preemption of state law in Chapter 4. In some areas—e.g., elevators and boilers—OSHA has not issued standards and states may therefore enforce their own regulations.

41. In *AFL-CIO v. Marshall*, 570 F.2d 1030 (D.C. Cir. 1978), the circuit court ordered OSHA to develop benchmarks for the hiring of state safety inspectors and industrial hygienists and adopt state funding criteria.

42. See John D. Blum, "Revealing the Invisible Tort: The Employer's Duty to Warn," in Richard H. Egdahl and Diana Chapman Walsh, eds., *Health Services and Health Hazards: The Employee's Need to Know* (New York: Springer-Verlag, 1978), pp. 173–181.

43. See 45 Fed. Reg. 35, 212 (May 23, 1980), effective August 21, 1981, codified at 29 CFR 1910. 20 (1980). Individual employees may have access to their own employer-held medical records under provisions of state law, but this is meaningful in only a small fraction of the states. See George J. Annas, "Legal Aspects of Medical Confidentiality in the Occupational Setting," *Journal of Occupational Medicine* 18:540 (1976). On organized medicine's opposition to even this least controversial aspect of the "right to know" proposals, see John Elliott, "Controversy in Medicine: Access to Employee Health Records," *Journal of the American Medical Association* 241:778 (1979). At least two states, New York and Connecticut, have worker "right to know" laws providing access to certain exposure data.

44. *New York Times* (national edition), 23 June 1981, p. 7.

11

Food and Drug Law

*This is a day of synthetic living, when to an ever-increasing
extent our population is dependent upon mass producers for
its food and drink, its cures and complexions, its apparel and
gadgets. These no longer are natural or simple products but
complex ones whose composition and qualities are often
secret. Such a dependent society must exact greater care than
in more simple days and must require from manufacturers or
producers increased integrity and caution as the only
protection of its safety and well-being. Purchasers cannot try
out drugs to determine whether they will kill or cure. . . .
Where experiment or research is necessary to determine the
presence or the degree of danger, the product must not be
tried out on the public, nor must the public be expected to
possess the facilities or the technical knowledge to learn for
itself of inherent but latent dangers.*
— Robert H. Jackson dissenting in *Dalehite v. United States*[1]

VIRTUALLY EVERYONE CONCERNED with human health agrees that the
foods people eat and the drugs they ingest play an important part in
determining their physical and mental well-being. It is hardly surprising,
then, that legislatures and courts have been deeply involved in efforts to
assure the safety and purity of the foods and drugs available to the
public.

This involvement takes several forms. On the simplest level, the common law of nuisance abatement has, in the past, been used to seize and
embargo (a sort of quarantine for inanimate objects) spoiled, contaminated, or adulterated foods, drugs, cosmetics, or other articles with the
potential to endanger public health. More recently, this common-law
approach has been replaced by statutory controls, both state and federal.
On the federal level, the Food, Drug, and Cosmetic Act and its various
amendments sets the standard for regulating the production and distribution of legal food and drugs, while the Comprehensive Drug Abuse

Prevention and Control Act deals with the control of illegal substance abuse. Parallel state statutes, provider practice acts, antisubstitution acts, and other legislation also affect food and drugs and, quite often, carry important implications for the health practitioner, but it is the work of the federal Food and Drug Administration (FDA) that dominates this area of health protection.[2]

Perceptions about the FDA vary markedly depending on the eye of the beholder and on particular issues in the news. The general public, which knows little about the agency's specific duties, nevertheless recognizes it as a defender of the nation's health; the food and drug industries, on the other hand, often claim its oversight of their operations burdensome and it standards of safety and purity rigid and excessive. Almost two decades ago, the FDA was widely applauded because its refusal to approve U.S. distribution of thalidomide saved thousands of newborns from the tragic deformities that followed that drug's use by pregnant women in England, Germany, and other countries. More recently, it has been depicted as a stumbling block to progress for its attempted ban on saccharin, after animal tests indicated that this substance could cause cancer.

Since drugs are basic to allopathic medicine, laws and regulations affecting their availability, safety, and quality are obviously important to practitioners. But they, too, have little sense of FDA legal authority or its function in relation to either food or drugs.

History

During the past one hundred years, as the United States grew in size and population, many of the products that had been produced and sold locally, including foods and medicines, became part of a national and international commerce. Because this increased the possibility of adulteration and mislabeling, many states enacted food and drug laws to protect the consumer.[3] But the problem was difficult to deal with on a state level, and a consensus developed for federal action under the commerce clause.[4] The first efforts to secure federal pure food and drug legislation began in the late 1800s, and the issue has remained a political football to this day, pitting consumer protection advocates against anti-regulation forces and against companies and industries eager to keep a free production and labeling hand in order to maximize profit. In the battle over the initial federal legislation at the turn of the century, as well as in later battles over major amendments in the 1930s and the 1960s, the balance was tipped by the revelation of existing horrors. In 1906 Upton Sinclair's moving novel, *The Jungle*, provided the public with a graphic—and accurate—picture of the filthy and hazardous conditions in the meat-packing industry, and won widespread backing for the energetic crusade by Dr. Harvey Wiley, chief chemist for the U.S. Department of Agriculture, to regulate the food industry. When tobacco states' congressmen succeeded in having tobacco eliminated from the official United States Pharmacopeia, so that it would not be defined as a drug, passage of the Pure Food and Drug Act of 1906, regulating the interstate commerce of misbranded and adulterated food and drugs, was assured. The act became the first significant piece of health and safety legislation ever enacted by Congress.[5]

Although the new law called for criminal proceedings and/or seizure of nonconforming items, its regulatory potential was quite limited. The government had the burden of proving fraud or adulteration, and could only act against deleterious substances added to foods in quantities injurious to health. Naturally occurring substances, however dangerous, and even poison, in small quantities, were beyond the reach of the act, as were cosmetics and medical devices; drugs were subject to regulation only after they came on the market. As the title of the law indicates, the primary concern of the new legislation was food (and secondarily, patent medicines). Attention to prescription drugs and medical devices evolved much later.

In addition to these limitations, a series of decisions by the U.S. Supreme Court further restricted the act's impact. The Court ruled, for example, that the law's ban on false and misleading statements did not extend to therapeutic claims.[6] To remove that restriction, Congress added the Sherley Amendment, in 1912, specifically prohibiting "false and fraudulent" therapeutic claims, but the prohibition came to require proof that a claim was both false *and* fraudulent and thus was ineffective against "the ignorant nostrum vendor who sold inefficacious drugs in good faith."[7]

Despite its shortcomings, the 1906 law did establish a federal role in regulating food and drugs to protect the public from misrepresentation and adulteration. This in turn led to the development of a food and drug expertise within the Department of Agriculture's Bureau of Chemistry, the predecessor of the present Food and Drug Administration (now part of the Department of Health and Human Services).

The first major revision of the 1906 statute came in 1938, with passage of the Food, Drug, and Cosmetic Act,[8] which remains the basic law today. It was adopted, after being bottled up in congressional committees for five years, following a tragic incident in 1937 in which more than one hundred people died from sulfanilamide that was manufactured with a poisonous solvent. The new legislation—like its predecessor, a compromise—placed cosmetics and medical devices under the jurisdiction of the Food and Drug Administration, expanded the agency's powers through an injunction process and increased penalties, and broadened the ban against deleterious substances to include not only food additives but also products that were inherently unsafe, such as poisons or carcinogens. Its most important provision, however, was to shift the burden of proof regarding drug safety from the government to the manufacturer; stipulating that new drugs could not be marketed until their safety had been investigated by the manufacturer and a report on safety submitted to the FDA. The act also required that drug labels give adequate direction for use, but permitted exemptions from this requirement where "not necessary for the protection of the public health."

Several important amendments have been added to the 1938 act over the years. The Humphrey-Durham Amendment of 1951,[9] prohibited the dispensing of drugs unsafe for unsupervised lay use, except on a physician's prescription. (Prior to 1938 any nonnarcotic drug could be purchased from a pharmacist without a prescription. Under the unamended 1938 act the drug companies decided which other drugs, if any, would require a prescription.) The Food Additives Amendment of 1958 and the Color Additive Amendements of 1960[10] included additives under the premarketing clearance previously required for new drugs. These amendments also contained what has become known as the Delaney clause (after the legislation's sponsor), which requires

> That no additive shall be deemed to be safe if it is found to induce cancer when ingested by man or animal, or if it is found, after tests which are appropriate for the evaluation of the safety of food additives, to induce cancer in man or animal. . . .[11]

Both amendments established grandfather clause exemptions for substances that had previously been sanctioned by the FDA. In addition, food additives generally recognized as safe (GRAS) do not fall under the food additive regulatory process.[12]

The Drug Amendments of 1962 (the Kefauver-Harris amendments),[13] followed closely upon the thalidomide tragedy and established new requirements previously rejected by Congress. Prior to marketing, manufacturers now had to establish—through scientific evidence—both the safety and the efficacy of new drugs. The amendments also allowed for removal of drugs already on the market, until their safety could be proved, if an imminent hazard to the public's health was suspected. The 1962 amendments also increased FDA authority in regulating prescription drug promotion and clinical testing of new agents. Finally, the Medical Device Amendments of 1976 extended the premarketing requirements that had evolved for drugs to medical devices, a broad category including everything from tongue depressors to pacemakers and X-ray machines.[14]

Today the Food and Drug Administration has authority over 80 percent of all processed foods (including food additives, but excluding red meat and poultry), drugs (including serums and vaccines, and both prescription and over-the-counter drugs), medical devices, and cosmetics. Over the years the agency has sought to shift its role from policing offenses to approving proper practices, preferring to view itself as a scientific research arm, like the National Cancer Institute, rather than as an FBI for food and drugs. The *FDA Annual Report, 1976* explains that

> FDA's regulatory strategy is anticipatory rather than reactionary: preventive rather than corrective. FDA will never have the physical or financial resources to continuously police every segment of the industrial community. The Agency's strategy, therefore, is to assure that safety is built into the products it regulates.[15]

However it views itself, the FDA has a plethora of critics. The food and drug industries routinely castigate the agency for excessive regulatory practices, and persistently lobby Congress to restrict its powers, while consumer groups just as persistently argue that "the FDA is over-influenced by the industries it is supposed to regulate" and that it is too understaffed and underfunded to do its job effectively so that "industry pressures gradually erode even the most vigilant FDA officials."[16] Nevertheless, as George McKray points out:

> The agency probably has more impact on the daily lives of Americans than any other regulatory body. It is responsible for 110,000 establishments that make and store the products it regulates. The retail value of these products is $200 to $300 billion a year, or 20 to 25 cents of every consumer dollar spent in this country.[17]

The individual states also have food and drug laws, although no state has a single agency responsible for regulating all aspects of food and drugs. Most state food and drug laws are based on the Uniform State Food, Drug, and Cosmetic Bill, which itself was patterned after the federal Food, Drug, and Cosmetic Act of 1938.[18] However, only a third of the states have updated their drug laws to parallel the provisions of the Kefauver-Harris Drug Amendments of 1962. The federal food and drug law, based on congressional authority to regulate interstate commerce and on the importance of a uniform national market for food, drugs, medical devices, and cosmetics, creates a clear basis for federal preemption of state food and drug laws.[19] But this generally has not been a problem area. On the one hand, states have not sought to impose laxer requirements than those adopted on the federal level (laetrile being a notable exception). On the other hand, Congress and the courts have frequently allowed more stringent state requirements, especially if there is no direct conflict between state and federal provisions.[20] Thus federal and state cooperation have predominated in this area. That, plus the fact that the courts have continually expanded the definition of interstate commerce, has meant that the Food, Drug, and Cosmetic Act is effectively applied to the vast majority of food, drug, medical device, and cosmetic transactions in the country.

The Act

An agency-prepared synopsis of general information on food and drug law explains the FDA's basic statutory authority as follows:

> The law is intended to assure the consumer that foods are pure and whole-some, safe to eat, and produced under sanitary conditions; that drugs and devices are safe and effective for their intended uses; that cosmetics are safe and made from appropriate ingredients; and that all labeling and packaging is truthful, informative, and not deceptive. Another law, the Fair Packaging and Labeling Act, affects the contents and placement of information required on the package.
>
> The Federal Food, Drug, and Cosmetic Act prohibits distribution in the United States, or importation, of articles that are adulterated or misbranded. The term "adulterated" includes products that are defective, unsafe, filthy, or produced under insanitary conditions (Secs. 402, 501, 601). "Misbranded" includes statements, designs, or pictures in labeling that are false or misleading, and failure to provide required information in labeling (403, 502, 602). Detailed definitions of adulteration and misbranding are in the law itself, and hundreds of court decisions have interpreted them.
>
> The law also prohibits distribution of any article required to be approved by FDA if such approval has not been given.[21]

The Food, Drug, and Cosmetic Act is well organized and fairly straightforward, so that it takes a close reading to appreciate its numerous exemptions and inconsistencies. The statute begins by defining basic terms, the most important of which are:[22]

- food, which "means (1) articles used for food or drink for man or other animals; (2) chewing gum; and (3) articles used for components of any such article."[23]
- food additive, which "means any substance the intended use of which results or may reasonably be expected to result, directly or indirectly, in its becoming a component or otherwise affecting the characteristics of any food (including any substance intended for use in producing, manufacturing, packing, processing, preparing, treating, packaging, transporting, or holding food; and including any source of radiation intended for any such use), if such substance is not generally recognized, among experts qualified by scientific training and experience . . . to be safe under the conditions of its intended use. . . ."[24]
- drug, which "means (A) articles recognized in the official United

States Pharmacopeia, official Homeopathic Pharmacopeia of the United States, or official National Formulary, or any supplement to any of them; and (B) articles intended for use in the diagnosis, cure, mitigation, treatment or prevention of diseases in man or other animals; and (C) articles (other than food) intended to affect the structure or any function of the body of man or other animals; and (D) articles intended for use as a component of any articles specified in clause (A), (B), or (C); but does not include devices or their components, parts, or accessories."[25]

- device, which "means an instrument, apparatus, implement, machine, contrivance, implant, in vitro reagent, or other similar or related article, including any component, part, or accessory, which is—(1) recognized in the official National Formulary, or the United States Pharmacopeia, or any supplement to them; (2) intended for use in the diagnosis of disease or other conditions, or in the cure, mitigation, treatment, or prevention of disease, in man or other animals; or (3) intended to affect the structure or any function of the body of man or other animals, and which does not achieve any of its principal intended purposes through chemical action within or on the body of man or other animals and which is not dependent upon being metabolized for the achievement of any of its principal intended purposes."[26]

- cosmetic, which "means (1) articles intended to be rubbed, poured, sprinkled, or sprayed on, introduced into, or otherwise applied to the human body or any part thereof for cleansing, beautifying, promoting attractiveness, or altering the appearance; and (2) articles intended for use as a component of any such articles. . . ."[27]

These definitions, which determine the scope of FDA's universe,[28] are followed by a listing of prohibited acts: adulteration, misbranding, and shipment of an unapproved drug or device.

The act prohibits "the adulteration or misbranding of any food, drug, device, or cosmetic in interstate commerce,"[29] as well as the introduction or receipt in interstate commerce "or the doing of any other act with respect to, a food, drug, device, or cosmetic, if such act is done while such article is held for sale . . . after shipment in interstate commerce and results in such article being adulterated or misbranded."[30] These very broad prohibitions obviously depend for their meaning on what constitutes adulteration and misbranding. In fact, one reason the 1938 law has not been superceded is that Congress has been able to effectuate major changes simply by revising the definition of adulteration or misbranding, without having to change the prohibited acts.

Foods are considered misbranded if the labeling or packaging is false or misleading. Food is deemed adulterated if it naturally "contains any poisonous or deleterious substance which may render it injurious to health" or if it contains or may have been contaminated by filthy, putrid, decomposed, or diseased substances.[31] A food is also considered adulterated if it "contains any added poisonous or added deleterious substance" other than pesticide chemicals, color additives, or food additives that have been approved as safe. The act also provides authority for the establishment of a "defintion and standard of identity" for food whenever this will "promote honesty and fair dealing in the interest of the consumer." This provision makes it possible for the FDA to take action against a food that is "economically adulterated"—made by substituting cheaper ingredients for those the consumer justifiably expects. Such a food is considered misbranded under the act.

A 1979 panel of the Institute of Medicine/National Academy of Sciences called these food requirements inflexible, confusing, and cumbersome.[32] One problem is that such standards are applied so rigidly that if a manufacturer uses a better ingredient than that cited in the standard, the product is considered misbranded, even if the deviation is listed on the package. Such rigidity tends to protect established products from the competition of improvement.

Additional confusion in this area revolves around food additives—substances that become components of food, either intentionally, or indirectly by leaching from packaging materials or other such means. A food additive may be dealt with in one of four ways:

1. The FDA may prohibit it as unsafe. For example, the Delaney clause declares that any food additive "found to induce cancer when ingested by man or animal" is by definition unsafe and must be prohibited. This provision is actually rarely used, the FDA more often relying on its discretionary authority to deny a petition seeking marketing approval for an additive.
2. The FDA may determine from scientific evidence that a food additive is safe and will issue an order permitting its use and regulating the specific foods in which it may be used, the amount that may be present in a food, and so on.
3. The additive may be excluded from the act's definition of "food additive" if it is "generally recognized, among experts qualified by scientific training and experience to evaluate its safety, as having been adequately shown through scientific procedures . . . to be safe under the conditions of its intended use."
4. The additive may be covered by a "grandfather clause" under the "prior sanction" of federal law.[33]

As far as drugs and devices are concerned, the law states that they are adulterated if not manufactured under sanitary conditions, according to current "good manufacturing practice." A drug is also adulterated "if it purports to be . . . a drug the name of which is recognized in an official compendium, and its strength differs from, or its quality or purity falls below, the standards set forth in such a compendium."[34] A drug or device is misbranded if its packaging does not meet various labeling requirements (narcotic and hypnotic substances, for example, must be labeled "Warning—may be habit forming," and nonprescription drugs must have "adequate directions for use").

Before a new drug can be marketed, the manufacturer must submit certain information to the FDA,[35] including "full reports of investigations which have been made to show whether or not such drug is safe for use and whether such drug is effective in use."[36] Marketing will be approved if adequate testing has shown that the drug is safe and that there is "substantial evidence that the drug will have the effect it purports or is represented to have. . . ."[37] "Substantial evidence" is defined as "evidence consisting of adequate and well-controlled investigations, including clinical investigations, by experts qualified by scientific training and experience to evaluate the effectiveness of the drug involved."[38] The new drug's labeling must also be approved from the perspective of meeting standards of safety and efficacy. Exemptions are provided for drugs used by qualified individuals for investigational purposes. Basically this is a licensing system, framed in terms of a new drug "application" that the government can either "approve" or reject.[39]

The act's prohibition of misbranding of foods, drugs, devices, and cosmetics is straightforward as a basic principle, but application of the requirement—the main thrust of which is aimed at product labeling—has produced complexity and ambiguity.[40] Among other things, there is not always a clear distinction between a product label and the promotional material surrounding the sale of the product.

The scope and definition of the labeling requirements under the act are the same for foods, drugs, devices, and cosmetics, but the main focus for applying the requirements varies according to the product involved. For foods, labeling requirements are aimed both at prohibiting representations that are "false or misleading in any particular" and at requiring disclosure of specified information. Just what must be disclosed remains an area of great unevenness, weakness, and confusion; ingredients need not be listed at all for some foods and some ingredients need not be disclosed in any food.[41] For drugs, labeling must include adequate directions for use, including FDA-approved descriptive and warning materials for prescription drugs.[42]

Under the 1938 statutory framework, the FDA had authority over labels and labeling, whereas the advertising of food, drugs, devices, and cosmetics came within the purview of the Federal Trade Commission (FTC). Over time, however, this distinction became blurred. Several courts supported the FDA's position that promotional material available to customers in connection with their purchase of a product constitutes labeling under the act. Since 1962 the FDA has had direct authority to regulate prescription drug advertising and the FDA and FTC have co-operated in regulating advertising of over-the-counter drugs, seeking in particular to limit advertising claims to those approved for package labeling.[43]

The Agency

Unlike many other federal regulatory bodies, which are headed by a quasi-autonomous group of commissioners appointed by the president for fixed terms and approved by the Senate, the Food and Drug Administration is not an independent agency. Its commissioner is appointed by, and responsible to, the secretary of Health and Human Services (HHS), who, in turn, serves "at the pleasure of the President." The FDA is not even specifically authorized in legislation—the Food, Drug, and Cosmetic Act and its amendments assigning implementation responsibility entirely to the secretary of HHS. Technically, therefore, both the FDA and its commissioner could be changed by simple administrative order, although this is unlikely.

The FDA has six divisions: the Bureau of Foods, the Bureau of Drugs, the Bureau of Biologics, the Bureau of Medical Devices and Diagnostic Products, the Bureau of Radiological Health, and the Bureau of Veterinary Medicine. The National Center for Toxicological Research also operates under its aegis.[44] In addition, the FDA makes extensive use of several dozen advisory committees as a source of expert information in making regulatory decisions. There is, for example, a Safety of Pesticide Residues in Food Advisory Committee, as well as a Device Good Manufacturing Practice Advisory Committee. The FDA has included consumer and industry liaison members on most committees. The Federal Advisory Committee Act[45] set guidelines for the establishment and operation of committees advising federal agencies and requires that their meetings be open. Advice is also sought from time to time from independent outside scientific groups.

Until 1940 the FDA was part of the Department of Agriculture. Today such organizational placement may seem strange, but that cabinet department still retains important food regulation authority, being responsible for meat inspection, meat quality grading, and standards for meat products.[46] This division of authority makes for less effective, more complicated food safety regulation, but given the politics involved the arrangement is unlikely to be altered.

The Food and Drug Administration is organized into ten regional offices (plus additional district offices), each with its own investigative, research, and compliance staffs. Because the act under which the FDA functions spells out its duties and jurisdiction in such detail, its investigators can carry out their work in an almost mechanical fashion, making on-site inspections, bringing suspect items to the research staff for analysis, and referring apparent violations to the compliance staff for possible action. All of this is done to carry out the mandate of the act in several general areas, which have been summarized as:

1. Establishing mandatory standards of identity, quality, and quantity for foods.
2. Regulating the safety of food additives.
3. Safety regulation of artificial colors added to foods, drugs, and cosmetics.
4. Enforcing the Fair Packaging and Labeling Act provisions which apply to food, drugs, devices, and cosmetics.
5. Regulating cosmetics, drugs, and devices, which includes insuring that drugs, cosmetics, and devices are not adulterated or misbranded, and that new drugs be shown to be safe and effective prior to marketing.
6. Regulating vaccines, blood and other biological products.
7. Regulating animal drug safety.[47]

Implementing the Act

Because it is virtually impossible to keep checking articles in transit, the FDA operates by measuring compliance at the source. The act authorizes the agency "to enter, at reasonable times, any factory, warehouse, or establishment in which food, drugs, devices, or cosmetics are manufactured, processed, packed, or held . . ." and to "to inspect . . . all pertinent equipment, finished and unfinished materials, containers, and labeling therein." If drugs or devices are involved, inspection of "records, files, papers, processes, controls, and facilities" bearing on possible adulteration or misbranding is also authorized.[48] In addition to random inspections based on listings of all known facilities under its jurisdiction, the FDA schedules inspections on the basis of consumer complaints, as well as advertising, news accounts, and anything else suggestive of possible violations of the act.[49]

When inspection uncovers noncompliance, the FDA can take several different steps to keep adulterated and misbranded articles from the public.[50] If the goods in question have not been shipped or distributed, the agency can go into federal court and seek an injunction to prevent shipment.[51] The injunction is an effective preventive measure, and the fact that it is a federal court, rather than the agency itself that issues the order, makes compliance more likely. If the goods have reached the market, the most effective way to prevent its use by the public is voluntary recall by the manufacturer of all the offending items, a halt in further distribution and, if necessary, a public warning of possible danger. There is some debate as to the FDA's authority to require a recall. Former FDA General Counsel Peter Barton Hutt has argued that

> Much has been made of the suggestion that the Food and Drug Administration has no authority to require or even to request recall or detention. I do not subscribe to that view. I know of nothing in the statute which prohibits this enforcement mechanism, and it obviously comports with the objectives underlying the statute.[52]

There is no doubt that the FDA can ask a federal court for permission to seize adulterated or misbranded goods, and it is this authority that puts teeth into any request or order for manufacturer recall. Adulterated and misbranded food, drugs, devices, and cosmetics may be seized according to a process begun with a libel of condemnation.[53] It is an enforcement action taken against the noncomplying items, rather than against an individual or corporation. The owner may contest the basis of the seizure, simply abandon the goods seized, or ask the court for permission to bring the items into compliance. There is nothing in a seizure proceeding, other than the risk of additional seizures, to prevent the manufacturer from producing and distributing more of the noncomplying articles.

Criminal penalties[54] of imprisonment of up to one year and a fine of up to $1,000, or both, are authorized for an initial violation, even if there is no evidence of deliberate intent to violate the act. Imprisonment for up to three years, a fine of up to $10,000, or both, are authorized for cases involving intent to defraud or mislead, and for repeated violations. The Supreme Court has upheld the conviction of a top-level manager of a food firm despite the defendant's argument that he himself was not aware that his company was not complying with the act, because the manager was in a position to know the facts and to take whatever action was needed to correct the situation.[55] Thus, the criminal penalties provision makes noncompliance with the act personally hazardous to top management of noncomplying businesses, while injunctions and seizure affect the ability to market goods already processed or produced.

The act also specifically authorizes publicity as an enforcement tool. Dissemination can be made of "information regarding food, drugs, devices, or cosmetics in situations involving . . . imminent danger to health, or gross deception of the consumer."[56] By publicizing its findings regarding adulterated and misbranded products, the FDA can both warn the public about possible hazards or fraud and bring pressure on the market-sensitive producer to make the necessary changes.

Other, nonpunitive, portions of the act deal with approval of marketing applications for new drugs, devices, and additives.[57] A new drug may not be commercially marketed until the manufacturer has completed a lengthy new-drug application process to prove to the FDA that it is safe and effective. Drug companies and researchers working with them often argue that this process is so detailed and slow that it keeps valuable new drugs off the market for a long time. On the other hand, there have been numerous instances when this careful process has saved lives and prevented serious injury.[58]

Regulation Through Rule Making

As with all major statutes, the Food, Drug, and Cosmetics Act is "unfinished law." For example, it is left to the agency to develop "a reasonable definition and standard of identity" for foods and to "promulgate regulations for exempting . . . drugs intended solely for investigational use." The act contains two provisions giving the FDA authority to promulgate regulations to implement and enforce the act. For certain types of regulations, including those involving food standards, dietary food labeling requirements, food and color additive petitions, and adjudicatory orders on new drug applications, the FDA is required to follow a formal rule-making process, including published notice, trial-type evidentiary hearings, written orders, and possible judicial appeal—a process that can drag on for many years before a regulation takes effect.[59] Yet until the 1970s the FDA relied on formal rule making, along with case-by-case court enforcement, to implement the act.

Another provision of the act, however, provides the FDA with a general authority "to promulgate regulations for the efficient enforcement of this Act."[60] In a series of cases, beginning in 1967 and reaching their peak in 1973, the U.S. Supreme Court and other federal courts upheld the agency's power to adopt industrywide regulations having the force of law using this informal rule-making process.[61] This significantly increased the FDA's power and flexibility by eliminating a great deal of procedural delay. It also made it more feasible for any interested parties, such as groups of health professionals, to become involved in the rule-making process. Under the informal rule-making process the agency publishes notice of a proposed rule, provides an opportunity for interested persons to comment, and then publishes a statement of the final rule, including an explanation of its basis and purpose.

FDA Information Policies

The FDA is the recipient and repository of vast amounts of information in which the public and health professionals have considerable interest.

Prior to the 1970s virtually none of this information was disclosed to the public. Under the agency's implementation of the Freedom of Information Act this situation has changed dramatically. Now such information as general agency correspondence, consumer complaints, minutes of meetings with trade associations, summaries of scientific conferences, and warnings issued to companies of violations disclosed through inspection can be obtained through the filing of a freedom of information request. Information that the FDA declines to release includes trade secrets, files on impending investigations, and internal memos. The area of most controversy has involved the extent to which safety and effectiveness data submitted in support of a new drug application will be released. After approval of an application the agency will provide summaries of safety and effectiveness data and the reasons for approval of the application, along with full information on adverse reaction reports, analytical methods used, correspondence, and the like. Safety and effectiveness data on food and color additives, antibiotics, and new drugs that failed to get approval is completely disclosed.[62]

Drugs, Drugs, and Drugs

Regulation of drugs is especially complicated because of the several different legal categories into which drugs can be grouped. The federal Food, Drug, and Cosmetic Act of 1938 stipulated that certain drugs could only be sold on prescription and had to be labeled as such. The drug companies decided which drugs would be included in this category, although if the FDA disagreed it could move against a drug as misbranded. Since 1951, however, the FDA has had authority to determine whether a drug will be placed in the over-the-counter or prescription categories. To be sold by prescription are those drugs that are habit forming or have a potential for toxic or other harmful effects.[63]

New drugs—and manufacturer-claimed new uses for established drugs—are approved for marketing by the FDA after the drug's sponsor has demonstrated safety and effectiveness "under the conditions of use prescribed, recommended, or suggested in the labeling thereof." The first step in this lengthy process requires that when the sponsor is ready to study the drug's effects in humans it submit to the FDA a Notice of Claimed Investigational Exemption for a New Drug (known as an IND), along with information on preclinical investigations. Without a proper IND, shipment of investigational drugs in interstate commerce would be a violation of the act. Clinical evaluation under an IND covers three phases, the first two studying pharmacological effects on small numbers of patients, the third being a large clinical trial. After this process is completed the sponsoring company files a New Drug Application (NDA) which, if approved, allows marketing of the drug.[64]

Although the drug marketing-approval process is under close FDA control, after a new drug is approved the FDA lacks control over actual use. The agency does determine approved usages for prescription drugs, but it is limited to assuring that physicians are informed about such approved usages through labeling, advertising, and package-insert requirements. If doctors choose to go beyond such approved use, however, nothing in the food and drug law prevents them from doing so on their own responsibility.[65]

There is another way to categorize drugs, and that is according to whether or not they have a "potential for abuse." Drugs of abuse are not substances taken to fight disease or, as with oral contraceptives, to produce other clearly physical effects (although they may have been manufactured for those purposes), nor are they used to reduce the symptoms of mental illness (although, again, they may have been manufactured for that purpose), but rather they are used to produce a pleasurable effect or decrease emotional discomfort through their impact on the brain. These drugs can be habit forming, and they are believed to require ever-larger doses to sustain their effect and/or stave off withdrawal symptoms. The drugs in this category include those that long have been illegal, such as heroin, cocaine, and marijuana, as well as the commercially available (and legal) psychoactive drugs.[66] The latter include prescription drugs, over-the-counter drugs, social drugs such as alcohol and nicotine, and nondrug compounds that are also used for psychoactive effect.

Over the years a number of laws have been passed to discourage drug abuse. The Pure Food and Drug Act of 1906 forced patent medicines to list cocaine or other drugs on their labels. The Jones-Miller Act of 1909 took specific action against narcotic drug abuse, and in 1914 Congress passed the Harrison Narcotics Act,[67] which remained the primary narcotics control law in the United States until 1971. The Harrison Narcotics Act required dealers and dispensers of narcotics (opium, cocaine, and their derivatives) to register annually with the Treasury Department, thus narrowing the channels through which an estimated 200,000 Americans[68] could legally receive their drugs. The Treasury Department was involved because the law was based on the federal government's taxing power and used an excise tax on narcotics as the device to exercise authority and control in this area.

Two basic legal approaches to the control of substance abuse have been relied on over the years. One is to restrict availability; the other is to punish use.[69] Both create what has been called a "crime tariff" by making the sale and use of the substance illegal. The laws drive trade undergound and prices up sharply. If, as is often the case, enforcement of the law is inadequate and/or corrupt, it is the increase in the price of the drug rather than a decrease in its use that is the main result of the legal controls.

Efforts to restrict availability can take several forms. One is to regulate, but not prohibit, sale. An example is alcohol. Its sale is closely regulated as to time and place, certain age groups are not allowed to purchase it, and sales are heavily taxed—purportedly to discourage consumption. A second type of restriction, the so-called vice model, makes it a crime to manufacture and sell the illegal substance, but does not make purchase or use itself illegal. A third restricting device, the "medical model," allows the medical profession to authorize what would otherwise be an illegal sale. (The Harrison Act permitted narcotic sales for curative—not maintenance—purposes when authorized with a prescription written by a physician, dentist, or veterinarian registered under the act.) Finally, there are the laws that prohibit a substance completely and penalize not only sale, but possession as well. Between the Civil War and World War I most states passed laws dealing with the opiates and cocaine, almost all of them prohibiting distribution rather than punishing use.

Laws aimed at punishing use are primarily a twentieth-century phenomena, although they recently have fallen from favor somewhat. A large number of states have enacted criminal penalties for the possession and use of controlled substances, and some even made it a crime to be in a place where drugs are used or to possess the hyperdermic syringes or other paraphenalia used in drug abuse. Under some laws, addiction was itself a crime: In 1962 the U.S. Supreme Court invalidated a California law that made it a criminal offense to "be addicted to the use of narcotics." The Court observed that

> It is unlikely that any state at this moment in history would attempt to make it a criminal offense for a person to be mentally ill, or a leper, or to be afflicted with a venereal disease. A state might determine that the general health and welfare require that the victims of these and other human afflictions be dealt with by compulsory treatment, involving quarantine, confinement, or sequestration. But, in the light of contemporary human knowledge, a law which made a criminal offense of such a disease would doubtless be universally thought to be an infliction of cruel and unusual punishment in violation of the Eighth and Fourteenth Amendments. . . . We cannot but consider the statute before us as of the same category.[70]

In 1968 the Court was asked to extend this logic by invalidating a state law that made public intoxication a crime. A five-to-four majority declared that "it is simply not yet the time" to take this further step.[71]

Unsuccessful attempts have been made to invalidate possession and use convictions by arguing that addiction deprived the defendant of the free will necessary to the commission of a crime.[72] It has also been argued—unsuccessfully—that treating marijuana in the same way as amphetamines and barbiturates was irrational and violative of constitutional equal protection.[73] Many people feel that all controlled substance laws that penalize the user should be invalidated as a violation of a constitutional right of privacy. The National Commission on Marijuana and Drug Abuse (established by the 1970 Controlled Substance Act), in its 1973 report, disagreed that punishing the user served as a deterrent to use, an aid in enforcement, or a meaningful way of indicating societal disapproval, and approved of a privacy-right based "zone of no law" to cover the private use of drugs.[74] This view is still a long way from being accepted; but with an ever-increasing proportion of the population, including white upper-middle-class adults trying and using mind-altering drugs, it is likely that laws punishing use will play less of a role in abuse-control efforts. There are no laws punishing the use of alcohol, which is as destructive and addicting as many illegal drugs.

For many years, efforts to control drug abuse were hampered by wide variations in state law and by confused jurisdiction on the federal level. For a long time, federal control efforts were concentrated in the Treasury Department, even though a large portion of the drugs of abuse were legitimately manufactured (and FDA-regulated) drugs diverted into illicit channels.[75] In 1965 Congress enacted the Drug Abuse Control Amendments to the Food, Drug, and Cosmetic Act,[76] vesting federal authority over amphetamines and similar stimulants, barbiturates and similar depressants, and hallucinogens (other than marijuana and narcotics) in the Food and Drug Administration's Bureau of Drug Abuse Control. And in 1968 President Lyndon Johnson took executive action to end this split enforcement by establishing a Bureau of Narcotics and Dangerous Drugs within the Justice Department to assume most of the authority and functions of the FDA's Bureau of Drug Abuse Control and the Treasury Department's Bureau of Narcotics.

All these changes were relatively minor, however, compared to the Comprehensive Drug Abuse Prevention and Control Act of 1970.[77] This law, usually refered to as the Controlled Substances Act, repealed and replaced all previous federal narcotics and dangerous-drug laws. This act (which does not preempt state drug control) emphasizes enforcement rather than education and treatment, and centralizes authority in the Department of Justice.[78] It is the Food and Drug Administration, however, that determines which drugs should be controlled. Oakley Ray, author of a leading text on drug use, observes that "this separation of enforcement from the scientific and medical decision of what should be controlled was a major victory for those arguing for a sane drug law."[79] In addition to scientific evidence on known pharmacological effect and psychic and physiological dependence, the FDA is instructed to consider the historical pattern, scope, duration, and public health significance of abuse. Drugs with a potential for abuse—except for distilled spirits, wine, malt beverages, and tobacco, which were specifically excluded by the act—are assigned by the FDA to one of five "schedules," or classifications, each of which is controlled differently. Abusable drugs with no safe and acceptable medical use, such as heroin, opiates, and hallucinogenic substances, fall into Schedule I: Their use is prohibited in all but government-approved research. Abusable drugs with safe and accepted medical uses fall into the remaining four schedules. Schedule II drugs, which include morphine, cocaine, methadone, codeine, and amphetamine-type stimulants, are the most tightly controlled of these drugs: Production is controlled; prescriptions cannot be refilled; special records must be kept; and penalties for illegal trafficking can be as high as for Schedule I drugs. Schedule III drugs, such as nonamphetamine-type stimulants and paregoric, and Schedule IV drugs, such as chloral hydrate, phenobarbital, and diazepam, are less rigidly controlled, reflecting lower potentials for abuse. Schedule V drugs, with the lowest potential for abuse, include some drugs that may be dispensed without a prescription. The FDA is also responsible for regular updating of drug assignments to the various schedules.

Everyone who manufactures, distributes, or dispenses any controlled substance must register with the government annually, and must conduct periodic inventories and keep detailed records. These requirements are designed to prevent legally produced drugs from being diverted into the illegal market.[80]

Although the 1970 act stipulates the harshest penalties for the large-scale dealer in illegal drugs, penalties still exist for possession as well as for distribution. Many states have enacted their own controlled substances acts, and many of them have also eased the penalties directed against the use and possession of small amounts of illegal drugs. In New York, which is notable for having taken the opposite approach under the hard-line law pushed through by then-governor Nelson Rockefeller, judges and juries have hesitated to convict small users and peddlers altogether because of the automatic harsh penalties.[81]

Despite an almost century-long effort to solve drug abuse by legal sanctions, the problem remains intractable. Ray argues that, given the realities of drug use today, "it is senseless to look to the law as a way of reducing our current and future drug problems." There are many reasons for this, especially the fact that such large profits are involved. Support for strict enforcement is limited not only by the spreading use of illegal drugs in all segments of the population, but also by the fact that alcohol, tobacco, and other harmful substances are treated far more leniently.[82] It may well be that simple prohibition and punishment can never work in the absence of effective education and treatment programs. But despite a growing attention to decriminalization, treatment, and education, the law is only moving slowly in this direction.[83]

For the health professional, substance abuse and treatment of the addict and the experimenter will remain an important concern. The practitioner's role may change slowly with time, but strict reporting requirements are likely to remain in effect for many years.[84]

Conclusion

Roughly twenty-five cents out of every consumer dollar is spent on items regulated by the Food and Drug Administration. Yet the current clamor to reduce regulation of business may well set the stage for a weakening of the Food, Drug, and Cosmetic Act—the Delaney clause and the new drug approval process in particular. Today, Americans take it so for granted that the food they eat, the medicines they use, the hair coloring, eye shadow, or cologne they apply are safe and effective, that many fail to make the connection between that safety and the monitoring mandated by federal statutes. Health professionals, who see the connection more clearly than most, have a responsibility to make sure that the protections developed over many decades are not destroyed.

NOTES

1. 346 U.S. 15 (1953), pp. 51–52.
2. At the same time there has been a shift to a strict liability standard in products liability suits, as well as a federal regulatory role under the Consumer Products Safety Act. See Chapter 12.
3. Laws aimed at assuring the purity of food and drugs are not new. For example, in India in about 300 B.C., there were fines for those found guilty of "adulteration of grains, oils, alkalis, salts, scents and medicinal articles with similar articles of no quality . . ." and in China, at about the same time, the supervisors of markets had agents "whose duty it was to prohibit the making of spurious products, including food, and the defrauding of purchasers." King John proclaimed the first English food law, The Assize of Bread, in 1202, making it illegal for bakers or others to adulterate bread by mixing in ingredients such as ground peas or beans. Harry Edward Neal, *The Protectors: The Story of the Food and Drug Administration* (New York: Julian Messner, 1968), pp. 11–12. Also see George McKray, "Consumer Protection: The Federal Food, Drug, and Cosmetic Act," in Ruth Roemer and George McKray, *Legal Aspects of Health Policy: Issues and Trends* (Westport, Conn.: Greenwood Press, 1980), pp. 173–174.
4. The growing interstate commerce in food increased the pressure for federal controls. Long-distance shipping took a good deal of time, and manufacturers, lacking refrigeration, resorted to chemicals such as borax, copper, salicylic acid, aluminum salts, and formaldehyde, to preserve foods and to cover up spoilage.
5. On the history of the 1906 Act, see C. C. Regier, "The Struggle for Federal Food and Drug Legislation," *Law and Contemporary Problems* 1:3 (1933). For a

history of federal food legislation in general, see "One Hundred Years of Food Protection," in United States Senate Committee on Agriculture, Nutrition, and Forestry, *Food Safety: Where Are We?* (Washington, D.C.: U.S. Government Printing Office, 1979), pp. 1–121. And for a brief history of federal food and drug regulation, with special emphasis on prescription drugs, see Arthur Hull Hayes, Jr., "Food and Drug Regulation after 75 Years," *Journal of the American Medical Association (JAMA)* 246:1223–1226 (1981).

6. *Johnson v. United States*, 221 U.S. 488 (1911).

7. David F. Cavers, "The Food, Drug and Cosmetic Act of 1938: Its Legislative History and Its Substantive Provisions," *Law and Contemporary Problems* 6:2–42 (1939). Also see David F. Cavers, "The Evolution of the Contemporary System of Drug Regulation under the 1938 Act," and James Harvey Young, "Drugs and the 1906 Law," both in John B. Blake, ed., *Safeguarding the Public: Historical Aspects of Medicinal Drug Control* (Baltimore: Johns Hopkins, 1970).

8. 52 Stat. 1040 (1938); now 21 U.S.C. Secs. 301–392. Most statutory references in this chapter will be to the act. The U.S. Code section number can often be derived by dropping the middle digit of the act section number and adding a 3 in front of the remaining two digits.

9. 65 Stat. 648 (1951).

10. 72 Stat. 1784 (1958) and 74 Stat. 397 (1960). The Color Additive Amendments apply not only to food, but also to drugs, devices, and cosmetics.

11. The language quoted is from Sec. 409(c)(3)(A), the food additives section of the act. Almost identical provisions are found in Sec. 706(b)(5)(B), from the Color Additive Amendments of 1960, and Sec. 512(d)(1)(H), from the Animal Drug Amendments of 1968. See materials on the Delaney clause in Richard A. Merrill and Peter Barton Hutt, *Food and Drug Law* (Mineola, N.Y.: Foundation Press, 1980), especially pp. 77–86.

12. "Grandfathering" means to exempt from a new restriction things, activities, or people by virtue of their existence prior to or at the time of enactment of the restriction. Food additives were grandfathered directly; color additives under a "provisional" listing of two decades' duration. On grandfathering and GRAS see Merrill and Hutt, *Food and Drug Law*, pp. 63–77, 115–134. In 1980 the United States General Accounting Office recommended to Congress that it eliminate the GRAS and grandfather exceptions. See *Need for More Effective Regulation of Direct Additives to Food*, HRD-80-90, (Washington, D.C.: General Accounting Office, August 14, 1980). Late in 1980 the FDA announced the results of a decade-long review of GRAS-listed substances carried out at government request by the Federation of American Societies for Experimental Biology. Of 415 GRAS ingredients, 305 were judged safe and 68 as safe as currently used but requiring study before any increase in level of use. The remainder lacked sufficient data to warrant being recognized as safe. See *The Nation's Health*, February 1981, p. 3.

13. 76 Stat. 780 (1962).

14. 90 Stat. 539 (1976). There also have been other, less sweeping, amendments to the 1938 act, not detailed here. These include the Animal Drug Amendments of 1968, 82 Stat. 342 (1968), giving the FDA premarketing approval

authority over any animal drug that is likely to leave residue in edible tissue of livestock, and the "Vitamin-Mineral Amendments of 1976," Title V of the Health Research and Health Services Amendments of 1976, 90 Stat. 401 (1976), restricting FDA authority over dietary supplements. The Food and Drug Administration also has authority under several other statutes in addition to the Food, Drug, and Cosmetic Act and its various amendments. These include the Fair Packaging and Labeling Act, the Radiological Control for Safety and Health Act (to regulate X-ray machines, microwave ovens, ultrasound equipment, and other sources of potentially harmful radiation), the Biologics Act (to regulate biologic products such as vaccines and products derived from human blood), and the Public Health Services Act (to control sanitation in food service establishments and on interstate carriers). The FDA also shares some authority with the Environmental Protection Administration under the Federal Insecticide, Fungicide, and Rodenticide Act and the Federal Environmental Pesticide Control Act. See Merrill and Hutt, *Food and Drug Law*, pp. 6–7, 945–951.

15. *FDA Annual Report, 1976*, DHEW, PHS, Washington, D.C., 1977, p. 3.

16. *Cancer Prevention and the Delaney Clause* (Washington, D.C.: Health Research Group, 1977), p. 14. The Nader Summer Project study of the FDA found "a kind of defeatist attitude which permeates every level of the FDA bureaucracy. There is little belief among the agency personnel that the FDA can really make any difference." James Turner, *The Chemical Feast* (New York: Grossman, 1970), pp. 250–251. Other critiques of FDA performance can be found in Samuel Epstein, *The Politics of Cancer* (San Francisco: Sierra Club, 1978), pp. 376–383, and M. M. Silverman and P. R. Lee, *Pills, Profits and Politics* (Berkeley: University of California Press, 1974). Also see chap. 11 in James R. Michael, ed., *Working on the System: A Comprehensive Manual for Citizen Access to Federal Agencies* (New York: Basic Books, 1974). A series of articles on the FDA in the *New York Times* of March 13–15, 1977, attempted to take a middle course, suggesting that underfunding forced the FDA to perform in a manner unsatisfactory to both consumers and industry. Daniel Greenberg has written extensively on FDA internal politics in the *New England Journal of Medicine (NEJM)*. See in particular "FDA: Poor Marks for Its Self-investigation," *NEJM* 294:1465–1466 (1976).

17. Roemer and McKray, *Legal Aspects of Health Policy*, p. 185.

18. The bill is recommended to the states by the Association of Food and Drug Officials of the United States. For the text, see Commerce Clearing House, *Food, Drug, Cosmetic Law Reports* All States, Sec. 10, 100 (1978).

19. See Chapter 4.

20. See Merrill and Hutt, *Food and Drug Law*, pp. 831–865, especially references collected in note 5, pp. 837–838.

21. *Requirements of Laws and Regulations Enforced by the U.S. Food and Drug Administration* (Rockville, Md.: FDA, 1979), p. 1 (HEW pub. No. (FDA) 79-1042).

22. This presentation is oversimplified; several exceptions or additions have been eliminated in order to present the general meaning of each term. For example, pesticides in unprocessed foods are excluded from the definition of food additive.

23. Sec. 201(f).

24. Sec. 201(s).
25. Sec. 201(g)(1). This definition encompasses biological products, including "any virus, therapeutic serum, toxin, antitoxin, vaccine, blood, blood component or derivative, allergenic product, or analogous product." Biological products are closely regulated, with registration and batch testing requirements. See *Requirements of Laws and Regulations Enforced by the U.S. Food and Drug Administration*, pp. 47–49.
26. Sec. 201(h).
27. Sec. 201(i).
28. Not only the scope, but the way in which a product is to be regulated. Is a wrinkle remover a cosmetic or a drug? The answer, which can depend on the way in which the product is marketed, is important because drugs are more closely regulated. See, for example, *United States v. An Article of Drug . . . 47 Shipping Cartons, More or Less . . . "Helene Curtis Magic Secret . . ." Helene Curtis Industries, Inc.*, 331 F.Supp. 912 (DC, Md. 1971).
29. Sec. 301(b).
30. Sec. 301(k).
31. Although the act does not specifically establish a good manufacturing practices standard for unadulterated food, the FDA has established a set of such practices as criteria for maintaining sanitary conditions in food establishments. The FDA has also developed what it calls "defect action levels" for foods, stating the amounts of contamination that will subject a food to enforcement action. These tolerances for filth and decomposition in foods are set on the basis of "no hazard to health."
32. See R. J. Smith, "Institute of Medicine Report Recommends Complete Overhaul of Food Safety Laws," *Science* 203:1221–1224 (1979).
33. The Delaney clause was invoked in 1967 to ban the food additive Flectol H and in 1969 against the additive 2-chloroanaline. In 1977 the FDA was stymied in its attempt to invoke the clause a third time, to ban saccharin, when Congress placed a moratorium on such a step. See "One Hundred Years of Food Protection," pp. 53–58. Also see notes 11 and 12, and Epstein, *Politics of Cancer*, pp. 376–377. There has been a voluminous debate over the value of the Delaney clause. See, for example, Frederick Coulston, ed., *Regulatory Aspects of Carcinogenesis and Food Additives: The Delaney Clause* (New York: Academic Press, 1979). Since 1977 Congress has specifically prohibited the FDA from enforcing the Delaney clause against saccharin. Opponents of the nondiscretionary Delaney provision hope to open it up to political give and take by inserting a qualifying term, "significant risk."
34. Sec. 501.
35. Actually, by the wording of the statute, to the secretary of Health and Human Services. See "Agency" discussion in this chapter.
36. Sec. 505 (b)(1).
37. Sec. 505(d)(s).
38. Sec. 505(e).
39. The drug approval system has been challenged most heatedly by the laetrile controversy. The FDA had moved under Sec. 505 of the act to prohibit the interstate distribution of laetrile because it was a new drug for which a new drug application had been neither submitted nor approved. The FDA's

position was critical because, although twenty-one states had specifically "legalized" laetrile, production and marketing of the substance in a manner that avoided the FDA's interstate commerce authority would be extremely difficult. Laetrile proponents therefore sought to enjoin the FDA from interfering with the interstate shipment and sale of laetrile. Their legal arguments, each of which was ultimately rejected, were as follows:

1. New drug approval is based on evidence of safety and effectiveness. The U.S. Court of Appeals for the Tenth Circuit concluded that "the 'safety' and 'effectiveness' terms used in the statute have no reasonable application to terminally ill cancer patients. . . ." and ordered the FDA to treat laetrile "as if" it had been found safe and effective. In a unanimous decision the U.S. Supreme Court rejected this implied exemption. No such exemption can be found or read into the statute. Moreover, said the Court, to do so could lead to needless suffering and death by "terminal" patients who might actually be helped by legitimate therapy. *United States v. Rutherford,* 544 U.S. 442 (1979).
2. It was also argued that laetrile should be exempt from the premarketing approval process because it was grandfathered under the 1938 act or the 1962 drug amendments. The district court rejected the 1938 claim but accepted the 1962 argument. The court of appeals rejected both grandfather arguments and the Supreme Court refused to intervene. *Rutherford v. United States,* 616 F.2d 455 (1980).
3. Finally, laetrile proponents argued that prohibiting the substance violated their constitutional right to privacy by denying them a free choice of treatment. The court of appeals ruled—the Supreme Court agreeing by refusing to intervene— that "the decision by the patient whether to have a treatment or not is a protected right, but his selection of a particular treatment, or at least a medication, is within the area of governmental interest in protecting public health. The premarketing requirement of the Federal Food, Drug and Cosmetic Act . . . is an exercise of Congressional authority to limit the patient's choice of medication." *Rutherford v. United States,* 616 F.2d 455 (1980), at 457.

The continuing clamor for laetrile legalization—fueled by the immense profits involved, abetted by widespread antidoctor suspicions, and politically orchestrated by the John Birch Society—forced the FDA into authorizing clinical trials of this substance. To do so the agency had to make exceptions to normal scientific and ethical standards, bypassing preliminary animal testing and using in the experimental treatment of human subjects a substance that the scientific community regarded as worthless. The results of these trials to date have merely confirmed the inefficacy of laetrile. See Charles G. Moertel et al., "A Pharmacological and Toxicological Study of Amygdalin," *JAMA* 245:591–594 (1981); Neil M. Ellison et al., "Special Report on Laetrile: The NCI Laetrile Review," *NEJM* 299:549–552 (1978); National Cancer Institute, *A Clinical Trial of Laetrile (Amygdalin) in the Treatment of Advanced Cancer,* March 1981; and James Harvey Young, "Laetrile in Historical Perspective," in Gerald E. Markle and James C. Peterson, eds., *Politics, Science and Cancer: The Laetrile Phenomenon* (Boulder, Colorado: Westview Press, 1980), pp. 11–60.

40. For example, close to 100 pages of a recent 950-page casebook on food and drug law are devoted to labeling. See Merrill and Hutt, *Food and Drug Law,* pp. 134–166, 311–360, 569–575, 642–646.
41. For approximately 275 standardized foods—accounting for 45 percent of

FDA-regulated foods—the agency has established standards of identity, which specify the name of the food product and list mandatory and optional ingredients. The mandatory ingredients need not be listed on the product labels, but any specified optional ingredients used must be. As for nonstandardized foods, all ingredients must be listed, in descending order of prominence. But spices, flavorings, and colorings need not be specifically identified. In addition to ingredients, food labels must include the name of the food (often the "common or usual" name as established by the FDA), the name and place of business of the manufacturer, and an accurate statement of the net amount of food in the package. See *Requirements of Laws and Regulations Enforced by the U.S. Food and Drug Administration*, pp. 10–12. The Fair Packaging and Labeling Act of 1966, 15 U.S.C. Secs. 1451–1461, strengthened FDA authority over labeling of foods, drugs, devices, and cosmetics by making more precise the requirements regarding truthful labeling of net contents. (The act also provided FDA authority to promulgate regulations aimed at the chronic problem of slack-filled, and therefore deceptive, packages, but the agency has not attempted to use this authority).

The most discussed food labeling issue in recent years has been the inability of consumers to determine from current labels which "flavorings," "colorings," and "spices" a product contains. During the Carter administration the FDA, the Department of Agriculture's Food and Consumer Service Office, and the Federal Trade Commission were actively and jointly pursuing regulations that would have required specific rather than generic identification of these ingredients. They were also interested in requiring labeling information regarding sugar, salt, and cholesterol content. At present it seems highly unlikely that any such new requirements will be implemented, with the possible exception of a voluntary salt labeling standard. For more on nutrition labeling and regulation, see Merrill and Hutt, *Food and Drug Law*, pp. 262–293, esp. pp. 265–272 and 290–293.

42. See Merrill and Hutt, *Food and Drug Law*, pp. 311–360. On patient package inserts—a concept the FDA is not likely to pursue vigorously under the current administration—see the references collected in ibid., p. 341.

43. See ibid., pp. 352–354. On earlier developments, see "Developments in the Law: The Federal Food, Drug, and Cosmetic Act," *Harvard Law Review* 67:632–722 (1954), a classic review of the basic 1938 statutory program.

44. See Steven Jonas and David Banta, "Government in the Health Care Delivery System," in Steven Jonas et al., *Health Care Delivery in the United States*, 2d ed. (New York: Springer, 1981), p. 327.

45. 86 Stat. 770 (1972).

46. However, fishery products and milk and milk products fall under FDA jurisdiction.

47. The Food and Drug Administration, in Michael, *Working on the System*, p. 637.

48. Sec. 704. Of course, such congressional authorization cannot override the Fourth Amendment prohibition on unreasonable searches and seizures. See Chapter 5.

49. A description of the consumer complaint process is contained in an FDA consumer memo, *Reporting Problem Products to FDA* (HEW pub. No. (FDA)

80-1066). Also see The Food and Drug Administration, in Michael, *Working on the System,* pp. 639–643.
50. Actually the Justice Department is asked by the FDA to initiate enforcement action. The Justice Department can, but rarely does, refuse.
51. Sec. 302.
52. Peter Barton Hutt, "Philosophy of Regulation under the Federal Food, Drug, and Cosmetic Act. *Food Drug Cosmetic Law Journal* 28:177 (1973). The point is at issue because the federal government, unlike the states, does not have broad constitutional police powers. Federal courts have issued injunctions sought by the FDA ordering product recalls. See, e.g., *United States v. K-N Enterprises, Inc.,* 461 F.Supp. 988 (1978).
53. Sec. 304. This is similar to traditional public health embargo, which is, in effect, a quarantine for goods. See Chapter 5.
54. Sec. 303.
55. *United States v. Park,* 421 U.S. 658 (1975). Also see Sam D. Fine, "The Philosophy of Enforcement," *Food Drug Cosmetic Law Journal* 31:324–332 (1976).
56. Sec. 705(b).
57. Sec. 505.
58. Compare Review Panel on New Drug Regulation, *Interim Reports,* Volume I (Washington, D.C.: Department of Health, Education, and Welfare, May 31, 1977), which found no persuasive support for the "drug lag" scenario, with *FDA Drug Approval—a Lengthy Process that Delays the Availability of Important New Drugs* (Washington, D.C.: General Accounting Office, HRD-80-64, May 28, 1980), which did. Similarly, compare Donald F. Kennedy, "A Calm Look at 'drug lag,'" *JAMA* 239:423–426 (1978), with William M. Wardell, "A Close Inspection of the 'Calm Look,'" *JAMA* 239:2004–2011 (1978). Also see Institute of Medicine, *Pharmaceutical Innovation and the Needs of Developing Countries* (Washington, D.C.: National Academy of Sciences, 1979), and Silverman and Lee, *Pills, Profits and Politics,* pp. 243–250.
59. Sec. 701(e) includes the formal rule-making requirement and enumerates the situations in which it must be used. Although open to all interested parties, participation in such formal hearings is extremely costly, in terms of both time and money, putting interested noncommercial parties, such as consumer or health professional groups, at a distinct disadvantage. The hearing requirement can also be used to effectively delay unwanted regulations. The most famous example of prolonged formal hearings involved the FDA's effort to establish a standard requiring at least 90 percent peanuts in peanut butter—rejecting an 87 percent standard. It took twelve years and 100,000 pages of hearing record before a final standard was promulgated. For a list of articles criticizing the FDA formal rule-making experience, see Merrill and Hutt, *Food and Drug Law,* pp. 895–896. For a general discussion of administrative rule making, see Chapter 3.
60. Sec. 701(a).
61. *Abbott Laboratories v. Gardner,* 387 U.S. 136 (1967), *Weinberger v. Hynson, Wescott and Dunning, Inc.* 412 U.S. 609 (1973); *Ciba Co. v. Weinberger,* 412 U.S. 640 (1973); *Weinberger v. Bentext Pharmaceuticals, Inc.,* 412 U.S. 645 (1973); *USA Pharmaceutical Co. v. Weinberger,* 412 U.S. 655 (1973); *National*

Nutritional Foods Association v. Weinberger, 512 F.2d 688 (1975). Also see Stephen Hull McNamara, "The New Age of FDA Rule-Making," *Food Drug Cosmetic Law Journal* 31:393–403 (1976), and Richard A. Merrill, "FDA and the Effects of Substantive Rules," *Food Drug Cosmetic Law Journal* 35:270–282 (1980).

62. See Robert M. Halperin, "FDA Disclosure of Safety and Effectiveness Data: A Legal and Policy Analysis," *Duke Law Journal* 1979:286–326 (1979). Also see Merrill and Hutt, *Food and Drug Law*, pp. 408, 919–926. The FDA receives 1,500–1,800 FOIA requests each month, most of them from industry. Fewer than 2 percent are denied.

63. See Peter Temin, "The Origin of Compulsory Drug Prescriptions," *Journal of Law and Economics* 22:91–105 (1979). More generally, see Peter Temin, *Taking Your Medicine: Drug Regulation in the United States* (Cambridge, Mass.: Harvard University Press, 1980).

64. See Oakley Ray, *Drugs, Society, and Human Behavior*, 2d ed. (St. Louis: Mosby, 1978), pp. 52–54, and Merrill and Hutt, *Food and Drug Law*, pp. 369–439. Also see William R. Rollins, "What Nurses Should Know about Administering 'New Drugs,'" *Nursing Law and Ethics* 1(6):1–2, 9–11 (June/July 1980). Few over-the-counter (OTC) drugs have been subjected to the new drug approval process, often because they fell under grandfather provisions of the 1938 and 1962 statutes. During the 1970s the FDA expended considerable energy attempting to classify OTC drug ingredients according to whether or not experts in the field: (1) found them to be safe and effective; (2) found them to be unsafe or ineffective; or (3) could make no recommendation because of insufficient data. See Merrill and Hutt, *Food and Drug Law*, pp. 439–461, as well as Roger A. Schultz, "The Changing Philosophy of OTC Review," *Food Drug Cosmetic Law Journal* 35:673–676 (1980). In *Cutler v. Kennedy*, 475 F.Supp. 838 (1979), a federal district court held that the FDA was acting illegally by continuing to allow the marketing of those OTC drugs for which there was insufficient data on safety and effectiveness. In September 1981 the FDA issued final rules (Fed. Reg., September 29, 1981) requiring proof of safety and effectiveness for all OTC drug ingredients as a condition of continued marketing, but allowing marketing during the course of the drug-approval process. At about the same time, the Nader-founded Public Citizen group and the National Council of Senior Citizens filed suit in federal court seeking to compel the FDA to ban immediately all OTC drug ingredients for which evidence of safety and effectiveness was lacking.

One subcategory of drugs, antibiotics, also receives special consideration under the act. Samples of production batches of antibiotics, as well as of insulin and color additives, must be submitted to FDA laboratories to be certified for purity, potency, and safety before being shipped in interstate commerce.

65. See Merrill and Hutt, *Food and Drug Law*, pp. 462–466. In Steven H. Erickson *et al.*, "The Use of Drugs for Unlabeled Indications," *JAMA* 243:1543–1546 (1980), "A chart review of 500 drug uses during a three-month period in a family practice clinic showed that 46 (9.2%) were for indications not included in the Food and Drug Administration-approved

labeling. . . . On no occasion did the chart show that patients were informed that a drug was being prescribed for an unlabeled indication."

There is another issue involved in prescribing, namely the legality of substituting a generically equivalent drug for a drug prescribed by brand name. During the 1950s and 1960s most states amended their antisubstitution laws—which originally were enacted to prevent a generically or chemically different drug from being substituted for the drug prescribed—so that it became illegal to substitute even equivalent drugs for a drug prescribed by brand name. But then in a remarkably quick turnabout, state laws were amended once again to allow generic substitution. In less than nine years, during the 1970s, some forty-five states and the District of Columbia adopted some version of a generic prescribing law, ranging from permissive laws, allowing the pharmacist to substitute unless the prescriber indicates to the contrary, to nearly mandatory laws, requiring the pharmacist to use the lowest price equivalent unless the prescriber indicates to the contrary. Most states also provide a drug formulary of varying degrees of authority, listing drugs that may or may not be substituted (or, as in Massachusetts and New Hampshire, must be substituted). See Note, Jillena A. Warner, "Consumer Protection and Prescription Drugs: The Generic Substitution Laws," *Kentucky Law Journal* 67:384–414 (1978–1979); "Drug Substitution Laws: A State-by-State Overview," *Drug Therapy* 9(12):15–34 (December 1979); and George J. Annas, Leonard H. Glantz, and Barbara F. Katz, *The Rights of Doctors, Nurses, and Allied Health Professionals* (New York: Avon, 1981), pp. 120–123. Also see H. G. Grabowski and J. M. Vernon, "Substitution Laws and Innovation in the Pharmaceutical Industry," *Law and Contemporary Problems* 43:43–66 (1979), and Carl T. DeMarco, *Pharmacy and the Law* (Germantown, Md.: Aspen Systems Corporation, 1975), chap. 4.

66. Thirty percent of all prescriptions are written for drugs that work on the brain. See Ray, *Drugs, Society, and Human Behavior,* p. 12.
67. 35 Stat. 614 (1909) and 38 Stat. 785 (1914). Both repealed 1970. For more on the history of drug abuse law, see Ray, *Drugs, Society, and Human Behavior,* pp. 32–46. Also see R. J. Bonnie and M. R. Sonnenreich, *Legal Aspects of Drug Dependence* (Cleveland, CRC Press, 1975), and R. L. Bogomolny, M. R. Sonnenreich, and A. J. Roccogrand, *A Handbook on the 1970 Federal Drug Act: Shifting the Perspective* (Springfield, Ill.: Charles C. Thomas, 1975).
68. See Ray, *Drugs, Society, and Human Behavior,* p. 35.
69. These approaches apply not only to substance abuse, but to other types of "vice" control efforts. See generally, John Kaplan, "Classification for Legal Control," in Blum et al., *Controlling Drugs* (San Francisco: Jossey-Bass, 1974).
70. *Robinson v. California,* 370 U.S. 660 (1962).
71. *Powell v. Texas,* 392 U.S. 514 (1968). But states can take this step by statute. For example, the state of Illinois has eliminated this crime, its statute also specifying that "no county, municipality, or other political subdivision may adopt or enforce a local law, ordinance, resolution, or rule having the force of law that includes drinking, being a common drunkard, or being found in an intoxicated condition as one of the elements of the offense giving rise to a criminal or civil penalty or sanction." 91½ ILL. STAT. ANN. Sec. 510 et seq. Sec. 518 (1).

72. See *Gorham v. United States*, 339 A.2d 401 (D.C.C.A. 1975).

73. See *State v. Rao*, 370 A.2d 1310 (Conn., 1976).

74. See *Drug Use in America: Problems in Perspective*, The Second Report of the National Commission on Marihuana and Drug Abuse, Washington, D.C., March 1973. The development and expansion of a constitutional right to privacy is discussed in Chapter 18.

75. A 1969 study by the former Bureau of Narcotics and Dangerous Drugs found that 92 percent of all stimulant and depressant drugs on the illicit market had been diverted from legitimate manufacturers. See Bogomolny et al., *On the 1970 Federal Drug Act*, p. 10.

76. 79 Stat. 226 (1965).

77. 84 Stat. 1242 (1970). See William W. Vodra, "Summary of the Controlled Substances Act," *Drug Enforcement* 2:2–7 (Spring 1975). Also see Annas, *et al., The Rights of Doctors*, pp. 114–120.

78. The Controlled Substances Act represents an abandonment of the long-favored tax mechanism, relying instead on direct proscription.

79. Ray, *Drugs, Society, and Human Behavior*, p. 40.

80. At least one observer has argued that this effort has succeeded only in shifting drug users to illegally manufactured drugs, not in decreasing overall drug abuse. See ibid., p. 42. Also see J. C. Anthony, "The Effect of Federal Drug Law on the Incidence of Drug Abuse," *Journal of Health Politics, Policy and Law* 4:87–108 (1979), and Richard C. Schroeder, *The Politics of Drug Abuse*, 2d ed. (Washington, D.C.: Congressional Quarterly Press, 1980), pp. 143–150.

81. See "Rockefeller Drug Law: After 6 Years, Officials Question Its Effectiveness—Carey and Legislative Chiefs Planning Changes," *New York Times*, 14 May 1979, p. B2.

82. See, for example, Tom Christoffel and Sandra T. Stein, "Using the Law to Protect Health: The Frustrating Case of Smoking," *Medicolegal News* 7(4):5–9, 20, 28 (Winter 1979).

83. In addition to the various books and articles on drug abuse control cited above, the reader may wish to consult the following: Rufus King, "'The American System': Legal Sanctions to Repress Drug Abuse," in, J. A. Inciardi and C. D. Chambers, eds., *Drugs and the Criminal Justice System* (Beverly Hills: Sage, 1974), pp. 17–37; Note, "Criminal Law—Recent Trends in State Drug Legislation," *Annual Survey of American Law* 1976:343–357 (1976); C. D. Chambers, J. A. Inciardi, and H. A. Siegel, *Chemical Coping: A Report on Legal Drug Use in the United States* (New York: Spectrum, 1975); Harford et al., "Effects of Legal Pressure on Prognosis for Treatment of Drug Dependence," *American Journal of Psychiatry* 133:1399–1404 (1976); J. Tyrone Gibson, *Medication Law and Behavior* (New York: John Wiley, 1976); Norman E. Zinberg and Risa G. Dickstein, "Prescribing Controlled Substances: Physicians' Rights and Responsibilities," in William J. Curran, A. Louis McGarry, and Charles S. Petty, *Modern Legal Medicine, Psychiatry, and Forensic Science* (Philadelphia: F. A. Davis, 1980), pp. 905–925.

84. While practitioners are required to report all prescriptions for controlled substances, substance abuse treatment records remain confidential. HEW issued specific guidelines on the confidentiality of alcohol and drug abuse patient records. See 40 Fed. Reg. 27802–27821 (July 1, 1975).

12 | Law and the Elimination of Health Hazards

*How can the passengers in a steamboat foresee the bursting
of a boiler? Or those on a railroad the neglect of a switch?
Or those in a street the falling down of a new wall from bad
mortar . . . ? The proverb says that a burned child will dread
the fire. But of what use of safety is its dread, after it has
burned to death? We dislike the modern system of free trade,
which leaves life and health and comfort and convenience of
consumers to the interest of suppliers, and should prefer a
return to the old system, which rendered suppliers responsible
to consumers. The world is not governed enough for the
benefit of the many, though governed too much in other
countries, too little in our own, for the benefit of the few.*
—*Philadelphia Public Ledger*[1]
August 1852

HEALTH AND LEGAL PROFESSIONALS generally share the conviction that
prevention of problems is preferable to dealing with them after they
develop. Unfortunately, when it comes to health, the principle is honored primarily in the breach.

Most health problems are preventable. A preventive approach to
health care is concerned with encouraging life-styles that may avoid
illness, detecting disease at an early stage, and reducing environmental
hazards that damage health. It is the last objective that is most likely to
involve the use of law. William Haddon, Jr., a physician, has organized
the standard measures for reducing health damage caused by environmental hazards into ten basic strategies:[2]

1. Prevent the creation of the hazard in the first place; e.g., prevent
   production of plutonium, thalidomide, LSD.
2. Reduce the amount of the hazard brought into being; e.g., reduce speed of vehicles, lead content of paint, mining of asbestos;
   make less beverage alcohol.
3. Prevent the release of the hazard that already exists; e.g., pas-

223

teurizing milk, bolting or timbering mine roofs, impounding nuclear wastes.

4. Modify the rate or spatial distribution of release of the hazard from its source; e.g., brakes, shutoff valves, reactor control rods.
5. Separate, in time or space, the hazard and that which is to be protected; e.g., isolation of persons with communicable diseases; walkways over or around hazards; evacuation.
6. Separate the hazard and that which is to be protected by interposition of a material barrier; e.g., surgeon's gloves, containment structures, childproof poison-container closures.
7. Modify relevant basic qualities of the hazard; e.g., altering pharmacological agents to reduce side effects, using breakaway roadside poles, making crib slat spacing too narrow to strangle a child.
8. Make what is to be protected more resistant to damage from the hazard; e.g., immunization, making structures more fire- and earthquake-resistant, giving salt to workers under thermal stress.
9. Begin to counter the damage already done by the environmental hazard; e.g., rescuing the shipwrecked, reattaching severed limbs, extricating trapped miners.
10. Stabilize, repair, and rehabilitate the object of the damage; e.g., posttraumatic cosmetic surgery, physical rehabilitation, rebuilding after fires and earthquakes.

One of the most notable things about this list of prevention strategies is that most of the called-for actions require the use of law. Earlier chapters dealt with the authority exercised by local, state, and federal governments to protect and promote the public's health, and various legal and regulatory measures adopted toward that end. This chapter will explain other legal avenues that are, or can be, employed to prevent or reduce environmental pollution and accidents and to promote healthy life-styles. Although the legal authority for government intervention in these areas is generally clear and straightforward, there is considerable controversy about when and to what degree government intervention to protect health is warranted, particularly in situations where scientific evidence of risk and benefit remains equivocal.

Environmental Law

Environmental influences have profound effects on health and disease. Cancer—which has been termed "the plague of the twentieth century"—is estimated to be 60 to 90 percent attributable to environmental causes,[3] and heart disease, trauma, and other leading causes of death and disability are also strongly environmentally based.

"Environment" is an ambiguous term. The word can be used globally to refer to "all the conditions, circumstances, and influences surrounding and affecting the development of an organism or group of organisms," or more narrowly to mean air, water, and land. Environmental law is concerned with the narrower use of the term.

The major roots of environmental law are found in the common law of nuisance. Traditionally, there have been two types of nuisance suits: private and public. Private nuisance relates specifically to a substantial and unreasonable interference with an individual's use and enjoyment of his or her land, as, for example, when sewage flows from one person's property to that of a neighbor. Public nuisance involves unreasonable interference with a right common to the general public. Originally the concept of public nuisance was entirely a creature of common law; but today state statutes define certain situations as public nuisances, and anyone affected by the nuisance, including public officials, can initiate a public nuisance lawsuit. In recent years, certain of the legal requirements that previously narrowed the impact of such suits have disappeared. As a result, the public nuisance suit has become a useful tool in dealing with environmental pollution.

The courts will not treat just anything that bothers someone or a group of extremely sensitive individuals, as a nuisance. However, evidence that some ongoing activity impairs or is likely to impair human health will be persuasive to a court. In a leading text on environmental law, William H. Rodgers, Jr. outlines four categories of remedies applied by courts in nuisance cases, including damages, land use accommodations, technological accommodations, and operational controls.

> The damages remedy obviously is aimed at making whole the plaintiff's losses by a money judgment. The land use remedy recognizes a fundamental incompatibility of the conflicting uses and anticipates that one or the other of the parties should relocate; typically, defendant either is forced to shut down or buy out the plaintiff. The technological remedy rejects a land use adjustment in favor of an approach normally requiring defendant to install the best control technology and operate it to the maximum efficiency. It is, in a sense, a technological alternative to a land use decision. The fourth remedy, that of operational controls, interferes least with defendant's enterprise. It usually requires no costly capital investments in technological solutions. It requires only that the actor conduct his enterprise with more skill or care or in a different manner or at a different time to minimize the harm.[4]

While the private lawsuit has long been a useful tool in protecting the environment from contamination, government is in the best position to develop environmental standards, determine compliance with those standards, and take action against violators. In many cases, however, government itself is guilty of environmental pollution, and other cases are complicated by government subsidies to the pollutor, or by government regulations that affect the pollutor's nonenvironmental operations.

Government officials can initiate public nuisance legal actions in behalf of the affected public. But in recent years Congress and the state legislatures have provided stronger statutory support for governmental environmental control efforts, establishing standards that tell potential pollutors in advance what they may and may not do. And because certain kinds of pollution—notably contamination of air and water—do not stop at state boundaries, the federal role in pollution control has grown dramatically over the past decade, as Congress increasingly shifted the responsibility for standard setting and oversight from the states to the federal government and moved from a policy of encouraging and assisting to one of mandating pollution control efforts. The major federal environmental protection laws include the National Environmental Policy Act, the Clean Air Act, the Clean Water Act, the Resource Conservation and Recovery Act, and the Toxic Substances Control Act.

The National Environmental Policy Act of 1969 (NEPA)[5] was intended as a mechanism for integrating environmental considerations into major federal decisions that might affect the environment. The statute declares "a national policy which will encourage productive and enjoyable harmony between man and his environment; to promote efforts which will prevent or eliminate damage to the environment and biosphere and stimulate the health and welfare of man. . . ." NEPA has been described as

> a seminal enactment that introduces federal courts to environmental questions comprehensively for the first time, expands the scope of judicial review of administrative action, injects new discipline and values into administrative decision-making, and strengthens the hand of the Congress in overseeing agency actions with adverse environmental effects. While NEPA can be credited with all these things and more, so too it can be written off as "a paper tiger."[6]

The reason for this widely divergent picture lies in the fact that, aside from its mandate to the federal government to prepare environmental impact statements with regard to its own proposed operations, NEPA is more of a declaration of objectives than a standard of enforcement.[7]

The environmental impact statement provision requires every agency that proposes legislation or "other major federal actions significantly affecting the quality of the human environment" to include with the proposal a detailed statement of

—the environmental impact of the proposed action,
—any adverse environmental effect which cannot be avoided should the proposal be implemented,
—alternatives to the proposed action,

—the relationship between local short-term uses of man's environ-ment and the maintenance and enhancement of long-term productivity,

—any irreversible and irretrievable commitments of resources which would be involved in the proposed action should it be implemented.[8]

NEPA also created a Council on Environmental Quality, which pre-pares an annual "Environmental Quality Report" for submission to Con-gress by the president. Although the task of the council is merely to gather information on the state of the environment—including an ap-praisal of the impact of various federal programs and activities—it had developed into an effective voice for the protection of the environment during the 1970s.

The Clean Air Act[9] is perhaps the leading piece of federal environ-mental legislation, particularly since it was strengthened by a series of amendments in 1970. The amendments signaled a change in federal air pollution control legislation, shifting from a policy of encouraging and assisting state pollution control efforts while allowing the states "wide latitude to determine both the air quality standards they would meet and the period of time in which they would do so . . ."[10] to setting federal air quality standards, which the states were required to meet within a spec-ified period of time. At the same time, states were allowed—in fact required—to develop their own plans for implementing the new air standards. The basic approach, then, consists of federal goal setting and state implementation, with federal backup and overview.

Under the 1970 amendments, the U.S. Environmental Protection Agency (EPA) was empowered to develop national ambient air quality standards for dispersed pollutants and to list those air pollutants that have a significant adverse effect on public health (primary standards) and welfare (secondary standards), along with the permissible acceptable level in the atmosphere. The standards are expressed in terms of goals for the air itself, not as limits on the sources of emissions, and are based on medical judgments regarding the limits necessary—with an adequate margin of safety—to prevent injury to the most sensitive individuals (such as those with bronchial asthma and emphysema).[11]

The amendments impose an obligation on the states to develop im-plementation plans to translate the air standards into reality. States must establish specific emission limitations for individual stationary sources of pollution, establish timetables and mechanisms for compliance, monitor-ing, and enforcement, and submit their plans to the EPA for approval. If a state fails to develop an acceptable plan within a fixed period of time, EPA is mandated to initiate its own air-quality control program in that state.

Although the states normally develop and enforce emission standards for existing sources of pollution, the federal government also sets specific emission standards in three important areas. The EPA develops new source performance standards aimed at requiring, where feasible, the best pollution control technology available for stationary sources of pollution, such as copper smelters, coal preparation plants, or superphosphoric acid plants and the like, which states must use in checking all new pollution sources. The EPA is also authorized to establish emission standards for "hazardous air pollutants."[12] Authority under the hazardous-air-pollutant provision is very broad; public-health considerations alone—without regard to costs or control feasibility—can be used to set an emission standard as low as zero. But this provision has been invoked, only with regard to beryllium, mercury, asbestos, and vinyl chloride. Motor vehicle pollution is dealt with under the amendments through congressionally established exhaust emission standards for new cars,[13] federal regulation of fuel additives, and by requiring states to develop transportation-control plans.

The Clean Air Act amendments also provide that the levels of air pollution in those sections of the country where the air is cleaner than the federal standards mandate may only be increased by a specified amount annually.

The Clean Water Act amendments of 1977 modified, but preserved, the Federal Water Pollution Control Act, adopted by Congress in 1972, which has been described as "one of the most complex and extensive pieces of environmental legislation ever passed, and perhaps the most difficult to administer."[14]

The Clean Water Act calls for state-set (but EPA approved) water quality standards and implementation plans, based on nationwide limitations set by the EPA in three areas. The EPA is empowered to establish technology-based effluent limitations for major "point sources"[15] of water pollution, requiring "application of the best available technology economically achievable" by the mid-1980s. In addition, a national permit system regulates all pollutant discharges into navigable waters. EPA may delegate management of the permit system to the states. Finally, EPA also has responsibility for developing effluent limitations for new sources of discharge and for existing and new sources of toxic pollutants. In a few instances—notably DDT and aldrin/dieldrin—zero effluent limits have been established. Prior to the current federal administration, considerable federal funding was provided under the Clean Water Act for the construction of improved municipal waste treatment facilities.

Many people argue that dealing with point sources of water pollution is not enough, because runoff from agricultural lands constitutes one of the most important sources of water pollution. Such nonpoint sources have only recently begun to receive attention under the Clean Water Act.[16] A related problem, pollution of groundwater, is not covered by the act; but the Safe Drinking Water Act of 1974 protects underground sources of drinking water from contamination by underground injection and regulates contamination levels in public drinking-water systems.

The Resource Conservation and Recovery Act of 1976 deals with solid wastes and is one of several recent federal laws that confront the major environmental pollution threat posed by hazardous and toxic wastes. Until the mid-1960s the federal role in this area was very limited. The Solid Waste Disposal Act of 1965[17] called for research into proper disposal methods and provided funding of demonstration projects and grants to the states to cover the costs of surveying solid-waste disposal practices and problems. Five years later Congress passed the Resources Recovery Act of 1970,[18] which shifted the emphasis from disposal to recovery of resources and energy from solid waste; however, little was done to implement the new act's provisions.

In 1976 Congress passed the Resource Conservation and Recovery Act,[19] the first real federal regulatory measure involving solid waste. The act limits the open dumping of solid or hazardous waste and authorizes the EPA to establish minimum criteria for such dumping. A permit system is established to control wastes considered hazardous from their point of origin to the point of disposal, and a system of performance standards governs owners and operators of hazardous waste treatment, storage, and disposal facilities. EPA can issue compliance orders and take action against imminent hazards. At the same time, the states are given broad potential authority; the act permits EPA-approved state control programs to take over most of the direct federal role and provides grants to help the states establish proper waste disposal programs. But six years after enactment of the act, regulations have not yet been fully promulgated.

The Toxic Substances Control Act of 1976 has been called "potentially the most important single preventive public health measure of the century,"[20] and marks congressional recognition of the strong association between cancer and environmental contaminants and its effort to exercise some control over the more than 44,000 chemical substances in commercial use in the United States. Although "toxic substances" is used in the title, the phrase does not appear anywhere else in the act. Basically the statute is designed to keep track of all commercial chemicals in use or about to be put in use, identifying and controlling those that present an unreasonable risk of harm to human health and the environment.[21]

The Toxic Substances Control Act (TSCA) was aimed at severe health and environmental threats typified by polychlorinated biphenyls (PCBs), fluorocarbons, and vinyl chloride, but Congress chose not to adopt a preclearance regulatory scheme of the sort applied to pharmaceuticals and pesticides, favoring instead a system that puts the burden of identification and restriction on government. The act includes five major requirements:

1. Inventory.   As a first step EPA has collected information from chemical manufacturers, importers, and processors, compiling "the nation's most comprehensive inventory of existing chemical substances in U.S. commerce." Substances on the Initial and Revised Chemical Substances Inventory, although subject to regulation under the act, will not be subject to the premarket notification requirement applicable to new substances. Pesticides, tobacco, drugs, cosmetics, food, and food additives (as well as firearms and ammunition) are completely exempted from coverage under the act.

2. Identify.   The act requires the EPA to identify, among the existing chemical substances in the inventory, those that may present an unreasonable risk to human health or the environment or for which it is known that there is substantial human exposure or environmental release. Such substances must be tested by, and at the expense of, the relevant manufacturers and processors.[22]

3. Control.   If EPA determines that manufacture, importing, processing, distribution, use, or disposal of a chemical substance "presents or will present an unreasonable risk of injury to health or the environment," it may apply a broad range of controls: "outright prohibitions against manufacture, processing or distribution of the product, bans against manufacture for a particular use, limitation on amounts that may be manufactured for a particular use, restrictions on labeling, monitoring and testing, commercial use, disposal, warnings, manufacturing quality controls and the like."[23] The only class of chemicals that has been subjected to actual banning under the act has been PCBs. And even with PCBs, although their manufacture has been substantially restricted, their use continues to be widespread under exempted categories.

4. Review.   Under a premarketing notification program that began in 1979, manufacturers and importers of new chemical substances must notify EPA at least ninety days before manufacturering or importing the new chemical and provide information on the substance, including any test data on health and environmental effects within the submitter's possession. The same notification requirement applies to significant new uses of chemical substances in the inventory. Commercial use of the substance may begin after ninety days unless the EPA moves to prohibit or limit its use, either indefinitely or pending acquisition of additional data.

5. Record Keeping. Manufacturers, processors, and distributors of chemical substances are required to keep records of "significant adverse reactions" to health and the environment which may have been caused by a chemical substance.[24] In addition, EPA must be apprised of any known or reasonably ascertainable study revealing "any effect of a chemical substance or mixture on health or the environment or on both, including underlying data and epidemiological studies, studies of occupational exposure to a chemical substance or mixture, toxicological, clinical, and ecological studies of a chemical substance or mixture, and any test performed pursuant to the Act." And health and safety information submitted under the act is specifically exempted from trade secret protection under the Freedom of Information Act, and is subject to public disclosure.

Implementation of TSCA has always been poorly funded, even relative to other environmental programs, and a General Accounting Office (GAO) report issued late in 1980 concluded that four years after TSCA was passed "neither the public nor the environment are much better protected." The GAO report stated that the EPA had been slow in collecting information on new chemical substances and had given a low priority to control of existing chemical substances.[25] On the same day this report was sent to Congress, the U.S. Court of Appeals for the District of Columbia ordered the EPA rapidly to strengthen its mandated rules for controlling PCBs. The court judged the existing rules to be ineffective: of the PCB-containing substances in use at the time TSCA was enacted, 99 percent were still in use four years later.[26] Little seems to have altered the assessment published in *Science* early in 1979:

> Despite a panoply of laws intended to protect society from hazardous chemicals, the regulatory road from discovery of a hazard to its control remains rough. Bureaucratic inertia and delay are permanent features of the process; pressure from affected industries is constantly applied; and statutes are often unworkable from the start. As a result, prompt regulatory action is virtually nonexistent, and when action does occur, it is usually at the prodding of outside citizen groups.[27]

Given the current federal administration's hostility to such regulatory programs, it seems unlikely that the toxic substances control picture will improve in the near future.

Many other federal environmental protection laws exist. One of the most critical is the Federal Environmental Pesticide Control Act of 1972, which amended the Federal Insecticide, Fungicide, and Rodenticide Act of 1947 to require a premarketing registration system for pesticides, similar to the FDA's drug-approval system.[28] The Atomic Energy Act regulates the processing, utilization, and distribution of nuclear materials. The Marine Protection, Research, and Sanctuaries Act of 1972 is concerned with ocean dumping. The Ports and Waterways Safety Act of 1972 is designed to prevent or mitigate damage from oil spills. The Hazardous Materials Transportation Act and related laws regulate the safe transportation in interstate commerce of hazardous materials. And the much ignored Noise Control Act of 1972 regulates new products that are "major sources of noise."[29]

Other Environmental Law Issues

With the increase in the number and complexity of environmental statutes a new area of environmentally related administrative law has evolved, the two most important aspects of which concern the scope of judicial review and standing to bring suit under environmental statutes.

Scope of Judicial Review. The EPA's major task is to reduce the risk of harm by applying its own expertise and the applicable environmental statutes to prevent conditions that could endanger the public health.[30] Since those statutes are broad and general, the agency has considerable discretion. However, the courts will invalidate EPA decisions they deem contrary to statute or in violation of required procedural rules, and although they have traditionally hesitated to review factual determinations, they are increasingly unwilling to defer automatically to agency expertise. In many cases the result has been to force the agency into a *more* protective stance.

A 1971 case, *Citizens to Preserve Overton Park, Inc. v. Volpe*,[31] challenged the administrative propriety of approval by the secretary of Transportation of interstate highway construction through a public park without full consideration of alternative routes. In reaching its decision, the U.S. Supreme Court called upon reviewing courts to engage in "substantial inquiry" into the procedural fairness, reasonableness, and good faith of agency decisions, including discretionary decisions. The Court explained:

> To make this finding the court must consider whether the decision was based on a consideration of the relevant factors and whether there has been a clear error of judgment. . . . Although this inquiry into the facts is to be searching and careful, the ultimate standard of review is a narrow one. The court is not empowered to substitute its judgment for that of the agency.

What is more, as one federal appellate court has observed:

> The more technical the case, the more intensive must be the court's effort to understand the evidence. . . . The immersion in the evidence is designed *solely* to enable the court to determine whether the agency decision was rational and based on consideration of the relevant factors. . . . It is settled that we must affirm decisions with which we disagree so long as this test is met. . . .[32]

The difficulty with even the limited review needed to ascertain whether formal agency decisions are supported by substantial evidence is the "uncertain" nature of the "facts," especially those involving effects on health. In *Ethyl Corp. v. Environmental Protection Agency,* a challenge to the EPA's decision to limit the lead content of leaded gasoline to an eventual average of 0.5 grams per gallon, the District of Columbia Circuit Court of Appeals noted:

> Even scientific "facts" are not certain, but only theories with high probabilities of validity. Scientists typically speak not of certainty, but of probability; they are trained to act on probabilities that statistically constitute "certainties." *See generally* T. KUHN, THE STRUCTURE OF SCIENTIFIC REVOLUTIONS. While awaiting such statistical certainty may constitute the typical modes of scientific behavior, its appropriateness is questionable in environmental medicine, where regulators seek to prevent harm that often cannot be labeled "certain" until after it occurs. . . .[33]

One member of this same court has noted elsewhere that the question goes beyond that of simply technical uncertainty; that "we are all becoming increasingly conscious of the extent to which many supposedly scientific or technical decisions involve painful choices, and pose difficult policy problems."[34]

Lawyers like finality and certainty; in many areas of law, courts require clear and convincing evidence, if not proof beyond a reasonable doubt. If the same standard were applied to environmental matters, the EPA would be required to prove that harm had occurred, or at least that its occurrence was quite likely, and the harm would have to be quantifiable. Obviously, such a standard would make it virtually impossible to deal with new or newly perceived health threats.

An alternative approach is to assess risk on the basis of reasonable conclusions rather than conclusive facts, and to demand "adequate reasons and explanations, but not 'findings' of the sort familiar from the world of adjudication."[35] A leading judicial discussion of this problem points out:

> Danger . . . is set not by a fixed probability of harm, but rather is composed of reciprocal elements of risk and harm, or probability and severity. . . . That is to say, the public health may properly be found endangered both by a lesser risk of a greater harm and by a greater risk of a lesser harm. Danger depends upon the relation between the risk and harm presented by each case, and cannot legitimately be pegged to "probable" harm, regardless of whether that harm be great or small. . . .[36]

As was observed in the Ethyl Corporation decision:

> Questions involving the environment are particularly prone to uncertainty. Technological man has altered his world in ways never before experienced or anticipated. The health effects of such alterations are often unknown, sometimes unknowable. While a concerned Congress has passed legislation providing for protection of the public health against gross environmental

modifications, the regulators entrusted with the enforcement of such laws have not thereby been endowed with a prescience that removes all doubt from their decision-making. Rather, speculation, conflicts in evidence, and theoretical extrapolation typify their every action. How else can they act, given a mandate to protect the public health but only a slight or nonexistent data base upon which to draw?

Thus, instead of holding the EPA to the impossible standard of certainty the courts have imposed upon it the burden to "justify the reliability of its methodology, to produce all supporting documentation necessary to an understanding of what the agency did, to explain fully the benefits expected from the administrative action, and to come forward with relevant evidence on alternatives (including the alternative of taking no action)."[37]

Two suggestions have been made as to how the courts might more effectively handle highly technical cases of the sort common to health prevention regulation. One has been to allow judges to appoint scientific aides in much the same way they now appoint and make use of law clerks. The other is to establish a specialized "science court." Both suggestions involve a limited abdication of responsibility and control by the judicial system, and neither has received substantial support.[38]

Standing To Sue.   Courts do not review EPA actions and decisions on their own initiative; someone must bring a lawsuit. In some instances an alleged polluter may challenge an EPA action in court, in others, the agency itself may ask a court to enforce the law against a violator. But can ordinary citizens—the apparent beneficiaries of a particular law— challenge EPA actions or inaction that they deem incompatible with that law's basic purpose?

Before 1970 the critical question was whether such citizens had enough of an interest in the matter to seek judicial action, and the answer was primarily based on the Administrative Procedure Act, which provides that "a person suffering legal wrong because of agency action, or adversely affected or aggrieved by agency action within the meaning of a relevant statute, is entitled to judicial review thereof."[39] The courts were often very narrow in their recognition of a legal wrong or adverse effect, and a general interest shared by many or all citizens would not, in many instances, have been enough to provide legal standing. The U.S. Supreme Court, however, in an important 1970 decision,[40] established a two-part test for determining the adequacy of standing to sue: First, that the complainant seeking standing be able to allege "injury in fact, economic or otherwise"; and second, that "the interest sought to be protected by the complainant is arguably within the zone of interests to be protected or regulated by the statute or constitutional guarantee in question." These tests have been broadly interpreted; the judicial guideline, simply stated, is that "one who is hurt by governmental action has standing to challenge it."[41]

The Clean Air, Clean Water, Toxic Substances Control, Safe Drinking Water, and Resource Conservation and Recovery acts contain "citizen suit" provisions that allow concerned individuals and groups, *without showing personal harm,* to sue any alleged violator of statutory standards and to sue the EPA for failing to carry out nondiscretionary duties under the various acts. The Clean Air Act, for example, provides that "any person," that is, an individual, group, corporation, etc., may bring such an enforcement lawsuit in the federal courts without having to meet the two tests for standing discussed above and without needing to meet the jurisdictional amount requirement of most federal civil suits. Moreover, the court may award the costs of attorney and expert witness fees in such litigation to successful plaintiffs. Before iniating such a suit, however, the potential plaintiff must give the EPA and relevant state authorities sixty days' notice, allowing them to initiate enforcement action. But because citizen groups rarely can muster legal and technical resources comparable to those of polluting corporations, and because EPA can be sued only for inaction—not inappropriate action—"citizen suit provisions have thus far proved relatively unsuccessful in stimulating private enforcement actions."[42]

State Environmental Action. Citizen suits and liberal rules on standing simply allow the courts to intervene more readily to make certain Congress's dictates are properly implemented. But where Congress has not legislated, the focus must shift back to state law and law enforcement. In addition to the common law governing nuisance, many states have adopted extensive environmental-protection legislation, sometimes to meet the provisions of federal law, sometimes because federal law did not go far enough. In many of the federal environmental-protection statutes Congress has specifically provided that state pollution-control laws are *not* precluded (preempted) as long as they are more stringent.[43] But Congress need not allow such parallel regulation; it could prohibit stricter state controls. The potential for conflict here may become increasingly important as public pressure moves some states to prohibit the very nuclear power plants (and waste disposal sites) that the Federal Nuclear Regulatory Commission regulates.[44]

It is only realistic to recognize that pollution-generated costs often surpass the resources that an individual state can bring to bear on a problem, as for example in the case of the Love Canal toxic waste problem in New York.[45] The Comprehensive Environmental Response, Compensation, and Liability Act of 1980[46] created a $1.6 billion "superfund" to finance federal and/or state cleanup of hazardous waste disposal sites and chemical spills in situations where the party responsible for the toxic threat is unwilling or unable to do so promptly. The super-fund has been criticized as being inadequate, given the magnitude of the problem, and as severely limited by its failure to provide strict liability for harm. Congress rejected proposals to clear away some of the legal obstacles currently facing individuals who sue chemical companies and others for harm caused by toxic waste contamination.[47]

Consumer Product Safety Commission

In today's highly industrialized, consumption-oriented society, poorly designed or poorly made consumer products present a serious risk of death, injury, or serious illness to large numbers of people. Like toxic wastes, this hazard is hard to control once it is released; but it is possible to take preventive action before the hazard is even created.

In 1969 the Department of Health, Education and Welfare estimated that household accidents, most of them involving unsafe consumer products, resulted annually in 30,000 deaths, 110,000 permanently dis-abling injuries, and 20,000,000 injuries serious enough to require medi-cal treatment. According to the congressionally authorized National Commission on Product Safety, some 20 percent of these accidents might have been prevented by mandatory consumer product safety stan-dards. It was in response to these data that Congress, acting under its commerce power, enacted the Consumer Product Safety Act of 1972.[48]

The act created the Consumer Product Safety Commission (CPSC), an independent regulatory commission with authority to administer sev-eral existing safety laws (the Federal Hazardous Substances Act, Poison Prevention Packaging Act, and Flammable Fabrics Act)[49] and to regu-late many additional hazards. The commission was authorized to collect and disseminate data on product hazards and resulting injuries, and to establish and enforce product safety standards. "Consumer product" was broadly defined to include any article produced or distributed for sale for a consumer's personal use, consumption, or enjoyment, in or around a household or school, in recreation, or otherwise. At least ten thousand products are so defined. Specifically excluded from commis-sion jurisdiction are products already regulated by other federal agen-cies, such as food, drugs, cosmetics, medical devices, motor vehicles, aircraft, and boats. Tobacco products, firearms, meat, poultry, and eggs are also specifically exempted.

The CPSC derives its hazard information from several sources, in-cluding the National Electronic Injury Surveillance System, which gathers injury information from participating hospital emergency de-partments. The commission may also conduct its own consumer product tests and receive information directly from consumers. Moreover, any interested person may formally petition the commission to develop a new safety standard or a rule banning a particular product. The commission cannot, however, require manufacturer-registration or notification concerning their products, as required in the production of pesticides and toxic substances.

In establishing standards, the CPSC follows a unique procedure, inviting business, consumer, professional, and academic groups to submit an existing nongovernmental standard or to offer to develop a new one for commission consideration. These outside standard developers must follow a designated procedure aimed at affording input from other interested groups. But because "a developer's resources must be sufficient to enable it to complete its task within a stipulated period of time, consumer groups find themselves at a distinct competitive disadvantage in relation to entities which are affiliated with private industry."[50]

The commission also has a broad range of enforcement options, ranging from voluntary notification compaigns to court-ordered product bans, and products that present such "an unreasonable risk of injury" that no safety standard is feasible, may be removed from the marketplace. But to invoke its regulatory authority the CPSC must prove that the existing hazard cannot be adequately dealt with by labeling or packaging changes. The commission can require a manufacturer to notify consumers and distributors of a hazard, to repair or replace the product, and/or to refund the purchase price. The act also permits consumers to initiate personal-injury suits in federal court where a knowing violation of a safety rule is involved. After a standard is developed, products that do not meet that standard may not be introduced into interstate commerce.

The commission's notable successes include regulation of crib design, which has reduced crib injuries by 44 percent and deaths by 33 percent since 1974, and poison prevention packaging rules, which have reduced the accidental ingestion of aspirin by children by roughly 50 percent since 1970.[51] However, Epstein criticizes both the statute and the Commission for not going far enough. He argues that the act

> is anachronistic in shifting the burden of proof from manufacturer to the government, which must prove hazard before it can regulate. These statutory limitations aside, the commission has not been an aggressive regulator. . . . In December, 1977, the General Accounting Office issued a report criticizing the commission for dragging its feet in developing and issuing safety standards, setting priorities, and for keeping inadequate records on product-related injuries.[52]

In addition to federal regulation, consumer product safety is affected by product liability lawsuits. Health-related questions often play a crucial role in this increasingly significant and complex area of private litigation, as, for example, DES and toxic shock syndrome lawsuits.[53]

Motor Vehicle Safety

In an article analyzing the incidence and economic costs of cancer, motor vehicle injuries, coronary heart disease, and stroke, published in the December 1980 *American Journal of Public Health,* motor vehicle injuries were cited as first in total numbers and second only to cancer in total estimated costs.[54] Motor vehicle deaths and injuries are also highly preventable.

The traditional approach to traffic safety, long followed by government, private safety organizations, and the automobile industry, concentrated on driver behavior and highway design. But in the late 1960s a series of new federal highway and motor vehicle safety laws focused attention on the safety of the vehicles themselves. The National Highway Traffic Safety Administration (NHTSA), since 1970 a subcabinet agency directly responsible to the secretary of Transportation, followed a course during the 1970s that increasingly shifted its focus toward automobile design safety standards.

Under the National Traffic and Motor Vehicle Safety Act, NHTSA is mandated to establish safety standards for new cars and authorized to issue used car and tire quality standards. Other motor vehicles, such as motorcycles, are covered as well. The act also requires auto companies to notify owners of safety defects.[55] The Highway Safety Act requires all states to adopt comprehensive highway safety programs and gives NHTSA the authority to develop uniform highway safety standards covering traffic laws, highway design and marking, state accident record systems, and the like.

The states also may act under their own police power to help reduce motor vehicle deaths and injuries, including the promulgation of traffic laws and the licensing of drivers. More recently, the federal government has played a dominant role in prompting state adoption of vehicle inspection programs, motorcycle helmet laws, and the 55 mph speed limit. Four areas of state intervention—drinking drivers, child restraint, seat belts, and helmet laws—have been the subject of discussion and legislation.

Drinking Drivers. Over half the fatal crashes in the United States involve a driver who has been drinking heavily. All fifty states have relatively stringent drinking-driving laws on the books, defining the drinking-and-driving offense in terms of blood-alcohol levels. In fourteen states exceeding this level is an automatic violation of the law; in the thirty-six remaining states, exceeding the level creates a rebuttable presumption of alcohol-impaired driving.

Recent studies have shown that it is the likelihood of being caught and convicted, not the severity of the punishment, that can make such laws effective. Unfortunately, drinking-driving laws have not proved very effective anywhere in the world, primarily because rigorous enforcement with certain punishment is never sustained.[56]

Child Restraints. Automobile accidents are the leading cause of death for children over one year old. It has been estimated that child restraints could reduce passenger deaths by over 90 percent (and injuries by 70 percent); but less than 10 percent of child auto passengers ride in child restraints—and in most cases the restraints are not properly used.[57]

Several states have considered—thirteen have passed—legislation making child-restraint use mandatory. The first to pass such a law was Tennessee, and it was the state chapter of the American Academy of Pediatrics that helped win its adoption. The law requires that all children under four ride in a federally approved and properly used child restraint. However, the law applies only to parents and legal guardians driving their own cars, and exempts recreational vehicles, vans, and trucks. The results, in terms of fewer child deaths, have been dramatic.[58]

Political and public support for such laws has not been strong, but is growing. Ten states have some form of child restraint law on the books.

Seat Belts. Passenger restraint for adults has garnered scant political support, despite a technology of proven effectiveness. Seat belts are required in all cars under federal law, but only 10 percent or less of the population use them.[59] Passive restraint systems—air bags and automatic seat belts—are available only in a few car models on the market, and while polls indicate that a majority of people favor a federal passive restraint requirement, the automobile industry has successfully staved off implementation of such a requirement since the early 1970s. States could encourage seat belt usage by penalizing nonuse or limiting the recovery of damages by nonwearers injured in accidents, but less than half the public supports such legislation, even though significant reductions in fatalities and injuries have been reported in countries that have enacted seat belt use laws.[60]

Motorcycle Helmets. The laws requiring motorcyclists to wear protective helmets point up both the difficulties and the advantages of using law to promote motor vehicle safety. Only three states had motorcycle helmet laws in 1967, when the federal government mandated such laws as a condition for receiving federal highway funds.[61] By 1969 forty states had adopted helmet laws and by 1975 the number had risen to forty-seven states. But in 1976 Congress removed the financial penalty, and by 1980 twenty-eight states had repealed their helmet laws.[62] One recent study—corroborated by others—concluded that "the repeals or weakening of motorcyclist helmet use laws were typically followed by almost 40 per cent increases in the number of fatally injured motorcyclists."[63]

Opponents of helmet laws argue that they are an improper government intervention in what should be an individual decision. But there is little legal support for such a view. Thus, for example, a federal district court in Massachusetts, upholding the constitutionality of the Massachusetts helmet-use law, noted:

> In view of the evidence warranting a finding that motorcyclists are especially prone to serious head injuries, . . . the public has an interest in minimizing the resources directly involved. From the moment of the injury, society picks the person up off the highway; delivers him to a municipal hospital and municipal doctors; provides him with unemployment compensation if, after recovery, he cannot replace his lost job, and, if the injury causes permanent disability, may assume the responsibility for his and his family's continued subsistence. We do not understand a state of mind that permits plaintiff to think that only he himself is concerned.[64]

Although laws restricting life-style risks, such as helmet laws, constitute a valid exercise of state police power, such legislation has actually been quite rare. When enacted, restriction of the individual has generally been justified on two grounds. The first, the weak paternalism rationale, is that low-level restrictions on the individual must be balanced against significant benefits in terms of avoidance of death, disease, disability, and discomfort. The second, the cost to society rationale, is that the cost of excess morbidity, lost production, etc., resulting from life-style-induced injury and disease is borne by society as a whole.[65]

Government's Health Promotion Role

Besides limiting environmental hazards and helping to prevent accidents, law is also used to foster healthy life-styles and discourage unhealthy behavior. Such efforts—which have long been the focus of state public health concerns and which, more recently, have received some attention on the national level—have not been characterized by dramatic success, but the salutory impact of governmental efforts can be seen in such things as decreased cigarette smoking rates and improvements in hypertension control.

Considering its demonstrated efficacy in these cases, government activity designed to promote healthy life-styles has been quite limited. The National Consumer Health Information and Health Promotion Act of 1976 and state health education efforts have never been well funded, and health and safety restrictions, whether they be seat-belt or helmet-use laws, or prohibition of harmful substances such as tobacco and other drugs, are generally weak to nonexistent. Cigarette smoking is the nation's primary preventable health risk, yet almost all efforts to use the legal system—public regulation as well as private litigation—to reduce smoking have been effectively stymied.[66] Nor can governmental efforts to deal with alcohol abuse be considered at all satisfactory.[67]

The debate over how far government should intrude in order to protect and promote good health, which is at heart a political issue, is often clothed in legalistic arguments centering either on the difficulty of proving the harm to be avoided or the efficacy of the government response, or on the high costs of implementing the measures in question. On the first issue there has been enough judicial review to make clear that reasonable and rational decision making, and not certainty, can be the guideline when public health and safety are at stake. The cost-benefit issue has taken on a new importance with recent challenges that have come before the courts.

Whether the benefits anticipated from health-related standards—for example, allowable exposure levels in the workplace or a limit on discharges into the atmosphere—must bear some reasonable relationship to the costs of implementation is a question determined by the legislature in enacting a statute. Congress could require administrative agencies to conduct cost-benefit analyses, but it does not have to. In the cotton dust case,[68] the Supreme Court held that such vague terms as "feasible" or "reasonably necessary and appropriate" in the Occupational Safety and Health Act did not imply a cost-benefit requirement; indeed, said the Court, the act's reference to "feasible" measures rules out any cost-benefit test in protecting employees from material health impairment. In February 1981, the Reagan administration imposed just such a test on the rule making of federal administrative agencies, but such a requirement could not validly apply where inconsistent with specific congressional mandates (as with OSHA).

The major difficulty with a cost-benefit approach is that in practice it is far from being a neutral tool. As a House of Representatives report on the subject noted, "It is easy for the analyst to manipulate the study to achieve virtually any desired conclusions." Most of the data needed in cost-benefit analyses is soft and suspect: Soft because it must include estimates on future developments and must attach dollar amounts to human life, productivity changes, pain and grief, and suspect because (especially as regards compliance cost estimates) it often comes from the very industry facing regulation.[69] And not insignificantly, the costs of compliance and the benefits from enforcement fall on different parties.

One result of these difficulties is that estimates of the costs and benefits of various regulatory programs vary widely. A 1980 report on the benefits of environmental, health, and safety regulation, prepared for the Committee on Governmental Affairs of the United States Senate by

the Massachusetts Institute of Technology Center for Policy Alternatives, "identified a large amount of evidence that substantial benefits
have been realized from federal environmental, health and safety regulations. The benefits . . . include direct economic gains, improvements
in public health and in the standard of living, and enhanced environmental quality."[70] At the same time, other studies have come up with lower
and higher estimates, and the report concludes that the "current primitive state-of-the-art of the assessment of benefits" makes a regulatory cost-
benefit approach inadvisable.[71] For better or worse, health professionals
are not given the responsibility of making such assessments. Rather, they
are asked to recommend such measures as are needed to protect and
promote health. Others—with legislative or regulatory authority—can
then weigh these recommendations against arguments that the costs are
too high.

Conclusion

Using the law to prevent or reduce health hazards is not easy. This is not
because the health professions do not know what changes in the environment and in personal life-styles would bring about significant improvements: Much more is known than has been implemented. Nor is it because legal principles limit governmental authority in this area. The
problem lies in inadequate support for the enactment and enforcement
of such laws.[72] The benefits of preventive health measures accrue to the
entire society, but compliance is frequently directed at the few: the industrial polluter, the seller of hazardous products, the motorcycle
daredevil whose accident may hurt others or result in a public burden.
Opponents of legal controls for public health purposes have had a clearer and stronger stake in the debate, and they have argued, quite effectively, that health prevention is a private matter and should not involve
public law. Yet that argument was answered over 130 years ago by a
Philadelphia newspaper: To the rhetorical plea, "Leave everybody to
regulate his own business, and let consumers take care of themselves.
Demand and supply will regulate everything, and those who *offer* the
best article cheapest will get all the custom," the newspaper responded:
"Yes! And after they are blown up, run over and crushed, knocked
down dead, or poisoned to death, they will discover they have made a
mistake. . . ."[73]

NOTES

1. "Who Benefits?," *Philadelphia Public Ledger*, 28, 30 August 1852; reprinted in
   the *New York Times*, 24 March 1981, p. 19.

2. William Haddon, Jr., "Advances in the Epidemiology of Injuries as a Basis for Public Policy," *Public Health Reports* 95:411–421 (1980). Also see William Haddon, Jr. and Susan P. Baker, "Injury Control," in Duncan Clark and Brian MacMahon, eds., *Preventive and Community Medicine* (Boston: Little, Brown, 1981).

3. Samuel S. Epstein, who uses the "plague" characterization, gives a 70 to 90 percent range, in *The Politics of Cancer* (San Francisco: Sierra Club, 1978), p. 23. The National Cancer Institute's estimate is 60 to 90 percent. See William H. Rodgers, Jr., *Handbook on Environmental Law* (St. Paul, Minn.: West, 1977), p. 899. Since most toxic substances were not introduced until after World War II, environmentally related disease is likely to increase significantly in coming years. It should be noted that these estimates are based on the broader use of the term "environment," as described in the paragraph that follows.

4. Rodgers, *Environmental Law*, p. 143. Other texts and casebooks on environmental law include Richard B. Stewart and James E. Krier, *Environmental Law and Policy: Readings, Materials and Notes*, 2d ed. (Indianapolis: Bobbs-Merrill, 1978); Frank P. Grad, *Environmental Law: Sources and Problems*, 2d ed. (New York: Matthew Bender, 1978); J. Gordon Arbuckle et al., *Environmental Law Handbook*, 6th ed. (Washington, D.C.: Government Institutes, 1979); and J. G. Arbuckle, S.W. Schroeder, and T. F. P. Sullivan, *Environmental Law for Non-Lawyers*, 2d ed. (Bethesda, Md.: Government Institutes, 1974).

5. 42 U.S.C. Sec. 4331 et seq.

6. Rodgers, *Environmental Law*, p. 697.

7. The significance of NEPA was potentially enhanced by regulations, effective 1979, requiring a plan for mitigation of environmental impact to accompany each environmental impact statement followed by monitoring of the actual impact. See 40 C.F.R. 1505.2(c) and 1505.3. But implementation of such requirements seems unlikely during the Reagan administration. A majority of states also have enacted state environmental policy acts, which require environmental impact statements.

8. Hugh J. Yarrington, "The National Environmental Policy Act," *Environmental Reporter* 4(36):3, monograph no. 17 (January 4, 1974). See 40 C.F.R. 1502.12–16, as well as 40 C.F.R. 1505. Also see note 7.

9. The Air Pollution Control Act of 1955 was amended by the Clean Air Act of 1963. But the current law is primarily the result of the Clean Air Act amendments of 1970, 42 U.S.C. Secs. 1857 et seq.

10. This policy shift is described in *Train v. Natural Resources Defense Council, Inc.*, 421 U.S. 60, 63 (1975).

11. See, for example, R. Jeffrey Smith, "Utilities Choke on Asthma Research—Polluting Industries Have Mounted a Major Campaign Against Protection for Sensitive Populations under the Clean Air Act," *Science* 212:1251–1252 (1981). National health standards are not established for all air pollutants, but only for those with significant adverse effects on health and the environment. "Health effect" and "adequate margin of safety" have never been clearly defined.

12. A hazardous air pollutant is an air pollutant "to which no ambient air quality standard is applicable and which in the judgment of the Administrator may

cause, or contribute to, an increase in mortality or an increase in serious irreversible, or incapacitating reversible, illness." Section 112(a)(1), 42 U.S.C. Sec. 1857c-7(a)(1).

13. Automobile emission standards are specified in the statute. In all other federal environmental legislation, actual standard setting is delegated to EPA.

14. Epstein, *Politics of Cancer*, p. 362. The Federal Water Pollution Control Act originated in 1948, but took its modern-day form as the result of extensive amendments in 1972. Further amendments in 1977 also introduced a new name, the Clean Water Act. See 33 U.S.C. Sec. 1251 et seq.

15. The 1972 legislation defines "point source" as "any discernible, confined and discrete conveyance, including but not limited to any pipe, ditch, channel, tunnel, conduit, well, discrete fissure, container, rolling stock, concentrated animal feeding operation, or vessel or other floating craft, from which pollutants are or may be discharged." 33 U.S.C. Sec. 1362(14).

16. Sec. 208 of the act calls for a nationwide regional planning effort to control nonpoint sources, such as storm runoff and agricultural runoff. However, those plans that have been developed have largely not been implemented. Many view the situation as presenting an intractable problem.

17. 79 Stat. 992.

18. 84 Stat. 1227.

19. 42 U.S.C. 6901 et seq.

20. Epstein, *Politics of Cancer*, p. 373. The act is codified as 15 U.S.C. Sec. 2601 et seq.

21. Problems created by harmful substances not in use and no longer needed, that is, hazardous waste, are primarily dealt with under the Resource Conservation and Recovery Act, but the tendency to refer to such waste as toxic as well as hazardous creates some confusion.

22. In order to require testing, EPA must determine not only that a chemical poses an unreasonable risk to health or the environment and/or that there may be substantial human or environmental exposure to the chemical, but that there is insufficient data and experience to determine or predict health effects and new test data would rectify this deficit. To assist in the burden of identifying chemicals for testing, the act established an Interagency Testing Committee, with representatives from the EPA, the Occupational Safety and Health Administration, the National Institute for Occupational Safety and Health, the Council on Environmental Quality, the National Institute of Environmental Health Sciences, the National Cancer Institute, the National Science Foundation, and the Department of Commerce. The committee is to develop an annual priority list of up to fifty chemicals for EPA to consider for required testing.

23. Rodgers, *Environmental Law*, p. 901, summarizing provisions of 15 U.S.C. Secs. 2605(a)(1)–(7), (b).

24. Records of alleged employee health effects must be kept for thirty years; all other alleged adverse reaction recordings, including those concerning effects on consumers and the environment, must be kept for five years. Exempted from this requirement are various small manufacturers and manufacturers of chemical mixtures and research chemicals.

25. *New York Times* (national edition), 11 November 1980, p. A16.
26. *New York Times* (national edition), 1 November 1980, p. 7.
27. R. Jeffrey Smith, "Toxic Substances: EPA and OSHA Are Reluctant Regulators," *Science* 203:28–32 (1979).
28. 7 U.S.C. Sec. 321, et seq. One academic study panel identified pesticides as the source of the world's foremost pollution problem. Rodgers, *Environmental Law*, p. 836 at note 12. But implementation of the act has been severely criticized, most notably by Dr. Samuel Epstein, *Politics of Cancer*, pp. 363–368. The premarketing approval system for drugs is discussed in Chapter 11.
29. Atomic Energy Act, 42 U.S.C. Sec. 2011, et seq. Marine Protection, Research, and Sanctuaries Act, 33 U.S.C. Sec. 1401, et seq.; Ports and Waterways Safety Act, 33 U.S.C. Sec. 1221, et seq.; Hazardous Materials Transportation Act, as amended, 49 U.S.C. Sec. 1801, et seq. (also see 18 U.S.C. Sec. 831, et seq., 46 U.S.C. Sec. 170, and 49 U.S.C. Sec. 1472(h)); Noise Control Act, 42 U.S.C. Sec. 4901, et seq.
30. In *Reserve Mining Co. v. EPA*, 514 F.2d 492 (8th Cir. 1975) (*en banc*), at 528, the Eighth Circuit Court of Appeals observed: "In the context of this environmental legislation, we believe that Congress used the term 'endangering' in a precautionary or preventive sense, and, therefore, evidence of potential harm as well as actual harm comes within the purview of that term."
31. 401 U.S. 402 (1971).
32. *Ethyl Corp. v. EPA*, 541 F2d 1 (D.C. Cir. 1976) (*en banc*), *cert. denied*, 426 U.S. 941 (1976).
33. Ibid., footnote 26.
34. David L. Bazelon, "Coping with Technology through the Legal Process," *Cornell Law Review* 62:817–832 at 819 (1977).
35. *Amoco Oil Co. v. EPA*, 501 F.2d 722 (D.C. Cir. 1974) at 741.
36. *Ethyl Corp. v. EPA*.
37. Rodgers, *Environmental Law*, p. 21; citations eliminated. Also see Paola F. Ricci and Lawrence S. Molton, "Risk and Benefit in Environmental Law," *Science* 214:1096–1100 (1981).
38. See Harold O. Leventhal, "Environmental Decision Making and the Role of the Courts," *University of Pennsylvania Law Review* 122:509–555 (1974) (science clerks); Howard Markey, "A Forum for Technocracy? A Report on the Science Court Proposal," *Judicature* 60:364–371 (1977); Richard E. Talbot, "Science Court: A Possible Way to Obtain Scientific Certainty for Decisions Based on Scientific Fact?" *Environmental Law* 8:827–850 (1978); Arthur Kantrowitz, "Proposal for an Institution for Scientific Judgment," *Science* 156:763–764 (1967); Task Force of the Presidential Advisory Group on Anticipated Advances in Science and Technology, "The Science Court Experiment: An Interim Report," *Science* 193:653–666 (1976); Scott C. Whitney, "The Case for Creating a Special Environmental Court Sytem," *William and Mary Law Review* 33:41–56 (1973); Also see Bazelon, "Coping with Technology," and Joel Yellin, "High Technology and the Courts: Nuclear Power and the Need for Institutional Reform," *Harvard Law Review* 94:489–560 (1981).

39. 5 U.S.C. Sec. 702. See Chapter 3 for a discussion of the Administrative Procedure Act.
40. *Association of Data Processing Organizations v. Camp*, 397 U.S. 150 (1970).
41. Kenneth Culp Davis, *Administrative Law Text* (St. Paul, Minn.: West, 1972), p. 419. Although the Court has held "that a party seeking review must allege facts showing that he is himself adversely affected . . . ," this merely means, for example, that a review of a decision affecting a public park must be requested by someone who makes use of that park. See *Sierra Club v. Morton*, 405 U.S. 727 (1972). Justice Douglas would not even have required this level of injury, arguing that suit should be allowed directly in behalf of the park.

> Inanimate objects are sometimes parties in litigation. A ship has a legal personality, a fiction found useful for maritime purposes. . . . The ordinary corporation is a 'person' for purposes of the adjudicatory processes, whether it represents proprietary, spiritual, aesthetic, or charitable causes.
> So it should be as respects valleys, alpine meadows, rivers, lakes, estuaries, beaches, ridges, groves of trees, swampland, or even air that feels the destructive pressures of modern technology and modern life. . . .
> The voice of the inanimate object, therefore, should not be stilled.

42. Steward and Krier, *Environmental Law and Policy*, p. 547.
43. See, for example, Sec. 116 of the Clean Air Act. But federal acceptance of more stringent state control may not be as true of state common law nuisance actions as of state regulatory limitations. See Stewart and Krier, *Environmental Law and Policy*, pp. 549–550. Also see discussion of *Huron* and *Ray* cases in Chapter 4 at note 10. The relationship of common law remedies to federal regulatory action is less than clear. Common law is generally applied when no statute is involved. Thus, for example, the Supreme Court held in 1972 that a state may resort to a federal common law of public nuisance to deal with polluters located outside the state. *Illinois v. Milwaukee*, 406 U.S. 91 (1972). But the Court ruled nine years later that subsequent passage of the Federal Water Pollution Control Act had made application of federal common law unwarranted in this situation; because the pollution was within the limits set by the act the complaining state could not get the federal courts to impose a higher standard. *City of Milwaukee v. Illinois*, 101 S.Ct. 1784 (1981). But it remains unclear as to whether or not the complaining state could invoke state common law public nuisance in the courts of the state in which the polluter is located.
44. See G. B. Henderson II, "The Nuclear Choice: Are Health and Safety Issues Preempted?," *Boston College Environmental Affairs Law Review* 8:821–872 (1980).
45. See Michael Brown, *Laying Waste: The Poisoning of America by Toxic Chemicals* (New York: Pantheon, 1980).
46. P.L. 96-510, 94 Stat. 2767.
47. S. Meyers, "Compensating Hazardous Waste Victims: RCRA Insurance and a Not So "Super" Fund," *Environmental Law* 11:689–720 (1981); Warren J. Hurwitz, "Environmental Health: An Analysis of Available and Proposed Remedies for Victims of Toxic Waste Contamination," *American Journal of Law and Medicine* 7:61–89 (1981); Joseph K. Brenner, "Liability for Generators of Hazardous Waste: The Failure of Existing Enforcement Mecha-

nisms," *Georgetown Law Review* 69:1047–1082 (1981); Note, "Allocating the Costs of Hazardous Waste Disposal," *Harvard Law Review* 94:584–604 (1981).

48. 15 U.S.C. Secs. 2051–2081. Although industry opposed a restrictive act, there was considerable support among industry spokesmen for the fundamental approach of the act, which basically expanded the existing system of voluntary standards. This was the case because: (1) growing products liability litigation put a premium on avoiding product-caused injury anyway; (2) efforts by individual companies to improve product safety put them at a competitive disadvantage, while cooperative efforts raised antitrust problems; and (3) state, local, and voluntary standards were creating confusion in nationwide markets. See *The Consumer Product Safety Act: Text, Analysis, Legislative History* (Washington, D.C.: Bureau of National Affairs, 1973), p. 7; also see Howard S. Kritzer and Charles E. Wilson: "Consumer Protection—II: The Consumer Product Safety Act," *Annual Survey of American Law* 1974/1975:429–456 (1975), and the casebook by Marshall S. Shapo, *Public Regulation of Dangerous Products* (Mineola, N.Y.: Foundation Press, 1980).

49. 15 U.S.C. Sec. 1261, et seq.; 15 U.S.C. Sec. 1471, et seq.; 15 U.S.C. Sec. 1191, et seq. The CPSC is also responsible for administering the Refrigerator Safety Act, 15 U.S.C. Sec. 1211, et seq.

50. Kritzer and Wilson, "Consumer Protection," p. 446.

51. Center for Policy Alternatives at the Massachusetts Institute of Technology, *Benefits of Environmental, Health, and Safety Regulation* (Washington, D.C.: Committee on Governmental Affairs, U.S. Senate, 1980), pp. 25–27.

52. Epstein, *Politics of Cancer*, pp. 374–375.

53. See, for example, Jonathan T. Zackey, Stanley Moslz, and Thomas F. Lambert, Jr., "Trends in Product Liability Litigation," *Trial* 16(11):82–89 (November 1980).

54. Nelson S. Hartunian, Charles N. Smart, and Mark S. Thompson, "The Incidence and Economic Costs of Cancer, Motor Vehicle Injuries, Coronary Heart Disease, and Stroke: A Comparative Analysis," *American Journal of Public Health* 70:1249–1260 (1980). A longer version of the same argument, by the same authors, is *The Incidence and Economic Costs of Major Health Impairments* (Lexington, Mass.: Lexington Books, 1981). But also see Edward J. Sondik and Marvin K. Kristein: "Estimating Costs of Illness and Injury: A Criticism," *American Journal of Public Health* 71:1392–1393 (1981). Estimated direct and indirect costs associated with these conditions in 1975 were: cancer, $23.1 billion; motor vehicle injuries, $14.4 billion; heart disease, $13.7 billion; and stroke, $6.5 billion. Of course the automobile also affects health through its impact on the environment and is therefore the focus of emission, noise, and solid-waste control regulation. See Frank P. Grad et al., *The Automobile and the Regulation of Its Impact on the Environment* (Normal: University of Oklahoma Press, 1975).

55. For a general description of NHTSA and the act see: "The National Highway Traffic Safety Administration," in James R. Michael, ed., *Working on the System: A Comprehensive Manual for Citizen Access to Federal Agencies* (New York: Basic Books, 1974), chap. 13. The act also authorized development of the Research Safety Vehicle, a safe, energy-efficient, moderately priced au-

tomobile embodying state-of-the-art engineering design and component parts. This prototype car has been on display for several years but never adopted for mass production by any of the major auto makers. For an examination of the "substantial reductions in car occupant deaths" associated with federal automobile safety standards, see Leon S. Robertson, "Automobile Safety Regulations and Death Reductions in the United States," *American Journal of Public Health* 71:818–822 (1981).

56. H. Laurence Ross, *Deterrence of the Drinking Driver: An International Survey* (Washington, D.C.: U.S. Department of Transportation, 1981) (report no. DOT-HS-805 820).

57. See Jerome A. Paulson, "The Case for Mandatory Seat Restraint Laws," *Clinical Pediatrics* 20:285–290 (1981), and Robert G. Scherz, "Fatal Motor Vehicle Accidents of Child Passengers from Birth through 4 Years of Age in Washington State," *Pediatrics* 68:572–575 (1981).

58. See, for example, Allan F. Williams and JoAnn K. Wells, "The Tennessee Child Restraint Law in Its Third Year," *American Journal of Public Health* 71:163–165 (1981); Allan F. Williams and JoAnn K. Wells, "Evaluation of the Rhode Island Child Restraint Law," *American Journal of Public Health* 71:742–743 (1981); Paulson, "Case for Mandatory Seat Restraint Laws"; Dianne B. Sontag, K. W. Heathington, and Mark Lo, *Enforcement of the Child Passenger Protection Law* (Washington, D.C.: U.S. Department of Transportation, 1980) (report no. DOT HS-805 802); Julie S. Howard et al., *Judicial Perspectives on Child Passenger Protection Legislation* (Washington, D.C.: U.S. Department of Transportation, 1980) (report no. DOT HS-805 803). The Tennessee law originally contained a "babes in arms" exception, allowing a child to be held by an older passenger—a practice more dangerous than no restraint at all. This "child crusher" exception was removed in 1981. See Robert S. Sanders, "Legislative Approach to Auto Safety: The Tennessee Experience," in Abraham B. Bergman, ed. *Preventing Childhood Injuries* (Columbus, Ohio: Ross Laboratories, 1982).

59. Recent surveys of manual belt usage in the United States found only about 11 percent of drivers and 3 to 7 percent of other occupants using them. *Five Year Plan for Highway Safety Research, Development and Demonstration* (Washington, D.C.: National Highway Traffic Safety Administration, 1981), p. 32. Canada, Australia, France, Israel, Japan, Sweden, and Great Britain have mandatory seat belt laws.

60. See, for example, *Task Force Report on Safety Belt Usage Laws* (Washington, D.C.: U.S. Department of Transportation, revised June 1978) (report no. DOT HS-804 088); *General Safety Belt Usage: Issue Paper* (Washington, D.C.: U.S. Department of Transportation, revised March 1980) (report no. DOT HS-803 824); Franklin G. Fisher, Jr., *Effectiveness of Safety Belt Usage Laws* (Washington, D.C.: U.S. Department of Transportation, 1980) (report no. DOT HS-805 490); and *Public Attitudes Toward Passive Restraint Systems: Summary Report* (Washington, D.C.: U.S. Department of Transportation, 1978) (report no. DOT HS-803 567).

61. The Highway Safety Standards, promulgated under the Highway Safety Act of 1966, faced states with a loss of 10 percent of their federal highway construction funds if they failed to legislate motorcycle helmet laws, a 0.10

percent blood-alcohol concentration for presumed intoxication, and periodic motor vehicle inspection.

62. Unlike the case with seat-belt usage requirements, failure to use a motorcycle helmet is a conspicuous act. Thus, for example, helmet usage in Kansas, while required by law, was estimated by law enforcement authorities to be in excess of 95 percent; after the law's repeal, usage fell below 50 percent. Norman E. McSwain, Jr., and Michael Lummis, "Impact of Motorcycle Helmet Law Repeal," *American Association for Automotive Medicine Quarterly Journal* 1(4):29–32 at p. 32 (October 1979).

63. Geoffrey S. Watson, Paul L. Zador, and Alan Wilks, "The Repeal of Helmet Use Laws and Increased Motorcyclist Mortality in the United States, 1975–1978," *American Journal of Public Health* 70:579–585 at p. 579 (1980). Also see Andreas Muller, "Evaluation of the Costs and Benefits of Motorcycle Helmet Laws," *American Journal of Public Health* 70:586–592 (1980); *A Report to Congress on the Effect of Motorcycle Helmet Use Law Repeal—A Case for Helmet Use* (Washington, D.C.: U.S. Department of Transportation, 1980) (report no. DOT HS-805 312); and "Impact of Helmet Law Repeal," *American Association for Automotive Medicine Quarterly Journal* 1(4):14–19 (October 1979).

64. *Simon v. Sargent*, 346 F.Supp. 277 (D. Mass. 1972), affirmed without opinion 409 U.S. 1020 (1972). There are other motor-vehicle-related regulatory measures not covered above. Perhaps most important are those that relate to young drivers; 16- to twenty-four-year-old drivers, while representing 22 percent of licensed drivers, are involved in 40 percent of all fatal crashes. Recently there has been some questioning of the value of high school driver education programs; while such programs may increase driving skills, they also usually allow for licensure at a younger age, when judgment may not yet be adequately developed. See Leon S. Robertson, "Crash Involvement of Teenaged Drivers When Driver Education is Eliminated from High School," *American Journal of Public Health* 70:599–603 (1980). A similar mature judgment–driving issue is involved in establishing the age of purchase for alcoholic beverages.

65. Beauchamp offers a third rationale, social justice, based on the John Rawls concept of justice. See Dan E. Beauchamp, "Public Health and Individual Liberty," *Annual Review of Public Health* 1:121–36 (1980). Also see Daniel I. Wikler, "Persuasion and Coercion for Health: Ethical Issues in Government Efforts to Change Life-Styles," *Milbank Memorial Fund Quarterly/Health and Society* 56:303–338 (1978).

66. See Tom Christoffel and Sandra Stein, "Using the Law to Protect Health: The Frustrating Case of Smoking," *Medicolegal News* 7(4):5 (Winter 1979), as well as responses by Daryl B. Matthews, "Where There's Smoke There's Ire," *Medicolegal News* 7(4):4 (Winter 1979) and Richard M. Gilbert, "Ethical Considerations in the Prevention of Smoking in Adults and Children," *Medicolegal News* 8(3):4 (June 1980). Also see Donald W. Garner, "Cigarette Dependency and Civil Liability of Cigarette Manufacturers: A Modest Proposal," *Southern California Law Review* 53:1422–1468 (1980); Harvey M. Sapolsky, "The Political Obstacles to the Control of Cigarette Smoking in the United States," *Journal of Health Politics, Policy and Law* 5:277–290 (1980); A.

Lee Fritschler, *Smoking and Politics: Policy-Making and the Federal Bureaucracy*, 2d ed., (Englewood Cliffs, N.J.: Prentice-Hall, 1975); Kenneth M. Friedman, *Public Policy and the Smoking Health Controversy* (Lexington, Mass.: Lexington Books, 1975).

67. See Don E. Beauchamp, *Beyond Alcoholism: Alcohol and Public Health Policy* (Philadelphia: Temple Univesrity Press, 1980), and Jan de Lint, "The Prevention of Alcoholism," *Preventive Medicine* 3:24–35 (1974).

68. *American Textile Manufacturers Institute v. Donavan*, 49 U.S.L.W. 4720 (U.S. June 16, 1981). See discussion of the case in Chapter 10.

69. See Daniel Swartzman, Richard Liroff, and Kevin Croke, eds., *Cost-Benefit Analysis in Environmental Regulation: Politics, Methods and Ethics* (Washington, D.C.: Conservation Foundation, 1981). The most notorious example of cost-figures-out-of-a-hat involved vinyl chloride. When the Occupational Safety and Health Administration issued exposure limits for vinyl chloride in the workplace, industry consultants warned that compliance would cost $65 to 90 *billion* and result in the loss of 1.7 to 2.2 million jobs. In fact, compliance cost $130 million and the loss of 375 jobs, with an increase in the cost of PVC resins of $0.005/pound. See David D. Doniger, *The Law and Policy of Toxic Substances Control: A Case Study of Vinyl Chloride* (Baltimore: Johns Hopkins, 1978).

70. "A 1978 estimate of the economic impact of environmental policies in the United States indicates that the annual benefits of improvements in air quality since 1970 have been $21.4 billion and that total annual benefits in 1985 due to improved water quality will be $12.3 billion. It is further estimated that by the end of 1980 U.S. environmental regulations will have added 0.1% to the consumer price index, reduced unemployment by 0.4%, and increased gross national production by $9.3 billion." Michael G. Royston, "Making Pollution Pay," *Harvard Business Review* 58(6):14, citing *Tenth Annual Report of the Council on Environmental Quality* (Washington, D.C., 1980), pp. 655–662.

71. *Benefits of Environmental, Health, and Safety Regulation*, pp. 38, 43.

72. Enforcement consists of apprehension or citation plus court adjudication. In most areas—child immunization, pollution control, drinking drivers, etc.—the main problem is lax enforcement. With drinking drivers it has been shown that certainty of enforcement is the key to effectiveness, and this is probably also true for most other areas. Nancy Milio is concerned with another aspect of the problem; that is, "This nation does not have a health policy." See her *Promoting Health Through Public Policy* (Philadelphia: F. A. Davis, 1981).

73. See note 1.

13

Death and the Law

Death and the law have always been intrinsically interrelated. This relationship, which began with society's interest in homicides and suicides, has transcended its origin and is now concerned with what is death and when it occurs; when and at whose order or with whose consent autopsies may be performed; and who can consent to the donation of organs for transplantation. —E. Donald Shapiro[1]

UNTIL QUITE RECENTLY, the accepted standard for ascertaining that someone had died was the determination, by a competent physician, that the individual's respiration and cardiovascular function had ceased.[2] But then came two major medical advances: the development of mechanical devices that can sustain circulation and respiration almost indefinitely, even if the brain is irreversibly destroyed, and the growing success in transplanting human corneas, kidneys, hearts, and other organs from cadavers, particularly those whose death was caused by accidents or illnesses that destroyed all brain function and whose circulation was artifically maintained in anticipation of transplantation. These developments have meant that a new, brain-related standard for determining death is required.

In 1968 the Ad Hoc Committee of the Harvard Medical School to Examine the Definition of Brain Death proposed three clinical criteria for determining permanent brain nonfunction and irreversible coma: unreceptivity and unresponsivity, an absence of movement or breathing, and an absence of reflexes, with confirmation by an isoelectric electroen-

251

cephalogram. The committee also recommended that all the tests be conducted by a physician in no way involved in any possible utilization of organs from the deceased for transplant purposes; that they be repeated twenty-four hours later with no change in results; and that determination and pronouncement of death be made before any mechanical support is discontinued. Finally, the committee stressed that the determination of death was a medical judgment based on objective clinical data, not a decision that would involve conferring with family members.[3]

There has been some debate regarding certain applications of the Harvard committee's recommendations, but by and large its definition and criteria have become well established,[4] and provide the physician the assurance that his or her clinical determination that someone has died is based on widely accepted standards.

The same need for assurance has led many states to enact statutes defining death. Such statutes are not really necessary. "The general rule," Annas et al., explain succinctly, "is that a person is dead when the doctor says he's dead."[5] As long as the doctor has made a reasonable determination based on usual and customary medical standards (such as the Harvard criteria) the law will accept that determination.[6] But a general desire to make an event as important as death as unambiguous as possible, and a lingering fear that the need for cadaver organs might lead to precipitous declarations of death, have encouraged state legislatures to establish their own legal definitions of death.

Such statutes take several forms. The earliest, enacted in Kansas in 1970, provides alternative definitions of death, one based on the traditional respiratory and cardiac criteria and the other based on "the absence of spontaneous brain function," and leaves it to the physician to decide which definition to apply in a specific pronouncement. This approach has been criticized for fostering

> the misconception that there are two separate types of death. This is particularly unfortunate because it seems to relate to the need to establish a special definition of death for organ transplant donors. These laws could lend support to the fear that a prospective transplant organ donor would be considered dead at an earlier point in the dying process than an identical patient who was not a potential donor.
>
> In addition, such laws suffer the legal disadvantage of possibly permitting a physician, either inadvertently or intentionally, to influence the outcome of a will.[7]

A second statutory approach provides for the use of brain death criteria only in "the event that artificial means of support preclude a determination that these functions have ceased . . . ."[8] A third approach, recommended by the American Bar Association in 1975, is a simple, one-sentence statement recognizing "irreversible cessation of total brain function" as constituting death for legal purposes.[9] In 1978 the influential National Conference of Commissioners on Uniform State Laws recommended a Uniform Brain Death Act to the states, which declares that:

> For legal and medical purposes, an individual who has sustained irreversible cessation of all functioning of the brain, including the brain stem, is dead. A determination under this section must be made in accordance with reasonable medical standards.[10]

Most recently, the President's Commission for the Study of Ethical Problems in Medicine and Biomedical and Behavioral Research, established by Congress in 1978, urged that the states achieve a true uniformity in defining death and proposed its own Uniform Determination of Death Act:

> An individual who has sustained either (1) irreversible cessation of circulatory and respiratory functions, or (2) irreversible cessation of all functions of the entire brain, including the brain stem, is dead. A determination of death must be made in accordance with accepted medical standards.

Most important, this proposal has been accepted by the American Bar Association, the National Conference of Commissioners on Uniform State Laws, and the American Medical Association as a substitute for their own earlier proposals.[11]

Over half the states have adopted brain-death statutes; it is likely that the others will follow suit, most likely adopting the president's commission proposal. The use of brain death criteria—in states with and without such statutes—have been uniformly upheld by the courts in cases where attorneys for murderers have argued that termination of artificial life support, and not their client's violence, was the actual cause of the victim's death.[12]

Since time is a crucial factor in organ transplants, some states have sought to avoid after-the-fact challenges by requiring independent confirmation of pronouncements of death by a second physician. And several states stipulate that physicians involved in pronouncing death may not be involved in any organ transplants that follow.[13]

The Death Certificate

Regardless of the definition used, when death occurs a death certificate must be issued. Death certificates are used as evidence in filing insurance claims, settling estates, and transferring property, as a basis for litigation, and, collectively, as an important source of public health data. A critical part of the completion of the certificate is specifying the cause of death. The physician who last attended the deceased must complete the certificate, unless the death seems to be a homicide, suicide, accident, or was unattended, in which case the death must be reported to the coroner or medical examiner.[14] It is up to the latter, and not the attending physician, to decide if further investigation is warranted. Most death certificates are signed by attending physicians, while many reported deaths have the certificate signed by a nonphysician coroner. One result is that many death certificates are signed without an actual cause of death being specified; instead, a mechanism of death—for example, cardiopulmonary arrest—is listed as the "cause." The resulting inaccuracy in death certificate information is particularly unfortunate from a public health perspective, for it destroys much of the usefulness of what could be an extremely valuable data source.[15]

Investigation of Death

It is certainly not true that "dead men tell no tales." Not only is there much to be learned from investigation of death, the knowledge gained can be of significant benefit to the public. Investigation of unnatural deaths, such as homicides and accidents, establish the cause and manner of death and can help locate killers or prevent future accidents. Ongoing study of natural death helps prevent, detect, and treat disease. And legal claims, especially those involving insurance, often depend on the results of postmortem examination, autopsy, and other investigations.

Because these are all ends that add to the public's health and welfare, the states' police power would presumably support a requirement for full investigation, including autopsy, of virtually all deaths. In fact, however, only a small number of deaths are studied by autopsy, either officially ordered or voluntarily agreed to by the family of the deceased. Even in those jurisdictions with effective death investigation systems, only 25 to 30 percent of all deaths will receive official attention. Of these, fewer than one-third (less than 10 percent of all deaths) become subject to autopsies. And despite the lurid public image of death investigation, only about 3 to 10 percent of investigated deaths are determined to be homicides.[16] The autopsy rate in hospitals was just over 20 percent of all hospital deaths in the mid-1970s, down from 40 percent for such unofficial autopsies a decade earlier.[17]

Official investigation of suspicious or unattended deaths dates far back in history.[18] Until recently it also constituted the major focal point of health law. Forensic medicine, as this specialty field is called, involves "the application of medicine to the administration of justice."[19]

When are deaths officially investigated? Although the medical examiner or coroner usually has a fair amount of discretion, such investigations are mandatory under certain conditions. Petty and Curran summarize these as follows:

- Deaths due, or suspected to be due, to violence, including accidents, suicides, and homicides.
- Deaths that occur in jails or prisons, or in hospitals less than twenty-four hours after admission.
- Deaths that are sudden, unexpected, and without apparent cause or physician in attendance.
- Deaths that may have resulted from a communicable disease or other public health hazard.[20]

Who conducts a death investigation? In the past the responsibility usually rested with elected coroners, most of them completely untrained in forensic medicine. Over the past century, however, some twenty states and many major metropolitan areas have replaced the lay coroners with medical examiners who are trained forensic pathologists appointed under a civil service system that protects them from undue political pressures. Medical examiners do not usually carry out the quasi-judicial functions of the coroner (hearings and inquests); responsibility for determining whether criminal charges should be pursued is left to prosecutors. Today, where the coroner system does remain, coroners may be physicians—although funeral home directors and professional politicians persist—but rarely are physician-coroners trained in forensic pathology. Shapiro and Davis point out that "the factor of significance is not so much whether, in a particular place, the traditional 'coroners' functions are still carried out by a 'coroner' or a 'medical examiner,' but rather who the 'coroner' or 'medical examiner' is and what his qualifications are."[21]

Whoever is "in charge," death investigation today includes such highly specialized fields as forensic pathology, forensic toxicology, forensic dentistry, forensic anthropology, forensic psychiatry, criminalistics, and various other investigatory and laboratory specialties.[22]

Official medicolegal autopsies are conducted to help determine the cause and manner of death, and, in some instances, the identity of the deceased, and to document these facts for possible legal action to follow. In some autopsies the cause of death may be very apparent, but the autopsy is still important for documentation purposes. Hospital autopsies, on the other hand, are performed to extend medical knowledge by learning more about the disease processes or other factors involved in the patient's death. (Unlike medicolegal autopsies, they are not concerned with external evidence, such as clothing.)

Autopsies are expensive to perform and often disconcerting to relatives and friends of the deceased. Thus the decision to conduct a medicolegal autopsy needs to be made with care, and it is most important that the autopsy be properly authorized. It is not unknown for relatives to bring suit to prevent an autopsy or to demand money damages for an autopsy performed without proper authorization.

Most state laws give medical examiners and coroners broad authority to order an autopsy whenever they judge it is necessary to determine the cause of death, and the courts have upheld such good-faith, non-negligent orders in the face of objections based on religious and other grounds.[23] But some statutes, reflecting their origins as homicide investigation laws, require the permission of the prosecutor and/or the existence of "suspicious" circumstances for an autopsy to be conducted, and there have been successful lawsuits brought against medical examiners and coroners who have acted precipitously in this area.[24]

The major goal of death investigation is to enforce the criminal law and make it harder for homicide to go undetected and unpunished. Most observers believe that achieving this goal depends, in large measure, on the amount of support provided those charged with doing the job.

A second goal of death investigation is to save lives by studying and learning more about the immediate and contributory causes of other deaths, including those related to motor vehicle accidents, drownings, poisonings, fires, suicide, inadequate hospital or nursing-home care, and environmental dangers. Often the medical examiner or coroner is in the best position to uncover vital facts regarding pollution effects or motor vehicle accidents, and to detect situations and unsuspected diseases that pose a threat to the general community. Michael Baden, former chief medical examiner for New York City, has suggested that it is the medical examiner's duty to help prevent such unnatural deaths by making the public aware of their physical—and social—causes.[25] And Philadelphia's medical examiner notes:

> During the episode of infection which occurred among visitors to Philadelphia in 1976, and which acquired the misleading name of "Legionnaire's disease," the Medical Examiner's Office was the principal source of information, both positive and negative, which was used by the Public Health Department to make decisions as to what, if any, measures should be taken to control the contagion during the early stages.[26]

A third purpose of death investigation is to provide information that may be of legal but noncriminal importance. Insurance companies and workers' compensation systems depend heavily on the findings of death investigations. And medical examiners and coroners frequently provide testimony in civil actions ranging from claims growing out of automobile accidents to controversial police killings.

Although improving health care is not a stated goal of official death investigation, it is sometimes a welcome result. In about 25 percent of autopsies performed, the findings contradict previous clinical diagnoses.[27] Thus, with the hospital autopsy rate falling steadily, medicolegal autopsies take on increasing importance.

Hospitals have become more and more involved with official death investigation, simply because they are so often the site of death. With improvements in resuscitation and emergency treatment and transportation, the number of deaths that occur on the way to or shortly after arrival at a hospital have significantly increased.[28] In addition, bodies are sometimes brought to hospitals for pronouncement of death. Although such cases usually do not call into question the medical care, if any, provided by the hospital, its personnel have an obligation to maintain the body in the same condition as at the time of death, and to document all relevant facts carefully (practices also important for deaths where health care is more directly implicated).[29] Thus care must be given to the documentation, collection, and preservation of potential evidence; for example, clothing and wound debris must be preserved undisturbed and therapeutic needle marks labeled. Hospital personnel should document both the origin and chain of possession of all potential evidence. Often these requirements are specified in local ordinances or in guidelines promulgated by the medical examiner.

Hospital Autopsies

Autopsies conducted in hospitals have declined from 50 percent of hospital deaths shortly after World War II to 22 percent in 1975. The purposes of the hospital autopsy have been summarized as follows:

> The autopsy is a check on the accuracy of the clinical diagnoses, historical data and "instruments of precision" used for diagnostic purposes.
> The autopsy is a check on the appropriateness of medical and surgical therapy . . . .
> The autopsy provides data on both new and old diseases, drugs and surgical procedures.
> The autopsy provides information beneficial to the deceased's family.
> The autopsy is a provider of organs . . ., tissues . . . and extracts . . . for the benefit of the living.
> And, finally, the autopsy clarifies real or potential medicolegal deaths.[30]

Unlike medicolegal autopsies, those not ordered by a coroner or medical examiner require permission, either from the deceased during his or her lifetime or from the appropriate relative. (Some state anatomy laws permit medical schools and hospitals to perform autopsies of unclaimed cadavers.) State laws that define the right of possession of the body of a deceased person differ as to who can provide valid permission for an autopsy. Some laws indicate which relatives are authorized to provide consent, others establish a priority order, and some provide for authorization by the decedent prior to death, although it is not unknown for relatives to override such authorization. In all cases it is possible for an autopsy authorization to be limited in scope. It is clear, however, that any hospital autopsy that is conducted without legal permission places the participants and the hospital at risk of civil and criminal liability.[31]

A related concern involves the donation of body parts for transplantation. The Uniform Anatomical Gift Act, which has been adopted, with some variation, in all states, allows adults to dispose of their bodies and body parts for transplantation, research, and educational purposes. The donation must be in writing and properly witnessed, and can be revoked at any time. The act also specifies a sequence of relatives and friends who may, in the absence of evidence of contrary intent, consent to such donation on behalf of a deceased who left no written instructions.

Forensic Science Beyond the Area of Death Investigation

Although forensic science is most often thought of in terms of death investigation—and then, most often in terms of homicide—there are other areas of criminal and noncriminal investigation in which its skills are applied.

Two areas in which the nonforensic health professional may become involved are rape and child abuse. In these situations, treating professionals have the dual obligation to assist the victim medically and to cooperate in whatever criminal and civil legal proceedings ensue. It is important for those treating the victim to understand that they may be called upon to present evidence in court at some later date, and to realize that there are specific protocols for the collection and retention of potential evidence (such as vaginal smears, photographs of bruises, etc.), with a clear and unbroken chain of custody of the physical evidence being very important.[32]

Forensic psychiatry, the utilization of psychiatric expertise by the legal and law enforcement systems, has traditionally been associated with criminal law, particularly in determining competency to stand trial and criminal responsibility (the insanity defense). But today psychiatrists are also being called upon in civil law proceedings, including personal-injury suits (where so-called traumatic neurosis may be claimed by a plaintiff); workers' compensation and disability determinations involving claims of mental illness; divorce; child custody; adoption; challenges to contracts, wills, and deeds; civil commitment; and legal competency and guardianship (see Chapter 19).[33]

NOTES

1. E. Donald Shapiro, "Forensic Medicine: Legal Responses to Medical Developments," *New York Law School Law Review* 22:905–924 (1977), at p. 905.
2. Hirsh offers as a traditional definition "a total stoppage of the circulation of blood, followed by a cessation of the vital functions consequent thereon, such as pulsation and respiration." Harold L. Hirsch, "Death as a Legal Entity," *Journal of Forensic Science* 20:159–168 (1975).
3. A definition of irreversible coma, Report of the Ad Hoc Committee of the Harvard Medical School to Examine the Definition of Brain Death. *Journal of the American Medical Association (JAMA)* 205:337–340 (1968).
4. See Frank J. Veith et al., "Brain Death: I. A Status Report of Medical and Ethical Considerations," *JAMA* 238:1651–1655 (1977); Frank J. Veith et al., "Brain Death: II. A Status Report of Legal Considerations," *JAMA* 238:1744– 1748 (1977); Paul A. Byrne et al., "Brain Death—An Opposing Viewpoint," *JAMA* 242:1985–1990 (1979); Peter McL. Black, "Brain Death," *New England Journal of Medicine* 299:338–344 (part I) and 393–401 (part II) (1978); Robert M. Veatch, *Death, Dying, and the Biological Revolution* (New Haven: Yale University Press, 1976); Alexander M. Capron, "Legal Definition of Death," *Annals of the New York Academy of Sciences* 315:349–362 (1978); Julius Korein, ed., *Brain Death: Interrelated Medical and Social Issues* (New York: The New York Academy of Sciences, 1978); Paul S. Rothstein, "The Citadel for the Human Cadaver: The Harvard Brain Death Criteria Exhumed," *University of Florida Law Review* 32:275–307 (1980); J. L. Bernat et al., "On the Definition and Criterion of Death," *Annals of Internal Medicine* 94:389–394 (1981); A. Earl Walker, *Cerebral Death*, 2d ed. (Baltimore: Urban and Schwarzenberg, 1981); and John I. Coe and William J. Curran, "Definition and Time of Death," in William J. Curran, A. Louis McGarry, and Charles S. Petty, *Modern Legal Medicine, Psychiatry, and Forensic Science* (Philadelphia: F. A. Davis, 1980), pp. 141–149. Debate regarding the original Harvard criteria has centered about the flat EEG test when young children, drugs, or hypothermia are involved, and suggestions that the twenty-four-hour waiting period is too conservative.
5. George J. Annas, Leonard H. Glantz, and Barbara F. Katz, *The Rights of Doctors, Nurses and Allied Health Professionals: A Health Law Primer* (New York: Avon, 1981), p. 224. Petty and Curran note, however, that while in some states only a physician or health officer can make a pronouncement of death, "in other states directors of hospitals are added to the list . . . . In still other instances, anyone can apparently make the pronouncement of death." Charles S. Petty and William J. Curran, "Operational Aspects of Public Medicolegal Death Investigation," in Curran, McGarry, and Petty, *Modern Legal Medicines*, p. 81.
6. Judicial consideration of the brain death concept has often occurred when a person charged with murder has argued that the victim, taken off a respirator after pronouncement of death according to brain death criteria, had actually been killed by removal from the respirator. William J. Curran discusses one state supreme court's rejection of such a defense in "The Brain-Death Concept: Judicial Acceptance in Massachusetts," *New England Journal*

of Medicine 298:1008–1009 (May 4, 1978). Also see Coe and Curran, "Definition and Time of Death," pp. 147–148. Other cases have involved physicians sued for removing organs from patients declared dead according to brain-death criteria. But since these judicial decisions have often been limited in their precedential value—either because of narrowly defined holding or because the decision was from a lower-level court—and are always retrospective determinations, legislative definition of death is considered preferable. See *Defining Death: A Report on the Medical, Legal and Ethical Issues in the Determination of Death* (Washington, D.C.: President's Commission for the Study of Ethical Problems in Medicine and Biomedical and Behavioral Research, 1981), pp. 47–51, 68–69, 133–146.

7. Veith et al, "Brain Death: II," p. 1747. Four states have modeled their own statutes on the Kansas law. See *Defining Death*, pp. 62–63.

8. This approach was suggested by A. M. Capron and L. R. Kass in "A statutory Definition of the Standards for Determining Human Death: An Appraisal and a Proposal," *University of Pennsylvania Law Review* 121:87–118 (1972); see Veith et al., "Brain Death: II." Ten states have adopted the Capron-Kass proposal. See *Defining Death*, pp. 63–64.

9. Five states have statutes similar to the ABA proposal. Unfortunately, Illinois adopted the proposal as an amendment to the state's Uniform Anatomical Gift Act, thus suggesting that it applies only when organ transplantation is contemplated. See *Defining Death*, p. 64.

10. Two states have adopted the Uniform Brain Death Act. See Coe and Curran, "Definition and Time of Death," p. 146. The National Conference's earlier proposal of a Uniform Anatomical Gifts Act was adopted in all fifty states. See discussion below, following note 31. The American Medical Association proposed its own model bill in December 1979; to date no state has adopted it. Seven states have "nonstandard" brain death statutes. The texts of all twenty-six state brain death statutes can be found at pp. 121–134 of *Defining Death*.

11. The proposal has also been endorsed by the American Academy of Neurology and the American Electroencephalographic Society. See *Defining Death*, pp. 72–84. All of these brain death definitions aim at what Annas et al., *Health Law Primer*, p. 226, have described as "*predictability* that traditional death criteria (i.e., cessation of spontaneous heartbeat and respiration) will inevitably occur soon . . ." (emphasis in original). It should be noted that none of them define as death the Karen Ann Quinlan situation, to be discussed in Chapter 14, in which respiration and brain activity exist in an individual with no prospect of ever being returned to a cognitive, sapient state. However, Robert Veatch has proposed a definition of death based on "irreversible cessation of spontaneous cerebral functions." Veatch, *Death, Dying, and the Biological Revolution*, pp. 71–76 (also discussed in Annas *et al*, *Health Law Primer*, p. 226). The president's commission considered but rejected this approach. See *Defining Death*, pp. 38–40. See a wideranging discussion, including this point, in Martin R. Ufford, "Brain Death/Termination of Heroic Efforts to Save Life—Who Decides?," *Washburn Law Journal* 19:225–259 (1980).

12. See note 6.

13. See the California statute, quoted in Shapiro, "Forensic Medicine," pp. 920–921. Coe and Curran, "Definition and Time of Death,", p. 146, point out that statutory stipulations that physicians involved in pronouncing death may not also be involved in any organ transplants that follow raise difficult questions regarding the validity of the pronouncement if the prohibition is violated (that is, it may well be an unethical conflict of interest, but if it occurs do you void the pronouncement of death and declare the deceased not to be legally dead?). The medical examiner's proper role in preventing this type of problem is outlined in J. H. Davis and R. K. Wright, "Influence of the Medical Examiner on Cadaver Organ Procurement," *Journal of Forensic Sciences* 22:824–826 (1977). The president's commission did not view this as a problem area, noting that the Uniform Anatomical Gift Act specifies that the physician who determines that death has occurred "shall not participate in the procedures for removing or transplanting a part."

14. Hirsch, Morris, and Moritz note that:

> In some states only those deaths that are believed to have resulted from the unlawful act of another person are required to be reported to the coroner. In others, all deaths caused by violence, regardless of the manner in which they are supposed to have occurred, and all deaths that have occurred unexpectedly or from unknown causes, must be reported to the coroner. Other circumstances that may require the reporting of death to the coroner include occurrence of death within 24 hours after admission to a hospital, death under general anesthesia or caused by complications of diagnostic or therapeutic procedures, cremation of the body or moving the body out of the state, the decedent's having been held as a prisoner at the time of his death, the possibility that death may have been related to occupation, and nonattendance by a physician during the last 3[0] days of the decedent's life.

Charles S. Hirsch, R. Crawford Morris, and Alan R. Moritz, *Handbook of Legal Medicine*, 5th ed. (St. Louis: C. V. Mosby, 1979), p. 4.

15. See Jurgen Ludwig, "About Death Certificates," *Mayo Clinic Proceedings* 55:347–348 (1980). Reporting today is done on the standardized U.S. medical examiner or coroner death certificate form, and in most jurisdictions must be completed within twenty-four to seventy-two hours after death. See, generally, National Center for Health Statistics, *Physicians' Handbook on Medical Certification: Death, Birth, Fetal Death*, (Washington, D.C.: DHEW, 1978) (DHEW pub. no. (PHS) 78–1108).

16. These figures, from the Chicago metropolitan area, seem to reflect the experience in other parts of the country. (Cook County Medical Examiner's Office, informal communication.) Also see Theodore J. Curphey, "Role of the Forensic Pathologist in the Medicolegal Certification of Modes of Death," *Journal of Forensic Sciences* 13:163 (1968); reprinted in William J. Curran and E. Donald Shapiro, *Law, Medicine, and Forensic Science*, 2d ed. (Boston: Little, Brown, 1970), at p. 186. Milton Helpern, "Forensic Medicine: Past, Present, and Future," *New York State Journal of Medicine* 72:801–804 (1972).

17. William C. Roberts, "The Autopsy: Its Decline and a Suggestion for Its Revival," *New England Journal of Medicine* 299:332–338 (1978).

18. On the historical background see William J. Curran, "History and Develop-

ment," in Curran, McGarry, and Petty, *Modern Legal Medicine*. Also see Cyril H. Wecht, "Legal Medicine: An Historical Review and Future Perspective," *New York Law School Law Review* 22:873–903 (1977); Russell S. Fisher, "History of Forensic Pathology and Related Laboratory Sciences," in Werner U. Spitz and Russell S. Fisher, *Medicolegal Investigation of Death*, 2d ed. (Springfield, Ill.: Charles C. Thomas, 1980), pp. 3–11; and "The History of Legal Medicine," in Francis E. Camps, ed., *Gradwohl's Legal Medicine*, 3d ed. (Chicago: Year Book Medical Publications, 1976), chap. 1.

On the early coroner's system see Shapiro, "Forensic Medicine,", and E. Donald Shapiro and Anthony Davis, "Law and Pathology through the Ages," *New York State Journal of Medicine* 72:805–809 (1972).

19. Shapiro, "Forensic Medicine," p. 905. "Forensic" derives from "of the forum, public, or court." Curran, in proposing a consistent terminology for health law, defined forensic medicine as "the specialty areas of medicine, medical science and technology concerned with investigation, preparation, preservation, and presentation of evidence and medical opinion in courts and other legal, correctional, and law-enforcement settings." William J. Curran, "Titles in the Medicolegal Field: A Proposal for Reform," *American Journal of Law and Medicine* 1:1–11 (1975).

20. Petty and Curran, "Operational Aspects of Public Medicolegal Death Investigation," p. 55.

21. Shapiro and Davis, "Law and Pathology Through the Ages," p. 807. States vary widely in their approach, some having statewide medical examiner systems, some giving local jurisdictions the option of establishing a medical examiner's system, and some having coroners on the local level along with a state chief medical examiner.

22. Criminalistics is concerned with analysis, identification, and comparison of bloodstains, clothing, firearms, etc. Forensic dentistry is concerned with victim identification through dental remains and suspect identification in homicide and child and sexual assault cases through bite marks. Forensic anthropology is concerned with identification of skeletal remains. Other forensic science specialties include questioned document examination, voiceprint and polygraph examination, ballistics, and fingerprinting. A medical examiner's or coroner's office will work closely with law enforcement agencies (and their laboratories), insurance investigators, prosecutors, courts, funeral home directors, and hospital pathologists and other hospital personnel. The point is frequently made that the medical examiner or coroner should not be allied with the prosecution in criminal proceedings, serving instead as a neutral, independent party; but obviously the pressures to favor the law enforcement apparatus are quite strong. Petty and Curran, "Operational Aspects of Public Medicolegal Death Investigation," pp. 83–84, note that, however organized, a death investigation system must have investigatory capability, autopsy facilities, and histology, photographic, and toxicology support.

23. For example, *Synder v. Holy Cross Hospital*, 30 Md. App. 317, 352 A. 2d 334 (1976). However, Petty and Curran, "Operational Aspects," p. 60, note that some courts have upheld religious objections when the cause of death

seemed reasonably apparent without an autopsy (citing *Weberman v. Zugibe*, 91 Misc. 2d 254, 394 N.Y.S. 2d 371 (1977)). Medical examiners and coroners have generally been afforded judicial immunity from liability, based on their adherence to the authorizing statute. The extent of immunity afforded will depend upon the specific statute. Lawsuits that do proceed despite statutory immunity will argue that the authorizing statute was not adhered to. The Supreme Court of Wisconsin recently held that the "statute granting immunity from suit did not bar parents' claim for alleged unauthorized performance of autopsy on body of deceased child where complaint alleged that medical examiner ordered autopsy either without any subjective determination as to whether there was any reason to believe that death was due to any of statutory circumstances authorizing autopsy or despite his subjective determination that there was no reason to believe that death was due to any of such statutory circumstances." *Scarpaci v. Milwaukee County* 96 Wis. 2d 663, 292 N.W. 2d 816 (1980).

24. The most famous case is *Rupp v. Jackson*, 238 So.2d 86 (Fla., 1970), in which a medical examiner was sued for having performed an autopsy in a case in which the cause of death was not apparent. The Florida Supreme Court interpreted the authorizing statute narrowly, holding that the medical examiner had authority to perform an autopsy—absent consent—only when the death involved violence or foul play or if an autopsy is requested by the prosecuting attorney. None of these conditions were met and the defendant was found liable.

25. Views of Dr. Baden as paraphrased in Shapiro and Davis, "Law and Pathology Through the Ages," p. 807.

26. Marvin E. Aronson, "Public Health Aspects of Medicolegal Death Investigation," in Curran, McGarry, and Petty, *Modern Legal Medicine*, at p. 616.

27. Roberts, "The Autopsy," pp. 332–333.

28. Petty and Curran, "Operational Aspects of Public Medicolegal Death Investigation," pp. 72–74, 84.

29. Deaths that are possibly related to the health care that the deceased had been receiving, including instances of negligent care, merit careful official attention, although usually only unexpected deaths or deaths involving diagnostic and therapeutic procedures that ordinarily do not result in death will generate such attention. Deaths of individuals receiving care in nursing homes, clinics, and practitioners' offices are even more deserving of official attention, but usually much more difficult to investigate adequately. For an overview of this subject see Earl F. Rose, "Deaths Related to Medical Care," in Curran, McGarry and Petty, *Modern Legal Medicine*. Although state laws vary, it is possible that death investigation records, including the hospital record, may be made public in court or via open record laws.

30. Roberts, "The Autopsy," pp. 332–333 (emphasis deleted).

31. See discussion in David G. Warren, *Problems in Hospital Law*, 3d ed. (Germantown, MD.: Aspen Systems Corporation, 1978), pp. 201–210. Also see Hirsch, Morris, and Moritz, *Handbook of Legal Medicine*, pp. 194–195.

32. See the relevant materials in Curran, McGarry, and Petty, *Modern Legal Medicine*. Some areas of forensic science, such as questioned document ex-

amination and ballistics, are particularly remote from the world of the health care practitioner, and a few, such as voice identification and polygraph technology, are only tangentially related.

33. See, generally, the *Bulletin of the American Academy of Psychiatry and the Law*, *Journal of Psychiatry and Law*, *American Journal of Forensic Psychiatry*, and *International Journal of Psychiatry and Law*. Also see A. H. Brooks, *Law, Psychiatry, and the Mental Health System* (Boston: Little, Brown, 1974); Seymour Pollack, "Psychiatry and the Administration of Justice," and Herbert C. Modlin, "Psychiatry and the Civil Law," in Curran, McGarry, and Petty, *Modern Legal Medicine;* Gerald Cooke, ed., *The Role of the Forensic Psychologist* (Springfield, Ill.: Charles C. Thomas, 1979); Walter Bromberg, *The Uses of Psychiatry in the Law* (Westport, Conn.: Quorum Books, 1979); J. E. H. Williams, "Legal Views of Psychiatric Evidence," *Medicine, Science, and the Law* 20:276–282 (1980); and a classic criticism of forensic psychiatry, Bruce J. Ennis and Thomas R. Litwack, "Psychiatry and the Presumption of Expertise: Flipping Coins in the Courtroom," *California Law Review* 62:693–752 (1974).

Part III | CLINICAL PRACTICE AND THE LAW

14 | Consent to Treatment/Refusing Treatment

The very foundation of the doctrine is every man's right to forego treatment or even cure if it entails what for him are intolerable consequences or risks, however warped or perverted his sense of values may be in the eyes of the medical profession, or even of the community, so long as any distortions fall short of what the law regards as incompetency. Individual freedom here is guaranteed only if people are given the right to make choices which would generally be regarded as foolish ones.

—Harper and James[1]

SEVERAL ASPECTS of the practitioner-patient interaction can be defined in legal terms. Patients have a legal obligation to pay practitioners for services rendered. There are some aspects of the practitioner-patient relationship that are privileged, while in other instances the practitioner is legally bound to report those aspects that the law insists on knowing. Perhaps the most troubling aspect of the legal relationship is the possibility of a lawsuit by the patient charging the practitioner with negligent treatment, that is, malpractice (see Chapter 16). However, this chapter and the one that follows deal with a critical preludial issue: the responsibility of the practitioner to obtain proper authorization—consent—from the patient. Few health law topics have received as much attention in recent years as the complex principles underlying consent to treatment. What constitutes valid patient consent and how is it obtained? What is "informed" consent? Who can authorize care for the incompetent patient and, perhaps even more important, who can approve termination of treatment for such a patient? And what consent rules apply to innovative and experimental procedures?

Authorization of Care

When a patient consults a health care professional, it is generally taken for granted that he or she wants the benefit of that professional's skills and knowledge. It is therefore easy to forget that such care, however necessary, beneficial, and well intentioned, must be authorized by the patient. In most cases, the availability and quality of the care provided are usually of far greater concern to the patient than his or her consent to treatment; indeed, most patients are unlikely to even note that their consent is required. But the law is very clear on the fact that, with certain exceptions, the patient is free to refuse diagnosis and treatment that others would deem desirable.

The law does more than merely protect the patient's right to refuse treatment; it demands that the practitioner secure explicit authorization of such treatment from the patient or a legally recognized surrogate. If such consent is lacking, has not been voluntarily, competently, or knowingly given, or is exceeded, any diagnostic procedure or treatment becomes an "unauthorized and offensive touching," which constitutes common law assault and battery or negligence.[2] Patient consent need not be written, but it must be clear and valid.[3]

In an assault and battery lawsuit against a physician, the question of whether the physician was negligent is not at issue. Thus there is no need for expert testimony regarding appropriate professional standards of care. Nor is it necessary to demonstrate that the patient was injured. The likelihood of the court or jury assigning more than nominal damages is relatively slight if the patient has suffered no real harm; but punitive damages are possible. If there has been no negligence, the practitioner had the patient's best interest at heart, and little or no harm was caused, why should a suit by the patient be recognized? The classic statement—invariably quoted in discussions of consent—was written by Judge Benjamin Cardozo in a 1914 New York decision involving just such a situation:

> Every human being of adult years and sound mind has a right to determine what shall be done with his own body; and a surgeon who performs an operation without his patient's consent commits an assault, for which he is liable in damages. . . . This is true, except in cases of emergency where it is necessary to operate before consent can be obtained.[4]

In order for patient consent to be valid, four tests must be met. First, the consent must be for what is actually done. If the patient agrees to a diagnostic procedure only, the practitioner is not free to extend an operation further, unless an emergency exists. Until recently, perhaps the largest category of consent lawsuits involved such an extension of the field of an operation. Second, consent must be voluntarily given. Thus, for example, if a physician threatens to abandon a patient, leaving the person without medical assistance unless he or she authorized a particular procedure, the consent so obtained would not be considered voluntary. Authorization from individuals especially vulnerable to pressure, such as the poor and the addicted, present special difficulties here. A third requirement of valid consent to treatment is that it be given by a person legally and mentally competent to do so. This means, among other things, that the patient is able to understand the nature and consequences of the treatment involved. The very young and the mentally infirm, therefore, may be unable competently to authorize their own treatment. Finally, a patient can only authorize treatment if he or she is given adequate information about it; in other words, there must be *informed* consent. This last requirement, long given only cursory attention by the courts—as well as by practitioners—has, in recent years, become a major focus of authorization of care.

There are a number of situations in every practitioner-patient relationship, where authorization may not be required, either because it involves an emergency that cannot wait for consent[5] or because the encounter is essentially nonmedical (such as a discussion of fees). However, where consent is required but not obtained, or the authorization is flawed, the practitioner is exposed to legal liability. What, then, must the practitioner keep in mind to meet the law's requirements in this area?

Authorization of What Is Actually Done

If the patient authorizes a particular procedure, and the practitioner does something other than, or in addition to, that procedure, the fact that the change is desirable does not alter the fact that it is unauthorized. Usually such situations involve patients who are anesthetized and cannot be consulted regarding the need to extend the scope of an operation or other procedure, although it might also involve an acute emergency in which there is simply no time for discussion. The general rule has long been that a surgeon can only extend an operation beyond the bounds that are authorized when there is an unforseen and critical emergency calling for immediate action. Waltz and Inbau argue that the "courts can probably be counted upon to accord a liberal interpretation to the concept of emergency" in such situations. In fact, some courts have been willing to support such extensions of an operation in the absence of an actual emergency when an abnormal condition is encountered during the procedure and the surgeon acts in a reasonable manner to deal with this unforeseen event. One factor in this judgment is the ease or difficulty with which consent could have been obtained from some member of the patient's family; another is the feasibility—and risk—of postponing the extension to a later operation. Obviously, too, the more likely that some permanent ill effect could result from the expanded procedure, the narrower the options for the surgeon.[6]

Voluntariness

A law dictionary defines consent as the "voluntary agreement by a person in the possession and exercise of sufficient mentality to make an intelligent choice to do something proposed by another."[7] Thus, it is clear that a "consent" that is not voluntary is not a consent at all. The question, then, is what might, in the eyes of a court, vitiate the voluntariness of a consent. One reason voluntariness is a problem is the fact that the patient is in a vulnerable position. He or she needs help and the health care practitioner can offer that help. Certainly for the practitioner to indicate that the patient must consent to a particular course of treatment or else forego any treatment would be coercive. Positive inducements would be equally inappropriate, as would misrepresentation.

It may well be, as some have argued, that real consent to treatment is an impossibility, because in most cases practitioners can influence a patient to agree to whatever the practitioner recommends.[8] But the more vulnerable the patient, the more open to question is the voluntary nature of the consent given. Thus, the poor, who may have limited options for treatment; prisoners and members of the military, whose life options are already severely limited; and addicts, who are subject to a special type of pressure, are particularly vulnerable to coercive pressures in medical situations. The careful practitioner should be able to show that recommendations were made to the patient without pressure and that consent was reasonably uncoerced. If no mutually acceptable course of treatment can be agreed upon the practitioner has the responsibility of helping the patient find other health professionals to take over the treatment.

Competence

Obtaining valid consent becomes a major difficulty when the patient is not competent to consent in his or her own behalf; that is, if the patient cannot adequately understand the nature and consequences of a proposed treatment. Children, for example, lack the requisite legal competency, but they still get sick. It would make little sense to dispense with the consent requirement in these instances; indeed, formal consent may be most important in such situations. The intuitive answer is to allow a proxy, a third party acting in the patient's best interests, to authorize care, with all the other tests of valid authorization applied to this third party. There is, of course, a danger that the proxy, be it a relative, a friend, or an officially appointed disinterested party, may misconstrue or misrepresent the patient's interest. Relatives may be more interested in appearances or inheritance than what is best for the patient or what he or she would want. The state may be unduly swayed by the recommendations of the treating professionals or weigh the cost in health resources more heavily than what the patient's free choice might be.

Since it is rare for assualt and battery charges to be lodged in connection with patient treatment, the validity of proxy consent is rarely tested. It seems clear that the much publicized cases in which courts are asked to authorize termination of treatment or life support for incompetent patients represent only a small portion of the instances in which families and physicians agree upon such a course. Nevertheless, there is legal risk to the practitioner when treatment is undertaken or halted without adequate authorization, and the practitioner should have some understanding of which situations involving incompetent patients require third-party consent. Yet one study, for example, found that only between 10 and 17 percent of physicians queried even knew that they had to have parental consent for treatment of all minors, including teenagers.[9]

There are a number of different categories of individuals incompetent to authorize their own care and treatment.

Minors. Children are in the process of developing the judgment and wisdom to take on adult responsibilities. In the eyes of the law they are presumed to be incompetent to consent to their own medical care. Until the age of majority, which in most states is set at eighteen, the consent of one parent is needed to authorize care. "The common-law rule was and is that treatment for a minor even without negligence and where the treatment led to a satisfactory result but for which the parents did not consent gave rise to an action for assault and battery brought by the parents," explains Angela Roddey Holder in *Legal Issues in Pediatrics and Adolescent Medicine.*[10] There are four major exceptions to this basic rule. Two relate to the minor's status: emancipated minors and mature minors may consent to their own treatment. Two other exceptions relate to the type of treatment involved: emergency care and treatment specifically included in minor treatment statutes—for example, treatment for drug abuse or sexually transmitted disease—do not require parental consent. Consent to medical treatment by minors is discussed at length in Chapter 20.

The mentally infirm. Individuals who are mentally impaired, either because of mental retardation, mental illness, senility, or emotional impairment, *may* lack the capacity to competently authorize their own care, but this is not always the case. But such persons lose the right and responsibility to consent or refuse to consent to their own treatment only if they have been declared legally incompetent by a court. This is true even of institutionalized individuals, including those committed against their will.[11] (See Chapter 19 for further discussion of the relationship between mental incompetency and legal incompetence.)

Intoxicated and addicted persons.   Unlike minors and individuals who have been declared legally incompetent, intoxicated and/or addicted persons have no special legal status that would affect their ability to consent to treatment. What of the person, obviously under the influence of alcohol and/or drugs, who refuses treatment? The law in many states empowers the police or other authority to detain such individuals and bring them to a treatment facility without their consent. But consent to treatment is a separate matter, and as with any competent adult, the individual's wishes and directions must be respected.

Unconscious persons.   An unconscious or semiconscious person brought to the emergency room or other medical facility should be provided with all treatment reasonably necessary to respond to the emergency situation, even though he or she cannot give consent. Obviously this does not extend to any elective procedure.

Informed

Case law in the United States on consent to medical treatment dates back to the turn of the century. For more than fifty years, the primary question at issue was the same: Did the patient freely and fully authorize the treatment? Beginning in the mid-1950s, however, the focus began to shift from the patient to the practitioner, and specifically the adequacy of the information he or she provided the patient. The courts began to take note of the unequal relationship between the practitioner and the patient. Since the practitioner has the advantage of training and experience, the courts declared, he or she has a positive duty to share relevant information with the patient.[12]

As one court observed, in a leading decision on this subject:

A reasonable revelation in these respects is not only a necessity but, as we see it, is as much a matter of the physician's duty. It is a duty to warn of the dangers lurking in the proposed treatment, and that is surely a facet of due care. It is, too, a duty to impart information which the patient has every right to expect. The patient's reliance upon the physician is a trust of the kind which traditionally has exacted obligations beyond those associated with armslength transactions. His dependence upon the physician for information affecting his well-being, in terms of contemplated treatment, is well-nigh abject.[13]

From this perspective, failure to provide adequate information—*even though the patient did authorize the treatment*—is viewed as negligent practice. "It is evident that it is normally impossible to obtain a consent worthy of the name unless the physician first elucidates the options and the perils for the patient's edification. Thus the physician has long borne a duty, on pain of liability for unauthorized treatment, to make adequate disclosure to the patient," this same court stated.

It is this requirement that the patient be provided with sufficient information regarding treatment risks and alternatives to make an intelligent decision that constitutes the doctrine of *informed consent.* Judicial decisions regarding informed consent are often vague in their rationale, but the underlying logic is one of self-determination and the encouragement of rational decision making.[14]

With growing judicial recognition of a positive duty to adequately inform the patient came a notable change in the way in which consent to treatment cases are dealt with, as explained in Prosser's classic text on torts: "The earliest cases treated this [lack of information] as a matter of vitiating the consent, so that there was liability for battery. Beginning . . . in 1960, it began to be recognized that this was really a matter of . . . negligence in failing to conform to the proper standard."[15]

In 1972 the California Supreme Court declared:

> The battery theory should be reserved for those circumstances when a doctor performs an operation to which the patient has not consented . . . . However, when the patient consents to certain treatment but an undisclosed inherent complication with a low probability occurs, no intentional deviation from the consent given appears; rather, the doctor in obtaining consent may have failed to meet his due care duty to disclose pertinent information. In that situation the action should be pleaded in negligence.[16]

Whether the wrong to the patient is battery or negligence is not without significance. The time limit on bringing suit is usually later for negligence than for battery, while the latter permits compensation, including punitive damages, for things other than actual injury. Negligence requires proof of actual harm. Expert testimony is not required to prove battery, but it is usually essential in a negligence suit.[17] Finally, malpractice insurance may not cover a situation involving battery.[18]

How is the adequacy of information provided to the patient to be measured? One author has outlined the standard under common law, which requires the physician to advise the patient regarding

A. Nature of the procedure;
B. Prospects for success;
C. Prognosis if not performed;
D. Diagnosis;
E. Risks and complications of the procedure; and
F. Alternatives.[19]

There must also be disclosure whenever it is obvious that serious injury may result from treatment, when the procedure is unorthodox or radical, and when a potentially lethal drug is involved. Common risks within the knowledge of most people need not be disclosed; nor is the practitioner required to discuss unexpected risks. Yet it is the last category—unexpected risks—that has led to the greatest number of lawsuits over informed consent.

The fact that there is only a remote chance that a particular complication will occur is not an adequate excuse for failure to disclose. If the potential harm is severe and there is a less risky alternative—including the option to do nothing—the patient has the right to know about it. How then, does a court decide whether a practitioner has been negligent, if a patient has not been warned about the possibility of a rare complication, and the complication occurs and the patient argues that he would have withheld consent had the warning been given? Traditionally, the courts have looked at the information other practitioners in the same specialty and/or community provide to their patients. Under such a *community-standard* approach, "due care" consists of disclosing those facts that one's colleagues routinely disclose. Only when it can be shown that a defendant fell below this professional standard of disclosure is there a presumption of negligence.

The issue of what other practitioners would have told this patient requires the expert testimony of other practitioners regarding their own practice; a jury cannot decide the matter on its own. A newer approach, followed by a minority of courts (and in a few cases, reversed legislatively), dispenses with expert testimony. It asks instead, would a reasonable and prudent patient faced with this treatment decision be influenced by the information at issue? In effect, the members of the jury decide whether they themselves might have foregone treatment if they had been given the information not given the plaintiff. As one court has put it: "The scope of the physician's communications to the patient, then, must be measured by the patient's need, and that need is whatever information is material to the decision."[20] This brings the focus of consent-to-treatment law back to the patient.

The *prudent-person* standard removes justification by hindsight. Once a nondisclosed risk has become a reality, it is neither surprising nor persuasive for the patient to assert that had the risk been disclosed he or she would have refused consent. And, as Annas et al. have pointed out,[21] it also makes it impossible for an idiosyncratic patient—even one who could *prove* his or her case—to argue successfully that because of this idiosyncrasy he or she would have been swayed by a risk that a reasonable, prudent person would have deemed inconsequential.

The purdent-person standard also has been extended by one of its original judicial proponents—the Supreme Court of California—to include a positive duty on the part of a physician to adequately inform a patient of the risks of a decision *not* to undergo treatment or *not* to submit to a diagnostic test. If a patient indicates an intention to decline a risk-free test, such as a pap smear, "then the doctor has the additional duty of advising of all material risks of which a reasonable person would want to be informed before deciding not to undergo the procedure."[22]

The law recognizes that there are some circumstances in which a practitioner is justified in withholding information of potential importance. A medical emergency obviously makes detailed discussion of alternatives impossible. And some patients may state expressly that they do not want to know about certain categories of risks or complication. These situations, if adequately documented, constitute fairly straightforward exceptions. A murkier situation exists when the practitioner concludes that the patient is unable to deal rationally with full disclosure. The courts have long recognized such a possibility under the doctrine of *therapeutic privilege*, and this portion of the community-standard test has been carried over to the prudent-person test. In the words of one leading court decision, an "exception obtains when risk-disclosure poses such a threat of detriment to the patient as to become unfeasible or contraindicated from a medical point of view . . . . The critical inquiry is whether the physician responded to a sound medical judgment that communication of the risk information would present a threat to the patient's well-being."[23]

The doctrine of therapeutic privilege has been attacked as paternalistic on the one hand and defended as a necessary and practical exception on the other. From a legal point of view, however, a significant aspect of the doctrine is that it takes an important question away from the jury and gives it back to the expert witnesses. In order to test the reasonableness of a therapeutic-privilege defense, the jury must rely on the expert testimony of the defendant's peers as to whether they would have withheld information under similar circumstances. Thus, while the defendant continues to bear the burden of defense, the plaintiff is forced to refute expert testimony.

Obviously, a crucial aspect of evidence in any informed-consent suit is the written consent form. There is considerable misunderstanding among practitioners about the role of this form. "By failing to distinguish between informed consent and its documentation," an editorial in the *New England Journal of Medicine* noted, "the legal profession has precipitated the most egregious misconception by physicians concerning informed consent—namely, that if a consent form is signed, informed consent is obtained."[24] The fact is that the signed consent form is simply a device used to document that the consent process described above—a voluntary assent based on the presentation of all relevant information—has taken place. If the patient can prove that the practitioner did not provide adequate information on which to base consent, the signed form often can be challenged. And what better proof is needed than evidence that signature was routinely secured by a clerk in the admitting office?

Since the consent form is not the consent itself but merely documentation that informed consent was obtained, the test of a good form is how well it records the interchange between practitioner and patient. A videotape of that discussion would perhaps be the best documentation (although it would introduce its own problems regarding spontaneity and confidentiality); but it is not usually feasible. Many experts recommend a form that describes the fact and nature of the practitioner-patient discussion and is signed by both parties. Not quite as desirable, but certainly superior to a signature obtained by a nonparticipant in the information communication process, is a note written by the practitioner in the patient's chart describing the matters discussed and the fact that the patient, on the basis of that discussion, authorized the proposed treatment. "Irrespective of the method of documentation—whether by consent form, progress notes or some combination of the two—informed consent should always be viewed in terms of the direct discussion between the doctor and patient."[25]

Footnote #18

Refusal to Authorize Treatment

Poor health usually makes people eager to receive whatever professional assistance the health sciences can offer. But there are exceptions when an individual will refuse to authorize recommended treatment. If the proposed treatment is not critical or life saving, such refusal is a logical component of the principles of authorization of treatment. Consent obviously means nothing if one can't say no.[26] If a patient rejects a recommended treatment, the practitioner has the choice of proceeding with an acceptable alternative or withdrawing from the relationship (after helping the patient find other care). But what if the disagreement is not merely over alternative treatment modalities but over survival itself? Does individual autonomy apply even when refusal of treatment is likely to mean death? The initial answer is yes. As the Kansas Supreme Court put it:

> Anglo-American law starts with the premise of thorough-going self-determination. It follows that each man is considered to be master of his own body, and he may, if he be of sound mind, expressly prohibit the performance of life-saving surgery, or other medical treatment.[27]

Categorical as this sounds, refusal to authorize life-saving treatment can be fraught with complications, especially with a patient who refuses treatment despite reasonable hope of recovery or significant improvement, or whose physical or mental condition renders him or her incompetent. Courts become involved when they are asked to force treatment on unwilling patients or to approve a refusal of treatment. At issue, usually, is the competency of the patient to make the decision alone and/or the potential for improvement in the patient's condition if treatment is given. When life itself is at stake, the courts have recognized a variety of exceptions to the self-autonomy rule, at times violating the rule without clearly articulating the basis for doing so.

When a competent adult refuses life-saving treatment that is virtually certain to cure or significantly improve the patient's condition, the refusal strikes most people (including judges) as irrational. The classic situation is the person who refuses a blood transfusion on religious grounds. A straightforward application of the principle of self-determination would require that such a refusal govern. However, courts have, in the past, been willing to order transfusions against the express wishes of competent individuals, but apparently only after these patients have made it clear that, although unable for religious reasons to authorize a transfusion, they could accept a court-ordered transfusion. But the language in some of these judicial opinions—especially the less recent ones—often seems to go further in restricting individual autonomy, describing a general state interest in preserving life and preventing suicide or reasoning that if the patient is a parent of young children or a pregnant woman the state has an interest in protecting the parent in behalf of the child. One court even seemed to suggest that the patient's refusal was less compelling than the need to permit "the hospital and its staff to pursue their function according to their professional standards."[28] But the clear trend is toward judicial recognition of patient autonomy in this area.[29]

When no religious beliefs are involved, some courts have used the very refusal of life-saving treatment as evidence of mental incompetency warranting judicial interference "for the patient's own good," while other courts have refused to intervene. Ken Wing has observed that judicial willingness to accept seemingly irrational refusals seems to increase with the age of the individual involved.[30]

Refusal of treatment by an incompetent patient is virtually impossible when health professionals hold out the promise of improving, perhaps even fully restoring, health and well-being. Even if the patient, before losing competency due to illness, had expressed a rejection of treatment, the court may question whether he or she would have remained firm in this refusal when directly confronting the reality of the situation. And if the patient is a minor, or is permanently incompetent, the court is likely to question whether any proxy can decide to forego treatment on the patient's behalf. Certainly if a minor agrees to treatment, no proxy refusal would be upheld. Courts have allowed refusals by the minor or incompetent *and* by parent or guardian to stand, but only if the medical situation was not life-threatening and, if the refused treatment could be postponed without critical consequences.[31]

When a terminal or vegetative condition is involved, so that treatment may prolong, but not improve, the patient's life, courts may view refusal to authorize treatment as a rational course, especially if patient and physician are agreed on the pointlessness of extraordinary measures. Problems arise, however, when the court must establish or verify the desires or best interest of an incompetent patient.

For competent adults the issue is to assure that their desire that extraordinary measures not be used in the face of a terminal illness or permanent vegetative state be observed even when illness has rendered them unconscious and/or mentally incompetent. Since the right to refuse treatment is recognized as a common law and, in many states, constitutional right, the critical requirement is that there be a directive clearly indicating the patient's wishes. In a recent well-publicized decision, New York State's highest court ruled that such a prior directive need not be in writing—although it must be sufficiently witnessed to meet a test of clear and convincing proof—and that it is not necessary for the courts to become involved—although health professionals worried about legal consequences may "apply to the courts for a ruling on the propriety of conduct which might seriously affect their charges."[32] Although they may be technically unnecessary, "right to die," "natural death," or "living will" statutes have been enacted in several states. They permit individuals to execute documents, before any disease process has raised questions concerning lack of competence (but in some states *after* terminal illness has been diagnosed), that instruct their families and those in medical attendance upon them that life not be artificially prolonged when death from incurable injury, disease, or illnesses is imminent. One purpose of such a directive is to provide assurance to the health professionals involved that they will not incur later civil or criminal liability for not having taken all possible steps to prolong life. Failure to do so for the patient who does want to be kept alive could constitute negligence or wrongful death.[33]

A different problem exists in the case of a minor, a mentally infirm patient, or one who did not earlier evidence a clear preference regarding artificial prolongation of life. Without guidance from the patient, to whom does the practitioner look for legally valid instructions? Can any third party provide proxy refusal of life-supporting measures? The highest courts in New Jersey, Massachusetts, and New York have confronted this question in recent years, and their answers have provided the primary guidance in the area.

In the much-publicized Karen Ann Quinlan case[34] the New Jersey Supreme Court confronted a comatose adult, who, doctors testified, could never be returned to a "cognitive, sapient state." Ms. Quinlan's breathing was being supported by a respirator; her parents requested that the respirator be disconnected, and—because the treating physicians refused to do so without court approval—the father of the patient asked a court to appoint him guardian of his adult daughter with authority to authorize termination of artificial life support.[35]

A lower court refused Mr. Quinlan's request; but that ruling was reversed by the New Jersey Supreme Court, which focused on the right to privacy developed by the U.S. Supreme Court in a series of contraception and abortion cases.[36] The court reasoned: "Presumably this right is broad enough to encompass a patient's decision to decline medical treatment under certain circumstances . ."; and that "Karen's right of privacy may be asserted in her behalf . . . by her guardian and family." The court went on to spell out the safeguards to be used in assuring that this and similar proxy decisions properly protect the best interest of the patient involved:

> Upon the concurrence of the guardian and family of Karen, should the responsible attending physicians conclude that there is no reasonable possibility of Karen's ever emerging from her present comatose condition to a cognitive, sapient state and that the life-support apparatus now being administered to Karen should be discontinued, they shall consult with the hospital "Ethics Committee" or like body of the institution in which Karen is hospitalized. If that consultative body agrees that there is no reasonable possibility of Karen's ever emerging from her present comatose condition to a cognitive, sapient state, the present life-support system may be withdrawn and said action shall be without any civil or criminal liability therefore on the part of any participant, whether guardian, physician, hospital or others.

The court also made it clear that this procedure could be followed in comparable cases, and that a decision regarding termination of treatment could be properly made within the institution, without involving the courts.[37]

The *Quinlan* decision provided health professionals with relatively specific guidelines to follow when confronted with a patient in a permanent vegetative state. But there was widespread consternation a year later when the Massachusetts Supreme Judicial Court confronted a related problem. The Massachusetts case, *Superintendent v. Saikewicz,* [38] involved a profoundly retarded 67-year-old man with acute myeloblastic monocytic leukemia. No medical treatment could cure him, but a prolonged and painful chemotherapy regimen might prolong his life for several months. The treatment would also be extremely confusing to a man who could not be made to understand what was happening. As in the Quinlan case, the question was who, if anyone, could validly decide whether to treat or not to treat, and what criteria should be used in reaching a decision. The Massachusetts court, like the New Jersey court, recognized the individual's right to refuse treatment, as well as the fact that an incompetent individual must be afforded "the same panoply of rights and choices it recognizes in competent persons." The court also agreed with the Quinlan approach in allowing a guardian to substitute his judgment in behalf of the incompetent individual and decide what the incompetent patient would have chosen, were he or she momentarily competent. But the Massachusetts court specifically rejected the *Quinlan* approach of affording immunity from civil and criminal liability without judicial involvement. While the New Jersey court had said, in effect, "Don't bother the courts with these matters again," the Massachusetts court ruled that legal immunity required the formal scrutiny of a court of law. According to the Massachusetts court:

> Such questions of life and death seem to us to require the process of detached but passionate investigation and decision that forms the ideal on which the judicial branch of government was created. Achieving this ideal is our responsibility and that of the lower court, and is not to be entrusted to any other group purporting to represent the "morality and conscience or our society," no matter how highly motivated or impressively constituted.

Although this decision provoked loud protests in the medical community, its message is hardly startling. What the court said is simply that those involved in terminating treatment for a hopelessly ill individual incapable of expressing his or her own refusal can only be certain of avoiding the risk of legal liability if a court of law oversees the decision making. And as Annas, Glantz, and Katz point out:

> Neither court requires recourse to either courts or ethics committees. One needs to consult these bodies only when one wants immunity from suit. Since no health care provider has ever been prosecuted for terminating treatment of such seriously ill individuals, the need for such immunity is highly questionable.[39]

In reaching their decisions, both the New Jersey and Massachusetts courts used a "substituted judgment" test. As the latter court explained it, "the decision in cases such as this should be that which would be made by the incompetent person, if that person were competent, but taking into account the present and future incompetency of the individual as one of the factors which would necessarily enter into the decision-making process of the competent person." In a third major case involving a terminally ill incompetent, New York State's highest court rejected this approach, saying its logic was similar to that in the statement: "If it snowed all summer would it then be winter?"

This case, *Storar v. Soper*,[40] involved a profoundly retarded and institutionalized fifty-two-year-old man with terminal bladder cancer and a life expectancy of three to six months. Without periodic blood transfusions, internal bleeding would lead to an even earlier death, but the patient was unable to comprehend the reason for the transfusions, which he found disagreeable. "His closest relative was his mother, a seventy-seven-year-old widow who resided near the facility. He was her only child and she visited him almost daily." She sought a court order discontinuing the transfusions. A lower court agreed, finding that she was in the best position to determine what her son would want and that she "wants his suffering to stop and believes that he would want this also." The Court of Appeals reversed the decision stating:

> Mentally John Storar was an infant and that is the only realistic way to assess his rights . . . . A parent or guardian has a right to consent to medical treatment on behalf of an infant . . . [but] . . . may not deprive a child of life-saving treatment, however well intentioned . . . .

Unfortunately such a principle seems misapplied in a case of terminal illness. Even more unfortunate is the court's failure to offer any means by which treatment could ever be discontinued for an incompetent who has left no prior directive and is terminally ill or in a vegetative state.

The *Storar* decision has been widely criticized, both for its failure to provide any means for treatment to be discontinued in such cases and for its seeming confusion regarding the medical facts involved. George Annas suggests:

> An overly cautious reading of the case by those who fear legal liability could subject children and incompetents to treatments that are ineffective and prolong agony . . . . It can be prevented, however, if the case is read and interpreted very narrowly . . . . The court treated John Storar *exactly* like a minor Jehovah's Witness who needed blood. And on this issue the court is unambiguous: under no circumstances can children be allowed to bleed to death. The analogy is to food, not to mechanical ventilators or major surgery.[41]

Do-Not-Resuscitate Orders

What about the related matter of do-not-resuscitate orders for hopelessly terminally ill patients? Need similar legal liability worries arise? This question was brought before a Massachusetts appeals court in 1978.[42] That court construed the requirements of *Saikewicz* to apply only when the possible treatment would be "administered for the purpose, and with some reasonable expectation, of effecting a permanent or temporary cure of or relief from the illness or condition being treated." Since this is not involved in "no code" orders for patients "on the threshold of death," the court held that the appropriateness of such orders were medical questions "to be answered in accordance with sound medical practice in consideration of the individual patient's condition and prognosis." Or as Annas, Glantz, and Katz put it: "The court states the obvious—where there is nothing to be done, nothing need be done."[43]

It is important that do-not-resuscitate orders be in writing by the responsible physician and be reviewed at least daily. The rationale for the order should be spelled out. Since curative therapy is not involved, this is not an informed consent situation. Nevertheless, communication with the patient's family is important and should be documented.[44]

NOTES

1. Fowler V. Harper and Fleming James, Jr., *The Law of Torts*, supplement to vol. 2 (Boston: Little, Brown, 1968), sec. 17.2.
2. Battery is the intentional and unauthorized offensive physical contact with a person by another. Assault is the apprehension of such contact. "The gist of the action for battery is not the hostile intent of the defendant, but rather the absence of consent to the contact on the part of the plaintiff." Prosser, William L., *The Law of Torts*, 4th ed. (St. Paul: West, 1971), p. 36. Negligence is discussed at length in Chapter 16.
3. See discussion of the consent form, below at note 24. In some respects the patient is in a situation like that of the boxer or football player who is subjected to a level of physical abuse which, had consent not been freely given, would constitute assault and battery (often of a rather aggravated kind). If it were shown that the athlete's consent had not been voluntary, or had been fraudulently obtained, assault and battery would be involved.
4. *Schloendorff v. Society of New York Hospital*, 211 N.Y. 125, 105 N.E. 92, 93 (1914).
5. See Jon R. Waltz and Fred E. Inbau, *Medical Jurisprudence* (New York: Macmillan, 1971), pp. 169–173.
6. Ibid., pp. 174–177. Also see George J. Annas, Leonard H. Glantz, and Barbara F. Katz, *The Rights of Doctors, Nurses, and Allied Health Professionals: A Health Law Primer* (New York: Avon, 1981), pp. 78–79.
7. *Black's Law Dictionary*, 4th ed. (St. Paul: West, 1951) p. 377.
8. See Bernard Barber, *Informed Consent in Medical Therapy and Research* (New Brunswick, N.J.: Rutgers University Press, 1980), especially chap. 4.
9. Leonard Glantz, Steven Feldman, Richard Parker, and Jonathan B. Weisbuch, "Medical Practice, Medical Education, and the Law," *Journal of Medical Education* 49:899–901 (1974).
10. (New York: John Wiley, 1977), p. 136. Also see George J. Annas, Leonard H. Glantz, and Barbara F. Katz, *Informed Consent to Human Experimentation: The Subjects' Dilemma* (Cambridge, Mass.: Ballinger, 1977), p. 68.
11. See Annas, Glantz, and Katz, *Informed Consent*, pp. 151–153. In a few states forced hospitalization automatically means legal incompetency, although the trend is toward a separation of the two determinations.
12. It is a duty based on an informal fiduciary relationship, with the physician acting in a position of trust for the patient. This can be contrasted to the simple duty of reasonable care that normally exists between strangers. For a

profile of the information disclosure practices of U.S. physicians, see the informed consent study report, pp. 313–457, in Arnold J. Rosoff, *Informed Consent* (Rockville, Md.: Aspen Systems Corporation, 1981). Also see Ruth F. Faden, Carol Lewis, Catherine Becker, Alan I. Faden, and John Freeman, "Disclosure Standards and Informed Consent," *Journal of Health Politics, Policy and Law* 6:255–284 (1980).

13. *Canterbury v. Spence,* 464 F.2d 772 (D.C. Cir. 1972).
14. See Annas, Glantz, and Katz, *Informed Consent,* pp. 33–38. Also see Jay Katz and Alexander Morgan Capron, *Catastrophic Disease: Who Decides What?* (New York: Russell Sage Foundation, 1975). Katz and Capron, pp. 82–90, list six functions of informed consent. These functions, which are frequently quoted, are: a) to promote individual autonomy, b) to protect the patient-subject's status as a human being, c) to avoid fraud and duress, d) to encourage self-scrutiny by the physician-investigator, e) to encourage rational decision making, and f) to involve the public. The individual autonomy rationale should not be taken too far, for as will be seen later, most courts have focused on the adequacy of the information provided, not on whether or not the patient actually understood that which was being consented to. On problems in patient understanding and recall see, for example, George Robinson and Avraham Merav, "Informed Consent: Recall by Patients Tested Postoperatively," *Annals of Thoracic Surgery* 22:209–212, (1976), and Barrie R. Cassileth et al., "Informed Consent—Why Are Its Goals Imperfectly Realized?," *New England Journal of Medicine* 302:896–900 (1980).
15. Prosser, *Law of Torts,* p. 165.
16. *Cobbs v. Grant,* 8 C.3rd 229, 502 P.2d 1 (1972).
17. But see discussion of *Canterbury,* below at note 20.
18. See Waltz and Inbau, *Medical Jurisprudence,* pp. 153–154.
19. Howard S. David, "Informed Consent—A Review and Analysis," *Trial Lawyer's Quarterly* 11:64 (Spring-Summer 1976). Also see Leslie J. Miller, "Informed Consent—Part I," *Journal of the American Medical Association (JAMA)* 244:2100–2103 (1980). So far no court has held that the duty to disclose risks should include data regarding the "track record" of the physician and hospital, although such information would be more relevant to the patient than aggregate risk data. George J. Annas suggested such an approach in "Public Access to Health Care Information: PSRO Data and Its Availability to Patients and Consumers," in Richard H. Egdahl and Paul M. Gertman, *Quality Assurance in Health Care* (Germantown, Md.: Aspen Systems Corporation, 1976), at pp. 157–159. E. A. Codman championed—and individually implemented—this type of disclosure duty prior to World War I.
20. *Canterbury v. Spence.*
21. Annas, Glantz, and Katz, *Informed Consent,* p. 31. Annas has pointed out elsewhere that a major flaw in using a hypothetical "prudent person" is that the individual autonomy basis of consent is effectively eliminated.
22. *Truman v. Thomas,* 165 Cal. Rptr. 308, 611 P.2d 902 (1980). The case involved a physician's failure to fully inform a patient of "the potentially fatal consequences of allowing cervical cancer to develop undetected by a pap smear."
23. *Canterbury v. Spence.* On the therapeutic privilege and other defenses (such

as common and remote risks), see Leslie J. Miller, "Informed Consent—Part II," *JAMA* 244:2347–2350 (1980).

24. James M. Vaccarino, "Consent, Informed Consent and the Consent Form," *New England Journal of Medicine* 298:455 (1978). Also see Rosoff, *Informed Consent*, chap. 10; Cassileth et al., *Informed Consent*; and T. M. Grundner, "On the Readability of Surgical Consent Forms," *New England Journal of Medicine* 302:900–902 (1980). Many state hospital associations publish consent manuals containing suggested consent forms.

25. Vaccarino, "Consent." The consent form itself may provide a complete defense (barring fraud or misrepresentation) if a state's legislature has specifically so provided by statute. This has happened in several states, while several others have statutorily adopted the community-standard test for measuring the adequacy of disclosure or, in a few cases, have actually specified what types of information must be disclosed. See Leslie J. Miller, "Informed Consent—Part III," *JAMA* 244:2556–2558 (1980). Also see Annas, Glantz, and Katz, *Informed Consent*, pp. 38–42. Annas, Glantz, and Katz also note that the number of informed consent cases is relatively small; they report approximately two hundred appellate decisions nationwide dealing with the informed consent. While often viewed as a device for collecting damages on a poor result when negligence cannot be demonstrated, it seems more likely that the modest increase in successful informed consent actions reflects the growing demand for access to information evidenced in society as a whole.

26. As explained in Chapter 5, this principle only applies if no overriding state interest exists, such as compulsory treatment for public health reasons. This usually involves treatment or preventive measures for communicable disease (flouridation of water being a notable exception).

27. *Natanson v. Kline*, 186 Kan. 393, 350 P.2d 1093 at p. 1104 (1960).

28. *John F. Kennedy Memorial Hospital v. Heston*, 58 N.J. 576, 279 A.2d 670 (1971).

29. See Leonard H. Glantz, "Legal Limits on the Rights to Refuse Treatment," in: Cynthia B. Wong and Judith P. Swazey, *Dilemmas of Dying: Policies and Procedures for Decisions Not to Treat* (Boston: G. K. Hall, 1981). Glantz points out that much of the judicial language suggesting limits on the right to refuse treatment predates judicial recognition of a constitutional right to privacy that could be applied to the refusal-of-treatment situation. Also see Annas, Glantz, and Katz, *A Health Law Primer*, pp. 82–85. The traditional judicially recognized state interests supporting limitations on refusal are the preservation of life, the prevention of suicide, the protection of innocent third parties, and maintaining the ethical integrity of the medical profession. They are discussed critically in the above two references, as well as in the *Saikewicz* decision, discussed in this chapter. For a discussion of release forms for such refusals, see Rosoff, *Informed Consent*, pp. 272–277.

30. Kenneth R. Wing, *The Law and the Public's Health* (St. Louis: C. V. Mosby, 1976), p. 28.

31. *In the Matter of Martin Seferth*, 309 N.Y. 80, 127 N.E.2d 280 (1955). See discussion in Wing, *The Law and the Public's Health*, pp. 24–25. Also see the discussion regarding nontreatment of defective newborns in Chapter 20 of this book.

32. *Eichner v. Dillon*, 420 N.E.2d 64, 52 N.Y.2d 363 (1981). See discussions in George J. Annas, "Help from the Dead: The Cases of Brother Fox and John Storar," *Hastings Center Report* 11(3):19–20 (June 1981), and John J. Paris, "The New York Court of Appeals Rules on the Rights of Incompetent Dying Patients," *New England Journal of Medicine* 304:1424–1425 (1981).

33. See Franklin J. Evans, "The Right to Die—A Basic Constitutional Right," *Journal of Legal Medicine* 5(8):17–20 (August 1977); Jane A. Raible, "The Right to Refuse Treatment and Natural Death Legislation," *Medicolegal News* 5(4):6–8, 13, 15 (Fall 1977); and Carla Dowben, "Prometheus Revisited: Popular Myths, Medical Realities, and Legislative Actions Concerning Death," *Journal of Health Politics, Policy and Law* 5:250 (1980). A related aspect of this matter, do-not-resuscitate orders, is discussed in this chapter.

34. *In the Matter of Karen Quinlan*, 70 N.J. 10, 355 A.2d 647 (1976).

35. Termination of life support seems to present fewer ethical and religious problems than it does legal difficulties. In the Quinlan situation, for example, it was made clear that disconnecting the respirator would not be inconsistent with the views of the Roman Catholic Church.

36. See Chapter 18.

37. However, unless the patient were a minor or already under a legal guardianship, a court would still be involved in order to authorize guardianship. But the court would not need to specifically consider the termination of treatment question.

38. *Superintendent of Belchertown State School v. Saikewicz*, 370 N.E.2d 417 (Mass. 1977). See George J. Annas, "Reconciling *Quinlan* and *Saikewicz:* Decision Making for the Terminally Ill Incompetent," *American Journal of Law and Medicine* 4:367–396 (1979), as well as other discussions of *Saikewicz* in the same journal at 4:111–130, 4:233–242, 4:337–365, and 5:97–117. Also see *In the Matter of Earle Spring*, 405 N.E.2d 115 (Mass. 1980), in which the Massachusetts Supreme Judicial Court clarified its *Saikewicz* reasoning, as well as George J. Annas, "Quality of Life in the Courts: Earle Spring in Fantasyland," *Hastings Center Report* 10(4):9–10 (August 1980); Leonard H. Glantz, "The Case of Earle Spring: Terminating Treatment on the Senile," *Medicolegal News* 8(4):14, 27 (1980); and Lee J. Dunn and Nancy E. Ator, "*Vox clamantis in deserto:* Do You *Really* Mean What You Say in *Spring?*" *Medicolegal News* 9(1):14–16, 27 (1981).

39. Annas, Glantz, and Katz, *A Health Law Primer*, p. 87.

40. *Storar v. Soper*, 420 N.E.2d 64, 52 N.Y.2d 363 (1981). The Storar and Eichner cases began in different lower courts, but were consolidated on appeal and decided together in one decision by the Court of Appeals of New York.

41. Annas, "Help from the Dead," p. 20. For more on critically ill patients, see: John A. Robertson, *The Rights of the Critically Ill: The Basic ACLU Guide to the Rights of the Critically Ill and Dying Patient* (Cambridge: Ballinger, Publication scheduled for 1982), and A. Edward Doudera and J. Douglas Peters, eds., *Legal and Ethical Aspects of Treatment for Critically and Terminally Ill Patients* (Ann Arbor: Health Administration Press, 1981).

42. *In the Matter of Shirley Dinnerstein*, 380 N.E.2d 134 (Mass. App. Ct. 1978). Also see Ronald B. Schram, John C. Kane, and Daniel T. Roble, " 'No Code'

Orders: Clarification in the Aftermath of *Saikewicz*," *New England Journal of Medicine* 299:875–878 (1978).

43. Annas, Glantz, and Katz, *A Health Law Primer*, p. 89.

44. See Robert J. Levine, "Do Not Resuscitate Decisions and Their Implementation," in Wong and Swazey, *Dilemmas of Dying*, pp. 23–41. A do-not-resuscitate order written when it should not have been was successfully challenged by a third party in *Hoyt v. St. Mary's Rehabilitation Center*, no. 774555, slip op. (Dist. Ct., 4th Jud. Dist., Hennepin Co., Minn., Feb. 13, 1981). The judge suspended the order, holding that it could only be renewed by a duly appointed guardian using a substituted judgment standard. See discussion in George J. Annas, "Orders Not to Resuscitate: The Sharon Siebert Case," *Nursing Law and Ethics* 2(5):3, 7 (May 1981).

15

Human
Experimentation

*Ordinary patients will not knowingly risk their health or
their life for the sake of "science." Every experienced
clinical investigator knows this. When such risks are taken
and a considerable number of patients are involved, it may
be assumed that informed consent has not been obtained in
all cases.*

—Henry K. Beecher[1]

THE PREVIOUS CHAPTER was predicated on two assumptions: that consent was being obtained for a standard diagnostic or treatment procedure and that the diagnosis or treatment proposed was in the best
interest of the patient. There are instances, however, when these assumptions are not valid. Authorization may be sought not only for accepted, standardized treatments, but also for innovative and experimental therapies, as well as for experimental procedures of no direct benefit
to the individual involved. In such situations special consent problems
are presented.

Consent to Innovative Therapy

Diagnostic and therapeutic procedures that deviate from the accepted
approach may be recommended to a patient if the physician feels that in
the given instance the innovation offers advantages over the standard
procedure. Whether such recommendation involves a procedure with

wide but minority acceptance or entails the first use of a particular approach to the problem at hand, special authorization problems are presented.

Most commentators view the area of innovative treatment as falling somewhere between standard therapy and experimentation,[2] and there is general agreement that the standards for consent underlying such treatment should be more stringent than for customary therapies. The standards must be stricter yet when the proposed procedure is frankly experimental and promises no direct benefit to the patient.[3]

Early U.S. court decisions tended to hold medical innovators to a standard of strict liability for an untoward result. Today, liability is more likely to be judged by a standard of reasonableness: While adhering to custom is evidence of reasonable and appropriate care, it is not an automatic and absolute requirement of such care. As Waltz and Inbau explain:

> It does not follow from the fact that a method of treatment is innovative that it is not reasonable medical practice to use it. Expert testimony on this issue can evaluate the defendant physician's innovative therapy on the basis of the condition of the patient, the probability of success of the therapy, and the nature, severity, and probability of collateral risks. Such expert testimony would be responsive to the fundamental and long-familiar inquiry: Did the defendant doctor conform to the standard of care of a reasonable practitioner under the circumstances confronting him?[4]

Patient authorization for innovative therapy raises more problems than with established treatment, both because less is known about the proposed procedure's efficacy and risks and because the law itself is unclear. As Williamson, Cochrane, and others have been demonstrating, relatively little is really known about the efficacy of most standard "accepted" medical practices.[5] But the patient needs to understand that even less is known about innovative approaches, particularly the attendant risks, if only because there has been less experience with them. It is especially important, in such instances, that the practitioner inform the patient as fully as possible regarding the recommended innovation.

One way to provide the patient with such information is to explain the nature of innovative procedures in general, including the greater possibility of unknown risks. It is not clear, however, what legal standard is to be used in judging the adequacy of disclosures regarding an innovative procedure. A comparison with other practitioners using the same innovative approach—if such other exists—or with what other practitioners tell their patients about innovation in general would seem to be appropriate legal benchmarks. But at least one analyst has pointed out that even when the prudent-person standard is used "it is not yet established that the innovative nature of a procedure must be disclosed."[6]

For want of any better guide, "any innovative practice in which the deviation from customary practice is substantive should be conducted so that it most closely approximates the standards of good research . . . should be reviewed by an [institutional review board, and] . . . the consent negotiation [should] indicate that the activity is being performed with—at least in part—research intent and so on."[7] Annas et al. suggest that "in such cases it may be appropriate to have a third party or group of persons who act as mediators or patient advocates to insure that the patient understands the procedure and its probable consequences before the patient-subject's consent is obtained."[8] At present, however, all of this is recommendation rather than a legal standard. One critical, and largely unsolved, problem is how to deal with a randomized controlled trial where it is necessary to provide consent without jeopardizing the double-blind nature of the experiment. Discussion of this problem is only in its infancy, and no dependable guidelines have emerged thus far.[9]

Consent to Nontherapeutic Experimental Procedures

The tremendous surge in medical research in recent decades—much of it federally funded—and the widespread use of human subjects in such research has focused public and government attention on the need to protect such subjects against abuse and exploitation. Revelations of unspeakable experiments carried out in the name of "science" by German doctors on hapless concentration camp inmates sent shock waves through the scientific community after World War II. In the years that followed, however, a review of a number of research projects in this country also brought to light a blatant disregard for the rights of subjects, some of whom did not even know they were being experimented on. The heightened concern about the ethics of human experimentation gave rise to a number of restrictions on such research, and to the creation by Congress, in 1974, of a National Commission for the Protection of Human Subjects of Biomedical and Behavioral Research.[10]

In a sense, of course, all therapy is experimental, particularly new diagnostic or therapeutic procedures and techniques. There is a sharp difference, however, between treatment, however new, applied in the therapeutic best interest of the patient, and experimentation, which offers no direct benefit to the individual involved. In the experimental situation, the individual is not a patient but a research subject. The contrast was spelled out in the Declaration of Helsinki:

> In the field of clinical research a fundamental distinction must be recognized between clinical research in which the aim is essentially therapeutic for a patient, and clinical research the essential object of which is purely scientific and without therapeutic value to the person subjected to the research.[11]

Today's stringent standards for subject authorization in connection with human experimentation were inspired in large measure by the horrors perpetrated by the doctors of the Third Reich. Paul Freund has pointed out that "the most striking thing about the Nazi episodes is the high standing of a number of the doctors involved and the medical science they represented."[12] When confronted with their atrocities at the Nuremberg war crimes trials, the doctors insisted that they had conducted their experiments within the ethical framework of the medical profession. The Nuremberg tribunal, in rejecting this defense, stressed that while "experiments yield results for the good of society that are unprocurable by other methods or means of study . . . certain basic principles must be observed in order to satisfy moral, ethical, and legal concepts."[13] The tribunal then set down ten such principles, which have come to be known as the Nuremberg Code. In brief, they provide that experiments involving human subjects should:

1. be based on voluntary consent;
2. yield fruitful results for the good of society, unprocurable by other methods;
3. be justified by earlier laboratory and animal tests and other studies;
4. be conducted in ways that minimize suffering and injury;
5. involve no risk of death or disabling injury;
6. involve risk proportionate to the anticipated benefit;
7. be based on proper preparation;
8. be conducted by qualified people;
9. permit the subject to stop the experiment at any time; and
10. be conducted by an experimenter prepared to terminate the study if injury, disability, or death seem probable.[14]

The first, and by far the longest, provision of the code is of particular concern here. It declares:

1. The voluntary consent of the human subject is absolutely essential.

This means that the person involved should have legal capacity to give consent; should be so situated as to be able to exercise free power of choice, without intervention of any element of force, fraud, deceit, duress, overreaching, or other ulterior form of constraint or coercion; and should have sufficient knowledge and comprehension of the elements of the subject matter involved as to enable him to make an understanding and enlightened decision. This latter element requires that before the acceptance of an affirmative decision by the experimental subject there should be made known to him the nature, duration, and purpose of the experiment; the method and means by which it is to be conducted; all inconveniences and hazards reasonably to be expected; and the effects upon his health or person which may possibly come from his participation in the experiment.

The duty and responsibility for ascertaining the quality of the consent rests upon each individual who initiates, directs or engages in the experiment. It is a personal duty and responsibility which may not be delegated to another with impunity.[15]

It should be noted that this provision adds another element to the three required for valid consent to diagnostic or therapeutic procedures. In addition to being voluntary, competent, and informed, consent to nontherapeutic experiments must include *understanding*. Under both the community standard and the prudent-person standard, the test of whether consent is "informed" is not whether the patient has understood what was involved, but whether enough information was provided for the average person to understand. This is not enough to constitute valid authorization for a subject's participation in an experiment.[16]

What does this mean to the health professional planning an experiment that involves human subjects? Obviously the Nuremberg Code provides important ethical guidelines; it is widely accepted as the definitive statement on the moral aspects of human experimentation. But for legal guidelines we must look elsewhere; the Nuremberg tribunal did not effectively establish precedent that controls U.S. courts.[17] Indeed, there seems to be only one court decision invoking the code[18]—which is not particularly suprising, because there are very few reported cases regarding human experimentation altogether. Annas et al. could find only one case, in Canada, involving consent to experimentation by an ordinary volunteer.[19] Nor have there been many more cases in the area that raises the greatest ethical and legal questions; namely, cases in which the subjects involved are members of disadvantaged subgroups of the population.

Three different types of court action are possible with respect to human experimentation: A court may be asked to approve of a subject's involvement in advance of the experiment; a court may be asked to stop an experiment because of the invalidity of subject consent; or damages may be sought after the fact, based on assault and battery. The possibility of such suits must be considered in all research; but because court intervention in the area of experimentation is rare, the actual effect is quite limited. Of far greater moment are the federal guidelines that have been developed regarding protection of human research subjects.

Federal involvement in this area goes back a number of years. The Department of Health and Human Services, which funds a large percentage of all the biomedical and behavioral research under way in the United States, has the authority to impose research guidelines as a condition of such funding. In 1953 the National Institutes of Health decreed that any research involving human subjects to be undertaken at its clinical center in Bethesda would have to secure the approval of a review committee responsible for the protection of human subjects. In 1966 the

U.S. surgeon general instituted the same prior review requirement for all extramural research supported by U.S. Public Health Service research or research training grants, extending it to intramural research a year later.[20] In 1971 the secretary of Health, Education and Welfare published an *Institutional Guide to DHEW Policy on the Protection of Human Subjects,* which became the basic guide for institutions hoping to receive HEW funding. (The *Guide* was codified in 1975 as *HEW Regulations on the Protection of Human Subjects.*)[21]

Meanwhile, in 1974, Congress adopted the National Research Act,[22] which created the National Commission for the Protection of Human Subjects of Biomedical and Behavioral Research and mandated it to recommend appropriate ethical research guidelines to the secretary of HEW, who was either to implement them as regulations or publish reasons for not doing so. When the commission expired in 1978, continuing study in this area was assumed by a new body, the Presidential Commission for the Study of Ethical Problems in Medicine and Biomedical and Behavioral Research.[23]

Between 1974 and 1978 the commission produced a series of reports and recommendations on the ethical and public policy issues involved in human experimentation. The commission studied the performance of institutional review boards and explored informed consent problems. An important ethical question of long standing has been whether there are any particular groups of people who should never be used as experimental subjects or who should be afforded special protection, such as minors, adult incompetents, institutionalized persons, prisoners, the poor, and the chronically ill. The commission spent much of its time considering some—but not all—of these groups. The commission's recommendations regarding research involving special subgroups of the population were intended for subsequent formal adoption by the secretary of Health and Human Services, but for the most part final regulations have not been implemented.

The issue with respect to minors and incompetent adults are the same as those discussed earlier in connection with therapeutic procedures, with several complicating factors added. Some courts have held that parents and guardians cannot authorize the invasion of a child's or an incompetent's body unless the procedure will be directly beneficial to the patient.[24] This requirement would completely exclude minors and incompetents from nontherapeutic experimentation. Annas et al. report "there are no decided cases or statutes that specifically deal with the problem of the validity of the consent of the parent or child to participation in nontherapeutic research."[25]

The desire to include adult incompetents in experiments is, in most instances, primarily based on convenience; but with children a real dilemma exists. Children are not simply little adults; new procedures and drugs intended for use on children cannot be tested on adult volunteers, nor can they always be adequately tested only with children who may derive some direct benefit. So a strong argument can be made that experiments involving children as subjects can "yield fruitful results for the good of society, unprocurable by other methods or means of study . . . ."[26] Nevertheless, many individuals—including some researchers—take the position that children should never be allowed to participate in nontherapetuic experiments.[27] The commission took the position that nontherapeutic research involving children as subjects is important, and can be conducted in an ethical manner as long as certain criteria are met. These include appropriate review by an institutional review board, parental authorization, and the assent of the minor when capable (generally seven years of age or older). Nor did the commission rule out research involving more than minimal risk to children.[28]

Prisoners present a different type of problem. They have been described as "the perfect human guinea pigs," offering researchers many advantages in terms of availability, motivation, control, and ease of observation. But a prison environment is inherently coercive, raising the question of whether any consent by a prisoner can be truly voluntary. In many countries the disturbing parallel to experiments conducted by the Nazi doctors (for which at least some of the concentration camp inmates were alleged to have "volunteered") has sharply limited the use of prisoners as research subjects. But in the United States, the practice—albeit recently curtailed—has continued, although certain prisoner motivations, such as the promise of favored treatment or consideration for parole, are now generally regarded as inappropriate to a voluntary decision. Those who favor the use of prisoners in research suggest other possible reasons why prisoners participate in such studies, including boredom and a desire to "pay back" society for misdeeds.

The National Commission for the Protection of Human Subjects made recommendations regarding prison-based research that could have a major impact on future studies. The commission approved such research in principle, as long as certain conditions, including prior approval by an institutional review board, are met. In order to minimize the coerciveness of the situation, the commission specified that adequate living standards must be provided in prisons used as a base for research—a requirement that, if enforced, is likely to mean that no prison research will be conducted in the future.[29]

The commission also issued recommendations on research involving individuals institionalized as mentally infirm, including "individuals who are mentally ill, mentally retarded, emotionally disturbed, psychotic, or senile, or who have other impairments of a similar nature and who reside as patients in an institution." Such persons present a dual problem: As with children, there are serious doubts about their legal capacity to consent. And as with prisoners, the use of institutionalized populations increases the possibility of coercion. Here, too, the commission approved participation of such persons in nontherapeutic experiments provided certain guidelines are followed. Besides prior approval by an institutional review board, the recommendations call for two additional safeguards. Where only minimal risk is involved, subjects incapable of consenting may be used if they do not expressly object to participating. If the research "represents a minor increase over minimal risk," individuals incapable of consenting may be used if they "assent," a commission term for a consent that would not meet the usual tests of comprehension.[30]

The commission issued special recommendations regarding psychosurgery and fetal research, the two topics that Congress, in establishing the commission, specifically singled out as areas of study and report. The commission concluded that institutions with an institutional review board that has evaluated the competency of the surgeon and the manner of patient selection and consent can ethically perform psychosurgery on children, prisoners, and involuntarily confined patients, provided a court has approved the procedure. The commission also recommended that the secretary of HEW conduct and support psychosurgery research.[31] As for fetal research, the commission stipulated that nontherapeutic research must impose "minimal or no risk on the fetus in utero," and that nontherapeutic research in anticipation of abortion, during the abortion procedure, or directed toward the nonviable fetus ex utero should be permitted only in special circumstances, and after approval of a national ethical review body.[32] The commission did not issue guidelines for research on poor and/or chronically ill subjects, although these groups have also been frequently cited as particularly vulnerable to research abuse.

Although the commission concentrated in particular on the ethics of experimenting on certain subgroups of the population, it also studied the overall question of how research subjects can best be protected from harmful research practices. The commission followed the basic thrust of the 1966–67 Public Health Service guidelines and the 1971 secretary's *Guide* in recommending (a) that all research involving human subjects conducted at an institution that receives federal funding be reviewed by an institutional review board before it is begun and (b) that there be informed consent by the subjects involved.[33]

Final regulations resulting from these recommendations were not issued until 1981. The regulations, now in effect, apply only to research involving human subjects that is conducted by the Department of Health and Human Services itself or funded in whole or in part by the department.[34] Specifically excluded from coverage is most research involving normal educational practices or use of educational tests, research involving survey or interview procedures, research involving the observation of public behavior, and research "involving the collection or study of existing data, documents, records, pathological specimens, or diagnostic specimens, if these sources are publicly available or if the information is recorded by the investigator in such a manner that subjects cannot be identified . . . ." Moreover, the secretary may waive application of the regulation to specific research or classes of research that would otherwise be covered.

Research to which the regulations do apply must be reviewed and approved by an institutional review board (IRB) and must be subject to continuing IRB review.[35] An IRB must have at least five members of varying backgrounds; at least one must be from a nonscientific area and at least one must be from outside the institution. However, if the research involves "no more than minimal risk" or "minor changes in previously approved research," approval—but not disapproval—can be given through an expedited review procedure under which "the review may be carried out by the IRB chairperson or by one or more experienced reviewers designated by the chairperson from among members of the IRB." Miminal risk is defined as not greater than "those ordinarily encountered in daily life or during the performance of routine physical or psychological examinations or tests." It specifically includes such things as collection of hair, nail clippings, excreta, and external secretions, recordings of data from adult subjects using noninvasive procedures, and the study of existing data, documents, records, and pathological and diagnostic specimens.

In order to approve research, the IRB must determine that each of the following requirements is satisfied:

1. Risks to subjects are minimized.
2. Risks to subjects are reasonable in relation to anticipated benefits, if any, to subjects, and the importance of the knowledge that may reasonably be expected to result.
3. Selection of subjects is equitable.
4. Informed consent will be sought.
5. Informed consent will be appropriately documented.
6. Where appropriate, the research plan makes adequate provision for monitoring the data collected to insure the safety of subjects.
7. Where appropriate, there are adequate provisions to protect the privacy of subjects and maintain the confidentiality of data.

No human subjects may be involved in research unless legally effective informed consent has been obtained, and "only under circumstances that provide the prospective subject . . . sufficient opportunity to consider whether or not to participate and that minimize the possibility of coercion or undue influence."

One way of maximizing informed consent is to specify the procedure that must be followed. Another is to require specific documentation that the consent process occurred. The regulations do both. In obtaining informed consent, the prospective subject must be provided with:

1. A statement that the study involves research, an explanation of the purposes of the research and the expected duration of the subject's participation, a description of the procedures to be followed, and identification of any procedures which are experimental;

2. A description of any reasonably foreseeable risks or discomforts to the subject;

3. A description of any benefits to the subject or to others, which may reasonably be expected from the research;

4. A disclosure of appropriate alternative procedures or courses of treatment, if any, that might be advantageous to the subject;

5. A statement describing the extent, if any, to which confidentiality of records identifying the subject will be maintained;

6. For research involving more than minimal risk, an explanation as to whether any compensation and an explanation as to whether any medical treatments are available if injury occurs and, if so, what they consist of, or where further information may be obtained;

7. An explanation of whom to contact for answers to pertinent questions about the research and research subjects' rights, and whom to contact in the event of a research-related injury to the subject; and

8. A statement that participation is voluntary, refusal to participate will involve no penalty or loss of benefits to which the subject is otherwise entitled, and the subject may discontinue participation at any time without penalty or loss of benefits to which the subject is otherwise entitled.[36]

An IRB may "approve a consent procedure that does not include, or which alters, some or all of the elements of informed consent . . . or waive the requirement to obtain informed consent," when the waiver or alteration "will not adversely affect the rights and welfare of the subjects," or when the research involves "no more than minimal risk" or "could not practicably be carried out without the waiver or alteration . . . ." This discretionary waiver provision has been the target of some criticism, but it is too early to tell how frequently—and in what circumstances—it will be invoked.[37]

The consent process must be documented, either by the signing of a written consent form embodying the elements of informed consent listed above or with a "'short form' written consent document stating that the elements of informed consent required . . . have been presented orally to the subject or the subject's legally authorized representative. When this method is used, there shall be a witness to the oral presentation." An IRB may waive the requirement of a signed consent form for research that "presents no more than minimal risk of harm to subjects and involves no procedures for which written consent is normally required outside of the research context" or if "the only record linking the subject and the research would be the consent document and the principal risk would be potential harm resulting from a breach of confidentiality." Although the regulations provide for consent by a "subject's legally authorized representative" they do not provide specific guidelines for research involving children or the institutionalized, although such guidelines are apparently forthcoming.

The question all of this poses for the health professional planning nontherapeutic research using human subjects is how to comply with federal, state, and professional standards for such research without jeopardizing the integrity of the subjects, the experiment, and the research design. The first step, clearly, is to establish contact with the appropriate institutional review board. Every institution subject to the federal guidelines must adopt and submit to HEW an "assurance" that establishes an IRB and describes review and implementation procedures. This document, plus the IRB's rules and regulations, should provide guidance for the investigator. In any research project, however, it is the investigator who bears the primary legal and administrative responsibility, and who must inform the institution if human subjects are involved in the research design—in which case the proposal must come before the IRB.[38]

Some states have also passed laws concerning conditions for human experimentation in situations not covered by federal regulations, which also require some manner of prior review and supervision. States also may have prohibitions on human experimentation in state institutions, such as prisons.[39]

Donation of Body Parts for Transplantation

Transplantation of body parts is a relatively new but expanding phenomena, and the law has not always kept up with the technology in this area. When transplantations involve a donation from one living person to another, consent by the transplant donor is to what is—for that person—a nontherapeutic procedure. Thus the legal issues are similar to those involved in informed consent to human experimentation.

Some observers maintain that agreement by a competent adult to donate part of his or her body for transplantation to another raises no large or unique legal questions,[40] because the individual has the autonomy and right to authorize such a nontherapeutic, often risky, procedure. But others suggest[41] that the severe psychological pressures usually involved in donor situations (donors and recipients are frequently related)[42] will cause courts to examine carefully the competency, voluntariness, and disclosure involved.

The situation is further compounded when the potential donor is a minor or an incompetent adult. The inherent ethical and legal question is whether a parent or guardian can validly consent on behalf of another to an invasive procedure of clear risk and no direct benefit to the person on whose behalf the consent is given. Clearly, if the parents refuse consent the unemancipated minor cannot become an organ donor. And a minor old enough to appreciate the situation cannot be made a donor against his or her will, regardless of parental consent. Thus only if the parents consent *and* the child either consents or is too young to express a view, does the question ever arise.

In the transplant situation, which often involves benefit to another family member, as in the case of a kidney donated by one sibling to another, a sacrifice is being asked of the child for reasons many people would view as reasonable. But the very reasonableness casts doubt on the voluntariness of the proxy consent: Not only is the minor under considerable family pressure, but the parents—to whom society entrusts protection of the child out of a belief that they have the best interest of their child at heart—have a competing, possibly stronger, interest in the sick child. For this reason, even when the minor who is a potential donor and both parents have authorized organ donation, the surgeon and hospital may hesitate to accept this authorization, and seek direction from a court, in order to be assured immunity from civil and criminal liability.

In overseeing parental proxy-consent to organ donation, the courts have applied one of three different tests. The first, generally referred to as the "substituted judgment" test, is one in which the court undertakes to decide what the minor (or other incompetent) would do in the given situation if he or she were competent to decide.[43] The second, or "best interest," test looks for (some might say invents) direct benefits to the donor. Courts have found direct benefits in the avoidance of psychological trauma from *not* donating, in the presumed ability of the recipient later to look after a permanently incompetent potential donor, and in the anticipation that positive feelings resultings from the donation might aid in the rehabilitation of an institutionalized prospective donor. Finally, there is the "fair and reasonable" test, under which the court, rather than making its own judgment, simply acts as an overseer to assure that the parental decision is made in a fair and reasonable manner.[44]

In 1970 the Michigan legislature confronted one aspect of this problem by enacting a statute that provides:

A person of 14 years of age or more may give one of his two kidneys to a father, mother, son, daughter, brother, or sister for a transplantation needed by him when authorized by order of the probate court which has jurisdiction of the person.[45]

The statute requires that the court determine whether or not the minor's consent is based on an understanding of the "needs and probable consequences of the gift." In such cases, parental consent is not required.[46]

NOTES

1. Henry K. Beecher, "Ethics and Clinical Research," *New England Journal of Medicine* 274:1354–1360 (1966).
2. In fact, John Robertson has applied the term "boundary activities" to the area of innovative therapy. See John Robertson, "Legal Implications of the Boundaries between Biomedical Research Involving Human Subjects and the Accepted or Routine Practice of Medicine," in *The Belmont Report: Ethical Principles and Guidelines for the Protection of Human Subjects of Research*, App. vol. 1 (Bethesda, Md: National Commission for the Protection of Human Subjects of Biomedical and Behavioral Research, 1978), pp. 16-1–16-54 (DHEW pub. no. (OS) 78-0013).
3. Others argue that innovative therapy presents the greater challenge to adequate authorization. Alexander Capron suggests: "The standard approach has it backwards, higher requirements for informed consent should be imposed in therapy than in investigation . . . patients who are offered new therapy often have eyes only for its novelty and not for its risks." Quoted in Robert J. Levine, "The Nature and Definition of Informed Consent in Various Settings," *The Belmont Report*, App. vol. 1, p. 3–40, citing Jay Katz, *Experimentation with Human Beings*, (New York: Russell Sage Foundation, 1972), p. 574.
4. Jon R. Waltz and Fred E. Inbau, *Medical Jurisprudence* (New York; Macmillan, 1971), p. 190. They also point out a "seemingly dangerous dilemma" owing to the fact that "the practicing physician has a duty to keep abreast of and apply new developments in his profession . . . . He now must determine when a particular procedure ceases being an innovation, for the use of which he may expose himself to strict liability, and becomes instead a new development which he will be required to use if he is to meet his duty of keeping abreast of his profession's advances" (p. 187).
5. A. L. Cochrane, *Effectiveness and Efficiency*, (London: Nuffield Provincial Hospitals Trust, 1972); John W. Williamson, *Improving Medical Practice and Health Care: A Bibliographic Guide to Information Management in Quality Assurance and Continuing Education* (Cambridge, Mass.: Ballinger, 1977). An important exception is drug therapy, due primarily to the 1962 amendments to the Food, Drug, and Cosmetic Act. See Chapter 11.
6. Robertson, in *The Belmont Report*, App., vol. 1, p. 16-21.
7. Robertson quotes—and then criticizes—Levine to this effect. See ibid., pp. 16-30–16-32.

8. George J. Annas, Leonard H. Glantz, and Barbara F. Katz, *Informed Consent to Human Experimentation: The Subject's Dilemma* (Cambridge, Mass.: Ballinger, 1977), p. 22.

9. See, for example, William J. Curran, "Reasonableness and Randomization in Clinical Trials: Fundamental Law and Governmental Regulation," *New England Journal of Medicine* 300:1273–1275 (1979).

10. For a general discussion of the ethical principles involved in human experimentation—including the importance of informed consent—see *The Belmont Report: Ethical Principles and Guidelines for the Protection of Human Subjects of Research* (Bethesda, Md.: The National Commission for the Protection of Human Subjects of Biomedical and Behavioral Research, 1978) (DHEW pub. no. (OS) 78-0012).

11. Declaration of Helsinki, World Medical Association, 1964. Endorsed in 1967 by the American Medical Association, American Federation for Clinical Research, American Society for Clinical Investigation, Central Society for Clinical Research, American College of Physicians, American College of Surgeons, Society for Pediatric Research, and American Academy of Pediatrics.

12. As quoted in *Medical World News* 8 June 1973, p. 40.

13. *United States v. Karl Brandt*, Trials of War Criminals Before Nuremberg Military Tribunals Under Control Council Law No. 10 (October 1946–April 1949). The military tribunal established at Nuremberg was almost entirely a project of the United States military, but the Nuremberg Code was subsequently adopted by the United Nations General Assembly. Considerable controversy surrounds the question of the precendential value of the code, either as U.S. common law or as international law. It would seem that U.S. courts could use the code as authority, but only one court has ever done so. See discussion in Annas et al., Informed Consent, pp. 6–9.

14. *United States v. Karl Brandt*.

15. Ibid.

16. Annas, Glantz, and Katz, *Informed Consent*, pp. 35–38, discuss two major purposes of informed consent in the experimental setting: promoting individual autonomy and encouraging rational decision making on the part of researchers. Thus the therapeutic privilege cannot apply to the non-therapeutic experimental situation.

17. See note 13.

18. *Kaimowitz v. Department of Mental Health*, Civ. No. 73-19434-AW (Cir. Ct. Wayne County, Mich., July 10, 1973).

19. The Canadian case is *Halushka v. University of Saskatchewan*, 52 W.W.R. 608 (Sask. 1965), discussed in Annas et al., *Informed Consent*, pp. 18–19. There are some classic instances of experimentation involving competent but disadvantaged adults that have been widely criticized as unethical and for which strong cases for liability on the part of the experimenters could be made. But in these instances, including the Tuskegee syphilis study and the Jewish Chronic Disease Hospital cancer study, voluntary settlements and mild punishments were the main final results. See Katz, *Experimentation with Human Beings;* Nathan Hershey and Robert D. Miller, *Human Experimentation and the Law* (Germantown, Md.: Aspen Systems Corporation, 1976), pp. 6–10; Public Health Service, *Final Report of the Tuskegee Syphilis Study Ad Hoc*

Advisory Panel (Washington, D.C.: Department of Health, Education and Welfare, 1973); and James H. Jones, *Bad Blood: The Tuskegee Syphilis Experiment* (New York: Free Press, 1981).

20. The effectiveness of these requirements is put into considerable question by the fact that the infamous Tuskegee syphilis study continued under U.S. Public Health Service auspices until 1971.

21. 45 C.F.R., Title 46 (1975).

22. 42 U.S.C. Secs. 2891-3(a).

23. Established under authority of 42 U.S.C. Sec. 1802 (1978).

24. See the discussion of consent on behalf of children to organ transplant donation, in this chapter.

25. Annas, Glantz, and Katz, *Informed Consent*, p. 93. They also discuss (pp. 77–79) the one decision that comes the closest to dealing with this type of proxy consent; *Bonner v. Moran*, 126 F.2d 121 (D.C. Cir. 1941). At the most Bonner would seem to establish the hypothetical that consent by a parent and fifteen-year-old child could free the physician from liability. But this case was decided before Nuremberg, the written opinion is confusing, and any lessons in it seem to be based on no more than speculation. Also see Edward T. Porcaro, Jr., "Experimentation with Children: The "Pawns" of Medical Technology," *Medicolegal News* 7(2):6–9, 16 (1979).

26. The quoted language is from the second provision of the Nuremberg Code. On using children as research subjects see "Why Children are Involved as Research Subjects," in *Report and Recommendations: Research Involving Children* (Washington, D.C.: National Commission for the Protection of Human Subjects of Biomedical and Behavioral Research, 1977) (DHEW pub. no. (OS) 77-0004), pp. 21–26.

27. In a sentence that has been quoted frequently in discussions of proxy consent by parents, the U.S. Supreme Court opined: "Parents may be free to become martyrs themselves but it does not follow that they are free in identical circumstances to make martyrs of their children before they have reached the age of full and legal discretion when they make choices for themselves." *Prince v. Massachusetts*, 321 U.S. 158, 1944. But this case actually had nothing to do with medical procedures—therapeutic or nontherapeutic—but rather, in a clash of child labor laws and the First Amendment, involved a nine-year-old selling Jehovah's Witness tracts.

28. See *Research Involving Children*, pp. 1–20, especially recommendations 1, 2, 5, and 7. Recommendation 5 provides, in part

> Research in which more than minimal risk to children is presented by an intervention that does not hold out the prospect of direct benefit for the individual subjects . . . may be conducted or supported provided . . . (A) such risk represents a minor increase over minimal risk; (B) such intervention or procedure presents experiences to subjects that are reasonably commensurate with those inherent in their actual or expected medical, psychological or social situations, and is likely to yield generalizable knowledge about the subjects' disorder or condition . . . .

It is unclear to this author what, if anything, (A) and (B) mean; but the recommendation clearly opens the door to risk-without-benefit experimentation involving children. The 1981 regulations, discussed below, did not include guidelines on experiments involving children as subjects, that issue left for future consideration.

29. See *Report and Recommendations: Research Involving Prisoners* (Washington, D.C.: National Commission for the Protection of Human Subjects of Biomedical and Behavioral Research, 1976) (DHEW pub. no. (OS) 76-131). Prisoners have been particularly involved in new drug testing, a practice that would have been effectively ended by FDA regulations scheduled to take effect June 1, 1981. But a lawsuit brought by four prisoners and the Upjohn Company caused the FDA to withdraw the regulations.

30. See *Report and Recommendations: Research Involving Those Institutionalized as Mentally Infirm* (Washington, D.C.: National Commission for the Protection of Human Subjects of Biomedical and Behavioral Research, 1978) (DHEW pub. no. (OS) 78-0006). See especially recommendations 2 and 4. The 1981 regulations, discussed below, did not include guidelines on experiments involving the institutionalized, that subject left for future consideration.

31. See *Report and Recommendations: Psychosurgery* (Bethesda, Md.: National Commission for the Protection of Human Subjects of Biomedical and Behavioral Research, 1977) (DHEW pub. no. (OS) 77-0001.) The secretary did not accept this psychosurgery recommendation.

32. See *Report and Recommendations: Research on the Fetus* (Bethesda, Md.: National Commission for the Protection of Human Subjects of Biomedical and Behavioral Research, 1975) (DHEW pub. no. (OS) 76-127). Of all of the commission's recommendations on special categories of research, this would seem to be the only area where regulations have been implemented with any finality.

33. In *The Belmont Report*, the commission also outlined more generalized principles for evaluating research involving human subjects: respect for persons, beneficence, and justice.

34. 46 Fed. Reg. 8366-92 (1981), codified at 45 C.F.R. Part 46. The federal regulations previously in effect applied to all research conducted at an institution receiving departmental funds, regardless of whether a specific research project was receiving federal funds or not. Since this meant that institutional review boards reviewed all human subject research, regardless of funding source, it is possible that some institutions will simply continue this practice. But they are no longer required to do so. The day after the departmental guidelines appeared, the FDA published very similar guidelines. See the *Federal Register* for January 27, 1981.

35. For a critical discussion of the performance of IRBs, see George J. Annas, Leonard H. Glantz, and Barbara F. Katz, *The Rights of Doctors, Nurses, and Allied Health Professionals: A Health Law Primer* (New York: Avon, 1981), pp. 143–144 and references cited therein.

36. In addition to these eight requirements, the regulations also provide six additional elements of informed consent that shall be provided "when appropriate." See 45 C.F.R. 46.116.

37. See, for example, Robert M. Veatch, "Protecting Human Subjects: The Federal Government Steps Back," *Hastings Center Report* 11(3):9–12 (June 1981).

38. The investigator must also be alert to ethical and legal concerns not covered

by the federal regulations. One such area is confidentiality. DHHS chose not to have "specific requirements describing how personal information must be maintained or to whom it may be disclosed." But see *Report and Recommendations: Disclosure of Research Information Under the Freedom of Information Act* (Bethesda, Md.: National Commission for the Protection of Human Subjects of Biomedical and Behavioral Research, 1977) (DHEW pub. no. (OS) 77-0003.) There is something of a dilemma as regards confidentiality, because effective protection of human subjects relies in good part on peer and public scrutiny. Except where individual subjects who are patients are identifiable, IRB records are usually not confidential. Institutional policy may well make such records open to the public; state open-meeting statutes may apply to IRB meetings and written materials; and IRB records may be subpoenaed in lawsuits. At the same time, disclosure of identifiable information without the subject's consent is to be avoided. Investigators therefore need to be extremely careful in how they record information. A related issue, access to existing medical records for epidemiological studies, is discussed in Chapter 17.

39. See, for example, Nathan Hershey and Robert D. Miller, *Human Experimentation and the Law* (Germantown, Md.: Aspen Systems Corporation, 1976), pp. 111–146.
40. See, for example, Waltz and Inbau, *Medical Jurisprudence* p. 219, note 24.
41. See Mark Kusanovich, "Medical Malpractice Liability and the Organ Transplant," *University of San Francisco Law Review* 5:223–279 (1971), especially the references listed in his note 18.
42. But see Robert Steinbrook, "Unrelated Volunteers as Bone Marrow Donors," *Hastings Center Report* 10(1):11–14, 20 (February 1980).
43. Annas, Glantz, and Katz, *Informed Consent*, p. 89, make the interesting point that, while courts using the substituted judgment test try to determine how a reasonable person would respond to the situation, at least one study has shown that most people actually deciding to donate organs to relatives did so on the basis of snap decisions, rather than on rational consideration.
44. See *Nathan v. Farinelli*, Civ. N. 74–87 (Mass. Super. Ct., July 13, 1974). Also see Charles H. Baron, Margot Botsford, and Garrick F. Cole, "Live Organ and Tissue Transplants from Minor Donors in Massachusetts," *Boston University Law Review* 55:159 (1975).
45. Michigan Code, Sec. 27.3178 (19b).
46. For more on the legal aspects of organ donation, see Norman P. Jeddeloh and S. N. Chatterjee, "Legal Problems in Organ Donation," *Surgical Clinics of North America* 58(2):245–259 (April 1978).

16

Malpractice

*If a physician operate on a man (i.e., gentleman) for a severe
wound with a bronze lancet and cause the man's death; or
open an abscess (in the eye) of a man with a bronze lancet
and destroy the man's eye, they shall cut off his fingers.*
—Code of Hammurabi[1]

MALPRACTICE is a poorly understood and emotional issue. Time was
when the notion of a patient suing a doctor or other health professional
was virtually unheard of.[2] Untoward outcomes were "unfortunate," and
unless there was unmistakable medical bungling—and often even then—
the practitioner was not called to task for a poor result. A number of
factors are behind the recent change in outlook. One is the vast oversell-
ing of the medical profession by the media, and the public's conviction
that no matter what was medically wrong with a patient, a good doctor
can put it right. Another was the realization, stemming from the revelations of Ralph Nader and other consumer advocates, that not all injuries,
medical and otherwise, were unavoidable, and that for some professionals the consumer's best interest might be a secondary concern. The
result has been an escalation in claims for personal injury in all areas,
including product liability and workers' compensation, during the
1970s. In no area has this phenomena been as pronounced as in the field
of medical practice.

Malpractice has long been a source of dread to health professionals.

Annas, Katz, and Trakimas report that even before the Civil War, "it was believed that some practitioners were stopping their surgical practices because of the threat of malpractice."[3] But the malpractice insurance "crisis" of the mid-1970s was the first to receive concerted attention by the medical profession and by state legislatures.

The precipitating events behind this "crisis" were the astronomical increases in malpractice insurance rates and the abandonment of this segment of the insurance market by several key companies. Just how many malpractice claims were made against practitioners and their insurers, how many actual malpractice suits against health care providers were filed, and how many awards—and in what amounts—were made, is not readily ascertainable.[4] There is no national reporting system that keeps track of all such information, and insurance companies, who are in the best position to supply such data, are generally reticent about providing it.[5] Given the increase in population, in medical personnel, and in the expense and complexity of medical care, it is reasonable to assume that the number of malpractice claims is increasing, and that, because of inflation and other factors, the size of settlements and awards has also gone up. But there are no dependable data as to the changeover time in the number of successful and unsuccessful malpractice claims and suits as a percentage of total provider-patient contacts and in the real (purchasing power) amount of money paid out.

The best source of information on all aspects of malpractice is the Department of Health, Education and Welfare's *Report of the Secretary's Commission on Medical Malpractice.*[6] Though the report was issued early in 1973, and predates the insurance-rate crisis of the mid-1970s, its data are significant. The commission found:

- Despite the publicity resulting from a few large malpractice cases, a claim-related medical malpractice incident remains a relatively rare event, with actual lawsuits even rarer, and trials rarer still.
- In 1970 a malpractice claim was asserted for one out of every 226,000 patient visits to doctors.
- Most doctors have never had a medical malpractice suit filed against them; even those who have rarely have been sued more than once.
- In 1970, 6.5 medical malpractice claim files were opened for every 100 active practitioners.
- Most hospitals, however large, go through the entire year without a single claim being filed against them.
- Most patients have never suffered a medical injury due to malpractice and fewer still have made a claim alleging malpractice.
- If the average person lives seventy years, he or she will have—based on 1970 data—approximately 400 contacts as a patient with doctors

and dentists. The chances that he or she will assert a medical malpractice claim are one in 39,500.

- An estimated 7,200 malpractice claims were asserted in 1970, of which approximately 40 percent resulted in payment to the claimant.
- Although payments ranged widely in amount, the typical (median) payment was $2,000. Half of all payments were for less than $2,000, and a significant number totaled between $5,000 and $20,000. Only 3 percent of all payments exceeded $100,000, but these contributed substantially to the aggregate cost of claims.
- Insurance carriers judged 46 percent of malpractice claims to have some validity, while lawyers for *both* plaintiffs and defendants estimated that only one-third of the claims involve actual malpractice.
- Eighty-six percent of the claims involved alleged injury due to improper treatment rather than to improper diagnosis. The alleged medical malpractice usually occurred in hospital settings (75 percent), especially the surgical suite (39 percent), or patients' rooms (34 percent). Emergency rooms and intensive care facilities accounted for only 13 percent of the incidents.

Several studies of malpractice claims, suits, and awards covering the mid-1970s—the period of malpractice "crisis"—indicate a continuation of this basic picture. The main changes seem to be a substantial increase in claims alleging improper diagnosis and significant increases in the size of awards. But the likelihood of a practitioner facing and losing a malpractice suit remains slight.[7] Malpractice litigation is simply not as pervasive as has been suggested. Furthermore, the screening of cases and their eventual settlement point to a more rational and ordered system than many health professionals believe. Yet while claims data fail to support a crisis view of malpractice, there is nothing to suggest that the current system is a very effective social mechanism.

What is the theory of malpractice law, and can such private litigation serve social ends?[8] The answer requires some background in the basic law of negligence.

The broad area known as private law concerns the competing legal rights and claims of private individuals and corporations (in contrast to public law—constitutional, criminal, and administrative law—which concerns the role of government). Private law includes disputes involving property rights, legal contracts,[9] and torts.

The law of torts—the focus of this discussion—determines when one person must pay compensation for injuries caused to another. A particular act may lead to both a tort action and criminal prosecution. The two systems are completely separate, however; in one case the liability is to the injured party, in the other, to society. Tort law also differs from contract law, because it is based not on an agreement between the parties but on the types of obligations the law says citizens have in their interactions with one another. These obligations are limited: A may harm B by beating him with a stick or by refusing to hire him for a job. Although B may be hurt more by the lack of work than by the beating, only the latter is recognized as a tort for which B may successfully sue A.

There is no general rule that a person causing an injury to another is automatically required to compensate the injured party. The injuries compensable under tort law include specific types of intentionally inflicted wrongs, such as assault and battery, defamation, and invasion of privacy, as well as injuries inflicted unintentionally through failure to exercise the care that could be expected of an ordinarily prudent person. An innocent, unavoidable accident creates no legal obligation.

Failure to exercise ordinary care is termed negligence, which is defined as "the omission to do something which a reasonable man, guided by those ordinary considerations which ordinarily regulate human affairs, would do, or the doing of something which a reasonable and prudent man would not do."[10] It is this model of "the reasonable man" that the courts use to determine whether conduct that has unintentionally resulted in injury constitutes negligence, and in such cases it is the task of the jury to serve as a collective "reasonable person." If they decide that a reasonable person would have been more careful than was the defendant, the defendant will be judged to have acted negligently, and the injury will be held compensable. If the jury decides a reasonable person would have acted pretty much as the defendant did, whatever harm was caused will not be considered negligence, and will not be compensable.

Two functions are served by recognizing negligence as a compensable tort. The most obvious is *compensation:* To make up, through money damages, for the harm the injured party suffered through no fault of his or her own. Since such harm cannot be undone, the victim attempts, by bringing a negligence action, to shift the continuing burden of that harm, at least in part, from the victim to the person who caused it (or, as is most often the case, to that person's insurance carrier).

Besides providing for compensation, the negligence suit serves a *deterrence*—or quality control—function. The basic concept here—and throughout American law—is to guide behavior by making certain undesirable actions so costly that they will be avoided; the realization that negligent behavior obligates an individual to compensate the victim of that negligence is expected to deter citizens from behaving negligently in their relations with others.[11] Negligence theory thus assumes that it would have been possible for the defendant to have avoided the injury inflicted, if he or she had only acted more prudently. The fact that the negligence lawsuit therefore centers on determining *fault* is a point often overlooked by health care providers—especially physicians—who view the process as a system designed simply to assign liability to those best able to bear the burden (although this technically inaccurate view may have some validity in practice).[12]

For a claimant to succeed in a lawsuit based on negligence the situation must meet four tests:

1. It must be shown that the defendant owed the plaintiff a *duty to act* in a particular way. This has a specific legal meaning, for there are many apparent or moral duties not recognized by the law. For example, there is generally no duty to take positive actions in behalf of others. A person walking by the river who sees a man drowing has a moral duty to throw him the lifebuoy conveniently at hand—especially if this can be done without any personal risk—but this is not a legal duty. Ignoring a drowing man, a burning house, or an injured person creates no risk of legal liability, unless some special relationship already exists, such as between bather and public lifeguard.[13] There is however, a duty to do whatever one is doing reasonably, so as not to inflict harm on others. This duty to act reasonably is owed to all—friend and stranger alike.

2. The plaintiff must prove that the defendant *failed to live up to the duty* owed the plaintiff. Was the defendant as careful as any reasonable person would have been? If not, the defendant has failed to exercise the due care expected of him.[14]

3. It must be shown that the plaintiff has *suffered real harm*, of a type recognizable to all, and not some trivial inconvenience the average person would shrug off. Hurt feelings would ordinarily not warrant compensation, nor would the fact that a duty breached almost led to harm. The tort negligence system involves compensation and implies a calculable loss.

4. The plaintiff must demonstrate that the defendant's breach of duty was the *actual cause* of the harm suffered by the plaintiff.

It is sometimes argued that a fifth element is also necessary in a negligence suit, namely that the harm be reasonably foreseeable. In most cases foreseeability is obvious enough to be assumed—a poorly attached car trailer, for example, might be expected to come loose and run into something. But that the trailer would hit a truck carrying explosives would not be considered reasonably foreseeable in terms of a duty to bystanders.[15]

In every negligence suit the plaintiff bears the burden of demonstrating the existence of all four elements outlined above. This need not, as in criminal prosecutions, be shown beyond a reasonable doubt, but simply by a preponderance of the evidence. But if the defendant can overcome this preponderance on any one element, the fact that the other elements have been satisfied will not matter; the plaintiff will lose.

How do these basic principles of negligence relate to malpractice? The answer is straightforward: Malpractice is negligent performance by a professional; and a malpractice suit is a negligence suit brought against a professional. Malpractice can be alleged regarding the performance not only of health professionals of all types, but of lawyers, architects, accountants, or any other practitioners. The four elements outlined earlier are basic to any malpractice suit.

1. A duty owed.   The professional does not owe a duty to the general public, but only to those with whom he or she has developed a professional relationship.[16] In terms of health care, the question of whether or not a provider-patient relationship existed is very important. For once such a relationship has been established, and unless it has been clearly terminated, the duty of the practitioner to the patient applies both to what he or she does and to what he or she does not do—actions and omissions. Thus a health professional can be negligent by doing nothing in the face of the patient's clear need for professional assistance. This need not be classical abandonment, in which the practitioner clearly intends to end the relationship, but also includes instances where the patient is not seen as often as due care dictates.[17]

The health professional has a duty to the patient to exercise reasonable care and skill, and, by implication, to possess the skills expected of such a professional. The classic statement of this duty appears in the court's observations in the 1898 case of *Pike v. Honsinger:*

> A physician and surgeon, by taking charge of a case, impliedly represents that he possesses, and the law places upon him the duty of possessing, that reasonable degree of learning and skill that is ordinarily possessed by physicians and surgeons in the locality where he practices, and which is ordinarily regarded by those conversant with the employment as necessary to qualify him to engage in the business of practicing medicine and surgery. Upon consenting to treat a patient it becomes his duty to use reasonable care and diligence in the exercise of his skill and the application of his learning to accomplish the purpose for which he was employed. He is under the further obligation to use his best judgment in exercising his skill and applying his knowledge. The law holds him liable for an injury to his patient resulting from want of the requisite knowledge and skill, or the omission to exercise reasonable care, or the failure to use his best judgment. The rule in relation to learning and skill does not require the surgeon to possess that extraordinary learning and skill which belong only to a few men of rare-endowments, but such as is possessed by the average member of the medical profession in good standing. Still, he is bound to keep abreast of the times, and a departure from approved methods in general use, if it injures the patient, will render him liable, however good his intentions may have been. The rule of reasonable care and diligence does not require the exercise of the highest possible degree of care; and to render a physician and surgeon liable, it is not enough that there has been a less degree of care than some other medical

man might have shown, or less than even he himself might have bestowed, but there must be a want of ordinary and reasonable care, leading to a bad result. This includes not only the diagnosis and treatment, but also the giving of proper instructions to his patient in relation to conduct, exercise and the use of the injured limb. The rule requiring him to use his best judgment does not hold him liable for a mere error of judgment, provided he does what he thinks is best after careful examination. His implied engagement with his patient does not guarantee a good result, but he promises by implication to use the skill and learning of the average physician, to exercise reasonable care and to exert his best judgment in the effort to bring about a good result.[18]

This statement should make it clear that professional negligence is broader than "carelessness." A practitioner may be negligent for undertaking a treatment for which he or she lacked the requisite skills, even though he or she was as careful as could be in carrying out the treatment. Some explanation of "that reasonable degree of learning and skill that is ordinarily possessed by physicians and surgeons" is in order. Because the logic of this standard is to hold practitioners to the level of competence of their peers, and because the trend toward specialization in all of the health professions has produced a multitute of peer groups, malpractice law takes specialty into consideration. Thus a general surgeon is expected to possess "that reasonable degree of learning and skill" of general surgeons, while the neurosurgeon will be compared to other neurosurgeons. A critical care nurse will be held to the standard of other critical care nurses, a nurse practitioner will be compared to other nurse practitioners. The principle is that professionals holding themselves out to have a certain level of skill and expertise will be held to that level. This means not only that someone practicing as a specialist will be judged by the standards of that specialty, but also that a nonspecialist who undertakes to treat a condition generally treated only by a particular specialty will be held to the level of that specialty.[19]

A duty breached.   Again, the concept is the same as in any other negligence suit. But while the same element is basic, the method of proof is different.[20] For while a judge and jury can put themselves in the position of any other reasonable person when considering possible negligence in an automobile accident, it is obviously impossible for them to decide on their own whether a surgeon who performed a Babcock-Bacon proctosigmoidectomy instead of an anterior resection for a lesion located above the peritoneal reflection had acted reasonably in meeting a duty of due care and skill. Nor can the proceedings be adjourned while they acquire enough medical education to qualify as competent surgeons. Therefore the courts rely on the testimony of other practicing surgeons as to what a reasonable, competent surgeon would do if faced with the patient's medical problem. The law says that in malpractice negligence suits the jury *must* be guided by the testimony of expert witnesses, rather than make their own judgments. "It is not enough," point out Law and Polan, "for the injured patient to present the court with facts and evidence that would allow the court to weigh and determine whether the doctor's conduct fell below that which would be expected of a reasonably prudent person. This represents legal recognition that medicine is a holistic art rather than a rulebook, formula science."[21]

There is one exception to this dependence on expert testimony, and that is the rule of evidence known as *res ipsa loquitor*—"the thing speaks for itself." Under this doctrine, the jury can decide on its own that damage was negligently caused if—and only if—(a) the injury was such that ordinarily does not occur unless someone is negligent, (b) the action or object that caused the injury was controlled solely by the defendant, and (c) the plaintiff did nothing on his own to contribute to the injury. There has been some concern that this doctrine places professionals unfairly at risk whenever there is mere circumstantial evidence of negligence. But the legal studies conducted by the Secretary's Commission on Medical Malpractice indicate that *res ipsa loquitor* is not widely used even in the minority of states where it is recognized.[22]

The need to base a lawsuit on the opinions of expert witnesses carries with it some rather obvious problems. If the plaintiff can provide an expert witness—or two or three—so can the defendant. It is then left to the jury to decide which witnesses were the most convincing. It is not unusual, however, for a plaintiff to have difficulty finding a cooperative expert witness, not because of any weakness in the malpractice claim, but because of the reluctance of professionals to testify against one another. No expert witness, no case.

How serious this problem is—the so-called conspiracy of silence—is not clear, since inability to secure witnesses may, in a large number of instances, reflect the dubious merit of a claim rather than the mutual-protection practices of the professionals. Thus, the HEW commission, while acknowledging the existence of the problem, was not willing to affirm the existence of a "conspiracy." It did recommend, however, "that organized medicine and osteopathy establish an official policy encouraging members of their professions to cooperate fully in medical malpractice actions so that justice will be assured for all parties. . . ."[23]

The commission and other observers agree that the apparent unwillingness of professionals to testify against one another is of less concern than it used to be, in part because of the decline in what is known as the "locality rule." The *Pike v. Honsinger* statement of duty owed, quoted previously, cited as a standard "that reasonable degree of learning and skill that is ordinarily possessed by physicians and surgeons *in the locality where he practices . . . ."* This narrow definition of peer may have made some sense in earlier decades, when communities were more isolated and many practitioners were effectively cut off from the centers of medical progress. But today, when health professionals are likely to take their training in one part of the country, apprenticeships in another, and subsequently practice in still another locality, and when an extensive communications network of professional journals and meetings and hospital connections makes it possible to keep abreast of the important advances in their field, the parochialism of the locality rule is hard to defend. Most jurisdictions are therefore moving away from it, either through direct judicial abolishment of the doctrine[24] or by simply ignoring it. This is especially the case as regards specialists. Locality then becomes simply one factor among many to determine the degree of care to be expected from a practitioner. Expert testimony may be allowed regarding the accepted standard of care in other, similar communities, or in the state as a whole, or—in the case of a specialist—nationwide. Thus plaintiffs rebuffed by professionals unwilling to speak out against colleagues and friends may call on the testimony of witnesses outside the defendant's community, who would be less reluctant to engender local professional hostility. Steven Polan suggests that this change in the locality rule has been a major factor in increasing malpractice litigation.[25]

3. Harm to the plaintiff. The harm involved in a malpractice suit is some type of injury. Unless such harm can be demonstrated there is no basis for a malpractice action, even if it is clear the health professional performed incompetently. This requirement is met if the plaintiff suffers even a very slight amount of damage; however, unless the harm is substantial—and there is therefore the possibility of substantial compensation—there is little incentive to undergo the expense and anxiety of bringing a claim (especially from the perspective of the attorney, whose fee is usually based on a percentage of the compensation won).

It must be stressed again that harm alone does not constitute malpractice. Some unfavorable outcomes of medical treatment are unavoidable (some operations will result in wound infection no matter how careful and correct the health professionals have been); to award malpractice damages in such cases would compensate the patient, but it would not serve to deter poor performance.

4. Causation. To succeed with a malpractice suit the plaintiff must show that the defendant's negligence or incompetence was responsible for, or substantially aggravated, the plaintiff's untoward medical outcome—that is, except for the defendant's negligence the unsatisfactory outcome would not have occurred. Obviously expert testimony plays an important role here. But when the harm could have been caused, for example, either by negligent action or by underlying disease or injury, the jury must decide which of the possible causes was actually involved.

Defenses

There are several legal doctrines that bar an action for malpractice or provide a recognized defense. The most important of these are the statute of limitations and the defense of contributory negligence.

Statutes of limitations bar private lawsuits after a specific period of time. The theory behind them is that with the passage of time the memories of all the parties involved dim, making proof difficult. It is also felt that after a certain time the disruptive effect of a "stale claim" on the life of a defendant must be weighed against the unfairness in denying to the plaintiff what might otherwise be a valid claim. All states have statutes of limitations, with the time period varying from state to state and from one type of legal action to another. Many states have a statute of limitations of two or three years for personal injury suits and six years for contract suits.[26] A number of states have a special limitation for malpractice claims, which is generally shorter than the time limit for personal injury suits.[27]

The most difficult issue regarding statutes of limitations in malpractice is when to start the clock running. Originally, all such limits were thought to refer to the time at which the negligence occurred. But another approach is to begin the statutory period when the practitioner-patient relationship or the particular course of treatment has come to an end. And a growing number of states are taking still another approach, known as the "discovery rule," which starts the statutory period at the time when a reasonable person, exercising reasonable diligence, would have discovered that negligence had occurred.[28]

While many states have not adopted the discovery rule as a general standard, most do apply it when the situation involves the discovery of a foreign object in the patient's body after surgery, even if this discovery occurs many years after the surgery took place. Some of these states have double time limits; a malpractice action must be begun within a certain time after discovery as well as within a certain time after the negligent act occurred.

There are two important exceptions to statutes of limitations. One is that the statutory period does not apply while the patient is incompetent to bring suit, either because of age or because of mental disability. For this reason pediatricians and others ministering to the health needs of children can face extremely long periods of malpractice jeopardy, since the time limit begins after their patients reach legal majority. However, several states have enacted statutes arbitrarily starting the time clock after a minor reaches age eight or ten.[29] The second exception involves deliberate concealment. If a health professional is aware of his or her own negligence and hides the true facts from the patient, the period of limitation will not begin until the patient has had an independent opportunity to discover the negligence. However, such fraudulent concealment is generally difficult to prove.

If a health professional sues a patient to collect an unpaid bill, a claim of negligence by the patient would be an acceptable defense. If, however, the patient was aware of the apparent negligence at the time of such a suit and does not raise this defense, a few states will not permit the patient to sue for malpractice later.[30] And in many states, if the negligent treatment involves an injury caused by a third person, such as the negligent driver in an automobile accident, a release signed by the patient as part of a settlement with that third person can also serve to release the treating health professional from malpractice liability, on the theory that any injury should have only one cause.[31]

Often, in a negligence action, the defendant will argue that the plaintiff is guilty of *contributory negligence*. This is less likely in a malpractice suit because it is the health provider who generally controls a treatment process. Traditionally, if the defendant in a negligence action could prove that the plaintiff contributed to his own harm, the plaintiff could not win, even if the defendant was proved to have been negligent as well. More recently, however, the trend is to apportion the damages on the basis of "comparative negligence" when the plaintiff's own negligence played some role in the outcome.

Contributory negligence is most likely to come up in a malpractice suit if a defendant claims that the patient's actions, before or after treatment, exacerbated the effects of the defendant's negligence. However, cases involving concurrent negligence by patient and provider are extremely rare. More often, what appears to be a claim of contributory negligence is really a denial of negligence on the part of the provider. If, for example, the provider argues that the patient really suffered a bad outcome because he or she waited too long before seeking treatment, or because he or she did not follow instructions for posttreatment self-care, the provider is really arguing that his or her own performance was not the cause of the bad outcome.[32]

Thus far the discussion has focused on what the law says about negligence and malpractice. Now attention can be shifted to some recent changes in the law and to other suggestions that have emerged from the malpractice "crisis" of the 1970s. In the mid-1970s, state legislatures were deluged with recommendations for changes in the law to deal with the inability of many physicians to obtain malpractice insurance. It is now known that this problem was primarily the result of insurance industry miscalculations, including bad investments, plus an intentional effort by the parent company of a key malpractice insurer to use this area of insurance underwriting to generate a beneficial tax credit.[33] Although there is little data supporting the view that increasing numbers of baseless lawsuits fueled the "crisis," the major thrust of the recommendations—and of the changes in the law that were adopted—was aimed at limiting the patient-plaintiff's ability to collect damages for negligently caused harm. Thus the losers in the malpractice crisis have been the injured patients, while the primary beneficiaries have been the insurance carriers. Health care professionals, especially physicians, have come out somewhere in the middle.

The legislative changes that were adopted varied from state to state; as might be expected, those states where insurance carriers threatened to pull out of the malpractice coverage market entirely enacted some of the most far-reaching changes. Some of these have since been invalidated by state courts; and to confuse matters further, the same or similar change has been nullified in one state while upheld in another.[34]

One popular legislative change has been to limit the period in which a malpractice suit can be filed by reducing the statute of limitations and/ or limiting the application of the "discovery rule." Some states have even reduced the extended time period for filing a claim allowed to minors.[35] A second popular change has been to establish an arbitrary ceiling on the amount of damages that can be recovered for negligence associated with a single course of treatment. These ceilings, or "caps," have varied from $150,000 to $750,000. Their legal status remains clouded; while the highest courts in at least five states have upheld such legislation, those in at least three other states have invalidated similar provisions. One basis for invalidating these statutes has been the argument that absolute limits on compensation eliminate a common law remedy and thereby deny constitutional due process. Another argument is that such laws violate state constitutional prohibitions barring special legislation that favors specific groups. And a third argument holds that compensation ceilings violate equal protection by creating an unjustifiably disfavored class of citizens.

Some state legislatures have adopted a related approach by acting to limit compensation for certain types of harm, such as awards made for pain and suffering and for punitive damages. Critics point out, however, that all such limitations or compensation are (a) unfair, in that it is those patients who have, in fact, established negligence who are affected, and (b) ineffective in reducing premiums, since only 25 to 30 percent of each premium dollar goes toward paying compensation.

Some states have dealt with the malpractice situation by increasing the burden of proof required to demonstrate that the defendant was negligent. Others have sought to restrict the use of *res ipsa loquitor*—a move that, according to Law and Polan, has had little, and possibly even a reverse, effect.[36] And some states have taken aim at the judicial trend broadening the health professional's obligation to disclose to the patient information regarding proposed treatment. The patient cannot give truly informed consent without adequate information, and failure to provide such information can constitute negligence. Law and Polan explain that changes in informed-consent standards were among the most popular legislative responses to the malpractice "crisis" of the mid-1970s. In 1975, for example, New York State adopted a new law that severely restricted a patient's right to be informed about proposed treatments. Such laws were supported by organized medicine, which felt that recent judicial decisions supporting the patient's right to know were at least partially responsible for the sharp increase in malpractice suits. Yet as Law and Polan point out, "the New York legislature had before it information showing that actions for failure to obtain informed consent have no measurable effect on malpractice premiums. In the entire history of New York, there had been only one case in which money was paid solely on an informed-consent theory."[37] And as one observer has noted about these reforms in general, an "examination of the legislation shows that, at most, the problems have been merely papered over and are likely to reappear all too soon."[38]

Several other "reforms" were widely suggested but not as readily accepted by state legislatures. These include abolishing the *ad damnum* clause—that (often inflated) part of the plaintiff's suit setting out a specific figure of requested damages—and abolishing the collateral-source rule, which bars a jury from taking into account a plaintiff's other sources of reimbursement, such as insurance, in determining damage awards. A recommendation strongly supported by medical groups is the abolition of the contingency-fee system, under which attorneys receive a percentage of the plaintiff's award instead of a set hourly fee. But such a measure is not likely to be voted by legislatures heavily populated with lawyers. (Those opposing such abolition argue that its burden would fall on poor patients, who cannot afford legal advice except on a contingency-fee basis.) Some states have imposed a sliding limit on contingency fees, reducing the percentage permitted the attorney as the size of the award goes up. Law and Polan point out that under the current malpractice system, lawyers as a group—that is, attorneys for both plaintiffs and defendants—get more than do patients from each malpractice dollar.[39]

There are other possible changes in malpractice law that are directed not at limiting the injured patient's ability to collect money damages, but at developing new machinery for dealing with malpractice claims. One suggestion calls for special screening panels of physicians, and, in some cases, lawyers and lay persons, to assess malpractice claims and determine if they have merit. If the panel decides a claim is without merit, the plaintiff can still pursue the lawsuit if he or she wishes, but many may be disuaded from doing so. At the height of the malpractice "crisis," some twenty-seven states established such screening panels, and some of these laws even allowed panel findings to be admitted in any subsequent trial. Two states require that plaintiffs who pursue a claim after a negative finding by a screening panel must post a bond to go toward covering the defendant's legal costs if the defendant wins. But a number of the screening panel statutes have been invalidated by courts as effectively depriving plaintiffs of jury trials, and the overall effectiveness of such panels to encourage pretrial settlements and reduce frivolous claims is in doubt.[40]

Another approach, which has the effect of removing malpractice from the courtroom, is the use of arbitration, based on an agreement by the patient and the health professional prior to the beginning of treatment to arbitrate any malpractice claim. Arbitration cannot be forced on a patient, since this, too, would deprive him or her of a trial by jury. Whether a patient can knowingly and voluntarily enter into a binding agreement to arbitrate future disputes is a question still to be definitively answered.[41]

A totally different approach championed in recent years is patterned after the workers'-compensation model and no-fault automobile insurance. Proponents argue that the no-fault concept provides a more efficient way of compensating patients for medical injury than the present system under which many injured plaintiffs fail to obtain redress and most of the insurance dollar is not spent as compensation to victorious plaintiffs.[42] Supporters of no-fault also argue that the present malpractice system is not really a deterrent.[43] Right or wrong, however, the no-fault advocates have thus far failed to develop detailed mechanisms to implement their concept. The biggest difficulty lies in trying to define a compensable event. What makes the no-fault program workable in automobile accident cases is the agreement by all the parties involved that such injuries should not have occurred and will therefore be compensated. But medical no-fault is not proposed as a mechanism to compensate *all* medical injuries (including those that were unavoidable), but only those that would presently be ascribed to malpractice; and there is simply no consensus regarding which injuries should be considered so avoidable that compensation should be automatic, without the trouble and expense of contested malpractice claims. Until this hurdle is overcome, the no-fault approach to claims of medical malpractice is not likely to make much progress.

Other efforts to sidestep the existing malpractice insurance system have ranged from the establishment of mutual insurance companies by health practitioner organizations to foregoing insurance protection altogether. Mutual insurance companies, which in some states were authorized through special legislation, were at first greeted with derision by the insurance industry. But by emphasizing practice records and risk management in accepting policyholders, these practitioner-run companies were able to reduce premiums. But in New York State a physician-run mutual company has recently run into difficulties with sharply escalating premiums.[44] Foregoing insurance protection completely—"going bare"—seems generally to be an ill-advised, emotional response. The transfer of assets to relatives can be set aside if a court views it as an attempt to frustrate future creditors, and future earnings may be reachable by successful malpractice plaintiffs.[45]

Law and Polan suggest that easier access to medical records by patients[46] would itself reduce the number of malpractice suits filed. They point out that suits alleging malpractice are sometimes brought simply to obtain information about their treatment that patients are unable to get in any other way, and that a review of the record would convince a substantial number of patients and/or attorneys that what they thought was an injury due to negligence really wasn't. These authors also suggest that advance notice be required before a malpractice suit can be filed, providing time for informal negotiation and compromise that might obviate a lawsuit.

The idea of suing plaintiffs or lawyers who initiate frivolous malpractice suits received widespread attention in the late 1970s, but such countersuits have practically no chance of actually succeeding. Countersuits based on defamation, malicious prosecution, abuse of process, or legal malpractice theories have not only proven difficult to win at the trial level, but those few that have succeeded—thereby garnering media attention—have generally gone on to be reversed by the appellate courts.[47]

Liability for the Negligence of Others

The discussion so far has assumed something that is rarely true—that medical services have been rendered to the patient in a setting that involves only one health care practitioner. More often, several individuals are involved in the treatment of a patient's disease or condition, each with a duty of exercising due care, and each liable for his or her own negligence. What is their relationship to one another? Can a health care professional be held responsible for the negligence of other professionals when they work together in treating the same patient?

Generally a commonsense standard of reasonableness applies. Obviously, before deciding if Professional A is responsible for the negligence of Professional B, it must be determined that B was negligent. If B was indeed negligent, it must then be determined what duty A had to the patient in regard to B, and whether he or she failed to carry out that duty. For example, a doctor making a referral to a consultant is expected to exercise due care in selecting that consultant. This is the full extent of the first doctor's duty; it is also the full extent of the liability involved. If A had every reason to expect B to do a good job, A is not liable, even if B fouls up. The same duty—and the same limitation— exists when arrangements are made for a substitute to take over care of the patient. In both cases, of course, the patient must consent to the referral. In another common situation, when a nurse supervisor assigns the care of a patient to a staff nurse, the supervisor does not assume legal responsibility for everything the staff nurse does. But if there was reason to know that the staff nurse could not adequately handle the tasks involved, the supervisor could be liable to the patient for any resulting harm.

When practitioners are working together, however, the duty owed the patient is a continuing one. Not only must Professional A exercise due care in the treatment of the patient; she or he is also obligated to observe the work of B and to take appropriate action if B exercises less than satisfactory care.[48]

When one professional is employed by another, the long established principles of "master" and "servant" apply, most notably the doctrine of *respondeat superior* ("let the master answer"). The employing professional's obligation to the patient is not limited to due care in selecting and supervising those employees who are involved in the patient's care; he or she is fully liable for the negligent acts of these employees even though that employer is without fault. The theory is that since the employee is working in the employer's behalf and advantage, an injured person should be permitted to avail himself or herself of the latter's greater resources in collecting damages.

The doctrine of *respondeat superior* can only be invoked if: (1) an employer-employee relationship existed (best demonstrated by the employer's authority to control the employee in the performance of his or her duties),[49] and (2) the employee's negligent act was within the scope of his or her employment, that is, it was part of what the employee had been hired to do.[50] The doctrine is especially significant with new health professionals, such as physician's assistants. Under *respondeat superior* the injured party can sue both the employer and the negligent employee. If the employer is forced to pay damages, he or she can sue the employee for indemnification.

Hospital Liability

A hospital, as a corporate entity,[51] is the employer under the doctrine of *respondeat superior* and is liable for torts its employees commit within the scope of their employment. A patient injured through the negligence of a hospital employee can therefore sue the hospital, which has greater financial resources, for compensation.[52]

An interesting situation arises when it comes to the physician, dentist, podiatrist, or other health professional who is allowed to treat patients within the institution but who is not an employee of the hospital. For many years courts allowed themselves to be persuaded that the hospital was merely a workshop for these independent practitioners: that since the institution could not control their performance—and therefore a *respondeat superior* situation did not exist—the hospital had no legal obligation in the event of malpractice and could not be held liable in the event of practitioner negligence. But beginning in the 1950s, some courts began to abandon this view, and by the 1970s there was a strong trend toward recognizing a broader duty on the part of the hospital. The most famous of these decisions is *Darling v. Charleston Community Memorial Hospital;*[53] it is discussed in Chapter 7, along with several other cases, which, together, represent a continuing judicial recognition of *corporate responsibility* on the part of hospitals.

The judicial trend is an important one. It does not mean that hospitals are held fully responsible for the negligence of nonemployee medical staff whose performance it does not control. Rather, the courts have held that hospitals owe their patients an independent and direct duty to exercise due care in such things as granting medical staff privileges and in establishing policies and procedures (a duty somewhat analogous to the referral duty discussed earlier). If Dr. Ben Casey, paragon neurosurgeon, negligently injures a patient, the hospital in which this occurred would not share in his liability because it could not have anticipated this unexpected misoccurrence. But if Dr. Casey has an unbroken record of twelve botched appendectomies, the hospital cannot honestly claim that it could not have predicted that the thirteenth was likely to have the same unfortunate results and/or that it could not have prevented the doctor from operating in that institution. It is this prediction and prevention that the hospital owes to all its patients, and because it has a governing body of recognized legal authority, an organized medical staff and a professional administration, the hospital can develop and implement privileging standards and procedures and protocols to assure that this duty is carried out.

Defensive Medicine

The threat of malpractice has led some health practitioners, physicians in particular, to defensive patterns of practice. Garg, Gliebe, and Elkhatib describe two such approaches:

The first arises when a test or procedure is performed not because it is perceived as essential but is done so that if the patient has a bad result the doctor cannot be accused of negligence for not having performed the test. This type, termed positive defensive medicine, is the major concern of those who argue that defensive medicine contributes to increased health care costs. The second type, termed negative defensive medicine, occurs when a physician avoids a potentially beneficial procedure because legal risks might arise from resulting complications. This does not contribute to costs but may compromise quality.[54]

Since practitioners do not always agree on which tests and/or procedures are necessary, it is hard to document instances of defensive practice; the Secretary's Commission on Medical Malpractice concluded, however, that such practice does occur and that it increases the cost of medical care. Hershey found the costs to be minimal,[55] but Garg et al. found that 8 percent of laboratory charges and 15 percent of X-ray charges could be attributed to defensive medical practice.[56]

Law and Polan make the following three points from the lawyer's perspective:

> First, it should be apparent by now that the tort law is intended to affect human behavior. It is supposed to encourage people to take precautions which a reasonable person would take to avoid risks of injury; and it is meant to have this effect on doctors just as it does on everyone else. Second, with . . . very limited exceptions . . . the tort law as applied to doctors is based entirely on the professional judgment of other doctors. Finally, and perhaps most usefully, in most situations in which a doctor might feel that he or she should modify treatment behavior because of a fear of a potential malpractice action, the doctor could as well, or better, deal with the situation by providing the patient with full information and allowing the patient to decide what is to be done.[57]

Conclusion

A patient who has suffered an untoward outcome may face a severe financial burden; if it can be demonstrated that the provider was at fault, it is only fair to shift this burden to him or her. But even when no such fault exists, many people consider it unfair for the blameless patient to carry both the physical and financial load alone. Other industrialized countries have socialized these costs through government-run insurance and social welfare programs. But in the United States such mechanisms are very limited, and persons facing large and on-going expenses as the result of a medical injury could well be pauperized. There is no doubt that some juries, and even some judges, are influenced by this realization when they weigh the conflicting claims of an injured patient-plaintiff and a (presumably insured) health professional defendant. This does not mean that totally groundless claims are likely to carry the day. But when the injury is real and the fault question clouded, need may well be given greater emphasis than fault. Nor is this situation likely to change unless some mechanism is adopted that relieves patients of the financial burden of medical injury.[58] Although it involved a suit against a pharmaceutical company for alleged vaccine-induced polio rather than a malpractice claim against a health services provider, the case of *Reyes v. Wyeth Laboratories*[59] makes the point clearly. The Federal Court of Appeals, quoting with approval from an earlier decision, stated that:

> "Until Americans have a comprehensive scheme of social insurance, courts must resolve by a balancing process the head-on collision between the need for adequate recovery and viable enterprises . . . . This balancing task should be approached with a realization that the basic consideration involves a determination of the most just *allocation of the risk of loss* between the members of the marketing chain." Helene Curtis Industries, Inc. v. Pruitt, *supra*, 385 F.2d at 862.
>
> Statistically predictable as are these rare cases of vaccine-induced polio, a strong argument can be advanced that the loss ought not lie where it falls (on the victim), but should be borne by the manufacturer as a foreseeable cost of doing business, and passed on to the public in the form of price increases to his customers.

Although many would argue that consideration of need is an abuse of the legal concepts underlying negligence law, emphasizing the traditional compensation function of tort law to the exclusion of everything else, it should be noted that the reverse distortion can occur when deterrence is emphasized above all else. Under what is called the Learned Hand rule, the failure to take steps to avoid some foreseeable harm— rather than noncompliance with professional standards—constitutes negligence. If the cost of avoiding harm would be greater than the harm itself, the rule is not applied. The 1974 Washington Supreme Court case of *Helling v. Carey*[60] provides the most notable example in the medical malpractice context. The question was whether it was negligent for defendant ophthalmologists to fail to routinely perform a pressure test for glaucoma on the thirty-two-year-old plaintiff. It was undisputed that it was the standard in this specialty not to perform such a routine test on patients under forty. But the court concluded:

> The issue is whether the defendants' compliance with the standard of the profession of ophthalmology . . . should insulate them from liability under the facts in this case where the plaintiff has lost a substantial amount of her vision due to the failure of the defendants to timely give the pressure test to the plaintiff . . . . We therefore hold, as a matter of law, that the reasonable standard that should have been followed under the disputed facts of this case was the timely giving of this simple, harmless pressure test to this plaintiff

and that, in failing to do so, the defendants were negligent, which prox-imately resulted in the blindness sustained by the plaintiff for which the defendants are liable.

This was, in effect, a judicial finding that an entire profession was negligent by not practicing to a higher standard of care. While not subsequently followed by other courts, the decision illustrates the type of strict liability role malpractice litigation could come to play.

But the fact is that as a quality maintenance device malpractice is terribly inadequate. Feedback is haphazard and often inappropriate. There is no assurance that the deterrent message will be effectively and clearly transmitted back to the large body of practitioners. There will be a considerable lapse of time between the medical encounter and the final decision. And because insurance spreads the financial burden, there is nothing to give the deterrent message any greater force for those practitioners most likely to perform negligently in the future.[61]

Possibly the greatest comfort to the health professional is the knowledge that a malpractice lawsuit is still the rare occurrence. Is there anything the practitioner can do to reduce the risk—and worry—of malpractice? Entire books have been written on the subject, with emphasis on due care, defensive practice, personalized treatment, responsiveness, proper demeanor, and the like.[62] The importance of practicing carefully, and within the limits of one's profession and expertise, goes almost without saying. Keeping abreast of advances in the field and following the professional literature regularly should be equally obvious, although busy schedules often make this difficult. Openness with the patient is viewed by many as asking for trouble; yet it hardly can be the case that withholding information and developing an adversary relationship will foster patient trust.

In the final analysis, the health professional must accept the fact that nothing short of abandoning practice can completely eliminate the threat of a malpractice suit, and even then the danger lingers for many years. Along with stress, heightened risk of infection, and chemical and radiation exposure, malpractice must ultimately be viewed as an occupational hazard for those engaged in patient care.

NOTES

1. Code of Hammurabi, ca. 1950 B.C., Sec. 218; as quoted in Ralph H. Major, *A History of Medicine*, vol. 1 (Springfield, Ill.: Charles C. Thomas, 1954), p. 27.
2. At least that is the persepctive today. Yet even in the days of far fewer malpractice suits, the professions worried about a malpractice crisis. See, e.g., George J. Annas, Barbara F. Katz, and Robert G. Trakimas, "Medical Malpractice Litigation under National Health Insurance: Essential or Ex-

pendable," in *Medical Malpractice: The Duke Law Journal Symposium* (Cambridge, Mass.: Ballinger, 1977), p. 162.

3. Ibid., note 4.

4. On the role of the insurance industry in the "crisis" see Tarky Lombardi, Jr., with Gerald N. Hoffman, *Medical Malpractice Insurance* (Syracuse, N.Y.: Syracuse University Press, 1978), esp. chap. 1, and discussion at note 33 of this chapter. A "claim" is an assertion by a patient that compensation for medical injury should be paid by the practitioner (which usually means by the insurance carrier). Some insurance companies open a claim file without such an assertion, merely on notification by the practitioner that a claim may ensue. But as many as 25 percent may be dropped in the face of the insurer's refusal to settle. (See Lombardi, p. 1.) A claim becomes a "suit"—that is, a lawsuit in a court of law—when the patient files the appropriate written materials with the clerk of court. A "settlement" is an agreement between patient and practitioner (insurer) by which the former agrees to forego, or drop, a suit in exchange for something else, presumably money. An "award" is an order of a court that payment be made to the patient by practitioner (insurer).

5. There is some reporting of jury awards nationally (e.g., Jury Verdict Research, Inc.), but claims data is less available. Some information is published by individual insurers, and the National Association of Insurance Commissioners recently published survey data. See William J. Curran, "Closed-Claims Data for Malpractice Actions in the United States," *American Journal of Public Health* 71:1066–1067 (1981).

6. *Medical Malpractice: Report of the Secretary's Commission on Medical Malpractice* (Washington, D.C.: Department of Health, Education and Welfare, 1973) (DHEW pub. no. (OS) 73-88). The report is relied upon by most observers as their major source of data. It should be noted, however, that despite its generally wide acceptance, there has been some criticism. The most notable and most immediate came from Herbert S. Denenberg, then Pennsylvania state insurance commissioner, who was highly critical of the commission's recommendations, although not necessarily of the data. *Medical World News*, 19 January 1973, pp. 18–19. Also see Lombardi, *Medical Malpractice Insurance*, chap. 6.

7. See Curran, "Closed-Claims Data"; George J. Annas, Leonard H. Glantz, and Barbara F. Katz, *The Rights of Doctors, Nurses, and Allied Health Professionals: A Health Law Primer* (New York: Avon, 1981), p. 242; and William J. Curran, "Malpractice Claims: New Data and New Trends," *New England Journal of Medicine* 300:26–27 (1979).

8. The role of private litigation to achieve social ends has received considerable attention from Professor Guido Calabresi. On malpractice see Calabresi, "The Problem of Malpractice: Trying to Round Out the Circle," *University of Toronto Law Journal* 27:131–141 (1977).

9. The contractual aspects of the physician-patient relationship are discussed in Sidney Shindell, *The Law of Medical Practice*, (Pittsburgh: University of Pittsburgh Press, 1966), chap. 2; Sidney Shindell, Jeffrey C. Salloway, and Colette M. Obembst, *A Coursebook in Health Care Delivery* (New York: Appleton-Century-Crofts, 1976), pp. 486–492; and Angela Roddey Holder, *Medical Malpractice Law*, 2d ed. (New York: John Wiley, 1978), chap. 1.

10. *Black's Law Dictionary*, 4th ed. (St. Paul, Minn.: West, 1951), p. 1184.
11. "The courts are concerned not only with compensation of the victim, but with admonition of the wrongdoer . . . [providing] a strong incentive to prevent the occurrence of the harm. Not infrequently one reason for imposing liability is the deliberate purpose of providing that incentive." William L. Prosser, *Handbook of the Law of Torts*, 4th ed. (St. Paul, Minn.: West, 1971), p. 23. Theoretically, the deterrence function of law could be served as effectively—and perhaps more equitably—even if the theory of negligence ignored the avoidability of the harm, instead of resorting to a prudent person standard. If A were legally responsible for all harm he or she caused B, A would presumably be just as careful as when his or her responsibility is limited to simply being prudent. But the law evolved differently. See Sylvia Law and Steven Polan, *Pain and Profit: The Politics of Malpractice* (New York: Harper & Row, 1978), pp. 1–6.
12. See discussion of *Reyes v. Wyeth Laboratories* and *Helling v. Carey*, in this chapter.
13. For an argument for a broader legal duty, see Marshall S. Shapo, *The Duty to Act: Tort Law, Power, and Public Policy* (Austin: University of Texas Press, 1977).
14. In addition to the type of negligence described here, more serious acts or omissions might constitute gross negligence (reckless disregard for the duty of care) or willful negligence (a conscious violation of the duty of care). As should be expected, it is an easier matter to hold a practitioner liable for more serious—and thus more apparent—negligence. For example, state good samaritan laws do not afford immunity against other than ordinary negligence.
15. A recent case in which foreseeability played a prominent role is *Renslow v. Mennonite Hospital*, 67 Ill.2d 348, 367 N.E.2d 1250 (1977). In that case, the plaintiff's prenatal injuries resulted from the negligent transfusion of blood into her mother *several years prior to plaintiff's conception*. The court allowed the claim, saying that such a medical result was reasonably foreseeable.
16. There are some limited exceptions to this general statement when harm to a third party is foreseeable. These would include a possible duty to warn the subject of threats of a psychiatric patient (see discussion in Chapter 19) and a duty to warn of communicable disease (see Chapter 5). Also see Harold L. Hirsh, "Physicians' Legal Duty to Third Parties Who Are Not Patients," *Medical Trial Techniques Quarterly* 23:388–400 (1977).
17. On the subject of abandonment, see Holder, *Medical Malpractice Law*, chap. 12, and Annas, Glantz, and Katz, *A Health Law Primer*, pp. 249–251. Holder points out:

> The physician may not withdraw in a pre-emptory manner from the treatment relationship or leave the patient stranded without medical attention. He must give the patient reasonable notice, which . . . should be in writing . . . [giving] the patient sufficient time to locate another physician who is willing to accept the case . . . [and must] provide sufficiently adequate records and information to his successor to insure proper continuing care (p. 373).

18. 155 N.Y. 201, 49 N.E. 760, 762 (1898).
19. It should be noted, however, that this is not always applicable to emergency

situations. Thus, for example, a nonspecialist who performs an emergency procedure for which he is untrained and in which he is inexperienced, but for which a better-qualified practitioner is not available, may actually be held to a lower standard of care than an emergency medical technician who, while not a physician, has had training and experience in the procedure. See Robert C. Scanlon, "The Malpractice Aspects of Emergency Care by Non-physicians," *Ganzaga Law Review* 12:676–690 (1977). The converse of this situation involves the new health professional, the emergency medical technician, physician's assistant, and the like, who, depending on the circumstances, may be held to the same standard as other members of the specific profession *or* to the standard of those who normally do the procedure, which might mean physicians. See Matthew W. Chapman and Jane Cassels Record, "Defensibility of New Health Professionals at Law: A Speculative Paper," *Journal of Health Politics, Policy and Law* 4:30–47 (1979).

20. In situations where there is an unexcused violation of an applicable statute, such as practicing without a license or beyond the scope of one's license, no other proof is called for; it is negligence per se. The violation is conclusive—or, in some states, allows a presumption—of negligence, and the issue is taken away from the jury.

21. Law and Polan, *Pain and Profit*, p. 101.

22. See Stephen K. Dietz, C. Bruce Baird, and Lawrence Berul, "The Medical Malpractice Legal System," in *Appendix: Report of the Secretary's Commission on Medical Malpractice*, (Washington D.C.: Department of Health, Education and Welfare, 1973) (DHEW pub. no. (OS) 73-89), pp. 128–129, as well as William J. Curran, *How Lawyers Handle Malpractice Cases: An Analysis of an Important Medicolegal Study* (Rockville, Md.: Health Resources Administration, 1976) (DHEW pub. no. (HRA) 76-3152). *Res ipsa loquitor* is used primarily in cases of foreign objects left in patients, burns, and injury to parts of the body not under treatment. See Annas, Glantz, and Katz, *A Health Law Primer*, pp. 252–253. The Secretary's Commission on Medical Malpractice did express concern over the way in which the doctrine has been expanded in California, where it has been used most liberally.

23. *Medical Malpractice: Report of the Secretary's Commission on Medical Malpractice* p. 37.

24. The leading example is *Brune v. Belinkoff*, 354 Mass. 102, 235 N.E.2d 793 (1968).

25. Polan, personal communication. But also see Dietz, Baird, and Berul, in *Appendix: Report of the Secretary's Commission on Medical Malpractice*, p. 124. That study, plus the follow-up analysis by Curran, *How Lawyers Handle Malpractice Cases*, suggests that the locality rule has not loomed large in the eyes of lawyers handling significant numbers of malpractice claims, although this may merely reflect their concentration in large cities. It is also interesting that a change in the locality rule was not—at least until quite recently—one of the medical profession's favored reforms for dealing with the malpractice "crisis." Law and Polan, *Pain and Profit*, pp. 100–101, note that a few states have stayed with, and reaffirmed, the locality rule.

26. Plaintiffs whose tort claim is "stale," that is, the two- or three-year period for bringing suit has run out, will sometimes attempt to sue for breach of contract. But only a limited number of such attempts have succeeded.

27. For more information on statutes of limitation in malpractice, see the references collected in the footnotes to p. 121 of Law and Polan, *Pain and Profit*.

28. If the patient happens to be a health professional, the standard could be more stringent and involve the time when a reasonable and diligent health professional would have discovered such negligence.

29. See Law and Polan, *Pain and Profit*, pp. 123–124.

30. Holder, *Medical Malpractice Law*, pp. 319–321, and Charles Kramer, *Medical Malpractice*, 4th ed. (New York: Practicing Law Institute, 1976), pp. 67–68.

31. Holder, *Medical Malpractice Law*, pp. 313–319, and Kramer, *Medical Malpractice*, pp. 68–69.

32. Holder, *Medical Malpractice Law*, pp. 301–310.

33. See Law and Polan, *Pain and Profit*, chap. 9, and Louise Lander, *Defective Medicine: Risk, Anger, and the Malpractice Crisis* (New York: Farrar, Straus & Giroux, 1978), chap. 8. Both discuss the Argonaut/Teledyne role in the malpractice "crisis." Also see Lombardi, *Medical Malpractice Insurance*, on Argonaut/Teledyne.

34. Because the impact of these changes on the practitioner may well be minimal, only the most common legislative changes are covered here. The reader is referred to Law and Polan, *Pain and Profit*, chap. 7, for a more comprehensive review. The discussion that follows relies heavily on their analysis.

35. See listing of states in notes to pp. 254–255 of Annas, Glantz, and Katz, *A Health Law Primer*.

36. Law and Polan, *Pain and Profit*, pp. 106–107.

37. Ibid., p. 113. Informed consent is the topic of Chapter 14 of this book.

38. Frank P. Grad, "Medical Malpractice and Its Implications for Public Health," in Ruth Roemer and George McKray, eds., *Legal Aspects of Health Policy: Issues and Trends* (Westport, Conn.: Greenwood Press, 1980), p. 404.

39. Law and Polan, *Pain and Profit*, p. 88. Claude Welch states that as little as 18 to 20 percent of the total malpractice dollar actually reaches the injured patient. "Medical Malpractice," *New England Journal of Medicine* 292:1372 (1975). For an overall review of legislative responses to the malpractice problem, see the report prepared for the Department of Health, Education and Welfare by the American Bar Association, *Legal Topics Relating to Medical Malpractice* (Washington, D.C.: Public Health Service, 1977).

40. On the constitutionality of a variety of malpractice reform techniques, see Martin H. Redish, *Legislative Response to the Medical Malpractice Crisis: Constitutional Implications* (Chicago: American Hospital Association, 1977). Also see Annas, Glantz, and Katz, *A Health Law Primer*, pp. 259–260, and William J. Curran, "Screening Panels in Malpractice Cases: Some Disturbing Progress Reports," *New England Journal of Medicine* 302:954–955 (1980). When he was attorney general, Griffin Bell suggested federal legislation requiring pretrial screening of malpractice cases in all states. *Medical World News*, 22 January 1979, p. 11.

41. For a review of state laws providing for binding arbitration, see *Statutory Provisions for Binding Arbitration of Medical Malpractice Claims* (Rockville, Md.: National Center for Health Services Research, 1976). Also see Irving Ladimer and Joel Solomon, "Medical Malpractice Arbitration: Laws, Programs, Cases," *Insurance Law Journal* 1977:335–365 (1977).

42. See, for example, C. C. Havighurst and L. R. Tancredi, "'Medical Adversity

Insurance'—A No-Fault Approach to Medical Malpractice and Quality Assurance," *Milbank Memorial Fund Quarterly* 51:125 (1973); Clark C.
Havighurst, "'Medical Adversity Insurance'—Has Its Time Come," in *Medical Malpractice: The Duke Law Journal Symposium*, pp. 55–105; Grad, "Medical
Malpractice," pp. 409–414.

43. Law and Polan, *Pain and Profit*, contest this view. See their chap. 8 for a more
detailed critique of medical no-fault.

44. Several state legislatures also authorized joint underwriting associations, a
pooling of insurance writers obligated to assume the malpractice burden.
On both approaches see ibid., chap. 10; Grad, "Medical Malpractice," p.
405; Lombardi, *Medical Malpractice Insurance*, pp. 104–107.

45. In contrast to "going bare," some states and some hospitals have required
practitioners to carry malpractice insurance. See C. K. Muranaka, "Compulsory Medical Malpractice Insurance Statutes: An Approach in Determining Constitutionality," *University of San Francisco Law Review* 12:599–654
(1979); "Constitutionality of Requiring Physicians and Other Health Care
Providers to Carry Malpractice Insurance," *Western State University Law Review* 7:75–90 (1979). On "going bare," as well as other aspects of malpractice
insurance (What types of liability does malpractice insurance cover? What
obligation does the insurer have to defend in a lawsuit?) see chap. 13 in
Annas, Glantz, and Katz, *A Health Law Primer*. Malpractice insurance policies
will often exclude abandonment, practice outside of certain settings, failure
to give information, and similar items. If a type of act or omission is not
covered by the policy, the insurance company will not defend against a claim
of that type—even though the claim may be completely without merit. Malpractice insurance usually covers nondeliberate acts, that is, errors.

46. See Chapter 17, for a discussion of this and other aspects of medical records.

47. See Annas, Glantz, and Katz, *A Health Law Primer*, pp. 285–289.

48. Elliot Sagall and Barry C. Reed, "Legal Responsibility for Negligence of
Assistants, Substitutes, Partners, Consultants, and Jointly Treating Physicians," in *The Law and Clinical Medicine* (Philadelphia: Lippincott, 1970), as
reprinted in N. Kittrie, H. Hirsh, and G. Wegner, *Medicine, Law and Public
Policy*, vol. 1 (New York: AMS Press, 1975), p. 218, point out: "Ordinarily,
the operating surgeon is not liable for the negligence of the anesthesiologist,
provided the latter is a qualified, competent, licensed physician and is not
acting under the control and direction of the operating surgeon."

49. There must first be an employer-employee relationship, however. *Respondeat superior* would not apply to a nurse supervisor, for example, for
while she controls the performance of staff nurses, she is not their employer.

50. "The requirement that the negligence must have been committed within the
scope of the employment seldom creates any problem since the indictable
acts most often are performed within the physician's office or at a patient's
home under the physician's orders. Such vicarious liability applies even
when the physician's employee or agent is another physician" (Sagall and
Reed, "Legal Responsibility for Negligence," p. 218). It should be noted that
the doctrine of *respondeat superior* applies not only to negligence, but to all
torts. Thus it could be used in imputing assault and battery or libel against
the employer.

51. See Chapter 7 for a discussion of the hospital's corporate identity, its liability under *respondeat superior* and for defective and inadequate equipment and the physical conditions of the premises, and its obligation to the patient to exercise due care in granting staff privileges and establishing policies and procedures.

52. They can also, of course, sue the employee. Thus salaried physicians (including housestaff and medical students), nurses (including student nurses), and other professional and nonprofessional staff are liable for their own negligence as well as is the hospital.

53. 33 Ill.2d 326, 211 N.E.2d 253 (1965), *cert. denied,* 383 U.S. 946 (1966).

54. Mohan L. Garg, Werner A. Gliebe, and Mounir B. Elkhatib, "The Extent of Defensive Medicine: Some Empirical Evidence," *Legal Aspects of Medical Practice* 6(2):25-29 (February 1978).

55. Nathan Hershey, "The Defensive Practice of Medicine: Myth or Reality," *Milbank Memorial Fund Quarterly* 50:69-98 (1972).

56. Garg eg al., "The Extent of Defensive Medicine."

57. Law and Polan, *Pain and Profit,* p. 115.

58. See Institute of Medicine, *Beyond Malpractice: Compensation for Medical Injuries* (Washington, D.C.: National Academy of Sciences, March 1978).

59. 498 F.2d 1264 (5th Cir. 1974), *cert. denied* 419 U.S. 1096. In *Reyes,* the jury— upheld by the courts—awarded $200,000 to the plaintiff after rejecting overpowering epidemiological evidence that the polio was most likely caused by that which was wild in the community—odds of 3,000 to 1 against odds of 5.9 million to 1.

60. 519 P.2d 981, 83 Wash. 2nd 514 (1974). Learned Hand (1872-1961) was a prominent federal judge best known for his First Amendment and tort decisions.

61. See William B. Schwartz and Neil K. Komesar, "Doctors, Damages and Deterrence: An Economic View of Medical Malpractice," *New England Journal of Medicine* 298:1282–1289 (1978). For other types of deterrents, see the discussion of "snitch" laws in Chapter 6 and of peer review systems in Chapter 7. As to the other side of the coin—patients unaware they have suffered negligent harm—see Joan Vogel and Richard Delgado, "To Tell the Truth: Physicians' Duty to Disclose Medical Mistakes," *UCLA Law Review* 28:52–94, (1980).

62. See, for example, W. J. Alton, Jr., *Malpractice: A Trial Lawyer's Advice for Physicians (How to Avoid, How to Win),* (Boston: Little, Brown, 1977), and Robert S. Pollack, *Clinical Aspects of Malpractice* (Oradell, N.J.: Medical Economics Co., 1980).

17

Medical Records

Society simply cannot accept the health professional's plea for unbounded data collection and full recording in data systems **unless** *there are iron-clad guarantees, enforceable at law, that the patient's rights, benefits, and opportunities in the larger society will not be harmed by production of his or her self-revelations from primary-care records.*

—Alan F. Westin[1]

THE KEEPING OF MEDICAL RECORDS is a practice almost as old as medicine itself. Spanish cave drawings dating back to 25,000 B.C., with silhouetts depicting the amputation of fingers and the perforation of the skull with surgical tools, provide, perhaps, the earliest examples of medical recording.[2] But only in this century has medical record keeping developed into a science of its own, providing the consistency, sophistication, completeness and accessibility that health professionals today take for granted. In earlier years, only the more important or instructive cases were recorded in detail; the remainder, if recorded at all, were disposed of in a line or two in a log book. Today's medical records, on the other hand, are likely to contain detailed, often voluminous reporting. And where earlier records were put to limited use—in part because of their inadequacies—medical records today have many and varied uses, and the number of persons and groups that need and have access to medical records is constantly increasing. At the same time, the advent of computerized record keeping has made such access very simple and has created serious problems of privacy and confidentiality with respect to patient information.

The two basic functions of medical recording are communication and documentation. The most obvious use of the medical record, or case history, is to centralize and communicate information about the individual patient during the course of treatment. Physicians use it to transmit information and instructions regarding the patient to nurses and other patient-care personnel as well as to other physicians. Nurses use it to provide physicians and others with information on the patient's vital signs and condition. Consulting personnel use it to indicate what they have done and/or observed. The medical record also helps the practitioners treating the patient to determine what is and should be happening with the patient.

The medical record is also an important teaching device, providing guidance and instruction for less experienced practitioners, and facilitates retrospective quality review and other record-based research. Such teaching and research functions do not directly help the patient whose record is involved, but they do contribute to general improvements in health and health care. Finally, by documenting the history of the patient's illness and treatment, the medical record serves a medicolegal function, helping to resolve any dispute that might arise concerning the outcome of such treatment.

Content

From a medical perspective the medical record should contain everything necessary to maximize the functions just outlined. Although there has been considerable standardization of structure and content in recent years, debate continues as to whether the report should be primarily problem-oriented or source-oriented.

From a legal perspective,[3] the medical record must meet requirements established under the authority of laws licensing health care institutions and health professional practice. Minimum requirements— usually in the form of administrative regulations propounded by the State Department of Public Health—exist in most states. In many cases the relevant regulation simply calls for a medical record that is "adequate," "complete," and/or "accurate." Some states require certain broad areas of information, such as patient identification information, history, diagnosis, treatment notes, and so on, and others require more detailed information, including medications, vital signs, pathologist's report, and the like. None, however, demand more than what would be expected in any professionally acceptable record today.[4]

The Joint Commission on Accreditation of Hospitals also imposes content requirements for medical records, specifying

- Identification data; when not obtainable, the reason should be entered in the record.
- The medical history of the patient.
- The report of a relevant physical examination.
- Diagnostic and therapeutic orders.
- Evidence of appropriate informed consent; when consent is not obtainable, the reason shall be entered in the record.
- Clinical observations, including results of therapy.
- Reports of procedures, tests, and the results.
- Conclusions at termination of hospitalization or evaluation/treatment.[5]

State statutes and regulations also set standards for completion, signing, maintenance, and retention of medical records. One important requirement is that records must be completed promptly; courts have upheld hospitals that have suspended staff privileges for physicians failing to do so. To provide proper authentication the record must be signed by the physician responsible for the patient's care. In describing this requirement, Southwick notes that "an automated authentication of entries in the chart is at present not legally acceptable in the majority of states. Fully computerized medical record systems are therefore not yet legally sanctioned."[6] Alterations should never be made in a medical record except according to a consistent policy, which should include crossing out inaccurate information in such a way as to leave it legible, adding new information, and initialing, dating, and explaining the reason for the change.

Ownership

The question of who owns the medical record can be answered in several different ways, depending on what "record" the questioner means. All states agree that the physical record—the actual paper on which patient data is recorded as well as X-rays and the like—belongs to the health practitioner or facility responsible for compiling it. But this clear ownership right to the physical record does not mean the right to do anything one pleases with it. For a medical record also includes the information contained in it, and there is increasing recognition of the patient's right to the information contained in his or her record. Since destruction of the record would affect the availability of the information in it, hospitals and practitioners, although owners of the physical record, are not free to destroy or deface it, to make it inaccessible, or to disseminate the information in the record any way they wish. Most states also require that patient records be retained for a certain length of time (usually ten to twenty-five years after discharge or death, or for time periods tied to various statutes of limitations), and some require that they be kept "permanently." State regulations may make special provisions for records of minors, for microfilming of records, and for certain portions of the record, such as nurses' notes. Some states also require approval by the state before records are destroyed.[7]

Access

At one time access to medical records may have been confined to the health professionals directly involved in delivering care, but that day is certainly gone. Today there is widespread and growing accessibility, with varying impact on the health professional, the patient, and third parties—which means everybody else.

Access to a patient's record by all who are directly involved in his or her treatment is beyond question, even though this "need-to-know" category has grown astronomically as hospital-based patient care has become more and more complex. It cannot realistically be said that patients have consented to access to their medical records by medical students not involved in treatment, researchers, administrative personnel, and similar individuals; but the issue is rarely raised because the patient or anyone else likely to protest is generally unaware of such access.

Westin points out that "people *not* involved in the patient's care may have access to the patient's record, including nurses on all three shifts, medical students, interns and residents, financial workers, ward secretaries, social workers and researchers of many kinds. All of this takes place on the 'implied consent' of the patient—that is, his/her very presence in the hospital is taken to imply consent for widespread in-house access . . . ."[8] On the other hand, Annas suggests that the "general rule is that only those persons directly involved in your care may read your record without your permission . . . . The AHA Bill of Rights demands that anyone viewing your record solely for teaching or learning purposes *must* have your *express* permission before doing so."[9]

Access by patients to their own medical records, although a relatively new and still quite rare practice, is receiving increasing attention.[10] A patient may want to see his or her medical record to check the accuracy of personal data, including the history; to learn what the record contains before authorizing its release to a third party; to aid him or her in making informed treatment decisions; to participate more fully in, and to judge the acceptability of, his or her care. Some health care providers have voluntarily begun to make medical records available to patients, but most still resist this trend. Patients, or their attorneys, could always obtain access to their records by filing a malpractice suit, but this is obviously not the most desirable mechanism from either the patient's or provider's perspective, (The attorney, of course, gets paid.)[11]

During the 1970s, the right of patient access to medical records gained some ground both in judicial decisions and, more frequently, state statutes. One state court held that since state law required the keeping of medical records they were quasi-public in nature and therefore accessible to patients. Other courts have focused on the fiduciary (trust) nature of the provider-patient relationship in requiring access. For example, an Illinois appellate court held:

> It is our opinion that the "fiducial qualities of the physician-patient relationship" . . . require the disclosure of medical data to a patient or his agent on request, and that the patient need not "engage in legal proceedings to attain a loftier status" in his quest for such information.[12]

Several states, but still a minority, have enacted laws that grant limited access by patients and/or their representatives to their medical records.[13] These laws vary considerably from state to state. Some apply only to certain types of medical records, such as only those kept by hospitals or only those kept in physician offices; some apply only to public hospital records, others only to private hospital records. Some apply only after the patient's discharge; others are not so restricted. Several states exclude certain categories of records (the two most common exclusions are mental-health records and those cases where the attending physician states that access could cause harm to the patient). Some statutes provide access by the patient directly; others only allow access to the patient's attorney, physician, or other representative. Some provide the right to make or obtain photocopies, other states only provide for examination, and still others permit examination or copying only of a summary of the record. Some statutes require a showing of "legitimate purpose and need," such as further health care or legal analysis, while others have no such restrictions.[14] However, statutory "rights" of access remain more theoretical than real, because few states impose any penalties if access is denied, despite the statutory provisions (and if there is a penalty it is usually limited to reimbursement of legal costs paid out to enforce statutory access).[15]

Since the Federal Privacy Act of 1974 makes no exception for health records, it does provide a right of access to patients of federal agencies providing health care such as the Indian Health Service and St. Elizabeth's Hospital in Washington, D.C., and of federal agencies maintaining health insurance and payment records, including Social Security and CHAMPUS. But Westin points out that "agency regulations have specified that if a federal physician or health-care provider believes it is in the patient's best interest, the disclosure of a record can be limited to a physician selected by the patient, who would then decide what to reveal to the patient."[16]

Access to medical records by third parties—and that means anyone other than patients and those involved in treating them—involves a variety of rules, exceptions, and problems.

Generally speaking there are three types of third-party access or disclosure: (1) that authorized by the patient; (2) that authorized by court order and other legal provisions; and (3) that which is not properly authorized at all. Certain portions of the medical record are not confidential and, at least as far as hospital records are concerned, are accessible to anyone. These include information as to name, address, age, marital status, date of admission, and the like. However, such information may not be as readily available—depending on local as well as federal law—with respect to patients receiving mental-health, alcohol, or drug-related treatment, or with respect to patients who specifically prohibit such disclosure.[17]

Patient-authorized third-party access is relatively straightforward. If the patient's authorization has been genuine and freely given, the provider is protected from subsequent liability for unauthorized release of information. This is the basis on which records are routinely released to insurance companies, to state welfare agencies, such as Medicaid, and to other physicians. Since patient-authorized release is an extension, by proxy, of the patient-access principles discussed above, whether such authorization is honored for other third parties, such as attorneys, friends, or relatives of the patient will depend on state law and on policy considerations.[18]

Where state law does not require it, providers may adopt policies restricting access to certain categories of third parties, despite the patient's authorization. For example, Southwick recommends that if the patient "requests transfer of the record or of information to a person known by the physician or hospital to be clearly unqualified or unlicensed there is probably a duty to refuse the request."[19] There is no legal requirement that patient authorization be fresh or current, although some providers impose such a standard on their own. Most applications for health or life insurance require that the applicant sign a blanket authorization, granting the company access to all medical information—whether specifically relevant or not—for all time. Many people do not realize how much they are authorizing when they sign such a form, nor have they much choice if they want the insurance protection. But so far there have been only limited judicial and statutory limitations of such authorization, and they continue to be required and honored. However, the amount of attention paid to blanket authorizations by government study commissions and both legal and lay commentators suggests that some modifications, either enforced or voluntary, are not far off. A sound authorization would include date of signature, expiration date, and specification as to what information is covered, who is to receive it, and what uses may be made of it. Practitioners do not have to comply automatically with information requests accompanied by authorizations that lack such crucial elements as a date.

Court-ordered access to medical records has been the focus of some attention in recent years, especially when such records—and record-based studies—are sought in efforts to demonstrate patterns of patient care. The most traditional court-ordered access, however, involves medical records needed in preparing or defending in malpractice and other lawsuits, or as evidence before the court.

The rules of evidence are a particularly complex and rigid part of the law. Written materials usually are not admissible into evidence in court proceedings because of the hearsay doctrine. This doctrine holds that courts should rely only on testimony of individuals directly involved in the events at issue, and not on oral or written evidence that rests on the credibility of individuals or items not available to the court (a lawyer can't cross-examine a document). But there are numerous exceptions to this rule, several of which have been applied to medical records. For example, Congress and almost all the states have passed laws allowing into evidence records compiled in the regular course of business, providing these records are contemporaneous with the transaction at issue, and were compiled by a party to that transaction.

Medical records have also been held admissible on the ground that they are public documents. In addition, a few states have enacted statutes that specifically make medical records admissible.[20] But the order to produce the record—called a *subpoena ducem tecum*—must reasonably define the data requested and cannot require any special kind of search to unearth the desired information. And, it is up to the lawyers requesting the information to prove (usually through the testimony of the medical records administrator) that the record in question is authentic and is relevant to the issues in the case.[21]

Most states have statutes that bar certain practitioners—most often only physicians—from disclosing in any judicial proceedings information acquired from patients as a necessary part of care and treatment, unless the patient has waived this privilege. This prohibition covers at least those portions of the medical record based on information obtained and entered by a physician.[22] But under these privileged communication statutes, the privilege is automatically waived if the patient brings his or her health into issue by initiating a lawsuit. In such cases the defendant can gain access to the record for pretrial fact-finding (called discovery) and both the defendant and the plaintiff can put the record into evidence at the trial itself. And nonprivileged production of medical information is routine in criminal cases and in divorce, custody, and commitment proceedings.[23]

The situation with respect to two related questions is less clear, despite growing judicial attention. The first involves attempts by a party to a lawsuit to gain access to the medical records of individuals unconnected to that suit. Such access is usually sought in an effort to demonstrate a pattern of negligence or failure to perform some duty on the part of the physician or hospital being sued or to uncover other damaging information. Most courts have refused to order such access; but there have been a few exceptions, and these have created a good deal of alarm in health care circles.

The second area of concern involves quality-assurance studies based on medical records. Because such documents do not identify specific patients, there is no issue of patient access or confidentiality. But the reason for seeking access to such documents, namely, to demonstrate patterns of neglect, is the same as in the attempt to gain access to the records of patients not involved in the lawsuit, and the legal principles involved are also similar.

Quality-assurance documents, such as studies and minutes compiled by patient-care audit or review committees, are not contemporaneous with the transactions they review; nor are they compiled as a routine part of hospital business by a party to those transactions. They therefore do not qualify for admissibility as evidence under the exception to the prohibition on hearsay that applies to business records.[24] But there remains the question of whether a party to a lawsuit can gain access to these materials for pretrial preparation and fact-finding (such documents can obviously be useful in determining whom to subpoena, what questions to ask, and what other records to look for). Courts generally favor liberal availability of information (discovery) as the best way to get at the facts behind a lawsuit. At the same time, many commentators[25] have argued that the confidentiality of quality review records merits an even higher priority in order to encourage open and frank participation in the review process. The majority of court decisions on the topic have favored discovery over confidentiality;[26] but statutes in most states have removed such records from the reach of the courts as a matter of public policy. However, such statutes often protect only specifically named committees—they may list "tissue committees" for example, but not "patient care audit committees." Records not expressly named in statutes barring discovery access thus remain potentially vulnerable to pretrial subpoena.

A related question, involving documents even more removed from actual medical records, concerns the availability of the findings of professional standards review organizations (PSROs). No one has seriously suggested that patient-identifiable PSRO data be made available to non-involved third parties. But under federal regulations, PSRO data permitting the identification of specific hospitals are available to the general public upon request.[27] But the Department of Health and Human Services, as well as individual PSROs, have consistently resisted attempts under the Federal Freedom of Information Act (FOIA) to obtain PSRO data permitting the identification of individual practitioners on the grounds that PSROs are private contractors, not government agencies, and are therefore not subject to the FOIA. Although one federal district court did rule that the FOIA did require release of all nonpatient-identifiable PSRO data, that decision was reversed on appeal.[28]

There are certain other limited circumstances under which third-party access to medical records information is authorized—indeed, required—by law. Various state-mandated reports of births and deaths, weapon-caused wounds, suspected child abuse, and certain communicable diseases must be made available to others.[29]

About one-third of the states have hospital-lien statutes giving hospitals a legal claim to reimbursement from any money damages patients may recover from third parties in personal-injury suits. In such situations the third party, in turn, is given access to the patient's medical record without his or her authorization.

Unauthorized access to medical records and to the information in them has been the focus of growing concern in recent years, in part because more and more record information is computerized, with access possible from several terminals. Keeping track of who needs to have (and in fact does have) access to patient records also becomes harder as health care becomes more complex and involves more and more health professionals. The problem is further complicated by the fact that information from the record is disseminated to so many places, especially for reimbursement purposes. Thus, even if access to the physical record is carefully limited to those with proper authorization, there is little certainty, and, indeed, a decreasing likelihood, that patient information can be kept from unauthorized eyes.[30]

Thus far, there is little that patients can do to prevent, or obtain compensation for, the unauthorized and inappropriate disclosure of their medical information, even if the disclosure is made by those treating the patient.[31]

The Hippocratic oath, as well as more modern principles of medical and nursing ethics, state that information divulged by a patient in the process of diagnosis and treatment must be held inviolate, and a number of states (but not most) incorporate this requirement in their licensing laws. Nevertheless, disclosure of such information is hardly uncommon. The testimonial privilege prohibitions apply only to judicial or quasi-judicial proceedings; and while a patient can, in theory, bring suit against a practitioner or hospital for unauthorized disclosure, there is no reported case of either having to pay money damages as the result of such a suit.[32]

The truth of the information disclosed is a complete defense against libel and slander in most states (certainly so if a reasonable motive for the disclosure can be shown). Lawsuits for invasion of privacy require proof that the recipient had no legitimate interest in the information disclosed. It is generally considered acceptable to release medical information to third parties if the provider has a legitimate purpose for the release, such as meeting requirements for insurance reimbursement.[33] Southwick argues that a suit for breach of an implied contract, based on the popular expectation that information disclosed to a physician is confidential, is likely to develop some legal force in the near future, especially if the recipient of the information is an adverse party. But there is little case law so far to support this view.[34] Ironically, one reason why there is little case law, and why the right to sue is so rarely exercised in connection with unauthorized disclosure, is that the patient is usually quite unaware that such disclosure has taken place.

During the 1970s, concern about records privacy in general, and health records privacy in particular, led to the formation of several national study commissions, the publication of a number of books and articles on the subject, and the initiation of a number of legal reforms aimed at assuring greater confidentiality of personal data. Several different approaches have been suggested and/or tried. The most direct is a statute or regulation prohibiting the release of any medical information except as specified in the law—an approach already applicable in many states to mental health records and, on the federal level, to drug-abuse and alcoholism treatment records and to certain Medicare patient information.[35] However, few such prohibitions are without exceptions, and some state laws allow any disclosure that is deemed in "the best interest of the patient" or that serve some public good.[36]

Most recently, concern has focused on how to protect the integrity of primary medical-care records[37] and of information in computerized data banks.

The Department of Health, Education and Welfare, in a position paper drafted in the mid-1970s, set down five components of desirable, fair information practices with respect to medical records:

1. The subject of the record should be aware of its existence; there should be no personal record-keeping systems whose very existence is secret to all but the data user.
2. The subject of the record should have access to it, and be informed about how the data in the record will be used.
3. Individual informed consent should be required before informa-

tion obtained for one purpose is made available for other purposes.

4. In creating, maintaining, using and disseminating record information, the data user must take reasonable precautions to assure accuracy and reliability, and to prevent misuse.

5. The subject of the record should be able to challenge and correct erroneous information.[38]

The most widely publicized recommendations on confidentiality were drawn up by the Privacy Protection Study Commission, which was established under the Federal Privacy Act of 1974 to study "personal privacy in an information society." With respect to medical records the commission recommended:

- That patients be allowed access to their records and be permitted to copy, amend, and correct them.
- That access to records compiled as part of the treatment process be based clearly on a need to know.
- That no patient-identifiable information be disclosed to third parties without patient authorization, except for patient care audit purposes or to meet the requirements of statute or court order.
- That disclosures to third parties include only the information needed for the purpose of the disclosure.
- That each time information is disclosed to a third party a copy of the authorization for such disclosure be made part of the record.
- That Medicare/Medicaid certification requirements, state legislation, and voluntary cooperation be employed to achieve these objectives.[39]

The commission's recommendations were well received, but attempts to translate them into legislation have not fared well.

An especially difficult confidentiality issue is the use of medical records for research purposes. Many researchers are afraid that tighter restrictions on disclosure of information could significantly hamper investigations based on data from patient records; including a wide variety of epidemiological studies that require the identification of individuals in order to follow their medical histories over time. Such studies often are retrospective, that is, they make use of records compiled in past years; hence it is rarely possible to secure informed consent from the patients involved.

One way out of this dilemma is to have someone other than those involved in the particular research—generally an institutional review board—review and approve both the need for the data requested and the way it is to be used. Thus, the National Research Act[40] requires that investigators justify to an appropriate institutional review board the need and method for subjecting research "subjects" to risk, and includes record-based research and possible invasions of privacy within those terms. The board must examine proposed methods for protecting the confidentiality of data as part of its review. Similarly, the report of the privacy protection commission recommends (a) that record-based bio-medical and epidemiological research not violate any limitation under which the information to be used was first compiled; (b) that patient-identifiable data be used in research only when it is clearly necessary to the research and when the research itself is clearly important enough to justify the risk of disclosure; (c) that the owners of the records satisfy themselves that proper research safeguards will be followed; and (d) that the owners of the records retain control over any subsequent re-disclosure of patient-identifiable information. The adequacy of such protections has not yet been tested. Given the widespread disclosure of patient information for nonresearch purposes, it is remarkable that the use of such information for research has received the attention that it has.[41]

NOTES

1. Alan F. Westin, *Computers, Health Records, and Citizen Rights*, Monograph 157, (Washington, D.C.: National Bureau of Standards, December 1976), p. 278.
2. The earliest known medical treatise, a papyrus on which are reported forty-eight surgical case histories, all entered according to a definite form, is associated with the Egyptian physician and statesman Imhotep, who lived during the Pyramid Age of about 3000–2500 B.C. See Ada P. Kahn, "History of Medical Record Science: From Hieroglyphics to Electronic Data Processing" (first in a series), *Medical Record News* (October 1969), pp. 20–31; and Enda K. Huffman, *Medical Record Management* (Berwyn, Ill.: Physician's Record Company), 1972, chap. 1.
3. A useful discussion of the legal aspects of medical records can be found in chap. 11 of Arthur F. Southwick, *The Law of Hospital and Health Care Administration* (Ann Arbor: Health Administration Press, 1978). Also see George J. Annas, Leonard H. Glantz, and Barbara F. Katz, *The Rights of Doctors, Nurses, and Allied Health Professionals: A Health Law Primer,* (New York: Avon, 1981), chaps. 8 and 9. David G. Warren, *Problems in Hospital Law*, 3d ed. (Germantown, Md.: Aspen Systems Corporation, 1978), pp. 167–178.
4. Incident reports are not normally required to be made part of the medical record and it is generally conceded to be bad practice to do so, since such reports are less likely to be made if they will eventually become available to malpractice plaintiffs, as would be the case if they were part of the medical record. It is also clearly inappropriate to include personal comments in the record—for example, patient is "a slob," "cute," "dishonest," etc.
5. Joint Commission on Accreditation of Hospitals (JCAH), *Accreditation Manual for Hospitals*, 1981 ed. (Chicago: The Commission, 1980), pp. 84–88.

6. Southwick, *The Law of Hospital and Health Care Administration*, p. 301.
7. See, for example, Stu Chapman, "How Long Should You Keep Your Patient's Medical Records?," *Legal Aspects of Medical Practice*, (August 1979), pp. 19–33. There are also numerous state and professional-body retention requirements and recommendations for other types of hospital records, such as patient indexes, occupational, physical, and respiratory therapy treatment records, pharmacy records (including narcotic receipts and narcotic dispensing), tracings and X-ray films, tumor registry, utilization review, etc. Except for those covered by federal law, such as narcotics, these will vary from state to state. Southwick notes (*The Law of Hospital and Health Care Administration*, p. 304) that requirements of permanent retention "would probably not effectively prohibit microfilming, and some regulations affirmatively permit it. In general, if local law says nothing about microfilming, the process is assumed to be permitted." Also see Annas, Glantz, and Katz, *A Health Law Primer*, pp. 162–165. When a practitioner sells a practice, retires, or dies, special precautions must be taken in dealing with medical records. See Annas, Glantz, and Katz, *A Health Law Primer*, pp. 164–165.
8. Westin, *Computers, Health Records, and Citizen Rights*, p. 22.
9. George J. Annas, *The Rights of Hospital Patients* (New York: Avon, 1975), p. 125 (emphasis in original).
10. See, for example, Judith Rensenberger, "The Right of Patients to Read Their Charts," in the "Style" section of the *New York Times*, (national edition), 29 August 1981, p. 28.
11. *Medical Malpractice: Report of the Secretary's Commission on Medical Malpractice* (Washington, D.C., Department of Health, Education and Welfare, 1973) (DHEW pub. no. (OS)73-88), p. 75, found that "the unavailability of medical records without resort to litigation creates needless expenses and increases the incidence of unnecessary malpractice litigation."
12. *Cannell v. Medical and Surgical Clinic*, 21 Ill. App.3d 383, 315 N.E.2d 278 (1974).
13. For example, Illinois provides that

> Every private and public hospital shall, upon the demand of any patient who has been treated in such hospital and after his discharge therefrom, permit the patient, his physician or authorized attorney to examine the hospital records, including but not limited to the history, bedside notes, charts, pictures and plates, kept in connection with the treatment of such patient, and permit copies of such records to be made by him or his physician or authorized attorney. This provision shall not apply to records relating to psychiatric care or treatment. Any such demand for examination of the records shall be in writing and shall be delivered to the administrator of such hospital. (ILL, REV. STAT. Chap. 51, Secs. 71 et seq. [September 19, 1976]).

14. See Melissa Auerbach and Ted Bogue, *Getting Yours: A Consumer's Guide to Obtaining Your Medical Record* (Washington, D.C.: Health Research Group, 1978), p. 10. Also see Annas, Glantz, and Katz, *A Health Law Primer*, pp. 157–159. None of the statutes authorize the patient to correct inaccuracies in the medical record—a practice recommended by the Privacy Protection Study Commission.
15. In a 1974 survey of sixteen large Boston-area hospitals, the Center for Law

and Health Sciences received only one response indicating that the hospital policy was to obey the Massachusetts patient-access-to-hospital-records law. See Annas, *The Rights of Hospital Patients,* pp. 119–120.

16. Alan F. Westin, "Medical Records: Should Patients Have Access?" *Hastings Center Report* 7(6):25 (December 1977). There undoubtedly are some limited circumstances in which disclosure of record information could be harmful to a patient, and advocates of patient-access accept denial of access in such cases if good cause is documented. The difficulty is the attitude, widespread among health professionals, that most patients requesting access fall into this category, that the very act of requesting access is a danger signal, a mark of maladjustment. Compare John H. Altman, Peter Reich, Martin J. Kelly, and Malcolm P. Rogers, "Patients Who Read Their Hospital Charts," *New England Journal of Medicine* 302:169–171 (1980), with George J. Annas, Daryl Matthews, and Leonard H. Glantz, "Patient Access to Medical Records," *Medicolegal News* 8(2):17–18 (April 1980). As one solution to the conflict between the patient's interest in reviewing his or her record and the health professionals interest in an uninhibited forum for communication and problem discussion and in avoiding increased patient anxiety, Alan Westin has suggested the creation of a two-tier, or "dual," system of medical records. One part, "the official record," would consist of "all personal data about the patient; social and family history; complaints, tests, and examination results; diagnoses recorded; treatment summaries, drug regimens, etc.; payment information . . . ." A second part would consist of "any especially sensitive judgments about a patient's emotional or psychological condition or speculative and tentative hypotheses . . . ." The first part would be freely accessible to the patient, the second would not. Westin notes that computerized record keeping would make it much easier to print out selective portions of the record. Westin, "Medical Records: Should Patients Have Access?," pp. 23–28.

17. See Annas, *The Rights of Hospital Patients,* pp. 115–116. Many state medical records and hospital associations publish guides on the release of medical records. Also see *Institutional Policies for Disclosure of Medical Record Information* (Chicago: American Hospital Association, 1979). Federal restrictions apply to alcohol and drug abuse treatment records; see note 34.

18. Access to employer-held employee health records by third parties, such as the employees' union or by OSHA, is discussed in Chapter 10. Also see "Controversy in Medicine: Access to Employee Health Records," *Journal of the American Medical Associations,* 241:777–780 (1979).

19. Southwick, *The Law of Hospital and Health Care Administration,* pp. 306–307.

20. Ibid., pp. 337–338.

21. Ibid., p. 301, recommends that incident and accident reports not be made a part of the medical record, so that they are not automatically available to malpractice plaintiffs who obtain their records. However, in some states incident reports are specifically and independently available as part of the pretrial discovery process.

22. See Jon R. Waltz and Fred E. Inbau, *Medical Jurisprudence* (New York: Macmillan, 1971), p. 243. There was no privileged communication between physician and patient under the common law, such privilege being tradi-

tionally recognized between husband and wife, attorney and client, and clergyman and parishioner. Federal courts provide this protection only to psychotherapists.

23. Trudy Hayden and Jack Novik, *Your Rights to Privacy* (New York: Avon, 1980), p. 70.

24. However, Reid F. Holbrook and Lee J. Dunn argue that it may still be possible to get medical review committee records admitted into evidence. See their discussion: "Medical Malpractice Litigation: The Discoverability and Use of Hospitals' Quality Assurance Committee Records," *Washburn Law Journal* 16:54–76, (1976), pp. 68–70.

25. See, for example, Charles M. Jacobs, Susan Weagly, and Tom Christoffel, "Objection Overruled," *Quality Review Bulletin* (January/February 1976), pp. 28–29, 35. A concise articulation of the public policy argument favoring nondiscoverability can be found in *Bredice v. Doctors Hospital, Inc.*, 50 F.R.D. 249 (D.D.C. 1970).

26. Holbrook and Dunn, "Medical Malpractice Litigation," pp. 64–65.

27. 42 C.F.R. 476.

28. *Public Citizen Health Research Group v. DHEW, et al.*, 449 F.Supp. 937 (D.D.C. 1978); 477 F.Supp. 595 (D.D.C. 1979); reversed, 668 F.2d 537 (D.C. Cir. 1981). Also see the related discussion in note 45, Chapter 7 of this book, and see Institute of Medicine, *Access to Medical Review Data: Disclosure Policy for Professional Standards Review Organizations* (Washington, D.C.: National Academy of Science, 1981).

29. On state vital statistics and communicable disease requirements, see Chapter 5. On child abuse reporting, see Chapter 20. On reporting of deaths, see Chapter 13. Related to these statutory requirements is the judicially created duty to warn those who might be harmed by a patient; see the discussion of the *Tarasoff* decision in Chapter 19.

30. See Westin, *Computers, Health Records, and Citizen Rights*, chap. 2, 3; Marc D. Hiller and Vivian Beyda, "Computers, Medical Records, and the Right to Privacy," *Journal of Health Politics, Policy and Law* 6:463–487 (1981); *Personal Privacy in an Information Society: The Report of the Privacy Protection Study Commission* (Washington, D.C.: July 1977), chap. 7; Fran Frieder Baskin, "Confidential Medical Records: Insurers and the Threat to Informational Privacy," *Insurance Law Journal* 1978:590–610 (1978); Arthur R. Miller, *The Assault on Privacy* (Ann Arbor: University of Michigan Press, 1971); National Academy of Sciences, *Databanks in a Free Society: Computers, Record-Keeping and Privacy* (New York: Quadrangle Books, 1972). The Privacy Protection Study Commission noted that only one-third of the hospital medical record is recorded by physicians.

31. See, generally, Hayden and Novik, *Your Rights to Privacy*, chap. 7.

32. George J. Annas, cited in Westin, *Computers, Health Records, and Citizen Rights*, p. 26. The special circumstances surrounding confidentiality and privileged communications in the mental health setting are discussed in Chapter 19.

33. Southwick, *The Law of Hospital and Health Care Administration*, pp. 317–330.

34. Ibid, pp. 331–333. One relatively recent court decision that did accept, in principle at least, legal liability for unauthorized disclosure is *Horne v. Patton*,

287 So.2d 824 (Ala. 1973). In *Horne* the Alabama Supreme Court said that a physician who released medical information to a patient's employer could be liable for violating confidentiality, invading the patient's privacy, and for breach of implied contract. On confidentiality and privilege in general, see pp. 18–27 of Westin, *Computers, Health Records, and Citizen Rights*. Also see Henry H. Foster, "An Overview of Confidentiality and Privilege," *Journal of Psychiatry and Law* 4:393–401 (1976); National Commission on Confidentiality of Health Records (NCCHR), *Health Records and Confidentiality: An Annotated Bibliography*, 2d ed. (Washington, D.C.: The Commission, 1979); James F. Holzer, "Patient Privacy and the Media," *Medicolegal News* 7(1):8–9, 11 (Spring 1979).

35. The drug and alcohol abuse protections are aimed at encouraging patients to seek treatment without fear of disclosure and repercussion. Regulations based on the Comprehensive Alcohol Abuse and Alcoholism Prevention, Treatment, and Rehabilitation Act of 1970, 42 U.S.C. 4582 (1970) and the Drug Abuse Office and Treatment Act of 1972, 21 U.S.C. 1175 (1976) provide strict confidentiality standards regarding the identity, diagnosis, prognosis, and treatment of drug and alcohol abuse patients in federally assisted treatment facilities. See 42 C.F.R. Secs. 2.1 et seq. (1976).

36. Westin, *Computers, Health Records, and Citizen Rights*, pp. 23–25. The Privacy Protection Study Commission reported: "Nineteen states have regulations, statutes, or case law recognizing medical records as confidential and limiting access to them. In 21 states, a physician's license may be revoked for willful betrayal of professional secrets. These statutes do not generally apply to medical care providers other than physicians . . . ." As cited in Hiller and Beyda, "Computers, Medical Records, and the Right to Privacy," p. 471. The practical effect of such laws, however, would seem to be extremely limited.

37. Westin, *Computers, Health Records, and Citizen Rights*, pp. xi–xiii, 9–10. Westin divides the kinds of uses of medical records into three different "zones": Zone I-Primary Health Care; Zone II-Service Payers and Health Care Reviewers (private health insurance companies, Medicare and Medicaid, public and private quality review); Zone III-Secondary Users of Personal Medical Data (the use of medical records in the nonmedical world, for example, schools, employment, life insurance).

38. John P. Fanning, David B. H. Martin, and Susan J. Bennet, "Fair Information Practice for Health and Medical Records," Conference on the Confidentiality of Health Records, Key Biscayne, Florida, November 6–9, 1974.

39. *Personal Privacy in an Information Society*. Also see Annas, Glantz, and Katz, *A Health Law Primer*, pp. 182–185.

40. 42 U.S.C. Secs. 2891-3(a).

41. See, for example, Leon Gordis and Ellen Gold, "Privacy, Confidentiality, and the Use of Medical Records in Research," *Science* 207:153–156 (January 11, 1980). Also Margaret Martin, "Statisticians, Confidentiality, and Privacy," *American Journal of Public Health* 67:165–167 (February 1977). Also see *Report and Recommendations: Disclosure of Research Information Under the Freedom of Information Act* (Bethesda, Md.: National Commission for the Protection of Human Subjects of Biomedical and Behavioral Research,

1977) (DHEW pub. no. (OS) 77-0003); *Washington Research Project, Inc. v. DHEW,* 504 F.2d 238, *cert. denied* 421 U.S. 963 (1975). Westin, *Computers, Health Records, and Citizen Rights,* pp. 76–78; "CDC and NIH see threat in Freedom of Information Act," *Medical World News* (August 20, 1979), pp. 40, 45; D. H. Cowan and B. R. Adams, "Ethical and Legal Considerations for IRBs: Research with Medical Records," *IRB: A Review of Human Subjects Research* 1(8):1–4, 8 (December 1979).

18 | Family Planning: The Supreme Court and Contraception, Abortion, and Sterilization

There is, of course, a sphere within which the individual may assert the supremacy of his own will and rightfully dispute the authority of any human government, especially of a free government existing under a written constitution, to interfere with the exercise of that will.

—Jacobson v. Massachusetts[1]

If the right of privacy means anything it is the right of the **individual**, *married or single, to be free from unwarranted governmental instrusion into matters so fundamentally affecting a person as the decision whether to bear or beget a child.*

—Eisenstadt v. Baird[2]

FAMILY PLANNING is the term currently used to encompass various aspects of human reproduction, including contraception, sterilization, fertility problems, genetic screening and counseling, and abortion.[3] The decision whether or not to bear children has received considerable judicial attention during the past decade, and the resulting body of law is best considered together under its connecting common theme, even though certain aspects involve general topics, such as authorization of treatment and malpractice, which are dealt with in other chapters. The major focus will be on a series of decisions in which the courts have evolved a right to various family planning services.

For many years, the courts—especially the U.S. Supreme Court—steered clear of cases involving such highly personal matters as contraception and abortion. This left the states free to institute restrictions in these areas, including laws prohibiting the use, prescription, and/or distribution of contraceptive materials as well as barring abortions under any circumstances.

Contraception

In 1965 the U.S. Supreme Court decided what has become a most influential case, *Griswold v. Connecticut*.[4] The case challenged a Connecticut law that declared:

> Any person who uses any drug, medicinal article or instrument for the purpose of preventing conception shall be fined not less than fifty dollars or imprisoned not less than sixty days nor more than one year or be both fined and imprisoned.

The executive director of the Planned Parenthood League of Connecticut and the medical director of its clinic were both convicted for assisting and abetting the violation of this law by giving contraceptive information, instruction, and medical advice to *married couples* and for prescribing contraceptive devices or materials. The case ultimately went to the U.S. Supreme Court, which, by a 7 to 2 vote, declared the Connecticut statute unconstitutional.

Members of the seven justice majority presented four separate rationales for this holding. In the opinion written for the Court, Justice William Douglas argued that the law infringed upon a constitutional right of privacy, which existed even though the Constitution nowhere explicitly speaks of such a right and the Court had never before recognized a privacy right. Justice Douglas pointed out that a number of stated constitutional rights, such as the freedoms of speech, press, assembly, and protection against unreasonable search and seizure, have been extended by Court decisions well beyond a literal reading of the Constitution. The guarantees in the Bill of Rights he declared, "have penumbras, formed by eminations from those guarantees that help give them life and substances. . . . Various guarantees create zones of privacy." Justice Douglas concluded:

> Would we allow the police to search the sacred precincts of marital bedrooms for telltale signs of the use of contraceptives? The very idea is repulsive to the notions of privacy surrounding the marriage relationship. We deal with a right of privacy older than the Bill of Rights—older than our political parties, older than our school system. Marriage is a coming together for better or for worse, hopefully enduring, and intimate to the degree of being sacred. It is an association that promotes a way of life, not causes; a harmony in living, not political faiths; a bilateral loyalty, not commercial or social projects. Yet it is an association for as noble a purpose as any involved in our prior decisions.

Justice Arthur Goldberg, in a concurring opinion joined by Chief Justice Earl Warren and Justice William Brennan, also noted that a right of privacy is not mentioned explicitly in the Constitution; but he read such a right into the Ninth Amendment provision that "the enumeration in the Constitution, of certain rights, shall not be construed to deny or disparage others retained by the people." Since the Ninth Amendment had been virtually ignored by the Court for almost two centuries, this argument was considered by many commentators as being as creative as Douglas's strikingly new penumbra analysis.

Justices John Harlan and Byron White each had different reasons for holding the Connecticut contraception law as unconstitutional. Justice Harlan maintained that it violated basic values "implicit in the ordered concept of liberty," while Justice White argued that it deprived married couples of liberty without due process of law. Thus only four of the nine justices accepted the right of privacy concept that the case has come to represent.

Justice Potter Stewart, in a dissent to the decision, protested the privacy argument:

> With all due deference, I can find no such general right of privacy in the Bill of Rights, in any other part of the Constitution, or in any case ever before decided by this Court.

Nevertheless, given judicial breath, the constitutional right of privacy took on a life of its own. It was further broadened in the 1972 case of *Eisenstadt v Baird*,[5] where—despite Justice Douglas's stirring language regarding marriage ("intimate to the degree of being sacred")—the Court found little trouble in using the equal protection clause to extend the privacy pinciple set down in *Griswold* to encompass the distribution of contraceptives to unmarried individuals.

The Court declared:

> If the right of privacy means anything, it is the right of the *individual*, married or single, to be free from unwarranted governmental intrusion into matters so fundamentally affecting a person as the decision whether to bear or beget a child.

Finally, in 1977, the Court invalidated a New York law[6] that made it a crime for anyone other than a licensed pharmacist to distribute contraceptives, and for anyone, including pharmacists, to advertise or display contraceptives.[7] "Read in the light of its progeny," the Court concluded, "the teaching of *Griswold* is that the Constitution protects individual decisions in matters of childbearing from unjustified intrusion by the state."

Thus, the *Griswold* decision not only removed legal restrictions to contraception that now seem almost medieval, it also established the principle that certain areas of human activity were impervious to governmental restriction—what some have called "zones of no law"—constitutionally protected from state and federal control. This principle has proved extremely far-reaching.

Abortion

The new right of privacy received its most important—and most controversial—application in the Supreme Court abortion decisions of 1973. Abortion was a social issue that the Court had avoided for many years; but since a majority of the states had laws making it a crime to procure or attempt an abortion (except for the purpose of saving the woman's life), the challenge to the right of privacy could not be ignored.[8]

The decision in *Roe v. Wade*[9] (and the companion case of *Doe v. Bolton*[10]), written by Justice Harry Blackmun,[11] began with an historical discussion of antiabortion laws. Under the common law, Blackmun observed, abortions performed prior to quickening (the first recognizable movement of the fetus in utero) had never been prohibited. In fact, it would "now appear doubtful that abortion was ever firmly established as a common law crime even with respect to the destruction of a quick fetus." This common law view predominated in the United States until the mid-nineteenth century; not until after the Civil War did states begin to adopt statutes restricting abortion, and these, too, focused on abortions performed after quickening. Eventually, however, "the quickening distinction disappeared from the statutory law of most states and the degree of the offense and the penalties were increased. By the end of the 1950's a large majority of the States banned abortion, however and whenever performed, unless done to save or preserve the life of the mother."

The purpose of Blackmun's historical essay was to emphasize the fact that the current abortion laws represented a highpoint of rigidity and prohibition, rather than a social control of long standing. This fact was important in determining the validity of such laws from a constitutional perspective. As Blackmun observed in concluding his historical discussion:

> It is thus apparent that at common law, at the time of the adoption of our Constitution, and throughout the major portion of the 19th century, abortion was viewed with less disfavor than under most American statues currently in effect. Phrasing it another way, a woman enjoyed a substantially broader right to terminate a pregnancy than she does in most States today. At least with respect to the early stage of pregnancy, and very possibly without such a limitation, the opportunity to make this choice was present in this country well into the 19th century. Even later, the law continued for some time to treat less punitively an abortion procured in early pregnancy.

The *Roe* decision went on to consider existing state abortion laws in light of *Griswold* and related cases, concluding:

> The Court has recognized that a right of personal privacy, or a guarantee of certain areas or zones of privacy, does exist under the Constitution. . . . This

right of privacy, whether it be founded in the Fourteenth Amendment's concept of personal liberty and restrictions upon state action . . . or . . . in the Ninth Amendment's reservation of rights to the people, is broad enough to encompass a woman's decision whether or not to terminate her pregnancy.

This did not conclude the matter, however, for two arguments had been made in support of the abortion laws that could, perhaps, be expected to override this privacy right. First, it was argued that a fetus is a "person," with its own competing constitutional protection under the Fourteenth Amendment.[12] Justice Blackmun responded that while the Constitution does not define "person," it does "citizens" as "persons born or naturalized in the United States," a phrase obviously not applicable to a fetus. He also reasoned that since, during most of the nineteenth century, "prevailing legal abortion practices were far freer than they are today," the word "person" in the Fourteenth Amendment would not have included the "unborn." Finally, Blackmun noted that the states had not really considered fetuses to be "persons," since all state abortion laws contained exceptions permitting abortions to save the life of the pregnant woman, and such an exemption was inconsistent with the view of a fetus as a person. Thus Blackmun and the Court rejected this challenge to the privacy right of a pregnant woman.

It was also argued that the states themselves had a legitimate countervailing interest in regulating abortion that was greater than the individual woman's right to privacy. The Court concluded that validity of the state's claims depended on the stage of fetal development:

(a) For the stage prior to approximately the end of the first trimester, the abortion decision and its effectuation must be left to the medical judgment of the pregnant woman's attending physician.

(b) For the stage subsequent to approximately the end of the second trimester, the State, in promoting its interest in the health of the mother, may, if it chooses, regulate the abortion procedure in ways that are reasonably related to maternal health.

(c) For the stage subsequent to viability the State, in promoting its interest in the potentiality of human life, may, if it chooses, regulate, and even proscribe, abortion except where it is necessary, in appropriate medical judgment, for the preservation of the life or health of the mother.

The underlying concept here is clear; the law will not ignore the distinction between a one-day-after-conception embryo and a nine-month old fetus. One might ask whether the Court's trimester and viability standards do not establish sharper distinctions than are medically justified. The answer is clearly yes. The Court reasoned that in setting constitutional restrictions for the states it must provide definite and fixed guideposts. Of course there may be new challenges as medical advances make it possible for ever-younger fetuses to survive; but the Court preferred its somewhat arbitrary framework to the chaos of allowing individual states to set abortion guidelines.

It should be noted that the *Roe* decision, after affirming a woman's right of privacy included the right to choose abortion, declared that "the abortion decision and its effectuation must be left to the medical judgment of the pregnant woman's attending physician."[13] Thus even during the first trimester, a state can regulate abortion to the point of requiring that only licensed physicians perform the procedure. But the state may not restrict or regulate the medical judgment of the pregnant woman's physician regarding termination of pregnancy. More extensive regulation is possible during the second trimester, up to the point of viability, but such regulation is permissible only in the interest of the patient. Nor may the state deal with abortion more strictly than it does other similarly serious medical procedures; crippling limitations "in the interest of the patient" would not be proper. After the fetus is viable, however, states are free to prohibit abortion if they choose, except where the woman's health would be jeopardized by continuing the pregnancy.

The companion case to *Roe*, *Doe v. Bolton*, dealt with some of the common restrictions placed on legal abortion by the abortion reform laws enacted in the 1960s. Justice Blackmun, who wrote the decision, reiterated the Court's view that the only appropriate restrictions on previability abortions were those necessary to protect the woman's health. This limitation precluded requirements that abortions be performed only in licensed, accredited hospitals, or only after approval by a review committee or consultants, because such requirements were not imposed on other medical or surgical procedures of equal complexity and hazard.

As one case after another in recent years have made clear, the Supreme Court's 1973 pronouncements have not settled the abortion issue. Despite the the Court's rulings, many states and the Congress have effectively limited the availability of abortion for significant groups of women. A number of state legislatures have sought to regulate the conditions under which they can be performed, including requirements for the husband's consent or prohibitions against particular techniques, such as saline injection. In addition, Congress and the states have both sharply restricted public funding for abortions.

The Supreme Court undertook to review the continuing efforts by the states to restrict abortion in 1976 in the case of *Planned Parenthood of Central Missouri v. Danforth*.[14] The Court's ruling, which dealt with a Missouri statute regulating abortion, appeared to many to represent the beginning of a pulling back from its more comprehensive decision in *Roe*. The Court pointed out that the *Roe* decision had not accepted the argument "that the woman's right is absolute and that she is entitled to terminate her pregnancy at whatever time, in whatever way, and for whatever reason she alone chooses," and that it had stated explicitly that this right "must be considered against important state interests in regulation." The sphere of state interest was expanded in the *Danforth* decision, written for the Court by Justice Blackmun. The *Danforth* ruling invalidated some provisions of the challenged Missouri law, including a requirement for written consent from the husband for first trimester abortions and prohibition against saline abortion techniques (the method used in 60 to 80 percent of all post-first-trimester abortions).[15] The Court also reviewed Missouri's legislatively defined standard of professional care. The law provided that "no person who performs or induces an abortion shall fail to exercise that degree of professional skill, care and diligence to preserve the life and health of the fetus which such person would be required to exercise in order to preserve the life and health of any fetus intended to be born but not aborted." Since this provision made no distinction regarding the stage of fetal development, the Court held it to be constitutionally improper.[16]

However, the *Danforth* decision did uphold the validity of some restrictions contained in the state law, including a statutory definition of viability: "that stage of fetal development when the life of the unborn child may be continued indefinitely outside the womb by natural or artifical life-supportive systems." The plaintiff had argued that the definition was too vague because it did not set a specific gestational age. The Court also upheld a requirement that a woman sign a written consent before obtaining a first trimester abortion, even though this treated abortion differently from other procedures; in the Court's view, this requirement was not burdensome. In addition, the Court upheld a special record-keeping and reporting requirement for abortions. While conceding that this requirement was "perhaps approaching permissible limits" by treating first trimester abortions differently from comparable medical and surgical procedures, Blackmun concluded that as long as confidentiality was maintained this requirement, too, was not unduly burdensome.[17]

Perhaps the most difficult issue presented by *Danforth* involved a minor's right to an abortion. The Missouri statute required the consent of at least one parent to a first trimester abortion for an unmarried woman under the age of eighteen.[18] The Supreme Court declared this to be an impermissible restraint: "The State does not have the constitutional authority to give a third party absolute, and possibly arbitrary, veto over the decision of the physician and his patient to terminate the patient's pregnancy." Thus, "the State may not impose a blanket provision . . . requiring the consent of a parent . . . as a condition for abortion of an unmarried minor during the first 12 weeks of pregnancy." But in holding this portion of the Missouri law invalid, the Court made it clear that this should "not suggest that every minor, regardless of age or

maturity, may give effective consent for termination of her pregnancy."
And, in fact, in another case decided the same day, the Court seemed to
hold the door open.

Bellotti v. Baird[19] represented a challenge to the Massachusetts abortion statute that also required parental consent but permitted mature
minors who were refused such consent to seek a Court order allowing an
abortion. The Court sent the case back to the federal district court and
the Massachusetts high court with questions regarding the exact meaning of the statute. In 1979 the Supreme Court finally invalidated the
Massachusetts statute and other nonabsolute parental abortion consent
laws because they required all minors, including mature minors, desiring an abortion to request parental consent before seeking a court order.
Said the Court: "Every minor must have the opportunity—if she so
desires—to go directly to a court without first consulting or notifying her
parents. If she satisfies the court that she is mature and well-informed
enough to make intelligently the abortion decision on her own, the
Court must authorize her to act."[20] On the other hand, if the Court does
not find sufficient maturity, it should authorize or refuse to authorize
the desired abortion according to the minor's "best interest." Since Massachusetts law did not meet these criteria, the Court seemed to many to
be spelling out the kind of parental consent statute it would uphold.

The Court's most recent decision in this area involved parental notice
rather than consent. Under consideration was a Utah statute that required physicians to notify, "if possible," the parents or guardians of a
minor upon whom an abortion is to be performed. The Court dealt with
the case on very narrow grounds, holding that when—as in the case
before it—the minor was neither emancipated nor mature, but rather
living with and dependent upon her parents, the requirement of the
statute could be constitutionally applied. "Although we have held that a
state may not consitutionally legislate a blanket, unreviewable power of
parents to veto their daughter's abortion," noted the Court, "a statute
setting out a 'mere requirement of parental notice' does not violate the
constitutional rights of an immature, dependent minor."[21]

After the landmark abortion decisions of 1973, a significant number
of abortions were publicly funded through Medicaid. But abortion opponents succeded in restricting such funding on both federal and state
levels. The Supreme Court was therefore confronted with the question
of whether such restrictions unconstitutionally deprived poor women of
this privacy right. The Court considered several aspects of this question
in a group of cases decided together in 1977. In Beal v. Doe[22] the Court
held that, despite the fact that the statute establishing Medicaid requires
payment for "necessary medical services," the states are free to exclude
services connected with elective, nontherapeutic abortion. In Maher v.
Roe[23] the Court held that such an exclusion did not violate either the

equal protection clause of the Fourteenth Amendment or the right to privacy. The majority reasoned that for a state to treat funding of abortions differently from the funding of other Medicaid-funded medical expenses did not infringe upon or unduly burden a fundamental right. And in *Poelker v. Doe*[24] the court held that a publicly owned and operated hospital could adopt a policy of not performing abortions, even though it provided maternity care.

Finally, in *Harris v. McRae*[25] the Court went even further, upholding the constitutionality of the Hyde Amendment prohibition on federal funding of medically necessary abortions.[26] Writing for the Court, Justice Stewart argued that the Hyde restriction, by means of unequal subsidization of abortion and other medical services, encourages alternative activity legislatively deemed in the public interest.

> Although government may not place obstacles in the path of a woman's exercise of her freedom of choice, it need not remove those not of its own creation. Indigency falls in the latter category. . . . Although Congress has opted to subsidize medically necessary services generally, but not certain medically necessary abortions, the fact remains that the Hyde Amendment leaves an indigent woman with at least the same range of choice in deciding whether to obtain a medically necessary abortion as she would have had if Congress had chosen to subsidize no health care costs at all.

Following this reasoning, the Court's majority rejected the district court's determination that the Hyde restriction violated (1) the constitutional right to privacy by limiting an indigent woman's decision to terminate a pregnancy, (2) the First Amendment free exercise clause for women whose religious beliefs favored abortion, and (3) equal protection by discriminatorily denying a particular group of citizens the ability to exercise a fundamental right in the absence of any legitimate countervailing governmental interest. Since the Court also concluded that the Medicaid Act "does not require a participating state to pay for those medically necessary abortions for which federal reimbursement is unavailable under the Hyde Amendment," this meant that public funding would be available to indigent women in need of abortions only in those states that voluntarily choose to fund the procedure. Needless to say, this conclusion sparked widespread protest, both popularly and from a four-man minority on the Court.[27] Justice Brennan argued in dissent:

> As a means of delivering health services, then, the Hyde Amendment is completely irrational. As a means of preventing abortions, it is concededly rational—brutally so. But this latter goal is constitutionally forbidden.

The main thrust of the minority's position was that for government to restrict a constitutionally protected right—in this case abortion—through indirect means is as illegitimate as the more direct achievement of that end. "By thus injecting coercive financial incentives favoring childbirth into a decision that is constitutionally guaranteed to be free from governmental intrusion, the Hyde Amendment deprives the indigent woman of her . . . right recognized in *Roe v. Wade*."

Abortion—and public funding of abortion—is as divisive an issue for the Supreme Court as it is for the rest of society. The law in this area in the future will depend very much on who sits on the Court, with age favoring the majority in *McRae*. It is risky to predict the outcome of current efforts to directly outlaw all abortions, but it does seem unlikely—given the strong public support for keeping abortion legal—that these efforts will succeed. The constitutional amendment effort seems close to being abandoned; the effort to statutorily define the beginning of human life is overwhelmingly opposed by constitutional scholars—including those opposed to abortion—as being unconstitutional and a dangerous precedent; the "states' rights" effort might succeed, but its impact would not be universal.

It is safe to say that the abortion picture will continue to change. One of the two major battlegrounds, public funding of abortions, involves the health professional indirectly. But the never-ending efforts to regulate the conditions under which abortions are performed will continue to be of concern to all who are professionally involved in family planning, because these regulations are often vague enough to create legal risks and uncertainty for the health professional. Just such an issue was involved in *Colautti v. Franklin,* [28] which reached the Supreme Court in 1978. Under a Pennsylvania statute, a physician was required to use the abortion technique most likely to produce a live fetus if "there is sufficient reason to believe that the fetus may be viable." A physician who did not try to save a potentially viable fetus could be subject to criminal charges. The Court found that "may be viable" was unconstitutionally vague language and that the statute intruded upon what is essentially a medical judgment. It held that the law was "little more than a trap for those who act in good faith," which could have a "profound chilling effect on the willingness of physicians to perform abortions near the point of viability in the manner indicated by their best medical judgment."

Despite this decision, however, antiabortion groups in several states have secured passage of laws that, although slightly differently worded, make abortions performed near the point of viability legally hazardous for the participating health professional. It is obviously important, therefore, for health professionals in this area to keep abreast of abortion laws in their state and to document carefully the basis for all estimates of fetal development.

For those health professionals who choose not to perform or participate in abortion procedures, the legal picture is considerably less cloudy. Several state have statutes expressly protecting the job rights of such persons[29]—although a service or clinic heavily devoted to abortions is unlikely to have to hire or retain individuals who refuse to take part in such procedures.

Sterilization

Sterilization may occur as an unwanted but unavoidable result of disease and/or surgery involving the reproductive organs, and except for malpractice, this is not an area of legal concern. On the other hand, surgical procedures conducted specifically for the purpose of rendering an individual sterile present a series of legal questions, since the ability to reproduce is such an important part of human existence and surgical sterilization is thus far, with few exceptions, not a reversible process.

Voluntary sterilization.   One group of legal questions involves the availability of sterilization to the individual who desires it. Because there are no state laws prohibiting sterilization, as there were in the case of contraception and abortion, the matter of availability relates largely to institutional policies prohibiting or discouraging sterilization. In one case[30] a U.S. court of appeals held that a public hospital may not restrict sterilization more closely than other comparable surgical procedures. However, in a similar suit against a hospital operated by a religious order,[31] another U.S. court of appeals held that receipt of Hill-Burton funds, tax-exempt status, and regulation by the state did not provide sufficient public involvement to require the hospital to make sterilization available. And as with abortion, some states—and Congress—protect the health professional who does not want to participate in a sterilization procedure for reasons of conscience.[32]

Civil liability for a failed sterilization operation could involve lack of adequate informed consent or negligence in performing the procedure, in postoperative testing, or in postoperative counseling. Some lawsuits have been brought alleging violation of a promised warranty that the operation would be—or had been—a success.[33] Since it has been estimated that in two-thirds to three-fourths of married white couples (slightly less for black couples) one spouse will obtain a contraceptive sterilization within fifteen years of the last wanted birth, the number of procedures (and possible unexpected births) is quite large.[34]

Involuntary sterilization.   Sterilizations performed without the voluntary and competent consent of the individual present the most serious legal difficulties. Such involuntary sterilizations can be the result of governmental compulsion, third-party proxy authorization, or coercion.

Compulsory sterilization laws had their origins in the writings of

Galton and Spencer and in the eugenics movement of the first decades of this century, which aimed at improving the human species by preventing the "unfit" from reproducing. By the 1930s almost thirty states had enacted eugenic sterilization laws, each of them authorizing sterilization of mentally deficient persons, and all but two including mentally ill persons as well. Seventeen states also authorized the sterilization of epileptics, two-thirds of the laws applied only to persons confined in institutions.[35] At least 65,000 persons are estimated to have been sterilized in the United States under these laws during the first half of the century. The 1930s and 1940s were the high point of forced sterilizations. It was not until the mid-1950s that states began to move away from eugenic sterilizations, either by repealing compulsory sterilization statutes or allowing them to fall into disuse. But some states still have such laws on the books.[36]

When the early eugenic sterilization laws were first challenged in state courts, they were declared invalid. But the tide soon turned. The landmark case, *Buck v. Bell*,[37] was decided by the U.S. Supreme Court in 1927, in a decision written by Justice Oliver Wendell Holmes. The case involved Carrie Buck, a seventeen-year-old-woman in a foster home who was committed to the Virginia State Colony for Epileptics and Feeble-Minded after bearing an illegitimate child. The state sought to have Carrie Buck sterilized under a law that provided for the forced sterilization of "mental defectives." It was asserted, and the U.S. Supreme Court accepted as fact, that Carrie Buck was "the daughter of a feeble-minded mother in the same institution," feeble-minded herself, "the mother of an illegitimate feeble-minded child," and "the probable potential parent of socially inadequate offspring." The Court upheld the law authorizing state-compelled sterilization against the challenge that it violated Fourteenth Amendment due process and equal protection provisions. Holmes's decision concluded that adequate due process was afforded by the law's requirement that all proposed sterilizations be reviewed by an internal hospital review board, with the patient given notice and an opportunity to appeal a sterilization order in court. As to whether such forced sterilization could ever be justified, however careful a procedure was observed, Holmes wrote:

> It is better for all the world, if instead of waiting to execute degenerate offspring for crime, or to let them starve for their imbecility, society can prevent those who are manifestly unfit from continuing their kind. The principle that sustains compulsory vaccination is broad enough to cover cutting the Fallopian tubes. . . . Three generations of imbeciles are enough.

Carrie Buck's daughter eventually entered school, where her teachers rated her as "bright," vividly demonstrating the bankruptcy of the eugenic theories on which compulsory sterilization laws were based. And over half a century later it was revealed that many victims of the law, including Carrie Buck's sister, had not been told they were being sterilized but, instead, were misled into thinking they were receiving appendectomies.[38] But the most shocking aspect of *Buck v. Bell* is not that it was decided on the basis of distorted facts, but that the legal principle established in the decision is still "good" law. *Buck v. Bell* has never been reversed. The decision has been narrowed—most notably by a 1942 Supreme Court opinion[39] invalidating a "habitual criminal" sterilization law because it did not apply equally to all classes of repeat felonies—but it is still constitutionally permissible for a state to compel sterilization of the "unfit" if done uniformly, and with adequate due process. Thus if there is "a sphere within which the individual may assert the supremacy of his own will and rightfully dispute the authority of any human government," it does not encompass state-compelled destruction of the individual's ability to reproduce. And if the right of privacy means freedom "from unwarranted governmental intrusion into matters so fundamentally affecting a person as the decision whether to bear or beget a child," that freedom does not extend to the mentally impaired. Part of the reason for this state of affairs is the long history of judicial paternalism toward those viewed as less than competent, including a readiness to define the best interest of such groups for them rather than to accept their own definition. In such situations the opinion of medical experts is afforded great respect, highlighting the legal power the patina of scientific legitimacy provides for the health professions.

Involuntary sterilizations authorized by third parties most typically involve a parent seeking sterilization of a retarded, sexually active child. Such involuntary sterilization is often considered less offensive than state-ordered sterilization, because the parent is presumed to have a greater interest in the child's welfare than does the state.[40] Against such sterilizations, it is argued that no benefit is conferred, that retardation is not highly inheritable, and that third-party monetary concerns can cloud the issue. Just as with *Buck v. Bell*, there is much to suggest that "facts" presented to justify need, as well as procedural safeguards, in proxy-authorized sterilizations are often far removed from reality.

Because of the serious, permanent effects of sterilization, physicians will often seek court approval before proceeding. In some states the legislatures have specifically authorized judicial review and approval of sterilization petitions, but in other states the courts do not have the specific authority to give such approval,[41] and may therefore refuse to allow sterilization of anyone unable to offer their own consent. Where judicial review is called for, the modern trend is likely to favor very strict application of review criteria. In a recent decision, the New Jersey Supreme Court ruled that only a court can appropriately decide whether sterilization is in the best interests of persons unable to offer their own consent because of legal disabilities. The court required a standard of clear and convincing evidence, the appointment of a *guardian ad litem* to represent the individual, and noted that "the ultimate criterion is the best interests of the incompetent person."[42]

In Oregon a seven-member State Board of Social Protection reviews sterilization petitions. "Any two persons or any person licensed to practice medicine and surgery . . . may file a petition . . . alleging that any other person within the state" should be sterilized. The board will order involuntary sterilization if convinced that any offspring would be children "(a) who would have an inherited tendency to mental retardation or mental illness; or (b) who would become neglected or dependent children as a result of the parent's inability by reason of mental illness or mental retardation to provide adequate care."[43]

A third type of involuntary sterilization involves individuals who are coerced; most such coercion has involved women. Coercion, as the leading court decision on the subject explained, can take several forms:

> There is uncontroverted evidence in the record . . . that an indefinite number of poor people have been improperly coerced into accepting a sterilization operation under the threat that various federally supported welfare benefits would be withdrawn unless they submitted to irreversible sterilization. Patients receiving Medicaid assistance at childbirth are evidently the most frequent targets of this pressure. . . . [One plaintiff] was actually refused medical assistance by her attending physician unless she submitted to tubal ligation after the birth.[44]

The last type of coercion described may constitute abandonment of the patient, but as a private action it is beyond governmental control.[45] Coercion under publicly funded programs, however, is clearly amenable to such control, and in 1979, the Department of Health and Human Services, in the wake of a lawsuit against the federal government, finally adopted guidelines to restrict such coercion in federally funded sterilizations.[46]

The 1979 rules totally prohibit funding of sterilization of mentally incompetent or institutionalized individuals and of individuals under twenty-one years of age. Mentally competent individuals over twenty-one may be sterilized if they have voluntarily given informed consent, signed a prescribed consent form, and waited at least thirty days after giving consent (except in the case of premature delivery or emergency abdominal surgery). The required consent form is headed with a notice that refusal to consent will not affect any federal benefits. It goes on to attest to a full discussion with doctor or clinic regarding the irreversible nature of the procedure, alternative birth control methods, and risks and benefits. It would seem, however, that compliance with these federal requirements has been far from adequate.

Fertility Problems

Infertility, and the measures taken to overcome this problem by couples desiring children, can also have legal consequences for the health professional. The oldest solution has been adoption. The physicians, nurses, or midwives involved in a childbirth should avoid any participation in bringing together the biological mother and would-be adoptive parent(s), because there could be severe legal difficulties if the contact is handled improperly. Social workers respresenting agencies involved in adoption need advice and counsel of a legal specialist to assure that necessary procedures are properly adhered to.[47] And it goes without saying that all health professionals must adhere to the same careful privacy and confidentiality standards with respect to inferility and adoption that are expected regarding all other patient information.

Artificial insemination homologous (ATH)—using the sperm of the husband—is not an area of legal concern; but artifical insemination heterologous (AID)—using the sperm of a donor—can create serious legal difficulties.[48] Time was when a child conceived through AID was considered illegitimate and the mother an adulteress, although this situation began to cease in the late 1960s as a result of new statutes and court decisions. At least fifteen states have laws that regulate artificial insemination by donor. Some states require that the procedure be performed by a physician, others require the written consent of both husband and wife, and still others provide civil immunity for the physician. All convey an irrefutable presumption of legitimacy to the child born within wedlock, as long as both wife and husband have consented in writing to the insemination procedure.[49]

One serious defect in most of these laws (the New York City Health Code is a notable exception) is the absence of any controls on who may serve as donors. There is nothing to prevent men with diseases that might be handed down from donating their sperm for AID, nor are there regulations requiring the maintenance of confidential files of donor names, addresses, and medical histories, which could be tapped if the needs of the child born as a result of AID urgently require it. George Annas has criticized existing law in this area as being "based primarily on protecting the best interests of the sperm donor rather than those of the recipient or resulting child."[50]

Two procedures for overcoming infertility have recently been creating controversy: in vitro fertilization and contracts to bear a child. The feasiblity of in vitro fertilization was demonstrated in England in 1978 with the live birth of a normal child conceived by this technique; a therapeutic in vitro fertilization clinic opened in Virginia in 1980.[51]

Legal argument and speculation continue to surround the procedure, which some people object to on moral grounds and others fear for the legal and social complications, but which many childless couples look to with renewed hope of becoming parents. It is an area where medical science has outdistanced the law; but, as with AID, it is reasonable to expect that solutions to the legal problems posed by in vitro fertilization will gradually be evolved as the technique comes into wider use.[52] Contracts to bear a child raise innumerable difficulties. What happens if either the surrogate mother or the sperm donor renege on the contract? If payment is involved, are state laws prohibiting "baby buying" violated? Does the whole process run counter to public policy?[53] Fortunately this is not a major area of concern for the health care delivery system.

Genetic Screening and Counseling

The technology for genetic screening, which can uncover certain non-evident diseases or a predisposition to them in screenees and their off-spring, has made tremendous strides in recent years. As is often the case, the law has been struggling to relate to these developments both in the legislatures and in the courts. In the 1960s, for example, in what is now viewed by many as overreaction,[54] many states mandated screening for phenylketonuria (PKU). In the 1970s, seventeen states enacted sickle cell anemia screening laws, some encouraging, others requiring, such screening.[55] More recently states have established genetic screening programs directed at galactosemia, homocystinuria, maple-sugar-urine disease, tyrosinemia, and histidinemia.[56]

The constitutionality of government-required screening programs is quite clear, and is based on the state's police power to promote the public's health. Genetic screening falls into the same category as screening for venereal disease, glaucoma, vision and hearing impairment, and other diseases and conditions (see Chapter 5). However, the present trend in state genetic screening legislation favors voluntary screening programs rather than mandatory requirements. Even so, it is relevant to ask whether laws establishing such programs are necessary, or even desirable. Criticism of PKU screening has focused on the damage caused by false positives, the failure of follow-up, and the success of screening without legislative mandate. Screening for carriers of sickle cell trait has been even more controversial, generating charges of racist attempts at eugenic control and, because the medical facts of this trait are so poorly understood by the lay public, many carriers face ostracism, job loss, and other disabilities.

However, even where physicians are mandated to provide genetic screening, there have been few, if any, efforts to enforce that duty, and the penalties for failure to comply with such laws are unclear. Realistically, therefore, the legal implications of genetics screening for the health care professional involve tort law, not criminal law. Waltz suggests four potential problems:

1. Medical malpractice (i.e., professional negligence), including incorrect diagnosis;
2. Failure to obtain informed consent to the screening procedure;
3. Failure to disclose the results of screening; and
4. Unauthorized disclosure of screening results to persons other than the screenee.[57]

Genetic counseling involves "information about the disorder or characteristic in question, its frequency, and its manifestations, if any, and about the probabilities for transmission to the next generation. It includes answers to all questions. . . ."[58] Genetic counseling can present serious and unique legal problems. The family practitioner, psychologist, nurse, social worker, obstetrician, or other professional involved in counseling would do well to become familar with some of the basic medicolegal discussions on the subject (such as the book by Reilly and the two volumes edited by Milunsky and Annas[59]) and to review any questions they have regarding counseling protocols with legal counsel.

The two major areas of legal concern in this area are malpractice and confidentiality. They apply when patients seek information to help them determine whether or not to attempt pregnancy or to terminate a pregnancy. Malpractice can involve either errors of commission, as when a wrong diagnosis was provided (or accepted by the counselor without verification), leading either to a birth or to termination of a pregnancy that would otherwise have been avoided, or errors of omission, such as failure to provide necessary information, lack of informed consent, or failure to make appropriate referrals for other studies, such as amniocentesis.[60]

Lawsuits may be brought by the parents or potential parents as well as in the name of a child. Damages for the child's pain and suffering can be sought by the child, but not by the parents; therefore a number of cases have been brought in recent years in behalf of children with genetic defects, alleging "wrongful life" (that is, wrongful conception). Most courts have not been receptive to this claim, recognition of which could require them to decide whether it would have been better never to have been born at all rather than to have been born with gross defects. For example, in two cases against physicians alleging inadequate information and erroneous advice provided prenatally to the parents, New York State's highest court rejected the possibility of wrongful life claims on behalf of children with birth defects, while recognizing as compensable the lesser injuries sustained by the parents.[61] More recently, however, the California Supreme Court has ruled that a child born with Tay-Sachs disease can bring suit for wrongful life against two testing laboratories that allegedly were negligent in incorrectly informing her parents that they were not carriers. Some worry that recognizing this type of claim opens a Pandora's box, because it also would encompass wrongful life suits by children against their parents.[62]

The second major area of legal concern regarding genetic counseling involves the confidentiality of information. Besides all the normal ethical and legal constraints regarding practitioner-patient confidentiality, there are two special considerations that can complicate this matter. One is when a patient is found to be a carrier of a serious genetic disease, and there is a high likelihood that his or her blood relatives are similarly affected. If the patient refuses to transmit this knowledge to the relatives, the patient's right to confidentiality comes into conflict with the practitioner's duty to warn. The legal situation in such instances is less than clear; but it may be that the public policy inherent in contagious-disease reporting statutes, and in some recent court decisions stipulating a psychiatrist's duty to warn individuals threatened by violent patients, would protect the practitioner who contacted the relatives, even if it did not actually require such contact.[63]

A second special situation arises when a family genetic study reveals that the husband could not possibly be the father of the child or children involved. Frankness on the part of the practitioner is likely to lead to an unpleasant confrontation, but silence could cause several types of damage, such as unfounded decisions regarding future pregnancies. As one commentator has noted, it is a situation of being damned if you do and damned if you don't,[64] and neither law nor ethics dictates a clear answer to such a dilemma.

Childbirth

Finally, although the birth of a child is not technically an aspect of family planning, it seems quite appropriate that this chapter conclude with a few observations on childbirth. It has long been observed that physicians see the individual into the world and out of it. A similar observation can be made regarding the requirements and constraints of law. No state requires that women give birth in a hospital or actually prohibits home birth. Actually, however, the choices regarding birth setting and practice are, in many ways, quite limited.[65] In many states delivering a child constitutes the practice of medicine (or midwivery), and only licensed practitioners can legally attend births. In addition, except for minimal due process requirements, the courts will generally uphold hospital procedures controlling obstetrical practice within the institution, including such policies as natural childbirth, the husband's presence in the delivery room, and "rooming in." Childbirth also involves various public health reporting, screening, and treatment requirements. Finally, Congress resolved the question of whether exclusion of childbirth coverage from health insurance programs constituted sex discrimination by protecting such coverage in a 1978 amendment to the Civil Rights Act.[66]

NOTES

1. 197 U.S. 11 (1905).
2. 405 U.S. 438 (1972).
3. *A Discursive Dictionary of Health Care* (Washington, D.C.: U.S. Government Printing Office, 1976), p. 58, defines family planning as "the use of a range of methods of fertility regulation to help individuals or couples to avoid unwanted births; bring about wanted births; produce a change in the number of children born; regulate the intervals between pregnancies; and control the time at which births occur in relation to the age of parents." Family planning is a broader term than birth control.
4. 381 U.S. 479 (1965).
5. 405 U.S. 438 (1972).
6. *Carey v. Population Services International*, 431 U.S. 678 (1977).
7. The advertising prohibition was invalidated on First Amendment free speech grounds. See *Virginia State Board of Pharmacy v. Virginia Citizens Consumer Council*, 425 U.S. 748 (1976). In the *Carey* case the Court also invalidated a provision in the same law that made it a crime for any person to sell or distribute any contraceptive of any kind to a minor under the age of sixteen, but the decision did not establish a clear privacy right in this area for minors. In *Doe v. Irwin*, 615 F.2d 1162 (6th Cir. 1980) a federal court of appeals held that the distribution of contraceptive devices and medication to unemancipated minors without notice to their parents did *not* infringe any constitutional right of the parents. (But see related question of parental notice of abortion in discussion of *H. L. v. Matheson*, below at note 21. Also see discussion of minor treatment statutes in Chapter 20.)
8. In *The Brethren: Inside the Supreme Court* (New York: Simon & Schuster, 1979), Bob Woodward and Scott Armstrong suggest that when they originally accepted the *Roe* and *Doe* cases for argument, the justices anticipated dealing with them without having to go beyond some technical jurisdictional issues. According to this account, the justices were as suprised as anybody when they found that they would have to face the substantive questions involved by virtue of their having cleared away the jurisdictional issues in a preceding case. Also see, Linda Greenhouse, "Rare Portrait of the Brethren as Traditional Male Parents," *New York Times*, New York edition, 29 March 1981, p. E7.
9. 410 U.S. 113 (1973).
10. 410 U.S. 179 (1973).
11. Justice Blackmun had, for many years, served as legal counsel for the Mayo Clinic, a fact thought to underlie his interest in writing the decision and his emphasis in that decision of the rights and interest of the physician.

12. This is a different question from that of when life begins. The Court avoided the latter question, observing: "When those trained in the respective disciplines of medicine, philosophy, and theology are unable to arrive at any consensus, the judiciary, at this point in the development of mans' knowledge, is not in a position to speculate as to the answer."

13. See note 11. The emphasis on the physician's role, the less-than-satisfying trimester approach, and lack of clarity regarding second trimester state action have all contributed to Blackmun's opinion being held in generally low esteem, even among those who support the abortion-right result.

14. 428 U.S. 52 (1976).

15. Although purporting to base the ban against the saline method on protecting the woman from risk, the Missouri act did not prohibit techniques many times more dangerous.

16. See discussion of *Colautti v. Franklin* at footnote 28.

17. The Missouri law provided that

> Every health facility and physician shall be supplied with forms promulgated by the division of health, the purpose and function of which shall be the preservation of maternal health and life by adding to the sum of medical knowledge through the compilation of relevant maternal health and life data and to monitor all abortions performed to assure that they are done only under and in accordance with the provisions of the law.

18. In Missouri a minor could legally consent to medical services for pregnancy (excluding abortion), venereal disease, and drug abuse. On consent by minors in general, see Chapter 20.

19. 428 U.S. 132 (1976).

20. *Bellotti v. Baird II*, 443 U.S. 662 (1979).

21. *H. L. v. Matheson*, 101 S.Ct. 1164 (1981).

22. 432 U.S. 438 (1977).

23. 432 U.S. 464 (1977).

24. 432 U.S. 519 (1977). A municipal welfare regulation prohibiting elective abortions in the public hospital was upheld in *Poelker* as not being in violation of the Fourteenth Amendment.

25. 429 U.S. 935 (1980).

26. The Hyde Amendment, as considered by the Court, was a rider to an appropriations bill providing that "none of the funds provided by this joint resolution shall be used to perform abortions except where the life of the mother would be endangered if the fetus were carried to term; or except for such medical procedures necessary for the victims of rape or incest when such rape or incest has been reported promptly to a law enforcement agency or public health service."

27. For critical commentary on *Harris v. McRae* see, for example, Catherine C. Sewell and Mary A. Wetterer, "*Harris v. McRae:* The Hyde Amendment Stands While Rights of Poor Women Fall," *Kentucky Law Journal* 69:359–391 (1980–1981), and Kris Palencia, "*Harris v. McRae:* Indigent Women Must Bear the Consequences of the Hyde Amendment," *Loyola University Law Journal* 12:255–276 (1981). To date, the effects of the Hyde Amendment and *Harris v. McRae* have not been felt, because several key states continue to

fund abortions for indigent women. Also see Jay A. Gold, "Does the Hyde Amendment Violate Religious Freedom? *Harris v. McRae* and the First Amendment," *American Journal of Law and Medicine* 6:361–372 (1980). Denial of Medicaid funding for abortions has been declared unconstitutional on the state level. See *Committee to Defend Reproductive Rights v. Meyers,* 172 Cal. Rptr. 866, 29 Cal.3d 252, 625 P.2d 779 (1981).

28. 439 U.S. 379 (1979).

29. These "conscience acts" are typified by the Illinois provision, which states, in part:

> It shall be unlawful for any person, public or private institution, or public official to discriminate against any person in any manner, including but not limited to, licensing, hiring, promotion, transfer, staff appointment, hospital or any other privileges, because of such person's conscientious refusal to receive, obtain, accept, perform, assist, counsel, suggest, recommend, refer or participate in any way in any particular form of medical care contrary to his or her conscience (ILL.REV. STAT. 111½, Sec. 5305).

Also see 42 U.S.C. Sec. 3009-7, "Prohibition on entities receiving Federal grant, etc., from discriminating against applicants for training or study because of refusal of applicant to participate [in abortions or sterilizations] on religious or moral grounds."

30. *Hathaway v. Worcester City Hospital,* 475 F.2d 701 (1st Cir. 1973). But subsequent Supreme Court decisions have seemingly undercut this holding.

31. *Chrisman v. Sisters of St. Joseph,* 506 F.2d 308 (9th Cir. 1974).

32. See note 27. Consent by a spouse to a sterilization procedure also is analagous to the abortion situation. Presently this type of impediment is proscribed by the Court's holding in *Danforth.* Raising the matter with the patient's spouse would conflict with the obligation of confidentiality due the patient. Yet practitioners understandably feel more secure when the sterilization is supported by both patient and spouse.

33. See Gerald Robertson, "Civil Liability Arising from 'Wrongful Birth' Following an Unsuccessful Sterilization Operation," *American Journal of Law and Medicine* 4:131 (1978), and Barbara R. Grumet, "Reproductive Freedom and the Prevention of Birth Defects: A New and Developing Standard of Medical Care," *Medicolegal News* 8(5):4–9 (October 1980).

34. Charles F. Westoff and James McCarthy, "Sterilization in the United States," *Family Planning Perspectives* 11:147 (May/June 1979).

35. Ralph Solvenko, *Sexual Behavior and the Law* (Springfield, Ill.: Charles C. Thomas, 1965), p. 101. Also see Philip Reilly, *Genetics, Law, and Social Policy* (Cambridge, Mass.: Harvard University Press, 1977), chap. 4. In 1922 a model eugenic sterilization law was proposed and was followed by many states. The model law included as potential recipients the feebleminded, the insane, epileptics, the blind and deaf, inebriates, the diseased (having, for example, leprosy, tuberculosis, syphilis, and chronic infections), the deformed, and persons "dependent on the State" (such as orphans, tramps, and paupers). U.S. eugenic laws served as a model for Nazi Germany's further extension of the practice. See Alan Chase, *The Legacy of Malthaus: The Social Costs of the New Scientific Racism* (New York: Knopf, 1977).

36. See "Procreative Rights: Involuntary Sterilization, Abortion, Contraception, and Voluntary Sterilization," *Harvard Law Review* 93:1296–1307 (1980), pp. 1297–1298.

37. 274 U.S. 200 (1927).

38. *New York Times*, 23 February 1980, p. 6; 7 March 1980, p. A16.

39. *Oklahoma v. Skinner*, 316 U.S. 535 (1942).

40. For a brief argument in behalf of such sterilization, see Reilly, *Genetics, Law, and Social Policy*, p. 131.

41. This did not stop the Indiana magistrate whose illegal approval of an inappropriate involuntary sterilization was protected from personal liability by the U.S. Supreme Court in *Stump v. Sparkman*, 435 U.S. 349 (1978).

42. *In the Matter of Lee Ann Grady*, 426 A.2d 467 (N.J. 1981). For a discussion of the case, see George J. Annas, "Sterilization of the Mentally Retarded: A Decision for the Courts,"*Hastings Center Report* 11(4):18–19 (August 1981). Also see, generally, Charles Baron, "Voluntary Sterilization of the Mentally Retarded," in Aubrey Milunsky and George J. Annas, ed., *Genetics and the Law* (New York: Plenum Press, 1976), pp. 267–284, and Ruth Macklin and Willard Gaylin, *Mental Retardation and Sterilization: A Problem of Competency and Paternalism* (New York: Plenum Press, 1981).

43. Reilly, *Genetics, Law, and Social Policy*, p. 130.

44. *Relf v. Weinberger*, 372 F. Supp. 1196 (D.C.D.C., 1974).

45. In 1973 a South Carolina lawyer associated with the American Civil Liberties Union spoke to a group of women who had been sterilized as a condition of receiving public medical assistance. The lawyer informed one of the women that free legal assistance was available from the ACLU to sue the physician who performed her sterilization operation. The response of the disciplinary board of the South Carolina Supreme Court was to charge the lawyer with "solicitation in violation of the Canon of Ethics" was to vote a public reprimand. This punishment was overturned by the U.S. Supreme Court as violating First Amendment rights of free expression and association. See *In re Edna Smith Primus* 436 U.S. 412 (1978).

46. 42 C.F.R. 441.250–59. California and New York City regulate all sterilization procedures, not just those that are publicly funded. It should be noted that while informed consent has long been an important concern in the sterilization area, it is now receiving more attention for abortions and some contraceptive methods. See Rosalind Pollack Petchesky, "Reproduction, Ethics, and Public Policy: The Federal Sterilization Regulations," *Hastings Center Report* 9(5):29–41 (October 1979), and Eve W. Paul and Giles Scofield, "Informed Consent for Fertility Control Services." *Family Planning Perspectives* 11:159 (May/June 1979).

47. Laurie Wishard and William R. Wishard, *Adoption: The Grafted Tree* (San Francisco: Cragmont, 1980), and John R. Ball and Gilbert S. Omenn, "Genetics, Adoption, and the Law," in Aubrey Milunsky and George J. Annas, ed., *Genetics and the Law II*, (New York: Plenum Press, 1980), pp. 269–79.

48. Although the procedure is simple, five individuals are involved: wife, husband, donor, physician, and baby. Legal issues include malpractice, perjury on birth records, consent, legitimacy, inheritance and support rights of children, adultery, and liability for defect in the child.

49. See Reilly, *Genetics, Law, and Social Policy*, pp. 200–201.

50. George J. Annas, "Artificial Insemination: Beyond the Best Interests of the Donor," *Hastings Center Report* 9(4):14–15, 43 (August 1979). Also see M. Curie-Cohen, L. Luttrell, and S. Shapiro, "Current Practice of Artificial Insemination by Donor in the United States," *New England Journal of Medicine* 300:585 (1979); W. G. Johnson, R. C. Schwartz, and A. M. Chutorian, "Artificial Insemination by Donor: The Need for Genetic Screening," *New England Journal of Medicine* 304:755–757 (1981); and J. M. Shaman, "Legal Aspects of Artificial Insemination," *Journal of Family Law* 18:331–352 (1979–1980).

51. The clinic received approval from the Committee on Human Experimentation and Research of Eastern Virginia Medical School. Since federal funds were not involved, federal regulations regarding human subjects were not a concern. See Frank H. Marsh and Donnie J. Self, "In Vitro Fertilization: Moving from Theory to Therapy," *Hastings Center Report* 10(3):5–6 (June 1980). Also see Reilly, *Genetics, Law, and Social Policy*, pp. 206–221.

52. See Barbara F. Katz, "Legal Implications and Regulation of *In Vitro* Fertilization," in Milunsky and Annas, *Genetics and the Law II*, pp. 351–367.

53. See George J. Annas, "Contracts to Bear a Child: Compassion or Commercialism?," *Hastings Center Report* 11(2):23–24 (April 1981); Katz, "Legal Implications"; N. P. Keane, "Legal Problems of Surrogate Motherhood," *Southern Illinois University Law Journal* 1980:147–170 (1980).

54. Philip Reilly, "State Supported Mass Genetic Screening Programs," in Milunsky and Annas, *Genetics and the Law*, pp. 159–171.

55. In the early 1970s several states passed laws mandating such screening, but federal sickle cell legislation called for voluntary programs, and the states revised their requirements accordingly.

56. Reilly, "State Supported Mass Genetic Screening Programs," p. 164.

57. Jon R. Waltz, "The Liability of Physicians and Associated Personnel for Malpractice in Genetic Screening," in Milunsky and Annas, *Genetics and the Law*, pp. 139–157, at p. 140.

58. Committee for the Study of Inborn Errors of Metabolism, *Genetic Screening: Programs, Principles and Research* (Washington, D.C.: National Academy of Sciences, 1975), p. 261.

59. See notes 35, 42, and 47 of this chapter.

60. Such errors of omission obviously involve the genetic counseling situation itself, as well as any encounter which concerns pregnancy. In addition, anything that may affect a future pregnancy and which the practitioner is aware of, or should be aware of, would be included in this area. Perhaps the most extreme version of this principle, which goes beyond the realm of genetic counseling, is a 1977 Illinois Supreme Court decision that held that an Rh incompatible blood transfusion of a young girl created a duty to warn of problems in future pregnancy, a duty owed to any child conceived in the future. *Renslow v. Mennonite Hospital*, 67 Ill.2d 348, 367 N.E.2d 1250 (1977). On information, consent, and patient autonomy, see Jay Katz, "Disclosure and Consent: In Search of Their Roots," in Milunsky and Annas, *Genetics and the Law II*, pp. 121–129.

61. *Park v. Chessin* and *Becker v. Schwartz*, 46 N.Y.2d 401, 413 N.Y.S.2d 895, 386 N.E.2d 807 (1978).

62. *Curlender v. Bio-Science Laboratories*, 165 Cal. Rptr. 477, 106 Cal. App. 3d. 811

(1980). See in Milunsky and Annas, *Genetics and the Law II:* Alexander M. Capron, "The Continuing Wrong of 'Wrongful Life,'" pp. 81–93; Joseph M. Healey, Jr., "The Legal Obligations of Genetic Counselors," pp. 69–76; and Margery W. Shaw, "The Potential Plaintiff: Preconception and Prenatal Torts," pp. 225–232. Also see George J. Annas, "Righting the Wrong of 'Wrongful Life,'" *Hastings Center Report* 11(1):8–9 (February 1981). And see, generally, Grumet, "Reproductive Freedom," and Alexander M. Capron, "Tort Liability in Genetic Counseling," *Columbia Law Review* 79:618–684 (1979).

63. George J. Annas makes this argument in "Problems of Informed Consent and Confidentiality in Genetic Counseling," in Milunsky and Annas, *Genetics and the Law*, pp. 111–122, at pp. 117–118. He notes that until this problem is dealt with through legislation, it is important that the practitioner make his or her policy on the matter clear to patients at the outset of counseling. On the other hand, the National Academy of Sciences' committee on the subject (see note 58) felt that "under current law, genetic screeners would be ill-advised to contact relatives without the screenee's explicit consent, in view of the sparse case law support for a 'public health' exception to the confidentiality rule." They felt, further, that individual autonomy should have priority over programs aimed at disease reduction. See Reilly, *Genetics, Law, and Social Policy*, p. 168. Also see Kurt Hirschhorn, "Medicolegal Aspects of Genetic Counseling," in Milunsky and Annas, *Genetics and the Law*, pp. 105–110.

64. Hirschhorn, "Medicolegal Aspects," p. 108.

65. See Barbara F. Katz, "Childbirth and the Law," *Colorado Medicine* 77:64–67 (February 1980); Eric M. Newman, "Family Law—Constitutional Right of Privacy: The Father in the Delivery Room,"*North Carolina Law Review* 54:1297–1307 (1976); George J. Annas, "Are Childbirth Laws Adequate?," *Women and Health* 2:23 (September/October 1977), reprinted in *Health Law Project Library Bulletin* 3(2):1 (February 1978), along with a commentary by Edward V. Sparer, "Inadequate Childbirth Care: A Different Perspective on Law and Lawyers"; Mary F. Forrest, "Natural Childbirth: Rights and Lia-bilities of the Parties," *Journal of Family Law* 17:309–332 (1979); Jennifer Jordan Tachera, "A Birth Right": Home Births, Midwives, and the Right to Privacy," *Pacific Law Journal* 12:97–120 (1980).

66. *General Electric Company v. Gilbert*, 429 U.S. 125; pregnancy sex discrimina-tion amendment to Title VII of the Civil Rights Act of 1964, 42 U.S.C. 2000e-2.

19

Mental Health and the Law

In 1968, when I first began representing mental patients, a few pages would have been sufficient to discuss judicial involvement in the public practice of psychiatry. Today, I could not adequately canvass that subject in several hundred. Even half a dozen years ago, I knew most of the significant cases by heart, and had personally participated in a majority of them. Today, I know only a small portion of what there is to know. The point, of course, is that judges, particularly federal judges, are now extensively involved in regulating the public practice of psychiatry.

—Bruce Ennis[1]

AS RECENTLY AS a decade or two ago, there was little overlap between the world of the mental health professional and the world of the law, outside of the area of criminal behavior. Involuntary commitments of individuals to mental hospitals were routine and rarely challenged in the courts; the right to receive or refuse treatment was, for the most part, a philosophical concept; and the legal implications of the professional-patient relationship in the mental-health arena were largely unexplored. Today, however, the situation has changed dramatically, and mental health professionals, both those employed in an institutional setting and those engaged in private practice, must give increasing consideration to the legal aspects of their practice and theory.

Even the term "mental illness" is a matter of considerable controversy. The medical model, which had served as the basis of most mental health law, is predicated on "the hypothesis that disordered behavior . . . is caused by an underlying physical abnormality or by an underlying psychological abnormality that is analogized to physical abnormality."[2] Yet as Ennis and Emery point out:

371

The belief that mental disorder is essentially a medical problem to be dealt with by doctors makes it easier to ignore the legal, ethical, and social issues raised by involuntary hospitalization and treatment . . . [and] . . . legitimizes practices that would be much more controversial if they were described in nonmedical terms.[3]

For years the medical model made it easier for judges and lawyers to escape responsibility for decisions affecting the freedom of persons alleged to be mentally ill by transfering responsibility—and substantial power—to the mental health professional, especially the psychiatrist. More recently, however, the trend has been away from automatic acceptance of the medical model of mental illness, a shift applauded by many mental health professionals uncomfortable with the expectation that they could serve the interests of the individual while acting in behalf of the state.[4]

Recent changes in mental health law have been nationwide in scope. But since mental health law is tied more closely to statutes than are many other fields of law, there is considerable variation from state to state. Local legal advice regarding specific applications is therefore important.

Admission/Commitment

With rare exception,[5] the patient receiving medical or surgical treatment can be assumed to have sought and freely agreed to that treatment. Not so in the mental health area. Admission to—and discharge from—a mental health facility can involve a complex set of controversial legal issues relating to the patient's willing presence and participation.

An individual becomes an inpatient in a mental health institution as a result of either an involuntary or voluntary admission. The latter situation involves fewer legal restraints; but a number of critics insist that many ostensibly voluntary admissions are not voluntary at all, but rather the result of coercion and ignorance on the part of the patient of his or her status and rights. (One study found that "only 8 of the 100 patients were rated as fully informed concerning the terms of their voluntary admissions.")[6] Under most state laws, too, persons voluntarily admitted to a mental institution are not completely free to leave; they can only discharge themselves from the institution after a waiting period (for example, five, ten, thirty days) following a request for release, and then only if the hospital does not initiate commitment proceedings during that waiting period.

The most controversial type of admission is involuntary civil commitment, which can occur under both emergency and nonemergency statutes (the former intended as a quick stopgap measure pending consideration of long-term, nonemergency commitment).[7] Both situations involve what the Supreme Court has termed a "massive curtailment of liberty," a loss of freedom hardly different from imprisonment for a crime.[8] The authority of the states to provide for such curtailment has long been accepted.

The typical state mental health statute provides for involuntary commitment of persons who are mentally ill and dangerous to themselves and/or others, or in need of help and treatment.[9] For persons considered dangerous to others, the state's justification for commitment is the protection of society from such danger under the state's police power.[10] For persons considered in need of help or treatment, the state's justification for commitment is protection of the individual, under the doctrine of *parens patriae*, which casts the state as "the general guardian of all infants, idiots, and lunatics."[11] And, for persons considered dangerous to themselves, the state's justification for involuntary commitment is rationalized on grounds of both *parens patriae* and police power.[12]

Critics of involuntary commitment, including many lawyers, mental health professionals and informed laymen, reject all three of the grounds cited. They argue that the mentally ill are no more dangerous, as a group, than the general population;[13] that society has no right to force treatment on an individual even "for his own good"; and that judgments concerning what constitutes irrationality are frequently subjective and unclear. What is surprising about this debate is the fact that lawyers got into it so late in the day. "Considering the number of persons affected," observed Justice Harry Blackmun in one of the important Supreme Court decisions dealing with the state's power to commit, "it is perhaps remarkable that the substantive constitutional limitations on this power have not been more frequently litigated."[14]

In recent years, however, the legal profession has made up for past neglect; and partly as a result of this attention, some two-thirds of the states have substantially revised their mental health laws. Under earlier statutes, involuntary commitment often took place on the simple assertion by one or two examining physicians that the individual was mentally ill and either dangerous or in need of treatment. Newer laws specify procedural rights and tighten the basis for commitment. (At the same time, deinstitutionalization has created its own legal problems. These will be discussed later in this chapter in the section on mental retardation.)

Substantive standards for involuntary commitment vary from state to state. The typical statute provides for civil confinement of persons who are mentally ill and dangerous to themselves or others, or in need of treatment; many require that a finding of "mental illness" be made before a commitment order can be issued. Some statutes call for more specific justification for commitment. Minnesota requires a finding "that [the individual] has attempted or threatened to take his own life or attempted to physically harm himself or others." "The clear trend," write Ennis and Emery, "is to require proof of physical danger to self or others, based on evidence of overt acts, threats, or attempts of a dangerous nature in the recent past, and to prohibit involuntary hospitalization if 'need for treatment' is the only reason for hospitalization."[15] Some believe the standards should be more rigid. Scott has suggested that involuntary commitment should be permitted only if: (a) the individual evidences serious mental disorder; (b) he or she is unable to make an informed decision about treatment; (c) there is likelihood of imminent serious harm to self or others as evidenced by recent behavior; and (d) commitment will make available treatment likely to benefit the individual.[16]

The Supreme Court has avoided appraisal of substantive standards for commitment:

> We need not decide whether, when, or by what procedures, a mentally ill person may be confined by the State on any of the grounds which, under contemporary statutes, are generally advanced to justify involuntary confinement of such a person—to prevent injury to the public, to ensure his own survival or safety, or to alleviate or cure his illness.[17]

But in *Addington v. Texas*[18] the Court did decide that, whatever the standard, there must be "clear and convincing" evidence before individuals can be involuntarily committed. This degree of proof lies somewhere between the traditional "preponderance of the evidence" standard, which adds up to more-probable-than-not, and the "beyond a reasonable doubt" standard of criminal law.

Another view with respect to involuntary commitment that has gained favor in recent years is the doctrine of the least restrictive alternative. Simply put, this holds that when government has a legitimate basis for limiting an individual's liberty, it should do so in the least restrictive way possible, throughout the course of confinement. The doctrine was cited in several lower court decisions, and it won Supreme Court support in *O'Conner v. Donaldson*, where the Court held:

> While the State may arguably confine a person to save him from harm, incarceration is rarely if ever a necessary condition for raising the living standards of those capable of surviving safely in freedom, on their own or with the help of family or friends.[19]

At least one court has gone even further, holding that where a statutory right to mental health treatment exists, alternatives to involuntary hospitalization must be created if they do not already exist.[20]

Chief Justice Warren Burger observed, in *O'Conner v. Donaldson*, that "there can be no doubt that involuntary commitment to a mental hospital, like involuntary confinement of an individual for any reason, is a deprivation of liberty which the State cannot accomplish without due process of law." More recently, in *Addington v. Texas*, the Court emphasized that procedural due process protections apply in such commitment decisions. But what specific procedural rights are constitutionally required? The Constitution requires that the states provide adequate notice to those whose liberty they seek to deny. While the timing, form, and content of the required notice varies from state to state, lower court decisions indicate that such notice must be written in plain language understandable to the individual and be provided far enough in advance of the required commitment hearing to allow the individual adequate time to prepare a response. The notice should state the time and place of the hearing, cite the applicable statute, and advise the individual of the specific reasons alleged in support of commitment, the names of opposing witnesses and the rights he or she is entitled to at the hearing.[21]

There are two types of civil commitment hearings. Some states call for an initial "probable cause" hearing to determine whether there is substantial evidence to warrant subjecting the prospective patient to involuntary hospitalization. According to Ennis and Emery: "Recent commitment statutes usually require a probable cause hearing within a few days after hospitalization and a final hearing approximately two weeks after the probable cause hearing."[22] The Supreme Court has not yet determined whether this type of hearing is constitutionally required. It is clear, though, that before actual commitment a patient has a constitutional right to a "final" hearing before an independent tribunal—either a court or a special commission (usually composed of two or more doctors and perhaps an attorney). And critics argue that the use of nonjudicial officials, even under some type of indirect court supervision, to deprive individuals of liberty is an unconstitutional extension of the medical model, and that individuals threatened with involuntary commitment should in all cases be afforded an actual judicial hearing.[23]

Most state statutes provide for legal representation in civil commitment proceedings, and some state courts have ruled that the state must provide such representation for indigents. However there is no uniformity as to just when in the commitment process a lawyer must be provided.[24]

The primary method of evaluating an individual's need for commitment is a mental examination conducted by either a state employee or some other selected professional. In criminal cases a defendant has a Fifth Amendment right not to talk to investigating officers, but the Supreme Court has never determined that the privilege against self-incrimination applies in civil commitment cases—although several lower courts have ruled that the privilege should apply.[25] Ennis and Emery maintain that, at a minimum, patients should be told that what they say in a precommitment session with a mental health professional may be used as evidence of mental disorder or dangerousness justifying hospitalization. In fact, they argue that involuntarily confined patients should have the right to have a lawyer present when interviewed by a psychiatrist, even if the interview is at the patient's request.[26]

Often the individual facing commitment is excluded from the hearing because it is believed that he or she will suffer trauma from hearing the evidence or will disrupt the proceeding. It can be argued that the individual's right to be present at a commitment hearing is so fundamental to the exercise of his or her other rights, that exclusion, if allowed at all, should be governed either by the standards used for removing defendants in criminal trials or by a specific showing that trauma is likely to occur.[27]

It has also been suggested that the individual may have a limited right to be free from medication at the time of the hearing. Nebraska has banned all prehearing treatment; Michigan permits drugging only when absolutely necessary to prevent physical injury; and several other states prohibit forced drugging that inhibits a meaningful opportunity to participate in the hearing process.[28]

Typically, a commitment hearing will include expert testimony by mental health professionals concerning the need to commit the individual in question. To balance this testimony the individual's attorney may need to present other experts to testify on behalf of the subject. The Supreme Court has not dealt with the question of whether equal protection and due process require the appointment of expert examiners and/ or expert witnesses for indigents, but several state courts and at least two legislatures have recognized such a right, although not necessarily the right of the individual (rather than the court) to select the expert.[29]

Most criminal and civil trials afford the participants the option of trial by jury, but this is usually not the case with commitment proceedings.[30] But implicit in the notion of due process is the right to confront and cross-examine adverse witnesses, and several courts have held that where personal liberty is at stake the state must summon witnesses for cross-examination in order to reduce factual error and permit the fact finder to observe the demeanor of witnesses.[31] Many states permit prospective patients to waive the rights discussed above, and some consider them automatically waived unless the individual affirmatively requests specific rights. This differs markedly from criminal cases, in which a judge must decide if any waiver proffered by a defendant is affirmative, voluntary, and "knowing and intelligent."[32]

It is not clear whether someone who has been committed has a constitutional right to appeal his or her commitment. Because, as a practical matter, such an appeal would take too long to offer a useful avenue of freedom from an unjustified commitment, lawyers representing involuntarily committed mental patients are more likely to rely on such legal measures as habeas corpus, which challenge the initial basis of confinement.[33]

Mental patients are usually committed for indefinite lengths of time. However, the Supreme Court, in *O'Conner v. Donaldson,* indicated that involuntary commitment could not constitutionally continue once the basis for the original commitment no longer existed. In a concurring opinion, Chief Justice Burger noted that commitment "must be justified on the basis of a legitimate state interest, and the reasons for committing a particular individual must be established in an appropriate proceeding. Equally important, confinement must cease when those reasons no longer exist." This ruling has not yet been translated into requirements that commitments be periodically reviewed, but many states require such review (at intervals ranging from three months to a year) and some specify that the review must be by a court.[34]

All of the substantive and procedural standards outlined above apply primarily with respect to nonemergency involuntary commitment to a mental health facility. The story is very different in the case of emergency (or short-term) hospitalization, where immediate steps are considered necessary either to provide help or to prevent danger. Emergency hospitalization allows the authorities to act first and ask questions afterward, with much lower standards and burdens of proof and far fewer procedural safeguards than commitment normally requires. Theoretically, such hospitalization is used only in true emergencies and for very brief periods, until the full panoply of standards and rights can be applied. But Ennis and Siegel assert that "the so-called emergency procedure is, in almost every state, the *standard* procedure and almost everyone is hospitalized, initially, under the emergency procedure, whether there is a true emergency or not."[35] And the duration of permissible "short-term" hospitalization varies among the states from two weeks to as much as two months.[36]

An important, although probably overemphasized, corollary to involuntary commitment is the so-called right to treatment. Although, as explained in Chapter 9, nothing in the U.S. Constitution provides sufficient basis for asserting a "right" to health care, a limited exception can be found in the mental health area, namely that if a nondangerous individual is involuntarily deprived of liberty by the state through civil commitment, the state should provide that person with some level of treatment. The leading case here is *O'Conner v. Donaldson,* a suit brought by a civilly committed mental patient challenging his confinement and seeking damages from the state. By the time the case reached the Supreme Court, the patient had been discharged and the lower courts had determined that (a) he had not been dangerous; (b) he was capable of "surviving safely in freedom"; and (c) he had not been receiving treatment, but merely custodial care. The question was whether his confinement in such circumstances had violated his right to liberty.

In considering Donaldson's claim for damages, the federal district court had instructed the jury that "a person who is involuntarily civilly committed to a mental hospital does have a constitutional right to receive such treatment as will give him a realistic opportunity to be cured." The court of appeals approved this phrase. But the Supreme Court, although upholding the general result, did not endorse this right to treatment. Instead the Court held:

> In short, a State cannot constitutionally confine without more a non-dangerous individual who is capable of surviving safely in freedom by himself or with the help of willing and responsible family members or friends. Since the jury found, upon ample evidence, that O'Conner, as an agent of the state, knowingly did so confine Donaldson, it properly concluded that O'Conner violated Donaldson's constitutional right to freedom.[37]

In so ruling, the Court gave strong support to the doctrine of the least restrictive alternative. But while the decision makes it clear that the state cannot confine without treatment, it does *not* say the state must provide treatment. There are several other notable things the decision does not do: It does not apply the same quid pro quo of treatment in return for confinement to patients commited as dangerous to themselves or others (nor does it define dangerousness, especially to self); it does not establish a treat-or-free "right" for voluntary patients; and it does not define a minimal level of treatment, although it holds the door open for lower courts to do so. Several lower courts, both before and after *Donaldson*, have sought to develop and enforce minimal treatment standards, including individualized treatment plans, qualified staff and humane physical and psychological environments.

Wald and Friedman[38] have observed that right-to-treatment suits have often been brought by a shaky coalition of civil libertarians, who want either to abolish involuntary commitment or to restrict it to those judged dangerous to others, and by service-oriented advocates eager to establish court-assured minimal levels of treatment. This coalition's most famous case is *Wyatt v. Stickney*,[39] in which a federal judge, after determining that constitutional due process required adequate and effective treatment in cases of involuntary commitment, set minimal requirements for the Alabama mental health system. The requirements, set with the advice of mental-health professional organizations, dealt with adequacy of physical plant and staffing ratios, prohibition of unpaid work, and the selection of the least restrictive treatment setting for each patient.

One of the arguments raised by defendant states in such suits—

which, as in *Wyatt*, often involve the mentally retarded as well as the mentally ill—has been lack of funds. But courts have never favored such a defense when constitutional rights were at stake. As with the welfare cases discussed in Chapter 9, the individual states can decide whether or not to have commitment laws and mental health facilities; but if they do operate a mental health system they must do so without violating individual rights.

The most recent decision in this area involved a lawsuit brought in federal district court in Pennsylvania by residents of Pennhurst, a state-run institution for the severely and profoundly retarded, an institution in which conditions were undisputedly inadequate and dangerous. The lawsuit asked that Pennhurst be closed and that community living arrangements be established for its residents. The district court agreed with the plaintiffs and, based on both constitutional and statutory grounds, ordered the facility closed.[40] The court of appeals avoided the constitutional issues by upholding the decision on the basis that the federal Developmentally Disabled Assistance and Bill of Rights Act of 1975[41] created a judicially enforceable substantive right to treatment under the least restricting setting possible. The act's "bill of rights" section states that "treatment, services, and habilitation for a person with developmental disabilities should be designed to maximize the developmental potential of the person and should be provided in the setting that is least restrictive of the person's liberty." Rather than see the facility closed, the appeals court ordered it kept open under district court supervision. The U.S. Supreme Court reversed this decision in *Pennhurst State School and Hospital v. Halderman.*[42] Although their decision does not deal directly with any constitutional right-to-treatment argument, neither does it provide much encouragement for such arguments in the future. The Court held that in enacting the "bill of rights" section of the act, "Congress intended to encourage, rather than mandate, the provision of better services to the developmentally disabled." Thus the act was simply a funding vehicle with no significant strings attached; it was not legislation that "required the States, at their own expense, to provide certain kinds of treatment." *Pennhurst* was a widely publicized legal challenge by reform advocates, with implications for both the mental retardation and mental illness systems. Although the Court's decision focused on statutory interpretation, the case has a broader significance because (a) it reflects the Court's unreceptiveness to legal actions based on right-to-treatment and least restrictive alternative grounds, and (b) the justices, including those who dissented from the major holding, were particularly inhospitable to the court supervision remedy, which would have put the courts in the position of overseeing the operation of hard-pressed institutions such as Pennhurst.

Refusing Treatment

The counterpart to a right to treatment is a right to refuse treatment. In the area of medical and surgical services the right to refuse treatment is the general rule; exceptions generally involve patients who, by reason of age or court order, are legal incompetents.[43] In most states, however, a mental patient—even an involuntarily committed patient—is not legally incompetent unless a separate incompetency determination has been made. This raises the question of whether legally competent, and thus presumably autonomous, individuals can be dealt with as if they were incompetent to make decisions regarding their own treatment. Most often these decisions involve medication, but they might also include other forms of treatment, such as electroshock therapy. Ennis and Emery point out that "although in almost every jurisdiction there is no express statutory or other legal authority to *force* treatment on committed persons, forced treatment occurs every day in every state."[44] Only in recent years has this common practice been challenged, first by mental patients and their advocates, and later by some courts.

There are several legal grounds on which such a challenge can be based. The first is simply the fact that, however incompetent the patient may be in the eyes of the mental health professional as well as in fact, there is no basis in law to force treatment on the unwilling patient, even one who has been involuntarily committed, except in an emergency or after a judicial determination of legal incompetency. As one court put it, "the *parens patriae* relationship does not materialize until a patient is judicially declared incompetent. We are persuaded that *parens patriae* is not broad enough to control medical decisions of a competent person."[45] The doctrine of the least restrictive alternative, discussed earlier, is another legal argument against forced treatment. This doctrine has been primarily applied to the site of treatment, but it could also mean the least intrusive form of treatment. Although it is not, in itself, a basis for refusing all treatment, it might well allow for refusal of the more intrusive of alternative treatments. The constitutional right to privacy (the relatively new constitutional doctrine described in the previous chapter) might also represent a legal argument supporting refusal of treatment. The doctrine holds that there are certain areas of individual, private concern into which government should not and may not intrude, and where law cannot require or prohibit private action. It is on this basis that a number of refusal-of-treatment cases in the medical and surgical areas, such as *Quinlan* and *Saikewicz*, have been decided. Applied to the mental health field, this would mean that the force of law, such as involuntary commitment statutes, could not be used to bring about changes in anything as intimate as an individual's thoughts and feelings.[46]

There have been some notable cases in this area recently. In 1978, in *Rennie v. Klein,* [47] a federal district court judge ruled that a patient's right to privacy included a qualified right to refuse treatment. The judge defined four factors to be considered by a court if nonemergency treatment were to be forced, including the patient's dangerousness to others at the institution, his or her capacity to decide on the particular treatment, the availability of a less restrictive alternative, and the risk of permanent side effects from the treatment. For involuntary patients the judge did not stipulate that such an evaluation required a judicial proceeding; but he did call for a hearing by an "independent psychiatrist" with provision for legal representation for the patient.

Another federal district court decision, *Rogers v. Okin,* [48] established for voluntary and involuntary patients alike an absolute right to refuse treatment in nonemergency situations (with emergency narrowly defined), unless there was a judicial determination of incompetency. Even in the latter instance, the court ruled, the constitutional right to privacy requires that consent be obtained from either a court or a court-appointed guardian before treatment can be undertaken. Alan Stone, speaking as president of the American Psychiatric Association, termed the decision "the most impossible, inappropriate, ill-considered judicial decision ever made in the field of mental health law,"[49] a judgment that did not stop the Oklahoma Supreme Court from ruling that in the absence of an emergency, "legally competent adults involuntarily admitted to a state mental hospital" have an absolute right to refuse nonemergency— "organic therapy"—treatments that "are intrusive in nature and an invasion of the body." For individuals found to be incompetent by a court, a guardian is to be appointed, who, the court seems to suggest, might apply "the substituted judgment doctrine," to ascertain what the patient would have done if he or she were competent.[50]

These decisions are not yet widespread enough to be considered a trend. Furthermore, despite their emphasis on individual liberty over professional efforts to treat, their impact on institutional practice may be quite limited. Treatment is still unimpeded when, as is usually the case, it is administered with the patient's consent. And treatment is still possible despite patient refusal when there is a substantial danger of the patient doing injury to self or others (but with such emergencies carefully defined). And even in the absence of consent or emergency, treatment is still possible if a court can be persuaded that the treatment program is in the best interest of the patient.

For psychiatric outpatients (and arguably for voluntary inpatients) the right to refuse treatment does not present the same dilemma. Such patients are in much the same situation as medical or surgical patients, and the basic rules of informed consent described in Chapter 14 theoretically apply, although there is greater likelihood that such exceptions as emergency, proxy consent for incompetents, and therapeutic privilege will be made use of. In those jurisdictions that follow the prudent-person approach, the standard is what information a reasonable person would need to know; in other jurisdictions, professional standards and custom apply.[51]

There are legal rights, in addition to the right to treatment and the right to refuse treatment, that are of importance to mental hospital inpatients. One is the right to periodic review of the need for confinement mentioned earlier.[52] Also, there is the right to notice and hearing before being transferred from an open ward to a locked one; the right to visits by persons from outside the institution; the right to unread and uncensored communication with lawyers, health professionals, and public officials; the right not to have personal assets, such as social security checks, appropriated by the hospital without a hearing; the right to refuse to perform labor that involves the operation and maintenance of the hospital; and the right to physical exercise.

The Special Status of the Minor

Because society and the law seek to balance the rights and interests of minors against those of their parents, young persons confronting the mental health system face special problems with respect to authorization of treatment, commitment, the right to treatment, and the right to refuse treatment.

The legal limitations on a minor's ability—and inability—to consent to medical treatment are discussed in Chapter 20. Similar limitations would seem to apply to psychiatric care, although there have been very few cases on the subject.[53] Some statutes dealing with the treatment of minors specifically provide for mental health care and counseling (although unless the statute speaks to the point, it may be that only psychiatric care provided by physicians would be authorized). In general, the statutes apply only to counseling and other noninvasive practices. Some limit the number of sessions minors can authorize on their own; many provide an age floor, such as fourteen or sixteen, for such authorization. There is no unanimity as to whether parents must be notified and/or given access to treatment records. Some states also authorize minors above a certain age to apply for admission to a mental health facility.[54]

The most controversial aspect of a minor's role in the mental health system involves involuntary commitment. A minor, like an adult, can be committed to a mental hospital against his or her will. But if the parents have authorized the commitment, the minor, despite his or her objections, is considered a voluntary patient and therefore denied many of the procedural rights afforded adults, including a judicial hearing. This practice persists despite a number of studies showing a parental decision to commit a child often results from factors other than the needs of the child, such as the parent's own illness.[55]

The legality of such involuntary admissions without juridical hearing was put to rest—at least for the present—by the Supreme Court's 1979 decision in *Parham v. J. R.*,[56] in which the Court overturned a determination by a lower federal court that the absence of an adversary-type hearing before an impartial tribunal violated the constitutional due-process rights of a minor facing involuntray commitment. Declared Chief Justice Burger, writing for the Court:

> Simply because the decision of a parent is not agreeable to a child or because it involves risks does not automatically transfer the power to make that decision from the parents to some agency or officer of the state. The same characterizations can be made for a tonsilectomy, appendectomy or other medical procedure. Most children, even in adolescence, simply are not able to make sound judgments concerning many decisions, including their need for medical care or treatment. Parents can and must make those judgments. . . . We conclude that the risk of error inherent in the parental decision to have a child institutionalized for mental health care is sufficiently great that some kind of inquiry should be made by a "neutral factfinder" to determine whether the statutory requirements for admission are satisfied. . . . It is necessary that the decisionmaker have the authority to refuse to admit any child who does not satisfy the medical standards for admission. Finally, it is necessary that the child's continuing need for commitment be reviewed periodically by a similarly independent procedure. . . . Due process has never been thought to require that the neutral and detached trier of fact be law-trained or a judicial or administrative officer. . . . Thus, a staff physician will suffice, so long as he or she is free to evaluate independently the child's mental and emotional condition and need for treatment. . . . It is not necessary that the deciding physician conduct a formal or quasi-formal hearing. A state is free to require such a hearing, but due process is not violated by use of informal, traditional medical investigative techniques.[57]

Parham makes clear that a minor faced with involuntary admission to a mental hospital has fewer individual rights than an adult. This presumably also applies to the minor's right to treatment and to refuse treatment while in the institution (since that right is in part predicated on *involuntary* commitment, while minors confined with parental consent are considered voluntary patients), but there is not enough judicial guidance to be certain just how a minor's claim to a right to treatment or to refuse treatment would fare.[58]

Civil Competence

The term "competency" is used in both the civil and criminal areas of mental health law. In both instances the term describes a legal concept regarding the mental capacity or ability of persons to perform certain acts.[59] At one time a person who was involuntarily committed often automatically became legally incompetent, but today it is standard for a separate determination to be required. In most instances, the determination of legal incompetence involves a judgment that a person is unable to manage his or her own life, both in terms of taking adequate care of himself or herself and of taking care of his or her property.[60] In such situations the legal authority to make such management decisions is taken away from the individual and transferred to someone else, who is charged with making these decisions in behalf of and in the best interests of the individual. This person—variously called a guardian, conservator, or committee—is usually appointed by a court.

A finding of legal incompetence usually results in a severe loss of legal rights; the individual is no longer able to vote, to marry or divorce, to make contracts or a will, to consent to or refuse medical treatment. At the same time, the guardian is often given unilateral authority to have the individual committed without a hearing and to disburse the individual's assets. Because some people obviously do not have the ability to make such decisions, there is nothing surprising or wrong in a legal mechanism that shifts authority to someone else. But many critics have objected to the almost cursory way this often is done.

Despite the substantial interference with individual autonomy involved, the criteria included in statutes authorizing legal incompetence are quite often vague. Definitions of incompetence, for example, include "mental weakness not amounting to unsoundness of mind";[61] or "any person, whether insane or not, who by reason of old age, disease, weakness of mind or other cause is unable, unassisted, properly to manage and take care of himself or his property, and by reason thereof is likely to be deceived or imposed upon by artful and designing persons."[62] The procedural criteria tend to be equally lax. Most statutes use a two-part test for determining whether guardianship is required. The first identifies the type of disability affecting an individual, such as mental illness, mental retardation, or senility; the second requires that the disability prevent the individual from caring for himself or herself or from managing property.[63] But despite the severe deprivation of autonomy involved in a finding of incompetence, the procedures actually employed are weak. Ennis and Emery note that in many states the alleged incompetent

> does not even receive notice of the judicial hearing to declare him incompetent. He may or may not be permitted to attend the hearing or cross-examine those who say he is incompetent. He may not have or be assigned a lawyer. The hearings usually last only a few minutes. The rules of evidence are ignored. And frequently there is absolutely no evidence that the person has, in fact, squandered or wasted any of his assets.[64]

Adding to these problems is the all-or-nothing nature of competency determination in most states. Some states do distinguish between guardians of property and income[65] and guardians for the person, who are concerned with decisions regarding domicile, education, and so forth. But Stone reports:

> Of the 41 jurisdictions which provide for some court-appointed guardianship, 35 have guardianship of the person as well as of property. . . . Lamentably, while in theory, fiduciary responsibility for the welfare of a person and surrogate management of his property are quite different, in practice they often become merged in the same person, and even the same state of mind. One major study concludes that separate guardianship of the person is unknown. The consequences of this fusing of functions can be anticipated. A recent national conference concluded: "Guardianship, as it is practiced in most states, does not adequately protect most impaired elderly persons in need of protection. When it is used, it safeguards property not the person."[66]

It should be kept in mind that guardianship requires someone willing to serve in that role and, often, funds adequate to pay the costs of administration. For people without the necessary funds and/or friends—primarily the aged poor—a system of public guardianship is necessary. Some states and localities have established such systems, but many have not. And, where established, the public guardianship system is obviously ripe for abuse unless carefully overseen.

The mental inabilities underlying legal incompetency cannot be assumed to be permanent, and therefore most states provide for some means of modifying the powers of the guardian or terminating the relationship altogether. A majority of states require an annual judicial review, while others leave the review period to the discretion of the court that first made the incompetency determination. In addition, there is generally some mechanism whereby the individual declared legally incompetent, or others in his or her behalf, can initiate a review for the purpose of altering the guardianship.[67]

Criminal Law and Mental Status

Although mental competency to stand trial and the insanity defense are much discussed in both the legal and mental health literatures, few mental health professionals are likely to find themselves involved in either of these determinations of legal status, especially the latter. Moreover, those who are so involved will require considerably more detailed information and understanding than can be afforded here. It may be useful, nonetheless, to summarize briefly the relevant issues.

It has long been an accepted legal doctrine—affirmed by the Supreme Court in 1975—that defendants in criminal cases must be able to understand the nature and consequences of the proceedings against them and be able to participate in presenting a defense. Inability to do so constitutes incompetency to stand trial.[68] Stone suggests that competency to stand trial is "the most significant mental-health inquiry pursued in the system of criminal law. Its significance derives from the numbers of persons to whom it is applied, the many points in the criminal trial process at which it can be applied, the ease of its being invoked, and the consequences of its application."[69]

Referral for evaluation of competency to stand trial has been criticized as a way for the state to delay trial, obtain information, prevent bail, and institute preventive detection without a commitment hearing. Very few of those evaluated are subsequently found incompetent to stand trial;[70] but all who are subjected to it suffer a period of confinement for evaluation, of up to three months, and are deprived of the opportunity for release on bail.

Individuals found incompetent to stand trial are generally committed for treatment aimed at restoring them to such competency. At one time this period of commitment could be longer than the maximum sentence for the crime involved, or even—especially for the mentally retarded—for an indefinite period. But in 1972, in *Jackson v. Indiana*, the Supreme Court held that the state "cannot constitutionally commit . . . for an indefinite period simply on account of . . . incompetency to stand trial. . . ."[71] Today, if the individual is not restored to competency after a specified period of time, confinement can continue only if the requirements for involuntary civil commitment are met.

Ennis and Emery point out that the real issues in competency to stand trial are legal ones, and that mental health professionals are not trained to deal with them.[72] They generally will not know, for example, whether the best strategy in a particular case may be a negotiated plea— in which case ability to participate in a trial is irrelevant—or whether, in case of a trial, it is a better strategy for the defendant to testify or not to testify. They concede, however, that these considerations are usually ignored. The result, it has been noted elsewhere, is:

> In practice, psychiatrists rarely disagree about present insanity or mental incompetency to stand trial, and if the psychiatrist called by defense counsel is prepared to testify that the defendant is incompetent to stand trial, his statements usually are not challenged by the district attorney and an agreement is made for civil commitment, at the termination of which the trial may be held.[73]

If, however, it is determined that the defendant cannot readily be made competent, the state must decide either to release the individual or to initiate civil commitment.[74]

The second major mental status issue in the criminal law involves the principle that conviction for a crime requires not only proof of the criminal act but also demonstration of criminal intent. This means that persons cannot be punished for acts for which they were not mentally responsible. Defining, let alone establishing, a standard of criminal responsibility is no easy matter—if, indeed, it is possible at all. Thousands of books, articles, and legal opinions have been written in attempts to evolve an acceptable standard, but disagreement continues. The major trends are represented in the following two definitions of criminal responsibility:

- An individual should not be held responsible if he was "laboring under such a defect of reason, from disease of the mind, as not to know the nature and quality of the act he was doing or, if he did know it, that he did not know he was doing what was wrong." (The McNaughtan rule—formulated in an 1843 English case.)[75]
- "A person is not responsible for criminal conduct if at the time of such conduct as a result of mental disease or defect he lacked substantial capacity either to appreciate the criminality (wrongfulness) of his conduct or to conform his conduct to the requirements of the law." (The American Law Institute Model Penal Code.)[76]

The evolution and application of a standard for criminal responsibility can be fascinating from both a psychological and philosophical perspective. Nevertheless, few defendants make use of the insanity defense and even fewer are successful in so doing; for example, 278 successful not-guilty-by-reason-of-insanity pleas were reported from the state of New York for the period from April 1965 through June 1976. In those cases where the defense is successful, the defendant most likely will be committed to a mental hospital—in some states automatically, in some states by decision of the same jury, and in some states through separate proceedings. A more recent variation in a handful of states is to allow the jury to find a defendant "guilty but insane," thus keeping supervision of commitment and treatment within the jurisdiction of the criminal courts.[77]

Individuals committed or imprisoned as the result of criminal prosecution can be confined in a variety of settings, often high-security state facilities for the "criminally insane."[78] Considerable controversy exists over the relative ease with which individuals can be transferred between such facilities and prisons and/or regular mental hospitals, since the states vary widely in the rights afforded individuals facing such transfer.[79]

A final aspect regarding mental status and the criminal law involves coercing people in trouble with the law into various mental health treatment programs under the threat of criminal sanctions. This procedure is used most heavily in connection with alcoholism and drug abuse, but also is applied to juvenile offenders and mental health patients. As with much else in these areas, this *diversion* from prison to treatment is made at the expense of numerous due-process protections.

Mental Retardation

By rights, mental retardation merits a chapter in itself. "Nowhere in the interaction between law and mental health," observes Stone, "is there more ambiguity, more confusion, and more failure to articulate and achieve goals than in the area of mental retardation."[80] At the same time, the law that is developing on mental retardation parallels that of mental illness in many respects, especially as regards commitment and treatment.

One widely accepted estimate is that some six million Americans will, at some time in their lives, function in the mentally retarded range. Of these, more than 275,000 are institutionalized. Yet despite the numbers, mental retardation is not so much a factual characteristic as it is a label or classification[81] based largely on IQ test score ranges. Friedman argues that the consequences of being labeled mentally retarded are so severe that "due process requires that such classification be accurate." But, in fact, only limited support for his position has emerged from courts and legislatures.

Being labeled mentally retarded will affect the individual profoundly, in a variety of settings and generally throughout his or her life. It may also lead to commitment to a state or private institution. The retarded individual, like one who is mentally ill, may voluntarily seek admission to an institution or may be involuntarily committed. In between is the "voluntary" admission of minors on the basis of their parents authorization, which may be the most common type of admission.[82]

The substantive standards employed in involuntary commitment are even vaguer for mental retardation than for mental illness. Some states require a finding of dangerousness to self or others, while other states rely on the *parens patriae* ground of need for care and treatment. And according to Friedman, "Other states allow commitment on the basis of mental retardation alone, without any requirement either of dangerousness or of need for care."[83] At the opposite extreme, a few states have abolished involuntary commitment of the mentally retarded altogether.

The procedural standards employed in involuntary commitment tend to be equally lax. While legislation and litigation have led to such procedural requirements as notice, hearing, and counsel, these procedural rights are still rarely honored.

As with mental illness, somewhere between the substantive and procedural standards that have been applied to involuntary commitment in recent years is the doctrine of the least restrictive alternative. A federal court applied the doctrine in a 1975 case in the District of Columbia involving the commitment of the mentally retarded,[84] and some states now follow a similar standard. A strong impetus for such an approach was thought to reside in the federal Developmentally Disabled Assistance and Bill of Rights Act of 1975; but as the earlier discussion of *Pennhurst State School and Hospital v. Halderman* indicated, the U.S. Supreme Court rejected such a view.

The legal rights of the mentally retarded can be considered in terms of their rights—or potential rights—in the institution, in the community (including education and marital and sexual relations), and in the criminal law system. Within the institution, the first basic right after the right to treatment in the least restrictive setting is the right to treatment itself. The most far-reaching recognition of such a right was stated in *Wyatt v. Stickney*, where the federal district court held that in "the context of the right to adequate care for people civilly confined to public mental institutions, no viable distinction can be made between the mentally ill and the mentally retarded." The court set minimal standards to assure a humane psychological and physical environment, individualized habilitation and training plans, and adequate staffing; in short, a basic right to habilitation analogous to the mentally ill patient's claim to a right to treatment.[85] In upholding this decision, the court of appeals emphasized that commitment to an institution without providing this level of care would violate the due process rights of those confined. Other courts have followed this same rationale.

In general, conditions in facilities for the mentally retarded are worse than those for the mentally ill. Thus while some courts have not gone as far as to uphold a right to habilitation, many have upheld a right to be protected from harm while in the institution. The leading litigation here is the Willowbrook case. *New York State Association for Retarded Children, Inc. v. Carey,*[86] an action brought on behalf of the five thousand residents of New York State's overcrowded, inadequately staffed Willowbrook State School for the Mentally Retarded. The federal district court found that conditions at Willowbrook were "inhumane." Beyond that, however, there is some confusion as to what the case stands for. There was a formal order and memorandum, but no actual court opinion, since the litigation had resulted in a consent decree that set out detailed plans for improving the operation of the institution and the movement of residents into less restrictive community settings, with an advisory board to oversee the changes. Moreover, funding for the board has dried up and litigation over placement continues. But the litigation does seem to establish a right to be protected from harm, a right based at least in part on the Eighth Amendment protection from cruel and unusual punishment.[87]

Various specific rights within the institution—such as the right to refuse medication, and to communications, visitation, etc.—parallel, but generally lag behind, those of the mentally ill.[88] In some states commitment of a mentally retarded individual to an institution automatically establishes legal incompetence, but most states require a separate competency proceeding. The current trend is toward item-specific legal incompetency and guardianship, using the logic of the least restrictive alternative. If a retarded individual can manage his or her own day-to-day affairs but may be unable to handle financial decisions, a guardian of the estate may be all that is necessary. A guardian is given general authority only when that is necessary.

The rights of the mentally retarded in the community begin with the basic right to live in the community. With the emphasis on deinstitutionalization, the acceptance or nonacceptance of group or foster homes for the retarded in residential areas becomes crucial. In many instances efforts have been mounted to keep such homes out of residential areas by invoking local single-family zoning regulations to exclude group or foster homes. The result is a conflict between a municipality's right under its police power to set standards for its neighborhoods and the individual rights of the mentally retarded (and other groups such as the mentally ill, the aged, drug and alcohol abuse patients, etc.) Many states have enacted statutes that override local zoning provisions and specifically allow group and foster care facilities. In addition, litigation has been used to challenge zoning laws on constitutional grounds, charging either that they violate due process because they are arbitrary, irrational, and bear no substantial relation to any legitimate governmental interest or that they violate equal protection by discriminating between groups without any legitimate governmental purpose.[89]

Another community-related right of the mentally retarded involves education, a subject that has received considerable emphasis in the past decade. In two class-action lawsuits in the early 1970s, *Pennsylvania Association for Retarded Children v. Pennsylvania* and *Mills v. Board of Education*,[90] the courts ruled that mentally retarded, and other handicapped or "exceptional" children capable of benefiting from it, have a legal right to publicly supported education. These cases led to similar right-to-education litigation elsewhere. In addition, in 1974 Congress enacted Education of the Handicapped Amendments,[91] which require the states, as a condition for federal financial aid to education, to provide appropriate education for all handicapped children.

Two other rights of the mentally retarded should be briefly mentioned. Sexual and marital rights are discussed by Friedman and others.[92] The most difficult legal dilemma, that of sterilization, is discussed in Chapter 18. The rights of the physically handicapped are especially relevant to the mentally retarded, because many are physically handicapped as well. Architectural-barrier legislation has been an important factor for all physically handicapped individuals.[93]

Mentally retarded individuals bear much the same relationship to the criminal law process as do the mentally ill. Competency to stand trial is an obvious concern; criminal responsibility—the insanity defense—is also relevant; each of the major definitions of criminal responsibility can be applied to the mentally retarded. An additional problem involves coercion and the ability of the retarded to resist police and prosecutorial pressure.[94]

The Professional-Patient Relationship

The previous pages of this chapter have dealt primarily with the legal status of the individual as a patient in a mental health facility and as a defendant in a criminal case whose mental health is open to question. A totally different issue is the relationship between the mental health professional and the patient or client.

The main legal issues embodied in that relationship are confidentiality, privilege, and malpractice. The principles involved are the same as in other health professional-patient relationships, but they are complicated by the sensitive information contained in patient communications and practitioner files in the mental health area.[95]

Confidentiality means the expectation that information communicated to a mental health professional, often information regarding innermost thoughts and feelings, will not be in turn communicated to others. The same expectation generally applies to the professional's observations and speculations as set down in his or her notes on the patient. The rationale for such confidentiality is not merely respect for the patient's privacy; it is considered absolutely vital to the frank and open communication essential for treatment in this area.

In a previous chapter it was noted that general patient-physician confidentiality is as much a set of ethical as legal principles; and that actually the legal basis for preventing disclosure or collecting damages for unauthorized disclosure is not particularly strong. In the mental health area, however, the situation is different, for there are statutes specifically protecting the confidentiality of mental health records in most states, in some cases with penalties for violation of such confidentiality. Many of these statutes provide exceptions, allowing disclosure of such information in involuntary commitment proceedings, child custody and divorce cases, and lawsuits in which the patient himself or herself introduces his or her mental or emotional condition as an issue. But some of the more narrowly drawn statutes limit disclosure except under tightly drawn circumstances. In describing the variation in statutory protection, Ennis and Emery note:

> Some statutes prohibit disclosure of the fact of hospitalization; others only prohibit disclosure of information about the patient's diagnosis and treatment. Most statutes permit disclosure to other persons within the hospital or state mental health system, and many permit disclosure to private physicians, police, welfare officials,and insurance companies. Some even permit disclosure to prospective employers. Other statutes prohibit disclosure to almost everyone, unless the patient or ex-patient consents to disclosure.[96]

The counterpart to disclosure to third parties is the accessibility of mental health records to the patient. The law regarding patient access to mental health records seems to be following the general trend toward increased access, but at a respectful distance. Thus where statutes and court decisions have supported the patient's right of access to medical records, mental health records have often been specifically exempted or, at a minimum, made only semiaccessible under special rules.

Privilege involves a particular type of confidentiality, which is relevant only when the health professional is called upon to provide information for a court of law. As explained in Chapter 17, the statutory physician-patient testimonial privilege gives patients the right to prohibit disclosure by their physicians in certain legal proceedings of information derived from the patient-physician professional relationship.[97] This privilege, however, usually applies only to physicians, does not apply in criminal cases, and includes other exceptions that sharply limit its impact. As a result, several states have enacted special statutes allowing the patient to prohibit disclosure of confidential communication between psychotherapist and patient. The privilege applies only in the judicial setting; it simply means that the psychotherapist cannot, without the patient's permission, provide to a court of law any information based on a professional relationship with the patient.

But even such specific laws do not establish absolute testimonial confidentiality, both because not all states have adopted such laws, and because individual statutes each determine which mental health professionals (still often only psychiatrists and psychologists) are covered by the privilege. Furthermore, the statutes usually contain several exceptions, although not quite as many as with standard physician-patient privilege statutes. Besides those mentioned already—commitment, child custody, divorce, and lawsuits where the patient raises the issue of mental status— these exceptions typically include reports required under other statutes and patients believed to be dangerous to themselves or to others. States with the strongest privilege provisions may specify other mental health professionals to whom the privilege applies and/or provide fewer exceptions, thus making the privilege much like the attorney-client privilege.[98]

In recent years one of the most heated confidentiality debates has concerned a possible duty on the part of the professional to warn third parties (including the police) of threats made by patients during the course of therapy. The controversy was fueled by a 1976 decision of the California Supreme Court: *Tarasoff v. Board of Regents of the University of California*,[99] which involved a patient receiving outpatient psychotherapy at a university hospital. During the course of his therapy the patient threatened to kill an unnamed but readily identifiable person, and the therapist viewed the threats as serious enough to warrant the initiation of involuntary commitment proceedings. This led the therapist to ask the campus police to take the patient into custody and make an independent determination of dangerousness, a police procedure called for under California law. The police, however, decided the patient was not dangerous and released him. When the object of the patient's threat returned to the city after a lengthy absence he killed her. And when the woman's parents sued the therapist and the university for negligence in failing to have warned their daughter of the potential danger she faced, the state supreme court agreed with this theory of liability, dismissing the defense of confidentiality. The court stated:

> We recognize the public interest in supporting effective treatment of mental illness and in protecting the rights of patients to privacy . . . and the consequent public importance of safeguarding the confidential character of psychotherapeutic communication. Against this interest, however, we must weigh the public interest in safety from violent assault. . . . We conclude that [confidentiality] must yield to the extent to which disclosure is essential to avert danger to others. The protective privilege ends where the public peril begins.[100]

The *Tarasoff* decision was viewed by many mental health professionals as presenting them with the impossible choice of either jeopardizing the therapist-patient relationship or risking liability to third parties for negligence. But two important aspects of the case have muted this concern somewhat: First, the limited applicability of the decision—the court simply held that in situations such as this one, where the therapist concluded that the patient was dangerous enough to invoke a custody and commitment process, a jury can consider whether the therapist's failure to warn a third party fell below the standard of care ordinarilly exercised by other therapists in similar circumstances.[101] Second, despite widespread fear that the *Tarasoff* decision would set off a wave of similar rulings around the country, only two other courts have followed the *Tarasoff* rationale in reaching decisions.[102]

Tarasoff, based on an allegation of professional negligence—malpractice—is the most controversial, but certainly not the only, basis on which a mental health professional can be sued for malpractice. From a legal perspective, malpractice charges against a health professional involve the same principles outlined in Chapter 16: harm suffered by the patient as a result of the professional's having negligently performed at a level below the standard followed by similar competent professionals. The most noteworthy aspect of malpractice suits against mental health professionals is that there were very few of them until quite recently. Stone notes that a 1973 review of the subject, *The Malpractice of Psychiatrists*, found few appellate cases. However, that situation has begun to change, and some commentators predict considerable acceleration in the number and kinds of malpractice suits brought against professionals.[103] A similar increase can be expected with lawsuits alleging lack of informed consent.[104]

In the past, the two most frequent types of malpractice suits against mental health professionals were those alleging sexual improprieties with the patient and those brought by next-of-kin after the suicide of a patient. In addition, there have been a number of cases in which patients who received electroshock therapy have asserted that they were not adequately apprised of possible side effects. And failure to diagnose medical illness associated with mental or emotional problems is perhaps one of the most "traditional" bases for malpractice against a mental health professional.

The two most widely discussed recent developments in mental health professional liability are suits charging improper confinement (as in *O'Conner v. Donaldson*) and suits involving failure to warn third parties (as in the *Tarasoff* situation).[105] Stone predicts that another likely development in the near future may be a dramatic increase in malpractice suits based on negligent prescribing of medications.[106] It also seems likely that mental health professionals will be paying increasing attention to the adequacy of the information they provide their patients and to the expectations held by those patients. Already there are some therapists who draft written contracts with their patients outlining the goals and prospects of therapy.

One of the biggest problems in predicting developments in this field is the ever-growing variety of talking therapists and therapeutic approaches. Much of the literature in the field focuses on psychiatrists, psychologists, and, in a few cases, social workers. It is very difficult to anticipate what a malpractice suit against a dance therapist might look like.

Conclusion

Mental health law has been generally fluid in recent years. Wald and Friedman point out:

Mentally handicapped persons have been successful in persuading federal courts that they have a right to treatment, to protection from harm, to treatment in the "least restrictive setting," to equal educational opportunity, to protection from forced administration of hazardous or intrusive procedures, to both procedural and substantive protections in the civil commitment process, to safeguards against indefinite confinement after a finding that they are incompetent to stand trial, and to liberty. The essence of these landmark judicial decisions has been incorporated into both state laws and federal legislation. . . .[107]

Large numbers of people have been profoundly affected by these changes in the law. The mental health professional may be apprehensive or opposed to many of these developments, but it is important to recognize that the legislative and judicial changes are so widespread and so deeply rooted that the tide will not be reversed.

NOTES

1. Bruce J. Ennis, "Judicial Involvement in the Public Practice of Psychiatry," in Walter E. Barton and Charlotte J. Sanborn, eds., *Law and the Mental Health Professions: Friction at the Interface* (New York: International Universities Press, 1978). p. 5.
2. John P. Wilson, *The Rights of Adolescents in the Mental Health System* (Lexington, Mass.: Lexington Books, 1978), p. 88.
3. Bruce J. Ennis and Richard D. Emery, *The Rights of Mental Patients* (New York: Avon, 1978), p. 22. The mental health system's interest in helping patients often seems at odds with the patient autonomy interest of the mental health law reform movement. Since many readers will be less familiar with the arguments—if not the impact—of the latter orientation, it is emphasized here (especially by reference to the Ennis and Emery handbook).
4. A major catalyst in these changes has been the mental health law advocates who have promoted litigation and legislation throughout the 1970s to safeguard the rights of mental patients. While some critics, most notably Thomas Szasz, argue that groups such as the Mental Health Law Project only have made a repressive system work more efficiently, there can be no doubt that the changes wrought by these lawyers during the past decade have altered the mental health system in the United States.
5. See the discussions of court-ordered treatment in Chapter 5 and of consent to treatment generally, in Chapter 14.
6. G. B. Olin and H. S. Olin, "Informed Consent in Voluntary Mental Hospital Admissions," *American Journal of Psychiatry* 132:938–939 (1975), as quoted by Ennis in Barton and Sanborn, *Law and the Mental Health Professions*, p. 13. Also see his references 13–18 on p. 17.
7. See discussion of emergency commitment, later in this chapter. For an early discussion of commitment see "Note: Developments in the Law of Civil Commitment of the Mentally Ill," *Harvard Law Review* 87:1190–1227 (1970). The "civil" designation distinguishes this process from criminal

proceedings. While the distinction is supposed to operate to the advantage of the individual by avoiding the stigmas and penalties of the criminal law, civil commitment also lacks the procedural protections of the criminal law and, much like the juvenile justice system (see Chapter 20 of this book), is based on the theory that a benevolent state will look out for the best interest of individuals judged incompetent to look out for themselves.

8. *Humphrey v. Cady*, 405 U.S. 504 (1972) at 509. This is where the lawyer's perspective and the mental health professional's perspective are likely to diverge most sharply. In oversimplified terms, the question asked is, Which should be valued most highly: personal freedom or mental health? Where the lawyer sees curtailment of liberty, the mental health professional—by virtue of training and dedication—may see an opportunity for help. Alan Stone, in what his students have dubbed the "Thank You Theory of Paternalistic Intervention," goes to the heart of the matter by endorsing as a major rationale for involuntary commitment the very factor lawyers have long considered the weakest justification: treatability. The patient's subsequent gratitude is used to justify intervention. See Alan A. Stone, *Mental Health and the Law: A System in Transition* (Rockville, Md.: National Institute for Mental Health, 1975), chap. 4.

9. While commitment is usually to a state mental health facility, many state statutes allow commitment to any approved public or private treatment facility willing to accept the patient. It is also important to note that in most states neither voluntary nor involuntary commitment carries with it the status of legal incompetency. To be declared legally incompetent requires an additional and separate judicial determination. See the discussion of competency and guardianship in this chapter.

10. See discussions of state police power in Chapters 4 and 5.

11. For example, a statute may provide that commitment of a mentally ill person is appropriate if he is "unable to provide for his basic physical needs so as to guard himself from serious harm." Critics of the *parens patriae* rationale point to the fact that society allows presumably "sane" individuals to smoke cigarettes, jump motorcycles through fiery hoops, squander their limited incomes on state lotteries, and court serious harm in many other ways without forced state intervention. See David B. Wexler, *Mental Health Law: Major Issues* (New York: Plenum Press, 1981), pp. 36–41. *Parens patriae* as applied to children is discussed in Chapter 20 of this book.

12. *Parens patriae* for obvious reasons; police power because the dire results of suicidal or other severely destructive behavior have considerable impact on others. Critics of this basis for commitment point out, first, that suicide is not always, or even frequently, an irrational act and that labeling it as such often reflects mainly on the value system and subjective judgments of the labeler. Second, it is noted that the suicide rate among those who talk about or attempt the act is so low that accurate prediction is impossible. Thus involuntary commitment on the basis of dangerousness to self would include several individuals not actually dangerous to self along with persons actually likely to cause themselves serious harm. Third, it is argued that there is little evidence that involuntary commitment will reduce the likelihood of suicide.

13. Criticism of the dangerousness rationale also points to the fact that prediction of dangerousness is notoriously unreliable. Since mental health professionals lose less by overpredicting than by underpredicting—it is argued—many harmless people will lose their liberty for every truly dangerous person who is confined. It is further argued that the treatment of "dangerousness" is unlikely to succeed. See American Psychiatric Association, *Clinical Aspects of the Violent Individual*, Task Force Report 8, (Washington, D.C.: American Psychiatric Association, 1974). Also see Ennis and Emery, *The Rights of Mental Patients*, pp. 20–22. In *Baxtrom v. Herold*, 338 U.S. 107 (1968), the U.S. Supreme Court held that a prisoner summarily transferred to a mental hospital with only a brief administrative hearing at the end of his prison sentence had been improperly denied the procedural protections normally made available to a person facing involuntary civil commitment. As a result of this decision the state of New York was forced to release 969 inmates who had been confined to state hospitals for the criminally insane on the basis of psychiatric predictions of dangerousness. A year later, 7 of the 969 had been returned to state criminal institutions. After four years 2.7 percent had acted out in dangerous ways and were in criminal facilities. See Bruce J. Ennis and Thomas P. Litwack, "Psychiatry and the Presumption of Expertise: Flipping Coins in the Courtroom," *California Law Review* 62:693–752 (1974).

14. *Jackson v. Indiana*, 406 U.S. 715 (1972).

15. Ennis and Emery, *The Rights of Mental Patients*, p. 57.

16. E. P. Scott, "Viewpoint: Another Look at the Crossroads," *Mental Health Law Project* 2:9 (June 1976), as cited in Robert L. Sadoff, "Indications for Involuntary Hospitalization: Dangerousness or Mental Illness?," in Barton and Sanborn, *Law and the Mental Health Professions*, p. 305.

17. *O'Conner v. Donaldson*, 422 U.S. 563 (1975), pp. 573–574.

18. 441 U.S. 418 (1979). See discussion of *Addington* in Wexler, *Mental Health Law*, chap. 3.

19. *O'Conner v. Donaldson*, p. 575. The Court went on to say: "Mere public intolerance or animosity cannot constitutionally justify the deprivation of a person's physical liberty. . . . In short, a state cannot constitutionally confine without more a nondangerous individual who is capable of surviving safely in freedom by himself or with the help of willing and responsible family members or friends." See further discussion at footnote 37.

20. *Dixon v. Weinberger*, 405 F.Supp. 974 (D.D.C. 1975).

21. Ennis and Emery, *The Rights of Mental Patients*, pp. 66–67. And see *Lessard v. Schmidt*, 349 F.Supp. 1078 (E.D. Wis. 1972), *vacated on procedural grounds*, 414 U.S. 473 (1974), *reinstated* 379 F.Supp. 1376 (E.D. Wis. 1974), *vacated on procedural grounds*, 421 U.S. 957 (1975), *reinstated* 413 F.Supp. 1318 (E.D. Wis. 1976).

22. Ennis and Emery, *The Rights of Mental Patients*, p. 65.

23. Ibid., pp. 64–66.

24. Ibid., pp. 60–64. See their discussion of the use of *guardians ad litem* in lieu of legal representation—a declining practice generally regarded as unconstitutional

25. For example, *Lessard v. Schmidt*, and *Suzuki v. Quisenberry*, 411 F.Supp. 1113 (D.Ha. 1976).
26. Ennis and Emery, *The Rights of Mental Patients*, pp. 74–76.
27. Ibid., pp. 71–72.
28. Ibid., pp. 72–73.
29. Ibid., pp. 67–70.
30. Since juvenile defendants are not guaranteed a right to a jury trial, it appears unlikely that the present Supreme Court will extend such a right to persons facing commitment. However, where state law grants a jury trial in situations closely analogous to commitment, it has been suggested that such a right might be based on equal protection grounds. See ibid., pp. 79–80.
31. Ibid., pp. 76–78.
32. Ibid., pp. 80–82.
33. See ibid., pp. 82–83, for a discussion of the strengths and weaknesses of "extraordinary writs" such as habeas corpus.
34. Ibid., pp. 127–131.
35. Bruce Ennis and Loren Siegel, *The Rights of Mental Patients*, (New York: Avon, 1973), p. 17.
36. Lynne N. Henderson, "We're Only Trying to Help: The Burden and Standard of Proof in Short Term Civil Commitment," *Stanford Law Review* 31:425–455 (1979).
37. Ibid., p. 576.
38. Patricia M. Wald and Paul R. Friedman, "The Politics of Mental Health Advocacy in the United States," in David N. Weisstub, ed., *Law and Psychiatry II* (New York: Pergamon Press, 1979), pp. 55–70.
39. 325 F. Supp. 781 (M.D.Ala. 1971), 334 F. Supp. 1341 (M.D.Ala. 1971), 344 F. Supp. 373 (M.D.Ala. 1972), *aff'd sub nom Wyatt v. Aderholt*, 503 F. 2d 1305 (5th Cir. 1974). The right to treatment concept originated with Morton Birnbaum; see his "The Right to Treatment," *American Bar Association Journal* 46:499 (1960). Volumes have been written on the concept since.
40. The district court based its decision on the Eight Amendment and equal protection clause of the U.S. Constitution, the Rehabilitation Act of 1973, 29 U.S.C. Sec. 794, and the Pennsylvania Mental Health and Mental Retardation Act of 1966, 50 P.S. Sec. 4201. As discussed below, the court of appeals based its decision on a different federal statute.
41. 42 U.S.C. Sec. 6000 et seq.
42. 448 U.S. 905 (1981). But see *Youngberg v. Romeo*, No. 80-1489 (6/18/82).
43. See Chapters 14 and 20. Also note the general public health exceptions discussed in Chapter 5.
44. Ennis and Emery, *The Rights of Mental Patients*, p. 133.
45. *In re the Mental Health of K.K.B.*, 609 P.2d 747 (Okla. 1980). See discussion of civil competence in this chapter. Also see *Winters v. Miller*, 446 F.2d 65 (2nd Cir. 1971), *cert. den.* 404 U.S. 985 (1971). Some argue that the situation is easier with the voluntary patient, who is considered to have consented to at least certain basic treatments by virtue of voluntary hospitalization.
46. Other bases for refusal of mental health treatment are the First Amendment freedom of speech protection applied to an underlying freedom of

thought (see *Rogers v. Okin,* discussed in this chapter) and the Eighth Amendment protection from cruel and unusual punishment. See Ennis and Emery, *The Rights of Mental Patients,* p. 132–135, for a fuller discussion of legal grounds for challenging forced treatment. See, generally, A. Edward Doudera and Judith P. Swazey, eds., *Refusing Treatment in Mental Health Institutions: Values in Conflict* (Ann Arbor: Health Administration Press, 1982).

47. 462 F.Supp. 1131 (D.N.J. 1978). The decision was substantially upheld in 653 F.2d 836 (3d Cir. 1981).
48. 478 F.Supp. 134 (D.Mass. 1979), 634 F.2d 650 (1st Cir. 1980). The court of appeals upheld the decision but limited its impact in several respects. The Supreme Court accepted an appeal of the case but then chose not to decide it because of a recent state court decision which may affect the outcome. *Mills v. Rogers,* No. 80-1417 (6/18/82).
49. *Boston Globe,* 21 November 1979, p. 13; quoted in George J. Annas, "Refusing Medication in Mental Hospitals," *Hastings Center Report,* 10(1):21–22 (February 1980). Also see Daryl B. Matthews, "The Right to Refuse Psychiatric Medication," *Medicolegal News* 8(2) 4–6, 16 (April 1980).
50. *In re the Mental Health of K.K.B.,* 609 P.2d 747 (Okla. 1980). Also see *Davis v. Hubbard,* 506 F.Supp. 915 (N.D. Ohio 1980).
51. See, in general, Henry H. Foster, Jr., "Informed Consent of Mental Patients," in Barton and Sanborn, *Law and the Mental Health Professions,* pp. 71–95. See discussion of prudent-person standard at note 20 of Chapter 14 of this book.
52. As will be discussed in this chapter, the Supreme Court has ruled that confinement for incompetence to stand trial can only be for a limited and reasonable period of time. *Jackson v. Indiana,* 406 U.S. 715 (1972). The Court applied the same limitation to confinement for observation. *McNeil v. Director, Patuxent Institution,* 407 U.S. 245 (1972). Ennis and Emery argue that the same time limit should be applied to those committed for treatment, because after a certain period of time confinement can no longer be expected to be productive. See Ennis and Emery, *The Rights of Mental Patients,* pp. 127–132.
53. See, generally, Angela Roddey Holder, *Legal Issues in Pediatrics and Adolescent Medicine* (New York: John Wiley, 1977), pp. 238–245. Also see Wilson, *The Rights of Adolescents,* especially pp. 16–23, 43–49, 193–231.
54. See Wilson, *The Rights of Adolescents,* pp. 125–129.
55. See "Mental Health Treatment for Minors." *Mental Disability Law Reporter* 2:460–472 (January/February 1978), footnote 20.
56. 442 U.S. 584 (1979).
57. The Court also considered the situation in which the minor is a ward of the state, so that it is the state, in the role of parent, that is applying for the child's admission. For this situation the majority announced: "We have already recognized that an independent medical judgment made from the perspective of the best interests of the child after a careful investigation is an acceptable means of justifying a voluntary commitment. We do not believe that the soundness of this decisionmaking is any the less reasonable in this setting." Justices Brennan, Marshall, and Stevens dissented. They

agreed that a preadmission hearing could be constitutionally dispensed with if the parents consented to the admission, but argued in behalf of a postadmission review hearing. In the case of state wards, the dissenters felt that a preadmission hearing was a necessary protection. For an interesting comparison of the *Parham* decision to the Court's determination in *Danforth* that the state could not require parental consent for a minor's abortion, see George J. Annas, "Parents, Children, and the Supreme Court," *Hastings Center Report* 9(5):21–23 (October 1979).

58. The right of minors to refuse treatment is especially unclear. It should be recalled that the *Rennie v. Klein* court made the right to refuse less formally required for involuntary patients, while the *Rogers v. Okin* court did not consider voluntariness relevant. It should be noted that in some states, such as Illinois, children can be admitted to a mental health facility on the basis of their parent's authorization, but those over twelve are then free to sign themselves out on their own authority.

59. Irwin N. Perr suggests, "Because competency at its hard core is a legal concept, psychiatrists and others would be best advised not to use the word other than to express an opinion directed to a legal issue." Irwin N. Perr, "The Many Faces of Competence," in Barton and Sanborn, *Law and the Mental Health Professions*, pp. 211–234, at 212. A variety of terms are used to refer to the legally determined inability to handle one's civil affairs. These include legal incompetence, civil incompetence, mental incompetence, and mentally disabled person. The former is used here to emphasize the legal nature of the concept.

60. The historical antecedants of modern-day legal incompetency determinations lie entirely with the protection of property. Since the English crown claimed a share of all estates, legal incompetency was a device to assure that a crazy aristocrat would not fritter away his—and therefore the crown's—wealth and property.

61. Stone, *Mental Health and the Law*, p. 164, describes this as a very common standard, citing R. C. Allen, et al., *Mental Impairment and Legal Incompetency* (Englewood Cliffs, N.J.: Prentice-Hall, 1968).

62. California Probate Code, Sec. 1460 (1976).

63. See Pickering, "Limitations on Individual Rights in Incompetency Proceedings," *University of California-Davis Law Review* 7:457 (1974).

64. Ennis and Emery, *The Rights of Mental Patients*, p. 175.

65. Also called guardians of the estate and conservators.

66. Stone, *Mental Health and the Law*, p. 167, quoting the National Council on the Aging, *Overcoming Barriers to Protective Services for the Aged* (1968), p. 37. Another type of guardian, *guardians ad litem*, may also be appointed for the specific purpose of conducting litigation on behalf of the individual.

67. The main obstacle to making this right a full reality is that the individual not only bears the burden of initiating the proceeding, but must also show that he or she is competent. This is an especially difficult task, since it requires overcoming judicial biases that tend to favor the initial judicial determination that imposed guardianship.

68. *Dusky v. United States*, 362 U.S. 402 (1960); *Drope v. Missouri*, 420 U.S. 162 (1975). Most states, as well as the federal government, have competency-to-stand-trial statutes. Pennsylvania's is representative: "Whenever a person

who has been charged with a crime is found to be substantially unable to understand the nature or object of the proceedings against him or to participate and assist in his defense, he shall be deemed incompetent to be tried, convicted or sentenced so long as such incapacity continues." See Gerald Cooke, "An Introduction to Basic Issues and Concepts in Forensic Psychology," in Gerald Cooke, ed., *The Role of the Forensic Psychologist* (Springfield, Ill.: Charles C. Thomas, 1979), pp. 5–15, at p. 8.

69. Stone, *Mental Health and the Law*, p. 200.
70. Ennis and Emery, *The Rights of Mental Patients*, p. 100, give Massachusetts as an example; 5 percent of those defendants committed for evaluation are found to be incompetent to stand trial.
71. *Jackson v. Indiana*, 406 U.S. 715 at 720 (1972). *Jackson* involved a mentally defective deaf-mute who could not read, write, or otherwise communicate except through limited sign language. He was charged with a crime, evaluated for competency to stand trial, and on the basis of a negative evaluation committed to the state's Department of Mental Health until such time as that department should certify to the court that "the defendant is sane." Since there was no evidence that such certification would occur, this was— argued Jackson's counsel—a life sentence without even having been convicted of a crime. The Supreme Court held that Jackson had thereby been deprived of equal protection and that his due-process rights had been violated. Said the Court;

> We hold, consequently, that a person charged by a State with a criminal offense who is committed solely on account of his incapacity to proceed to trial cannot be held more than the reasonable period of time necessary to determine whether there is a substantial probability that he will attain that capacity in the foreseeable future. If it is determined that this is not the case, then the State must either institute the customary civil commitment proceeding that would be required to commit indefinitely any other citizen, or release the defendant. Furthermore, even if it is determined that the defendant probably soon will be able to stand trial, his continued commitment must be justified by progress toward that goal.

72. Ennis and Emery, *The Rights of Mental Patients*, pp. 101–102.
73. Robert L. Sadoff, *Forensic Psychiatry* (Springfield, Ill.: Charles C. Thomas, 1975), p. 79. It is important that treating personnel and evaluators steer away from inquiring into the alleged crime. It should also be clear that the purpose of the confinement is to prepare the individual for participation in defense, not to assess the individual's mental status at the time of the alleged crime. Yet these two separate functions—evaluation and/or treatment relative to incompetence to stand trial and evaluation of mental status at the time of the alleged crime—are often merged; in some states, courts will refer individuals for simultaneous pretrial evaluations for both purposes.
74. A third alternative, trying the incompetent defendant, is discussed with approval in Ennis and Emery, *The Rights of Mental Patients*, pp. 107–108.
75. There have been several modifications of the McNaughtan rule, including the addition of an "irresistible impulse" test. See materials collected in Alexander D. Brooks, *Law, Psychiatry and the Mental Health System* (Boston: Little, Brown, 1974), pp. 135–160.
76. A third definition of criminal responsibility, the Durham rule, was formu-

lated in 1954 by the District of Columbia Court of Appeals—*Durham v. United States*, 214 F.2d 862. It was abandoned in 1972. This controversial—and unworkable—test held that "an accused is not ordinarily responsible if his unlawful act was the product of mental disease or mental defect." There long has been a popular movement to do away with the insanity defense completely, a position apparently supported by the Reagan administration. Aside from other difficulties, this would require changing virtually all of the existing state and federal criminal laws to remove the required element of intent.

77. See Richard A. Pasewark, Mark L. Pantle, and Henry J. Steadman, "The Insanity Plea in New York State: 1965–1976," *New York Bar Journal* 51:186–189 (1979). Also see Scott L. Sherman, "Guilty but Mentally Ill: A Retreat from the Insanity Defense," *American Journal of Law and Medicine* 7:237–264 (1981).

78. Two other groups of people, "sexual psychopaths" and "defective delinquents," are also confined to these facilities, often for an indeterminant period of time. Both are controversial categories, with seemingly little to do with dangerousness. See Stone, *Mental Health and the Law*, chap. 11, and Ennis and Emery, *The Rights of Mental Patients*, pp. 110–112.

79. Subject to the overall requirements imposed by *Baxtrom v. Herold* (see note 13). On criminal commitment generally, see Wexler, *Mental Health Law*, chap. 5.

80. Stone, *Mental Health and the Law*, p. 119. He goes on to note:

> The mentally retarded individual presents an ongoing set of legal problems throughout his life. First, there is the problem of the label, how it is applied, and the criteria for its application. Second, there is the problem of protecting the labeled individual as to whether he is to be institutionalized or not, and at what age. Third, there is the protection of his rights while institutionalized. Fourth, for the mentally retarded outside total institutions there is the need to protect and supervise the exercise of their constitutional rights, and to insure that they are provided a decent living situation and are not exploited (p. 124).

81. Paul R. Friedman, *The Rights of Mentally Retarded Persons* (New York: Avon, 1976), pp. 14–15, citing Philip Roos, "Basic Facts about Mental Retardation," in Bruce J. Ennis and Paul R. Friedman, eds., *Legal Rights of the Mentally Handicapped*, vol. 1 (New York: Practicing Law Institute, 1973), pp. 19–31. Friedman notes, however, that this figure is artificially high in the sense that probably no more than two million people are technically mentally retarded at any given time. Stone, *Mental Health and the Law*, p. 119, notes: "Perhaps there is no other place in the mental health system where labels are more odious and more invidious. . . . These labels are, of course, applied to a disproportionate number of disadvantaged and minority children."

82. See Friedman, *The Rights of Mentally Retarded Persons*, pp. 24–27, 33, 36–38.

83. Ibid., p. 34.

84. *Dixon v. Weinberger*, 405 F.Supp. 974 (D.C.D.C. 1975).

85. Habilitation is aimed at maximizing personal functioning. The Court, in *Wyatt v. Stickney* (see note 39), defined it as "the process by which the staff of the institution assists the resident to acquire and maintain those life skills

which enable him to cope more effectively with the demands of his own person and of his environment and to raise the level of his physical, mental, and social efficiency. Habilitation includes but is not limited to programs of formal, structured education and treatment." 344 F.Supp. 373 (M.D.Ala. 1972) at 395. Also see *Youngberg v. Romeo,* No. 80-1489 (6/18/82).

86. No. 72 Civ. 356/357 (E.D.N.Y. January 2, 1980).

87. *Horacek v. Exon,* 375 F.Supp. 71 (D. Nebraska, 1973) is specifically premised on the Eighth Amendment.

88. See Friedman, *The Rights of Mentally Retarded Persons,* pp. 57–95.

89. See Penelope A. Boyd, "Strategies in Zoning and Community Living Arrangements for Retarded Citizens: *Parens Patriae* Meets Police Power," *Villanova Law Review* 25:273–316 (1980); J. E. Reiner, "A Review of the Conflict between Community-Based Group Homes for the Mentally Retarded and Restrictive Zoning," *West Virginia Law Review* 82:669–686 (1980); "The Rights of the Mentally Ill to Receive Treatment in the Community," *Columbia Journal of Law and Social Problems* 16:193–268 (1980).

90. 334 F. Supp. 1257 (E.D. Pa. 1971) and 348 F.Supp. 866 (D.D.C. 1972). The *Mills* court also ruled that the school system's mental retardation diagnosis and assignment process must include notice, hearing, review, and a written record of the process and that the right-to-education applied to institutionalized retarded as well.

91. 20 U.S.C. Secs. 1401 et seq. (Supp. IV, 1974).

92. Friedman, *The Rights of Mentally Retarded Persons,* pp. 112–124.

93. Section 504 of the Rehabilitation Act of 1973; the Architectural Barriers Act of 1968, as amended, 42 U.S.C. Secs. 4151–4156 (1970). The legal rights and problems of the handicapped are not dealt with in this book. Recent literature on the subject includes Kent Hull, *The Rights of Physically Handicapped Persons* (New York: Avon, 1979); "Special Report: The Supreme Court and the Handicapped," *AMICUS* 4:170 (July/August 1979); W. R. Tate, "The Education for All Handicapped Children Act of 1975: In Need of an Advocate," *Washburn Law Journal* 19:312–329 (1980); Kent Hull, "Limiting *Davis:* Educating Handicapped People for Health Care Professions," *Medicolegal News* 8(1):11–13, 28 (February 1980).

94. See Friedman, *The Rights of Mentally Retarded Persons,* pp. 138–140.

95. Confidentiality and privilege are discussed in Chapter 17, malpractice in Chapter 16.

96. Ennis and Emery, *The Rights of Mental Patients,* p. 176. One particularly serious and unresolved confidentiality problem involves insurance reimbursement for mental health services. Because the very fact that a person is in therapy can be damaging, and because no effective safeguards exist to prevent redisclosure of information in the hands of insurance carriers, many therapists and patients simply forego insurance reimbursement, even though mental health services are covered.

97. The right belongs to the patient, who can refuse to claim it, leaving the therapist no choice but to testify. But, when claimed, this patient's right is a meaningful protection for the therapist, who on his or her own could not refuse to testify without facing contempt of court charges. In *In re Lifschutz,* 467 P.2d 557, 2 Cal.3d 415 (1970), the California Supreme Court rejected a

psychotherapist's attempt to claim the privilege on his own. However, there has been some movement of late toward establishing the privilege as a right of the therapist as well, the rationale being that even when the patient authorizes testimony, the confidentiality of therapist communications and notes should be preserved. Such a change must be legislative; see *In re Lifschutz*. In Illinois, for example, a psychiatrist, other physician, psychologist, social worker, or nurse providing mental health or developmental disabilities services may assert the privilege "contrary to the express wish" of the patient, but the judge can require a closed, in camera hearing to "establish that the disclosure is not in the best interest" of the patient—provided that "other admissible evidence is sufficient to establish the facts in issue." ILL. REV. STAT. ch. 91½, sec. 810(b). Presumably a fair number of therapists keep a private second set of "personal notes" on patients, intended only for their own use. But if the existence of such notes is known they may be reachable in legal actions—unless there is specific statutory protection for therapist personal notes. See ILL. REV. STAT. ch. 91½, sec. 803 "Records and Communications—Personal Notes of Therapist."

98. Sadoff, *Forensic Psychiatry*, pp. 213–214, points out that the communications between patients in group therapy sessions do not constitute a therapist-patient relationship and would not be protected by any privilege statute. A particularly difficult issue arises when a therapist treats a family group, such as husband and wife, and in subsequent litigation, such as a child custody hearing, one party invokes the privilege and the other requests testimony. At least one court has excused such testimony because it would have been a violation of a professional code of ethics. See "Professional Ethics Code Upheld—Therapist Excused from Testifying," *Behavior Today* 12(24):1–2 (June 22, 1981).

99. 551 P.2d 334 (1976).

100. In addition to addressing the question of whether a duty of due care, that is, duty to warn, was owed to the threatened individual, the court also addressed the workability of such a legally imposed duty given the inability of therapists to predict dangerousness. The court concluded that the therapist need only exercise that reasonable degree of skill, knowledge, and care ordinarily possessed and exercised by other therapists under similar circumstances. The problem here—and a major criticism of the decision—is that it may be difficult to the point of impossibility to define a standard of care in an area, such as psychotherapy, where there are so few measurables. (These considerations, but not confidentiality, also come into play in lawsuits against mental institutions that have released a patient who subsequently injures or kills someone. In such lawsuits it is usually alleged that the institution knew, or should have known, that the patient was dangerous, and therefore had a duty either to not release or to warn certain individuals.) See discussion of *Tarasoff* in Wexler, *Mental Health Law*, chap. 7.

101. The jury would also have to decide whether the therapist's negligence caused the injury to the third party by the patient. In actual fact there was no jury verdict in *Tarasoff*; the damage suit was ultimately settled out of court. See Paul S. Applebaum, "Tarasoff: An Update on the Duty to Warn," *Hospital and Community Psychiatry* 32(1):14–15 (January 1981).

102. The New Jersey Superior Court in *McIntosh v. Milano*, 403 A.2d 500 (N.J. Super. Ct., 1979) and a federal district court in *Lipari v. Sears, Roebuck and Co. (Neb.)*, 49 U.S.L.W. 2120 (August 19, 1980). Some states have sought to encourage third-party warnings by granting practitioners statutory immunity from defamation liability.

103. Data on trends in psychiatric malpractice is presented in Chester L. Trent, "Psychiatric Malpractice Insurance and Its Problems: An Overview," in Barton and Sanborn, *Law and the Mental Health Professions*, pp. 101–117. Also see Daniel B. Hogan, *The Regulation of Psychotherapists, Volume III: A Review of Malpractice Suits in the United States* (Cambridge, Mass.: Ballinger, 1979) and Seymour L. Halleck, *Law in the Practice of Psychiatry: A Handbook for Clinicians* (New York, Plenum, 1980). See Allen Stone's analysis of possible new types of malpractice suits: "New Liability for the Mental Health Practitioner," in Allen Stone, *Mental Health and Law: A System in Transition* (New York: Jason Aronson, 1976), chap. 15. On mental health malpractice in general, see Ronald Jay Cohen, *Malpractice: A Guide for Mental Health Professionals* (New York: Free Press, 1979).

104. See Chapter 14 for a general discussion of informed consent. In the mental health field, failure to disclose medication side effects would seem to be a critical informed consent area.

105. "I should sue you on behalf of two groups of clients. . . . The first group are the people you evaluate who you would not release from prison. They should sue you because psychological knowledge is still so inadequate that you cannot competently predict that they would harm anyone or themselves or commit crimes. . . . The second group that should sue you are the families of the victims of the crimes committed by those you released from prison." David Seth Michaels, quoted by Stanley L. Brodsky, "Buffalo Bill's Defunct Now: Vulnerability of Mental Health Professionals to Malpractice," in Barton and Sanborn, *Law and the Mental Health Professions*, pp. 119–132, at p. 123.

106. Stone, *Mental Health and Law*, pp. 252–253.

107. Wald and Friedman, in Weisstub, *Law and Psychiatry II*, p. 55 (footnotes deleted). The changes have been frequent and important enough that the American Bar Association's Commission on the Mentally Disabled—itself established in 1973—began bimonthly publication of the *Mental Disability Law Reporter* in 1977. Wexler, *Mental Health Law*, chaps. 8–10, views behavior modification as an important additional area for future legal flux.

20

Children and the Law

Our jurisprudence historically has reflected Western Civilization concepts of the family as a unit with broad parental authority over minor children. . . . Surely, this includes a "high duty" to recognize symptoms of illness and to seek and follow medical advice. The law's concept of the family rests on the presumption that parents possess what a child lacks in maturity, experience and capacity for judgment required for making life's difficult decisions. More important, historically it has recognized that natural bonds of affection lead parents to act in the best interests of their children.

—Parham v. J. R.[1]

PEDIATRICIANS are fond of pointing out that children are not merely little adults. This also has been a guiding principle of the law, which treats children differently than it does adults—sometimes to their benefit, sometimes to their distinct detriment. Some of these differences, as they involve consent and mental health, have been discussed briefly in the chapters dealing with those subjects; other areas that can involve the health professional include abuse and neglect, child custody, and child advocacy.

It is generally agreed that "the child, by reason of his physical and mental immaturity, needs special safeguards and care, including appropriate legal protection. . . ."[2] Usually it is the parents' responsibility to provide this protection; but when parents, for whatever reasons, fail in this task, government may exercise its authority to intervene. *Parens patriae* is a doctrine adopted by the American legal system from English law for this purpose; it expresses the right and the responsibility of the government to look out for the interests of minors and others who cannot legally take care of themselves. The doctrine is used (a) to compel obedience of a child to his parents, (b) to compel a child's duty to the state, through compulsory education, for example, and (c) to protect children from their own parents, when necessary.[3] The latter purpose gives the state enormous powers to intervene in the parent-child relationship. Brian Fraser explains that the doctrine of *parens patriae* was specifically cited

> in 1839 in the case of *Ex Parte Crouse* (". . . rights guaranteed to the parent are granted by the grace of the state . . ."), and . . . it became firmly entrenched in the case of *Prince v. Massachusetts* (. . . parents may make martyrs of themselves but they are not free to make martyrs of their children . . .).[4]

The doctrine creates an on-going tension among the three parties involved, especially between parents and state.[5] When should the state step in between parent and child? At one extreme, parents are afforded absolute control; in earlier societies they could kill, maim, and sell their children without having to answer for their actions. Even fairly recently they have been allowed to beat, exploit, and imprison their children with a relatively free hand.[6] At the other extreme, government can and does intervene in disagreements with parents regarding what is best for their children; the danger being the imposition of governmental standards of "proper" upbringing.[7]

Society has never been quite certain how far its authority over children ought to reach. For the most part, parental authority is regarded as sacrosanct; only in recent decades have the interests of the child come to be recognized and championed as distinct from those of the parent and the state, particularly in such areas as juvenile justice, medical treatment, child abuse and neglect, and child advocacy.

The Juvenile Court System

One way the state exercises its control over children is through a special judicial mechanism, the juvenile court (or, in some states, children's court, family court, domestic relations court, or probate court). Some health professionals—especially physicians and social workers—may well, in the course of their professional work, find themselves involved with the juvenile justice system.

Under the common law, an individual achieved adult status at the age of twenty-one; before that, he or she was a minor—an infant, a child, or a juvenile—with reduced legal rights and duties. In most states this age of maturity was later established by statute as twenty-one for males and eighteen for females, but after ratification of the Twenty-sixth Amendment in 1971 gave eighteen-year-olds the right to vote in federal elections, all but a few states lowered the age of majority to eighteen.

However, states often also set varying ages for the exercise of specific rights and privileges. A state where the age of majority is eighteen, for example, may nonetheless prohibit persons under twenty-one from purchasing alcohol. Thus there may be separate and differing age requirements for

> obtaining a drivers license
> marrying without parental consent
> obtaining medical care without parental consent
> curfew
> employment
> juvenile court treatment
> making contracts
> suing and being sued
> supervision by child welfare agencies
> statute of limitations on malpractice and other torts

Perhaps the most important of these age requirements is that which determines whether individuals are subject to the adult or the juvenile justice system. Under early common law, children under seven were deemed incapable of criminal intent. The same presumption was made of children aged seven through fourteen, but in such cases the prosecution could attempt to prove otherwise. After fourteen, young people were subject to the same laws, criminal and civil, as were adults.

During the later half of the 1800s, however, concern over the brutalizing effect of exposing children to the adult criminal-justice process led to a series of reforms that culminated in the creation of special juvenile courts,[8] first in Illinois in 1899 and eventually in all states. The goal was to replace the adversarial, punitive criminal-justice system with one devoted to the care, protection, and education of children. The Illinois Juvenile Court Act of 1899 provided that

> the care, custody, *and discipline* of a child shall approximate as nearly as may be possible that which should be given by its parents, and in all cases where it can properly be done the child be placed in an improved family home and become a member of the family by legal adoption or otherwise.[9]

The current Uniform Juvenile Court Act declares it the purpose of the juvenile court "to provide for the care, protection, and wholesome moral, mental, and physical development of children coming within its provisions . . . consistent with the protection of the public interest to remove, from children committing delinquent acts the taint of criminality and the consequences of criminal behavior and to substitute therefor a program of treatment, training, and rehabilitation."[10] Juvenile courts are therefore considered civil, not criminal, courts.

This system casts the state in the role of benevolent—and interventionist—parent. When a child comes before the juvenile court, the primary question is not whether he or she has committed a particular crime, but rather whether the situation requires the active intervention of the state in his or her behalf. This can have advantages for a young person in trouble, but as with all benevolencies, it includes certain risks.

Specifically, the juvenile justice system has long been criticized for differing in two important ways from the adult criminal-law system. First, children can be brought before the juvenile court not only for committing crimes, but also for so-called status offenses. Such children have not done anything that would constitute a crime if they were adults; they come under court supervision as "children in need of supervision," "incorrigibles," "sexually promiscuous," "delinquent," or "unruly children"[11]—all vague terms incapable of objective disproof.

Second, the juvenile court functions quite differently from an adult criminal court. Because it is supposed to be a decriminalized process, the proceedings are generally informal. In the past, proceedings were often conducted in judges' chambers, eliminating not only the formal trappings of robe, bench, and baliff; but also, in many instances until quite recently, active attorney participation, open confrontation of an accusation, cross-examination of witnesses, protection from self-incrimination, and even a transcript of the proceedings. In short, the child brought before the juvenile court was assured none of the due-process rights that are guaranteed the adult criminal defendant, and their omission was justified as being in the best interest of the child.

As Patrick Murphy, a crusader for reform of that system, has written:

> When a child is convicted of an offense and his removal from society is deemed necessary, he is not imprisoned with a correctional agency but, instead, committed to a Youth Commission or a State Juvenile Correctional Division—where, of course, he may not be punished. He is sent not to a jail but to a training school or camp where he learns from his kindly parent the state how to lead the good life.[12]

These euphemisms are part of the assumption that the juvenile court is looking out for the welfare of the child. Not until 1970 did the U.S. Supreme Court require that the criminal conduct of juveniles, like that of adults, be proved beyond a reasonable doubt.[13]

The juvenile court system is a busy one; every year one million children across the country get into trouble with the law. One out of nine children will pass through a juvenile court before the age of eighteen. Yet it was not until 1967, in the case of *In re Gault,* that the Supreme Court held that juveniles must be afforded some of the procedural rights guaranteed to the adult criminal defendant. These include benefit of counsel (including assigned counsel), timely written notice of charges, the right to confront the accusation and cross-examine witnesses, protection from self-incrimination, and notification that these rights exist.[14] Two years later the Court, in deciding a case involving the free-speech rights of children, declared that "Students in school as well as out of school are 'persons' under our Constitution. They are possessed of fundamental rights which the state must respect."[15]

Yet the Court has not been willing to pursue this logic very far. In fact, a contradictory position can be found in more recent Supreme Court decisions.[16] Children may be "persons" with some rights, but the law still treats them primarily as children—in need of the protection and control of parents and/or state. Nor has the tension between parent and state as to who is most able to represent the child's best interest been noticeably eased. In fact, as the Supreme Court noted in *Kent v. United States,*[17] "there may be grounds for concern that the child receives the worst of both worlds: that he gets neither the protection accorded to adults nor the solicitous care and regenerative treatment postulated for children." Despite the trend of Supreme Court decisions toward use of adult criminal procedure standards, juvenile courts may still make "nondelinquency" or noncriminal determinations, such as whether a child is in need of supervision, based simply on a preponderance of the evidence rather than proof beyond a reasonable doubt.

A leading current concern is how to deal with adolescents who commit serious adult crimes but whose age—in most states below eighteen—places them under the jurisdiction of juvenile court. In several states there is a range, such as the period from sixteen to eighteen years of age, when both juvenile and adult criminal courts have jurisdiction. States differ on how to determine which jurisdiction should apply in individual cases, but the Supreme Court has encouraged leaving the determination to the juvenile court, although there have been strong pressures during the past decade to reduce the age at which the adult criminal court jurisdiction prevails.[18]

Medical Treatment of Children

The United Nations Declaration of the Rights of the Child, adopted in 1959, states:

> The child shall enjoy the benefits of social security. He shall be entitled to grow and develop in health; to this end special care and protection shall be provided both to him and to his mother, including adequate pre-natal and post-natal care. The child shall have the right to adequate nutrition, housing, recreation and medical services.[19]

This is, of course, merely a statement of what should be, not what must be.[20] Transforming a declared right to adequate health care for children into an enforceable right requires statutory action, and unfortunately, many child health programs enacted into law—notably Early and Periodic Screening, Diagnosis, and Treatment (EPSDT)—have provided much less than their original promise. A 1976 Brookings Institution study concluded that the only federal children's programs that have been justified and administered adequately are certain categorical grants to children with obvious physical and mental needs.[21] Cuts in social programs under the current federal administration make this picture even more dismal.

Perhaps more significant than any "right" to health care for children are the various government measures that have special impact on the health of children. As explained in Chapter 5, state governments have authority to require immunization, newborn and school health-screening, flouridation of drinking water, and communicable-disease reporting—all of which are important components of children's health.

In many states the definition of parental neglect of children includes the failure to provide proper medical care.[22] The parental role in medical diagnosis and treatment is crucial, because under the traditional common law rule minors are incompetent to authorize their own care and treatment, making parental consent a necessary precondition of most medical care. Without such consent, treatment of a minor—even with his or her own consent—could constitute assault and battery, and the treating professional could become liable to the parents for damages.

The legal incompetency of minors in this regard is part of the general attempt to fit children into the legal framework. Children are in the process of developing the judgment and wisdom to take on adult responsibilities. Until they acquire these capacities, society does not hold them to the same rules as adults. For many—although not all—purposes, legal responsibility is related to the age of majority—an arbitrary age, fixed by state statute, at which an individual legally becomes an adult. Until the past decades, the age of majority in most states was twenty-one; today it is generally eighteen. Medical treatment illustrates the utility and the drawbacks of such an arbitrary point.

Most twenty-five-year-olds are able to decide for themselves whether or not to undergo a recommended appendectomy; most four-year-olds are not. But the age in between at which that capacity develops differs from one individual to another. Some sixteen-year-olds, for example, are mature and responsible; some twenty-year-olds are not. For the practitioner, however, this poses a serious problem. The surgeon who plans to operate on a four-year-old will automatically ask for parental consent. But what about a seventeen-year-old? If the surgeon judges that the young person is able to decide responsibly, and proceeds without consulting the parents, should society allow them to recover damages? The age of majority provides some certainty for the treating professional. Yet strict adherence to the traditional parental consent rule would create problems for great numbers of young people in need of health care. The law's response has been to keep the basic rule that parents (or legal guardians) must consent to treatment for a minor, but to allow four major categories of exceptions.[23] Two relate to the minor's status and two to the type of treatment involved.

Emancipated minors.   Since the purpose of a fixed age of majority is to establish an objective level of certainty, the law will allow exceptions if other objective factors can be relied upon. One such exception applies to minors who are effectively emancipated from their parents—that is, they do not live with them; they are not financially dependent on them; and, in most cases, the parents have agreed to the independent status. Marriage, military service, judicial decision, parental consent, and the failure of parents to meet their legal responsibilities result in their offspring's emancipation. College students, even though they may be financially dependent on their parents, are also generally considered emancipated. And runaways who refuse to identify their parents are emancipated in a de facto way.[24] Emancipated minors can authorize their own treatment without the practitioner incurring liability to the parents.[25]

Mature minors.   Under an exception known as the mature-minor rule, courts have also accepted a minor's own authorization of treatment when three conditions are met:

1. The minor is near the age of majority and appears fully to understand the nature and importance of the proposed treatment.
2. The treatment is for the minor's own benefit.
3. The treatment does not pose any serious hazard and can be justified as necessary by conservative medical opinion (as evidenced, for example, through a consultation).

Although there is no specific age limit for the mature-minor rule, Holder reports, "No decision can be located within the past 20 years in which a parent recovered damages . . . for treatment of a child over the age of 15 without parental consent."[26] Unlike the exception for emancipated minors, whose objective status, such as marriage, establishes their independence, the mature-minor rule requires a subjective judgment on the part of the practitioner that the minor's consent alone is adequate. It is important, therefore, that the practitioner in such cases document the basis for accepting such authorization.

Emergency care.   In the face of a genuine emergency, the requirement of parental consent is generally waived; but determining whether an emergency exists is often a subjective judgment, and the practitioner could, theoretically, be second-guessed by a court if the parents challenge the necessity of the care. However, since there is an obvious societal interest in having emergencies dealt with promptly, courts are likely to be liberal in construing emergency. The test is generally whether it was reasonably feasible to obtain parental consent without endangering the minor's health.

Minor treatment statutes.   Another category of exceptions is also based on the type of treatment involved. There are state statutes specifically dispensing with parental consent in instances where: (a) minors may forego treatment because they do not want their parents to know about the necessity for such treatments; (b) the effects of nontreatment can be severe, both for the individual and for society; and (c) the medical problem is widespread. Venereal and other communicable diseases, birth control, pregnancy, abortion, and alcohol and drug abuse are examples that meet these criteria.[27]

State statutes may also specify a basis for emergency consent by minors. And, as Holder notes, "Many statutes also provide that a minor who is a parent may consent to medical treatment of his own child without the consent of his parents, but this right also should be assumed to exist in all states, with or without a special statute."[28] In all such instances the legislature is seeking to assure that treatment can be obtained when needed. Obviously the careful practitioner would do well to become familiar with the relevant minor-treatment statutes.

Goldstein, Freud, and Solnit argue that absent refusal by the minor himself:

> Refusal by parents to authorize medical care when (1) medical experts agree that treatment is nonexperimental and appropriate for the child, and (2) denial of that treatment would result in death, and (3) the anticipated result of treatment is what society would want for every child—a chance for normal healthy growth or a life worth living—should be a ground for intervention.[29]

The courts have generally agreed with this perspective. But a significantly more difficult problem arises when a healthy life is not possible, especially where newborns suffer from major birth defects (often of a lethal nature). Nontreatment decisions are commonly made in such situations. Although ethical controversy exists, the courts have rarely been involved in this area and there is therefore little case law. As John Robertson points out:

> In recent years the courts have occasionally reviewed these decisions when doctors who have disagreed with parents' refusal to treat or agreed but feared legal liability have sought guidance on the legality through custody and guardianship proceedings. While these cases have rarely gone beyond the trial court level, they almost uniformly result in decisions requiring treatment, thus making clear the existence of a legal duty to treat the child.[30]

Technically, ignoring this duty can lead to criminal and civil liability for those involved—parents and health professionals. But this very rarely occurs.[31] All in all, this important legal and ethical problem area has been poorly dealt with.[32]

Another difficult problem arises when a minor—at least a minor old enough to understand what is happening—refuses recommended medical treatment. Even when the parents join in the refusal, many courts have intervened to authorize life-saving treatment when petitioned to do so by a hospital, physician, or social agency. When parents do provide consent in the face of a minor's refusal, much depends on the minor's age: The older the patient is, the more likely it is that his or her refusal will be adequate to block treatment. Holder suggests a young child probably has no legal right to refuse, but that it is extremely risky to treat a teenager under such conditions. She suggests as "not at all unlikely" the emergence of a new type of lawsuit, in which a minor who unsuccessfully refused treatment brings an assualt and battery action against the practitioner after reaching majority.[33] Under the mature-minor rule, as Annas et al. point out, "if you can understand the risks you can consent to them."[34] The same right would seem to apply for refusal of treatment.

The most difficult area in this regard involves mental treatment. The Supreme Court has ruled, in 1979, that due process does not require notice and hearing when parents seek to commit their child to a state mental care facility. Chief Justice Burger, speaking for the Court, wrote:

> Simply because the decision of a parent is not agreeable to a child or because it involves risks does not automatically transfer the power to make that decision from the parents to some agency or officer of the state. The same characterizations can be made for a tonsillectomy, appendectomy or other medical procedure. Most children, even in adolescence, simply are not able to make sound judgments concerning many decisions, including their need for medical care or treatment. Parents can and must make those judgments.[35]

The special implications of consent to treatment by and for minors with respect to experimental therapies and family planning are discussed in Chapters 15 and 18.

Special Protection for Children

The main rationale for state intervention in behalf of a child (and against the child's parents) is that "children have a special right to the protection of the state by reason of their dependency."[36] This is the basis for a wide variety of interventions, including authority over familyless children (custody, foster care, adoption), public health measures, parental requests for assistance, and child-abuse and neglect laws.

Under the early common law, children were simply chattel of their parents and owed them strict obedience. State intrusion into the parent-child relationship, when it occurred, would take place in support of the parent.[37] The move toward state intervention on the part of children in the United States did not come until the end of the nineteenth century. In a landmark episode in 1874, a small child, Mary Ellen, was discovered by a church worker, seriously ill, beaten, having been kept chained to a bed and fed only bread and water, yet there was no established legal basis on which some agency of government could intervene in her behalf. Eventually it was the American Society for the Prevention of Cruelty to Animals that succeeded in having Mary Ellen "removed from her parents on the ground that she was a member of the animal kingdom and that therefore her case could be included under the laws against animal cruelty."[38]

Even today, not all physical mistreatment of children is illegal; the government itself may, under certain conditions, be involved in the corporal punishment of children. This may be part of the reason why child abuse and neglect only recently has been recognized as the serious social problem it is.

Under *parens patriae* the authority of the individual states to intervene on the part of an abused and neglected child is clear, and such intervention can take many forms, most of which involve proceedings in juvenile court. The most extreme step is to remove the child from the custody of parents (or other caretakers), and to authorize state social service agencies to arrange for institutional or foster care. Less drastic measures can include psychological and educational programs for the parents, homemaker services, regular home visits by social workers, and the like.

All of these steps, however, require some mechanism to bring such children under the state's protection. The child-abuse reporting acts passed by most states during the past decade and a half represent just such a mechanism. These laws contain no provisions for punishing abusive parents; their sole purpose is intervention in aid of the child. Nevertheless, there is an ongoing, and perhaps insoluble, debate regarding child-abuse intervention, which reflects the classic parent-state tension. On one side are those who favor aggressive state intervention in behalf of the child; on the other are those who consider such intervention dangerous to family autonomy and integrity.[39] Markham describes aggressive intervention as the medicolegal model and family autonomy as the privacy model. She notes:

> The privacy model is expounded largely by those who deal with the court aspects of child protection. Lawyers who specialize in juvenile law and parent defense have martialed the privacy attack through legal teaching, writings,

and the courts. By contrast, the campaign for greater intervention has been led largely by physicians, lawyers, and social workers who are involved in the day to day treatment and observations of disturbed families. Ironically, the juvenile justice advocates emerge as the most vociferous proponents of "parents' rights" while the family-oriented professionals most strongly advocate a policy of "children's rights."[40]

Child-abuse reporting laws generally contain a series of definitions. "Child" may be defined as any person under eighteen (or some younger age). "Abuse" was at one time defined simply as a nonaccidental injury; today the term carries a much broader meaning and, although statutory definitions vary, "all are a combination of two or more of the following elements: a non-accidental physical injury; sexual molestation; emotional abuse or mental injury; and neglect."[41] "Neglect" may include such elements as failure to provide proper and necessary support, education, medical, or other remedial care; abandonment; or subjecting a child to an environment injurious to the child's welfare.

The trend in recent years has been to expand the coverage of reporting laws, both by specifically adding neglect, sexual abuse, and mental injury to the definition of abuse and by leaving these terms undefined, and therefore broad. This trend, criticized by those who favor the privacy model, is consistent with increased state intervention in behalf of the child.[42]

Reporting laws generally specify who is to report, as well as when, how, and to whom reports are to be made. Federally sponsored model state child-abuse reporting legislation includes among those required to report "any physician, intern, hospital personnel engaged in the admission, examination, care, or treatment of persons, nurse, osteopath, chiropractor, podiatrist, medical examiner or coroner, dentist, optometrist, or any other medical or mental health professional, Christian Science practitioner, religious healer, school teacher or other school official or pupil personnel, social service worker, day-care worker or other child care or foster care worker, or any peace officer or law enforcement official [who] has reasonable cause to suspect" abuse.[43] Twenty states go even further and mandate reports from anyone with knowledge or suspicion of such abuse; in the other states, reports by neighbors, relatives, and friends will be accepted, although with a low investigatory priority, but are not specifically mandated. (About half of all reports do, in fact, come from concerned private citizens.)[44] To encourage reporting, most states also allow for anonymous reports. But it is only the professional mandated to report who must be concerned with the penalty provisions and possible civil liability discussed below.

Reports must be made whenever the professional *suspects or believes* that a child has been abused; it is not required that the reporter *know* abuse has occurred.[45] Generally such a report is to be made "immediately" or "promptly" by phone, with a written report to follow in one to seven days. Many states have established twenty-four-hour reporting hotlines. The report usually must contain, if known, the names and addresses of the child and of his or her parents or other persons having custody; the nature and extent of any injuries; information on previous injuries and/or neglect; and "any other information that the person making the report believes may be helpful in establishing the cause of the injury . . . and protecting the child."

Most often the report must be made to a state social service agency, such as the Department of Social Services or Department of Children and Family Services, which is authorized by the reporting statute to investigate the situation.[46] If that investigation confirms serious abuse, the agency either will arrange with the parents for some kind of mutually acceptable voluntary intervention, to be monitored by an agency caseworker, or will go before the juvenile court to request involuntary protective action, to be implemented and monitored by the court. The latter may include, but is not limited to, removal from parental custody.[47]

As Brian Fraser, executive director of the National Committee for Prevention of Child Abuse, has pointed out, dealing with child abuse requires background in medical pathology, psychiatry, social work, and the law:

> It is unrealistic to expect any one individual to have substantive expertise in all of these areas. In almost all states and state delivery systems, however, there is a presumption that there is one individual who has all of this expertise. In most states it is an individual social worker who must resolve the issues of diagnosis, prognosis and treatment once the investigation has been completed.[48]

To overcome this unrealistic approach, some state statutes have mandated the creation of multidisciplinary child protection teams, organized on a community, district, regional, or statewide level.

Many potential reporters are afraid that filing a child-abuse report will make them vulnerable to suits for libel, slander, or invasion of privacy, but the fear is groundless; both the common law and the courts favor good-faith reporting of this kind, and there is no record of a U.S. court finding a reporter liable in such situations. To provide additional reassurance, however, all state child-abuse reporting laws contain an explicit grant of immunity from any liability for good-faith reporting by persons, institutions, and agencies. Many, but not all, states also explicitly provide that communications that may be privileged under other laws, such as those between physician and patient, social worker and client, or even husband and wife, lose that privilege in situations where child-abuse reports are called for.[49]

These assurances—and the basic humanitarian concerns of the potential reporter—are relied upon to make the reporting system work. Some state laws do not even include penalties for failure to report; where such provisions do exist, they are mild, and according to the National Center on Child Abuse and Neglect, "there are no reported cases of a criminal prosecution for failure to report an abused or neglected child."[50]

There are those who feel there should be penalties for nonreporting. Douglas Besharov, first director of the National Center on Child Abuse and Neglect, notes:

> Penalty clauses tend to assist mandated reporters in working with parents by making it easier to explain to parents why a report must be made. In addition, experience shows that a penalty clause is invaluable to staff members of agencies and institutions who often must persuade their superiors of the necessity of making a report.[51]

A somewhat different approach is to tie the reporting requirement to state health professional practice acts. For example, a recently enacted Illinois statute provides for the refusal to issue or renew or for the suspension or revocation of licenses to practice dentistry, medicine, nursing, podiatry, psychology, or social work for "willfully failing to report an instance of suspected child abuse or neglect" as required by law.[52]

In the mid-1970s a different type of enforcement emerged: the penalty of civil liability. Two lawsuits were brought against health care professionals and institutions in California in behalf of children who had been severely abused and permanetly injured. In both cases it was argued that the defendants had negligently failed at the time of earlier emergency room visits to report allegedly obvious instances of abuse, and that had such reports been made, the state's protective mechanisms would have prevented the subsequent more serious abuse. Under the common law, the violation of any statutory duty such as mandatory child abuse reporting requirements automatically constitutes negligence. Thus, all that needed be proven to establish liability was the existence of symptoms of abuse that were not reported. In one of the two cases there was an out-of-court settlement of over half a million dollars; in the other, the California Supreme Court decided that a valid legal cause of action had been stated.[53]

The impact was widespread; coming at a time of a nationwide malpractice litigation "crisis," the two cases strongly suggested that there was far greater risk in not reporting suspected abuse than in doing so. The two lawsuits also supported an approach favored by many lawyers: using civil liability to enforce social responsibility where direct penalties either do not exist or do not work. Whether the California lawsuits fostered more rigorous reporting is impossible to tell; certainly many thought other such lawsuits would follow, although this has not come to pass.

About one-third of state reporting laws also provide authority for medical examination of a possibly abused child, including X-rays and color photographs, without the permission of—and even in the face of clear refusal of permission by—the parents. Many states also give law enforcement officials, child protection agencies, and physicians in hospitals the power to take protective custody of a child for a limited period of time (generally ranging from twenty-four to seventy-two hours) if an imminent danger to his or her life or health is reasonably believed to exist, without incurring any liability from such action. This is, of course, an emergency measure and must be reviewed by a court as soon as possible. Some states permit such protective custody only if there is no time to apply for court intervention. The time limit, which protects the rights of the parents, gives the state social service agency little time to investigate the situation and prepare evidence before taking the matter to court. Since the state must prove that the child's home is a dangerous and inadequate environment in order to retain custody, some children could be returned to abusive parents because of an incomplete investigation, rather than a ruling on the full facts.

Most reporting laws establish a statewide registry of reports. This can be a useful resource in cases where a child's symptoms suggest the possibility of abuse but are not conclusive; past reports of suspicions regarding the same child at least suggest the need for further investigation (to be effective the registry must include reports of suspected as well as proven cases of abuse). But many registries are so underfunded that their records are unreliable and little used. Another problem concerns privacy and confidentiality—whether efforts are made to verify and update information in the registry and who has access to the information. Besharov explains that

> the necessity of storing this information should not forestall efforts to prevent its misuse. . . . All of the civil libertarian criticisms of central registries, except for the one based on a fear of data banks in general, can be met by intelligent planning.
>
> Yet, in most states, the subjects of reports are not informed that their names have been entered in the central register; they are not permitted to see the file that alleges derogatory things about them; they cannot have removed from the register charges that have proven to be untrue or unfounded; and they have no right to appeal to a higher administrative authority. Often, there is no provision to ensure the security or confidentiality of the data collected, although the state eligibility requirements of the Federal Act have begun to change this. . . .
>
> In general, states take three approaches to access to records. Some statutes prohibit access to anyone outside the child protective agency; others make the records confidential, but authorize the responsible state agency to

issue regulations allowing some persons access; and others enumerate who has access in the statute itself.[54]

Finally, most states provide that a *guardian ad litem* be appointed whenever a child comes before the juvenile court as the result of a suspected abuse report. This is a person, who may or may not be a lawyer, appointed by a court to represent only the child's interest (and not the parents' or the state's) in any suit to which he or she may be a party. The *guardian ad litem* has no standing or authority with regard to the child aside from the particular court proceeding.[55]

The federal government took a major step into the child-abuse area with passage of the Child Abuse Prevention and Treatment Act of 1974. The act provided funds to the states for the identification, treatment, and prevention of child abuse. To be eligible for such funds, a state must:

1. Have in effect a child abuse and neglect law that provides legal immunity for persons who report.
2. Provide for the reporting of known and suspected child abuse.
3. Provide that upon receipt of a report of known or suspected child abuse an investigation must be made promptly and, if there is a finding of child abuse, immediate steps must be taken to protect the health and welfare of the abused or neglected child or any other child in the same house.
4. Demonstrate that there are in effect administrative procedures, trained personnel, training procedures, institutional and other facilities, and multidisciplinary programs and services sufficient to assure that the state can deal effectively and efficiently with child abuse.
5. Preserve the confidentiality of all records.
6. Provide for the cooperation among law enforcement officials, courts of competent jurisdiction, and appropriate state agencies providing human services.
7. Ensure that in every case of child abuse that results in a judicial proceeding a *guardian ad litem* is appointed to represent the child.
8. Provide that the aggregate of state support for programs or projects related to child abuse are not reduced below the level provided during the fiscal year 1973.
9. Provide for dissemination of information to the public on the problem of child abuse and the facilities and prevention and treatment methods available to combat it.
10. To the extent feasible, ensure that parental organizations combating child abuse and neglect receive preferential treatment.[56]

The federal law prompted the states to amend their child abuse laws, placing greater emphasis on treatment and prevention. Improved state laws and the availability of federal moneys and guidelines have strengthened efforts to combat child abuse in most states;[57] but significant problems remain. The biggest is a shortage of resources: There are simply not enough treatment programs for child and family; many child-protective workers are undertrained and overworked; and prevention—possibly the most promising avenue in this area—is often totally absent. Laws can establish reporting mechanisms and can give juvenile courts the authority to intervene in the parent-child relationship. But these mechanism do little good without the necessary follow-up. Fraser suggests that the resources needed for this purpose can never be adequate and argues that "it is too costly to continue to react after the fact. The new focal point must be a commitment to primary prevention."[58]

Such a shift in focus runs contrary to the current legal approach, which rejects prediction. As Newberger and Bourne explain:

> Attorneys are proudly unwilling to accept conclusions or impressions lacking empirical corroboration. To lawyers, the law and legal institutions become involved in child abuse when certain facts fit a standard of review. To clinicians, the law may be seen as an instrument to achieve a particular therapeutic or dispositional objective (e.g., the triggering of services or of social welfare involvement) even if, as is often the case, the data to support such objectives legally are missing or ambiguous. The clinician's approach to the abuse issue is frequently subjective or intuitive (e.g., a *feeling* that a family is under stress or needs help, or that a child is "at risk"), while the lawyer demands evidence.[59]

Thus, for example, it is up to the state to prove that a child's home is inadequate (although in many states, once this is done, parents must prove it is safe for the child to return).[60] Also, while the health professional may view the matter solely in terms of the child, the juvenile court cannot ignore the jeopardy faced by the parents, who stand not only to lose custody or have their parental rights terminated, but to face separate criminal prosecution in addition to the noncriminal juvenile proceeding. At the same time, most lawyers continue to view involuntary intervention as a last resort.[61] Thus while both legislatures and courts have become increasingly sophisticated regarding child abuse, many problems remain that are unlikely to be resolved quickly.

Advocacy

Children face social and health problems other than abuse and neglect. One approach to dealing with a wide range of such problems is child advocacy, which has been defined as "intervention on behalf of children in relation to those services and institutions that impinge on their lives."[62] Advocacy, which first emerged in the late 1960s, is primarily a strategy. Knitzer explains:

> Child advocacy is a helping strategy, but it is different from traditional helping strategies. How is it different? The intervention is not directed to the child and his family (for example, as in hands-on pediatric care, psychotherapy, or tutoring). Rather, a main target of intervention is the institutional barriers that prevent individuals from getting the help that they need. It is directed at structural and social factors, administrative procedures, statutory constraints, budgetary restrictions, and the denial of due process for children.[63]

Knitzer distinguishes between case advocacy "on behalf of individual children" and class advocacy "on behalf of groups of vulnerable children." The latter involves efforts to bring about legislative and administrative changes, the monitoring of existing programs and agencies, and class-action litigation.

The child advocate concerned with health care for children must not only understand the health care delivery system and the health needs of children, but must also have legal, political, and communications skills as well. Child advocate groups, such as the Children's Defense Fund, have concerned themselves with such issues as medical care decision making for children and the expansion and monitoring of government health entitlement programs.

> There is a vital role for health professionals in working with advocacy groups, the groups that function independently of agencies and organizations: consumer groups, special children's councils, citizen's investigating and monitoring groups, and interested legislators and their committees. All these people need information about where the system breaks down. Professionals know where the system breaks down. They know where the skeletons are. They know where children are abandoned by service systems, and what the consequences are. They can share their information.[64]

Conclusion

During the past decade there has been increasing recognition of law as a useful tool in protecting the health and well-being of children. But little has happened to alter the long-standing conflict between state intervention and family autonomy, each claiming the mantle of the best interest of the child. As three of the leading analysts of this problem area have observed:

> We have been constantly aware of a pressure within us to use the legal system to meet every situation in which a child needs help. We had to remind ourselves that neither law, nor medicine, nor science has magical powers and that there is no societal consensus about what is "best" or even "good" for all children.[65]

NOTES

1. *Parham v. J. R.*, 442 U.S. 584 (1979).
2. United Nations Declaration of the Rights of Children, General Assembly Resolution 1386 (XIV), November 20, 1959, published in the *Official Records of the General Assembly, Fourteenth Session, Supplement No. 16*, 1960, p. 19.
3. At one time, parental authority was enforced with a vengeance. For example the Stubborn Child Act of the Massachusetts Bay Colony, echoing biblical injunctions, prescribed the penalty of death for older children who cursed or struck their parents. More recent "child in need of supervision" laws provide similar, albeit less severe, legal support for parental discipline. See John P. Wilson, *The Rights of Adolescents in the Mental Health System* (Lexington, Mass.: Lexington Books, 1978), pp. 16–20.
4. Brian G. Fraser, "The Child and His Parents: A Delicate Balance of Rights," in Ray E. Helfer and C. Henry Kempe, *Child Abuse and Neglect: The Family and the Community* (Cambridge, Mass.: Ballinger, 1976), p. 326. Frazer goes on to explain that "although the doctrine was roundly criticized in the *In Re Gault* case as a vehicle used to deny due process in juvenile delinquency cases ('. . . its meaning is murky and its historical credentials of dubious relevance . . .'), this was revived a year later by the same court in the case of *Ginzberg vs. the United States.*"
5. See Andrew Jay Kleinfeld, "The Balance of Power among Infants, Their Parents and the State,"*Family Law Quarterly*, part I, 4:319 (1970); part II, 4:409 (1970); and part III, 5:63 (1971). All three parts are reprinted in Sanford N. Katz, ed., *The Legal Rights of Children* (New York: Arno Press, 1974).
6. See Donald N. Bersoff, "Child Advocacy: The Next Step," *New York University Education Quarterly* 7(3):10–17 (Spring 1976).
7. Perhaps the most notorious current example of governmental definition of "proper" upbringing involves a Chicago juvenile court's denial of custody to the parents of a twelve-year-old Soviet citizen, Walter Polovchak, solely because they planned to return with him to their native country. Custody battles based on parental life-style, such as vegetarian diet, are not unheard of.
8. See generally, S. J. Fox, "Juvenile Justice Reform: An Historical Perspective," *Stanford Law Review* 22:1187–1239 (June 1970); Frank A. Orlando and Jerry P. Black, "The Juvenile Court," in Nicholas Hobbs, ed., *Issues in the Classification of Children*, vol. 1 (San Francisco: Jossey-Bass, 1975), pp. 349–376; Patricia M. Wald, "Introduction to the Juvenile Justice Process: The Rights of Children and the Rites of Passage," in Diane H. Schetky and Elissa P. Benedek, eds., *Child Psychiatry and the Law* (New York: Brunner/Mazel, 1980), pp. 9–20; and Peter S. Prescott, *The Child Savers: Juvenile Justice Observed* (New York: Knopf, 1981).
9. Emphasis added.
10. *Uniform Laws Annotated: Matrimonial, Family and Health Laws*, vol. 9A (St. Paul: West, 1979), p. 5.
11. See Alan N. Sussman, *The Rights of Young People* (New York: Avon, 1977), pp. 55–56.

12. Patrick T. Murphy, *Our Kindly Parent—the State: The Juvenile Justice System and How It Works* (New York: Viking Press, 1974), p. 5.

13. *In re Winship*, 397 U.S. 358 (1970).

14. *In re Gault*, 387 U.S. 1 (1967). The *Gault* decision did not include transcript of the hearing, statement of grounds for a decision, appeal, Miranda warning, exclusionary rule, or jury trial. Two other differences from adult criminal practice—both of which are supposed to aid the juvenile—are exclusion of the press and public from many juvenile courts and confidentiality of juvenile court records. See Sussman, *The Rights of Young People*, pp. 100, 108–112.

15. *Tinker v. Des Moines Independent School District*, 393 U.S. 503 (1969).

16. For example, *Goss v. Lopez*, 419 U.S. 565 (1975), providing due-process rights—but limited ones—to students facing school suspensions. Also note *Baker v. Owen*, 395 F. Supp. 294 (M.D.N.C. 1975), *affirmed* 423 U.S. 907 (1975), upholding constitutionality of school corporal punishment regardless of parental objections.

17. 383 U.S. 541 (1966).

18. See Sussman, *The Rights of Young People*, pp. 88–89. Health professionals directly involved in the criminal justice process—for example, the physician examing detained juveniles or the social worker doing a social investigation—must be alert to the legal status of juveniles with whom they have contact. See Angela Roddey Holder, *Legal Issues in Pediatrics and Adolescent Medicine* (New York: John Wiley, 1977), chap. 8, especially pp. 228–232.

19. See note 2.

20. As one commentator has put it: "A legal right is an enforceable claim to the possession of property or authority, or to the employment of privileges or immunities. In the field of children's rights, we are not dealing primarily with existing legal rights but with children's needs and interests and attempts to transform these into enforceable rights." Hillary Rodham, "Children's Rights: A Legal Perspective," in Patricia A. Vardin and Ilene N. Brody, eds., *Children's Rights: Contemporary Perspectives* (New York: Teachers College Press, 1979), p. 21.

21. See Gilbert V. Steiner and Pauline H. Milius, *The Children's Cause* (Washington, D.C.: Brookings Institution, 1976).

22. See Robert Bennett, "Allocation of Child Medical Decisionmaking Authority," in Harvard Child Health Project Task Force, *Developing a Better Health Care System for Children* (Cambridge, Mass.: Ballinger, 1977), p. 241.

23. In instances where only one parent is available or if the parents disagree, it is generally the parent with actual custody of the minor who prevails. See Holder, *Legal Issues*, pp. 137–138. On the age of majority, see Wilson, *The Rights of Adolescents*, pp. 20–23. On consent to treatment by minors, generally, see Rowine Hayes Brown and Richard B. Truitt, "The Rights of Minors to Medical Treatment," *DePaul Law Review* 28:289–320 (1979); Arnold J. Rosoff, *Informed Consent* (Rockville, Md.: Aspen Systems Corporation, 1981), chap. 4; Wilson, *The Rights of Adolescents*, chap. 4; George J. Annas, Leonard H. Glantz, and Barbara F. Katz, *Informed Consent to Human Experimentation: The Subject's Dilemma* (Cambridge, Mass.: Ballinger, 1977), pp. 64–75; Holder, *Legal Issues*, chap. 5; George J. Annas, Leonard H. Glantz, and Barbara F.

Katz, *The Rights of Doctors, Nurses, and Allied Health Professionals: A Health Law Primer* (New York: Avon, 1981), pp. 91–95.

24. It is crucial that the runaway's refusal to identify parents be documented in the record.

25. Holder, *Legal Issues*, pp. 139–141; Annas, Glantz, and Katz, *Informed Consent*, pp. 70–71.

26. Holder, *Legal Issues*, p. 145; also Annas, Glantz, and Katz, *A Health Law Primer*, pp. 92–93.

27. Some states, such as Illinois, allow pregnant minors to give their own consent to all types of care, whether related to the pregnancy or not. Thus pregnancy becomes another type of emancipation. Some minor treatment statutes are very broad; "Alabama, for example, permits any minor who is fourteen or older to give effective consent to medical, dental, or mental health services. . . ." Wilson, *The Rights of Adolescents*, p. 129.

28. Holder, *Legal Issues*, p. 141. Ironically, however, this does not necessarily mean that the minor who is a parent will be emancipated and able to consent to his or her own care.

29. Joseph Goldstein, Anna Freud, and Albert J. Solnit, *Before the Best Interests of the Child* (New York: Free Press, 1979), p. 91. Limiting such intervention to situations in which *death* will result seems unduly narrow.

30. John A. Robertson, "Dilemma in Danville," *Hastings Center Report* 11(5):5–8 (October 1981).

31. Most recently with the case of Siamese twins in Danville, Illinois. See ibid. However, Robertson feels that "additional prosecutions, though infrequent, could occur."

32. See Raymond S. Duff, "Counseling Families Deciding Care of Severely Defective Children: A Way of Coping with 'Medical Vietnam,'" *Pediatrics* 67:315–320 (1981); Norman Fost, "Counseling Families Who Have a Child with a Severe Congenital Anomaly," *Pediatrics* 67:321–324 (1981); Anthony Shaw, "Dilemmas of 'Informed Consent' in Children," *New England Journal of Medicine* 289:885–890 (1973); William G. Bartholome, "Proxy Consent in the Medical Context: The Infant as Person," *Appendix to Report and Recommendations: Research Involving Children* (Washington, D.C.: National Commission for the Protection of Human Subjects of Biomedical and Behavioral Research, 1977), pp. 3-23 to 3-54 (DHEW pub. no. (OS) 77-0005); Raymond Duff and A. G. M. Campbell, "Moral and Ethical Dilemmas in the Special-Care Nursery," *New England Journal of Medicine* 289:890 (1973); John Robertson and Norman Fost, "Passive Euthanasia of Defective Newborns: Legal Considerations," *Journal of Pediatrics* 88:833 (1976); John Robertson, "Involuntary Euthanasia of Defective Newborns: A Legal Analysis," *Stanford Law Review* 27:213 (1975); Robert A. Burt, *Taking Care of Strangers: The Rule of Law in Doctor-Patient Relations* (New York: Free Press, 1979).

33. Holder *Legal Issues*, pp. 151–157.

34. Annas, Glantz, and Katz, *Informed Consent*, p. 72.

35. *Parham v. J. R.* (see note 1).

36. This specific theme is discussed in Bernard J. Coughlin, "The Rights of Children," in Albert E. Wilkerson, *The Rights of Children: Emergent Concepts in Law and Society* (Philadelphia: Temple University Press, 1973), pp. 7–23,

quoted at p. 7. This protection can mean very different things. For example, compare Richard Farson, *Birthrights* (New York: Macmillan, 1974) and Richard Farson, "The Children's Rights Movement," in LaMar T. Empey, ed., *The Future of Childhood and Juvenile Justice* (Charlottesville: University of Virginia Press, 1979), pp. 35–65, with the widely noted essay by Judge Lindsay G. Arthur, "Should Children Be As Equal As People?," *North Dakota Law Review* 45:204–221 (1969). ("Should children be as equal as people? Certainly not. They should not have equal liberty: they should have less. Neither should they have equal protection—they should have more.") Also see Henry H. Foster, Jr., *A "Bill of Rights" for Children* (Springfield, Ill.: Charles C. Thomas, 1974).

37. See note 3.

38. D. P. Wilcox, "Child Abuse Laws: Past, Present, and Future," *Journal of Forensic Science* 21:71–75 (1976), at p. 72, citing Ray E. Helfer and C. Henry Kempe, eds., *The Battered Child* (Chicago: University of Chicago Press, 1968), p. 13. On the history of child abuse and child abuse laws, also see Stephen J. Pfahl, "The 'Discovery' of Child Abuse," in Joanne V. Cook and Roy T. Bowles, eds., *Child Abuse: Commission and Omission* (Toronto: Buttersworth, 1980), pp. 323–329, and Samuel X. Radbil, "Children in a World of Violence: A History of Child Abuse," in C. Henry Kempe and Ray E. Helfer, eds., *The Battered Child*, 3d ed. (Chicago: University of Chicago Press, 1980), pp. 3–20.

39. See Barbara A. Caulfield, "Legal Questions Raised by Privacy of Families and Treatment of Child Abuse and Neglect," *Child Abuse and Neglect* 1:159–166 (1977).

40. Barbara Markham, "Child Abuse Intervention: Conflicts in Current Practice and Legal Theory," *Pediatrics* 65:180–185 (January 1980). Similar debates revolve around punish versus nurture, civil versus criminal, and social workers versus police.

41. Brian G. Fraser, "A Glance at the Past, A Gaze at the Present, a Glimpse at the Future: A Critical Analysis of the Development of Child Abuse Reporting Statutes," *Chicago-Kent Law Review* 54:641–686 (1978), at p. 643.

42. The Federal Child Abuse Prevention and Treatment Act of 1974, U.S.C. Secs. 5101–5106, required qualifying states to provide for the reporting of neglect as well as abuse. Child abuse and neglect is defined in the act as "physical or mental injury, sexual abuse, negligent treatment, or maltreatment. . . ." According to Douglas J. Besharov, "The Legal Aspects of Reporting Known and Suspected Child Abuse and Neglect," *Villanova Law Review* 23:458–520 (1978), at p. 472–473, sexual abuse reporting is required in thirty-nine states, while reporting of emotional abuse and neglect ("mental injury") is required in at least thirty states. Also see Joseph J. Costa and Gordon K. Nelson, *Child Abuse and Neglect: Legislation, Reporting, and Prevention* (Lexington, Mass.: Lexington Books, 1978). Densen-Gerber and Hutchinson have called attention to the special area of "exploitative abuse." See Judianne Densen-Gerber and S. F. Hutchinson, "Medical-Legal and Societal Problems Involving Children—Child Prostitution, Child Pornography and Drug-Related Abuse; Recommended Legislation," in Selwyn M. Smith, *The Maltreatment of Children* (Baltimore: University Park Press, 1978).

An overview of reporting legislation can be found in Vincent J. Fontana and Douglas J. Besharov, *The Maltreated Child: The Maltreatment Syndrome in Children—A Medical, Legal and Social Guide* (Springfield, Ill.: Charles C. Thomas, 1979), chap. 8.

43. 42 U.S.C. Sec. 5103(6)(2); regulations at 45 C.F.R. Sec. 1340.3-3. Also see Costa and Nelson, *Child Abuse and Neglect*, p. 23.

44. Douglas J. Besharov reports that "private citizens—friends, neighbors, and relatives—though not subject to a mandatory reporting law in 30 states, make about 50% of the nation's reports." Besharov, "What Physicians Should Know about Child Abuse Reporting Laws," in Norman S. Ellerstein, ed., *Child Abuse and Neglect: A Medical Reference* (New York: John Wiley, 1981), p. 26.

45. The terms used include "cause to believe," "reasonable cause to suspect," and "reasonable cause to know or suspect."

46. Early reporting statutes often identified police departments as the agency to receive reports. And some critics argue that the juvenile court should receive the reports. But social and child welfare agencies are currently most likely to be identified by statute as the recipient of reports and the instigator of follow-up investigation. See Fraser, in *Chicago-Kent Law Reviews*, pp. 660–663.

47. Besharov, "What Physicians Should Know," p. 37, outlines these crucial first steps assigned to the child protective agency:

1. Providing immediate protection to children, through temporary stabilization of the home environment or, where necessary, protective custody.
2. Verifying the validity of the report and determining the danger to the children.
3. Assessing the service needs of children and families.
4. Providing or arranging for protective, ameliorative, and treatment services.
5. Initiating civil court action when necessary, to remove a child from a dangerous environment or to impose treatment on his family.

Also see Claudia A. Carroll, "The Function of Protective Services in Child Abuse and Neglect," in Kempe and Helfer, *The Battered Child* (1980), pp. 275–287, and Hortense R. Landau et al., *Child Protection: The Role of the Courts* (Washington, D.C.: National Center for Child Abuse and Neglect, 1980) (DHHS pub. no. (OHDS) 80-30256). On parental custody, see note 60 of this chapter.

48. Fraser, *Chicago-Kent Law Review*, p. 676.

49. See Table D in National Center on Child Abuse and Neglect, *Child Abuse and Neglect: State Reporting Laws* (Washington, D.C.: U.S. Government Printing Office, May 1978).

50. *State Reporting Laws*, sec. II.

51. Besharov, "What Physicians Should Know," p. 32.

52. Illinois Public Act 81-784.

53. The settlement came in *Robinson v. Wical*, No. 70-37607 (Cal. Super. Ct; San Luis Obispo, filed September 4, 1970). In commenting on the case, the editors of the *American Society of Hospital Attorneys Newsletter* observed: "Apparently counsel for the defendants felt that failure to comply with the statutory reporting requirement created a presumption of negligence." The

California Supreme Court decision is *Landeros v. Flood*, 17 Cal. 3d 399, 131 Cal. Rptr. 69, 551 P.2d 389 (1976). For a discussion, see Adrianne C. Mazura, "Negligence—Malpractice—Physician's Liability for Failure to Diagnose and Report Child Abuse," *Wayne Law Review* 23: 1187–1201 (1977).

54. Besharov, "Legal Aspects of Reporting," pp. 505–506, 508. Also see Douglas J. Besharov, "Putting Central Registries to Work: Using Modern Management Information Systems to Improve Child Protective Services," *Chicago-Kent Law Review* 54:687–752 (1978).

55. The *guardian ad litem*'s role is one of representing the child's interest, something that neither the district, county, city, or state's attorney representing the social service agency nor the lawyer representing the parents can be depended upon to do. Yet in some states the district, county, city, or state's attorney also fills the *guardian ad litem* role. And where the *guardian ad litem* is not a lawyer, he or she is limited in protecting the child's legal rights. Thus neither approach is as satisfactory as an attorney *guardian ad litem*. See Brian G. Fraser, "The Concept of *Guardian Ad Litem*," *Child Abuse and Neglect* 1:459–468 (1977); Brian G. Fraser, "Independent Representation for the Abused and Neglected Child: The *Guardian Ad Litem*," *California Western Law Review* 13:16–45 (1976–1977). Also see Donald N. Duquette, "Liberty and Lawyers in Child Protection," in Kempe and Helfer, *The Battered Child* (1980), pp. 316–329.

56. 42 U.S.C. Sec. 5103(b)(2); regulations at 45 C.F.R. Sec. 1340.3-3. States may satisfy these requirements in ways other than by state statute. For criticism of the laws implementation, see Abraham B. Bergman, "Abuse of the Child Abuse Law," *Pediatrics* 62:266–267 (1978).

57. See Hearings on Child Abuse Pevention and Treatment Act, National Advisory Board on Child Abuse and Neglect, Eli Newberger, hearing chairman, Fifth National Conference on Child Abuse and Neglect, Milwaukee, Wisconsin, April 6, 1981.

58. Fraser, *Chicago-Kent Law Review*, p. 685. Prevention can include identification of high-risk mothers in the delivery suite, identification of high-risk families in acute care and well-child care settings, supportive services for siblings of abused children, anticipatory guidance on matters such as discipline, junior high school education on normal child development, access to contraception and abortion to prevent unwanted births, and efforts to reduce social encouragement of violence (as, for example, on television). See Kempe and Helfer, *The Battered Child* (1980), chaps. 22–26.

59. Eli H. Newberger and Richard Bourne, "The Medicalization and Legalization of Child Abuse," in Richard Bourne and Eli H. Newberger, *Critical Perspectives on Child Abuse* (Lexington, Mass.: Lexington Books, 1979), p. 146.

60. But often this is too easy, since the law "sets relatively vague and imprecise limits upon authority to intrude and thus fails to provide fair warning." Goldstein, Freud, and Solnit, *Before the Best Interest of the Child*, p. 16. See their discussion and examples, pp. 72–86. In 1981 the U.S. Supreme Court held that Fourteenth Amendment due process does *not* require the appointment of counsel for indigent parents in every parental status termination proceeding. *Lassiter v. Department of Social Services*, 452 U.S. 18 (1981). In

1982, however, the Court rejected a fair preponderance of evidence standard in terminating parental rights, holding that before a state may completely and irrevocably sever the rights of parents in their natural child, due process requires that the state support its allegations by at least clear and convincing evidence. *Santosky v. Kramer*, 50 U.S.L.W. 4333 (U.S. March 23, 1982).

As the introductory principle of their latest work, Goldstein, Freud, and Solnit state that "so long as the child is part of a viable family, his own interests are merged with those of the other mer bei s. Only *after* the family fails in its function should the child's interests become a matter for state intrusion." For a review of the impact of Goldstein, Freud, and Solnit's earlier work (*Beyond the Best Interests of the Child* [New York: Free Press, 1973]) see Richard E. Crouch, "An Essay on the Critical and Judicial Reception of *Beyond the Best Interests of the Child*," *Family Law Quarterly* 13:49–103 (1979). Also see Robert E. Buckholz, Jr., "Constitutional Limitations on the Scope of State Child Neglect Statutes," *Columbia Law Review* 79:719–734 (1979).

61. See Edward J. Rolde, "Negative Effects of Child Abuse Legislation. *Child Abuse and Neglect* 1:167–171 (1977).

62. Alfred J. Kahn, Sheila B. Kamerman, and Brenda G. McGowan, *Child Advocacy: Report of a National Baseline Study* (New York: Columbia University School of Social Work, 1972), pp. 10–11.

63. Jane Knitzer, "Concepts of Advocacy: Definition and Levels of Professional Action," in *Child Advocacy and Pediatrics* (Columbus, Ohio: Ross Laboratories, 1978), p. 13. Also see Jane Knitzer, "Advocacy and Community Psychology," in Margaret S. Gibbs et al., *Community Psychology* (New York: Gardner Press, 1980), pp. 293–309.

64. Knitzer, "Concepts of Advocacy," p. 16. Also see Bersoff, "Child Advocacy"; Richard F. Tomkins, "Children's Advocacy and Primary Health Care," in Harvard Child Health Project Task Force, *Developing a Better Health Care System for Children*, vol. 2 (Cambridge, Mass.: Ballinger, 1977), pp. 193–230; Richard F. Tompkins, "Understanding Children's Advocacy in the Health Sector," *Pediatrics* 65:172–179 (1980); Jack C. Westman, *Child Advocacy: New Professional Roles for Helping Families* (New York, Free Press, 1979); American Academy of Pediatrics, *Handbook on Child Advocacy* (Evanston, Ill.: The Academy, 1977).

65. Goldstein, Freud, and Solnit, *Before the Best Interests of the Child*, p. 133.

Afterword

THE PRECEDING CHAPTERS have provided an overview of the major areas within which health care and law interact. Because contact with the law is an important element in the work of many health professionals, the general information provided in these pages and the specific statutes, regulations, and court decisions governing their professional endeavors are all of more than academic interest to the men and women engaged in this constantly changing field.

A general understanding of how the law sanctions or restricts the day-to-day functioning of the health professional can make it easier to avoid legal problems, to recognize such problems when they arise, and to work effectively with legal counsel.

Most health professionals, even those who work in a hospital or clinic, do not have regular and expense-free access to legal counsel. It is important, therefore, to know when such help is needed. Obviously an attorney must be consulted when an adverse legal proceeding, such as a lawsuit, has been initiated. And it may be wise to do so whenever such an action is threatened, however absurd the ground on which the threat is based. But there are other instances, too, where legal help is called for, such as when one is meeting with parties with potentially adverse interests, when a prediction or interpretation of legal developments is advisable, and even, at times, to provide an objective framing of issues.

How does one choose an attorney? Lawyers, like other professionals, vary widely in competence, and there is no established system for evaluating the quality of legal services. Thus, reputation and the recommendations of satisfied clients are often the most dependable guides. Equally important is the relationship that is established between client and attorney. Does the lawyer take the time to listen to the potential client's questions and to answer them in language free of jargon? Is he or she prepared to tackle the issue promptly and diligently, to keep careful records, to be available when needed, to discuss legal fees frankly and hold as closely as possible to the costs agreed upon? Is he or she someone the client can feel comfortable with over what could be a prolonged, difficult period of time?

No attorney can be expert in all fields of law. A specialist in medical staff law may know little about taxation; an expert on environmental law is not likely to know much about informed consent. Thus, it is not unreasonable for one's lawyer to consult with another attorney in connection with a question that requires specific expertise. Indeed, it is the attorney who purports to know everything who should arouse some doubts in the client's or potential client's mind.

Finally, it is important to remember that lawyers provide legal *advice*—specialized information upon which decisions can be based. It is up to the client to make the ultimate decisions, and to ask the questions necessary to understand fully what his or her options are. The situation, explains Ken Wing, is analogous to that involved in informed consent. Just as it is the job of the physician to outline treatment alternatives, likely outcomes and risks, even to make recommendations, and it is the responsibility of the patient to make the final decision, so it is the job of the lawyer to predict legal risks and outline alternatives, and the responsibility of the client to make the final choice.

Sometimes, what is most needed is not legal advice, but information. Often this can be obtained easily and without fee, from professional associations, appropriate regulatory agencies, or the constituent service offices of elected representatives. Many professional newsletters also include regular updates on legal developments in their field, and there are a number of other periodicals that focus exclusively on health law, politics, ethics, and related issues. (Such as *Law, Medicine and Health Care, American Journal of Law and Medicine, Journal of Health Politics, Policy and Law, Hastings Center Report, Journal of Legal Medicine,* and *Legal Aspects of Medical Practice.*) And when these fail to come through, there is a wealth of information available at the nearest law library. Many law libraries, including those operated by government agencies and some law schools, are open to the general public. And most law librarians are helpful to the nonlawyer.

While it would be a mistake for a nonlawyer to decide on his or her own precisely how a statute or judicial decision applies to a particular situation, it is often extremely useful to have the full text to study. The *Federal Register* or the *Code of Federal Regulations,* for example, can be invaluable guides to new federal rules, and law review articles can cast light on judicial decisions that may have been inadequately covered in professional journals or the mass media. Often such articles, setting particular litigation in perspective, appear even before a final decision has been handed down by the appellate courts.

In recent years, a growing number of books and articles on legal topics have been written for health professionals. Some focus on specific topics, for example, informed consent or how to testify in court. Others seek to acquaint health workers with the conceptual and ethical underpinnings of health law. Many of these materials have been cited in the preceding chapters. While they often encompass more than the health professional must know, many readers will welcome the added dimension such background provides. If used creatively, the law can be an important tool for improving health and health care services.

Appendix: Using the Law Library

THE MAIN THING to understand in making use of a law library is what the different categories of legal material—the "literature of the law"—contain. These categories include primary sources (statutes, regulations, and judicial decisions), finding tools, and secondary materials.

Statutes, the enactments of federal and state legislative bodies, are made available in several different forms. The first variation in form depends on how recent the statute is. Immediately after it becomes law, a statute will be made available to law libraries as a separately published slip law. Several commercial publications, including the weekly looseleaf *U.S. Law Week,* provide the texts of all or the most important new federal statutes. At the end of a legislative session, all of the new statutes enacted during that session will be published in numerical order in one volume: the *United States Statutes at Large* for federal statutes and what are most commonly called session laws on the state level. Then periodically—every six years for federal statutes—recently enacted statutes will be integrated into a statutory code arranged by topic. For federal laws this is the *United States Code,* which is arranged under fifty titles. The reference 42 U.S.C. 1320c-1 et seq. is to a statute found in Title 42 of the *United States Code* in sections 1320c-1 and those that follow (et sequentia). Another variation in form exists between officially and unofficially published versions of statutes. Commercial publishers are faster in completing their unofficial versions of statutory codes and offer several advantages over the official government-published versions, including better indexing, annotation to relevant court decisions, and during-the-year updates added as back-of-the-book "pocket part" supplements. Statute-related materials, such as constitutions, treaties, interstate compacts, and simple legislative resolutions, will also be found in law libraries. Local ordinances vary widely in form and availability.

Regulations, the formal rules issued by administrative bodies, are easily accessible at the federal level. The *Code of Federal Regulations* is a codification of all federal regulations arranged by topic into fifty titles, only partially paralleling the titles of the *United States Code*. The reference 42 CFR 478.4 is to section 478.4 of Title 42 of the *Code of Federal Regulations*. The CFR includes an index to its contents by subject as well as listings according to authorizing statute. The *Federal Register*, published several times a week, contains all federal administrative regulations as they are issued, along with executive orders, presidential proclamations, and the like. It thus provides a continual updating to the CFR, and monthly tables based on CFR titles and section numbers indicate which regulations have been altered during that month. Cumulative monthly lists of changes also accompany sets of the CFR. In addition, many commercially published looseleaf services and newsletters are available for keeping up-to-date on federal regulations in particular subject areas. Unfortunately, in most states it is difficult to impossible to locate published regulations, and on the local level published texts often simply don't exist.

Judicial decisions from the federal courts and the higher level state courts are published in several different forms. For the U.S. Supreme Court and some state supreme courts, individual slip opinions are issued as they are decided by the courts, and an accumulation of decisions are published as "advance sheets" from time to time during the year. Commercially published services, such as *U.S. Law Week*, also make U.S. Supreme Court decisions available soon after they are issued. Ultimately all of these decisions are published in bound volumes in which they are arranged in the order in which they were issued. The U.S. Supreme Court decisions currently constitute three or four volumes each year. When first issued, U.S. Supreme Court decisions bear the number the case was first assigned by the Court, for example, no. 80-732. Ultimately, however, a Supreme Court decision will be cited and located by volume and page number. Thus 410 U.S. 113 refers to a Supreme Court decision that can be found beginning on page 113 of volume 410 of the officially published decisions, *United States Reports*. There are also two commercially published sets of volumes of Supreme Court decisions, the *Supreme Court Reporter* and *Lawyers Edition, United States Supreme Court Reports*, which would identify this same case as 93 S.Ct. 705 and 35 L.Ed.2d 147. (The 2d in the last reference indicates that after a certain number of volumes, a second series of volumes was begun with a new volume 1, 2d series.) Only the more important decisions of the lower federal courts are published, and only in a commercial series. Court of appeals decisions are published in the Federal Reporter series, where a case citation—for example, 562 F.2d 280 (4th Cir. 1977)—will indicate which of the appellate courts issued the decision (here the Fourth Circuit Court of Appeals). Federal district court decisions are published in the Federal Supplement series, where a case citation—for example, 473 F.Supp. 147 (S.D.N.Y. 1979)—will indicate the district court involved (here the Federal District Court for the Southern District of New York).

State court decisions are published in official volumes in about two-thirds of the states, the remaining states relying on the National Reporter System, published by the West Publishing Company, which publishes state appellate opinions from all states. The West volumes combine states into seven regional reporters. Often a citation to a state court decision will give only the West series number, for example, 498 P.2d 136 (Montana, 1972) for a decision of the Montana Supreme Court published in the *Pacific Reporter*. But it is also common to provide parallel citations for a case, for example, 229 Ga. 140, 189 S.E.2d 412 (1972) for a decision of the Georgia Supreme Court, which can be found in both the official Georgia volumes and in the *South Eastern Reporter*.

After locating a judicial opinion, presumably one will want to read it. This can be a profitable experience for the nonlawyer, provided it is approached in the appropriate way. One will want to note who the parties to the legal case were, what type of relief was sought, what lower court decisions—if any—were involved, what legal issues—questions— are presented, what the court's general holding and specific decision is, and the rationale for that result. A common mistake made by non-lawyers in reading a judicial decision is to become bogged down in procedural history and frequent references. These portions of the decision may be of interest to the lawyer studying the case, but the nonlawyer should concentrate, instead, on approaching a judicial decision as one would any written essay, factual or fictional. It is also useful to keep in mind that if judicial language seems impenetrable this is most likely due to bad writing rather than sophisticated reasoning or arcane insight. Some judges might do better to hire editors rather than law school graduates as their clerks.

"*Finding tools*" consist of the many indexes, digests, looseleaf services, popular name tables, computerized research services, and the like, which make it possible to locate specific statutes, regulations, and judicial decisions from among the mountains of primary materials. Legal research depends on a wide array of these finding tools, which are critical to the lawyer whose brief must be exhaustive and up-to-date. The non-lawyer will be less dependent upon finding tools, but with the assistance of the law librarian and a little practice, locating legal materials can become a straightforward enterprise.

Secondary material, on the other hand, may be of more importance to the nonlawyer than to the practicing attorney. There are numerous types of secondary materials, but from the nonlawyer's perspective three categories are noteworthy: encyclopedias and looseleaf services, periodicals, and texts.

Legal encyclopedias are not considered particularly scholarly or authoritative. Such an assessment is not surprising, since encyclopedias attempt the perhaps impossible task of providing a general, noncritical introductory review of all areas of the law. The two general legal encyclopedias are *Corpus Juris Secundum* and *American Jurisprudence 2d.* There are also encyclopedias devoted to the law of each of several of the more populous states. Looseleaf services, like encyclopedias, attempt to be comprehensive, but they have the dual advantages of dealing with only a single area of law and of being continually updated. At the same time, looseleaf services are published only in those areas where there will be a market for such high-priced services. Since encyclopedias and looseleaf services provide such a broad, general coverage, many people view them as being primarily finding tools.

Legal periodicals are published by law schools, special interest subgroups within the law (for example, health law), and bar associations. They consist of scholarly articles, usually written by law professors, which often play a role in influencing subsequent court decisions, along with law student analyses of leading court decisions. They can be of considerable value to the nonlawyer as thorough reviews of a narrow area of law, often putting major judicial decisions in wider perspective and predicting future legal trends. Indexing of legal periodicals is poorly done as compared to biomedical journal indexing. The *Index to Legal Periodicals* has long been the standard index to U.S. legal periodicals, but a newly introduced microfilm system, the Legal Resource Index, provides a more complete guide to this literature. These indices are compiled by people with legal, not health, backgrounds, and it often proves difficult to guess under which broad heading they will place a health-related topic. Useful starting points are Health, Hospitals, Medical Jurisprudence, Mental Health, and Physicians and Surgeons.

Finally, there are innumerable legal texts and treatises providing exhaustive reviews of specific legal topics. Such books have no official place in the law, but those by particularly outstanding legal scholars will often be given considerable recognition by courts. The many volumes of *Restatements of Law,* developed by panels of legal scholars, have been very persuasive in courts. These volumes, which cover the major areas of law—contracts, property, torts, for example—present "blackletter" summary statements distilling the law on a specific point and then add commentary by the restatement panel. For more details on legal research, consult J. Myron Jacobstein and Roy M. Mersky, *Fundamentals of Legal Research* (Mineola, N.Y.: Foundation Press, 1977); Miles O. Price and Harry Bitner, *Effective Legal Research,* 4th ed. (Boston: Little, Brown, 1979); William P. Statsky, *Legal Research, Writing and Analysis: Some Starting Points* (St. Paul: West, 1974); or Morris L. Cohen, *Legal Research in a Nutshell* (St. Paul: West, 1978). Of particular use to nonlawyers is *Using a Law Library,* published in 1982 by HALT/Americans for Legal Reform, 201 Massachusetts Avenue, N.E., Suite 319, Washington, D.C. 20002.

Bibliography

General, Especially Chapters 1–5

GEORGE J. ANNAS, LEONARD H. GLANTZ, and BARBARA F. KATZ. *The Rights of Doctors, Nurses and Allied Health Professionals: A Health Law Primer*. New York: Avon, 1981.

MORRIS L. COHEN. *Legal Research in a Nutshell*. St. Paul, Minn.: West Publishing Company, 1978.

WILLIAM J. CURRAN and E. DONALD SHAPIRO. *Law, Medicine, and Forensic Science*, 3d ed. Boston: Little, Brown, 1982.

FRANK GRAD. *The Public Health Law Manual*. Washington, D.C.: American Public Health Association, 1975.

STEVEN JONAS ET AL. *Health Care Delivery in the United States*, 2d ed. New York: Springer, 1981.

Regulations and Health: Understanding and Influencing the Process. New York: National Health Council, 1979.

FRED RODELL. *Woe Unto You, Lawyers!* New York: Berkley, 1981.

RUTH ROEMER and GEORGE MCKRAY, eds. *Legal Aspects of Health Policy: Issues and Trends*. Westport, Conn.: Greenwood Press, 1980.

RAND E. ROSENBLATT. "Health Care Reform and Administrative Law: A Structural Approach." *Yale Law Journal* 88:243–336, 1978.

KENNETH WING. *Law and the Public's Health*. St. Louis: C. V. Mosby, 1976.

Chapter 6

FRANK P. GRAD and NOELIA MARTI. *Physicians' Licensure and Discipline: The Legal and Professional Regulation of Medical Practice*. Dobbs Ferry, N.Y.: Oceana Publications, 1979.

VIRGINIA C. HALL. *Statutory Regulation of the Scope of Nursing Practice*. Chicago: National Joint Practice Commission, 1975.

STEVEN JONAS. *Medical Mystery: The Training of Doctors in America*. New York: Norton, 1978.

RUTH ROEMER. "Regulation of Health Personnel." In Ruth Roemer and George McKray, eds., *Legal Aspects of Health Policy: Issues and Trends*. Westport, Conn.: Greenwood Press, 1980.

Chapter 7

GEORGE J. ANNAS. *The Rights of Hospital Patients.* New York: Avon, 1975.

LOUISE LANDER. "Licensing of Health Care Facilities." In Ruth Roemer and George McKray, eds., *Legal Aspects of Health Policy: Issues and Trends.* Westport, Conn.: Greenwood Press, 1980.

IRA M. SHEPARD and A. EDWARD DOUDERA, eds. *Health Care Labor Law.* Ann Arbor, Mich.: Health Administration Press.

ARTHUR F. SOUTHWICK. *The Law of Hospital and Health Care Administration.* Ann Arbor, Mich.: Health Administration Press, 1978.

DAVID G. WARREN. *Problems in Hospital Law,* 3d ed. Germantown, Md.: Aspen Systems Corporation, 1978.

Chapter 8

DAVID S. ABERNATHY and DAVID A. PEARSON. *Regulating Hospital Costs: The Development of Public Policy.* Ann Arbor, Mich.: AUPHA Press, 1979.

DREW ALTMAN. "The Politics of Health Care Regulation: The Case of the National Health Planning and Resources Development Act." *Journal of Health Politics, Policy and Law* 2:560–580, 1978.

ANDREW K. DOLAN. "Antitrust Law and Physician Dominance of Other Health Practitioners." *Journal of Health Politics, Policy and Law* 4:675–690, 1980.

MARTIN J. THOMPSON. *Antitrust and the Health Care Provider.* Germantown, Md.: Aspen Systems Corporation, 1979.

Chapter 9

KAREN DAVIS AND CATHY SCHOEN. *Health and the War on Poverty: A Ten-Year Appraisal.* Washington, D.C.: Brookings Institution, 1978.

Institute of Medicine. *Health Care in a Context of Civil Rights.* Washington, D.C.: National Academy Press, 1981.

WILLIAM RYAN. *Equality.* New York: Pantheon, 1981.

KENNETH WING. "Title VI and Health Facilities: Forms Without Substance." *Hastings Law Journal* 30:139–190, 1978.

Chapter 10

NICHOLAS A. ASHFORD. *Crisis in the Workplace: Occupational Disease and Injury, A Report to the Ford Foundation.* Cambridge, Mass.: MIT Press, 1976.

MARK A. ROTHSTEIN. *Occupational Safety and Health Law.* St. Paul, Minn.: West Publishing Company, 1978 (with supplements).

Chapter 11

GEORGE McKRAY. Consumer Protection: The Federal Food, Drug, and Cosmetic Act. In Ruth Roemer and George McKray, eds., *Legal Aspects of Health Policy: Issues and Trends.* Westport, Conn.: Greenwood Press, 1980.

RICHARD A. MERRILL and PETER BARTON HUTT. *Food and Drug Law.* Mineola, N.Y.: Foundation Press, 1980.

OAKLEY RAY. *Drugs, Society, and Human Behavior,* 2d ed. St. Louis: C. V. Mosby, 1978.

Requirements of Laws and Regulations Enforced by the U.S. Food and Drug Administration. Rockville, Md., FDA, 1979 (HEW Publication No. (FDA) 79-1042).

Chapter 12

DON E. BEAUCHAMP. *Beyond Alcoholism: Alcohol and Public Health Policy.* Philadelphia: Temple University Press, 1980.

A. LEE FRITSCHLER. *Smoking and Politics: Policy-Making and the Federal Bureaucracy,* 2d ed. Englewood Cliffs, N.J., Prentice-Hall, 1975.

WILLIAM H. RODGERS, JR. *Handbook on Environmental Law.* St. Paul, Minn.: West Publishing Company, 1977.

DANIEL SWARTZMAN, RICHARD LIROFF, and KEVIN CROKE, eds. *Cost-Benefit Analysis in Environmental Regulation: Politics, Methods, and Ethics.* Washington, D.C.: Conservation Foundation, 1981.

Chapter 13

WILLIAM J. CURRAN, A. LOUIS McGARRY, and CHARLES S. PETTY. *Modern Legal Medicine, Psychiatry, and Forensic Science.* Philadelphia: F. A. Davis, 1980.

Defining Death: A Report on the Medical, Legal and Ethical Issues in the Determination of Death. Washington, D.C.: President's Commission for the Study of Ethical Problems in Medicine and Biomedical and Behavioral Research, 1981.

Chapter 14

JOHN A. ROBERTSON. *The Rights of the Critically Ill: The Basic ACLU Guide to the Rights of the Critically Ill and Dying Patient.* Cambridge, Mass.: Ballinger (in press).

ARNOLD J. ROSOFF. *Informed Consent.* Rockville, Md.: Aspen Systems Corporation, 1981.

CYNTHIA B. WONG and JUDITH P. SWAZEY. *Dilemmas of Dying: Policies and Procedures for Decisions Not to Treat.* Boston: G. K. Hall, 1981.

Chapter 15

GEORGE J. ANNAS, LEONARD H. GLANTZ, and BARBARA F. KATZ. *Informed Consent to Human Experimentation: The Subject's Dilemma.* Cambridge, Mass.: Ballinger, 1977.

The Belmont Report: Ethical Principles and Guidelines for the Protection of Human Subjects of Research. Bethesda, Md.: The National Commission for the Protection of Human Subjects of Biomedical and Behavioral Research, 1978 (DHEW Publication No. (OS) 78-0012).

Chapter 16

FRANK P. GRAD: "Medical Malpractice and Its Implications for Public Health." In Ruth Roemer and George McKray, eds., *Legal Aspects of Health Policy: Issues and Trends.* Westport, Conn.: Greenwood Press, 1980.

LOUISE LANDER. *Defective Medicine: Risk, Anger, and the Malpractice Crisis.* New York: Farrar, Straus & Giroux, 1978.

SYLVIA LAW and STEVEN POLAN. *Pain and Profit: The Politics of Malpractice.* New York: Harper & Row, 1978.

TARKY LOMBADI, JR., with GERALD N. HOFFMAN. *Medical Malpractice Insurance.* Syracuse, N.Y.: Syracuse University Press, 1978.

ANGELA RODDEY HOLDER. *Medical Malpractice Law,* 2d ed. New York: Wiley, 1978.

Chapter 17

TRUDY HAYDEN and JACK NOVIK. *Your Rights to Privacy.* New York: Avon, 1980.

MARC D. HILLER and VIVIAN BEYDA. "Computers, Medical Records, and the Right to Privacy. *Journal of Health Politics, Policy and Law* 6:463–487, 1981.

Personal Privacy in an Information Society: The Report of the Privacy Study Commission. Washington, D.C.: The Commission, 1977.

ARTHUR F. SOUTHWICK. *The Law of Hospital and Health Care Administration.* Ann Arbor, Mich.: Health Administration Press, 1978, chap. 11.

ALLAN WESTIN. *Computers, Health Records, and Citizen Rights.* Washington, D.C.: National Bureau of Standards Monograph 157, 1976.

Chapter 18

AUBREY MILUNSKY and GEORGE J. ANNAS, eds. *Genetics and the Law.* New York: Plenum Press, 1976.

AUBREY MILUNSKY and GEORGE J. ANNAS, EDS. *Genetics and the Law II.* New York: Plenum Press, 1980.

PHILLIP REILLY. *Genetics, Law, and Social Policy.* Cambridge, Mass.: Harvard University Press, 1977.

Chapter 19

WALTER E. BARTON and CHARLOTTE J. SANBORN, eds. *Law and the Mental Health Professions: Friction at the Interface.* New York: International Universities Press, 1978.

BRUCE J. ENNIS and RICHARD D. EMERY. *The Rights of Mental Patients.* New York: Avon Books, 1978.

PAUL R. FRIEDMAN. *The Rights of Mentally Retarded Persons.* New York: Avon Books, 1976.

ALAN A. STONE. *Mental Health and the Law: A System in Transition.* Rockville, Md.: National Institute for Mental Health, 1975.

Chapter 20

DOUGLAS J. BESHAROV. "The Legal Aspects of Reporting Known and Suspected Child Abuse and Neglect." *Villanova Law Review* 23:458–520, 1978.

BRIAN G. FRASER. "A Glance at the Past, a Gaze at the Present, a Glimpse at the Future: A Critical Analysis of the Development of Child Abuse Reporting Statutes." *Chicago-Kent Law Review* 54:641–686, 1978.

JOSEPH GOLDSTEIN, ANNA FREUD, AND ALBERT J. SOLNIT. *Before the Best Interests of the Child.* New York: Free Press, 1980.

ANGELA RODDEY HOLDER. *Legal Issues in Pediatrics and Adolescent Medicine.* New York: Wiley, 1977.

ALAN N. SUSSMAN. *The Rights of Young People.* New York: Avon Books, 1977.

JOHN P. WILSON. *The Rights of Adolescents in the Mental Health System.* Lexington, Mass.: Lexington Books, 1978.

Index

442